Mastering VMware Horizon 8

An Advanced Guide to Delivering
Virtual Desktops and Virtual Apps

Peter von Oven

Apress®

Mastering VMware Horizon 8

Peter von Oven
Wiltshire, UK

ISBN-13 (pbk): 978-1-4842-7260-2
https://doi.org/10.1007/978-1-4842-7261-9

ISBN-13 (electronic): 978-1-4842-7261-9

Copyright © 2022 by Peter von Oven

This work is subject to copyright. All rights are reserved by the Publisher, whether the whole or part of the material is concerned, specifically the rights of translation, reprinting, reuse of illustrations, recitation, broadcasting, reproduction on microfilms or in any other physical way, and transmission or information storage and retrieval, electronic adaptation, computer software, or by similar or dissimilar methodology now known or hereafter developed.

Trademarked names, logos, and images may appear in this book. Rather than use a trademark symbol with every occurrence of a trademarked name, logo, or image we use the names, logos, and images only in an editorial fashion and to the benefit of the trademark owner, with no intention of infringement of the trademark.

The use in this publication of trade names, trademarks, service marks, and similar terms, even if they are not identified as such, is not to be taken as an expression of opinion as to whether or not they are subject to proprietary rights.

While the advice and information in this book are believed to be true and accurate at the date of publication, neither the authors nor the editors nor the publisher can accept any legal responsibility for any errors or omissions that may be made. The publisher makes no warranty, express or implied, with respect to the material contained herein.

Managing Director, Apress Media LLC: Welmoed Spahr
Acquisitions Editor: Aditee Mirashi
Development Editor: James Markham

Cover designed by eStudioCalamar

Cover image designed by Freepik (www.freepik.com)

Distributed to the book trade worldwide by Springer Science+Business Media New York, 1 New York Plaza, Suite 4600, New York, NY 10004-1562, USA. Phone 1-800-SPRINGER, fax (201) 348-4505, e-mail orders-ny@springer-sbm.com, or visit www.springeronline.com. Apress Media, LLC is a California LLC and the sole member (owner) is Springer Science + Business Media Finance Inc (SSBM Finance Inc). SSBM Finance Inc is a **Delaware** corporation.

For information on translations, please e-mail booktranslations@springernature.com; for reprint, paperback, or audio rights, please e-mail bookpermissions@springernature.com.

Apress titles may be purchased in bulk for academic, corporate, or promotional use. eBook versions and licenses are also available for most titles. For more information, reference our Print and eBook Bulk Sales web page at http://www.apress.com/bulk-sales.

Any source code or other supplementary material referenced by the author in this book is available to readers on GitHub via the book's product page, located at www.apress.com/978-1-4842-7260-2. For more detailed information, please visit http://www.apress.com/source-code.

Printed on acid-free paper

This book is dedicated, first and foremost,
to my family as well as friends and colleagues
who have supported me along the way.

Table of Contents

About the Author

 **Peter von Oven** is an experienced technical consultant working closely with customers, partners, and vendors in designing technology solutions to meet business needs and deliver outcomes. During his career, Peter has presented at key IT events, such as VMworld, IP EXPO, and various VMUGs and CCUG events across the UK. He has also worked in senior presales roles and presales management roles for Fujitsu, HP, Citrix, and VMware and has been awarded VMware vExpert for the last seven years in a row and vExpert EUC for the last two consecutive years. In 2016, Peter founded his own company specializing in application delivery. Today, he works with a number of partners helping drive and deliver innovative technology solutions. He is also an avid author, having now written 16 books and made videos about VMware end-user computing solutions. In his spare time, Peter volunteers as a STEM Ambassador, working with schools and colleges, helping the next generation develop the skills and confidence in building careers in technology.

About the Technical Reviewer

Tom Howarth is an IT executive with over 20 years of experience. He consults to private and public sector companies; he has a vast amount of experience with a number of IT systems, but specializes in virtualization and infrastructure design utilizing VMware technology to provide efficient and highly available cloud-based platforms that are also cost-effective and more importantly support resilient application delivery in the data center and public cloud. Tom's previous customers have included large IT support providers and technology integrators, government departments, and NGOs with whom he has earned a reputation for being diligent in solving problems in a timely and cost-effective manner.

He has been awarded VMware vExpert every year since inception (currently 13 years), VMware vExpert NSX (4 years), vExpert PRO (2 years), and vExpert Cloud Provider (2 years). Further, he has been awarded HashiCorp Ambassador for 2020 in its inaugural year and again for the second time in 2021.

When he is not whispering clouds, he likes to spend time with his family at the cinema, or in and around Gibraltar.

He can be reached via Twitter at @tom_howarth.

Acknowledgments

This is now book number 16! I would like to say a big thank you to the team at Apress for giving me another opportunity to write this book with them. As I've said before, the whole process of planning, researching, and writing a book still presents a huge challenge and undertaking. Given the current situation we all find ourselves in at this time of writing, authoring this book has come as a welcome distraction.

There are also a number of people I would like to acknowledge for sparing me the time to help in preparing this book. Firstly, to Aditee at Apress for making sure I kept on track and answering questions about the process. Secondly, a big thank you to industry colleagues for their help and guidance and invaluable insight into the digital workspace of today. In particular, Darren Hirons from VMware and Ben Ward and Simon Townsend from IGEL.

Last but by no means least, a huge thank you to Tom Howarth for providing his valuable skills in reviewing the technical content, which, as you will see, is a lot.

Finally, I would like to acknowledge you, the people that read this. Without you, this whole project would not be possible, so again, thank you. I would also love to hear from you with any suggestions or questions regarding the solutions covered in this book or any other end-user computing solutions for that matter. You can find me on Twitter at @pvo71.

Foreword

The global pandemic, a change in how we work and innovate, especially in the cloud, continues to drive change in the world of end-user computing (EUC) and impacts how we deliver digital workspaces.

This book assists those new to VDI and those already familiar with the VMware solutions, providing an up-to-date reference for those organizations and individuals looking at deploying VDI and DaaS.

Peter is a well-known subject matter expert in VMware solutions and has spent many years deploying solutions, educating many through his previous books, and contributing much to the EUC community. This latest book provides an informative update in the fast-paced world of EUC.

Congratulations and thank you Peter...

—Simon Townsend
Chief Marketing Officer
IGEL

Introduction

The VMware Horizon solution is the foundation for delivering the digital workspace. The term virtual desktop infrastructure, or VDI, was coined back in 2002, where end users simply connected, on a one-to-one basis, to a desktop operating system that was running as a virtual machine on a hypervisor on servers in the data center. Wind the clock forward to today, and although the basic principle remains the same, the technology behind the scenes to deliver a desktop or app experience has advanced massively.

This book will focus on how to get started with VMware Horizon and how to deliver virtual desktop machines and RDSH-based applications and desktop sessions to end users. Throughout this book, we will work through the solution to enable you to design, install, configure, and manage a Horizon deployment, using step-by-step instructions with real-life screenshots as you follow the test lab that is used throughout the book to demonstrate each key feature.

Starting with a high-level overview of remote desktop solutions, followed by an introduction into VDI specifically, this book will then provide an in-depth overview of VMware Horizon and where the solution fits within the market, and its key features. We will then move on to explaining the architecture and components and then look at how to design an optimized solution.

Once you have understood the architecture, the next step is to start installing and configuring Horizon, including best practices for building your virtual desktop gold image and optimizing it in order to deliver the best end-user experience possible.

Note It's worth highlighting that because some chapters are task oriented, they are a fair bit longer than others in order to do the subject justice and to enable you to understand each step in more detail. Additionally, a comprehensive reference guide explaining the API commands is available online at `https://github.com/Apress/delivering-virtual-desktops-apps-vmware-horizon8`.

INTRODUCTION

Throughout the chapters in this book, you will be given hints and tips, along with best practices, all seen from the eyes of somebody who works with this technology day in, day out, and in many different types of environments and scenarios. By the end of this book, you will have acquired the skills to build a Horizon environment for a proof of concept, a pilot, or in a live production environment. The following are some key topics we will cover in this book:

- Learn how the VMware Horizon solution can enhance the management and delivery of virtual desktops and applications within your environment

- Design a real-life Horizon solution, using best practice and following the recommended sizing and configuration guides

- Install, configure, and deploy Horizon ready to start delivering virtual desktop machines and applications to your organization

- Learn about some of the other components of the overall Horizon solution such as App Volumes, ThinApp, and Dynamic Environment Manager

- Understand how Horizon can be used as a cloud-based solution to deliver desktops and apps from a cloud platform

- Understand some of the more advanced management tasks using APIs and command-line tools

I hope that you enjoy reading the chapters and that they help you learn all about VMware Horizon and how to deploy and manage the solution.

CHAPTER 1

Remote Desktop Solutions

Welcome to Chapter 1 of *Mastering VMware Horizon 8.*

We are going to start this book by discussing the different technology solutions available on the market today that are designed to deliver an end-user experience. In this context, the end-user experience is the ability for an end user to access either a full desktop operating system or access individual applications, all of which are delivered remotely, as the desktops and applications are running on server infrastructure. They are either hosted on-premises, delivered from a cloud provider, or delivered via a hybrid model, combining the two.

Collectively, the technologies that deliver the end-user experience have more commonly become known as **digital workspace** solutions.

In This Chapter

In this chapter, we are going to cover the core methods and technology for delivering the end-user experience, before focusing on the VMware-specific technology stack, in the form of VMware Horizon.

In the following sections, we are going to start by discussing each type of technology solution, from a generic perspective, rather than as a VMware-specific product. We will discuss where each one is used, how each one works, and the key benefits that it offers.

Having then described each of the different technology solutions, we will also look at how you would decide which one is appropriate for your organization. In reality, it may not be a single technology that is required to cover all your organization's different use cases. It will likely be a mixture of delivery methods. However, the key point would be that in the case of VMware Horizon, these different delivery methods are all managed from a single management platform.

© Peter von Oven 2022
P. von Oven, *Mastering VMware Horizon 8*, https://doi.org/10.1007/978-1-4842-7261-9_1

Finally, in this chapter, we will introduce the VMware Horizon solution and its associated technology for delivering the end-user experience.

Why Deliver Desktops from a Data center or Cloud?

As we have just established, remote desktop solutions deliver the end-user experience remotely, from a data center or cloud platform, but the question is: Why would you consider deploying this type of solution?

There are several benefits that deploying a remote solution can deliver to both your organization and your end-user population. We are going to discuss these in the next sections; however, they are in no particular order, as priorities will be different depending on the specific requirements and use cases for your organization.

Cost Savings

A key reason to deliver end-user computing using a remote solution is to save costs. Cost savings can be realized in several ways. The first of these is the costs in managing end users.

Delivering desktops and applications centrally from a data center or cloud provider enables your organization to reduce the management overheads and deskside visits. However, you just need to be aware that the different models typically use different expenditure models.

If you deploy an on-premises solution, then while in the long run you will reduce management and support costs, or your operational expenditure (OPEX), there will be an up-front capital expenditure (CAPEX) cost to deploy the servers, storage, and networking required to host the solution in the first place. You also need to factor in environmental factors, such as increased power requirements and additional cooling for the new hardware.

Migrating to a cloud-based solution using one of the many "as a service" type solutions available will certainly reduce your CAPEX costs, as you will be essentially using somebody else's hardware. But what does that look like for the OPEX budget, and what savings will you make?

One thing to be aware of with delivering cloud-based solutions, charged via a subscription-based model where you only pay for what you use, is to calculate the hours that end users will be using the service. Another trap to watch out for, which also applies to on-premises solutions to a certain degree, is to only provide the resources that are required. Do not get carried away with adding unnecessary CPU, memory, and storage resources, as you will end up paying a lot more than you budgeted for. In my experience, I have seen many customers receive a monthly bill that was much higher than they expected it to be.

Security

As the desktop or application that the end user is accessing is running in a secure data center, no data will leave that data center, unless the IT department has specifically configured a policy to allow end users to copy data to their local device. On the flip side, that also means that end users cannot copy data from their local device into the data center, ensuring that they cannot introduce malware or other malicious content.

When the end user connects to their remote session, the only data transmitted to their endpoint device are the screenshots of the application or desktop they are connected to. Keyboard keypresses and mouse movements are then sent back securely to the session. Think of it as picking your PC up, placing it in the data center, and then running very long cables back to your screen, keyboard, and mouse.

This process is the same regardless of whether you are running in your on-premises data center or a public cloud provider. The connection between the session and the endpoint device will be secured.

To enable end users to log in to their sessions, you can also deploy additional security solutions, such as two-factor authentication.

The final point is with the endpoint device. Because there is no data on the endpoint from the session, then if the device is lost or stolen, there is no risk of data falling into the wrong hands or getting lost.

Easy to Manage and Support

We have already touched on the fact that you can reduce the costs of management. But the question is, how?

Centralizing your desktops and applications by default means that you have also centralized the management. This is especially true if you have migrated to a cloud-based desktop solution because the only way to manage the solution is by using a centralized web portal.

So, now that you have all your desktops and applications virtualized and hosted in a data center, performing management tasks is much simpler and quicker. Updating operating system gold images, to add the latest patches and security updates, is much easier; you will need to only do this once and then roll this out across the environment. Being centralized means that your end user will receive these updates the very next time they connect. In some cloud-based solutions, this could even be managed for you with the service provider, ensuring that the operating systems are patched and up to date.

When it comes to support and troubleshooting issues, then this is also much simpler to undertake. You can shadow the user's desktop or application session to understand the issue, resulting in this task being a simple case of the desktop admins logging on to the same session as the end user. This also has the potential to proactively update the rest of the end-user environment. If you identify an issue, you can easily fix this and then update gold images, ensuring that the issue is quickly fixed before other end users report the same issue.

There is a long-running joke in IT where the support team tells the end user to "turn it off and then on again!" However, this really is the case with remote desktop and application sessions. As desktops will typically be non-persistent, when the end user logs out, then the virtual desktop they were using is automatically deleted. Then, when they log on again, they receive a brand-new virtual desktop that will not have the issue they reported. Their personal data and application will all be kept and delivered to the new virtual desktop.

It is the same for applications. The end user simply logs out of the current application session and then logs in again to start a new one.

Disaster Recovery (DR) and Business Continuity (BC)

As with the previous sections, by moving to delivering end-user computing services from a data center, DR and BC all become default parts of how the solution is architected and built.

When it comes to disaster recovery, the fact that the virtual desktops and applications are running on server infrastructure enables them to become highly available. Deploying standard virtualization techniques, such as vMotion, enables desktops and applications to be moved and restarted on different servers, and even different data centers, in the event of a data center failing or becoming unavailable. This enables you to deliver an always-on end-user environment, regardless of where it is being delivered from.

You would naturally employ all this protection technology, given the fact that if a server should fail, it could now affect hundreds of users, in comparison to a single physical desktop machine failing, which would only affect an individual end user.

The same can be said for BC. Rather than failing over an entire data center, individual virtual desktops and applications can be restarted on different servers, ensuring they are always available.

If we look at support again briefly, if the system administrators need to perform maintenance on a particular server, they can very quickly and easily move workloads onto another server, ensuring there is no disruption to the end users. It also means that maintenance windows can be scheduled during office hours, rather than having to wait for when the office is closed in the evening or at weekends. This also has an impact on cost, reducing the extra hours that administrators must spend working. This also reduces the cost of the pizza bill, when working out of hours!

Of course, moving to a cloud-based solution means that there is no maintenance on hardware required.

Scalability

Scalability, or elasticity, as it is sometimes referred to, allows you to scale up or down resources dynamically. This concept is ideal for delivering end-user services.

You can easily add additional desktop or application resources to cope with the demands of your business, whether that is on a seasonal basis, where you need to add temporary resources or to address your overall growth plans. You just need to ensure that your on-premises infrastructure can support the increase in capacity.

Additional capacity can be added to the centrally hosted infrastructure, allowing end users to very quickly be onboarded. This can further be expedited if the end user is using their own device, which we will cover in the next section.

When it comes to cloud-based solutions, you can then scale up and down, as and when required. You can also only pay for what you use. So, if you add additional resources and capacity for a six-month period, then you will only be billed for this period. This solution is perfect if you have an element of unpredictability within your organization, as you are not reliant on having to add infrastructure capacity.

Bring Your Own Device (BYOD)

Finally, end users can bring their own device. The benefits of this model are numerous and fit into some of the points already highlighted.

End users can be quickly onboarded, as they already have a device that they can use. You simply need to allocate them desktop and application access and resources, then point them to the appropriate login pages. They can either download a specific client to use the services or just use the browser on their device.

As the end user is now using their own personal device, your organization saves the cost of having to provide them with a company-owned device. And as it belongs to the end user, you then do not have to support it. You just need to make sure that it can run the remote sessions.

There is no security risk. Data from the remote session is not stored on the end user's personal device. They are merely accessing a remote session, hosted in the data center or the cloud. This is an ideal solution for contractors as you do not need to purchase hardware just for a few months of a project while also keeping control of data access.

Virtual Desktop Infrastructure (VDI)

Let us start by defining what exactly we mean when we talk about VDI solutions.

VDI is a solution, consisting of a virtual desktop machine, running a desktop operating system (Windows or Linux) that is running on a hypervisor, which, in turn, is running on server hardware. This is in a central data center on-premises, or a cloud-based data center, such as Amazon or Azure.

End users then connect to the virtual desktop machine over the network or over the Internet. The desktop of that virtual desktop machine is displayed on their local endpoint device, using a display protocol, enabling them to interact with the virtual desktop machine using their local keyboard and mouse. For the end user, the experience is that they have a *full* Windows or Linux desktop to use. It just happens to be a virtual desktop machine, running in the data center.

Although VDI is the common term used for this type of solution, it can also sometimes be referred to as a hosted virtual desktop or HVD, as the virtual desktop machine is being hosted on data center infrastructure.

The Architecture of VDI

In the previous section, we described, at a high level, what VDI is. In this section, we are going to take a closer look at what that looks like from a high-level architecture perspective and how it works.

Let us start with the end user. After all, we are talking about end-user computing, and so the end user should always be the focus.

To initiate the connection to the virtual desktop machine, from their endpoint device, the end user launches the client software for their chosen VDI vendor. In this case, as we are talking about VMware Horizon, this would be the Horizon Client software. Equally, they could just use their normal web browser.

The client software contains the details of the infrastructure hosting the end user's virtual desktop machine or applications, which the end user needs to connect to. In particular, the address details will point the end user to a connection broker. The job of the connection broker is to authenticate the end user against Active Directory and then manage the available resources that the end user is entitled to use and that are available. It is the connection broker that is the core component to any VDI solution, orchestrating resources and ensuring they are delivered to the end user.

Before the concept of the connection server came into being, you would only be able to connect to a machine on a 1:1 basis, just like we do today when managing individual servers when we simply connect directly to the desktop of the server using the Microsoft Remote Desktop Protocol (RDP).

Figure 1-1 illustrates the connection process.

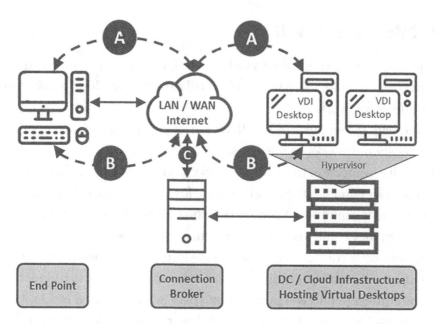

Figure 1-1. *The architecture of a VDI solution*

Once the end user has been authenticated, the Connection Server allocates a virtual desktop machine to that end user, based on what they are entitled to use. This is shown by the arrow labeled C in the previous diagram. This could be a ready built virtual desktop machine or a virtual desktop machine that is built on demand and configured dynamically to that specific end user. The connection server will orchestrate this communicating with the back-end infrastructure. In VMware terms, the connection server will communicate with your vCenter Server to create, build, and configure virtual desktop machines.

The screenshots of the virtual desktop machine are then sent over the LAN, WAN, or Internet, using a display protocol (A) that is optimized for delivering remote solutions, to the end user's endpoint device, and then displayed in either the client software, or the browser, depending on how the end user connected. The end user then interacts with the virtual desktop, using their local keyboard and mouse, with the keystrokes and mouse movements sent back to the virtual desktop machine, over the LAN, WAN, or Internet, using the same display protocol (B). We will discuss the display protocols in more detail in Chapter 2.

Now that we have discussed the high-level role of a connection broker, and how the virtual desktop is delivered to the end user's device, you will remember that one of the roles of the connection broker in delivering resources to the end users is to create, build, and configure virtual desktops on demand.

One of the early mistakes made in deploying VDI solutions that also impacted costs was the way in which the deployment was approached. Organizations deployed virtual desktops in the same way as they had with physical desktops. That meant that every end user was given their own dedicated virtual desktop, complete with a virtual hard disk of a similar size as the hard disk they had in their physical desktop. This resulted in terabytes of disk space being unnecessarily deployed.

The real big benefit that VDI enables is in the fact that you do not need to build a machine up front and dedicate to every end user in your organization. Virtual desktops can be created, built, and configured on demand, all from the same starting point. That starting point is a fresh clean copy of the gold image every time the end user logs in. Of course, there may well be a use case where an end user needs to have their own dedicated virtual desktop machine; however, those use cases will be few and far between.

VDI can deliver both use cases. A non-persistent virtual desktop model allows you to deploy the former. An end user does not own their virtual desktop, and a new desktop will be built or allocated to them each time they log in. Essentially, they receive a brand-new desktop every time they log in. When they have finished with the virtual desktop machine for that session, it then gets shut down and deleted. This also means that you do not need to create more virtual desktops than is required, which potentially means less infrastructure is required to host them. But what about their applications and user data? If the virtual desktop is deleted when they log out, do they lose their data?

The answer is of course they do not. This is where other solutions come into play within a virtual desktop solution. These ecosystem solutions are designed to manage applications and end-user data and settings to ensure that although the end user receives a newly created virtual desktop machine when they log in, as far as they are concerned, it looks and feels like it is the same virtual desktop each time. That means all their applications, files, settings, and any personalization are delivered at the same time.

This model is often referred to as the composite desktop model. The component parts of the desktop are abstracted from each other, so the OS, the apps, and the user data are treated and managed as separate entities. The following diagram illustrates the composite desktop model:

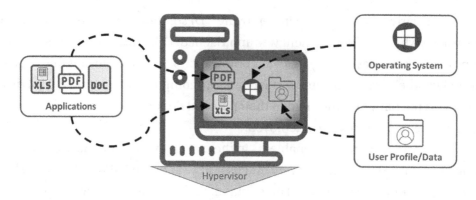

Figure 1-2. *The composite virtual desktop model*

Now that you understand the composite desktop model that is typically used for deploying non-persistent virtual desktop machines, we are going to discuss non-persistent and persistent desktop models in more detail, as deciding on which method you are going to use, or if you need to use both depending on your use cases, will have an impact on your overall design and architecture.

Non-persistent Virtual Desktop Machines

As the name suggests, a non-persistent virtual desktop machine is one that is not persistent. That means that it is effectively a disposable virtual desktop machine that is built and created on demand when an end user logs in and requests a virtual desktop machine to use and then deleted when they log out and have finished working.

Or it could be that when they log in to a virtual desktop machine, their apps and user settings are all applied for the duration of their session, and then when they log out, the virtual desktop machine is returned or reset back to where it was before the end user logged in. It is like performing a factory reset.

When the end user logs in, they could be connected to a completely different virtual desktop machine every time they connect. As they have just logged on to a brand-new vanilla virtual desktop machine, their applications, user data, and personal settings are all applied, as we described previously, using the composite desktop model.

A big advantage to building and deploying virtual desktop machines using the non-persistent model is that you do not necessarily need to build all the virtual desktop machines in advance and have them sitting there not being used, depleting valuable infrastructure resources. You only build what you need as the end users demand them.

This is referred to as concurrency, where you share resources intelligently, and hence there is a concurrent licensing model.

So how does this work? Take an example environment where you have 2000 end users in your organization. As the nature of your business is shift worker based, you will then only ever have a maximum of 1000 users logged in at the same time. Therefore, you would only create that pool of 1000 virtual desktop machines and effectively share them across your end-user estate.

Non-persistent enables this, as each end user will have their own desktop, built on demand for them as they connect. For IT, it means less infrastructure to purchase and manage.

Previously, there were several use cases that meant that a non-persistent model was not viable and the delivery of apps and data was clunky at best. However, with the advances in application layering solutions, such as VMware App Volumes or Liquidware FlexApp, and these technologies becoming a more mainstream technology, applications can be delivered to the end users seamlessly. The same is true when it comes to end-user personalization and end-user data, all of which can now be seamlessly integrated into the overall solution. We will cover these later in this book.

Persistent Virtual Desktop Machines

A persistent virtual desktop machine is the opposite of a non-persistent virtual desktop machine. Rather than an end user being allocated a random desktop or a new one that is built on demand, with the persistent model, the end user not only owns their own desktop, but they also use the same machine every time they connect and log in. The applications, end-user profile, and end-user data are all stored on the virtual desktop. Think of it in the same was as you would by having a PC on your desk. However, now, the PC has been virtualized and moved to a data center.

The use cases where an end user needs this kind of model are few and far between as we discussed in the previous section with the advances in solutions that deliver all aspects of the composite desktop model. However, there may be use cases where a specific piece of hardware is required by the virtual desktop machine, and therefore it makes sense to have a separate desktop pool designed specifically for this use case due to the configuration requirements. You could of course still deliver applications via layering and manage their end-user profile independently of the operating system.

Now that we have given you an overview of VDI, its use cases, advantages, and deployment models, in the next section we are going to look at an alternative way of delivering a desktop experience, but without the need to provide the end user with a full virtual desktop machine.

Server-Based Computing

The concept of VDI is not something new. Server-based computing, an early incarnation of VDI, has been around since the days of early mainframe solutions. If you look at what a mainframe is, it is a technology that centralizes the compute power in a data center, with end users connecting via a client device, typically a green screen terminal, with the applications running on the mainframe.

If you define server-based computing today, it is pretty much the same concept. Rather than mainframe computer resources, today you have x86-based servers, with multiple servers being referred to a server farm, running in a data center, enabling end users to connect with pretty much any endpoint device.

What do the end users connect to, and how is that different to VDI? As we have discussed previously, in a true VDI solution the end user had their own dedicated full version of the operating system as if they have their own desktop machine. With SBC, or Server Based Computing, they do not have their own copy of an OS. Neither do they have a full version of the OS. Instead, they get what is called a **session**.

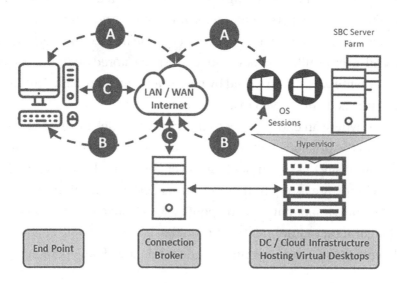

Figure 1-3. *Server-based computing*

In an SBC server environment, the operating system of the server itself can deliver multiple sessions of that operating system, enabling a multi-user environment. It is like the server carving out chunks of resources for end users to connect to and use. Each session of the server's operating system is unique. It is unique in that each unique user has their own dedicated session for the time that they are connected.

So, what we have discussed so far is the ability for end users to have an operating system experience delivered remotely, using the resources of server infrastructure to deliver that operating system, but what if they do not need an operating system and instead need access to one or two applications? The concept of SBC can also be applied to the delivery of applications in much the same way. This solution is called application publishing.

Application Publishing

Application publishing is server-based computing for applications. That means that rather than an end user having an operating system experience from where to launch their applications, the end user has access to *just* their applications and does not see the operating system. These applications are installed directly onto the server's operating systems running in the data center but delivered remotely as shown in the following diagram:

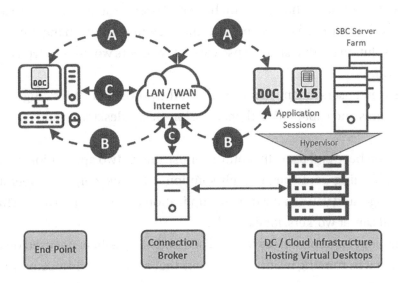

Figure 1-4. *Application publishing*

As you can see in the previous diagram, the applications are installed directly onto the server's own operating system. Unlike the applications on an individual end user's PC or virtual desktop machine, the applications on the server are installed using a multi-user mode to enable multiple users to access the applications at the same time with each end user having a unique application.

Applications are then delivered, or published, to the end user's endpoint device using a display protocol which is responsible for displaying the application session as well as sending the keyboard strokes and mouse movements back to the application session. All the end user will see is the icon to launch the app and then the app running as if it were running locally on their endpoint device.

So, the question is, which technology solution should I use? VDI or SBC?

VDI or SBC?

Now that we have covered the different technology solutions for delivering the end-user experience, the question is which one should you deploy in your organization?

Not wanting to give the standard presales answer of "it depends," the answer comes down to the use cases that you are looking to address as to which you would deploy. In fact, it is highly likely that you could deploy more than one technology, knowing that they are all managed using the same infrastructure and management consoles.

To answer the question though, if you have end users that need access to a full operating system experience where they can make configuration changes etc., then VDI would be the solution for that specific use case. Developers would be a typical user base for this solution.

If you have end users that need only some of the power of an operating system but not all the features and capabilities, then a session-based desktop would be the solution of choice.

Finally, if you have end users that only ever use one or two applications, then application publishing would be the likely solution. It means there is no operating system to manage, and you can ensure the application is always up to date. This would be ideal for call center workers, for example.

The technology solutions we have just discussed have all been focused on running on-premises, that is, running inside data centers that are physically located within your office environment. That means you would have to also manage and maintain a level of hardware and operating systems. If you wanted to negate this, then all the solutions we have discussed so far can also be delivered and consumed from the cloud.

Cloud-Based Desktops

The easiest way to describe cloud-based desktops, often referred to as Desktop as a Service (DaaS), is that your organization consumes virtual desktops and applications using a third-party infrastructure. This is illustrated in the following diagram:

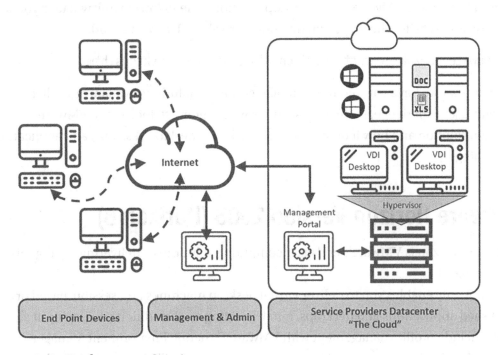

Figure 1-5. *Desktop as a Service*

One of the key advantages to this model of deploying virtual desktops and applications is that you do not need to deploy any on-premises infrastructure. All hardware is owned by the service provider which also means you do not need to worry about maintenance and support. This will be included in your payments.

About payments, using the "as a service" model means that you pay for services on a subscription-based model, or pay as you go. You only pay for the resources that you consume.

This could mean that for a basic virtual desktop machine, you could pay $50 per user per month, for example. For a higher-spec virtual desktop machine, maybe the cost could be $75 per user per month.

End users can be simply allocated resources by the IT admins via the service provider's management portal. It is a simple case of logging on and creating resource. This platform will also show current resource usage and more importantly the billing so you can monitor costs.

Most service providers will also provide session-based desktops and published applications as well as full virtual desktop infrastructure.

This book focuses on building on-premises infrastructure; however, for more information on the VMware cloud desktop solutions, the following link will take you to the VMware website where you can find out more about Horizon Cloud:

`www.vmware.com/uk/products/horizon-cloud-virtual-desktops.html`

Now that we have covered the general technology solutions available to deliver the end-user experience, in the next sections we are going to look at the VMware Horizon solution and how it delivers virtual desktops, desktop sessions, and application publishing.

VMware Horizon Version 2006 (Horizon 8)

VMware Horizon is VMware's end-user computing solution for delivering the digital workspace.

It not only enables you to deliver virtual desktop machines and session-based or published applications and desktops, but depending on the edition you deploy, it also could include profile management with VMware Dynamic Environment Manager and application layering with VMware App Volumes. We will give you an introductory overview of these other technologies later in this book; however, we will focus on the core application and virtual desktop delivery elements.

What Is New?

VMware Horizon Version 2103 (or Horizon 8.2) was released on March 23, 2021. As you will see from the version naming convention, this is the first version of Horizon to use the new year and month of release as the version numbers.

In this version, 2103, the 2103 part of the version number relates to 2021 (the year of release) and 03, the month of release, so, in this example, March 2021. However, you will also notice that the component parts, such as the connection server installer etc., will have the 8.2.0 version number as part of the filename.

Horizon 2103 (8.2) includes some brand-new features, which at the core bring the on-premises and cloud solutions closer together in the form of easy-to-manage and easy-to-deploy hybrid solutions. The highlights of this latest release are listed here:

- Support for the latest hybrid and multi-cloud architectures such as AWS and Microsoft Azure.

- Intelligent image and application management across all environments using the Horizon Control Plane.

- Introduction of a Universal Broker enabling global entitlements regardless of where the resource exists. This enables intelligent provisioning of end users to virtual desktops or applications hosted in any cloud environment.

- Real-time performance monitoring and security.

- Updated Instant Clone features such as smart provisioning.

- Blast Extreme Protocol improvements including 3D graphics workloads using the new HEVC H.265 codecs with GPU support for both 4K and 8K monitors.

- Improved unified communications with optimization packs for Zoom, WebEx, and Microsoft Teams.

- High-end graphics support from NVIDIA and AMD.

In the next section, we are going to look at the different editions of VMware Horizon as well as the licensing options.

Horizon Licensing and Editions

VMware Horizon is available to purchase in three different licensing models:

- **Subscription**: A subscription license is paid for on either a monthly or annual basis, allowing users to pay a per-user fee. Customers typically pay an initial subscription up front and are then entitled to use the software only during the subscription period for which they have paid, whereas with a perpetual license, the end user can use the software indefinitely.

- **Term**: A term license is the right to run the software for a fixed term, typically for one or two years. Each year you pay the annual fee again, but continue to receive updates and support.

- **Perpetual**: A perpetual license is paid for up front, and you own the license forever. A perpetual license will typically include 12-month support and maintenance, and then you have the option to purchase additional support for any subsequent years at a percentage of the original cost of the perpetual license.

In the next sections, we are going to look at the different features that are available with each license model, starting with perpetual licenses.

Perpetual Licensing Options

With the perpetual licensing option, Horizon is available in five different editions:

- Horizon Standard Edition

- Horizon Advanced Edition

- Horizon Enterprise Edition

- Horizon Apps Standard Edition

- Horizon Apps Advanced Edition

The following table highlights the key features available with each edition of Horizon:

	Horizon for Linux	Horizon Standard	Horizon Advanced	Horizon Enterprise	Horizon Apps Standard	Horizon Apps Advanced
Core Horizon Features						
Windows Virtual Desktops		✓	✓	✓		
Linux Virtual Desktops	✓			✓		
Non-Persistent Instant Clone Virtual Desktops	✓	✓	✓	✓		✓
Persistent Full Clone Virtual Desktops	✓	✓	✓	✓	✓	✓
Cloud Pod Architecture with Global entitlement	✓	✓	✓	✓	✓	✓
Help Desk Tool	✓	✓	✓	✓	✓	✓
Support for Blast Extreme, PCoIP, and RDP protocols	✓	✓	✓	✓	✓	✓
Session Collaboration				✓		
Optimized experience for Microsoft Teams			✓	✓		✓

Figure 1-6. *VMware Horizon perpetual licensing model*

With the perpetual licensing model, you also have access, included as part of the license, to other VMware products to enable you to build a complete digital workspace. These are highlighted in the following table that shows the feature/product and which edition of Horizon it is included with.

	Horizon for Linux	Horizon Standard	Horizon Advanced	Horizon Enterprise	Horizon Apps Standard	Horizon Apps Advanced
Horizon Complimentary Product Solutions						
VMware App Volumes - real-time app delivery/layering				✓		✓
VMware ThinApp - App virtualization/isolation		✓	✓	✓	✓	✓
VMware Dynamic Environment Manager - user profiles				✓	✓	✓
VMware Workspace ONE - unified workspace			✓	✓	✓	✓
VMware Unified Access Gateway	✓	✓	✓	✓	✓	✓
Vmware vSphere & vCenter for Desktops	✓	✓	✓	✓	✓	✓

Figure 1-7. *Perpetual licensing model included products*

In the next section, we are going to look at the Horizon subscription licensing options.

Subscription Licensing Options

With the VMware Horizon subscription licensing model, organizations can take advantage of a single and flexible entitlement to all the available Horizon technology solutions and deployment options.

This licensing model offers the following licensed options:

- **Horizon Universal**: Virtual desktop and application delivery designed for on-premises or cloud deployments

- **Horizon Apps Universal**: Application delivery designed for either on-premises or cloud deployments

- **Horizon Subscription**: Virtual desktop and application delivery exclusively for cloud deployments

- **Horizon Apps Subscription**: Application delivery exclusively for cloud deployments

- **Horizon Enterprise Edition Term License**: Allows you to run the Horizon Enterprise Edition and the feature contained within that version for either three-month or one-year terms

It is also worth noting that these license options are also available for either named users or concurrent users as described in the following:

- **Named user license**: This is an exclusive license that is assigned to a single named user of the software. The user will be named in the license agreement. In this model, you would need to purchase a license for every end user that would be using the software.

- **Concurrent user license**: This license model refers to the total number of people that are simultaneously, or concurrently, using the software. Ideal for organizations that have shift workers, for example, where you may have 100 end users but only 50 will be using the software at any one time. In this example, you would purchase 50 concurrent user licenses rather than purchasing 100 named user licenses.

The following table lists the Horizon subscription and term license options and the different features that are available in each of these editions:

Type of License	Horizon Universal	Horizon Apps Universal	Horizon Subscription	Horizon Apps	Horizon Enterprise
	Subscription	Subscription	Subscription	Subscription	*Term
Cloud & multi-cloud deployment	✓	✓	✓	✓	
On-premises deployment	✓	✓	✓	✓	✓
VMware vSphere & vCenter	On-Premises	On-Premises			On-Premises
Windows & Linux virtual desktops with instant/full clones	✓		✓		✓
RDSH published apps & desktops with instant/full clones	✓	✓	✓	✓	✓
Linux hosted apps	✓	✓	✓	✓	✓
Microsoft WVD	✓	✓	✓	✓	
VM hosted apps with Windows 10	✓	✓	✓	✓	✓
Remote access to physical Windows 10 PCs	✓	✓	✓	✓	✓
Support for non-vSphere based VDI & RDSH	✓	✓	✓	✓	✓
VMware-managed, multi-tenant DaaS deployment option	✓	✓	✓	✓	
Horizon Control Plane services including Universal Broker	✓	✓	✓	✓	
Rest API	✓	✓	✓	✓	✓
VMware Helpdesk Tool	✓	✓	✓	✓	✓
VMware App Volumes - real-time app delivery/layering	✓	✓	✓	✓	✓
VMware ThinApp - App virtualization/isolation	✓	✓	✓	✓	✓
VMware Workspace ONE - unified workspace	✓	✓	✓	✓	✓
VMware Unified Access Gateway	✓	✓	✓	✓	✓
Unified catalog of published/packaged apps, VDI, SaaS, and web apps with SSO	✓	✓	✓	✓	
Blast Extreme, PCoIP, RDP protocol	✓	✓	✓	✓	✓
Optimized video and audio experience for Teams, Zoom, WebEx	✓	✓	✓	✓	✓

Figure 1-8. *Subscription licensing model features*

Summary

In this chapter, we have given you a comprehensive introduction to delivering the end-user experience. That could be with a virtual desktop machine or a published desktop session or application. We discussed the use cases of which solution would be the best for each individual use case.

Next, we focused on virtual desktop infrastructure, its architecture, and how it works along with the deployment methods of on-premises, cloud-hosted, or a hybrid approach of the two. We completed the chapter by introducing you to the VMware solution for delivering the digital workspace: VMware Horizon. With the introduction of VMware Horizon, we looked at what is new in this latest version and the various licenses, editions, and features.

In the next chapter, we are going to build on this introduction to VMware Horizon and take a closer look at the architecture and components that make up the entire solution stack and what role they perform.

CHAPTER 2

Getting Started with VMware Horizon

In the first chapter, we took you through an overview of the different technology solutions available today that deliver the end-user experience, from virtual desktops, published desktops, to application delivery solutions.

As part of the introductory overview, we started to discuss VMware Horizon in greater detail by covering some of the various components that make up the complete Horizon environment. In this chapter, we will pick up from where we left off with that chapter and start to take a deeper look into each of these components by looking at the role they perform and how they work.

We are going to focus on the following Horizon components:

- Horizon Connection Server

- Horizon Replica Server

- Horizon Enrollment Server

- VMware Unified Access Gateway

- Horizon Agent

- Horizon Client

As part of this chapter, we will also look at how Horizon delivers the best possible end-user experience by using display protocols that are not only designed to provide the best visual experience possible but also allow end users to continue using external peripherals with their remote desktops and applications.

Finally, we will look at how to build virtual desktop machines using VMware vSphere solutions and cloning technologies.

© Peter von Oven 2022
P. von Oven, *Mastering VMware Horizon 8*, https://doi.org/10.1007/978-1-4842-7261-9_2

Horizon Digital Workspace

Let us start at the highest level and look at how the core Horizon components and additional end user–focused solutions all come together to deliver the digital workspace.

When we talk about the digital workspace and what that means, we are not talking about a single point solution. By that I mean we are not focusing on just VDI. We are talking about delivering applications and data to end users to enable productivity wherever they are physically located, whenever they need to use it, and on whatever device they choose to use. Horizon is an enabler for delivering that end-user experience.

The following diagram is a high-level view of the different components of the VMware Horizon solution:

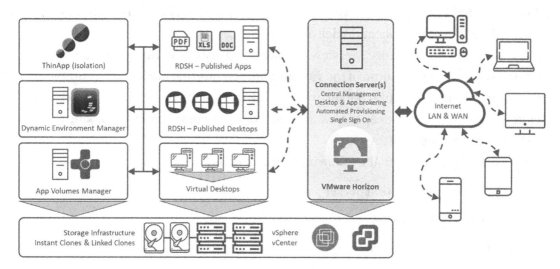

Figure 2-1. *VMware Horizon high-level solution overview*

The availability of the different components described in the preceding high-level overview is dependent on the edition and version of Horizon that you deploy save for the Horizon Connection Server which is the central point of management included in every version and edition.

For this book, we are going to focus on the Enterprise Edition so that we can include all the components and features, and we will start with concentrating on delivering virtual desktops in the first instance.

Horizon VDI Architecture

In this section, we are going to look at how VMware Horizon delivers virtual desktop machines to end users and the architecture behind how that delivery works.

The Horizon solution centers around a key component: the Horizon Connection Server. The Connection Server is the central point for all management tasks as well as the first point of contact for the end user when they connect to their available resources. It is the orchestrator that brings together all the component parts to deliver the end-user experience – from orchestrating the vSphere infrastructure to create virtual desktops to communicating with Active Directory to ensure that the end users are only presented what they are entitled to.

In fact, the Connection Server performs several different roles; we will cover each one of those roles in depth throughout this chapter.

The following diagram illustrates the Horizon architecture, centered around the Connection Server:

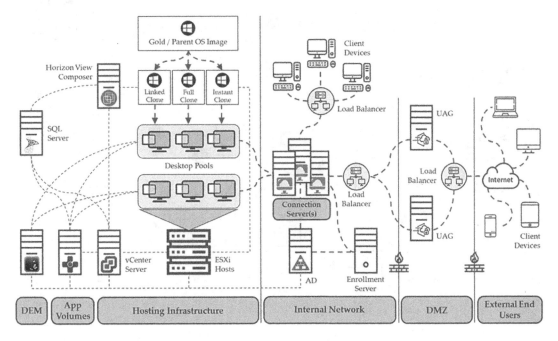

Figure 2-2. *VMware Horizon VDI architecture diagram*

The core component in Horizon is the Connection Server and the different roles that it performs. The Connection Server itself is an application that is installed on a Windows Server operating system. In the upcoming sections, we are going to look at each of those roles in more detail, starting with the core Connection Server role.

Horizon Connection Server

The Horizon Connection Server performs the role of the connection broker and has previously been referred to as the Horizon View Manager.

The primary role of the Horizon Connection Server is to connect end users to their virtual desktop machines, published desktops, and published applications. The Connection Server is the first part of the solution that the end users interact with by connecting to it and then being asked to provide their credentials so that they can be authenticated with Active Directory.

Once authenticated, the end user is presented with a list of the resources to which they are entitled. From here, they simply click and launch the resource they want to use, either a VDI desktop, a published desktop, or an application. The Connection Server initiates that connection and then delivers the resource to the end user's device. The following diagram illustrates the process in more detail:

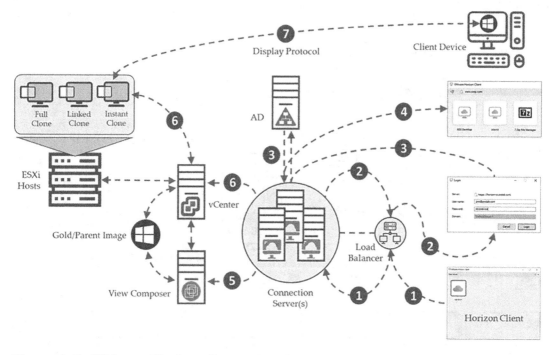

Figure 2-3. *VMware Horizon Connection Server*

Let us put some more detailed explanations or "animation" together around what is happening in the diagram.

The first step is for the end user to launch the Horizon Client on their chosen end point device. This could also be initiated from a supported browser. With the Horizon Client running, the end user would enter the details of the Connection Server they want to connect to. The details of the Connection Server may have already been configured, and so the end user would double-click the server's name to initiate the connection. This is shown as step **(1)** in the preceding diagram.

Once a connection has been established to the Connection Server, it will respond to the end user with a login box allowing them to enter their credentials. In this case, their credentials would be their login details for Active Directory. The same as they would use to log in to any other domain-joined desktop. This is shown as step **(2)** in the diagram.

The end user now enters their credentials, that is, their username, password, and the domain name that they are logging in to.

The list of available domains is no longer sent to the client by default; however, you can enable this in the Horizon Console should you want to. Alternatively, end users can use their userPrincipalName (UPN), which is essentially the user's name, to log in with.

The credentials are now passed back via the Connection Server for authentication with Active Directory, shown as step **(3)** in the diagram. Once the end user has been successfully authenticated, the Connection Server then updates the Horizon Client by showing a list of the available resources **(4)** the end user has access to. These resources are based on the end user's entitlements, and so they will only be able to access what they have been granted access to.

Now the end user can launch the resource they require. In this example, that resource is a virtual desktop machine, so they simply double-click the icon of the virtual desktop machine they want to use. So, what happens next?

Depending on how you have configured the Horizon infrastructure, the next step, now that an end user has requested a virtual desktop machine, is that they will be connected to an existing virtual desktop machine, or a virtual desktop machine will be created on demand. This could be done by the Connection Server making a call to vCenter to create an Instant Clone or to View Composer to create a Linked Clone virtual desktop machine. A third option would be to connect to a Full Clone that is already available.

In this example, we have shown the virtual desktop being created by either using Instant Clones **(5)** or via View Composer creating a Linked Clone **(6)**.

With the virtual desktop machine created and available for use, it can now be delivered to the end user and displayed in the Horizon Client or the browser **(7)**. Delivery is done using the display protocol, either Blast Extreme, PCoIP, or RDP which we will come on to later.

As part of the delivery and creation of the virtual desktop machine, the end-user profile could be delivered using VMware DEM, along with applications being delivered using VMware App Volumes. We will cover this in more detail later in the book. But for now, we will just look at how the core solution components work.

Next, we are going to look at the Horizon Replica Server role.

Horizon Replica Server

The Horizon Replica Server is another copy or replica of the original or first Horizon Connection Server that you installed in your environment and performs two key roles in addition to the normal Connection Server.

The first of these additional roles is to enable high availability or business continuity for the existing Connection Server. As the Replica Server is an exact copy of the first Connection Server, should that Connection Server fail or be unavailable, then end users will not be able to connect to their resources. However, having a Replica Server in your environment means that it would take over from the failed Connection Server and allow end users to continue to connect.

The second role that the Replica Server plays is in scalability. Each Connection Server can support a certain number of connections. In Horizon 2006, the recommended number of active sessions is 2000 with a maximum limit of 4000 sessions.

You can have a maximum of seven Connection/Replica Servers configured together in what is called a Pod, with a Pod supporting a recommended maximum of 10,000 sessions. We will talk more about Pod configurations and how to size them correctly and look at how to size for high availability in the next chapter.

How Does It Work?

In the previous section, we discussed what the Replica Server is, so let us now look at how it works.

The Replica Server is a copy of the first Connection Server that you installed in your environment, but does that mean it is just a copy of the Connection Server application or is there more to it than that? The answer is yes, there is a little more to it than it being just another instance of the Connection Server software. For a start, it must be a unique instance and so cannot be installed on the same server that is running as the first Connection Server in your environment.

When you install the Replica Server, although, as you will see when we come to the installation chapter, Chapter 4 you launch the same installer, you must select the Replica Server option from the drop-down list. This is so you install the replication components and hence why it is called a Replica Server.

As part of the original installation of the Connection Server, you also installed an Active Directory Application Mode (ADAM) database. This database was created to store the configuration information from the Connection Server – information such as end-user entitlement, desktop pool configuration, virtual desktop machines, and other Horizon-related information. When creating a Replica Server or second instance of a Connection Server, this information needs to be replicated to any subsequent servers that would perform the role of a Connection Server. This is so the information is present on all the servers should one of them fail.

The database is the replicated component and is copied to the Replica Server using the Lightweight Directory Access Protocol (LDAP) protocol like how Active Directory replicates information across Domain Controllers.

Once replication has completed, all Replica Servers will hold the same information as the original Connection Server. Should a server fail, an end user can connect to another server and still be able to connect to their resources. This is also why a load balancer is important in this configuration. Horizon by default does not load balance across Connection Servers, so when deploying multiple Connection/Replica Servers, you need to factor in a load balancer as part of your design.

In terms of how it works when an end user logs in, the Replica Server works in the same way as we have described in the previous section.

Next, we are going to look at the security side of Horizon, starting with the final role performed by the Connection Server, the Enrollment Server.

Horizon Enrollment Server

The Horizon Enrollment Server is the final role that is part of the Connection Server installation and is the newest part of the core Horizon components.

It provides the Horizon elements of a wider solution that allows end users to log in via Workspace ONE, and then when they need to connect to a virtual desktop or application being delivered by Horizon, there is no need to log in again. This feature in Horizon is called True SSO (Single Sign-On).

The Horizon True SSO feature allows end users to authenticate using their standard domain credentials, but without having to type them in again as they have already done this when logging in to Workspace ONE. They could also log in using a smart card or token without the need to physically type anything in at all. Before True SSO, if the end user launched a virtual desktop or application delivered by Horizon, then they would have to enter their credentials all over again. It sits between the Connection Server and the Microsoft CA, and its job is to request temporary certificates from the certificate store. The process is illustrated in the following diagram:

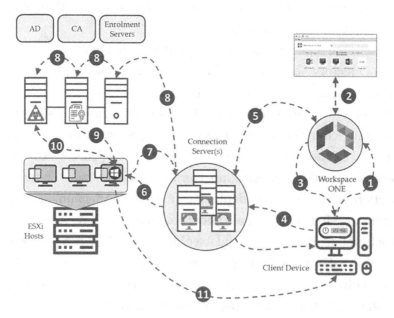

Figure 2-4. *VMware Horizon Enrollment Server*

Let us put some more detailed explanations or "animation" together around what is happening in the diagram:

1. The first thing that happens is that the end user logs in to Workspace ONE. They could do this by typing in their domain credentials, or they could use some form of two-factor solution such as token-based solution or a smart card.

2. From the list of available resources, the end user double-clicks and launches a virtual desktop machine from the list of their entitlements.

3. A SAML (Security Assertion Markup Language) token is generated and then sent to the end user.

4. The SAML token is then passed on to the Connection Server.

5. In step 5, the SAML token is verified with Workspace ONE, and then, once verified, an assertion is sent back to the Connection Server.

6. At this point, a virtual desktop machine is allocated to the end user.

7. The Horizon Agent running on the virtual desktop machine that has been allocated to the end user sends a request to the Connection Server for a certificate.

8. The Connection Server, in turn, forwards the certificate request to the Horizon Enrollment Server and then onto the Certificate Authority (CA).

9. The CA generates a short-lived certificate that is then sent to the virtual desktop machine.

10. Using the short-lived certificate, the end user is logged on to the virtual desktop machine.

11. Now that the end user is logged on to the virtual desktop machine, it can now be personalized, applications added, and then delivered to the end user via the display protocol.

In the next section, we are going to look at the VMware Unified Access Gateway to enable external users to connect from the Internet.

VMware Unified Access Gateway (UAG)

The Unified Access Gateway (UAG) is a platform that delivers secure edge services and end-user access to resources on the internal network. It allows authenticated end users to have access to their resources, such as virtual desktop machines and applications, that are running on servers within the local network.

In previous versions of Horizon, this role was one that was performed by the Connection Server and was called the Security Server. However, in the last versions of Horizon, the Security Server role no longer exists and has been replaced by the Unified Access Gateway.

Unlike the Security Server it replaced, the UAG is a hardened, locked-down, preconfigured Linux-based virtual appliance rather than being installed on a Windows server as a Windows application.

This means that it is much simpler to deploy, with very little ongoing management required. It also removed the need to pair with a Connection Server, which was how the Security Server was configured. Removing this requirement means that you can scale UAG appliances quickly and easily.

The following diagram shows the UAG architecture:

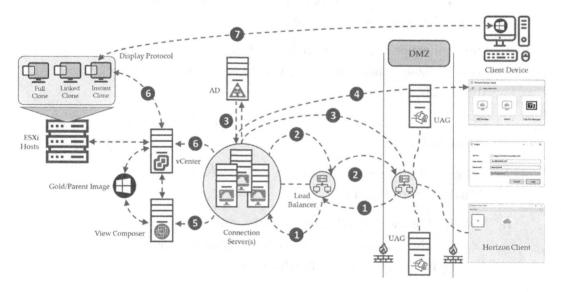

Figure 2-5. *VMware Horizon Unified Access Gateway*

As you can see in the diagram, the UAG simply passes the end-user login through to the Horizon Connection Servers. It can also be configured to perform the authentication.

Now that we have discussed the infrastructure side of Horizon, in the next section we are going to focus on the Horizon components for the virtual desktop machines in the form of the Horizon Agent.

Horizon Agent

The Horizon Agent is installed on the virtual desktop machine or application delivery server in an RDSH Server farm. It can also be installed on physical PCs to allow them to be managed by Horizon.

The role of the Horizon Agent is to communicate with the Connection Server, allowing the machine on which it is installed to be allocated as a resource to the end users.

You have several options during the installation and configuration of the Horizon Agent which we will cover in more detail in the installation chapter.

Direct Connection

Throughout this book, we have focused on virtual desktops being delivered by the Horizon Connection Server; however, there are some use cases where you have a large number of remote sites, like a retailer with hundreds of shops and warehouses.

Deploying a Horizon Connection Server in every store is probably not the best or most economical solution. Also, from a management perspective, it would not make sense to deploy it in that way. Of course, you would have a centralized data center hosting your desktop infrastructure that all the end users connected back to, but what if that connection failed? In a retail environment, that could affect sales.

There is a solution with Horizon that can solve this issue, and that is using the Horizon Agent Direct Connection. This specific version of the Horizon Agent allows the virtual desktop machines to be connected to without the need of a Connection Server.

It enables the Horizon Client to connect directly to virtual desktop machines or applications without the need of the Connection Server. Going back to the retail example previously highlighted, there could be several local virtual desktop machines that could be available in the event of a connection failure that could be used. End users would simply connect directly to the virtual desktop machine or application.

The final piece of the solution is the client.

Horizon Client

The Horizon Client is the part of the solution that the end users interact with. It is where the display protocol delivers the screenshots of the virtual desktop machines and applications to, and it is responsible for communicating back with keyboard strokes and mouse movements.

There are several different Horizon Clients available for the various device platforms. We will cover the client side options in Chapter 13.

Building Non-persistent Virtual Desktop Machines

In Chapter 1, we introduced you to the idea of building non-persistent virtual desktop machines. As a quick reminder, a non-persistent virtual desktop machine is effectively a disposable virtual desktop machine and is created on demand and then configured and personalized to the end user as they log in. When they log out, the virtual desktop machine is then deleted.

In this section, we are going to discuss how to build virtual desktop machines for the non-persistent use case. It is worth noting that we are now talking about how the virtual desktop machines are built using cloning technologies built into the Horizon solution rather than talking about how the end users are assigned to a virtual desktop machine. For example, you could still have a Full Clone desktop that has a non-persistent assignment.

So how do you configure Horizon to deliver non-persistent virtual desktop machines? The core solution for delivering non-persistent virtual desktop machines is by using Instant Clones. You can still use the Linked Clone feature with Horizon View Composer, but it would be a recommendation to use Instant Clones for any new deployments.

Instant Clones

Rather than being a specific Horizon feature, Instant Clones are a feature that is built into the vSphere platform, with availability from the vSphere 6.0 U1 release.

Instant Clones use a technology called VMware VM Fork to very quickly provision already powered on virtual desktop machines. The Instant Clone is created from a parent virtual desktop machine, an image which is your gold master image.

So how does it work? As we already discussed, the cloning process creates an already powered on parent VM from the replica VM. When the Instant Clone is created, it shares its memory with the running parent VM from which it was created. Instant Clones use a copy-on-write method for memory and disk management.

When an Instant Clone is created from a running parent virtual desktop machine, any reads of unchanged information come from the already existing running parent virtual desktop machine, but any changes made to the Instant Clone get written to a delta disk, and not back to the running parent.

This enables security and isolation between the Instant Clone virtual desktop machines by ensuring that each Instant Clone can be used immediately. Any changes that are made do not affect the shared data and memory of the running parent virtual desktop machine from which all other Instant Clones are based.

Sharing the memory of a running parent virtual desktop machine at the time it was created means that they are created immediately and already in a powered on state rather than having to wait for it to power on and boot.

Once the Instant Clone has been created, it is linked to the replica virtual desktop machine and not to the running parent virtual desktop machine. That means that you can delete the running parent virtual desktop machine without affecting the Instant Clone.

The speed in which Instant Clone virtual desktop machines can be created and delivered to end users allows for the non-persistent desktop model to be achievable without affecting end-user productivity as virtual desktop machines are spun up very quickly.

Depending on the number of spare virtual desktop machines you configure, a brand-new Instant Clone virtual desktop machine may be created immediately after a used machine is deleted. This enables end users to receive a newly created desktop every time they log in.

This approach also means that the end users will receive any updates much quicker than they would normally. If you update the master image, that is, the master virtual desktop machine snapshot that you used to create the desktop pool from, then when the end user next logs in, they receive the new image.

For read operations, the Instant Clone virtual desktop machine shares its memory and its disk with the parent virtual desktop machine and is created immediately and in an already powered on state.

As well as sharing the memory and disk with the parent virtual desktop machine, the Instant Clone also has its own unique memory and the delta disk for saving any changes.

The following diagram shows a high-level overview of the Instant Clone architecture with the replica being stored on its own datastore:

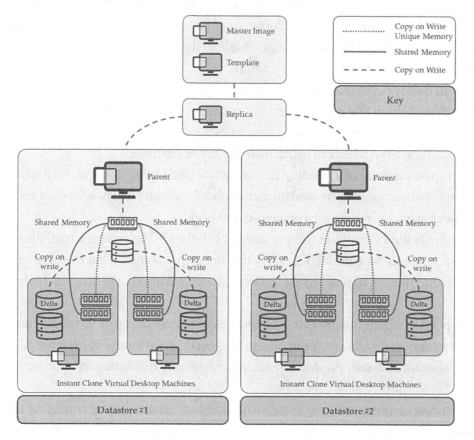

Figure 2-6. *Instant Clone architecture*

In the previous diagram, the Replica was stored on its own datastore using the tiered storage approach with the Replica datastore typically running faster SSD type storage devices. The following is an example with the Replica on the same datastore as the parent and the virtual desktop machines:

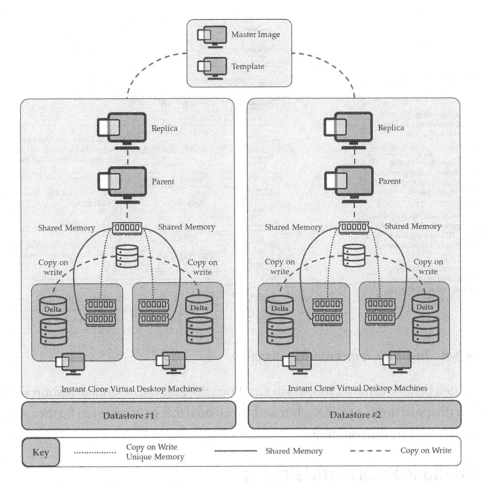

Figure 2-7. *Instant Clone architecture*

In the diagrams shown previously, we have highlighted several different steps or stages during the build process of a virtual desktop machine built using Instant Clone.

Let us look at that process in a bit more detail and describe those steps in a bit more detail and exactly what gets created and why. The following diagram shows each of the steps:

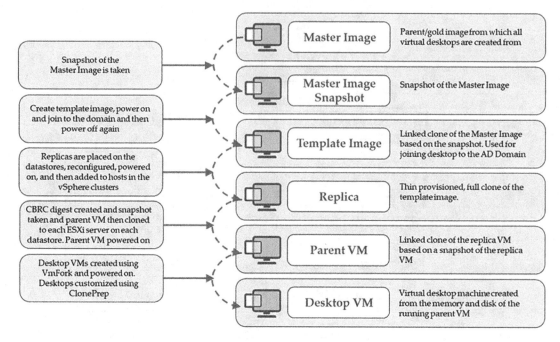

Figure 2-8. *Instant Clone creation process*

The idea behind Instant Clones is to cut down the amount of storage resources and speed up the provisioning process, but with Horizon 8 this goes one step further with Instant Clone Smart Provisioning.

Instant Clone Smart Provisioning

Instant Clone Smart Provisioning allows Horizon to choose the best and most appropriate method for deploying Instant Clones depending on your environment.

If you need fast provisioning of virtual desktop machines, then Horizon will deploy Instant Clones using a parent virtual desktop machine configured on each of the hosts that host the virtual desktop machines. This is the model we discussed in the previous section. However, if you do not need the speed and want to save on resources, then Horizon can create Instant Clone virtual desktop machines without the parent. One point to note is that this method will be slower than having the parent in place.

Smart provisioning is enabled by default with Horizon choosing the best method of deployment based on the following:

- Instant Clone created *with* a parent for

  - High density of virtual desktop machines per cluster

  - vGPU

  - vTPM

  - Linux virtual desktop machines

- Instant Clone created *without* a parent for

  - Low density of virtual desktop machines per cluster (when the number reaches 12 virtual desktops, then a parent will be created)

  - Horizon on AVS (Azure VMware Solution)

  - Mixed vCenter/vSphere versions

You can, if you need to, override the default behavior of the smart provisioning by editing the ADAM database on the connection server. There you will see the **pae-ProvisionScheme** attribute which will be currently configured as **<not set>** which is the default setting of having smart provisioning enabled. You can then change that setting by changing it to one of the following:

- **ModeA**: Standard Instant Clones where smart provisioning is disabled, and Instant Clones are built as they would normally be built.

- **ModeB**: Instant Clones are built with no parent virtual desktops.

We will look at editing the ADAM database in more detail in Chapter 16.

If you now look at the architecture where Instant Clones are built without a parent virtual machine, then this will look like the following diagram:

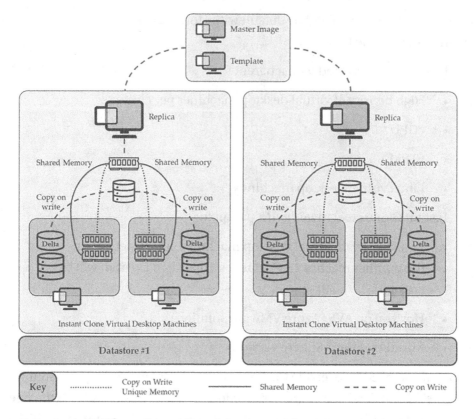

Figure 2-9. *Instant Clone Smart Provisioning without a parent*

Having now described the features and functionality of Instant Clones and how the technology works, in the next section we are going to discuss Linked Clones.

View Composer and Linked Clones

Building Linked Clone virtual desktop machines was the first solution available for building virtual desktop machines on demand. Although this particular part of the Horizon solution is still available in the Horizon 2006 edition, it is no longer available in Horizon 2012, and it is recommended for new deployments that Instant Clones are used. If you are already running Linked Clones, then you should consider migrating to Instant Clones.

So how do Linked Clones work? Like Instant Clones, Linked Clones rely on snapshot technology built into the vSphere platform.

With Linked Clones, a delta disk is created which is used by the newly created virtual desktop machine to store differences in data between its own OS and the OS of the original master image. Having this delta disk means that the Linked Clone virtual desktop machine is not a full copy of its parent. This is how the name Linked Clone was derived since the Linked Clone will always have that link to its parent to function and will continue reading from the replica disk, the replica being a copy of the snapshot taken on the original master image.

Although, as we just discussed, the Linked Clone uses a delta disk to store its differences, as it continues to read from the replica there is the potential that the Linked Clone virtual desktop machine could grow to the same size as the replica. To manage this, you can set limits on the size of the disk along with carrying out some of the Linked Clone maintenance, such as refreshing the Linked Clones which is like resetting them back to where they started where the delta disk was very small in size.

Therefore, Linked Clones, when managed correctly, are very efficient when it comes to disk space requirements.

Although the core technology driving Linked Clones is based on taking snapshots using the vSphere platform, as we are now talking about virtual desktop machines which have a different workload profile in that they are built and destroyed more often and managed differently, an additional component is required to take care of this. That component is called View Composer.

View Composer enables you to have more than one active snapshot linked to the master image giving the ability to create multiple virtual desktop machine images using that single master image.

Given that the Linked Clone virtual desktop machines that get created are going to use this single master image or the replica, then this will require a storage system that can deliver a high level of IOPS (Input/Output Operations Per Second) on the datastore where the replica lives. We will look at the storage considerations more closely in the design chapter, Chapter 3, as one of the things to think about is where to place replica disks or whether you should look at accelerated storage platforms. Regardless, the replica should be stored on a high-performing storage solution.

Horizon does employ some of its own technology to assist with the storage demands. This is called Content-Based Read Cache (CBRC). If you enable CBRC (which, by the way, is used by default with Instant Clones), you can allocate 2 GB of memory from the ESXi server hosting the virtual desktop machines to act as a cache for caching the most commonly read blocks. As we are building multiple virtual desktop machines all from the same image, then typically it is going to be the same blocks that are going to be needed. These blocks, now hosted in memory, can be accessed much faster and therefore speed up the Linked Clone build process.

Now we have described what a Linked Clone is, we can now look at how the build process works.

The starting point, as with any other rollout of a virtual or physical desktop solution for that matter, is to build the master image – the image that will be used to create all your virtual desktop machines from. A master image should be built using the operating system and configuration settings, any core applications, and, more importantly, the Horizon Agent so that the image can be managed by the Connection Server. Do not forget that the image can be made much smaller by delivering apps and end-user data using App Volumes and DEM, respectively. We will detail the master image build later in this book.

With the master image built and configured, it can then be used to start creating your virtual desktop machine pools as shown in the following diagram:

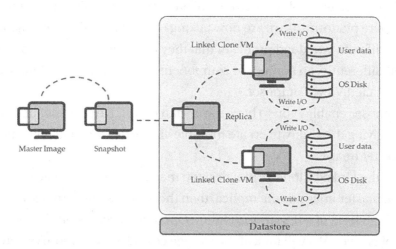

Figure 2-10. *Linked Clone creation process*

From the master image, you then take a snapshot. Then, when you create and configure your desktop pools in the Horizon Console on the Connection Server, you select this snapshot.

Once you have created the configuration of the desktop pool, the pool will be created, the replica will be created in read-only mode on the selected datastore, and then the number of virtual desktop machines will be created from the replica. End users can now log in and start using the newly created virtual desktop machines.

The Anatomy of a Linked Clone

Now that you have created your master image, created and configured desktop pools to use this new image, and the replica disk has been created, what else happens behind the scenes?

For a start, it is not just the replica disk that gets created. View Composer creates several other disks:

- Linked Clone disk

- Persistent disk or user data disk

- Disposable disk

- Internal disk

We will discuss what each of these disks is used for in the following sections.

Linked Clone Disk (Delta Disk)

As you would expect from the name, the core disk that gets created is the Linked Clone disk, but what does it contain?

The Linked Clone disk is an empty disk that is attached to the virtual desktop machine that the end user is logging in to, as the machine powers on and boots up. At first, this disk starts off small in size, but over time it will grow as more and more delta changes between the Linked Clone and the replica need to be stored.

As a maximum, the Linked Clone disk will only ever grow to the size of its parent virtual desktop machine or C: drive, as by that point there will be no more changes as they are effectively copies of each other. Typically, though, you should expect the Linked Clone to only increase by a few hundred MBs in size.

The replica disk that gets created from the snapshot of the master image is set as read-only and is used as the primary disk, so any disk writes that are requested by the virtual desktop machine are automatically written/read directly from the Linked Clone.

When it comes to designing your solution using Linked Clones, it is a recommended best practice to allocate tier 1 storage for storing the replica. The reason is due to the performance that is required. With all the virtual desktop machines being hosted within the same cluster, they will be continually referencing a single read-only VMDK virtual disk file. Low-performing storage would possibly create a bottleneck that would result in a delay for the end user accessing their virtual desktop machines.

Persistent Disk or User Data Disk

The next disk that gets created is the persistent disk. The persistent disk is used to store end-user data and settings and no operating system components. As this disk is persistent, it will not be deleted should you choose to perform something like a recompose or refresh operation which would wipe the Linked Close disk and would delete end-user data if they were stored on that disk.

The persistent disk is referenced by the virtual desktop machine name and not the end-user name should you need to mount this disk to a different virtual desktop machine.

This disk could also be used to store the end user's profile; however, typically, you would now deploy a user environment management solution such as VMware DEM to manage end-user data and settings.

Disposable Disk

With the disposable disk, View Composer creates a temporary disk that is used to store temporary system files. A temporary system file could be a Windows pagefile, temporary Internet files, or other files and data that are not necessary to keep between sessions.

These file types are redirected to this disposable disk, and then when the end user logs out and powers off the virtual desktop machine, the disk is deleted and therefore saves disk space.

Temporary files created by an end user should remain stored on the user data disk allowing them to be kept – particularly if these files relate to application installers that may keep files in a temp directory and could be required if the end user needs to update the configuration of the application.

Internal Disk

The final disk that gets created by View Composer is what is called the internal disk. This is used to store configuration information that is required when the Linked Clone virtual desktop machine is created and is hidden from the end user so it does not get accidentally deleted.

The main thing that is stored on the internal disk is the computer account password. This is the password that is required to join the virtual desktop machine to the Active Directory domain as it gets created and if you refresh the Linked Clone. It is also used to store the configuration information that is used by Sysprep or QuickPrep in configuring the operating system.

Full Clones

A Full Clone, as the name suggests, is a Full Clone of the parent image. Therefore, it is an exact copy and will take up the same size as the parent from which the copy is taken. This means that Full Clones are not the most efficient way of deploying virtual desktop machines. However, there may be use cases within your environment where you may need to deploy Full Clones.

The Benefits of Cloning

The purpose of cloning is twofold. First, it helps with the cost of deploying a virtual desktop solution in that you do not need to deploy as much storage. Instead of allocating storage to each virtual desktop machine, virtual desktop machines are now intelligently built on demand making use of the same shared files or master image wherever possible. This dramatically cuts down the cost of purchasing physical storage to store virtual desktop machines.

Storage requirements were always seen as one of the sticking points to wide-scale adoption of virtual desktops, as the cost benefits did not stack up in the amount of storage that was seemingly required.

Part of that problem was also down to the way that organizations approached the solution. They deployed virtual desktop machines in the same way as they did with physical desktops, and quite often each virtual desktop machine was configured with its own dedicated hard disk. Not only that, but the virtual hard disk was also of a similar size as it would have been in a physical desktop.

The second core benefit is the reduction in management costs. It has always been something of a nirvana to be able to have just a single image; however, with cloning technology and the other desktop personalization solutions that integrate, this is now achievable.

Going back to the management of the solution, this approach means you can very quickly scale your environment to address the demands of the business. You can quickly spin up additional virtual desktop machines when required and power them off when they are no longer needed. This enhances the overall end-user experience with resources being delivered to end users much quicker than before.

Delivering Applications

Once a virtual desktop machine has been created and configured from an operating system perspective, then one of the next things that needs to happen is the applications need to be delivered.

One of the key advantages to delivering non-persistent virtual desktops is that applications can now also be dynamically delivered based on user policy. This also aids being able to have a single master image. One of the barriers to the single image was applications. You would need the image to have every application installed into it, which would make it large in size, difficult to manage, and expensive as you could well be paying for application licenses that are not required.

Now you can deliver applications on demand and based on the user requirements. In VMware terms, the solution that enables this is called **App Volumes**, and we will cover a more detailed introduction to this solution in a later chapter.

The other element to application delivery is how to deliver isolated applications. These are applications that may not run on the virtual desktop operating system as they are no longer supported. VMware has a solution for this use case with a product called **ThinApp**. ThinApp allows you to package an application in its own bubble, consisting of the application files and the OS files required, all delivered in a sandbox, presented as a single file on the end user's desktop machine.

Delivering End User–Specific Data and Settings

The final part of delivering the non-persistent virtual desktop machine is making it personal to the end user. By that we mean configuring the desktop with the user's personal data and settings, as well as specific configurations for the applications that they use.

The VMware solution for this is **Dynamic Environment Manager** which we will discuss in more detail in a later chapter.

Delivering the End-User Experience

Now that the virtual desktop operating system is built and configured, the applications have been deployed. The desktop environment is configured for the specific end user that is logging in to use it. The next step in the solution is how to deliver the virtual desktop, or at least its screenshots, to that end user, allowing them to interact with it.

This is the job of the display protocol, although it does a lot more than just display the contents of the virtual desktop screen on the end user's device.

Display Protocols

VMware Horizon supports three different display protocols: VMware's proprietary protocol, Blast Extreme, Teradici's PCoIP protocol, and, finally, Microsoft's RDP.

Blast Extreme

Blast Extreme is a VMware developed protocol that uses the H.264 video codec, and the latest H.265 video codec with Horizon 8, as an option if you have the required GPU acceleration hardware in your ESXi host servers.

The latest H.265 codec, also known as High-Efficiency Video Coding (HEVC) or MPEG-H Part 2, allows Horizon to support both 4K and now 8K monitors.

The Blast protocol was first introduced back in Horizon 5.2, where it was used to deliver HTML5 access to virtual desktop machines, delivering the screenshots into a browser on the client. With the continuous improvements and innovation of the Blast protocol, it can now deliver an exceptional end-user experience with additional features being added beyond the other supported protocols – features such as session collaboration.

When compared with PCoIP, which will be discussed in the next section, Blast Extreme now adds significant improvements over PCoIP. Both support similar functionality, such as Client Drive Redirection, USB, unified communications, and local printing, but Blast Extreme is far more efficient using far fewer CPU cycles. This is an important factor when it comes to sizing the infrastructure.

Blast Extreme is also more flexible. It can compensate for an increase in latency or a reduction in bandwidth with the ability to dynamically adjust to compensate. Unlike PCoIP, it can also leverage both TCP and UDP, again depending on the network environment conditions at the time.

Blast Extreme also supports the following features:

- **Blast Adaptive UX**: Enables Horizon virtual desktops, desktop sessions, and published applications to be delivered to the end user using the Horizon Client or a browser with the ability to automatically adapt dynamically to the current network conditions.

- **Blast 3D Services**: Enables hardware-accelerated graphics with support for NVIDIA, Intel, and AMD solutions. This allows Horizon to support two 4K monitors running at a resolution of 3840 x 2169 or two 8K monitors running at a resolution of 7680 x 4320.

- **Blast Live Communications**: Delivers full access to headsets and webcams, for rich audio and video. Supports applications such as MS Teams, Google Hangouts, and Cisco WebEx.

- **Blast Unity Touch**: Enables the use of devices such as smartphones and tablets by delivering a more intuitive user interface, ensuring that Windows desktops, applications, and files are more usable on non-native Windows devices.

- **Blast Local Access**: When enabled by policy, allows end users to connect external peripheral devices such as USB flash drives, printers, smart card devices.

Now that we have introduced you to Blast Extreme and some of its features, in the next section, we are going to look more closely at how it works. We are going to look at three connection scenarios: connecting internally, connecting externally, and tunneled connections.

Blast Extreme for Internal Connections

In this section, we are going to discuss how Blast Extreme works when used over an internal network connection.

Internal connections are those connections that do not leave the confines of the network within your organization. All components such as the host servers, Connection Servers, and the client devices being used to connect are internal and inside the corporate firewall.

The following diagram shows the ports used for an internal Blast Extreme connection from the end-user client device to the Connection Server:

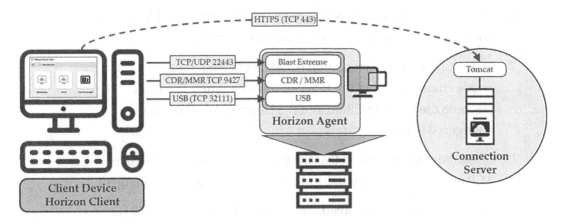

Figure 2-11. *Blast Extreme for internal connections*

So how does the process work? Let us describe what is illustrated in the preceding diagram:

1. The Horizon Client that is running on the end user's client device is launched and then connects to a Connection Server on TCP port 443 or via a load balancer in front of the Connection Servers in enterprise environments. This starts the end user authentication process which in turn makes a request for the resource the end user selected. The resource is either a virtual desktop machine or an application.

2. The Connection Server returns the connection information, on TCP port 443, for the allocated resource.

3. Next, a TCP WebSocket connection is made between the Horizon Client and the allocated resource. This connection is on port 22443. At this point, the VMware Blast service, which is running on the Horizon Agent, proxies the incoming TCP connection. The Blast Worker process determines whether UDP is enabled on the Horizon Agent and whether it is allowed on the client.

4. If UDP is enabled on the Horizon Agent, then the Blast Proxy process running on the Horizon Agent attempts to make a UDP WebSocket connection to the client using port 22443.

5. If UDP is either disabled or blocked, then the initial TCP connection is used instead.

6. If a local area network (LAN) is detected, then the initial TCP connection is used instead of the UDP connection.

7. When Client Drive Redirection (CDR) is enabled, then the traffic is side channeled from the Blast Extreme channel. The traffic between the Horizon Client and the Horizon Agent can be configured to use a separate port – in this case, TCP port 9427.

8. If multimedia redirection (MMR) is enabled, this traffic will use TCP port 9427 between the Horizon Client and the Horizon Agent.

9. If USB redirection is enabled, this traffic will use TCP port 32111 between the Horizon Client and the Horizon Agent. As with CDR, USB redirection traffic can also be side channeled using the Blast Extreme port.

In the next section, we are going to look at the connection process for external Blast Extreme connections.

Blast Extreme for External Connections

In this section, we are going to discuss how Blast Extreme works when used over an external network connection.

External connections are those connections where the end users are connecting from outside the corporate network, such as connecting over the Internet. As they are external to the corporate network, then they will first connect to a Unified Access Gateway or a Horizon Security Server if you still have this model deployed in your environment. If you do still use Security Servers, then it is recommended that you upgrade to a UAG appliance as Security Servers will no longer receive any updates or patches.

The Unified Access Gateway directs the traffic to the correct port and location on the Horizon Connection Server and the Horizon Agent running on the virtual desktop machine or RDSH Server.

The following diagram shows the ports used for an external Blast Extreme connection from the end-user client device to the Connection Server, via the Unified Access Gateway:

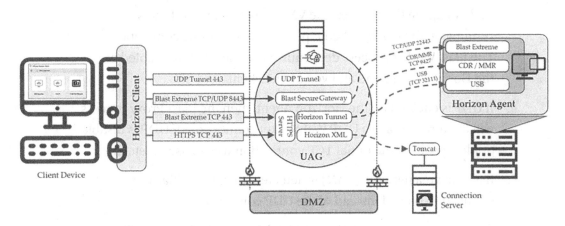

Figure 2-12. *Blast Extreme for external connections*

So how does the process work? Let us describe what is illustrated in the preceding diagram:

1. The Horizon Client that is running on the end user's client device is launched and then sends the authentication and resource request first to the Unified Access Gateway on TCP port 443. The Unified Access Gateway then sends the request on to the Connection Server on the same TCP port, port 443. This starts the end-user authentication process which in turn makes a request for the resource the end user selected. The resource is either a virtual desktop machine or an application.

2. The Connection Server returns the connection information, on TCP port 443, for the allocated resource.

3. Next, a WebSocket connection is made from the Horizon Client to the Blast Secure Gateway using TCP port 8443. The Blast Secure Gateway is a component of the Unified Access Gateway. Then a connection from the Blast Secure Gateway is made between the allocated resources on TCP port 22443. If you need to change the port used between the Blast Secure Gateway and the Unified Access Gateway, then this is configurable to suit your environment.

At this stage in the process, the VMware Blast service that is running on the Horizon Agent proxies the incoming connection. The Blast Worker process determines whether UDP is enabled on the Horizon Agent and allowed on the client.

4. If UDP is enabled on the Horizon Agent, then the Blast Proxy process will attempt to make a UDP WebSocket connection. If UDP is disabled or blocked, then the initial TCP connection will be used instead.

5. If a local area network (LAN) is detected, then the initial TCP connection is used instead of the UDP connection.

6. This connection is on UDP port 8443 between the Horizon Client UDP Tunnel on the Unified Access Gateway. Then from UDP port 22443 from the Unified Access Gateway to the Horizon Agent.

7. The VMware Virtual Channel is opened between the Horizon Agent and the Blast Secure Gateway on port 22443 and between the Blast Secure Gateway and the Horizon Client on port 8443. Communication over this virtual channel could use TCP or UDP. The remote experience traffic will also use this channel. This is the traffic for USB redirection and Client Drive Redirection (CDR).

8. With Client Drive Redirection (CDR) enabled, CDR traffic will go through the Horizon Tunnel on the Unified Access Gateway using TCP port 443. This traffic is then side channeled on the Blast Extreme channel to the Horizon Agent. You can also configure this to use a separate port.

9. If multimedia redirection (MMR) is enabled, then this traffic will also use TCP port 443 between the Horizon Client and the Horizon Tunnel on the Unified Access Gateway. TCP port 9427 is then used from the Unified Access Gateway to the Horizon Agent.

10. If USB redirection is enabled, this traffic will use TCP port 443 from the Horizon Client to the Horizon Tunnel on the Unified Access Gateway. TCP port 32111 is then used between the Unified Access Gateway and the Horizon Agent. USB redirection traffic can also be side channeled in the Blast Extreme port between the Unified Access Gateway and the Horizon Agent.

In the next section, we are going to look at tunneled connections using Blast Extreme.

Blast Extreme for Internal Tunneled Connections

In this section, we are going to discuss how Blast Extreme works when used over an internal tunneled network connection.

Internal tunneled connections are used in scenarios when the end point device used by the end user, the hosting infrastructure such as the Connection Servers, and the virtual desktop machines or RDSH Servers are all inside the corporate network. However, the end point devices could be on a different subnet from that of the virtual desktop machines or RDSH Servers.

In this scenario, you would not want to open any ports between the end point devices running the Horizon Client and virtual desktop machines and RDSH Servers running the Horizon Agent. Therefore, you can tunnel the traffic through the Horizon Connection Server. This allows for ports to be opened between the Horizon Connection Server and the Horizon Client and then between the Horizon Connection Server and the Horizon Agent.

The Horizon Client does not communicate with the Horizon Agent directly. This connection process is shown in the following diagram:

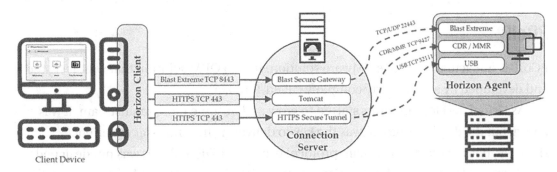

Figure 2-13. *Blast Extreme for tunneled connections*

So how does the tunneled connection process work? Let us describe what is illustrated in the preceding diagram:

1. The Horizon Client connects to the Connection Server using TCP port 443. Once connected, the end user is authenticated, and a request is made for a resource, either a virtual desktop machine or an application.

2. The Horizon Connection Server returns the connection information for the requested resource. This information is sent on TCP port 443.

3. A TCP WebSocket connection is made from the Horizon Client to the Blast Secure Gateway running on the Horizon Connection Server, using port 443. The connection is then established from the Blast Secure Gateway to the requested resource. This uses port 22443.

4. If you use MMR, CDR, or USB redirection, then the traffic for this will pass through the HTTPS Secure Tunnel on the Horizon Connection Server using TCP port 443. From there, each remote experience feature will use its default network port from the Horizon Connection Server to the Horizon Agent running on the resource:

    a. MMR uses TCP port 9427.

    b. CDR uses TCP port 9427.

    c. USB redirection uses TCP port 32111.

In the next section, we are going to look at another display protocol, PCoIP.

PCoIP

PCoIP is not actually a native VMware solution. It is an OEM solution that was designed and developed by a third-party company called Teradici.

As virtual desktop solutions started to grow and become more mainstream, it was found that the display protocol was the key to delivering the end-user experience. However, back in the day, the main protocol used was RDP, and that was not designed with large-scale virtual desktop environments in mind, especially with the requirements of modern end users and their need for high-end graphics and USB devices.

Therefore, a new purpose-built display protocol was required to cater for these specific use cases with the brief to deliver virtual desktop machines over the network, providing end users with the best feature-rich desktop experience possible and as near native to a physical desktop as possible.

PCoIP works by taking the entire screen contents (pixels) compressing them, encrypting them, and then transmitting just the pixels across a standard IP network (either internal or external) to the end point device.

When it comes to an end point device, these could be a standard client running the PCoIP software-based client, such as the standard Horizon Client, or in the case of using PCoIP, a purpose-built hardware-based client device called a zero client can be used. A zero client uses Teradici-specific hardware to decode the traffic, and as it is hardware based, then performance is much greater.

As PCoIP was designed from the ground up to specifically support virtual desktop machines, it supports high-resolution, full frame rates, 3D graphics, HD media, multiple displays, and high-definition audio, as well as USB peripheral redirection.

One of the key advantages of using PCoIP is its ability to dynamically adapt based on the current network conditions and what the end user is doing. To manage the network and use the bandwidth available in the most intelligent way, PCoIP used adaptive encoders. These encoders can automatically adjust the image quality should the network become congested and can be further defined using different policies to ensure that specific users in specific locations get the best experience, for example. Then, when the network congestion eases, PCoIP can revert to delivering the maximum image quality.

Another feature of PCoIP is that it uses the User Datagram Protocol or UDP protocol rather than TCP which is used by the likes of RDP. UDP is a real-time protocol and typically used for things such as Voice over IP (VoIP). The reason is that UDP traffic does not wait for an acknowledgment or then tries to resend, all of which make for a poor user experience and appear to the end user as a jerky screen.

In the next sections, we are going to discuss the different connection types: internal, external, and tunneled.

PCoIP for Internal Connections

Internal connections are those connections that do not leave the confines of the network within your organization. All components such as the host servers, Connection Servers, and the client devices being used to connect are internal and all sit inside the corporate firewall.

The following diagram shows the ports used for an internal PCoIP connection from the end user client device to the Connection Server:

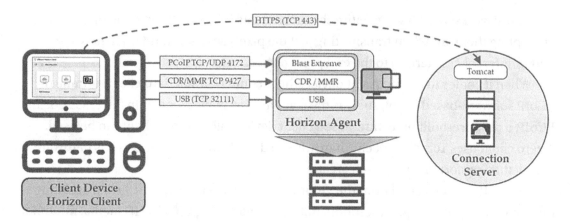

Figure 2-14. *PCoIP for internal connections*

The connection process works in the same way as we described for the Blast Extreme protocol; however, now we are using PCoIP on TCP/UDP port 4172.

In the next section, we are going to look at external PCoIP connections.

PCoIP for External Connections

In this section, we are going to discuss how PCoIP works when used over an external network connection, using the Unified Access Gateway.

External connections are those connections where the end users are connecting from outside the corporate network, such as connecting over the Internet. As they are outside of the corporate network, then they will first connect to a Unified Access Gateway or a Horizon Security Server if you still have this model deployed in your environment.

The Unified Access Gateway directs the traffic to the correct port and location on the Horizon Connection Server and the Horizon Agent running on the virtual desktop machine or RDSH Server.

The following diagram shows the ports used for an external PCoIP connection from the end user client device to the Connection Server, via the Unified Access Gateway:

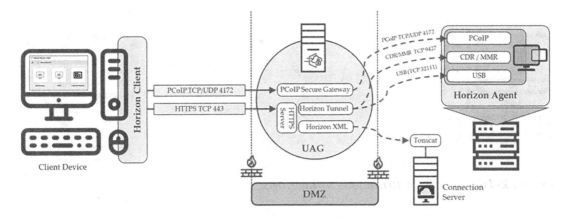

Figure 2-15. *PCoIP for external connections*

Again, as with the Blast Extreme process, the PCoIP connection process works in the same way but now using PCoIP as the protocol and TCP/UDP port 4172. This connects to the PCoIP Secure Gateway that is running on the UAG.

In the next section, we are going to look at the process for tunneling PCoIP connections.

PCoIP for Tunneled Connections

In this section, we are going to discuss how PCoIP works when used over an internal tunneled network connection.

Internal tunneled connections are used in scenarios when the end point device used by the end user, the hosting infrastructure such as the Connection Servers, and the virtual desktop machines or RDSH Servers are all inside the corporate network. However, the end point devices could be on a different subnet from that of the virtual desktop machines or RDSH Servers.

In this scenario, you would not want to open any ports between the end point devices running the Horizon Client and virtual desktop machines and RDSH Servers running the Horizon Agent. Therefore, you can tunnel the traffic through the Horizon Connection Server. This allows for ports to be opened between the Horizon Connection Server and the Horizon Client and then between the Horizon Connection Server and the Horizon Agent.

The Horizon Client does not communicate with the Horizon Agent directly. This connection process is shown in the following diagram:

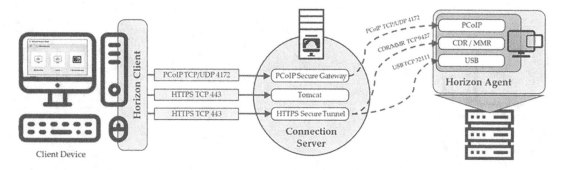

Figure 2-16. *PCoIP for tunneled connections*

The tunneled connection process is again the same process as used by the Blast Extreme protocol but using PCoIP as the protocol and therefore TCP/UDP port 4172.

Note   Although PCoIP is still very much available, the Blast Extreme protocol, VMware's own protocol, is now very much on feature parity, if not more advanced than PCoIP. However, you can continue to deploy PCoIP today, especially if you have it in place already.

In the next section, we are going to look at connecting using just a web browser.

Web Browser

In some use cases, an end user may not be able to, or want to, install the Horizon Client onto their device. In these cases, then they can connect to their virtual desktops and apps using an HTML-enabled web browser which needs no additional software to be installed on the device.

In the next sections, we are going to look at the different connection types for using the browser as the client. We will show internal, external, and tunneled browser connections.

Browser-Based Internal Connections

As we have discussed with the other protocols, the following diagram shows the connection process using a web browser rather than the Horizon Client and either Blast Extreme or PCoIP.

However, you will notice that Blast Extreme is used in the Horizon Agent on the virtual desktop machine and the Blast Secure Gateway feature of the Connection Server as shown:

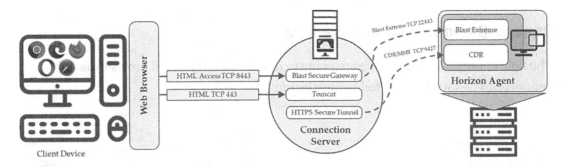

Figure 2-17. *Browser-based internal connections*

We have already described the connection process in the previous two sections, and this is no different other than now using a web browser rather than the Horizon Client.

In the next section, we are going to look at the browser-based external connection process.

Browser-Based External Connections

The next connection type we are going to look at is for using a web browser from outside the corporate network. As with the process we discussed in the previous sections, this configuration makes use of the Unified Access Gateway.

This is shown in the following diagram:

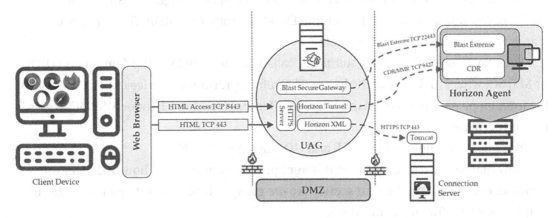

Figure 2-18. *Browser-based external connections*

In this connection process, the browser communicates with the UAG to provide the resources to the end user.

Finally, in the next section, we are going to look at browser-based tunneled connections.

Browser-Based Tunneled Connections

The final connection process we are going to look at is for tunneled browser-based connections as shown in the following diagram:

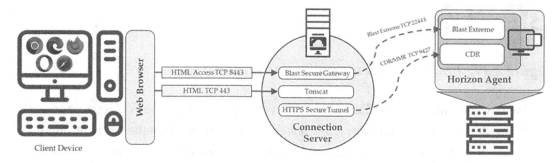

Figure 2-19. *Browser-based tunneled connections*

As with the other browser-based connections, Blast Extreme is used on the Connection Server and the Horizon Agent.

In the next section, we are going to look at the Microsoft Remote Desktop Protocol.

Microsoft Protocols

There are a few different versions of the Microsoft protocol. Originally, and within Horizon, you will see it called the Remote Desktop Protocol or RDP. This really is the standard name by which it is referred to.

You may also see it, in other solutions, called the Remote Desktop Connection (RDC) or MSTSC, where in the latter the letters TSC refer to Terminal Services Client. The latest incarnation or version is called the Microsoft Remote Desktop Client or MSRDC to give it the correct acronym.

The Microsoft client is both TCP and UDP, using port 3389.

Now that we have discussed the different protocol options and how to deliver the end-user experience, in the next section we are going to look at how to enable high-end graphics support for virtual desktops.

Choosing the Protocol

Having now discussed the different display protocols available, which one should you use in your environment? PCoIP, Blast Extreme, or RDP?

PCoIP used to be the default protocol of choice, but Blast Extreme has now caught up and overtaken it in terms of performance, features, and functionality. In fact, to take advantage of some of the newest features in Horizon, you can only use Blast Extreme.

The most compelling reason to go with these protocols is the fact that they use the UDP protocol, which is much better suited to streaming video and high-end graphics. This is because UDP is not worried about how the data ends up on the endpoint device. It is only worried about how quickly the data (screenshots in this case) are delivered to the end point.

However, these protocols can also use TCP as the protocol, and as we have discussed, these protocols can flex between which protocol they use depending on the network conditions at the time.

The reason for this is that TCP is more about how accurately the data is being received rather than how fast it is being delivered. To ensure that the data has arrived, TCP sends an acknowledgment from the endpoint device as to whether all the data packets sent have been successfully received. If this is not the case, and the endpoint device does not receive all the data packets it was expecting, then the end point responds by asking TCP to either stop sending packets or to slow down the number of packets that it receives. From an end user's perspective, the screen display will become "jerky" as the updates slow or fail to be delivered. The jerkiness is caused by parts of the display that are essentially missing, like watching TV when the picture becomes all pixelated due to poor signal.

With UDP, it is the opposite. It continues sending packets regardless of whether they arrive and does not request any form of acknowledgment from the end point device that they have arrived. Hence the reason UDP, for the end user, delivers a far better experience on a good connection.

About user experience, and in particular the performance, Blast Extreme will also use fewer resources on the endpoint device. This is even more the case if you offload the decoding using physical GPU cards in the host servers. The only consideration with the high-end graphics is that when using TCP as the delivery protocol, it may consume additional bandwidth, as the protocol compensates for packet loss.

We have just discussed why you might choose one protocol over another, but there are also reasons why you might not want to use a particular protocol within your environment. This is the reason that within the configuration of Horizon desktops, you can allow the end user to choose which protocol they connect with.

The most common issue is that the network ports that are used to connect a virtual desktop machine to a client are being blocked, especially those ports that involve external connectivity such as Internet connections.

Let us take an example using PCoIP as the protocol. You launch the client on your end point device and log in to your virtual desktop machine. The login process works as expected and with no errors, but all you can see is a black screen. This is down to PCoIP using UDP port 4172 which is being blocked and cannot send the pixels of the virtual desktop machine to your end point. You can log in with seemingly no issue because at that point you are using a different port that is typically a standard port and therefore is not blocked.

The PCoIP port is not blocked because it could cause a compromise. It is typically blocked because it is not one that has been used previously.

If, as in this use case, the end user sees the black screen, the quickest workaround is to log in again, but this time change the display protocol to RDP which does not use the same port. They should then be able to connect to their virtual desktop machine. In reality, you should work closely with your networking and security teams when designing your Horizon solution and the different scenarios of how users connect to their virtual desktop machines.

For example, I have seen many a design where the UAG has been factored in and included in the design, along with the resources required to run it. However, the customer does not actually have any external users connecting to virtual desktops, so there is no need for the UAG. Unless it is a future roadmap plan to have external access. But you get to the point.

In this section, we have discussed how to deliver the end-user experience to the end point. In the next section, we are going to look at how to further enhance the end-user experience and look at delivering high-end, hardware accelerated graphics for virtual desktop machines.

Hardware-Based High-End Graphics Capabilities

When it comes to delivering a virtual desktop machine with the ability to deliver a high-end graphics experience using dedicated graphics hardware, then VDI has not always been the solution and was often a use case that halted the adoption and rollout of VDI.

The core reason for this is simple when you think about it. Virtual desktop machines are running on server hardware, and server hardware was never designed to deliver high-end graphics. All it needed was the ability to deliver a basic, often text-based, management console.

As with nearly all use cases that were not initially best suited for a VDI environment, the ability to deliver high-end graphics now has a solution which addresses this use case, which has evolved over the years.

The first graphics-based solution was designed to support 3D graphics and was introduced with vSphere 5 and View 5.0. It delivered a software-based rendering solution that was able to support more graphically intense workloads such as the Windows Aero feature; however, it was still limited to some of the high-end use cases and added additional load on the infrastructure as CPU cycles were now being taken up for graphics rendering processes. What was needed was a hardware-based solution.

The first hardware-based graphics solution used the GPU virtualization solution that was introduced with vSphere 5.1. GPU virtualization allowed virtual desktop machines to share a physical GPU by allowing them to pass through the hypervisor layer and access the physical graphics card installed inside the host server directly.

When View 5.2 was released in 2013, hardware accelerated graphics became a standard feature with the introduction of two different techniques. The first, Virtual Shared Graphics Acceleration, or vSGA, delivered a solution whereby a GPU card could be shared across multiple virtual desktop machines.

This was then followed by Virtual Dedicated Graphics Acceleration, or vDGA, which enabled a virtual desktop machine to have a dedicated, one-to-one relationship with a graphics card.

The latest solution for delivering high-end graphics, Virtual GPU, or vGPU, is a solution that virtualizes the GPU card enabling the GPU to be virtualized and then shared across multiple virtual desktop machines. As far as the virtual desktop machines are concerned, they have their own dedicated, hardware-based graphics card.

In the following sections, we are going to look at all three of these high-end graphics solutions in more detail.

Virtual Shared Graphics Acceleration (vSGA)

vSGA allows multiple virtual desktop machines to all have access to a physical GPU card installed inside the ESXi host server on which they are running.

As the name suggests, virtual desktop machines do not have direct access to the physical GPU card inside the server. vSGA works by installing a graphics driver which is supplied by the graphics card vendor. This driver is delivered and installed on the ESXi host server as part of a vSphere Installation Bundle, or VIB.

Then, on the virtual desktop machine, you install the standard VMware SVGA 3D graphics driver that gets installed as part of VMware Tools installation. This driver is a VMware driver and provides DirectX 9.0c and OpenGL 2.1 support to the virtual desktop operating system. It is worth pointing out here that as vSGA uses this standard VMware video driver, this driver may not be compatible with some of the high-end graphics packages. Often, these apps need direct access to something like an NVIDIA driver as this is the supported and, more importantly, certified option.

When a user makes use of the accelerated graphics using the desktop capabilities of the VMware driver, these graphics commands are intercepted by the driver in the VIB and directed to the hypervisor. In turn, the hypervisor controls the physical GPU card installed inside the ESXi server.

In terms of delivering the experience to the end user's device, their virtual desktop machine is delivered using the chosen display protocol along with the VMware Virtual Audio driver, or DevTAP.

The following diagram shows a high-level overview of the vSGA architecture for delivering shared graphics:

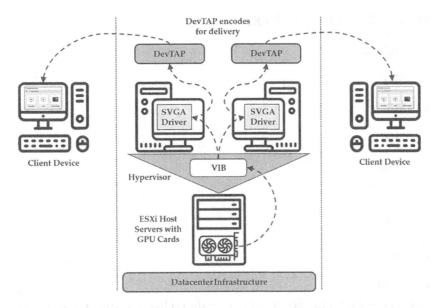

Figure 2-20. *Virtual Shared Graphics Acceleration (vSGA)*

There are several supported configurations and options to consider when deploying vSGA.

Supported Graphics Cards for vSGA

vSGA will support OpenGL 2.1 and DirectX 9.0c SM3 only running with one of the following supported GPU cards:

- AMD FirePro

  - S7000

  - S9000

  - S9050

  - W7000

- Intel HD Graphics P4700

- Intel Iris Pro Graphics

  - P6300

  - P580

- NVIDIA GRID KI and GRID K2
- NVIDIA Tesla
  - M10
  - M6
  - M60
  - P100
  - P4
  - P40
  - P6
  - V100

For the latest compatibility guide and an updated list of supported graphics cards, see the following link:

`www.vmware.com/resources/compatibility/search.php?deviceCategory=vsga`

In the next section, we are going to look at some of the configuration elements you need to bear in mind when deploying vSGA.

vSGA Configuration

As vSGA uses a shared approach to deliver hardware-based graphics acceleration to virtual desktop machines, the question is how many virtual desktops it can support. It is like the typical VDI question of how many users you can configure per CPU.

The best practice would be not to give all users access to a hardware-based GPU solution unless it works out cost-effective to do so.

As with the tip earlier, you would only configure those users that really need a hardware-based graphics experience, and so you would likely configure a dedicated desktop pool for this specific use case and deliver the solution to those users that really need it.

The number of virtual desktop machines that you can allocate a GPU resource to, or allocate to your desktop pool, is dependent on the amount of video memory (VRAM) that you configure for each virtual desktop machine. Do not forget that these hardware-based GPU resources are shared, and if you end up over-allocating resources, then as this is a virtual environment, and as would happen with any other virtual machine configuration, the virtual machine will not power on if the resources are not available.

So, when it comes to video memory, how is it shared? Half of the video memory allocated to a virtual desktop machine is actually allocated from the physical GPU card's memory. The other half is allocated from the host server's RAM. You need to bear this in mind when you size your host servers, ensuring that you configure enough memory for the server to allocate to a virtual machine to be used as both normal RAM and then for video memory. Using this, you will be able to work out the number of virtual desktop machines that can be supported.

For example, the default amount of video memory that gets allocated to a virtual desktop machine is 128 MB. Using the way that video memory is shared between the host server's RAM and the GPU card, 64 MB of that memory will be delivered by the GPU card, and the other 64 MB will be delivered from the host server. This gives you the total 128 MB of video memory.

Now let us say that the GPU card is configured with 8 GB of its own memory; you will be able to support 128 virtual desktop machines (8 GB or 8192 MB total GPU card memory divided by 64 MB required for each virtual desktop machines = 128 virtual desktop machines). As you can see, the number of virtual desktops supported is dependent on the amount of video memory that the GPU card can provide. Do not forget that you will need to ensure that the host server can deliver the amount of RAM required for each virtual desktop machine.

So, taking that number of 128 virtual desktop machines from the previous example, and configuring 8 GB of memory for each virtual desktop machine, the host server will need over 1 TB of memory just for the virtual desktop machines in addition to the 8 GB required for the graphics delivery.

In terms of maximum configurations, Horizon allows you to allocate a maximum of 512 MB of video memory to each virtual desktop machine. Going back to our example GPU card with 8 GB of video memory, the number of supported virtual desktop machines will be down to 32 virtual desktop machines (8 GB or 8192 MB total GPU card memory divided by 256 MB required for each virtual desktop machine = 32 virtual desktop machines).

The exception to the rule is when using AMD-based graphics solutions where the maximum number virtual desktop machine per GPU is 15.

Do not forget that if the resource requests for GPU cannot be met, then the virtual desktop machine will not boot or power on. However, if you do configure a desktop pool that contains more virtual desktop machines than you can guarantee GPU resource availability for, then Horizon has an automatic setting that means that Horizon can revert to a software-based 3D rendering model so that at least the virtual desktop machine can be delivered to the end user, albeit with limited and basic graphics capabilities.

Virtual Dedicated Graphics Acceleration (vDGA)

vDGA allows for an individual virtual desktop machine to have access to its own dedicated physical GPU card installed in the ESXi host server. This enabled the virtual desktop machine to have workstation levels of graphics performance, making it ideal for use cases such as CAD/CAM applications.

It supports OpenCL and NVIDIA CUDA. The following diagram shows the architecture for vDGA:

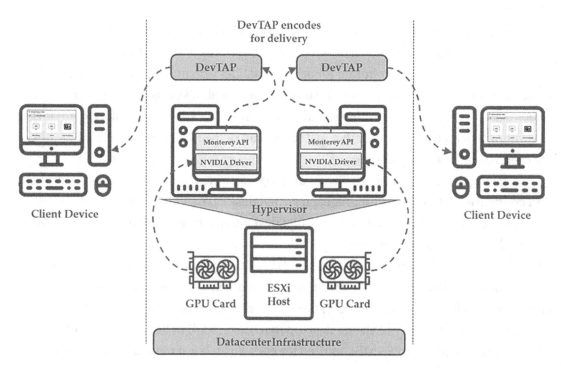

Figure 2-21. *Virtual Dedicated Graphics Acceleration (vDGA)*

To access the GPU directly, vDGA uses a feature called VMDirectPath I/O pass-through, or PCI pass-through. As the name suggests, this allows the virtual desktop machines to pass through the hypervisor layer and directly access the GPU card in the host server. As this is a direct one-to-one mapping between the virtual desktop machine and the GPU card, you cannot use vMotion.

Also, unlike vSGA, as the native video card driver is exposed to the virtual desktop machine, then vDGA has a higher compatibility with the high-end graphics applications as they can now use the certified drivers.

There are several supported configurations and options to consider when deploying vDGA.

Supported Graphics Cards for vDGA

vDGA supports several physical GPU cards including

- NVIDIA GRID

- NVIDIA Tesla

- NVIDIA Quadro

- AMD FirePro

- Intel

For the latest compatibility guide and supported graphics cards, please click the following link:

www.vmware.com/resources/compatibility/search.php?deviceCategory=vdga

In the next section, we are going to look at some of the configuration elements you need to bear in mind when deploying vDGA.

vDGA Configuration

vDGA is not limited by the amount of memory the physical GPU card has, it is limited only by the number of physical GPU cards that can be physically installed in the host servers. This is due to the one-to-one dedicated relationship between the virtual desktop machine and the GPU card.

For example, if you install a GPU card that has two GPUs onboard, then you can support two users. If you installed a second card of the same type, then you can support four end users with hardware accelerated graphics. If at this point you are concerned about end-user consolidation ratios and potentially having just four end users on a single server, then do not be. You can still configure other desktop pools of virtual desktop machines running on the same server that do not have access to a hardware-based GPU.

Therefore, the limiting factor is your host server and the number of GPU cards it can support. For these configurations, the server vendors offer a pre-built and preconfigured server via the OEM channel. That means the server has all the required GPU hardware installed and is ready to go.

One of the reasons for this is that for some of the GPU cards, due to the high-end requirements that they deliver, the host servers need additional power and cooling components to support the GPU cards.

Having now looked at both the vSGA and vDGA solutions, you can see that each has their own advantages and disadvantages; however, the ideal solution would be the shared approach to deliver a higher number of end users, but with the ability to use the native video driver to deliver the compatibility. This is where Virtual Shared Pass-Through Graphics Acceleration, or vGPU, comes into play as we will discuss in the next section.

Virtual Shared Pass-Through Graphics Acceleration (vGPU)

vGPU was launched as part of Horizon 6 and the 6.1 release. It combines the scalability that vSGA delivers in terms of the number of supported end users, plus it also allows the native GPU vendors' video drivers to be installed on the virtual desktop machines to enable maximum compatibility.

For example, if you have NVIDIA GPU cards physically installed in the host server, then you would install the native NVIDIA drivers on the virtual desktop machines.

The GPU is then virtualized, hence the name vGPU, and time-sliced, with each virtual desktop machine having a slice of that time where it can make use of the GPU hardware.

vGPU is only available with VMware vSphere 6 and Horizon View 6.1 and later.

The following diagram shows the architecture for vGPU:

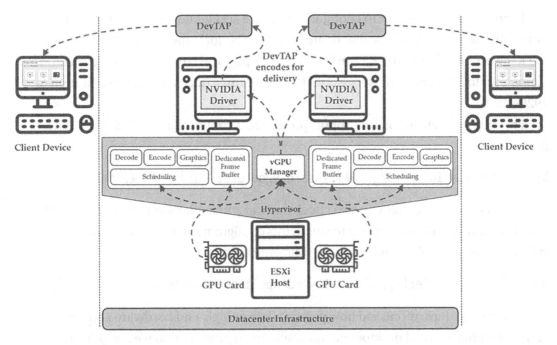

Figure 2-22. *Virtual Shared Pass-Through Graphics Acceleration (vGPU)*

There are several supported configurations and options to consider when deploying vGPU.

Supported Graphics Cards for vGPU

vGPU supports several physical GPU cards from AMD and NVIDIA. For the latest compatibility guide and supported graphics cards, please click the following link:

`www.vmware.com/resources/compatibility/search.php?deviceCategory=sptg`

In the next section, we are going to look at some of the configuration elements you need to bear in mind when deploying vGPU.

vGPU Configuration

With vGPU, the number of supported end users or virtual desktop machines is based on a profile setting that is configured on different profiles. When you configure the physical card in your host server, you will add the card itself as a PCI device, with the next configuration option allowing you to select the profile you want to use.

For example, if you want to configure hardware accelerated graphics for knowledge-based end users, that is, those that do not need the performance, then you could select the K100 profile and a GRID K2 card that has four physical GPUs, and then you could support up to 32 users. End users would be able to run a dual screen at a resolution of 1920x1200.

For an up-to-date list of the support profiles and configurations, click the following link:

https://docs.nvidia.com/grid/4.3/grid-vgpu-user-guide/index.html

It is recommended that you also check that the applications you want to run with vGPU are supported and certified to run in this configuration. For an up-to-date list of vGPU-supported applications, click the following link:

www.nvidia.com/object/grid-isv-tested-applications.html.

Now that we have discussed how you can deliver high-end hardware accelerated graphics within a virtual desktop environment, in the next section we are going to continue the media theme and discuss how to deliver unified communications and other audio-based applications.

Unified Comms, Video, and Audio Support

As we discussed at the beginning of the Hardware-Based High-End Graphics Capabilities, delivering unified communications using a virtual desktop machine was typically seen as another use case too far. The process worked fine, and you could make and receive video and voice calls, but the more people you added to calls, then the performance deteriorated.

The reason was twofold. The amount of traffic generated by the calls and the number of resources required meant that servers struggled to cope, resulting in a poor end-user experience.

What is the cause of these poor performance issues? The main reason is the way in which calls are initiated. The traffic created by the call is being transmitted using the same protocol that is being used to deliver the actual virtual desktop machine itself to the end user's end point device, causing a potential bottleneck when it comes to data traversing the network. All calls are going via the data center.

The next issue is that the host server that is running the virtual desktop machine now also has the added overhead of having to process the video call. The pinch point for performance becomes the data center and the network. What was needed was the ability to make peer-to-peer calls rather than this perceived hairpinning effect that meant video calling was not a great use case for VDI.

The following diagram shows the issue before and then the solution:

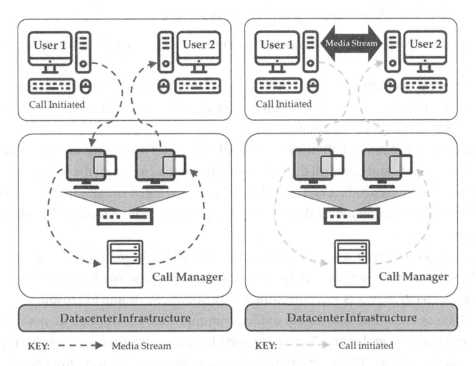

Figure 2-23. *Before and after – delivering VoIP with Horizon*

To create a working solution and remove the issues, VMware focused on three key areas to make the solution work:

- Offload the media processing from the virtual desktop machine to the end point device. This reduced the load on the server hosting the virtual desktop machines. This fixed the server resource issue as it no longer had to process the additional resources required for the video call.

- Create an optimized delivery between the end point devices rather than traverse traffic across the data center, thus freeing up bandwidth and congestion. Once the call is established, then traffic is directed between the end point devices and not via the data center. It also means it does not affect the protocol delivering the virtual desktop machine to the end point device.

- Enable a high-quality UC VoIP and video with QoS.

Considering those three focus areas, how does the ability to make a voice call work now?

A remote procedure call uses a virtual channel to allow the different components of a video call, running on a virtual desktop machine, to communicate and pass voice and video data to the recipient end point device.

The call control stack (a SIP stack if using SIP signaling) communicates with a call manager to initiate and establish the call. Then, the media engine on the end point device performs the encoding and decoding of voice and video streams into native voice and video codecs and then directly to the other end point device based on the call setup by the call manager.

The call is now a peer-to-peer call, and once the call has been initiated and established, the call data goes directly to the end point devices. No more hairpin effect. This methodology supports solutions from Cisco, Mittal, Avaya, and Microsoft.

With these issues now addressed, unified communications solutions are now able to be delivered to your end users. There has always been a strong use case to deploy unified communications with VDI. For example, call center users now can work from home during a snowy day and still be able to make and answer calls as if they were in the office.

Now that we have covered the infrastructure side of setting up and making video calls, there is another subject that often comes up with video calling and that is plugging in USB headsets and cameras. We will discuss this in the next section.

Real-Time Audio Video (RTAV)

As we just discussed in the previous section, delivering video calls used to be an issue in a VDI environment. We talked about the infrastructure side, but another issue with this type of solution was with using a webcam along with the bidirectional audio that is required to make the calls in the first place and how these connect to the end point device and are passed through to the virtual desktop machines.

The first problem was that using audio-in and audio-out on a virtual desktop machine was not supported. It did however work in theory, but in practice it was unusable. This was due to the high bandwidth requirements that were needed, without which it resulted in a poor end-user experience. The reason for this was down to the redirection of the device from the end point device to the virtual desktop machine. Redirection was the responsibility of the display protocol. So now the display protocol had to manage the delivery of the virtual desktop machine, manage the traffic generated by the call, and at the same time manage the traffic from the webcam and audio device.

If your solution used audio-in by plugging in a microphone via a 3.5 mm jack socket, then this did not work at all, but you could use audio-out with PCoIP and the audio redirection feature. This was a much better solution as the end point device was unable to split out a USB audio device, resulting in the audio-out functionality remaining local to the end point device. The audio-in on the other hand was redirected to the virtual desktop machine.

With this setup, a USB headset with both microphone and headphones would require the entire headset to be forwarded to the guest. This would have a negative effect on the bandwidth and cause a poor end-user experience. A new approach was needed which came in the form of the Real-Time Audio Video, or RTAV, feature of Horizon.

RTAV does not use USB to forward audio and webcam devices. Instead, USB devices remain connected to the local end point device. The audio stream data, both audio-in and audio-out, along with the webcam image data is encoded and delivered to the virtual desktop machine. Once received, the data streams are decoded and delivered to new virtual device hardware within the virtual desktop machine. These virtual hardware devices are for a virtual webcam and a virtual microphone which then play back the audio and video data streams received by the virtual desktop machine. They are also visible in the device manager of the virtual desktop machine.

Using this new method, RTAV supports the following features:

- Connecting webcams and audio devices such as headsets simultaneously for VoIP-based video conferencing apps

- Support for audio-in-only apps that do not require video, for VoIP-based voice-only apps

- Support for webcam-only apps. Ideal for webcam monitoring–type apps such as CCTV where audio might not be required

Now that we have solved the issue of how to set up and initiate a call, plug in a USB headset to enable audio, and use a webcam for video conferencing, you can now take advantage of solutions such as Microsoft Teams which we will discuss in the next section.

Microsoft Teams

With Microsoft Teams, the solution brings together the video calling elements as well as the need to use cameras and audio devices to make and receive video calls. However, the RTAV feature sends a substantial amount of data traffic over the network with the virtual desktop machine processing the audio and video data ready to make the call. While this is happening, the virtual desktop machine still has to process the display protocol, so that the virtual desktop machine can be displayed on the end point device.

To enable Microsoft Teams running inside a virtual desktop machine, VMware has released the Media Optimization for Microsoft Teams. This optimization pack works with Horizon 8 (2006) and Horizon 7 version 7.13. The following diagram shows how the optimization pack works:

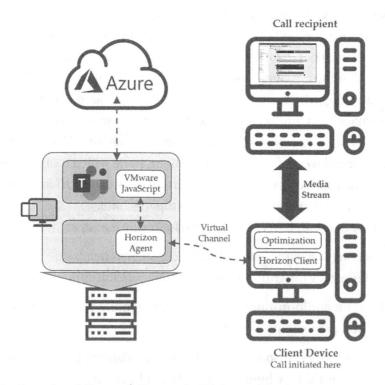

Figure 2-24. *Running Microsoft Teams in VMware Horizon*

You will also need to ensure that you are running the version of the Horizon Agent and Horizon Client for Windows that supports Microsoft Teams and the optimization pack. So, what does the optimization pack provide?

When an end user initiates a Teams call from their virtual desktop machine, a channel is opened on their local physical end point which then starts the call. The Microsoft Teams window that opened then draws over the Microsoft Teams window on the virtual desktop machine, effectively hiding it. In terms of the end-user experience, it appears that they are running Teams on the virtual desktop machine. However, the data traffic is going straight to the Internet from the local end point device. This means that the data traffic no longer travels across the network, and any processing of the audio and video data streams no longer happens in the data center but instead is processed on the end point device.

Although you can use most of the features of Microsoft Teams within a virtual desktop machine, at the time of writing this book there are still several limitations as listed in the following table:

Type of Limitation	Microsoft Teams or VMware Limitation
RDS hosts and application pools are not supported.	VMware limitation
HID buttons to answer and end calls are not supported.	VMware limitation
Outgoing application sharing is not supported.	VMware limitation
Virtual backgrounds are not supported.	Microsoft and VMware limitation
Live events are not supported.	Microsoft and VMware limitation
Pop out chat is not supported	Microsoft limitation

Figure 2-25. *Teams limitations*

In the next section, we are going to look at another feature that also raises several questions, printing from virtual desktop machines.

Printing

The main question that gets asked about printing from a virtual desktop machine is where the print job actually prints. Given that the virtual desktop machine is running in the data center, does that mean that the print job prints there too?

The answer is of course not, and the solution to this comes in the form of the VMware Integrated Printing solution that is a standard part of Horizon.

The VMware Integrated Printing feature enables end users to print from their virtual desktop machine to either a printer attached locally to their end point device or to a network printer.

It supports features such as

- **Client printer redirection**: Enables end users to print from their virtual desktop machine to a local or network printer. Printers that are redirected from a Windows client to a virtual desktop machine use a Native Printer Driver (NPD) which is installed on the virtual desktop machine, which must also be the same printer driver as the driver for the client printer. NPD supports only v3 printers. Or you can install the Universal Printer Driver (UPD) instead which means you do not have to install a printer driver on the virtual desktop machine. By default, if you install the native driver on the Horizon Agent computer, NPD is used. Otherwise, UPD is used.

- **Location-based printing**: Enables the mapping of printers that are physically nearer to your end point device.

- **Persistent print settings**: Print settings are kept when the end user logs out so that when they log in again, the print driver used and any print settings are applied again.

The VMware Universal Print Driver is installed as part of the Horizon Agent installation on the virtual desktop machine. Once installed, you will see an entry for VMware Universal EMF driver under your printer settings. The UPD supports the following features:

- **Orientation**: Enables you to select either portrait or landscape orientation for the print job.

- **Print on both sides**: Enables duplex printing as long as your printer supports this feature.

- **Multiple pages per sheet**: Allows you to print multiple document pages onto one physical page.

- **Paper source**: Allows you to select the paper tray in order to choose the type of paper and size of paper if you have multiple paper trays on your printer.

- **Color**: Enables you to choose to print in color or black and white/grayscale.

- **DPI**: Allows you to specify the printer resolution.

- **Print and preview**: Allows you to select print directly or print preview.

- **Number of copies**: Allows you to specify the number of copies to print.

- **Print as image**: Allows you to print each page as an image.

- **Compression**: Allows you to specify how the images in the printed document are to be compressed.

- **Stapling and hole punching**: If your printer supports stapling pages and hole punching, then this allows you to choose that option. It is dependent on the page orientation setting.

As part of the discussion on printing, we talked about plugging in a local printer into the end point device. We also touched on this when we talked about the USB headsets and RTAV, so in the next section we are going to discuss these and other devices and how they work with virtual desktop machines.

External USB Device Support

When it comes to external USB devices connecting to virtual desktop machines, then most USB devices should work without issue. The reason we say most is that there are so many different types of devices, models, and vendors, and it is impossible to test that every available device will work with Horizon.

Most devices should work without any issue, as when you plug a device into your end point device and it is recognized as a USB device, the display protocol will automatically redirect it to the virtual desktop machine.

As we discussed previously, even devices such as USB headsets and webcams can now be used within a virtual desktop environment. However, there may be some devices that do not work because they check the presence of a physical machine or other pieces of physical hardware inside the machine to enable them to work. It is always worth checking the compatibility first.

One device that has its own solution is the redirection of scanners. End users can use their physical scanners and other imaging devices that they can connect to their end point device and enable the scans to appear on their virtual desktop machines. The scanner redirection feature is installed as part of Horizon Agent and supports both TWAIN and WIA scanners.

We started this section by talking about plugging in USB devices, but what if you want to allow certain types of devices and not allow others? The answer to that is with the USB filtering option.

Filtering Supported USB Devices

Although USB redirection is supported, one of the reasons you deploy virtual desktops is to enhance security, and, in some circumstances, you might not actually want end users to plug in external USB devices and use them with their virtual desktop machines.

However, there may be a requirement for certain types of devices or devices that are approved by the corporate IT and security teams.

So, the first solution is to prevent USB devices from being redirected to the end user's virtual desktop machine. They can plug the device in locally if they so wish; however, the device does not get redirected and therefore does not appear on the virtual desktop machine. This can be managed by use of an Active Directory Group Policy where you define whether devices are redirected.

You can also manage this at a more granular level by creating specific filters. These filters could be configured to enable a specific device manufacturer or even more granular than that and configure specific devices from that manufacturer, with only these devices being able to be redirected.

For example, you may have a corporate standard for a specific device manufacturer and device type that end users should use. This device would be allowed, but any other device would be blocked.

So maybe it is a specific headset, or security device, which leads us to using multifunction USB devices.

Managing Multifunction USB Devices

A multifunction USB device is a device that has several different components integrated into it but has a single USB connector. For example, you may have a keyboard that also has an integrated mouse or pointing device, as well as a fingerprint reader or smart card reader.

Horizon allows you to split the device into its component parts. This feature allows you to redirect individual components of that integrated device rather than redirecting the entire device to the virtual desktop machine.

Going back to the example of the multifunction keyboard, you leave the mouse or pointing device as a local device on the end point device, but you could redirect the fingerprint reader or smart card reader to the virtual desktop machine.

Summary

In this chapter, we have given you a comprehensive introduction to VMware Horizon and how it delivers virtual desktop machines to end users. We started the chapter by discussing the core Horizon components, how they work, and what they are used for. Next, we discussed the different virtual desktop models, talking about the difference between persistent and non-persistent virtual desktop machines and their use cases. This was followed by how to build the different models using Instant Clones and Linked Clones.

The final section discussed how to deliver the best end-user experience. We covered the display protocol for delivering the virtual desktop machine experience to the physical endpoints and some of the technologies that enhance that user experience and how they work – things such as hardware accelerated graphics, unified communications solutions, and connecting external USB devices.

In the next chapter, we are going to discuss the best practice for designing a VMware Horizon virtual desktop environment.

## CHAPTER 3

Architecting Horizon for Deployment

In this chapter, we are going to take what we learned in Chapter 2 around the different Horizon components and features and start looking at how to design and architect a production-ready solution for delivering virtual desktop machines to end users.

Before you start any project for delivering end user–based solutions, it is recommended to create a business case, which is typically what drives you toward the project in the first place. From this, you can start to look at the requirements, but as this is an end-user solution, then end-user experience is key to success, and therefore the approach is to work closely with end users to help define the project.

Once you have understood the end-user requirements and understood the current environment, then you can start to map technology solutions to the use cases and work through the process of testing and selecting.

In the following sections, we are going to break this down into individual tasks that you should complete before embarking on your final design. Then, once we have all the information to hand, we will look at some example use cases and design best practice.

The Starting Point

Quite often, IT lead projects start in the IT team and are based around shiny new technology and flashing LEDs. However, with digital workspace or end-user computing projects, you need to turn the project on its head and start with the end user. I have seen far too many projects start with purchasing servers and storage without understanding what you will need to deliver. While you will obviously need the supporting infrastructure and hardware, how will you know how much and what spec and configuration you need if you do not understand what it is you need to deliver?

© Peter von Oven 2022
P. von Oven, *Mastering VMware Horizon 8*, https://doi.org/10.1007/978-1-4842-7261-9_3

So, with that said, let's look at why there is a need for change and what that change is going to look like to the business and ensure that the project delivers against those requirements.

Business Drivers and Requirements

There could be several reasons for delivering a digital workspace solution. It could be to allow end users to work from home or allow them to use their own devices.

You may have an organization dispersed across several sites that you want to centralize the end-user desktops for to simplify management and lower costs. Maybe you have a large contractor base whereby you need to deploy company apps to end users outside of the corporate domain. Often, you will have all these requirements, and you need to deploy a flexible and agile platform for delivering end-user services.

Whatever the reasons for deploying digital workspace solutions, once you understand the business drivers you can then start to approach the project, but still wearing that end-user hat.

But before you start designing or recommending any technology, you first need to understand the current landscape, and by that I mean looking at what the user environment looks like today. Where are end users working from? What devices are they using? What applications are they running? Do they have a specialist requirement such as high-end graphics or other bespoke and specialist peripherals? The only way you are going to build an accurate picture of what the environment looks like today is by conducting an assessment.

Assessments

There are two core elements to assessments. There is the physical side of an assessment where you focus on gathering data and other metrics and understanding what is currently deployed in terms of hardware and software, and then there is the human element where you speak to people to look at how end users work, with a particular focus on what is good and what is bad and what they expect from a new solution. After all, you could deploy a solution that ticks every box for the IT department, but when an end user logs on and starts using the solution and they have a bad experience, then all your hard work will be for nothing. Again, this is the reason why you need to focus on end users rather than the data center.

However, the assessment phase always seems to be done reactively and retrospectively, and in theory you should already have a picture of your current environment from which to work. This would form part of an end-user lifecycle management solution where you monitor the end-user experience continually so you can ensure end users are getting the best end-user experience. It can also allow you to provide proactive management and understand and fix issues before the end user picks up the phone to log a support call.

As you are embarking on a new project, then now is an ideal time to deploy a solution that manages the end-user experience and onboard your end users to guarantee the best possible experience.

If this is a new solution for your organization, then what we are looking to achieve is to build a baseline of what the end-user experience is like today. It will also serve as an inventory as well as build a picture of resource usage. This type of information is critical in getting your VDI solution designed correctly.

In terms of resources, the key things you need to look at are

- Applications (what is being used, what is not being used, and how often are certain apps used?)

- Resource consumption (CPU, memory, disk, and network are key)

- Operating systems, key if you are also migrating to a new OS

- Hardware inventory of specialist devices

- Machine boot times and login process breakdown

Without this physical data, designing your environment will be much more difficult, and likely you will best guess the requirements on a set of standard data for a typical virtual desktop machine. That might be OK for standard users, but what about the others?

You could easily fall into the trap of oversizing your virtual desktop machines, allocating more resource than is required or needed. The end users will likely be happy with this outcome as they get powerful virtual desktop machines, but think about the amount of infrastructure that you will need to deliver those oversized virtual desktop machines. That means more management and higher costs.

The other trap is to undersize the virtual desktop machines. This may reduce the cost of infrastructure and management overheads, but you could end up delivering a poor end-user experience. That has an impact on end-user productivity and ultimately the bottom line.

A desktop assessment takes away the guess work when it comes to understanding the resource requirements. It will not only quantify those resources in terms of the amount of CPU and memory that is being used, for example, but it will also paint a picture of when those resources are being consumed. It would identify peaks and troughs throughout the working day – things such as login storms which will tell you when most end users log in or what time they finish for the day so you could maybe look at powering off some of the resources to save power or to carry out updates.

So now you understand what your current desktop environment looks with some physical data defining the number of resources being consumed, the next step is to map that data to what end users are doing. This will help you understand the data you have collected and to design a solution that is appropriate to your use cases.

Assessing Your End Users

As an IT admin, you will have a deep understanding of how to deliver desktops and operating systems and manage the infrastructure behind the scenes. That is your specialty. But do you understand every role in your organization and some of those more specialist roles?

For example, I have seen cases where IT have seen an end user in their organization using a huge number of resources and then have decided that they do not really need that amount of resources and have reduced it. But if they have not engaged with that end user, how do they know that they do not need that amount of resources and by now removing it that end user can no longer work productively?

By interacting with end users, you will build a much more comprehensive picture of what they do and how they do it. So that end user that was reported to be using huge amounts of resources now turns out to be a high-powered workstation used for CAD/CAM work and connected to a full-size plotter. It also gives you the opportunity to see how they work, what devices they use, and what requirements they have and understand any new things that need to be considered for your design. They may be rolling out a new application that needs higher spec desktops. About applications, your interaction will give you a much better understanding on how these applications behave and will also help with your design. Maybe the way they store data does not lend itself to a non-persistent desktop. Maybe the application has dependencies that mean it cannot be virtualized or delivered as an application layer.

It also allows you to gain sponsorship for the project – by talking to the end users about what the new solution would look like and answering questions around concerns they have. If they have been involved from the start, then the design is less likely to fail or to end up with negative end-user feedback.

By now, you will have a physical set of data as well as all the information you were able to get by interacting with end users. The next step is to look at what the new solution needs to deliver. We do that by defining a set of success criteria which we will use to measure how successful the solutions we select are in delivering the end-user requirements.

Success Criteria

The success criteria are a documented definition of what a successful solution should look like. The criteria are made up from the key points that must have deliverables from the solution and should be clearly documented right from the start. They can then be used to demonstrate that the chosen solution can deliver against each one. For example, you may need the solution to be able to deliver high-end graphics to a tablet device.

An important factor when defining success criteria is to ensure you get the end users and sponsors to sign up to them. You are going to need their help in understanding whether the criteria have been met. This is also a common mistake I see. The IT team installs an application onto a virtual desktop, opens it, carries out a few basic tasks, and then closes the application and signs it off as being successful and working. However, when the end user launches the same application and then tries out some more advanced features, they fail! Again, I have seen this with CAD solutions where the CAD application opens without issue and you can load a drawing; however, when you start to rotate the drawing as a 3D model, for example, the performance is poor.

The other thing that success criteria do is to set the boundaries so that you do not experience scope creep. Scope creep is when other criteria are added to the list after it has been signed off. You need to stick to the list of success criteria. If it is not defined, then it does not get tested. The danger of adding new criteria is that the project will be delayed. It could also highlight that you need to revisit the end-user engagement as there should not be any surprises at this stage.

Your success criteria will also influence the technology that you deploy in that you will need to work with solutions that can deliver the success criteria. You would only consider solutions that satisfied the needs and requirements of the end user.

Selecting the Solutions

You can now start to select the solutions that will deliver against the set of success criteria.

VMware Horizon is not just a single solution that just delivers virtual desktops. The VMware portfolio of products goes much further. The core to Horizon is its ability to deliver virtual desktop machines which may well be the main part of your solution, but should those be virtual desktops or published desktops?

You also need to think about how applications are going to be delivered. Should they be part of the gold image and therefore installed in the operating system of the virtual machine, or should they be published? Should they be virtualized using ThinApp or delivered as application layers using VMware App Volumes?

Then there is the question of delivering non-persistent desktops and how you are going to manage the end-user environment in terms of Windows profiles. These are all considerations for selecting the components for your deployment and should be taken forward to the testing phase.

The Testing Phase

When it comes to the testing phase, there are three types of testing we are going to discuss:

- Proof of concept (POC)

- Proof of technology (POT)

- Pilot

We are going to discuss these in more detail in the following sections.

Proof of Concept

A proof of concept is typically a small-scale test setup that remains within the confines of the IT team and does not involve end users. It is used to demonstrate whether the solution works and for the IT teams to become familiar with the solution.

Quite often, a proof of concept is not really required. This is particularly true with VMware Horizon which has been around as a technology for a long time now and is no longer a concept. However, some organizations will still want to conduct a POC as the technology is new to them.

If you can bypass the proof-of-concept stage altogether and move straight to a pilot, then this will aid the speed of the project but will also get end users engaged earlier on in the testing phase. Maybe a demo or an extended hosted demo would suffice to get a feel for the solution.

There is also a risk that at the end of the POC, the project stalls as there was not really a business case or project, and it was just the IT teams testing technology for technology's sake. This will happen if the proof of concept is not aligned with the requirements or the success criteria.

Proof of Technology

A proof of technology is used to determine whether the proposed solution or technology that you are looking to deploy integrates and is compatible with your current environment. It is typically used when you have nonstandard or bespoke technology and systems within your organization. The proof of technology would be designed to demonstrate that these solutions all work together and therefore should be limited to just these niche use cases.

For example, you may have an expensive piece of manufacturing hardware that needs to be connected, and the proof of concept will need to demonstrate that this works correctly and as expected.

You should think of a proof of technology as a technical validation exercise; however, do not just limit this to the IT teams. If you are dealing with bespoke systems, then getting the user validation is even more critical.

Pilot

Ideally, and if possible, you should try and jump straight to the pilot phase. The reason is that during the pilot stage, you are working with real-life end users. This will give you the most valuable feedback and ensure better progress of the project.

The pilot is going to provide you the feedback you need to see if the project will be a success as you are essentially going to be rolling out a small-scale deployment rather than testing in the confines and safety of the IT department or just testing a particular niche use case.

Although the pilot is going to be a small-scale version of what you are likely to deploy in production, you should limit the scope of the pilot to a small number of end users from each of the departments that are going to be using the production solution. This ensures you get a good coverage of the different business areas and how they work while at the same time limiting the risk and exposure to the business.

As we have previously discussed, your sponsors will play a key role in the pilot and should be on hand to answer questions from the end users as well as gain valuable feedback that can be fed back into the design team to ensure the new solution delivers on all end-user requirements. Taking this feedback directly from those end users that are using the solution will ensure that the project does not fail. Just so long as you take that feedback onboard and make any necessary changes.

Just like the final production design, the pilot needs to be properly scoped, sized, and implemented. There is no point delivering a pilot that does not match what the end solution looks like. If that is the case, you may need to run the pilot again. There are several reasons why you should approach the pilot in this way, which we will discuss in more detail in the next sections.

Designing and Deploying the Pilot Environment

When designing and deploying the pilot environment, you should, as much as you possibly can, use the same hardware platforms (servers, storage, networking) that you are planning on using in your production solution. As much as you are testing the end-user experience during the pilot, it is also important to ensure you test the infrastructure.

There are a couple of common issues I see with the design and deployment of pilot environments. The first is that the IT team uses any old unused hardware that is lying around on which to install the pilot. Although cost-effective, it is not going to give you an indication of how the production environment will perform. You might then go on to purchase new and different hardware for production only to find there is an issue due to the platform differences or something is not supported. You need to pilot end users and infrastructure.

The second issue I see is that once the pilot has been completed successfully, you just keep on using it so as not to cause disruption to your end users. While this may seem like a good thing to do, as a pilot is a small-scale deployment, how will it cope with scaling? The pilot will have been sized for a limited number of users only. I have seen examples where more and more users are added to a pilot deployment, up until the point where it then breaks and no longer works.

If the plan is to take the pilot deployment straight into production, then you should design it for production from the start. This again goes back to ensuring you are using the right infrastructure foundations.

Reviewing the Pilot

It may sound obvious, but once the pilot phase has concluded, then you now need to measure the results against the success criteria to ensure that the solution is fit for purpose and delivers on all the end-user requirements. This often gets overlooked, and, as we described earlier, the solution just continues being used as is, given that end users are using it.

First, you need to ensure that it delivered against those success criteria. If it did not, then you need to understand the reasons why not. Was some particular use case missed, or has some of the end-user requirements changed since the pilot was designed and deployed?

Perhaps, it is nothing more than a perception issue that can be fixed by talking to the end user, although this should not happen if you have your sponsors in place. Regardless, the issue needs to be fixed, and once fixed, the pilot rerun for that particular use case to ensure it is now successful.

Once proved as successful, you need to get sign-off and agreement that all the end-user requirements have been met. Then, and only then, can you move on to the next steps in the project.

Defining the Next Steps

With the success criteria now signed off, you can start to design the production environment.

The testing phases will have proved which components you need for production, so now you can take those and build them into your design along with the end-user interactions that demonstrate how the solution will be used.

You also have the data from the assessment, so you can also start to size the hosting infrastructure ensuring that you have the resources required, which we will start to look at in the next section.

Designing the Production Environment

To help the design and build of your solution, VMware has a reference architecture that is designed to provide a blueprint for scaling Horizon. Not only scaling up in terms of the number of users but also scaling out in terms of different locations and geographies.

This is particularly useful for multisite environments that can now be managed as one and provides end-user mobility in that resources can be intelligently delivered based on the end users' physical location.

This reference architecture is called the pod and block architecture.

Horizon Reference Architecture: Pod and Block

The pod and block reference architecture takes a modular building block approach when it comes to designing and building out your Horizon environment. The key to this approach is in its ability to scale, with this architecture enabling you to easily add the components to support additional end users, up to a maximum of 12,000 users in a single block.

You can of course deploy multiple pods using the Cloud Pod Architecture which we will talk about later in this chapter.

As part of the design, this architecture also separates out the management infrastructure that hosts the Horizon components such as the connection server.

In the following sections, we will look at the architecture individually and then bring it all together at the end.

Horizon Block

A Horizon View block is a self-contained set of infrastructure that is designed to host up to 2000 end-user sessions if you are using RDSH-delivered published desktops or published applications and 2000 provisioned virtual desktop machines.

This number is based on the number of active sessions that a single connection server can manage. We will discuss the connection server in the "Management Block" section.

Although the actual theoretic limit of end-user sessions is 4000 active sessions, VMware recommends that you only deploy 2000 end-user sessions and virtual desktop machines.

As the Horizon block is effectively self-contained, it therefore has its own vCenter Server that is responsible for managing the ESXi host servers and the virtual desktop machines within the block. It would be responsible for the building of the virtual desktop machines using Instant Clones, for example. Do not forget that the connection servers are part of the management block and so are not part of this configuration.

When it comes to the number of ESXi host servers that are required within the block, this is decided based on the amount of resources you need to allocate to the virtual desktop machines.

For example, if you are delivering several hardware accelerated graphics–based virtual desktop machines using vGPU, then you will likely need a higher number of host servers to accommodate the physical graphics card, whereas if you have only task workers, then you will likely need less host servers.

We will cover the sizing elements of the block in the "Architecting Horizon Infrastructure" section.

The following diagram shows the Horizon block design consisting of a vCenter Server, ESXi host servers, up to 2000 virtual desktop machines, and up to 2000 end-user sessions:

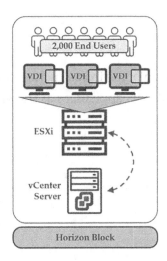

Figure 3-1. *Horizon block design for up to 2000 end users/sessions*

One question that often comes up is whether you must deploy your solution using the pod and block architecture. The answer is yes; you should follow this methodology wherever you can so that you deploy a supportable solution, and in fact you will be doing it by default in most cases.

The only time you might not follow the reference architecture design to the letter is during the pilot, although we have already discussed the reasons why the pilot should closely match your production solution.

In this case then you could have the connection server within the Horizon block rather than build a dedicated management block. That would reduce the number of vCenter Servers required and maybe the number of ESXi host servers, as the same ESXi host servers will host everything, including the virtual desktop machines and connection servers.

The other question is around the size of your environment. With the pod and block architecture, we talk about thousands of users, but what if you only have hundreds of end users, or less? Why would you build a small environment based on something that scales to so many users?

It may make sense to create a block based on a use case where you can separate out the different workload profiles. This would help with management, plus would also give you the ability to deploy DR and allow you to move users from one block to another should you need to, maybe for upgrades or in the event of a hardware failure. This would also apply when looking at the management block which we will talk about in the next section.

Management Block

The management block is made up of the infrastructure components such as the Horizon Connection Servers and UAG appliances as shown in the following:

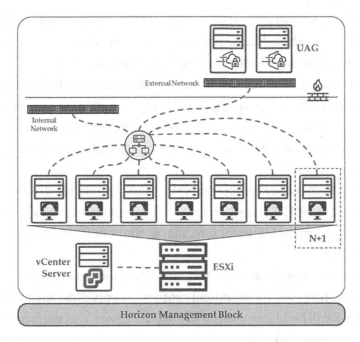

Figure 3-2. *Horizon management block design*

The key consideration within the management block is the number of connection servers that are supported. As we previously touched on, a single pod can support up to 12,000 end users. This figure is derived from the number of connection servers that you deploy, with each connection server supporting up to 2000 sessions and virtual desktops.

In a single pod, the management block can support a total of seven connection servers in an N+1 configuration, configured in a cluster. That means six connection servers will manage the active sessions and virtual desktops, while the remaining connection server provides redundancy.

In Chapter 2, we talked about the connection server being the master and any subsequent servers being referred to as replica connection servers. That means within the management block, you effectively configure one connection server and six replica servers.

We also previously talked about the fact that all the connection servers replicate their data, the ADAM database, using Microsoft's lightweight directory services along with the Java Message Service (JMS). This replication process is where the number of connection servers is derived from with seven being the number where best performance is achieved. This in turn dictates the number of end user's sessions and virtual desktop machines that are supported in a pod configuration.

Redundancy is an important part too, as should a connection server fail, you could not only affect 2000 users but also the performance of the remaining users as the remaining connection servers in the cluster will have to take on the additional load.

Going back to the earlier comment about not needing to apply the pod and block reference architecture when deploying a smaller number of users, you should still deploy N+1 connection servers to cater for failure. Having one connection server is a single point of failure, and when you are delivering services to end users, you do not want to prevent them from working.

When it comes to the other components, the management block will also have its own vCenter Server and ESXi host servers. In the management block, these will be supporting the management infrastructure, that is, the connection servers and replica servers, for example.

You could in theory use the vCenter Servers in the block to manage the hosts in the management block; however, the workload profiles are very different, and the vCenter Servers in the block will be highly utilized in creating clones and performing power operations on the virtual desktops.

If you are worried about the licensing of what is seemingly a high number of vCenter Servers, then do not be. The Horizon license includes vSphere for Desktop which allows you to deploy as many ESXi hosts and vCenter Servers as you need to support your virtual desktop workloads.

Now we have looked at the block and management block, we can now bring those components together to form a pod.

Horizon Pod

A Horizon pod configuration supports up to 12,000 end users and is made up of six blocks hosting the virtual desktop machines and a management block as shown in the following diagram:

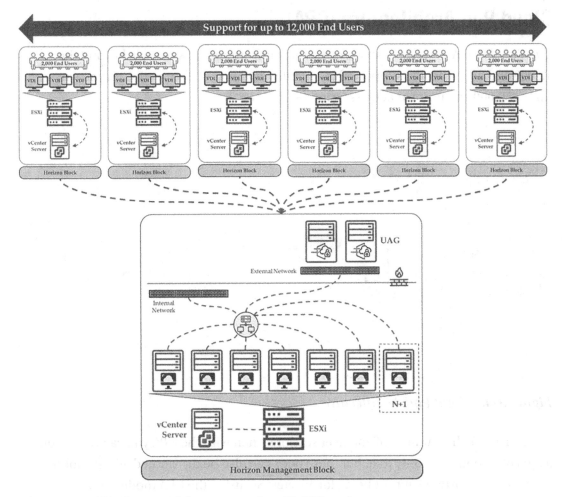

Figure 3-3. *Horizon pod for supporting 12,000 end users*

We will go to the next level and look at how to size the individual components such as the host servers and connection servers later in this chapter, but before we do, we need to answer another question which follows on from the pod and block architecture. That question is what to do if you have more than 12,000 end users within your organization, and can you deploy multiple Horizon pods?

The answer to that question is called the Cloud Pod Architecture which we will discuss in the next section.

Cloud Pod Architecture (CPA)

The Cloud Pod Architecture answers the question around how to scale beyond the 12,000 end users that are supported in an individual pod. In fact, with CPA you can scale up to 250,000 end users or active sessions.

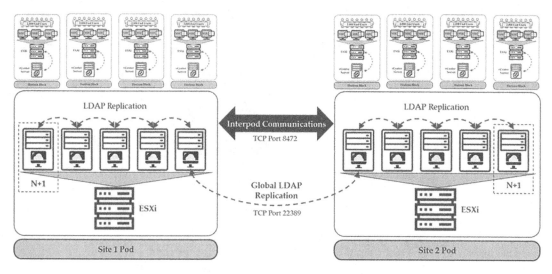

Figure 3-4. *Cloud Pod Architecture*

To achieve this number of end user sessions, then with the CPA you can deploy up to a total of 50 pods. Not only that, but these pods can also be distributed across multiple sites, with the current support being for 15 sites. So, using the CPA model, you can obviously scale the total number of end users, but it also means you can create a global deployment that is managed as a single entity using the global end-user entitlement layer.

Having multiple pods all connected to form a Cloud Pod Architecture enables you to entitle end users across desktop pools that reside across both different pods and sites.

CPA achieves this by using the Microsoft Active Directory Lightweight Service and the new Horizon Interpod API (VIPA) for communicating between the pods. VIPA is enabled when you enable the Cloud Pod Architecture in the Horizon Administrator console.

A question that often gets asked when using CPA is that if you have users that travel between sites, where does their desktop resource get allocated from? For example, if an end user is based in the UK and then they travel to the United States, does their virtual desktop get delivered from the UK?

To answer this question, CPA has several configuration options that allow you to configure where resources are delivered from. The default setting is that the end user will have a global entitlement. A global entitlement means that the preference would be for the end user to be allocated a virtual desktop machine from the local site. That local site is defined as where the end user is currently located, rather than using a virtual desktop machine from a secondary site.

However, with the scope configuration option, the IT administrators can configure where Horizon delivers the virtual desktops or applications to satisfy the end user request for resource. The following configuration options are available:

- **All sites**: Horizon looks for virtual desktops or applications on any pod that is configured within the federation.

- **Within a site**: Horizon looks for virtual desktops or applications that are only on pods that are in the same site as the pod that the end user connects to.

- **Within a pod**: Horizon looks for virtual desktops or applications that are only in the same pod as the one that the end user is connected to.

- **Home site**: Enables you to configure a site that is the end user's default site. When they log in, Horizon will only look for virtual desktops and applications from within that end user's home site, regardless of their location.

We will configure an example Cloud Pod Architecture environment later in this book. Having now looked at the reference architecture and how to start designing your Horizon environment, in the next section we are going to look a bit deeper into the pods and blocks and look at sizing the host servers and connection servers that support this reference architecture.

Architecting Horizon Infrastructure

The first thing to say is that while it is technically possible to run all your Horizon infrastructure, virtual desktop machines, and other virtual machine environments from a single set of infrastructure, so a single vCenter Server, and several ESXi host servers and clusters, this would not be recommended.

The reason why you would not do this is because in doing so you are creating several points of contention. By this we mean the different workload profiles between server and desktop operating systems and how those environments operate.

First, you have the way in which a virtual server works. Once powered up and booted, a server typically will stay in that state and is not powered on and off or restarted very often. On the flip side, desktops are powered on and off often as end users log in and log out. This means that they are built and destroyed on demand which is the job of the vCenter Server to manage these build and power operations. Therefore, you want to focus all vCenter Server resources to this task and not add any additional workloads.

When it comes to mixing server and desktop workloads, this could potentially cause end-user experience and performance issues. For example, you have a rather large database running as a virtual machine on the same infrastructure as your virtual desktop machines. If you ran a large database query, then this could potentially take a large amount of resource to run that query. All the time that is happening you are potentially taking away resources from running the virtual desktop machines.

It works the other way round too. If, for example, you have several high-end virtual desktop users consuming large amounts of resources, then any other server-based workloads running on the same infrastructure might take a lot longer to complete.

So, the answer, as we have already seen, is to not only separate your Horizon infrastructure from your normal virtual infrastructure but to also create two separate blocks to reflect the different workloads.

General Design Guidance

It is recommended, as it would be with any physical server-based infrastructure, to ensure that redundancy is at the top of your list. This means configuring the physical servers with redundant power supplies, RAID hard disks, mirrored SD cards, and multiple network cards. Note here that we have said multiple network cards.

The reason for calling this out specifically is that most servers will have multiple network connections on the motherboard already, and you may well add a dual-port card. Although the ports themselves may be able to fail over, if the card or motherboard fails, then that is not going to help.

When configuring your ESXi host servers, bear in mind that you should not stick to having just a single host regardless of the resource requirements as this will be a single point of failure. This is important in both management and desktop blocks, but critical in the desktop blocks.

Physical Host Servers

When it comes to choosing physical hardware–based servers for hosting the vSphere infrastructure, you need to think about the different workloads that are going to be hosted on these servers. For example, with the standard server type of workloads such as file servers or database servers, then you may not need extremely high-spec servers. In contrast, the servers hosting the virtual desktop machines may need specific hardware requirements such as the ability to host graphics cards or higher amount of memory and CPU.

We will look at these differences later in this section when we come to look at the management block and desktop block in more detail.

The next consideration is scale out or scale up. By this we mean whether you would consider deploying fewer higher-spec servers vs. more lower-spec servers. This decision would most likely depend on how you deploy high availability, but also may be budget driven too.

Networking

As we discussed in previous sections, one of the key requirements for networking is ensuring you deploy high availability to prevent any downtime resulting in end users being unable to connect. So multiple physical network cards for each host server should be connected to different switches, for example.

The next thing to consider is the network speed or bandwidth. This will likely be governed by the server and network hardware that you deploy and will be supplied with a particular speed network card. This could be from 1 Gbps all the way up to the latest 200 Gbps network cards depending on your switch infrastructure.

We will discuss the specific requirements in the following sections and how networking should be approached for the management block and the desktop block as each has different requirements when it comes to sizing correctly and what you need to focus on delivering.

Storage

As with networking, when looking at storage for Horizon you need to look at high availability, both in the local host servers that are likely to be running ESXi from local-based storage to a highly available SAN (physical or virtual) for the individual workloads.

Again, the storage requirements between the management block and the desktop block will be different due to the different workloads. The storage within the management block has a fairly static performance profile as once the virtual machines that are supporting the management functions have booted, then storage requests will be fairly static.

When it comes to the desktop block however, the storage performance profile is exactly the opposite. If you are using cloning technology to build your virtual desktop machines, either linked clones or Instant Clones, the storage performance now becomes critical as virtual desktop machines are spun up and down as end users log on and log off. Do not forget that with Instant Clones the virtual desktop machine and its disk will be deleted when the end user logs off.

We will discuss the specific storage requirements in the following sections and how storage should be approached for the management block and the desktop block given the different requirements. We will also look at some sizing examples.

vSphere Design for the Management Block

In this section, we are going to look deeper into the considerations, best practice, and what to focus on when building out your management block that is going to host the connection servers and replica servers.

Let us start with the ESXi host servers.

ESXi Host(s)

The ESXi host servers in the management block are going to be used for hosting the infrastructure components that will manage the connection servers and replica servers. As such, there is a fairly standard maximum configuration given that a pod only supports up to seven connection servers, six UAG appliances, and the associated vCenter Server requirements to manage the management block.

In theory, you could configure a single ESXi host server to deliver the resources required for the management components; however, as we have mentioned several times throughout this chapter, you want to design your solution with high availability built in as a standard. Therefore, although possible, it is not recommended to deploy just a single ESXi host server, and so we will base our design example in this chapter on delivering high availability.

We are going to start by looking at the CPU requirements.

ESXi Host Server CPU Requirements

As we highlighted in the previous section, the CPU requirements for the ESXi host servers in the management block need to provide the resources required to support the connection servers, replica servers, and the UAG appliances. So, what is required?

The following lists each individual component and the CPU resources that each one needs:

- **Connection Server**: 4 x vCPU

- **Replica Server**: 4 x vCPU

- **vCenter Server (small environment)**: 4 x vCPU

- **UAG appliance**: 2 x vCPU

Based on the preceding requirements for each individual solution component, if you were to build a management block to support an entire pod, complete with external access for all end users, so that is 6+1 connection servers, vCenter Server, and 6 UAG appliances, you would need a total of 44 x vCPUs.

The minimum physical server would have to be configured with a dual-core CPU as a minimum given that ESXi supports 32 x vCPUs per physical CPU core. Do not forget you will also need to allocate CPU cores to the underlying ESXi hypervisor.

However, it is recommended that you do not deploy a single physical server as this would be a single point of failure. Therefore, if you deployed two physical boxes to enable high availability, each configured with a dual CPU containing 12 cores, you would have a total of 48 cores available to use across the two host servers. With that, you can allocate vCPU to a physical CPU on a 1:1 basis.

Having now discussed the CPU requirements and consideration, in the next section we are going to look at the memory requirements.

ESXi Host Server Memory Requirements

The next resource we are going to look at is how much memory we need to configure in the ESXi host servers.

The following list details the memory requirements for each of the individual components:

- **Connection Server**: 10 GB

- **Replica Server**: 10 GB

- **vCenter Server (small environment)**: 19 GB

- **UAG appliance**: 4 GB

Based on the preceding requirements for each individual solution component, if you were to build a management block to support an entire pod, complete with external access for all end users, so that is 6+1 connection servers, vCenter Server, and 6 UAG appliances, you would need a total of 114 GB for the hosted virtual machines, plus an additional 8 GB for the ESXi host itself.

Again, this falls into the configuration realms of deploying a single ESXi host server; that is of course if you are not concerned about having a highly available solution.

Storage

The storage requirements for the management block are minimal, in terms of capacity and performance. Once the management block is built and deployed, then it will not require any additional storage capacity due to the static nature of the components it hosts.

The same is true for the performance of management block storage, as again due to the static nature, there is no requirement to build and delete virtual disks at scale, unlike the desktop block.

You could easily opt for a single host server with internal storage for storing both virtual machine disk files and the ESXi operating system disk. However, the best practice would be to make use of SAN infrastructure and maybe consider using a lower tier of disk for the management block that does not deliver the high-performance requirements.

Configuring for High Availability

We have touched on the subject of high availability several times already, but now we are going to look at the options for making the host servers hosting the management block resilient. Considering how to deploy high availability is a critical component of the management block as it hosts the connection servers. If connection servers become unavailable, then it will prevent end users from logging in to virtual desktop machines.

The obvious option is to have more than one ESXi host server. So even though the resource requirements suggest one server is sufficient, you should consider scaling down the specification of one server and to instead spread those resources over a vSphere cluster.

One thing to remember when doing this is to make sure that if one host server fails, the remaining server has sufficient resources available to be able to take all the workloads. So that is the answer for having two ESXi host servers, but there is a use case for deploying three host servers. That use case is for deploying high availability for your vCenter Servers.

vCenter Server

The vCenter Server for the management block is responsible for managing the virtual machines that form part of the management of the solution, namely, the connection servers, replica servers, and the UAG appliances. Therefore, as we have discussed, the workload is static in nature, and the vCenter requirements are not huge.

Typically, a vCenter Server Appliance configured for a small environment will suffice in terms of resource requirements, so that means 4 vCPUs and 20 GB of memory, plus 480 GB internal storage for the integrated PostgreSQL database. Note for these examples we are using a vCenter appliance.

Then there is the consideration of enabling high availability for your vCenter Server in the management block.

High Availability for vCenter Server

To enable high availability for vCenter, you will need to deploy three vCenter appliances as a vCenter HA cluster consisting of the following three nodes:

- **Active node**: Runs an active vCenter Server Appliance instance with a public IP address for management and a dedicated vCenter HA network for replication to the passive node and the witness node.

- **Passive node**: A clone of the active node which continually synchronizes with the active node using the vCenter HA network. It will automatically take over the role of the active node if the active node fails.

- **Witness node**: A lightweight clone of the active node that provides a quorum to protect against split-brain situations.

The following diagram shows the vCenter HA cluster architecture:

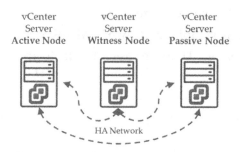

Figure 3-5. *vCenter Server HA cluster*

Now that we have covered the individual aspects of the design of the management block, in the next section we are going to bring all of this together and look at an example management block.

Example Management Block Design

In this section, we have brought together the individual components and considerations to demonstrate what a management block could look like.

For this example, we have gone with the maximum configuration, coupled with the maximum high availability features, designed to support an entire pod configuration of 12,000 end users.

This means that the management block consists of the following:

- vSphere cluster containing three physical ESXi host servers

- vCenter HA cluster with three vCenter Server Appliances (one per ESXi host)

- 1 x Horizon Connection Server

- 5 x Horizon Replica Servers

- 1 x Redundant Replica Server for failover should the Connection Server or a Replica Server fail

- 6 x UAG appliances for supporting 12,000 external end users, configured on their own separate, secure network to act as DMZ

This configuration is shown in the following diagram:

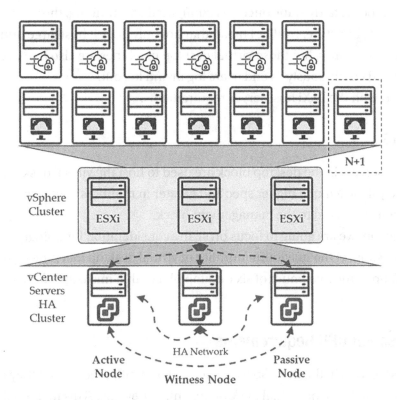

Figure 3-6. *Example management block configuration*

In the next section, we are going to turn our attention to the desktop block and look at the sizing considerations and best practice for building, deploying, and managing the virtual desktop machines.

vSphere Design for the Virtual Desktop Block

In this section, we are going to look deeper into the considerations, best practice, and what to focus on when building out your desktop block that is going to host the virtual desktop machines and vCenter Servers to support them.

The desktop block is going to be used for hosting the virtual desktop machines that the end users will connect to, along with the vCenter Server requirements for managing those desktops, particularly when it comes to creating the Instant Clones.

The desktop block is the opposite to the management block. Whereas the management block is fairly static once it is configured and running, the desktop block is far more dynamic in nature. By that I mean that not only does it host large numbers of virtual desktop machines, but those virtual desktop machines are also built, configured, and then deleted continuously as end users log in and log out.

Let us start with the ESXi host server requirements.

ESXi Hosts

The ESXi host servers in the desktop block are used to host the virtual desktop machines and therefore will be a much higher spec and greater in numbers of physical servers deployed when compared to the management block.

In this section, we are going to focus on sizing consideration for a single desktop block that can support the maximum number of virtual desktop machines. That can then be scaled out up to the maximum of six desktop blocks that make up a fully configured pod.

ESXi Host Server CPU Requirements

The ESXi host servers in the desktop block need to be configured so that they can provide the resources to the virtual desktop machine they host. This means CPU requirements are going to be far greater and not delivered all the same. By this we mean that there will be potentially different end-user use case requirements.

You may have some light users as well as some heavy end-user requirements that will mean the resources required will differ. This is where your desktop pool design is key; however, in this section, we are just going to talk about resources required.

One of the questions that always comes up when sizing the ESXi host servers hosting the virtual desktop machines is how many virtual desktops will fit on each host server. It may also be asked in a slightly different way, and the question now becomes how many virtual desktop machines can I fit on each CPU core?

In answer to that question, we do not really have an exact answer that covers all environments. What we mean is there is not a de facto standard answer, and it will depend on several factors, such as the speed and type of the CPU in your host servers, the number of cores each CPU has, and the number of sockets. There is then the question of what your end users are doing which will dictate the amount of resources you will need to allocate.

So, in some instances, you may be able to have a lot more end users supported on each server, remembering that each ESXi host can only support 200 virtual desktop machines as a maximum. Then, in other cases, you may have a host server with a physical GPU card installed and therefore just a handful of users on that server depending on the hardware accelerated graphics model you deploy.

The other consideration is whether again you scale up and have higher-spec servers to host more users on fewer physical servers, or you scale out and have more lower-spec physical servers with fewer end users. A lot of this decision will also be based on the price, as well as your model for deploying high availability. We have already seen in the management block that three ESXi host servers were used to deliver a vCenter HA cluster.

In this section, we are going to work through some examples to show you how you can calculate the potential number of users you can support. We are going to use some average figures for end-user CPU resource requirements; however, you should have some actual data for your calculations, collected from your assessment phase of the project.

We are going to cover three typical use case scenarios and the possible resource requirements for each use case based on light usage, medium usage, and then finally heavy usage. Also, for these examples, we are going to base the physical hardware servers on a typical type of server. In this case, a 2U rack mount server configured with two Intel Xeon Gold 5218 2.3 GHz, 16-core processors, giving a total of 32 cores and over 70 GHz.

One point to note in the calculation is that we are going to subtract two cores from the total number of cores available. These cores are going to be allocated to running the ESXi hypervisor.

So, what is the calculation we are going to use to work out the maximum number of virtual desktop machines per ESXi host server? The calculation is shown as follows:

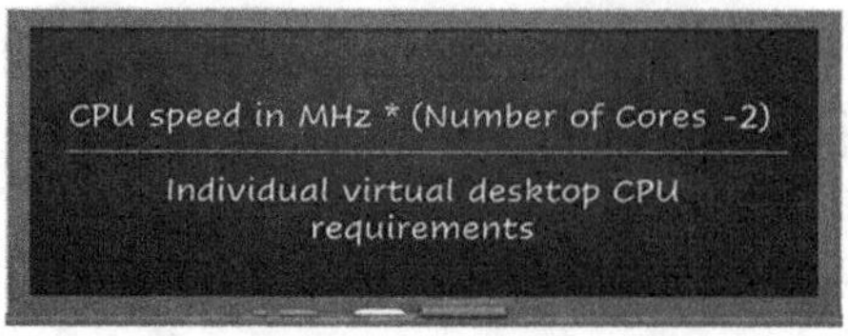

$$\frac{\text{CPU speed in MHz} * (\text{Number of Cores } -2)}{\text{Individual virtual desktop CPU requirements}}$$

Figure 3-7. *Calculation for the number of virtual desktops per server*

Now that we understand how we are going to work out the number of virtual desktop machines per ESXi host server, let's look at those example use cases.

Light User

A light user would be classified as somebody who would be working in a call center, for example. An end user that performs basic web browsing or general office suite type tasks including email. These desktops are likely only used during office hours and as such have low utilization.

For the light user example, we are going to put the CPU utilization at 500 MHz; however, your assessment data will help you derive the utilization for your specific environment. You may want to also consider adding additional CPU resources to cover any peaks in workload as your assessment data will be an average figure, and it is always good practice to allow some scope to cover any upgrades to applications and not deliver the exact number that may restrict performance. So, for this example, we will add 10% to the CPU usage.

You may also need to add sound or connecting external USB devices which may also require additional CPU cycles. If we use our calculation for this use case, and our example server hardware with its Intel Xeon Gold 5218 2.3 GHz, 16-core processors, then the CPU requirements will look something like the following:

$$\frac{2300 \text{ MHz} * (32-2)}{500 \text{ MHz} * 10\%} = \frac{69000 \text{ MHz}}{550 \text{ MHz}} = 125$$

Figure 3-8. *Light users per server example*

In this example, an individual ESXi host server could support approximately 124 virtual desktop machines. If you break this down to the number of virtual desktop machines per core, then we simply divide the 124 total by 30 which gives you approximately 4 virtual desktop machines per core.

So, let us look at this from a desktop block perspective.

If you are looking to build a desktop block to support the maximum number of end users, based on the light user profile, then we just take the maximum number of virtual desktops supported in a block configuration and divide that by the number of virtual desktop machines you can support on a single ESXi host server. That equates to approximately 16 ESXi host servers.

In the next section, we are going to look at another example use case.

Medium User

A medium user would be classified as somebody who would be working in data entry and a more advanced office suite user, for example. These virtual desktop machines will mainly be used during business office hours and sometimes longer but are not heavily utilized.

For the medium user example, we are going to put the CPU utilization at 750 MHz, but again your assessment data will guide you on a use case, and it may be that you only have one use case or maybe more than a handful. We will also add 10% to the CPU usage to cover any performance peaks.

If we use our calculation for this use case, and our example server hardware with its Intel Xeon Gold 5218 2.3 GHz, 16-core processors, then the CPU requirements will look something like the following:

$$\frac{2300 \text{ MHz} * (32\text{--}2)}{750 \text{ MHz} * 10\%} = \frac{69000 \text{ MHz}}{825 \text{ MHz}} = 83$$

Figure 3-9. *Medium users per server example*

In this example, an individual ESXi host server could support approximately 83 virtual desktop machines. If you break this down to the number of virtual desktop machines per core, then we simply divide the 83 total by 30 which gives you approximately 3 virtual desktop machines per core.

So, let us look at this from a desktop block perspective.

If you are looking to build a desktop block to support the maximum number of end users, based on the light user profile, then we just take the maximum number of virtual desktops supported in a block configuration and divide that by the number of virtual desktop machines you can support on a single ESXi host server. That equates to approximately 24 ESXi host servers if we use our example server hardware configuration.

In the next section, we are going to look at one final example use case. This time for heavy users.

Heavy User

A heavy user would be classified as somebody who would be working as a developer, IT admin or DB admin, or an engineer running high-end graphical applications, for example.

As such, these desktops will more than likely be heavily utilized throughout the day and potentially outside of the normal office hours to cater for projects and running out of hours admin tasks.

For the heavy user example, we are going to put the CPU utilization at 1500 MHz, but as we have discussed previously, your assessment data will guide you on a use case, and it may be that you only have one use case or maybe more than a handful. We will also add 10% to the CPU usage to cover any performance peaks.

If we use our calculation for this use case, and our example server hardware with its Intel Xeon Gold 5218 2.3 GHz, 16-core processors, then the CPU requirements will look something like the following:

$$\frac{2300 \text{ MHz} * (32-2)}{1500 \text{ MHz} * 10\%} = \frac{69000 \text{ MHz}}{1650 \text{ MHz}} = 41$$

Figure 3-10. *Heavy users per server example*

In this example, an individual ESXi host server could support approximately 41 virtual desktop machines. If you break this down to the number of virtual desktop machines per core, then we simply divide the 41 total by 30 which gives you approximately 1 virtual desktop machine per core.

So, let us look at this from a desktop block perspective.

If you are looking to build a desktop block to support the maximum number of end users, based on the light user profile, then we just take the maximum number of virtual desktops supported in a block configuration and divide that by the number of virtual desktop machines you can support on a single ESXi host server. That equates to approximately 48 ESXi host servers if we use our example server hardware configuration.

In the next section, we are going to look at the memory requirements for hosting the virtual desktop machines.

ESXi Host Server CPU Requirements

In this section, we are going to look at the memory configuration of the ESXi host servers for hosting the virtual desktop machines. Calculating the amount of memory required for each virtual desktop machine is straightforward as you can take your assessment data for memory usage and apply the multiples to give you the total memory requirement.

The question is then choosing the right server configuration in terms of balancing CPU and memory. By that we mean that an ESXi host may be able to provide the CPU resources for all your virtual desktop machines; however, it may not be able to accommodate the amount of memory that may be required. This comes down again to the scale-up or scale-out question.

Let us look at an example configuration, using our medium profile user type we used for the CPU calculations.

In this example, we have calculated, by using our assessment data, that a medium profile end user will need a virtual desktop machine configured with 4 GB of memory. In our CPU calculations, we calculated that each individual ESXi host server could support 83 virtual desktop machines. Therefore, that ESXi host server will need to be configured with 332 GB of memory to support this number of virtual desktop machines.

Do not forget you will also need to add the additional memory requirements for the ESXi host to run the hypervisor, plus memory to support the vCenter Server Appliances.

The other important factor to remember when designing the amount of memory required is not to overcommit the memory and to also configure the memory reservation to 100%. This obviously means you would need your host servers to be configured with enough memory to satisfy the amount that the virtual machines will require. By doing this, you stop the VSWP swap file from being created which in turn saves storage space and, as with any desktop machine, helps performance as memory will not need to be swapped to disk.

Overcommitting CPU and Memory Resources

In a typical virtualization environment, you can easily overcommit resources as the workloads are static, and therefore these overcommitments can easily be met. The same is not true of a virtual desktop environment. You should not overcommit memory in a virtual desktop environment.

The reason why you should not do this is down to the performance impact on the desktop which could result in poor performance and a negative user experience. If you overcommit memory, then a virtual desktop could try and take resources from another virtual desktop machines. However, given the workload profile of a desktop being dynamic, this is where the negative performance impact could be felt by the end user, by trying to take already utilized resources from one virtual machine to another.

If we talk about CPU and overcommitting CPU resources, it would be useful not to have to overcommit CPU resources, but the only way to do that is provide a 1:1 relationship between the CPU resources on the virtual desktop and the physical CPU in the host server. For small-scale deployments, this may be possible due to the large core count found in modern servers; however, for larger-scale deployments, this would not work due to the costs of deploying large amounts of physical CPU resources.

However, if you take a conservative approach to overcommitting CPU resources and not take it to the extremes, then you can balance the resources without having a negative impact on the end users.

How far you can configure an overcommitment depends on the workload profiles of your end users. It again comes down to that question of how many end users per host server/CPU/core which, as we have discussed many times before, will come from your assessment data. Do not search the Internet for this figure and come back with what is described as an average. There is no such thing, and it all depends on your actual environment.

Once you have worked out what the CPU overcommitment would be, then you can easily measure this by reviewing the CPU Ready figure on your ESXi hosts. This can easily be done using your vCenter Server, ESXTOP, or better still the same tool that you used for your assessment which is now being used as a monitoring tool comparing the baseline to real-time measurements.

The CPU Ready figure should be below 5% per vCPU. You may well find that in your environment a slightly higher figure could be acceptable without having an impact on performance, but you should test this out in your pilot before you deploy the solution into production.

Generally speaking, if your CPU Ready figure is as high as 10% per vCPU, then you will likely find that performance and the end-user experience will be negatively impacted.

Hardware Accelerated Graphics

One thing that will change the number of end users or virtual desktop machines you can support on an individual host is by adding hardware accelerated graphics and having a physical GPU card in the host server.

For a start, you would need to ensure that the server supported the graphics card. As we covered previously, the physical servers often need additional hardware in the form of cooling fans and uprated power supplies to support some of these graphics cards, plus a number of free PCI slots for the cards to plug into.

Then it would depend on the model of graphics you are going to deploy. With vSGA then the amount of memory in the host servers becomes an important configuration factor as half the video memory is allocated from the RAM in the host server.

With vDGA then the number of users per server is going to be much smaller due to the 1:1 relationship between the virtual desktop machine and GPU.

Finally, with vGPU, you can strike the balance between GPU compatibility and the number of supported virtual desktop machines. In this model, the number of users supported on each individual host server is dictated by the profile. For example, the K100 profile and a GRID K2 card with four physical GPUs will support up to 32 users. However, the actual server itself may be able to support a higher number of users whereby you would look to configure different desktop pools on the same server.

High Availability

When it comes to high availability with the ESXi host servers that are supporting the virtual desktop machines and the associated vCenter Server Appliances, then you absolutely need to factor in high availability. By default, if you are deploying the maximum of 2000 virtual desktop machines, then you will need more than one host server given the 200 limit of the maximum number of virtual desktop machines supported on a single ESXi host server.

Each host server needs to be configured with full redundancy, that is, multiple power supplies, network cards, RAID drives for the ESXi host operating system, etc.

You should also configure N+1 for the actual host servers. So, with our CPU calculations, for example, where we had 125 light users supported by an individual host server, then although one host server can easily support this workload, you should consider deploying two host servers. Then, should the first host server fail, you have a second server resource to take on the entire load of the failed server.

This also helps for maintenance tasks where you can move the virtual desktop off the host you want to work on and move them to the spare host. Just remember that with something like the high-end graphics solutions, vMotion will not work if you have a 1:1 relationship between a virtual desktop and GPU.

vCenter Servers

The vCenter Servers in the desktop block are going to be far busier than those in the management block. The reason is that they are dealing with far more power requests and are also responsible for creating Instant Clone disks as end users log in.

There are also more virtual machines to manage, and so you would likely opt for the medium environment configuration of 8 vCPUs and 28 GB of memory. You need to bear this in mind when sizing the ESXi hosts and that you have enough resource for vCenter Server Appliances as well as the virtual desktop machines.

From a storage requirement perspective, you will need a minimum of 700 GB of disk space for each vCenter Server Appliance to host the integrated PostgreSQL database.

In theory, you could get away with a single vCenter Server Appliance to support the 2000 virtual desktop machines in the desktop block; however, as we have previously discussed, that does not give you any protection against failure.

This is even more important when it comes to managing the virtual desktop machines. As the vCenter Server Appliance will also be managing linked clones, should it fail then your end users will not be able to log in, although existing users will be OK if virtual desktops have already been built and are being used.

With that in mind, you should configure high availability for your vCenter Server Appliances. Given the likely number of ESXi hosts within the desktop block, then you will easily be able to configure the nodes across the vSphere cluster without the need to add additional hosts just to support a vCenter HA cluster.

Next, we are going to look at the storage requirements for the desktop block and what is required to support the virtual desktop machines.

Storage Requirements for Virtual Desktop Machines

When it comes to storage considerations, we are going to look at these from a two-dimensional perspective: performance and capacity. We will start by looking at the capacity requirements and how much disk space you may need for your virtual desktop machines.

Storage Capacity

In this book, as we are talking about the latest version of Horizon, we are going to focus on Instant Clones rather than linked clones. To calculate the amount of storage you will need, there are several calculations that you can use to work this out. Before we look at that, let's recap on what Instant Clone disks consist of and more importantly how much space it will take up.

When an Instant Clone is created and starts up, it will take twice the size of its configured memory size. If you have not configured the 100% memory reservation as per the recommendation, then an ESXi swap file is now created. The size of the virtual desktop OS's paging file will also affect the growth of a clone's OS disk.

You also need to factor in disk space for storing two replicas on each datastore. The first replica is created when the desktop pool is created. Then, when the desktop pool is updated or patched the first time, a second replica is created on the same datastore and anchors the clones to this newly updated replica. Then, if no other clones are using the original snapshot, the original replica will be deleted. Therefore, the datastore must have the capacity to store two replicas during the recompose operation until one is deleted.

Finally, you will need space for the master image, template image, although these will be small in comparison to the other requirements.

So, let us look at the calculation for working out how much disk space you will need, starting with the minimum requirements.

Minimum Disk Space Requirements

The following calculation is used to work out the minimum disk space requirements for our example Instant Clone desktop pool:

Figure 3-11. *Calculation for minimum disk requirements for Instant Clones*

Let us take an example configuration where we have a desktop pool of 100 virtual desktop machines, each configured with 4 GB of memory. The master image or replica is 20 GB in size. In this example, the calculation for the minimum amount of disk space is shown in the following:

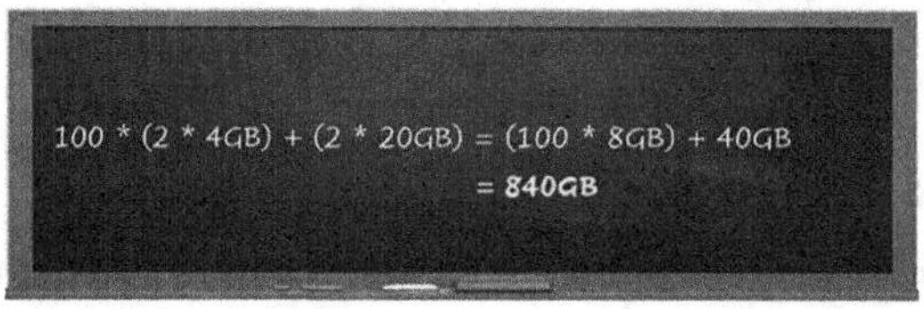

Figure 3-12. *Minimum disk requirements for the Instant Clone example*

The next example is for calculating the disk space if the disk space used grows to 50% of the maximum size.

Disk Space Requirements for 50% Utilization

We are now going to look at what happens when the clone starts to grow. For this example, we are going to look at the amount of disk space required should the Instant Clone grow to half the size of its maximum size.

The following calculation is used to work out the disk space requirements for our example Instant Clone desktop pool if it were to grow to half of its maximum size. This is half the size of the replica or master image:

Figure 3-13. *50% disk utilization calculation for the Instant Clone example*

Let us take our example configuration where we have a desktop pool of 100 virtual desktop machines, each configured with 4 GB of memory and the master image or replica is 20 GB in size. In this example, the calculation for working out the amount of storage required should the clones grow to 50% utilization of the replica is shown in the following:

$$100 * ((0.5 * 20GB) + 4GB) + (2 * 20GB) = (100 * 14GB) + 40GB$$
$$= 1,440GB \text{ or } 1.44TB$$

Figure 3-14. *50% disk utilization requirements for the Instant Clone example*

The next example is for calculating the disk space if the disk space used grows to its maximum size.

Disk Space Requirements for 100% Utilization

We are now going to look at what happens when the clone grows to its maximum size.

The following calculation is used to work out the maximum disk space requirements for our example Instant Clone desktop pool if it were to grow to its maximum size. This is half the size of the replica or master image:

# of desktops * (100% of replica + desktop memory) + (2 * replica)

Figure 3-15. *100% disk utilization calculation for the Instant Clone example*

Let us again take our example configuration where we have a desktop pool of 100 virtual desktop machines, each configured with 4 GB of memory and the master image or replica is 20 GB in size.

In this example, the calculation for working out the amount of storage required should the clones grow to the full size of the replica is shown in the following:

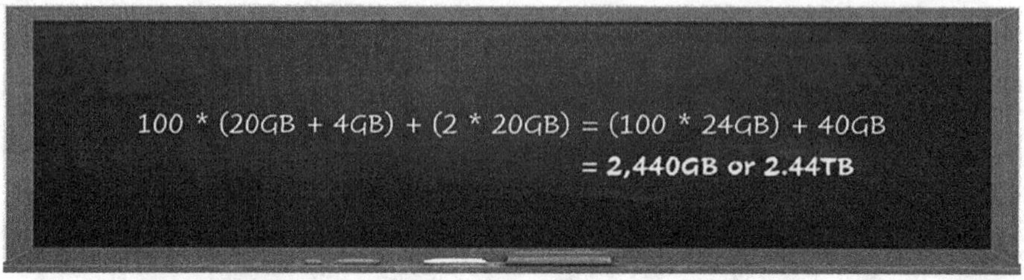

$$100 * (20GB + 4GB) + (2 * 20GB) = (100 * 24GB) + 40GB$$
$$= 2,440GB \text{ or } 2.44TB$$

Figure 3-16. *100% disk utilization requirements for the Instant Clone example*

You should now have a good understanding of Instant Clones and the potential storage requirements and how to calculate these.

Desktop Block Storage Example

The calculations that we have worked through in the previous sections are based on delivering just a non-persistent virtual desktop machine to the end users. That means that when the end user logs out, the disk that gets created will now be deleted. This means that we have shown, via the calculations, the maximum amount of disk space that will be required, based on a desktop pool of 100 virtual desktop machines.

Just as an example, and as we are looking at the sizing of the desktop block, let's take our example desktop specification of 4 GB per virtual desktop machine and a 20 GB replica and see what the storage requirements would be for a complete desktop block with the maximum of 2000 end users. The calculation would look like the following:

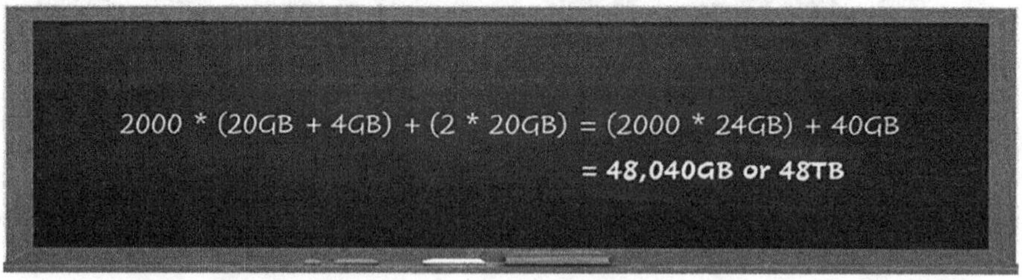

$$2000 * (20GB + 4GB) + (2 * 20GB) = (2000 * 24GB) + 40GB$$
$$= 48,040GB \text{ or } 48TB$$

Figure 3-17. *Maximum desktop block example storage requirements*

As you can see, the maximum amount of storage required for a fully configured desktop block would be approximately 48 TB. If you then scaled this out to a maximum pod configuration, then you would need six times the amount of storage, so a total of 288 TB.

Just to caveat that figure, this would be an absolute maximum amount of storage, which you are not likely to use, but this serves as a useful example to see the kind of storage you may require. The key reason you will not need this is that all the examples we have covered in this section have been based on non-persistent virtual desktop machines. That means that when the end user logs out, then the virtual desktop machine gets deleted.

That leads us on to the next section and what happens if you configure persistent disks.

Persistent Disks

In the previous section, we focused on non-persistent virtual desktop machines with Instant Clones. As we have described, with non-persistent virtual desktop machines, the Instant Clone gets deleted when the end user logs off. But what happens when the end user needs to save something?

The answer is that you can configure a persistent disk in addition to the Instant Clone OS disk. The other alternative is to use VMware App Volumes and the Writable Volume feature. The sizing of the App Volumes server would affect the sizing of the management block if you were to host them there. However, we will, in this section, focus on creating a persistent disk.

In this example, we are going to create a 5 GB persistent disk for end users to store their files and data.

Persistent disks will be kept on a different datastore to the Instant Clones. Not because the persistent disk needs the performance but more the opposite to ensure maximum performance for the Instant Clones. You would also use a different type of storage medium. So Instant Clones would be on fast SSD flash-based storage, whereas the persistent disks could quite happily live on spinning disks.

As the persistent disk will be thin provisioned, then you will not need all the disk space to be allocated up front, but bear in mind that these disks could end up being filled as end users save their files and data. It is worth monitoring this using your VDI monitoring tools.

The calculation for disk space required for persistent disks is simple and is shown in the following:

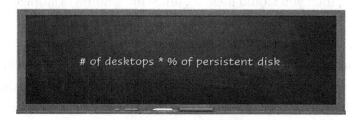

Figure 3-18. *Calculation for persistent disk storage requirements*

If we take our example desktop pool of 100 end users and configure them to all have a 5 GB persistent disk, then we can work out that the maximum amount of storage required if the persistent disks all grow to their maximum size would be 500 GB as shown in the following:

Figure 3-19. *Example calculation for 100% persistent disk storage requirements*

The actual amount of storage you will require for a persistent disk, if you need to deploy persistent disks, will come from your assessment data. Of course, you could use App Volumes or even a simple mapped network drive for end users to save their files and data.

Having now discussed the capacity aspect of storage, in the next section we are going to look at the performance requirements.

Storage Performance

In the previous section, we looked at how much storage capacity you need for your linked clone desktops, as well as configuring persistent disks.

For Instant Clones, the performance of the storage is a critical factor as the Instant Clone is basically creating a brand-new virtual desktop machine as the end user logs in.

The end user will expect their virtual desktop machine to be available almost instantly, and so the storage needs to be able to meet this requirement.

But how much performance is required? You can search the Internet and find figures that state a virtual desktop will require 25 IOPs, but while that figure might be right, does it reflect your end-user environment, and is that figure a steady-state figure? What about when the machine is being created?

The only way to answer this question is by looking at your assessment data. This should tell you the disk performance, and from there you can build and select a storage platform that can meet these requirements.

When considering the storage platform, you need to look at keeping the read and write latency to as low a figure as possible. The latency is the total time it takes to complete a requested operation and the requestor receiving a response. This is referred to as the IOPS latency. This will ensure that your end users do not see any drop in performance. What constitutes an actual latency figure will again depend on your environment and the workload profile of your end users. Also, the applications themselves will have some form of tolerances and requirements to run properly.

For example, 25 ms of latency may be a good starting point.

So, the objective is to provide as much storage performance or IOPs as you can with your chosen storage platform. However, Horizon can also help with the ability to tier different types of disk and place them on different datastores. The datastores themselves may then be underpinned by different types of storage. For example, you could have an all-flash array as tier one storage onto which you place the Instant Clone OS disks, and then persistent disks on a datastore that is underpinned by spinning disks.

The only exception to that rule is if you use vSAN as that only delivers a single datastore. We will look at this in the next section.

vSAN

vSAN is a software-defined storage solution that is part of the native vSphere hypervisor. It pools the server attached SSD disks to create a distributed and shared datastore for hosting your virtual desktop machines and Instant Clone OS disks. vSAN aggregates all local capacity devices into a single datastore that is shared by all the ESXi hosts in the vSAN cluster.

vSAN is included within the license for VMware Horizon Enterprise and Horizon Advanced Editions.

So, when it comes to the amount of resources required to run VSAN, VSAN does not require any dedicated host servers, and it does not require you to deploy virtual appliances to make it work. Typically, vSAN will consume around 10% of the ESXi host resources, so when you are sizing your ESXi hosts, bear this in mind and add 10% to cover VSAN resources.

In terms of capacity, we have already calculated some examples of how to calculate your requirements, and vSAN does not change this. When it comes to performance, if you deploy an all-flash vSAN deployment, then this could deliver up to 150,000 IOPS for each ESXi host server with submillisecond response times.

Since VSAN only creates a single datastore, Horizon now only needs to create a single replica virtual desktop machine for each gold image. This is shown in the following diagram:

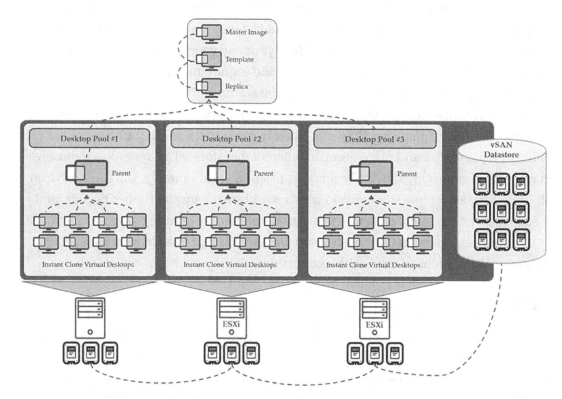

Figure 3-20. *vSAN example for deploying Instant Clones*

To help with enhancing and delivering the required performance, Horizon has integrated features of its own, as does vSAN.

The first solution is called the View Storage Accelerator, or VSA. This is also referred to as the Content-Based Read Cache, or CBRC.

The View Storage Accelerator provides an in-memory caching feature on the ESXi host server and takes advantage of the Content-Based Read Cache (CBRC) feature. This means that CBRC uses up to 2 GB of memory from the host server, to help reduce the read I/O requests from the storage and place them in memory, on the host.

As we are talking about virtual desktop machines that are obviously running a desktop OS and are being scaled to hundreds, if not thousands, of virtual desktop machines, there are a lot of commonalities across those blocks. This means that the cache will be accessed more than disk.

The second option is a vSphere feature of vSAN and is the vSAN Client Cache. It works by allocating 0.4% of the ESXi host server memory, up to a maximum of 1 GB, and uses this as an additional read cache in a similar way that CBRC does; however, the vSAN Client Cache extends DRAM caching of CBRC to your clones.

CBRC and the vSAN Client Cache will happily work together. When data is cached in CBRC, a read will be served out of the CBRC, and the request will never hit vSAN. If there is a CBRC miss, then the vSAN Client Cache will be checked before then going out to disk. This means that the vSAN Client Cache becomes an L2 cache for CBRC. This double cache helps improve the workload of the virtual desktop machines.

In the next section, we are going to look at some of the things you need to consider when designing your network stack to support the virtual desktop machines.

Networking

When it comes to networking, the key things we think of first are often bandwidth availability and how fast the network speed is and, linked with that, the latency of the connection. Latency is important when we start looking at WAN-based sites and Internet connections.

However, before we look at those elements, we are first going to touch on IP addressing requirements along with configuring subnets and DHCP scopes. This is often overlooked in favor of the network speeds, but without an IP address, then the virtual desktop machines will not be able to connect to the network in the first place.

Do not forget desktop pools and desktop blocks or the entire pod could be made up of thousands of virtual desktop machines that can quickly exceed the 256 address limit of using a 24-bit subnet if you use IPv4.

In an enterprise environment, there are going to potentially be multiple subnets and different VLANS to take into consideration. This is important as when you start to scale out the number of virtual desktop machines, you could quite quickly run out of addresses and subnets, and your DHCP scopes may not have been configured to cope with the number of IP addresses required.

You could of course use IPv6 which uses a 128-bit address, rather than the 32-bit addressing used in IPv4. Horizon supports IPv6, but you need to be aware that you cannot mix addressing schemes across the infrastructure components. For example, you cannot have a connection server using an IPv6 address and then a replica server using an IPv4 address.

Of course, you could create one large subnet that could cover all the virtual desktop machine in your environment; however, think of the size of this in terms of a broadcast domain. Imagine having a pod that is configured with the maximum of 12,000 virtual desktops that were part of this broadcast domain and all talking to each other. The amount of network traffic would have a negative impact on the rest of the network traffic, resulting in a poor end-user experience.

The best practice would be to create subnets made up from a smaller number of virtual desktop machines. So, for example, a subnet could be made up of 500 virtual desktop machines. However, if you are using an IPv4 address scheme and a 24-bit subnet, then you still have the issue of not being able to assign enough IP addresses. But luckily, Horizon has a resolution to this too with the network label feature.

Virtual desktop machines within your desktop pool will take the network interface card configuration and the network label from the parent virtual desktop machine. To do this, you can configure your desktop pool to use multiple network labels. These are selected from the network labels that you defined for your ESXi host server, and then associate those network labels with the network cards that were taken from the parent virtual desktop machine. You can then specify the maximum number of IP addresses that can be assigned to the virtual desktop machines from each network label.

When you then create the desktop pool and the virtual desktop machines start to get provisioned, Horizon will distribute the network labels across the virtual desktop machines in the desktop pool. Network labels are assigned in alphabetical order. Horizon then used the next label once all the IP addresses assigned to the first label have been assigned.

So now we have talked about the IP addressing considerations, the next thing you need to consider is that each of those virtual desktop machines will need a network connection via a virtual switch. In the next section, we are going to look at virtual switches for Horizon environments.

Virtual Switches

The first thing to say is that you should use distributed switches for your Horizon environment. This is required for ease of management and if you are going to use the network label feature. The following diagram shows an example network configuration:

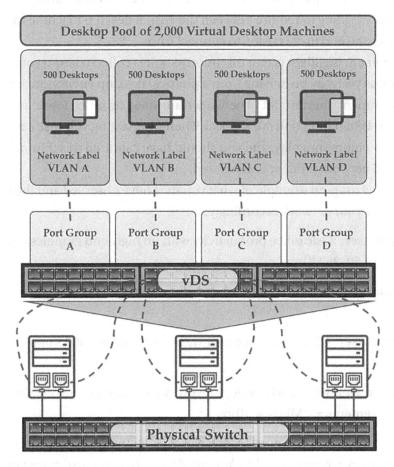

Figure 3-21. *Example networking configuration*

In this example, we have taken a desktop block with 2000 virtual desktop machines and then divided that into four subnets, each containing 500 virtual desktop machines. We have then created four port groups on the virtual distributed switch, labeled A to D, and given each subnet a VLAN tag too.

The configuration to create this is done from the command line, and so we will cover that in Chapter 6.

Network Bandwidth Considerations

Now that we have discussed the more physical requirements from the network design, such as switches and IP addresses, the next thing you need to think about is how much bandwidth you are going to require between the virtual desktop machines and the endpoint device the end user is using to connect from.

The first point to highlight is that this information is collected from your assessment data; however, as you may be moving from a physical desktop environment to a virtual desktop environment, the amount of network traffic may be much lower as graphics, keystrokes, and USB redirection are all local. Therefore, testing your use cases during the pilot phase now comes into play, and you should have captured this information to see what additional network traffic was generated.

The following list is an example of what you may have observed and the detail that will help you size your network accordingly:

- **Light user**: Basic office productivity with no high-end graphics or video = 50–250 Kbps

- **Medium user**: Heavier office user with web browsing = 250 Kbps–1 Mbps

- **Heavy user**: Advanced office user with 3D graphics = 500 Kbps–2 Mbps

- **Power user**: High-end developer with video and high-end graphics requirements = 2 Mbps–4 Mbps

As part of this process, you need to look closely at network optimization to deliver the best end-user experience possible. You need to look at your use cases and pilot data as well as understanding where your end users connect from. Are they connecting across the LAN, a WAN, or over the Internet?

Although there is not much you can do for Internet users, you could consider applying policies that limit some of the features and capabilities that could potentially consume more bandwidth and not work well over an Internet connection.

There are tools you can use to help optimize the network and the end-user experience. For example, there is a PCoIP tuning tool which can be used to optimize the delivery of the end user experience across the network.

Although bandwidth is important, latency can be the real killer when it comes to delivering the end-user experience across the network.

Typically, the maximum tolerance level for latency is around 250 milliseconds. Again, this is where you need to consider where your end users are connecting from. Over the LAN or WAN, you might be able to optimize it enough to be acceptable, but the Internet is going to be a tough call.

As part of your assessment, you would be able to understand from where your end users are going to connect.

The final part of the network discussion is around load balancing and what the requirements are.

Load Balancing

As you are likely to deploy at least two connection servers in an N+1 configuration, and probably more as you scale up the number of end users and virtual desktop machines, then you will need to spread the connections across the connection servers rather than have everyone log on to the same connection server.

As users will connect to the server via its name or IP address, you will also need some form of global namespace, so the logical solution is to deploy a load balancer in front of the Connection Servers. If you have external users, then you would also need to do the same for the UAG appliances.

Horizon does not come with an integrated load balancer; however, you should consider deploying VMware NSX for Horizon. There are other benefits of running NSX within your Horizon environment which we will cover in the next section.

NSX for Horizon

NSX is VMware's software-defined networking solution. It not only provides the virtual networking features, such as the load balancing, we talked about in the previous chapter, but it also improves the security of the virtual desktop machines.

It does this by addressing east-west threats enabling administrators to define a central policy. Once defined, the policy is distributed across the hypervisor on each of your ESXi host server. The policy is then automatically applied to each virtual desktop machine as each one is created by the Instant Clone process.

Virtual desktop machines can be isolated from virtual desktops running adjacent to them using microsegmentation. Microsegmentation enables each virtual desktop machine to have its own perimeter defense system using the NSX distributed virtual firewalling feature.

We have now discussed the networking considerations. In the next section, we are just going to recap on the specification and configuration of the Horizon components.

Horizon Component Sizing Requirements

Throughout this chapter, we have covered some of the requirements of the connection server, replica server, and UAG appliance. In this section, we are going to look at all those requirements or prerequisites together for both the hardware and software required.

Connection Server Sizing

The Connection Server is a Windows application that is installed on a Windows Server OS. This Windows server would be hosted as a virtual machine on an ESXi host server in the management block. We will start with the hardware requirements.

Connection Server Hardware Requirements

The following table outlines the recommended hardware configuration for running the connection server:

Hardware component	Required	Recommened
CPU	Pentium IV 2GHz or higher	4 CPUs
Network	100 Mbps NOC	1 Gbps NIC
Memory	4GB	10GB

Figure 3-22. *Connection server hardware requirements*

Next, we are going to look at the supported operating systems.

Connection Server Software Requirements

The following table outlines the recommended software configuration for running the connection server:

OS	Supported Editions
Windows Server 2012 R2	Standard (64-bit) Datacenter (64-bit)
Windows Server 2016	Standard (64-bit) Datacenter (64-bit)
Windows Server 2019	Standard (64-bit) Datacenter (64-bit)

Figure 3-23. *Connection server OS requirements*

In addition to the supported operating systems, Horizon also supports the following Active Directory domain functional levels as shown in the following table:

AD Domain Functional Level	Supported
Windows Server 2012 R2	☑
Windows Server 2016	☑
Windows Server 2019	☑

Figure 3-24. *Connection server AD functional level support*

In the next section, we are going to look at the requirements for the replica server.

Replica Server Sizing

As the replica server is essentially just another copy of the original connection server and acts as a backup or for scaling out the number of end users supported in a desktop block, then its requirements are identical to those we have covered in the previous section.

In the next section, we are going to look at the configuration maximums for deploying Horizon.

Configuration Maximums

When designing your Horizon environment, there are several configuration maximums. These maximums should not be seen as a target that you should aim for, unless of course you have that number of end users that you need to support, but instead provide guidance as to what the Horizon components support as a maximum configuration.

We will start by looking at the Cloud Pod Architecture maximums.

Cloud Pod Architecture Maximum Configurations

First, we are going to look at the maximum configuration for a single pod as shown in the following table:

CPA Maximum per pod	Limit
Active RDSH host servers in a single pod	20,000 (10,000 recommended
Active VDI sessions in a single pod	12,000
Maximum # of connection servers in a pod	7
Maximum end user login per pod	6 users per second
Maximum conncetion servers with HA in a pod	6 + 1
Maximum # of provisioned desktops in a pod	12,000

Figure 3-25. *CPA configuration maximums for a single pod*

Next, we are going to look at the configuration maximums for a pod federation as shown in the following table:

CPA Maximum per federation	Limit
Maximum # sessions for a pod federation	250,000
Maximum # pods in a federation	50
Maximum number of site in a federation	15

Figure 3-26. *CPA configuration maximums for a pod federation*

Next, we are going to look at the maximum configuration for the connection server, starting with the maximum number of supported sessions.

Connection Server Maximum Configurations

In this section, we are going to look at the configuration maximums for the connection server, highlighting the maximum number of sessions and then the desktop pool configuration limits.

First, we are going to look at the maximum session configuration as shown in the following table:

CPA Maximum per federation	Limit
Maximum # sessions per connection server	4,000
End user login rate	1 user per second

Figure 3-27. *Connection server maximum sessions*

Next, we are going to look at the desktop pool maximum configuration as shown in the following table:

Connection server pool maximums	Limit
# Desktops in a single instant clone pool	4,000
# Desktops in a single linked clone pool	4,000
# Desktops in a single full clone pool	4,000
# of RDSH host servers in a single farm	500

Figure 3-28. *Connection server desktop pool maximums*

In the next section, we are going to look at the vSphere maximum configurations.

vSphere Configuration Maximums

In this section, we are going to look at the maximum configurations for the vSphere infrastructure that supports your Horizon environment. So, this is for vCenter, ESXi, and storage datastores.

We will start with vCenter Server.

vCenter Server Configuration Maximums

The following table shows the vCenter Server configuration maximums:

vCenter Server Appliance maximums	Limit
# Powered on virtual desktop machines	12,000
# Registered virtual desktops per vCenter	12,000
# Hosts per cluster	64

Figure 3-29. *vCenter Server configuration maximums*

Next, we are going to look at the datastore configuration maximums.

Datastore Configuration Maximums

The following table shows the datastore configuration maximums:

Datastore maximums	Limit
# Virtual desktops per vSAN datastore	6,400
# Virtual desktops per VMFS datastore	500
# virtual desktops per NFS datastore	500

Figure 3-30. *Datastore configuration maximums*

Next, we are going to look at the ESXi host server configuration maximums.

ESXi Host Server Configuration Maximums

The following table shows the ESXi host server configuration maximums:

ESXi host server maximums	Limit
# vCPU's per CPU core	8
# Virtual desktops per ESXi host server	200

Figure 3-31. *ESXi host server configuration maximums*

Now that we have discussed the maximum configurations, the final part of the infrastructure we are going to cover is the UAG appliance.

UAG Sizing

The UAG, as it is an appliance, is available in three different configuration sizes as it not only supports external Horizon end users but also Workspace ONE users up to a maximum of 50,000 end users.

However, as Horizon connection servers only support a maximum of 2000 end users, then there is no point looking at either the large or extra-large configuration options.

For Horizon, use the standard UAG configuration as described in the following table:

UAG standard appliance	Required
CPU's	2
Memory	4GB
Minimum disk space	20GB

Figure 3-32. *UAG configuration requirements*

In the next section, we are going to look at capacity planning to help test your Horizon solution as you deploy it and more importantly to test that you have configured the appropriate resources before moving into production and enabling end-user access.

Capacity Planning

There are several solutions available to assist with capacity planning. In this section, we are going to introduce you to the VMware View Planner solution.

The View Planner is a capacity planning tool that has been designed to simulate real-world workloads for the VDI environment to assist with scalability and sizing. More importantly, it will ensure that you are going to deliver the end-user experience.

It works by capturing the end-user experience by simulating workloads on the virtual desktop machines. This workload is then measured against the infrastructure to identify any performance issues that could negatively impact the end-user experience.

The View Planner is simple to install by installing the following two components:

- **View Planner harness appliance**: Used for collecting and measuring the data from the virtual desktop machines

- **View Planner agent**: Installed on the desktop OS of the virtual desktop machine to generate simulated workloads

You can download the View Planner by following this link:

https://my.vmware.com/web/vmware/downloads/info/slug/other/vmware_view_planner/4_6

In the next section, we are going to look at how the end users are going to connect to their virtual desktop machines and understand if there is anything that may affect the overall design.

How End Users Connect

We are going to cover the end-user client options in Chapter 13; however, when it comes to the design considerations, it is worth understanding what the end users are going to use to connect to their virtual desktop machines. The reason is that the chosen display protocol could have a bearing on your configuration.

For example, if you are going to deploy zero clients, then they are going to be using PCoIP as the display protocol. You then need to design your solution bearing in mind the requirements of that protocol.

In the next section, we are going to look at how you would consider protecting your Horizon environment.

Protecting Your Horizon Infrastructure

In this section, we are going to briefly touch on protecting your Horizon environment. However, the majority of what we have covered in terms of your design already has an element of protection built in.

By this we are referring to the fact that you will have deployed multiple ESXi host servers in a cluster, with each individual host server being configured to withstand hardware failures that will not take the entire environment offline.

We have also deployed multiple connection servers to take over from failed servers, as well as to aid scalability.

In fact, most of what we have deployed has been designed with high availability in mind and is deployed by default as the solution scales.

However, let us briefly touch on DR.

DR

DR is something you should consider now that you have deployed virtual desktops. With physical desktops, DR was always hard to deploy, and organizations would buy empty office space, complete with desks and cupboards full of desktop PCs. Then, in the event of having to invoke DR, it would still take weeks to get everything set up and configured.

With virtual desktop infrastructure, DR is not only now possible but also much easier to invoke should you need it.

If you have deployed the Cloud Pod Architecture in your design, then you have already deployed DR, even though the objective of deploying CPA was to increase and scale up the number of supported end users.

With CPA, you will have deployed multiple pods; however, you may want to consider deploying those pods in different physical locations so that should an entire site go offline or fail, then the other sites can take over.

CPA works either in an active-active configuration or active-passive. Either way, you may want to consider deploying a second site to manage DR.

Backup

When it comes to backing up your Horizon environment, then there are a few key parts that you need to back up.

Typically, you would not back up things like your ESXi host server or connection servers; however, these do contain critical components, and that critical component is the database on each server.

The following lists the components that should be backed up:

- Horizon View ADAM database

- View Composer database (if you have linked clone desktops)

- vCenter Server database

- Events database

Depending on the other components you have deployed, such as App Volumes, that too will have a database that will need to be backed up.

About App Volumes, if you have deployed this within your environment, then you should also back up the packaged applications as you having to go back and run through the capture process again would be very time-consuming. Plus, any Writable Volumes that you have entitled for end users to install their own apps.

If you use ThinApp, you should also back up any ThinApp packages as again you would want to save time in not having to run the setup capture process again to rebuild the packages.

There is no need to back up virtual desktop machines as these will be delivered by Instant Clones and therefore are deleted as end users log out; however, if you have persistent disks, then you should back these up as they will contain user-specific data. You may, however, want to make sure you have a backup of your gold image.

Now we have covered all the key Horizon components, but what other infrastructure do you need, which may already be in place, to support your Horizon environment? We will discuss this in the next section.

What Other Infrastructure Is Required?

In addition to the Horizon-specific components that you will deploy, there are also several other considerations around support infrastructure and any potential additions or changes you might need to support your end users and their virtual desktop machines.

We will start with file server requirements.

File Servers

You are more than likely to have a file server already deployed within your existing environment to support your end users. The key here is to consider things that may require additional storage space – things like end-user profiles.

We have not yet talked about end-user environment management (UEM), which we will in a later chapter; however, for now you need to consider that configuration files and end-user files and profile information will need to be stored on a replicated file system.

You can start to think about how much storage you will need to deploy in advance of deploying a UEM solution as your assessment data should tell you the size of your end-user profiles. From here, you can size any additional storage requirements.

Database Servers

To support the Horizon and vSphere infrastructure, you will also need several different databases. You can use your existing database infrastructure to host these, but you need to ensure the database servers have enough resource available, both CPU and disk storage resources.

It is also worth considering high availability enterprise-class database infrastructure. The reason I say that is because I have seen several occasions where the pilot has gone straight into production and is still using a database such as SQL Server Express. While this is fine for POC and pilot environments, when you start to scale you could soon run out of resources.

Some of the database requirements for Horizon are internal, such as the ADAM database that sits on the connection and replica servers. But you should use external databases for the following:

- View Composer database (if you have linked clone desktops)

- Events database

- App Volumes

Do not forget that as we are using the vCenter Server Appliance, we are using the integrated PostgreSQL database on the appliance.

In the next section, we are going to look at the sizing implications for the database requirements for the events database and App Volumes. Linked clones are no longer part of this latest version of Horizon, and so we will not cover those.

Database Sizing Requirements

In this section, we are going to look at the different database requirements for each of the key Horizon components. We will start with the Horizon Events Database.

Events Database

The events database, which is still referred to as the View events database, stores all the Horizon event logs for any actions that take place on the connection servers.

The size is very much dependent on the number of users and the retention period that you configure. Although there are not any published figures, the typical size would grow by around 1–2 MB per month, for each individual end user.

If we take an example of a desktop block of 2000 end users and keep the data for just one year, then you should ensure that you have a minimum of 48 GB of storage available. This is simply calculated using the following:

Figure 3-33. *View event database requirements*

Next, we are going to look at the database requirements for App Volumes if you are considering including this in your deployment.

App Volumes Database Requirements

For completeness, we are going to add in the App Volumes database requirements just so that we have covered all the database requirements for an entire Horizon solution, starting with the configuration database storage requirements as shown in the following table:

Configuration Element	Space Required
Static configuration for App Volumes Manager	5MB
Storage per registered virtual desktop machine	1KB
Storage per ESXi host server	1KB
Storage per AD end user, group, OU	4KB
Storage per vSphere datastore	3KB
Storage per AD domain controller	1KB
Storage per Writable Volume ZIP file	ZIP file size + 30%

Figure 3-34. *App Volumes static configuration storage requirements*

In the next table, we have the database storage requirements for the App Volumes assignments:

Assignments	Space Required
Storage per package	16KB
Storage per package assignment	6KB
Storage per app in the package	2KB
Storage per Writable Volume	22KB
Storage per VMDK or VHD virtual disk file	5KB

Figure 3-35. *App Volumes assignment storage requirements*

Finally, in the following table, we have the database storage requirements for the App Volumes auditing and dynamic session information:

Auditing Information & Dynamic Data	Space Required
Activity log events per operation	0.5 - 1KB
System messages per message	0.5 - 2KB
Administrator sessions per session	1KB
Pending tasks and delayed jobs per job/task	1KB

Figure 3-36. *App Volumes auditing and dynamic storage requirements*

Now we have looked at the database requirements from a storage capacity perspective, but to finish off, in the next section, we are going to look at which database solutions are supported.

Supported Databases for Horizon

The following list details the supported database versions for Horizon:

- Microsoft SQL Server 2014 (32- and 64-bit) No SP and SP1, Std and Ent

- Microsoft SQL Server 2012 (32- and 64-bit) SP2, Exp, Std, Ent

- Microsoft SQL Server 2008 R2 (32- and 64-bit) SP2 and SP3, Exp, Std, Ent, Data center

- Oracle 12c   Release 1 (any release up to 12.1.0.2)   Standard One, Standard, Enterprise

In the final section, we are going to look at the AD requirements for Horizon.

Active Directory

You will already have an existing AD infrastructure, and Horizon does not really change that. All that is really required is configuration around end-user accounts and computer accounts.

The best practice is to create an organizational unit (OU) dedicated to virtual desktop machines. This is to ensure that you do not apply the wrong policies from your standard physical desktop policies if you have a mixed environment. Virtual desktops are heavily optimized to ensure they perform and deliver the best end-user experience. You are also sharing resources with other virtual desktop machines.

Physical desktops are stand-alone and have their own dedicated resources, and so policies may not be so focused on optimization.

These OUs could also be created for different use cases. For example, you could configure an OU for the sales team that focused on delivering policies since you know they are mobile and will be connecting remotely across the Internet. The policy in this instance would ensure that the delivery was optimized for the Internet by switching off things that would consume large amounts of bandwidth.

You should also be aware that with Instant Clones, computer accounts are going to be dynamic as virtual desktop machines get built and destroyed on a regular basis.

Whatever the case, you should review your AD configuration and ensure it is configured optimally for your Horizon environment.

Summary

This chapter is probably one of the most important chapters in this book. That is because in this third chapter, we have given you a comprehensive and detailed overview of what to consider when architecting a VMware Horizon solution for production. We have guided you first through how to approach a project and look to conduct an assessment to understand your current environment. Next, we looked at how you would set out to prove the technology was fit for purpose and how to test it and get engaged with the end users that are going to use it.

Armed with that information, the rest of this chapter has provided you with the information needed to architect your own solution. We have looked at how to size your environment and how to scale it out, from the host servers, networking, storage, and other infrastructure components as well as how to protect against events that could prevent end users from working. Not only that, but we have also highlighted the other factors that you need to consider for your design.

In the next chapter, we are going to take the design considerations and now start the first part of the deployment phase and install the Horizon components.

CHAPTER 4

Installing and Configuring Your Horizon Environment

In the previous chapter, we discussed, in detail, the design considerations for building your Horizon environment to enable you to understand the end-user requirements and design an environment to cater for those requirements.

Now that we have completed the design phase, and we have our design documented, the next step is to start installing the Horizon software.

This fourth chapter is going to take you through the installation and configuration of a VMware Horizon environment either for your pilot testing phase or for production.

We will cover each installation step in detail, discussing the configuration options as well as showing actual screenshots as we work through the installation process.

Before we start the actual installation, there are a few things that we need to ensure are in place first. We will discuss these in the next section.

Before You Start

Before starting the installation, you need to ensure that you have completed a couple of administration tasks. These tasks are to set up management or service accounts for the Horizon components and vCenter to have access to the resources required. These resources are used by the different components to authenticate and to ensure the correct permissions are set.

We will start with configuring Active Directory.

Configuring Active Directory

With Active Directory, there are two main tasks that we are going to complete. The first of these tasks is to create a few user accounts.

145

© Peter von Oven 2022
P. von Oven, *Mastering VMware Horizon 8*, https://doi.org/10.1007/978-1-4842-7261-9_4

AD User Accounts

You will need AD accounts to act as service accounts for the Connection Server. This is to enable Horizon to log in and manage components within vCenter Server. The first account to create is a login to the Horizon Administrator console. This is used to manage Horizon. In this example, we have created an account called **Horizon-Admin@pvolab.com**.

An account is also required for creating Linked Clones and Instant Clones. This is to enable the creation process to create a computer account for the newly created virtual desktop machine.

Organizational Units (OUs) for Horizon Desktops

We have already discussed the need for specific OUs for your Horizon desktops, so now is the time to create those OUs ready for installation and ready for when we work through optimizing the end-user experience in Chapter 7. The following screenshot shows an example of a Horizon Desktops OU that will be used in this chapter.

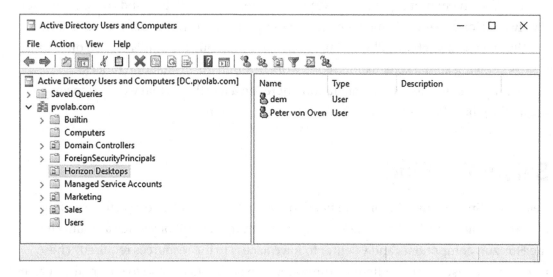

Figure 4-1. *Horizon Desktops organizational unit in AD*

Next, we are going to look at the vCenter Server accounts needed.

Configuring vCenter Accounts

You will need an Active Directory user account to allow the Horizon Connection Server to connect to the vCenter Server.

In this example, we have created a user account called **horizon-vc-user@pvolab.com** as shown in the following screenshot:

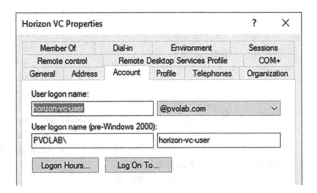

Figure 4-2. *vCenter Server user account in AD*

The vCenter Server account should be added as a local admin on the vCenter Server. Once you have created the vCenter user account, you will need to give it the user permissions as shown in the following table:

Required	Privilege #1	Privilege #2
Folder	Create Folder	
	Delete Folder	
Datastore	Allocate Space	
	Browse Datastore	
	Low Level File Operation	
Virtual Machine	Configuration	All
	Inventory	All
	Snapshot Management	All
	Interaction	Power Off
		Power On
		Reset
		Suspend
		Customize
	Provisioning	Deploy Template
		Read Customization Specifications
		Clone Virtual Machine
		Allow Disk Access
Resource	Assign Virtual Machine to Resource Pool	
	Migrate Powered Off Virtual Machine	
Global	Act as a vCenter Server	
	Enable Methods	
	Disable Methods	
	System Tag	
Host	Configuration	Advanced Settings
Network	All	

Figure 4-3. *vCenter Server user account privileges*

Now that we have created the account in Active Directory and looked at the vCenter-specific privileges that are required in vCenter, the next step in the process is to create a role for this user, along with these privileges, on the vCenter Server.

To do this, follow the steps described:

1. Log in to the vSphere Client using your administrator account.

    In this example, we are using the administrator@vsphere.local account as shown in the following screenshot:

Figure 4-4. *Log in to vSphere Client*

2. Enter your credentials and click **LOGIN**.

3. You will now see the vSphere Client home page screen as shown
    in the following screenshot:

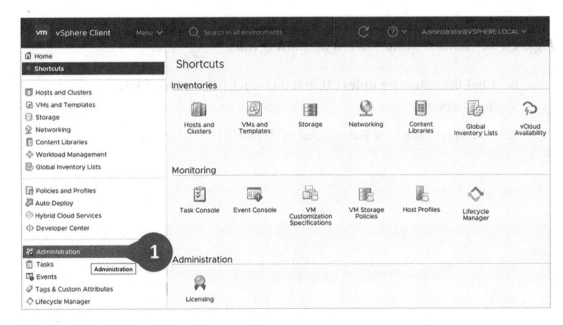

Figure 4-5. *vSphere Client home page screen*

4. Click **Administration** (1).

5. You will see the Administration configuration screen as shown in the following screenshot:

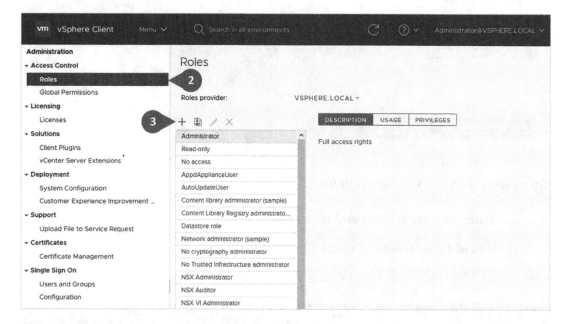

Figure 4-6. *Administration screen for adding roles*

6. Click the option for **Roles** (2), and then click the + button (3) to add a new role.

7. You will see the **New Role** screen as shown in the following:

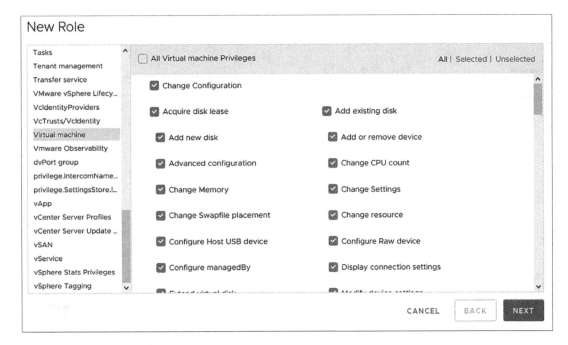

Figure 4-7. *Creating a new role – configuring privileges*

8. Using the table from Figure 4-3, add all the required privileges and then click **NEXT**.

9. You will now be able to add a role name as shown:

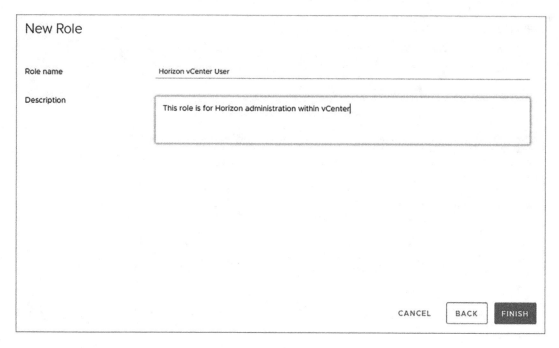

Figure 4-8. *Creating a new role – role name and description*

10. In this example, we have called the role **Horizon vCenter User** and then, in the description box, typed in a description for the role.

11. Click **FINISH.**

12. You will return to the **Roles** screen as shown:

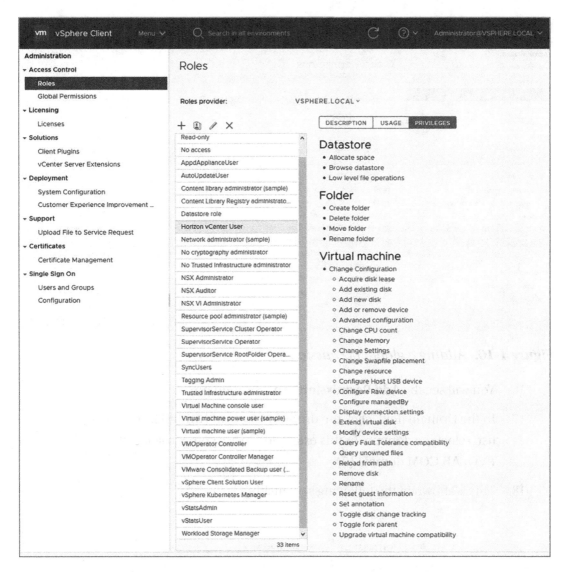

Figure 4-9. *New role successfully created*

13. Here, you will see the newly created role, and if you click the **PRIVILEGES** button, you will see the privileges that you configured.

14. Next, we are going to configure the permissions for this role.

15. From the **Administration** screen, click **Global Permissions** (4), and then click the + button (5) to add a new permission as shown in the following screenshot:

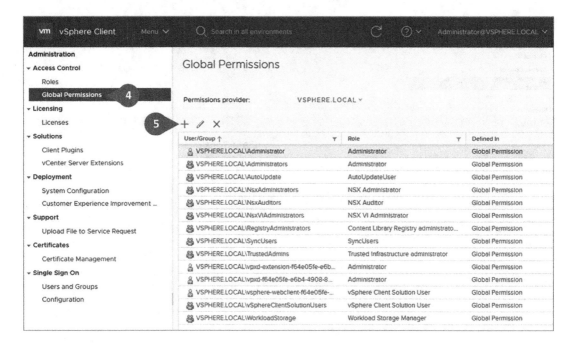

Figure 4-10. *Adding a global permission*

16. You will see the **Add Permission** configuration box.

17. In the Domain field, click the drop-down arrow (6), and from the list, select the domain. In this example, we are going to select the PVOLAB.COM domain (7).

18. This is shown in the following screenshot:

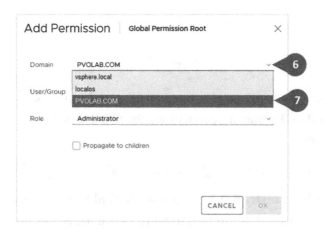

Figure 4-11. *Adding a global permission*

19. Next, in the **User/Group** field (8), start to type in the name of the user that was created in AD to be the vCenter and Horizon user. In this example, we have started to type in **Horizon** as the first part of the name as shown:

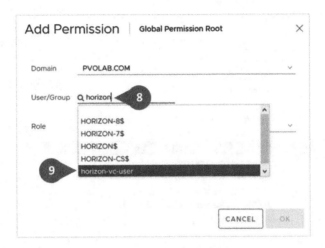

Figure 4-12. *Adding a global permission*

20. As you type, a drop-down list will appear with the results.

21. Click **horizon-vc-user** (9).

22. Finally, click the drop-down arrow for Role (10), and from the list of roles, select the Horizon vCenter User role (11) that you just created a role for as shown in the following:

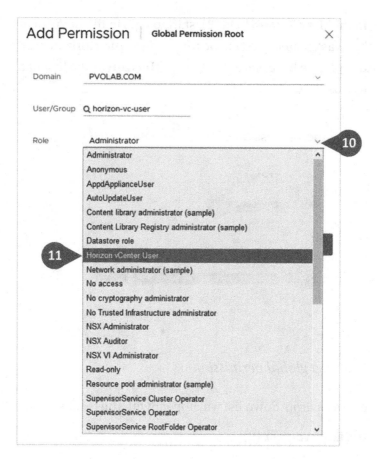

Figure 4-13. *Adding the new role to the global permission*

23.   Once configured, you will see something like the following screenshot:

Figure 4-14. *Global permission ready to save*

24. Click the **OK** button to complete the configuration.

25. You will return to the main **Administration** screen and the **Global Permissions** section. Here, you will see the newly configured global permission as shown:

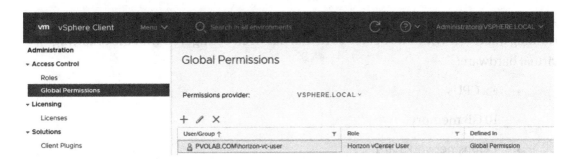

Figure 4-15. *Global permission successfully added*

You have now successfully created an AD user for Horizon and vCenter, configured the vCenter role and privileges, and assigned them to the AD account.

In the next section, we are going to install the Horizon Connection Server.

Installing the Horizon Environment

In this section, we are going to start installing the Horizon infrastructure components. These are the components that are going to form the management block: Connection Server, Replica Server, Enrollment Server, and Unified Access Gateway.

Installing the Horizon Connection Server

There are two parts to the Connection Server installation. The first part is to install the Connection Server software on a server, and the second part is to complete the initial configuration of the Connection Server.

In the initial configuration, we will add a license and configure things like the events database, vCenter Server, and Instant Clone domains, to name just a couple of these tasks.

First, we are going to have a quick refresh on the prerequisites before we start the actual installation process.

Prerequisites and Requirements

To serve as a reminder, the Connection Server is going to be installed on a virtual server running Microsoft Windows Server 2016 that has been configured with the following virtual hardware:

- 4 x CPUs
- 10 GB memory
- 1 Gbps network card
- 60 GB of free hard disk for the installation files

Next, we are going to work through the installation, step by step.

Performing the Installation

To install the Connection Server, follow the steps described:

1. Open a console or connect to the desktop of the server onto which you are going to install the Connection Server. In this example, we have pre-built a server and given it the hostname of **horizon-8.pvolab.com.**

158

2. Navigate to the location of the Horizon 8 software that you downloaded. This is shown in the following screenshot:

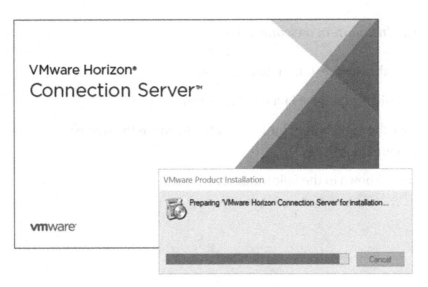

Figure 4-16. *Navigating to the Horizon 8.1 installer*

3. Double-click the **VMware-Horizon-Connection-Server-x86_64-8.1.0-17351278** to launch the Installer.

4. You will see the following splash screen along with the **VMware Product Installation** pop-up box:

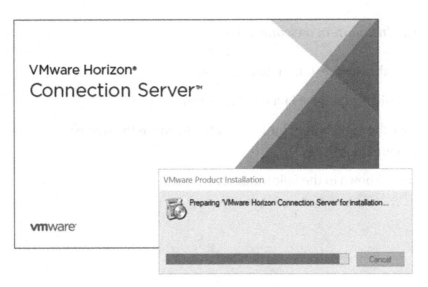

Figure 4-17. *Connection Server installer splash screen*

5. Next, you will see the **Welcome to the Installation Wizard for VMware Horizon Connection Server** screen as shown in the following screenshot:

Figure 4-18. *Installation welcome screen*

6. Click the **Next ➤** button to continue.

7. You will now see the **License Agreement** screen.

8. Click the radio button for **I accept the terms in the license agreement**.

9. This is shown in the following screenshot:

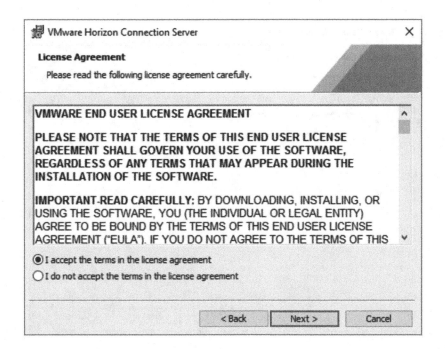

Figure 4-19.   *License Agreement screen*

10.   Click the **Next ➤** button to continue.

11.   You will see the **Destination Folder** screen as shown:

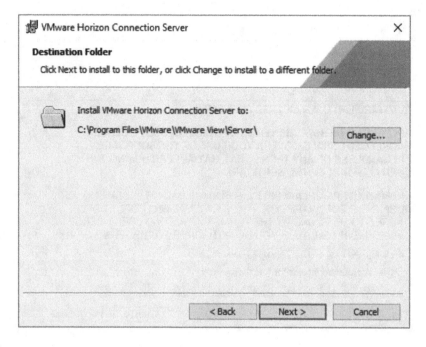

Figure 4-20. *Destination Folder screen*

12. Accept the default folder location and then click the **Next ➤** button to continue.

13. You will see the **Installation Options** configuration screen as shown in the following screenshot:

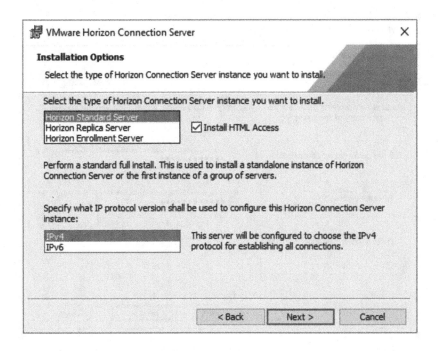

Figure 4-21. *Installation Options configuration screen*

14. This is the first Connection Server that we are installing, so from the list of Connection Server instance types, click the option for **Horizon Standard Server**.

15. We are also going to allow end users to access their virtual desktop machines using a browser, so check the **Install HTML Access** button. This will ensure the components for browser access will be installed with the Connection Server.

16. Finally, on this screen, select the IP protocol version you are going to use. In this example, we are going to select **IPv4** as the protocol. As this is the first Connection Server, then any other Horizon components that you install will also need to be configured to use IPv4.

17. Now click the **Next ➤** button to continue.

18. The next configuration screen is for Data Recovery as shown in the following screenshot:

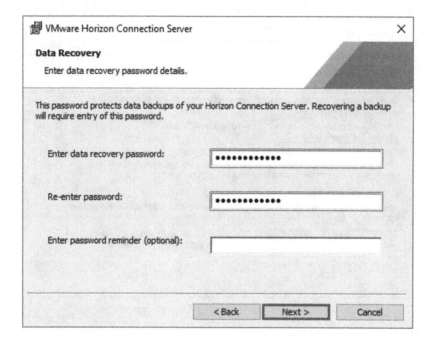

Figure 4-22. *Data Recovery screen*

19. On this configuration screen, you need to enter a password that will be used to protect data backups of the Connection Server. In the **Enter data recovery password** box, type in the password you want to set.

20. Then, in the Re-enter password box, type the password in again as a check.

21. Finally, in the Enter password reminder box, you can optionally add a reminder or a hint for this password.

22. Now click the **Next ➤** button to continue.

23. You will now see the **Firewall Configuration** screen as shown in the following screenshot:

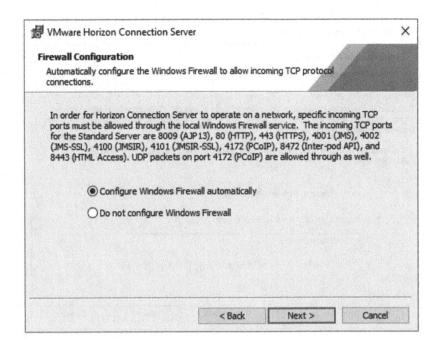

Figure 4-23. *Firewall Configuration screen*

24. Click the radio button for Configure Windows Firewall automatically. The recommended best practice is to allow the Windows Firewall to be configured automatically by the Horizon installer. You can then take a note of the ports that have been opened as they are listed on the screen.

25. Now click the **Next ➤** button to continue.

26. The next screen is for **Initial Horizon Administrators**. On this screen, you can add the user or group of users that are going to administer the Connection Server to begin with. Once installed, you can configure, via the Horizon Console, any new or additional administrators.

27. In this example, we are going to authorize a specific domain user and add the administrator account.

28. Click the radio button for **Authorize a specific domain user or domain group** as shown in the following screenshot:

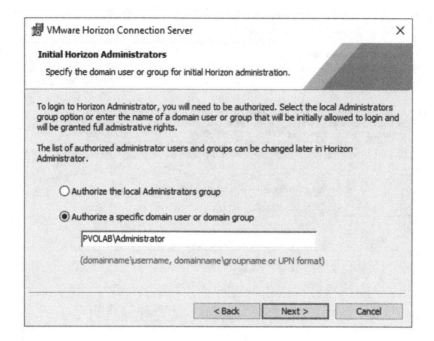

Figure 4-24. Initial Horizon Administrators configuration

29.   Click the **Next ➤** button to continue.

30.   The next screen is for the **VMware User Experience Improvement Program**. Checking the Join the VMware Customer Experience Improvement Program provides VMware with information that helps to fix problems and to get the most out of the products. It is optional and is not used to check licensing.

In this example we are going to ensure that the box is unchecked as shown in the following screenshot:

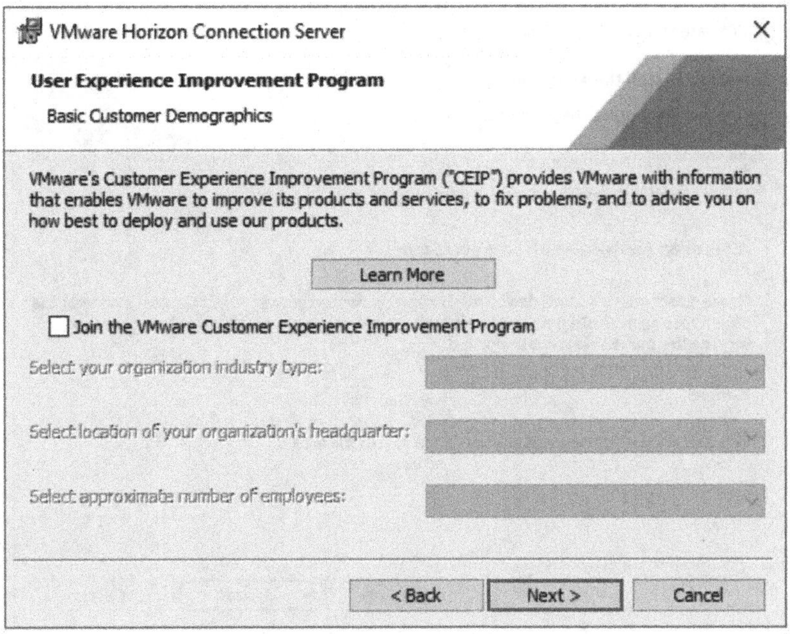

Figure 4-25. *Customer Experience Improvement Program*

31. Click the **Next ➤** button to continue to the **Ready to Install** screen as shown in the following screenshot:

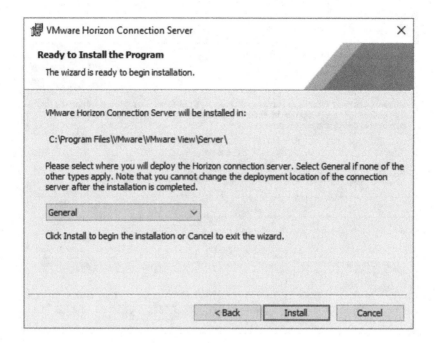

Figure 4-26. *Ready to install the Connection Server*

32. On this screen, you have the option of selecting where this Connection Server is going to be installed. In this example, we are installing the Connection Server on-premises, so we are going to click the option for **General**. If you are installing Horizon on a cloud platform, choose your platform from the list as shown in the following screenshot:

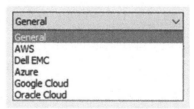

Figure 4-27. *Selecting where Horizon will be deployed*

It is worth noting that you cannot change the deployment location after you have installed the Connection Server.

---

33. Click **Install** to start the installation process.

34. You will see the **Installing VMware Horizon Connection Server**
     screen as shown in the following screenshot:

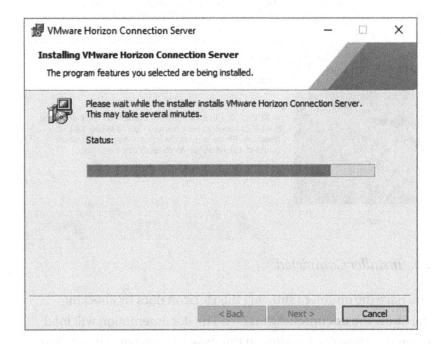

Figure 4-28. *Connection Server installation progress and status*

35. Once the installation has completed, you will see the **Installer**
     Completed screen as shown in the following:

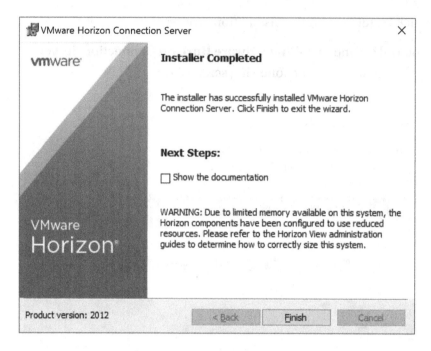

Figure 4-29. *Installer Completed*

36. You have the option of showing the Horizon docs by checking the **Show the documentation** box. The documentation will load when you close the Installer. In this example, we have unchecked the box.

37. Click the **Finish** button to complete the installation.

38. You will return to the desktop where you will see the following icon for the Horizon Administrator Console:

Figure 4-30. *Horizon Administrator Console desktop icon*

You have now successfully installed the Connection Server.

In the next section, we are going to log in to the Horizon Administrator Console for the first time and complete the second part of the installation, and that is to complete the initial configuration tasks.

Completing the Initial Configuration Tasks

Before you can start using the Horizon Administrator Console to build desktop pools and deliver virtual desktop machines to end users, there are a few initial administration and configuration tasks that you need to complete.

The first step is to log in to the Horizon Administrator Console. To do this, follow the steps described:

1. Double-click the **Horizon Administrator Console** icon.

2. You will see the following login screen:

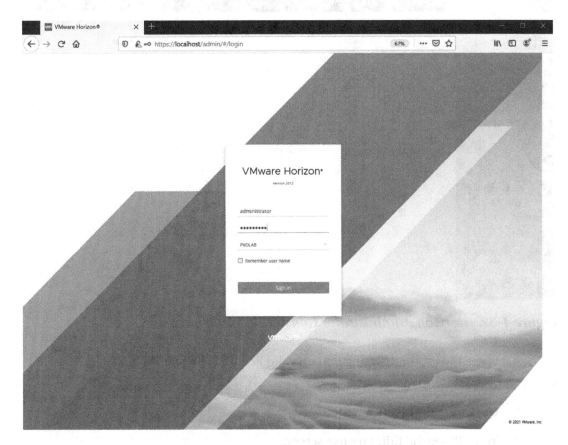

Figure 4-31. *Horizon Administrator Console login screen*

171

3. Type in the user's name and the password and then, from the
    drop-down arrow, select the domain this user resides in.

4. Now click the **Sign in** button.

You will now be signed in and will see the Horizon Administrator Console home
page, and, as this is the first time you have logged in, you will be taken directly to the
licensing page so that you can add your license key. In the next section, we will add a
license key.

Adding the License Key

The first task to complete on initial login is to add a license key as shown in the following
screenshot:

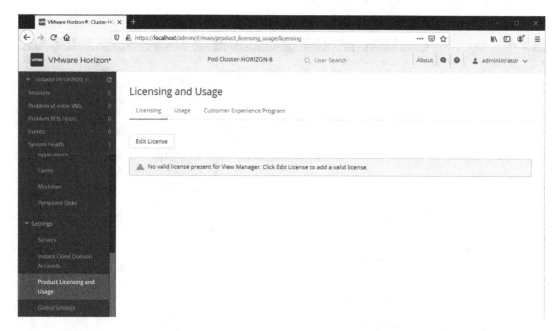

Figure 4-32. *Horizon Administrator Console licensing page*

You will see the message stating that no valid license is present. To add a license,
follow the steps described:

1. Click the **Edit License** button.

2. You will see the **Edit License** screen.

3. In the * License Serial Number box, type in your license key as shown in the following screenshot:

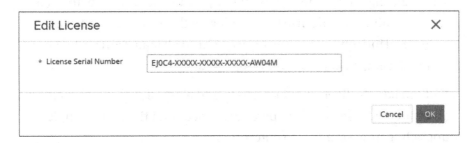

Figure 4-33. *Adding a serial number*

4. Click **OK**.

5. You will now see the **Licensing and Usage** screen as shown:

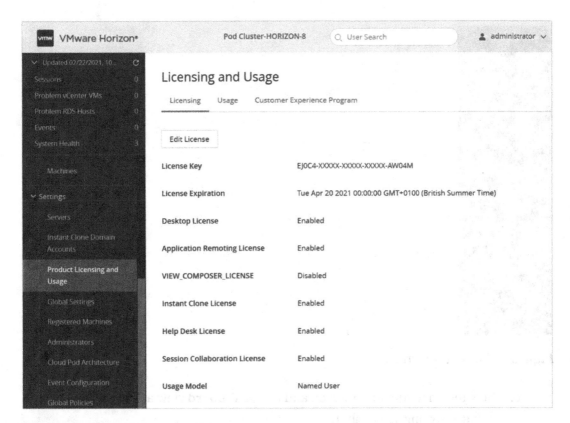

Figure 4-34. *Licensing and Usage screen*

Once you have successfully added the license key, you will see information relating to the license details and the current usage.

The licensing information shows the expiration date along with what specific features the license key enables. In this example, we have entered a Horizon Enterprise license, and so all features have been enabled using the named user usage model.

You can edit the license if you need to add a new license to replace an expired license or if you upgrade to a better edition, for example, upgrading from standard to enterprise.

Also, on this screen, you have the **Usage** tab which will show you the number of end users that are using Horizon, as shown in the following screenshot:

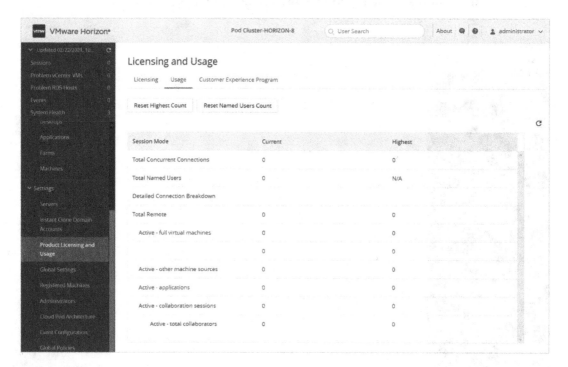

Figure 4-35. *Usage screen*

6. Now return to the home screen and the **Dashboard** view as shown in the following screenshot:

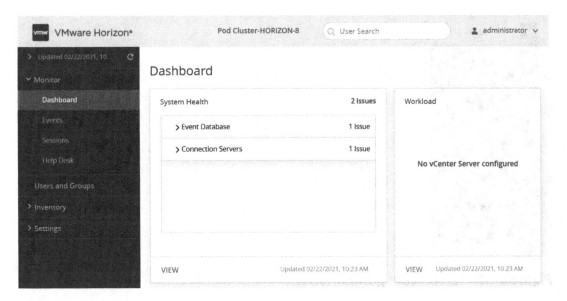

Figure 4-36. *Dashboard screen*

As you can see in the **Workload** section, there is no vCenter Server configured, so the next task to complete is to add the vCenter Server.

Adding a vCenter Server for Desktop Management

In this section, we are going to add the vCenter Server to the Horizon Console so that Horizon can manage the virtual desktop machines.

To do this, follow the steps described:

1. From the **Dashboard** screen, expand the option for **Settings**, and then click **Servers**.

2. Ensure that the first tab for **vCenter Servers** is selected as shown in the following screenshot:

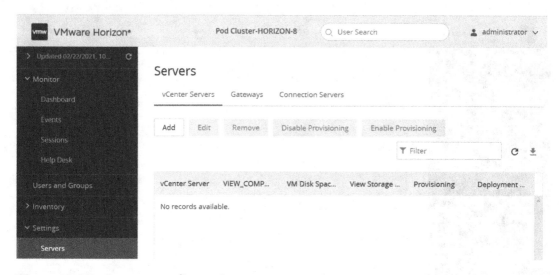

Figure 4-37. *Servers configuration screen*

3.   Click the **Add** button.

4.   You will see the **Add vCenter Server** screen, with the following
     screenshot showing the first part of that screen:

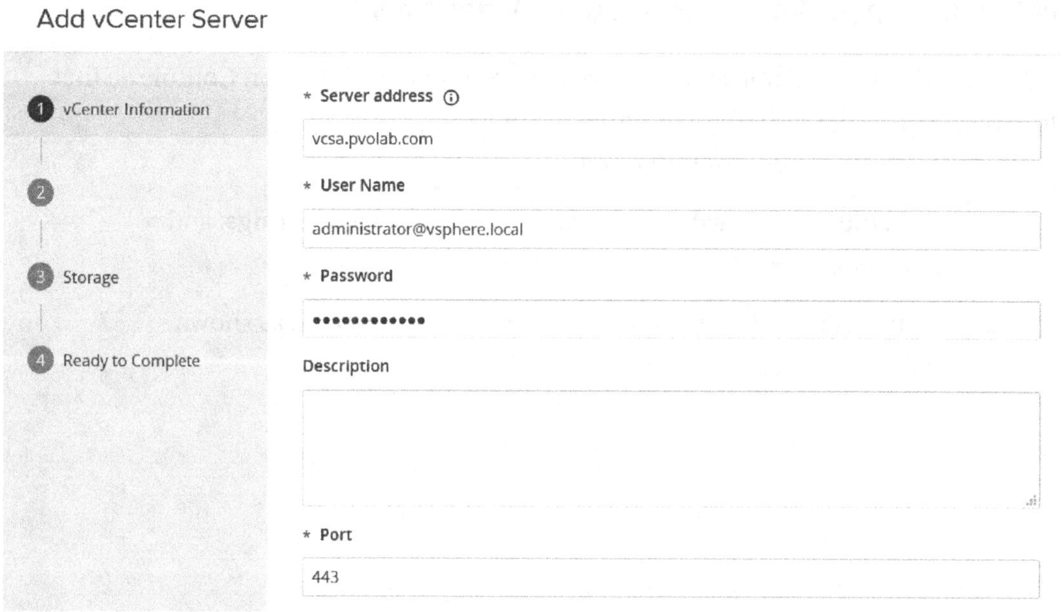

Add vCenter Server

* Server address ⓘ

vcsa.pvolab.com

* User Name

administrator@vsphere.local

* Password

••••••••••••

Description

* Port

443

1 vCenter Information

2

3 Storage

4 Ready to Complete

Figure 4-38. *Adding the vCenter Server screen*

5. In the **Server address** box, type in the name of the vCenter Server
    that is managing these specific virtual desktop machines. In this
    example, the vCenter Server is called **vcsa.pvolab.com**.

6. Next, in the **User Name** box, type in the username. This is the new
    vCenter user account that we created previously.

7. Then, in the **Password** box, type in the password for this account.

8. Optionally, in the **Description** box, you can type in a description
    for this vCenter Server.

9. The final configuration option in this part of the screen is the port
    that will be used for this connection. The default port is port 443
    as shown.

10. Now scroll down to the **Advanced Settings** section as shown in
    the following screenshot:

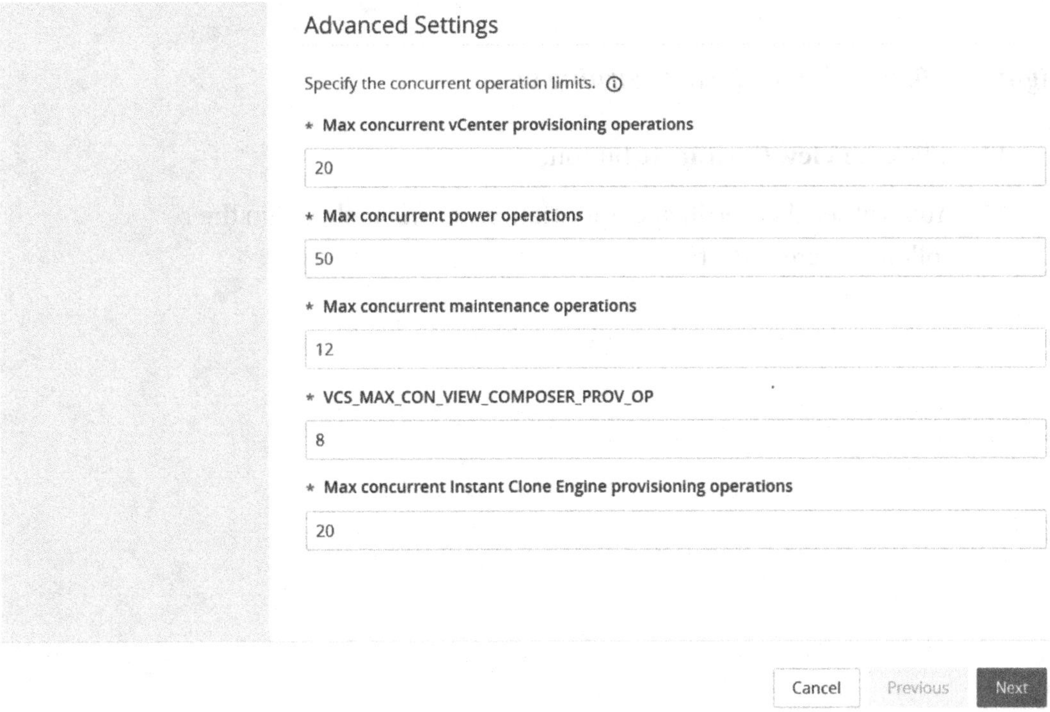

Advanced Settings

Specify the concurrent operation limits. ⓘ

* **Max concurrent vCenter provisioning operations**

```
20
```

* **Max concurrent power operations**

```
50
```

* **Max concurrent maintenance operations**

```
12
```

* **VCS_MAX_CON_VIEW_COMPOSER_PROV_OP**

```
8
```

* **Max concurrent Instant Clone Engine provisioning operations**

```
20
```

Cancel   Previous   Next

Figure 4-39. *Advanced Settings for vCenter Server configuration*

11. In this example, we are going to leave the advanced settings as the current defaults.

12. Once you have completed this configuration screen, then click the **Next** button.

13. If you have not yet set up a signed certificate for vCenter, then you will see the following **Invalid Certificate Detected** warning box:

Figure 4-40. *Invalid certificate warning box*

14. Click the **View Certificate** button.

15. You will see the Certificate Information screen as shown in the following screenshot:

Figure 4-41. *Certificate Information screen*

16. Click the **Accept** button.

17. The next screen is for View Composer as shown in the following screenshot:

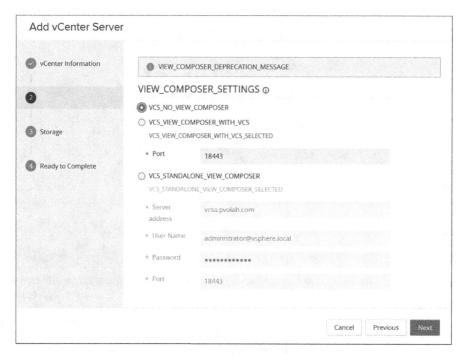

Figure 4-42. *View Composer deprecation message*

18. In Horizon 8.1 (2012), Linked Clones have been deprecated, and so as this is a new installation, we will not configure anything on this screen. Instead, you should use Instant Clones.

19. Click the **Next** button to continue.

20. You will see the **Storage Settings** screen as shown in the following screenshot:

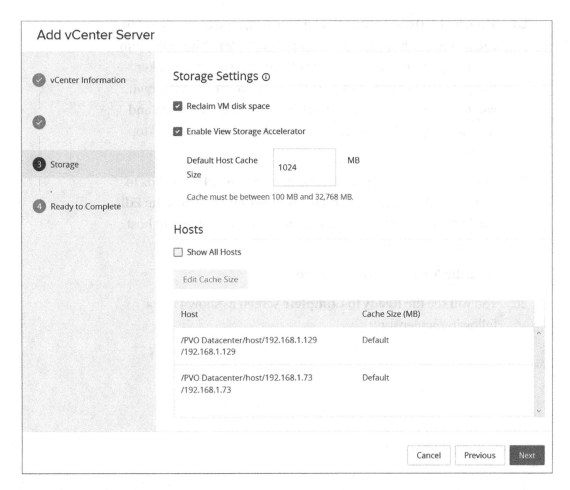

Figure 4-43. *Storage Settings screen*

21. Check the **Reclaim VM disk space** box. This allows the virtual
desktop machines to use a space-efficient virtual disk format. This
works by reclaiming unused disk space, such as space taken up by
deleted files, and therefore uses less disk space.

22. Next is the option for **Enable View Storage Accelerator**. Check
the box to enable it. This allows the ESXi host servers to cache the
most commonly read data blocks to memory instead of reading
them from disk. This improves the disk I/O performance. The
storage accelerator is required for Instant Clone replica disks.

23. Then in the **Default Host Cache Size** box, type in the size of the cache that will be used. The default is **1024 MB**. The maximum size is 32,768,768 MB. The higher the cache size, the quicker things like smart provisioning will be. However, do not forget, whatever size you select, this will be taken from memory, and that memory will no longer be available to the virtual desktop machines.

24. In the **Hosts** section, you can check the **Show All Hosts** box to display all ESXi hosts. You then have the option to click the **Edit Cache Size** to configure different cache sizes on different host servers.

25. Click the **Next** button to continue.

26. You will see the **Ready to Complete** screen as shown in the following screenshot:

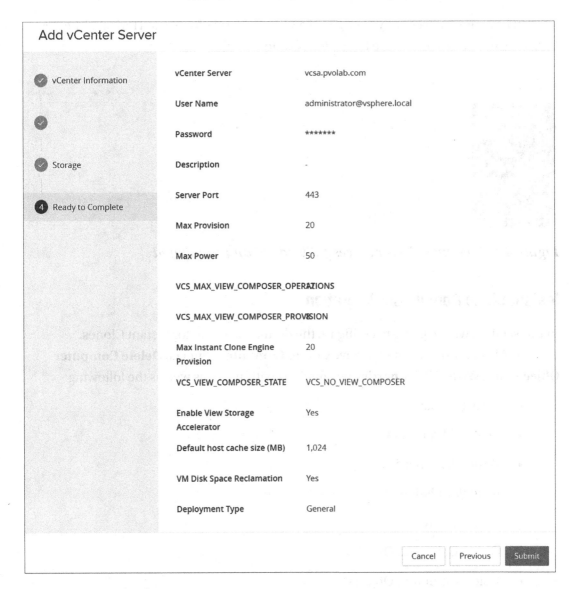

Figure 4-44. *Ready to complete the configuration screen*

27. Click the **Submit** button to complete the configuration.

28. You will now return to the **Servers** screen where you will see that the vCenter Server has been successfully added. You will also see the features that have been enabled, such as disk reclamation and storage accelerator. It will also show that the server is enabled for provisioning, meaning virtual desktop machines can be created.

29. This is shown in the following screenshot:

You have now successfully configured a vCenter Server for use in Horizon. The next task to complete is to configure the Instant Clone domain.

Figure 4-45. *vCenter Server successfully added and configured*

Instant Clone Domain Configuration

In this section, we are going to configure the domain account for Instant Clones.

This AD account will need to have **Create Computer Objects**, **Delete Computer Objects**, and **Write All Properties** permissions within AD, as well as the following:

- List Contents

- Read All Properties

- Write All Properties

- Read Permissions

- Reset Password

- Create Computer Objects

- Delete Computer Objects

To configure the domain account, follow the steps described:

1. From the left-hand menu, expand the option for **Settings** and then click **Instant Clone Domain Accounts**.

2. You will see the following screenshot:

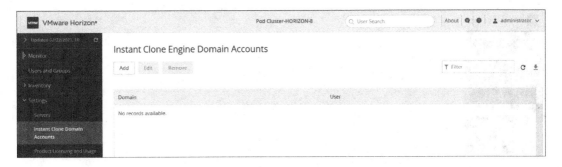

Figure 4-46. *Instant Clone configuration screen*

3. Click the **Add** button.

4. You will see the **Add Domain Admin** box as shown in the following screenshot:

Figure 4-47. *Add the domain admin account*

5. In the **Full domain name** box, click the drop-down menu and select the domain from the list.

6. Then in the **User Name** box, type in the user's name followed by the password for that user in the Password box.

7. Click **OK**.

8. You will now see the following screenshot showing the account has now been configured:

Figure 4-48. *Instant Clone domain account successfully configured*

You have now successfully configured the Instant Clone domain admin account. In the next section, we are going to add the Horizon events database.

Horizon Events Database Configuration

The Horizon events database is used to store the events that Horizon generates. The database can be either a Microsoft SQL database or an Oracle database and needs to be configured beforehand.

In this example, we have preconfigured a Microsoft SQL database and created a database called **HorizonEvents** and then have also created a user account for this database using SQL authentication.

Remember that when using SQL Server for the Horizon events database, it only supports SQL Server authentication mode.

We have also created a SQL username of **horizonevents**.

To configure the events database, follow the steps described:

1. From the left-hand menu, expand the option for **Settings** and then click **Event Configuration**.

2. You will see the following screenshot:

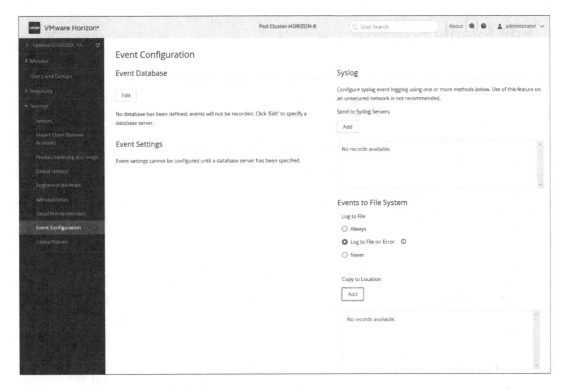

Figure 4-49. *Event Configuration screen*

You will also see the options for creating event details to be logged to a Syslog server and a file system which we will also cover in this section.

3. Under the **Event Database** heading, click the **Edit** button.

4. You will see the **Edit Event Database** configuration screen as shown in the following screenshot:

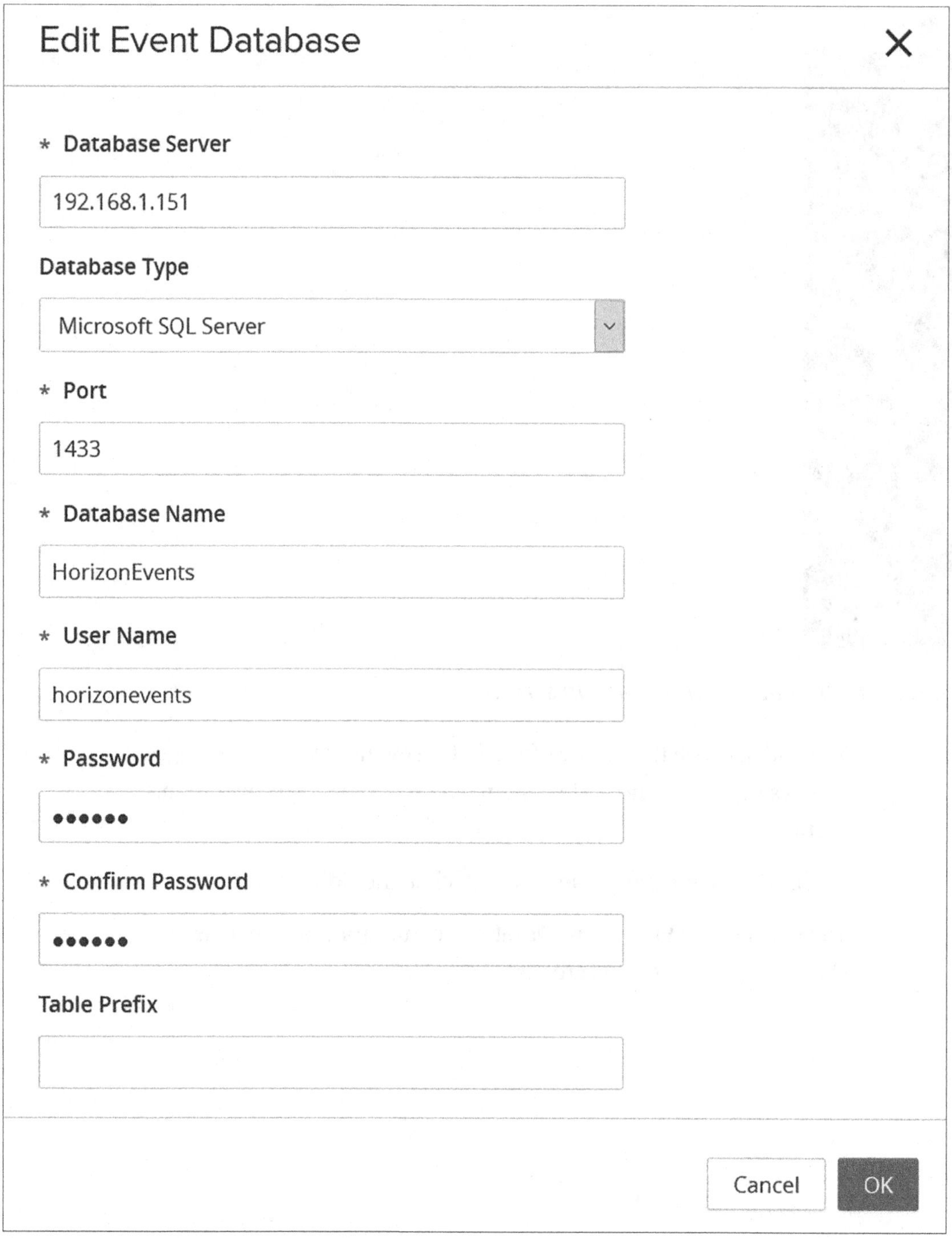

Edit Event Database   ✕

* Database Server

192.168.1.151

Database Type

Microsoft SQL Server

* Port

1433

* Database Name

HorizonEvents

* User Name

horizonevents

* Password

••••••

* Confirm Password

••••••

Table Prefix

Cancel   OK

Figure 4-50. *Edit Event Database configuration screen*

5. In the **Database Server** box, type in the address of the database.
    In this example, this is the Microsoft SQL Server.

6. From the **Database Type** box, click the drop-down arrow and
    select **Microsoft SQL Server**.

7. In the **Port** box, type in the port used to connect to SQL Server. In
    this example, we are using port 1433,

Depending on your version of SQL Server, you might want to check that the port
numbers match.

---

8. Enter the name of the database you created in the **Database
    Name** box. In this example, the database is called **HorizonEvents**.

9. Now enter the **User Name** to enable Horizon to log on to the
    database. In this example, we have created a SQL user account
    called **horizonevents**.

10. Then, in the **Password** box, type in the password for the user's
    name you entered and type it again in the **Confirm Password** box.

11. If you have one, enter the table prefix in the **Table Prefix** box.

12. Click **OK** once you have completed the configuration. You will see
    the following screenshot:

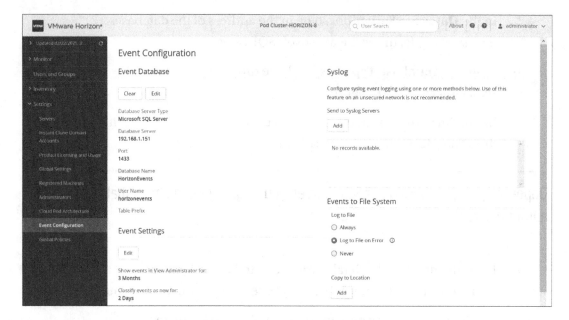

Figure 4-51. *Event configuration successfully completed*

With the events database now configured, you can now edit the settings for the length of time that events are displayed. If you remember from Chapter 3, the length of time that these logs are kept for will have an impact on the amount of storage required to keep them.

To change the default event settings, follow the steps described:

1. Under the **Event Settings** heading, click **Edit**.

2. You will see the **Event Settings** screen as shown in the following screenshot:

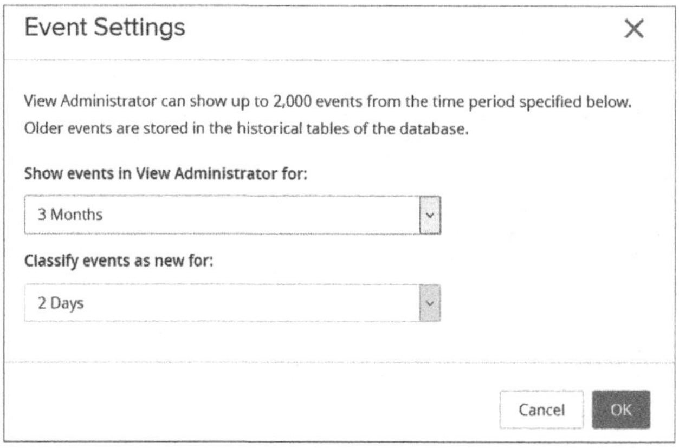

Figure 4-52. *Event Settings – editing the configuration*

On this screen, you can configure the length of time that events are shown in the administrator console and also how long a new event is classified as new.

3. Click **OK** to accept the settings.

    As previously mentioned, there are two other ways that events can be captured and recorded. The first of these is the use of a Syslog server.

To configure Syslog event logging, follow the steps as described:

1. Under the **Syslog** section, click the **Add** button.

2. You will see the following screenshot:

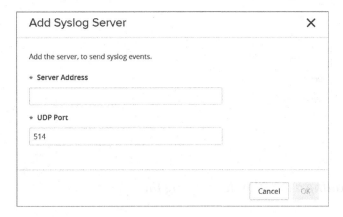

***Figure 4-53.**   Configuring a Syslog server*

3. In the **Server Address,** type in the address to the Syslog server that you are going to use.

4. Then, in the **UDP Port** box, type in the port number to use for communication to the Syslog server. The default port is shown as 514.

5. Click **OK** to save the changes and return to the main event configuration screen.

The final option on this screen is to configure a file location for log files. To do this, follow the steps described:

1. First, click the radio button to select when the log to file action will happen. You can choose **Always**, **Log to File on Error**, or **Never**.

2. Then click the **Add** button.

3. You will see the **Add File Location** configuration box as shown in the following screenshot:

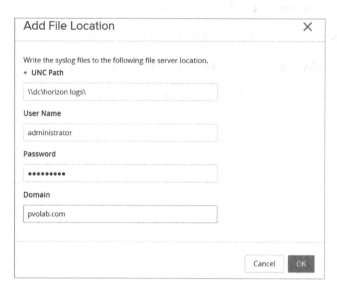

Figure 4-54. *Adding a location to store log files*

4. In the **UNC Path**, type in the path to the location of where the logs will be stored. In this example, we have a shared folder on the domain controller called **logs**.

Note   The path is a UNC path, so \\server_name\folder_name format.

---

5. Then enter the **User Name** for the user that has access to this folder, followed by the password for this account in the Password box.

6. Finally, in the **Domain** box, type in the name of the domain.

7. Click **OK** to save the configuration.

You have now successfully configured the recording of Horizon events. In the next section, we are going to look at configuring Horizon administrators.

Horizon Administrators

In this section, we are going to configure Horizon administrators by adding the user account we created in AD for this purpose.

To do this, follow the steps described:

1. From the left-hand menu, expand the option for **Settings** and then click **Administrators** as shown in the following:

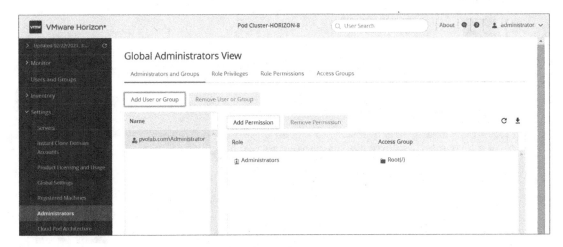

Figure 4-55. *Configuring Horizon administrators*

2. Now click the **Add User or Group** button.

3. You will see the **Add Administrator or Permission** configuration screen as shown in the following:

Figure 4-56. *Add Administrator Or Permission configuration screen*

4. Click the **Add** button.

5. You will see the **Find User or Group** screen as shown in the following:

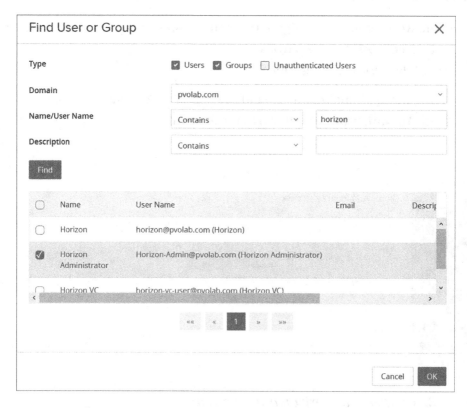

Figure 4-57.   Find a user or group screen

6. In the **Type** section, check the boxes for either **Users**, **Groups**, or **Unauthenticated Users** depending on what you want to add.

7. Now, in the **Domain** box, click the drop-down arrow and select the domain from those listed.

8. In the **Name/User Name** box, first, select the filter you want to search against. In this example, we are going to search for something that **Contains** the word **horizon**. Horizon is entered in the box next to the chosen filter and is the username we created in AD as the Horizon admin account.

9. Now click the **Find** button.

10. You will see the results listed below.

11. Check the box next to the account you want to use. In this example, it is the Horizon Administrator user.

12. Click OK.

13. You should see the account as shown in the following screenshot:

Figure 4-58. *Add Administrator Or Permission select role screen*

14. Click the **Next** button.

15. You will now see the **Select a role** screen.

16. Click **Administrators** as shown in the following screenshot:

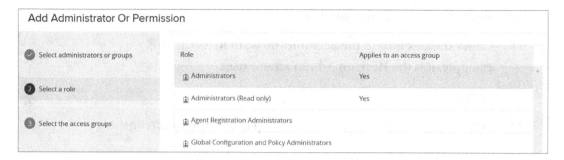

Figure 4-59. *Select a role screen*

17. Click the **Next** button.

18. You will see the **Select the access groups** screen as shown in the following screenshot:

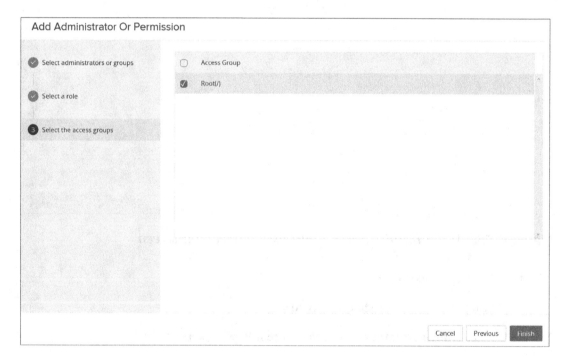

Figure 4-60. *Select the access groups screen*

19. Select the access group for this account and then click the **Finish** button.

20. You will now return to the Global Administrators View screen as shown in the following screenshot:

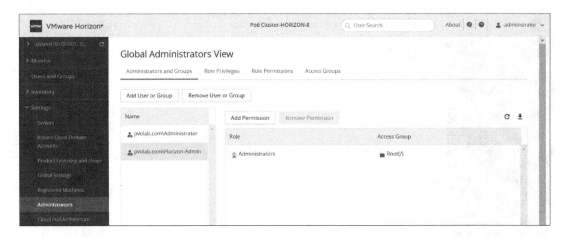

Figure 4-61. *Administrator account successfully added*

In the next section, we are going to look at the general settings.

General Settings

The general settings are a group of settings that define a number of configuration options including SSO configurations and how end users log in.

To configure the general settings, follow the steps described:

1. From the left-hand menu, expand the option for **Settings** and then click **Global Settings** as shown in the following:

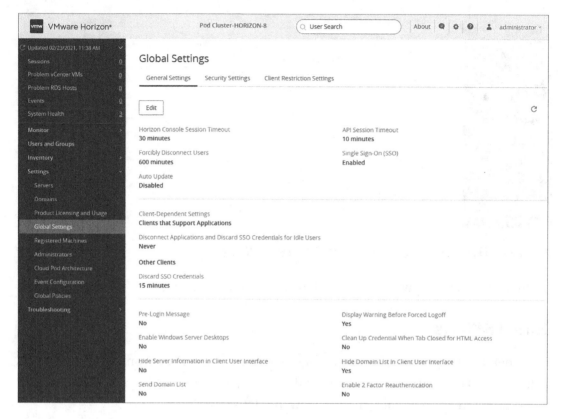

Figure 4-62. *Global Settings configuration screen*

2. Click the first tab for **General Settings**, and then click the **Edit** button.

3. You will then see the **General Settings** configuration screen. The first setting is to set the **Horizon Console Session Timeout**. This allows you to set the time limit on when a session times out. You will receive a warning message followed by a 60-second countdown timer. The session will continue if you click somewhere within the console. When the 60 seconds has expired, you will see a message stating that the session has expired, and you will need to log in again. The minimum session timeout is 2 minutes with a maximum session timeout of 72 hours.

4. Next is the **API Session Timeout**. With this setting, you can define how long an API session can remain idle before the session times out. The default is ten minutes.

5. The **Forcibly Disconnect Users** setting will disconnect all users
    once the specified time has elapsed since the end user logged in.
    All sessions will be disconnected at the same time regardless of
    when the end user opened them.

6. **Single Sign-On (SSO)** needs to be enabled, from the drop-down
    menu, if you are using True SSO. True SSO means that when an
    end user logs in using another form of authentication other than
    AD credentials, True SSO generates a short-term certificate rather
    than using cached credentials, after the end user logs in.

7. The next setting, under the heading of **Client-Dependent
    Settings**, is for **Disconnect Applications and Discard SSO
    Credentials for Idle Users**. This is used to protect application
    sessions when there is no end-user activity for a period of time. If
    you select the **After** option from the drop-down menu, then you
    can specify a time limit after which the SSO credentials will be
    discarded, as shown in the following screenshot:

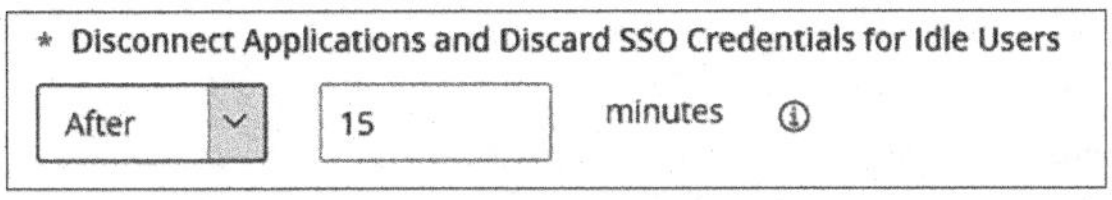

Figure 4-63. *Discard SSO credentials after a specified time*

The other option is to **Never** discard the SSO credentials.

8. Next, under the **Other Clients** heading, you have the option to
    Discard SSO Credentials as per the previous setting. This is
    for clients that do not support application remoting. You can
    configure a time limit with the **After** setting or select the **Never**
    setting.

9. These configuration options are all shown in the following
    screenshot that shows the first half of the General Settings
    configuration screen:

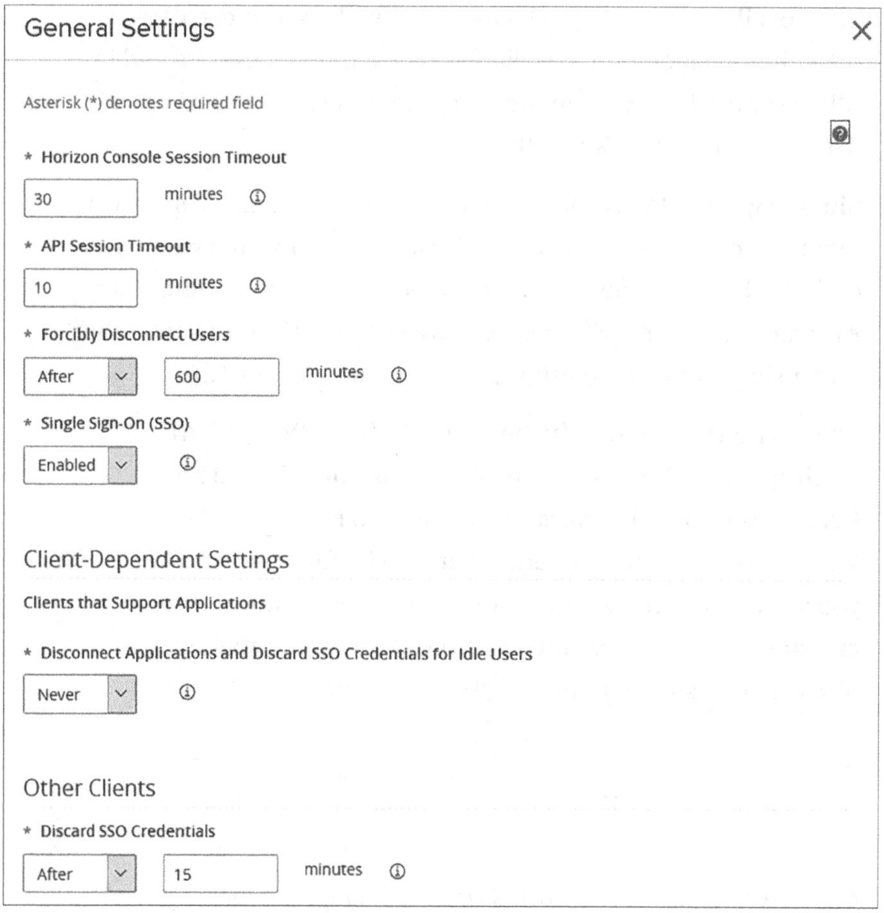

Figure 4-64. *General Settings configuration screen*

We are now going to scroll down to the second half of the General Settings screen and discuss the configuration options.

1. The **Enable automatic status updates** feature, enabled by checking the box, enables the global status area situated in the top left-hand corner of the application window. It will update both the app and the Horizon Dashboard every five minutes.

2. Next is the **Display a Pre-Login Message** option. Check the box to enable this feature, and then in the box below, type in the message. This message will be displayed when the user connects and before they log in. This message could be some form of

disclaimer or telling an end user about planned maintenance and when Horizon is not available to use.

3. The **Display Warning Before Forced Logoff** feature is used to display a message to end users before they are forcibly logged off. You then have the option to set a time for when they are actually logged off in the **After Warning, Logoff After** box. Then, in the box below, you can type in the message you want to be displayed.

4. Next, you can check the box to **Enable Windows Server Desktops**. This allows servers to be used as desktop machines and so will now display servers as well as desktops. This will include Horizon servers; however, the Horizon Agent can only be installed on servers that are not already running other server-based software.

5. The **Clean Up Credential When Tab Closed for HTML Access** option, when enabled, is used to remove an end user's credentials from cache when they close the tab that they are using to connect to their session using the HTML client.

6. Next is the **Hide Server Information in Client User Interface** option. Enabling this option means that the Horizon Connection Server address is not shown within the client.

7. You can also hide the list of domains being displayed to the end user by enabling the **Hide Domain List in Client User Interface** option. If you enable this option, then the end user will need to log in using a User Principal Name or UPN, for example, user@ domain.com or domain\user format.

8. The **Send Domain List** option allows the Connection Server to send a list of user domain names to the client before the end user authenticates.

9. Finally, the **Enable 2 Factor Reauthentication** option, when enabled, means that the end user will need to use two-factor authentication when they log back in to their session after they have been logged out due to the idle timeout being reached.

These settings and options are shown in the following screenshot:

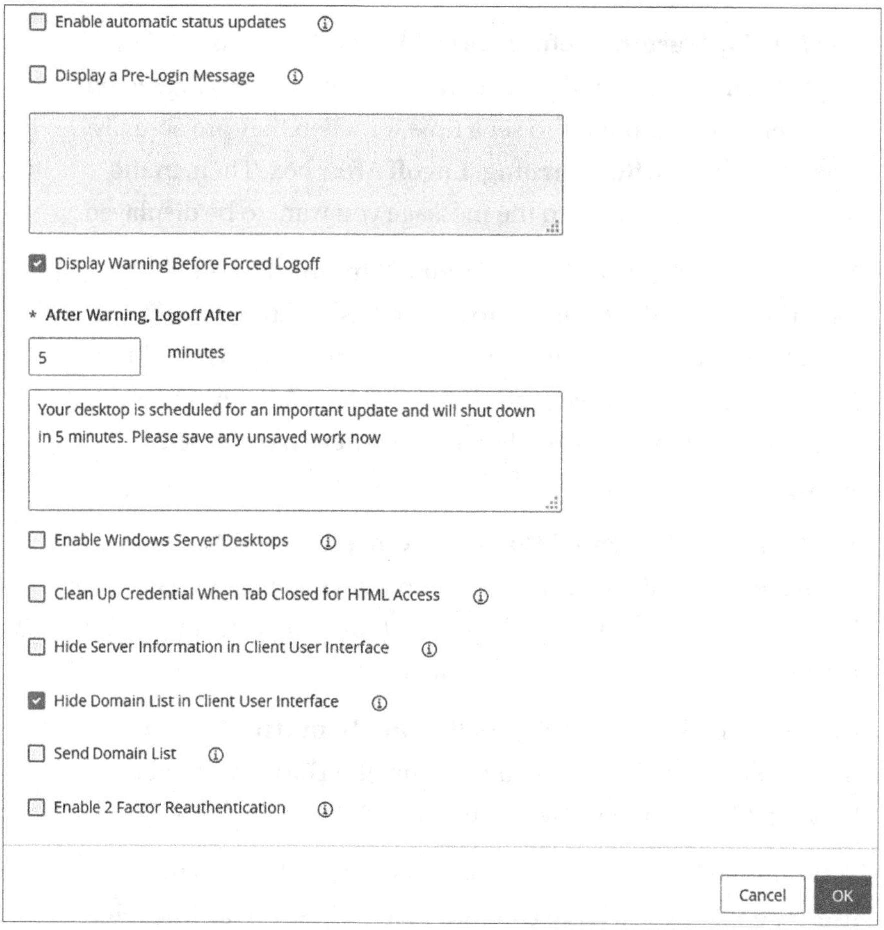

Figure 4-65.   *General Settings configuration screen – part 2*

Once you have configured your global settings, click **OK**. You will return to the Global Settings main screen.

Next, we are going to look at the Security Settings under the Global Settings configuration screen. To do this, follow the steps described:

1. From the **Global Settings** screen, click the **Security Settings** tab as shown in the following screenshot:

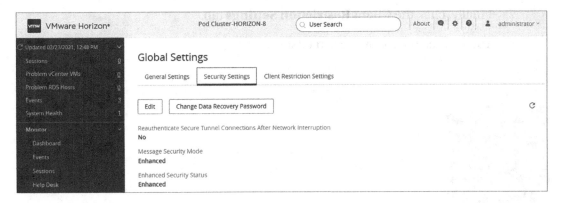

Figure 4-66. *Global Settings – Security Settings screen*

2. Click the **Edit** button.

3. You will see the Security Settings screen as shown in the following screenshot:

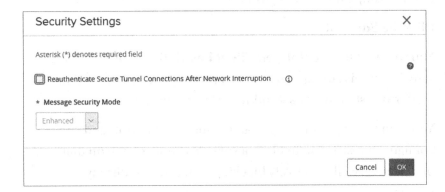

Figure 4-67. *Configuring security settings screen*

4. Enabling the **Reauthenticate Secure Tunnel Connections After Network Interruption** option means that if an end user is connected using a secure tunnel and that connection drops, then they will need to reauthenticate in order to reconnect. This adds an additional level of security.

5. Click OK once you have configured the security settings.

6. You will return to the **Global Settings** screen and the **Security Settings** tab.

7. Finally, click the **Client Restriction Settings** tab.

8. You will see the following screenshot:

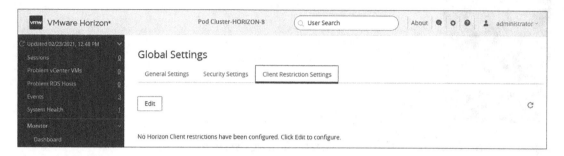

Figure 4-68. *Client Restriction Settings screen*

The client restrictions configuration screen allows you to block end users from connecting to Horizon if they are using an older or an unsupported version of a client. To configure a restriction, follow the steps described:

1. Click the **Edit** button.

2. You will now see the **Horizon Client Restrictions** configuration screen. On this configuration screen, you will see all the various platforms listed, such as Windows, Mac, Linux, etc.

3. You then have the option to enable a specific platform and configure a restriction to block a specific client version on that platform. As well as actively blocking, you can also display a warning.

Let's take the following example.

We want to configure a restriction for the Windows client which blocks any client version earlier than that specified, but we want to just warn end users about a different version as it is about to be restricted. So, to configure this scenario, we have completed the following steps:

1. Check the **Windows** box to enable the restriction for Windows clients.

2. In the **Block Connections from Client Versions** box, from the drop-down menu we have selected **Earlier Than**. The other option is for **Specific**. Then in the next box, we have typed in the

version number of the client to block. In this example, version **4.6.0**, so that means any client version trying to connect that is older than 4.6.0, the end user will not be able to connect.

3. In the **Warn Users Connecting from Specific Client Versions** box, we have typed in 4.7.0, meaning that end users connecting with this version will just receive a warning message.

4. This is shown in the following screenshot:

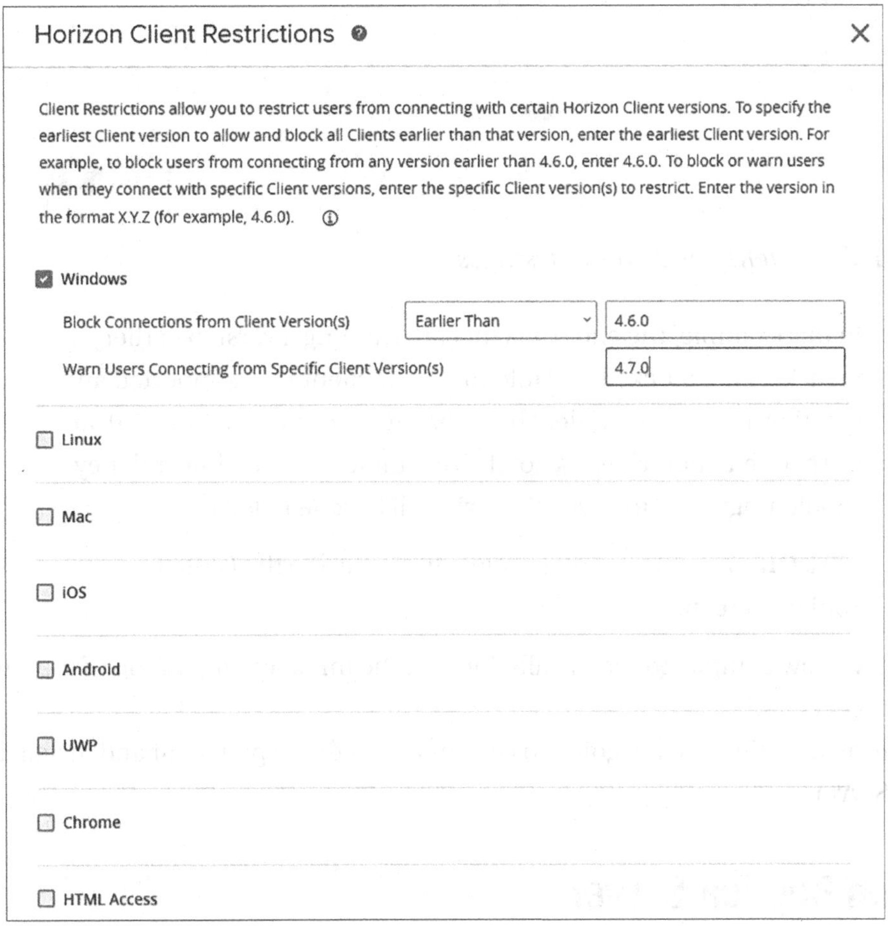

Horizon Client Restrictions ●   ✕

Client Restrictions allow you to restrict users from connecting with certain Horizon Client versions. To specify the earliest Client version to allow and block all Clients earlier than that version, enter the earliest Client version. For example, to block users from connecting from any version earlier than 4.6.0, enter 4.6.0. To block or warn users when they connect with specific Client versions, enter the specific Client version(s) to restrict. Enter the version in the format X.Y.Z (for example, 4.6.0). ⓘ

☑ Windows

　　Block Connections from Client Version(s)　　　| Earlier Than ⌄ | 4.6.0 |

　　Warn Users Connecting from Specific Client Version(s)　　　| 4.7.0| |

☐ Linux

☐ Mac

☐ iOS

☐ Android

☐ UWP

☐ Chrome

☐ HTML Access

Figure 4-69. *Client Restriction settings screen*

5. Next, we are going to configure the messages that are displayed to the end users.

6. Scroll down to the **Message for Blocked Client Versions** as shown in the following screenshot:

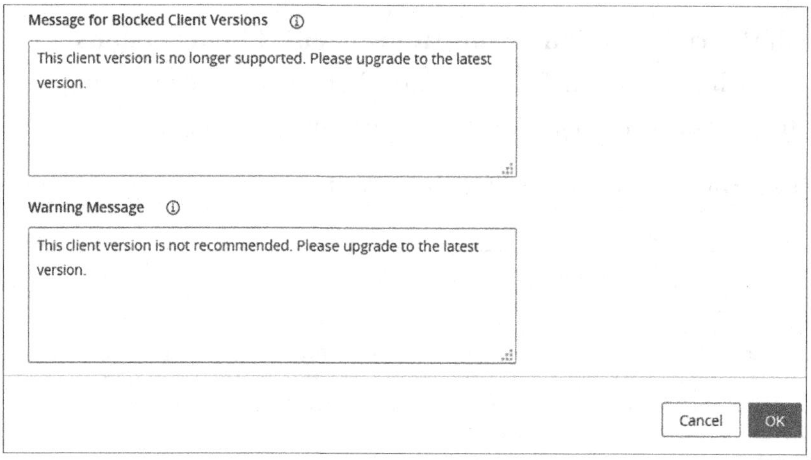

Figure 4-70. *Client Restriction messages*

In this example, the end users that are running a version earlier than 4.6.0 are blocked and told that their client is unsupported and that they need to upgrade. Those that are running version 4.7.0 are warned that their client is not the recommended version and they should upgrade. However, they will still be able to log in.

7. Click **OK** to save the configuration and return to the Global Settings screen.

We have now completed the installation and the initial configuration of the Horizon Connection Server.

In the next section, we are going to continue with the deployment and install a Replica Server.

Horizon Replica Server

The Horizon Replica Server, as we have already discussed, is just another version of the Connection Server; therefore, the installation process is almost identical to the process we followed for the Connection Server, up until the point where you select the server role.

Prerequisites and Requirements

To serve as a reminder, the Replica Server, being almost identical to the Connection Server, will be installed on a virtual server running Microsoft Windows Server 2016 that has been configured with the following virtual hardware:

- 4 x CPUs

- 10 GB memory

- 1 Gbps network card

- 60 GB of free hard disk for the installation files

Next, we are going to work through the installation, step by step.

Performing the Installation

To install the Replica Server, follow the steps described:

1. Open a console or connect to the desktop of the server onto which you are going to install the Connection Server software. In this example, we have pre-built a server and given it the hostname of **horizon-8-rep.pvolab.com**.

2. Navigate to the location of the Horizon 8.1 software that you downloaded. This is shown in the following screenshot:

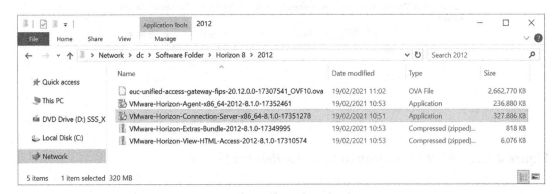

Figure 4-71. *Navigating to the Horizon 8.1 installer*

3. Double-click the **VMware-Horizon-Connection-Server-x86_64-8.1.0** to launch the Installer.

The first few installation steps are identical to the Connection Server installation, so we are not going to cover these in any detail, just highlight each step up to where the process is different for the Replica Server.

4. On the **Welcome to the Installation Wizard for VMware Horizon Connection Server**, click the **Next ➤** button.

5. Click to accept the license agreement and click **Next ➤**.

6. Click **Next ➤** to accept the default folder location.

7. You will now see the **Select the type of Horizon Connection Server to install** screen. In this example, click to select the option for **Horizon Replica Server** as shown in the following screenshot:

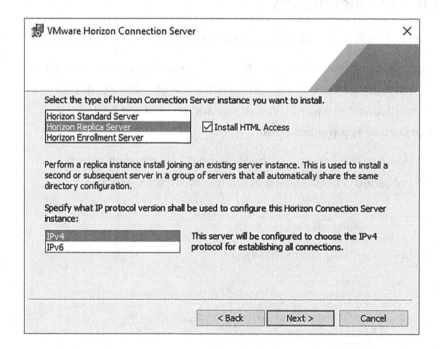

Figure 4-72. *Select the option to install a Replica Server*

8. Also ensure you check the **Install HTML Access** box and select **IPv4** as the protocol. Do not forget that you cannot mix the IP versions between the Horizon components, and as we selected IPv4 for the first Connection Server, we will need to also select it for the Replica Server.

9.   Click **Next ➤** to continue.

10. You will now see the **Source Server** screen. As this is a Replica
     Server, then you need to enter the details of the existing
     Connection Server from which to replicate the information. This is
     shown in the following screenshot:

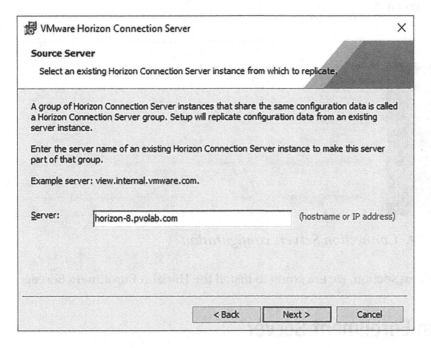

Figure 4-73. *Configuring the source server*

11. In the **Server** box, we have entered the details of the first
     Connection Server. In this example, that server is called
     horizon-8.pvolab.com.

12. Click **Next ➤** to continue.

13. Click to select the option for configuring the Windows Firewall
     automatically and then click **Next ➤** to continue.

14. On the **Ready to Install the Program**, click **Install**.

15. You will now see the progress status.

16. Once the Installer has completed, click the **Finish** button to close
     the Installer.

The Replica Server has now been successfully installed.

Log back in to the Horizon Admin Console on the original Connection Server and then expand the option for **Settings** and then click **Servers**.

17.   Now click the **Connection Servers** tab as shown in the following screenshot:

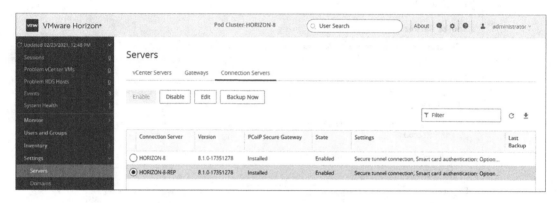

Figure 4-74. *Connection Servers configuration*

In the next section, we are going to install the Horizon Enrollment Server.

Horizon Enrollment Server

The Horizon Enrollment Server is also just another version of the Connection Server; therefore, the installation process is almost identical to the process we followed for the Connection Server and Replica Server up until the point where you select the server role.

Prerequisites and Requirements

To serve as a reminder, the Enrollment Server, being almost identical to the Connection Server, will be installed on a virtual server running Microsoft Windows Server 2016 that has been configured with the following virtual hardware:

- 4 x CPUs

- 10 GB memory

- 1 Gbps network card

- 60 GB of free hard disk for the installation files

Next, we are going to work through the installation, step by step.

Performing the Installation

To install the Enrollment Server, follow the steps described:

1. Open a console or connect to the desktop of the server onto which you are going to install the Enrollment Server. In this example, we have pre-built a server and given it the hostname of **horizon-8-sso.pvolab.com**.

2. Navigate to the location of the Horizon 8.1 software that you downloaded. This is shown in the following screenshot:

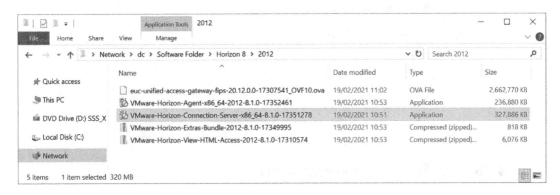

Figure 4-75. *Navigating to the Horizon 8.1 installer*

3. Double-click the **VMware-Horizon-Connection-Server-x86_64-8.1.0** to launch the Installer.

   The first few installation steps are identical to the Connection Server and Replica Server installation. We will not cover these in detail, highlighting each step to the point where the process is different from the Connection or Replica Server.

4. On the **Welcome to the Installation Wizard for VMware Horizon Connection Server**, click the **Next ➤** button.

5. Click to accept the license agreement and click **Next ➤**.

6. Click **Next ➤** to accept the default folder location.

7. You will now see the **Select the type of Horizon Connection Server to install** screen. In this example, click to select the option for **Horizon Enrollment Server** as shown in the following screenshot:

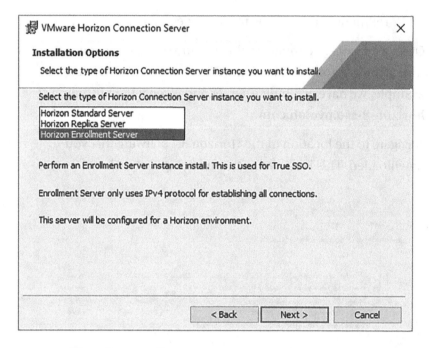

Figure 4-76. *Installing the Enrollment Server*

8. You will also see that the Enrollment Server only supports IPv4, so there is no option to select a protocol as there was with the Connection Server and Replica Server installs.

9. Click **Next ➤** to continue.

10. You will see the **Firewall Configuration** screen. It is worth noting that the ports required by the Enrollment Server are different to those used by the Connection Server and Replica Server, so make a note of these ports and ensure they are not blocked by anything.

11. Click the radio button for **Configure Windows Firewall automatically** as shown in the following screenshot:

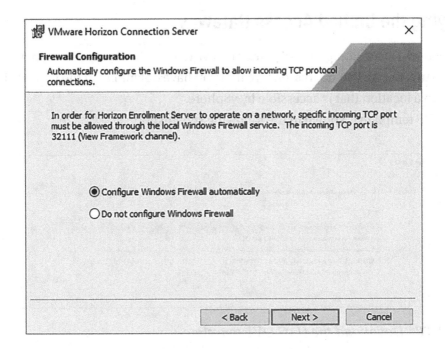

Figure 4-77. *Firewall configuration screen*

12. Click **Next ➤** to continue.

13. On the **Ready to Install the Program**, click **Install**.

14. You will now see the progress status.

15. Once the Installer has completed, click the **Finish** button to close the Installer.

The Enrollment Server has now been successfully installed.

In the next section, we are going to install the final component, the Unified Access Gateway appliance.

Unified Access Gateway

The UAG is a pre-built virtual appliance that is installed on your vSphere infrastructure and then configured to your environment once the appliance has been deployed.

We have already discussed that the UAG is available in different sizes depending on the number of end users you want to support, so let us start by deploying the virtual appliance.

Deploying the Unified Access Gateway

In this section, we are going to deploy the UAG virtual appliance on our vSphere infrastructure. Before you do this, ensure that you have downloaded the UAG OVF template to a location that is accessible by vSphere.

The OVF template is shown in the following screenshot:

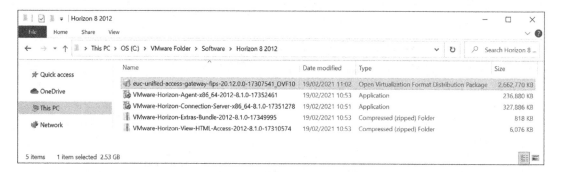

Figure 4-78. *Download the UAG OVF template*

To deploy the UAG virtual appliance, follow the steps described:

1. Log in to the vSphere Client.

2. Click to select the data center onto which you want to deploy the UAG virtual appliance and then right-click. In this example, we are going to deploy the appliance on the data center called **PVO Data center**.

3. Right-click the **PVO Data center,** and from the contextual menu options, click **Deploy OVF Template...** as shown in the following screenshot:

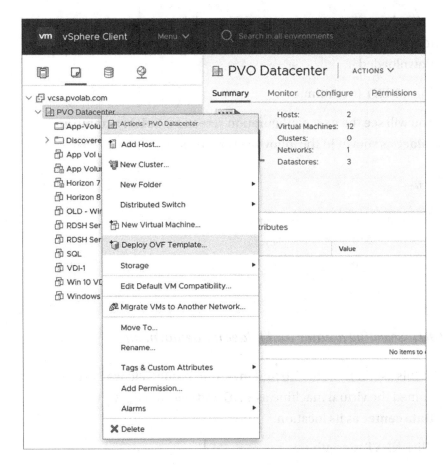

Figure 4-79. *Deploying the UAG OVF template in vSphere*

4. You will now see the **Deploy OVF Template** screen and the first part of the configuration for **Select an OVF template** as shown in the following screenshot:

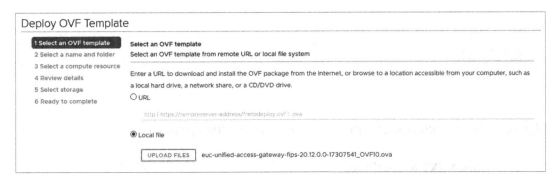

Figure 4-80. *Selecting the UAG OVF template for deployment*

5. Click the radio button for **Local file** and then navigate to the
    location where you saved the OVF template file when you
    downloaded it.

6. Click **NEXT** to continue.

7. You will see the next configuration screen for **Select a name and
    folder** as shown in the following screenshot:

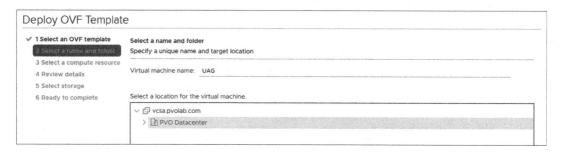

Figure 4-81. *Selecting a name and folder for deployment*

8. In this example, in the **Virtual machine name** field we have
    named the virtual machine as **UAG** and selected the **PVO
    Data center** as its location.

9. Click **NEXT** to continue.

10. You now need to select a compute resource to host the UAG
    virtual appliance. This is the ESXi host server on which it will run.
    In this example, we have selected the ESXi host server with the IP
    address of **192.168.1.129** as shown in the following screenshot:

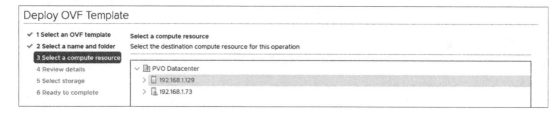

Figure 4-82. *Selecting a compute resource to host the appliance*

11. Click **NEXT** to continue.

12. You will now see the **Review details** screen as shown in the following screenshot:

Figure 4-83. *Deploying the UAG OVF Template*

13. Click **NEXT** to continue.

14. You will now see the **Configuration** screen as shown:

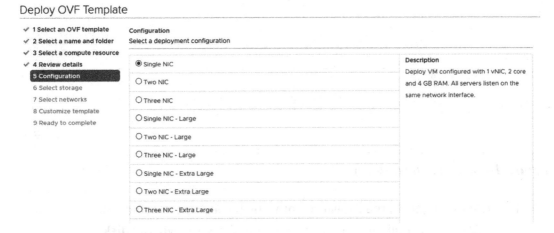

Figure 4-84. *Selecting a deployment configuration*

15. On the configuration screen, you can select the size of the UAG virtual appliance that you want to deploy. In this example, we are going to click the radio button option for **Single NIC**. This will automatically configure the CPU and memory requirements as per the pre-configured appliance sizes we discussed in Chapter 3.

16. Click **NEXT** to continue.

17. You will see the **Select Storage** screen as shown:

Figure 4-85. *Selecting a storage*

18. Click to highlight the datastore onto which you want to deploy the UAG virtual appliance. You can also, from the **Select virtual disk format** drop-down menu, choose the provisioning method. In this example, we have chosen to **Thin Provision** the appliance virtual hard disk and to store it on the **Virtual Machine Store** datastore.

19. Click **NEXT** to continue.

20.   The next configuration screen is the **Select networks** as shown in
the following screenshot:

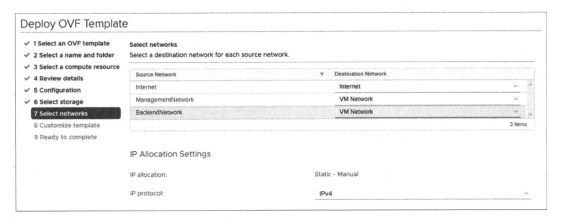

Figure 4-86. *Selecting networks*

21.   On the **Select networks** screen, you need to configure each
network source to its destination. On the **Destination Network**
drop-down, select the network you want to connect to.

22.   Then, in the **IP protocol** field, click the drop-down menu and
select the IP version you want to use – in this example, **IPv4**.

23.   Click **NEXT** to continue.

24.   The next configuration screen is the **Customize template** screen.
This is where you customize the virtual appliance template for
your environment. As there are several configuration options, we
have broken the configuration screen into four sections, with the
first section shown in the following screenshot:

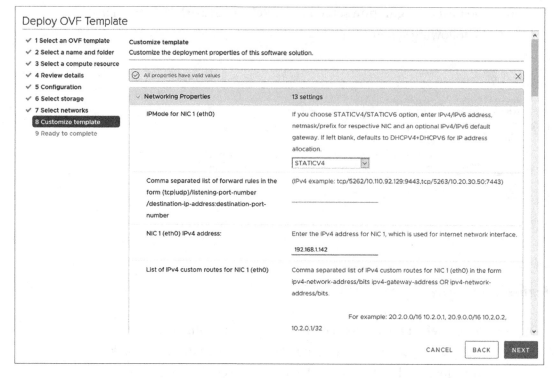

Figure 4-87. Customizing the template – part 1

25. On the first part of the customization screen, in the **IPMode for NIC 1(eth0)** section, from the drop-down box select the IP mode. In this example, we have selected the option for **STATICV4** so that we have a static IPv4 address.

26. Next, in the **NIC 1(eth0) IPv4 address** box, as we are using IPv4, type in the IP address for the UAG virtual appliance. This will be the address that is used to manage the appliance.

27. Now scroll down to the **DNS server addresses** section as shown in the following screenshot:

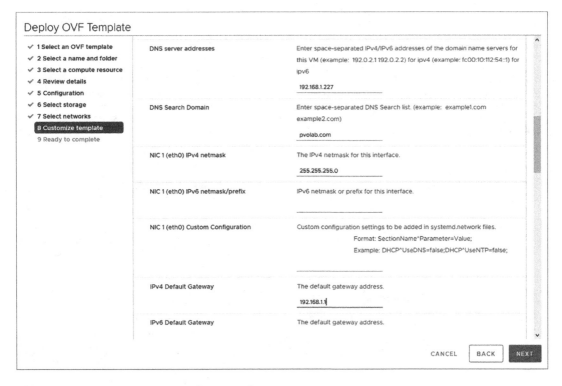

Figure 4-88. *Customizing the template – part 2*

28. In the **DNS server addresses** field, type in the address of your DNS server. In this example, the address is **192.168.1.227.**

29. Then, in the **DNS Search Domain** field, type in the name of the search domain. In this example, our domain is **pvolab.com**.

30. Next, in the **NIC 1(eth0) IPv4 netmask** field, type in the netmask. In this example, the netmask is **255.255.255.0**.

31. Finally, on this section of the configuration screen, in the **IPv4 Default Gateway** field, type in the IP address of your default gateway. In this example, the IP address is **192.168.1.1**.

32. Now scroll down to the **Unified Gateway Appliance Name** section as shown in the following screenshot:

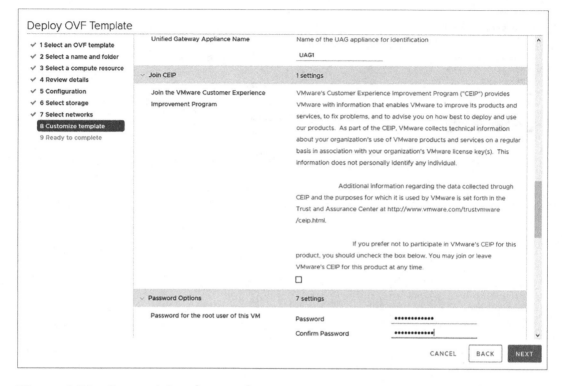

Figure 4-89. *Customizing the template – part 3*

33. In the **Unified Gateway Appliance Name** field, type in a name for
     this appliance. This will be the virtual machine name which we
     have called **UAG1**.

34. Next, in the **Join CEIP** section, remove the check from the box so
     as not to join the customer experience program.

35. Now scroll down to the **Password Options** section.

36. In the **Password for the root user of this VM** and the **Password**
     field, type in a password you want the root user to use, and then in
     the **Confirm Password** field, type the same password in again.

37. Now scroll down to the **Password for the admin user** as shown in
     the following screenshot:

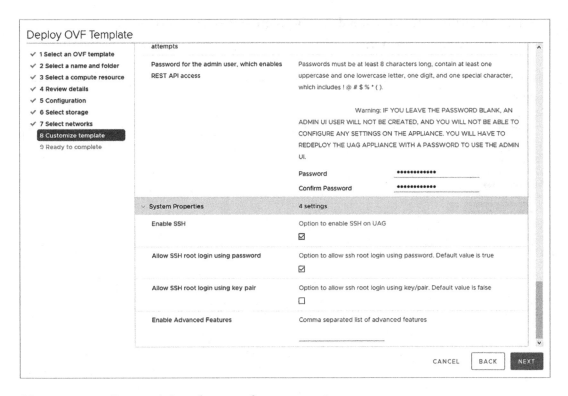

Figure 4-90. *Customizing the template – part 4*

38. In the **Password for the admin user, which enables REST API access** section and the **Password** field, type in a password you want the admin user to use, and then in the **Confirm Password** field, type the same password in again. This is the password that will be used to log in to the web-based console to configure and manage the appliance.

39. Next, you have the options to **Enable SSH**, **Allow SSH root login using password**, and **Allow SSH root login using key pair**. If you want to enable any of these features, then check the corresponding box.

40. Finally, in the **Enable Advanced Features** field, you can configure any advanced features you want, listing multiple features by separating them with commas.

41. Click **NEXT** to continue.

42.   You will now see the **Ready to complete** screen as shown in the following screenshot:

Figure 4-91.   *Ready to complete screen for template deployment*

43.   Click the **FINISH** button.

44.   You will see the deployment progress in the **Task Console** of the vSphere Client as shown in the following screenshot:

Task Name	Target	Status	Details	Initiator	Queued For	Start Time ↓	Completion Time	Execution Time	Server
Deploy OVF tem...	UAG	57%		VSPHERE.LOCAL...	8 ms	02/23/2021, 4:16...			vcsa.pvolab.com
Import OVF pack...	192.168.1.73	57%		vsphere.local\Ad...	63 ms	02/23/2021, 4:13...			vcsa.pvolab.com

Figure 4-92.   *Template deployment task in vSphere Client*

You have now successfully deployed the UAG virtual appliance, and the next step, in the next section, is to log in and configure the Horizon-specific settings.

Initial Unified Access Gateway Configuration

In this section, we are going to log in to the UAG virtual appliance and configure the Horizon settings.

To do this, follow the steps described:

1. Open a browser and enter the address of the UAG virtual appliance. In this example, the address we would type in is

    `https://192.168.1.142:9443/admin/index.html`

2. You will now see the UAG login screen as shown in the following screenshot:

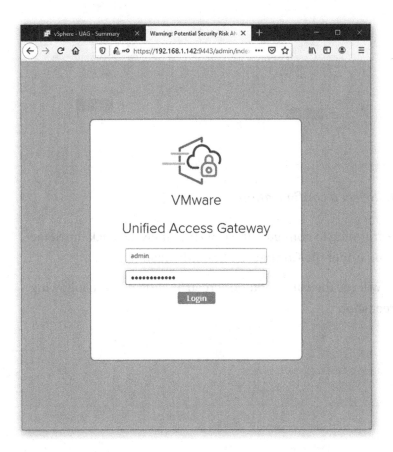

Figure 4-93. *UAG login screen*

3. Type in the username of admin and then the password that you configured for the admin user, and then click the **Login** button.

4. Once you are logged in, the first screen you see is to either Import Settings or Configure Manually as shown in the following screenshot:

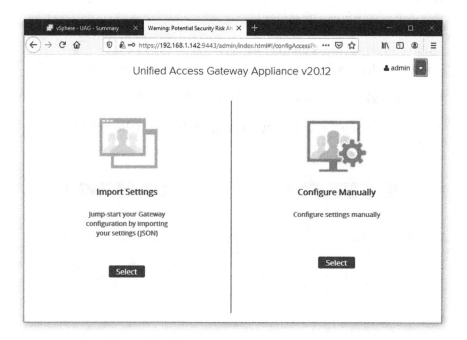

Figure 4-94. *Select a configuration*

5. We are going to configure the UAG manually, so click the **Select** button under the **Configure Manually** heading.

6. You will see the configuration screen as shown in the following screenshot:

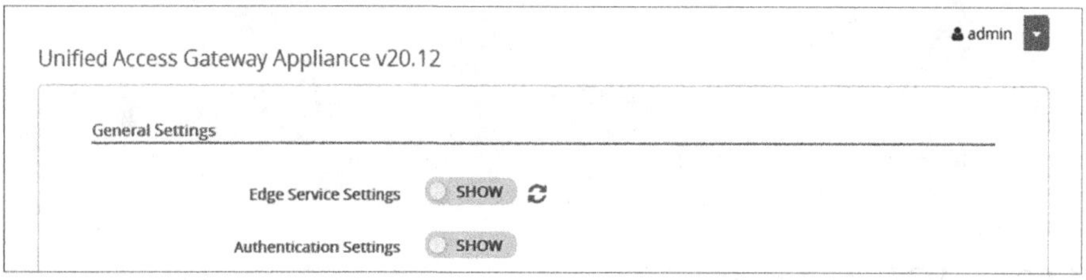

Figure 4-95. *UAG configuration settings screen*

7. Click the **SHOW** button next to the entry for Edge Service Settings.
   You will see the following screenshot:

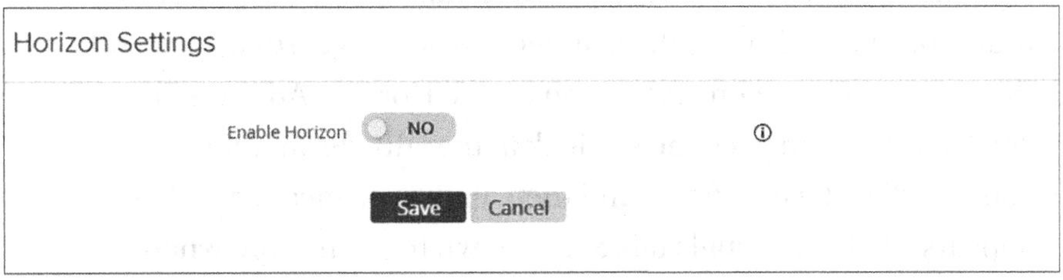

Figure 4-96. *Enabling Horizon settings*

8. Click the **Enable Horizon** button so it turns green and says **YES**.
   You will see the **Horizon Settings** screen as shown:

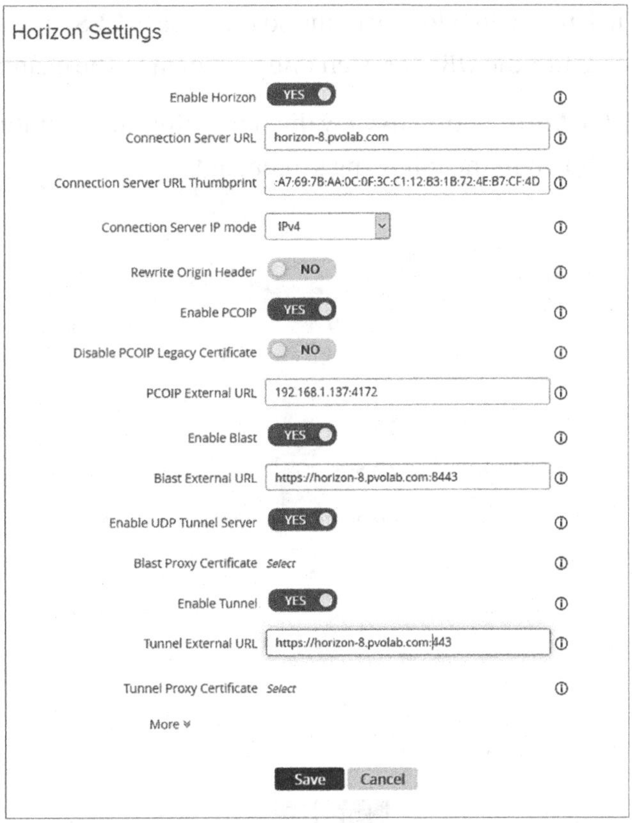

Figure 4-97. *Enabling Horizon settings*

9. In the **Connection Server URL** box, type in the address of the Connection Server. In this example, this is **horizon-8.pvolab.com**.

10. Next, in the **Connection Server URL Thumbprint** box, enter the thumbprint details from the Connection Servers certificate. To do this is to switch to a browser, open up the Horizon Administrator console, and then click the padlock in the URL. From there, you can click the certificate and then, in the certificate box that appears, click the Details tab. Scroll down to the bottom where you will find the thumbprint. Now cut and paste this into the box.

11. In the **Connection Server IP mode** box, from the drop-down menu, select **IPv4**.

12. The next task is to enable the protocols that you are planning on using in your environment, along with the tunneled connections option. Click the switch for each one so that it says **YES** to enable it, and then enter the URL for each one as shown in the examples.

13. Now click the **More** button to view the remaining configuration options as shown in the following screenshot:

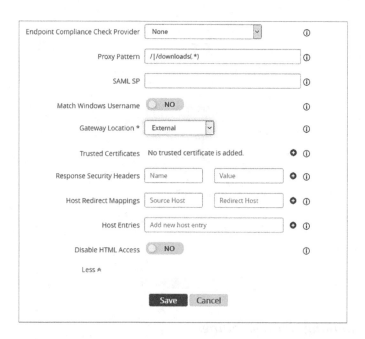

Figure 4-98. *Enabling Horizon settings*

14. In the **Gateway Location**, click the drop-down menu and select the location. In this example, we have selected the option for **External**.

15. Click **Save** to complete the configuration.

16. You will return to the main **General Settings** screen as shown in the following screenshot:

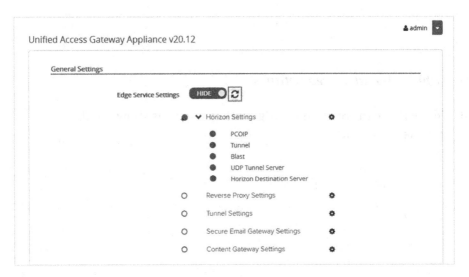

Figure 4-99. *Horizon settings enabled*

You will see all the options that you configured are now shown with a green button. If they do not appear straightaway, then you may need to wait or click the refresh button next to the HIDE button.

The final option is to rename the UAG appliance to something more friendly as you will need this name when you configure the Horizon Console in the next section.

To do this, follow the steps described:

17. From the admin screen in the UAG, under the **Advanced Settings** section, click the gear cog for **System Configuration** as shown in the following screenshot:

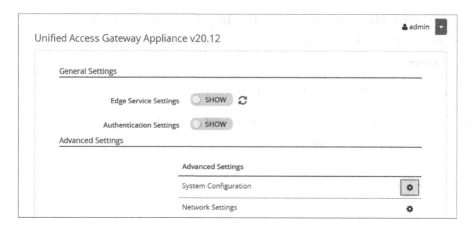

Figure 4-100. *UAG Advanced Settings*

18. You will see the **System Configuration** screen as shown in the following screenshot:

Figure 4-101. *UAG System Configuration settings*

19. In the **UAG Name** box, type in a name for this appliance. In this example, we have called it **UAG001**.

20. Then, in the **Locale** box, type in the code for your location. In this example, we have entered **en_GB** for the UK. Click the **i** button to see the available locales.

21. Now click **Save**.

You have now successfully deployed and configured the UAG virtual appliance. In the next section, we are going to add this appliance to the Horizon Console.

Configuring the Unified Access Gateway for Horizon

In this section, we are going to add the newly configured and deployed UAG virtual appliance to the Horizon Administrator Console.

To do this, follow the steps described:

1. Log in to the Horizon Console.

2. From the left-hand menu pane, expand the option for **Settings**
   and then click **Servers** as shown in the following screenshot:

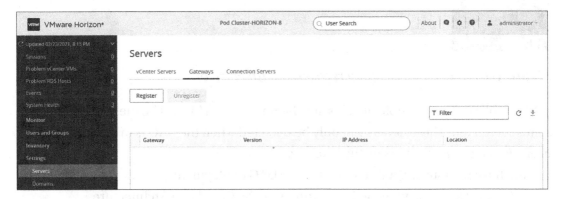

Figure 4-102. *Adding the UAG in the Horizon Console*

3. Now click the **Gateways** tab.

4. You will see the **Register Gateway** box as shown in the following
   screenshot:

Figure 4-103. *Registering a new gateway*

5. Enter the name of the UAG virtual appliance that you configured.
   In this example, we have called it **UAG001**.

6. Click **OK** to complete the configuration.

7. You will return to the Servers screen as shown in the following
   screenshot:

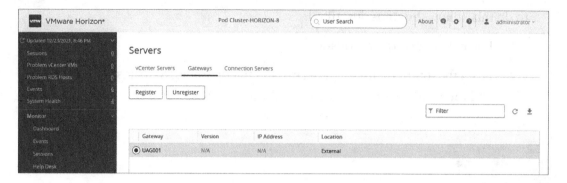

Figure 4-104. *UAG successfully registered with Horizon*

You will see that a couple of fields are shown as N/A. This will be the same in the status screen too. These details will only be detected when the UAG is in use and an end user connects to Horizon using the gateway.

You have now successfully completed the UAG deployment.

In the next section, we are going to configure the Cloud Pod Architecture.

Deploying Cloud Pod Architecture (CPA)

In this section, we are going to configure an example Cloud Pod Architecture deployment using two Connection Servers that are in different locations.

We will use the original Connection Server that was installed earlier in this chapter, the server with the hostname **horizon-8,** and we will create a pod federation with another Connection Server with a hostname of **horizon-8-cpa**.

To start the configuration, we are going to initialize CPA on the first Connection Server.

Initializing the CPA Feature

The first task to complete is to initialize the CPA feature on the first Connection Server to create the pod federation.

To do this, follow the steps described:

1. Log in to the Horizon Administrator Console.

2. From the left-hand menu pane, expand **Settings** and then click **Cloud Pod Architecture**.

3. You will see the following screenshot:

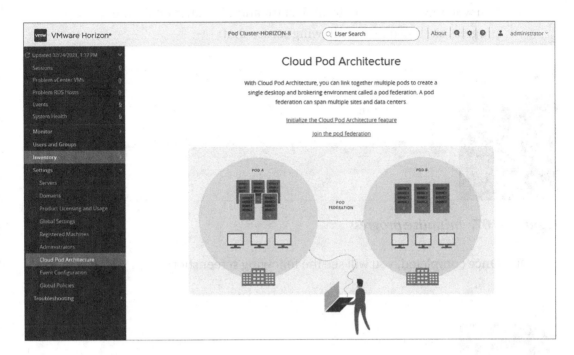

Figure 4-105. *Cloud Pod Architecture configuration screen*

4. Click the **Initialize the Cloud Pod Architecture feature** link above the graphic.

5. You will see the **Initialize** box as shown in the following screenshot:

Figure 4-106. *Initialize the Cloud Pod Architecture feature*

6. Click **OK**.

7. You will now see the initialization start, and you can monitor the progress as shown in the following screenshot:

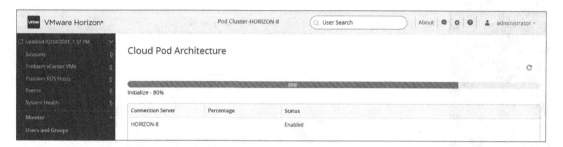

Figure 4-107. *Initialize progress*

8. Once completed, you will see the following screenshot:

Figure 4-108. *CPA successfully initialized*

The next task, in the next section, is to switch to the second Connection Server with the hostname **horizon-8-cpa** in this example and join it to this federation.

Joining a Pod Federation

Now that we have created a pod federation, the next task is to add your additional Connection Servers to that federation. In this example, we are going to add the Connection Server with the hostname **horizon-8-cpa** to the federation.

To do this, follow the steps described:

1. Log in to the Horizon Administrator Console.

2. From the left-hand menu pane, expand **Settings** and then click **Cloud Pod Architecture**.

3. You will see the following screenshot:

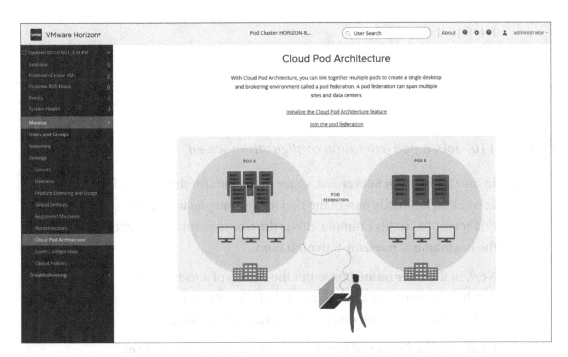

Figure 4-109. *Cloud Pod Architecture configuration screen on the second server*

4. Click the **Join the pod federation** link above the graphic.

5. You will see the **Join** box as shown in the following screenshot:

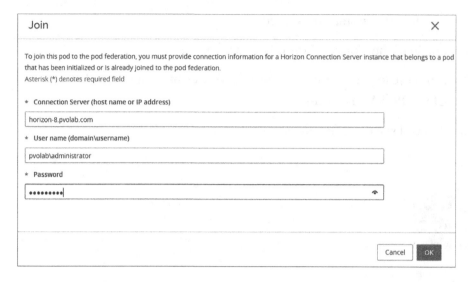

Figure 4-110. Join a pod federation configuration screen

6. In the **Connection Server** box, enter the details for the connection server that is already part of the pod federation you want to join this server to. In this example, this is the Connection Server with the hostname of **horizon-8.pvolab.com**.

7. Next, in the **User name** box, enter the details of a user account that has the permissions to join the pod – in this case, the administrator account, entered in the format of domain\user.

8. Finally, in the **Password** box, type in the password for the user account name you entered.

9. Click **OK**.

10. You will see the progress of the Connection Server being joined to the pod federation in the following screenshot:

Figure 4-111. Progress of the join process

11. Once the process has successfully completed, you will see the
following screenshot:

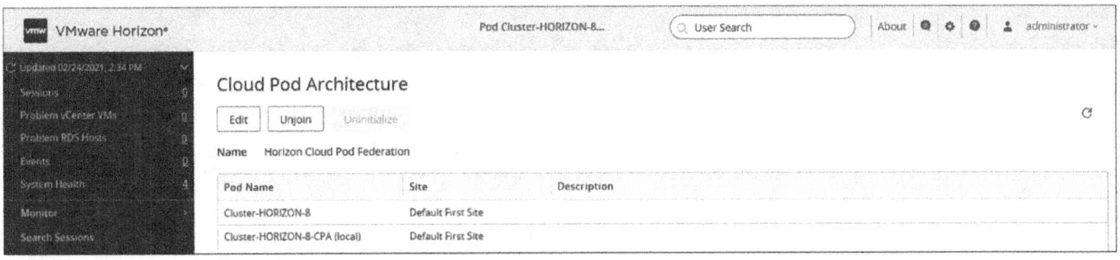

Figure 4-112. *Server successfully added to the pod federation*

As you can see from the screenshot, both Connection Servers have now been added
to form a pod federation.

You have now successfully configured a Cloud Pod Architecture. We will look at the
global entitlements that come with CPA in the next chapter.

Summary

We have given you a comprehensive overview with step-by-step instructions and
screenshots on how to install and deploy a VMware Horizon environment. We have
worked through the process of installing the first Connection Server in your environment
and then completing the initial configuration tasks such as adding license keys, a
vCenter Server, and an events database.

With the initial Connection Server built and deployed, we then worked through the
process of building and deploying a Replica Server and then an Enrollment Server. The
next step was to deploy and configure a Unified Access Gateway virtual appliance and
then integrate it into the Horizon environment to enable end users to log in securely
from outside of the corporate network or from the Internet. The final section of this
chapter showed how to create a pod federation for Cloud Pod Architecture to allow you
to scale or deliver high availability to your Horizon environment.

In the next chapter, we are going to switch our focus from the Horizon management
components to the virtual desktop machines and work through the process and best
practice for building a gold image from which to deploy virtual desktop machines.

CHAPTER 5

Creating Virtual Desktop Images for Deployment

At this stage of the book, you should have a good understanding of the Horizon architecture and have installed and deployed the software in an example environment.

The next step, covered in this chapter, is to build the virtual desktop gold image, or base image, that Horizon is going to use to create a virtual desktop machine to deliver to the end users.

This base image will contain the operating system, patches and updates, configuration settings, and potentially any applications. It will also have the Horizon Agent installed, plus any additional agents such as App Volumes.

Before we start to actually build and install an operating system, we are going to cover the build steps and the process for creating a gold image.

Defining the Build Process

The process for building an operating system image for a virtual desktop machine is not too dissimilar to how you would build a standard desktop OS image in that once you have built the image, it is then pushed out via some form of desktop management platform such as Microsoft Endpoint Configuration Manager to provision the desktop machines.

However, the key difference is in the deployment model. As we are talking about virtual desktop machines, once built either a snapshot or template will be created from that image. Then, depending on how you deploy your virtual desktop machines, the snapshot will be used to create Instant Clones or linked clones, and the template will be used to create Full Clones. So, in this example, the cloning process is taking on the provisioning process.

239

© Peter von Oven 2022
P. von Oven, *Mastering VMware Horizon 8*, https://doi.org/10.1007/978-1-4842-7261-9_5

When it comes to building the image, the best practice is to build a brand-new virtual desktop image from scratch. Do not take an existing physical desktop image and use a physical-to-virtual, or P2V, solution to create a virtual desktop machine image from the physical image.

This image needs to be designed as a virtual desktop machine from day one, and there are a couple of reasons why this is the best practice.

The first is in regard to the size of the image. If you take a physical desktop image, it is likely to be bigger than it needs to be. It will have been patched, updated, and have all the old files such as the windows.old folder still in place. With the size of physical hard disks in PCs today, it was not an issue, but now you are potentially using expensive, high-performance storage, and you want to keep costs down.

You also need to ensure the image contains the correct device drivers. Drivers that are VMware drivers or specifically for virtual desktop machines and are not hardware-based drivers for specific hardware that is present on the motherboard of the physical desktop. This could have a potential performance impact on the virtual desktop machine.

With all of this in mind, the following graphic depicts the build process that we are going to follow in order to build our virtual desktop OS image:

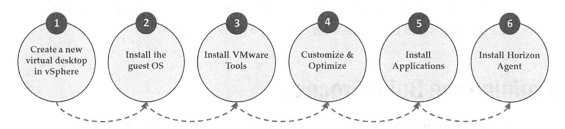

Figure 5-1. *Virtual desktop build process*

Now that we have described the steps that are involved in building the virtual desktop machine image for deployment, the next step is to start that process and build an image for Windows 10 virtual desktop machines first, and then a Linux-based virtual desktop machine.

Building the Virtual Desktop Gold Image for Windows

The first step of the process is to create the virtual desktop machine from a virtual hardware perspective, but before we do that, we are going to look at the specification and configuration of that virtual desktop machine.

The actual configuration of the virtual desktop that you build may need to be different to reflect the different use cases and therefore the different desktop pools; however, this can be changed as required once the image has been built, by taking copies or clones of the image from which to create these different configurations. In this example, we are going to build a standard configuration with the following configuration:

Virtual Hardware Component	Setting / Configuration
CPU	2 x vCPU
Memory	4 GB
SCSI Controller	LSI Logic SAS
Graphics card	N / A - defined by pool settings
Diskette drive	Disabled
Network card	VMXNET 3
Optical drive	Client device
Serial port	Disabled
Parallel port	Disabled

Figure 5-2. *Virtual desktop configuration*

As we discussed back in Chapter 3, do not get into the habit of overprovisioning resources, and ensure that the virtual desktop machines are configured appropriately.

In this example, we are configuring for a requirement that needs more resources and so have opted for two vCPUs and 4 GB. For lower workload resource requirements, then a single vCPU would suffice and maybe 2 GB of memory.

Now that we have the virtual desktop machine configuration requirements, we can start the build process.

Creating the Virtual Desktop Machine

In this section, we are going to create the virtual desktop machine using vCenter. To do this, we are going to follow the steps described:

1. Log in to the vCenter Server Appliance. In this example, we are using a vCenter Server that is managing the virtual desktop machines and so is part of a desktop block. The login screen is shown in the following screenshot:

Figure 5-3. *Logging in to the vCenter Server Appliance*

2. In this example, we have logged in as the local administrator using the administrator@vsphere.local account.

3. Click the **Login** button.

4. You will now see the vSphere Client Home page as shown in the following screenshot:

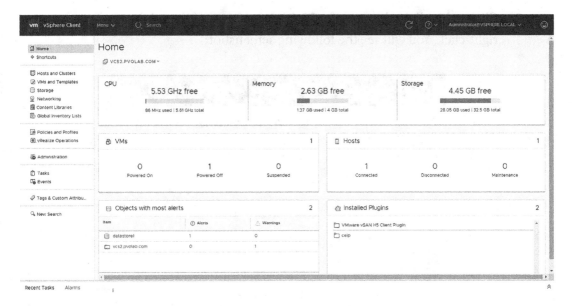

Figure 5-4. *vCenter Client Home page*

We are now going to create a new virtual machine following the steps described:

1. From the left-hand navigation pane, under **Home**, click **VMs and Templates** (1) as shown in the following screenshot:

Figure 5-5. *Select the VMs and Templates option*

2. Click to highlight the entry for **PVO's Data center** (2), and then right-click. You will see the following screenshot:

Figure 5-6. *Creating a new virtual machine*

3. From the contextual menu that appears, click the option for **New Virtual Machine**.

4. You will now see the **New Virtual Machine** box and the first option for **Select a creation** type as shown in the following screenshot:

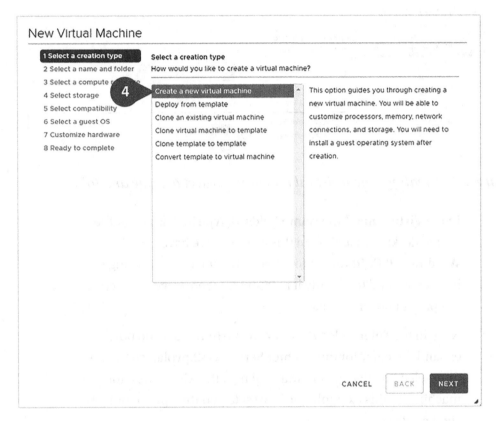

Figure 5-7. *Creating a new virtual machine – creation type*

5. Click **Create a new virtual machine** (4).

6. Now click the **NEXT** button to continue.

7. You will now see the next field for **Select a name and folder** as shown in the following screenshot:

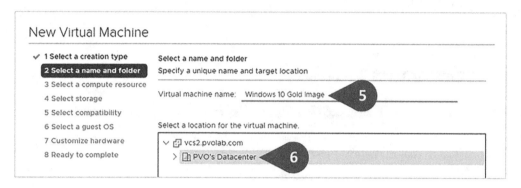

Figure 5-8. *Creating a new virtual machine – Select a name and folder*

8. In the **Virtual machine name** field (5), type in a name for the virtual desktop machine. In this example, we have called it **Windows 10 Gold Image** to reflect what the image is going to be used for and to identify it in vCenter when we come to create templates and snapshots.

9. Next, in the **Select a location for the virtual machine** box, expand the entry for the vCenter Server, vcs2.pvolab.com, and then select the data center that will host this virtual desktop machine. In this example, we have selected the option for **PVO's Data center** (6).

10. Now click the **NEXT** button to continue.

11. You will see the next section for **Select a compute resource**.

12. Expand the entry for **PVO's Data center** (7) and then select the host server that is going to host the virtual desktop machine. In this example, we are going to select the host server with the IP address **192.168.1.73** (8). Although ultimately the images that get created from this gold image for end users will reside on the desktop block, for the build of the gold image you can use any host server and move the image later. It would be a good practice to use the same platform versions so as to avoid any potential conflicts with virtual hardware compatibility at a later stage.

13.   Before you can continue, the vSphere will check the compatibility and whether this virtual machine can be created. You will see the **Compatibility** box at the bottom of the screen and the message **Compatibility checks succeeded** (9). This is shown in the following screenshot:

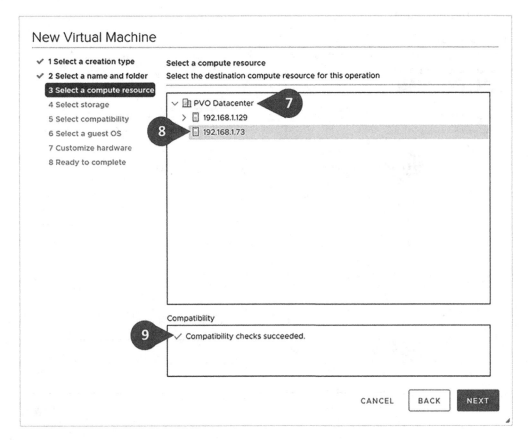

Figure 5-9. *Creating a new virtual machine – Select a compute resource*

14.   Click **NEXT** to continue.

15.   You will see the next section for **Select storage**.

16.   On this configuration screen, you select the datastore that will be used to store the virtual disk for the virtual desktop machine. In this example, we have created a datastore for storing virtual machines called VM Datastore. Click to select this datastore (10).

17.   Again, vSphere will check the compatibility and whether this
virtual machine can be created. You will see the **Compatibility**
box at the bottom of the screen and the message **Compatibility
checks succeeded** (11). This is shown in the following screenshot:

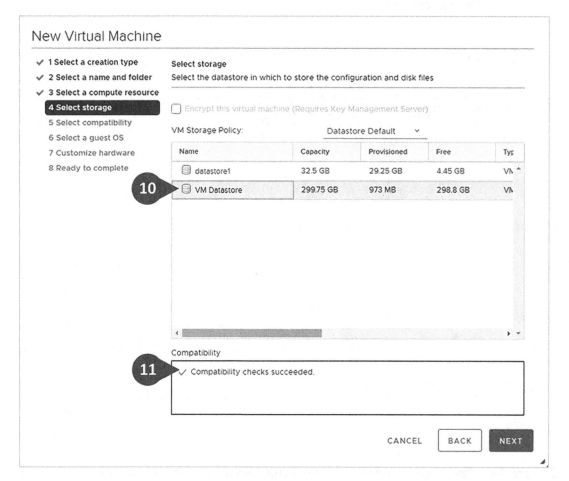

Figure 5-10. *Creating a new virtual machine – Select storage*

18.   Click **NEXT** to continue.

19.   You will see the next section for **Select compatibility**.

20.   From the **Compatible with:** drop-down box, select the compatibility
      level. In this example, we are going to select the option for **ESXi 7.0
      and later (12)** to reflect the version of ESXi running on our host
      servers. This is shown in the following screenshot:

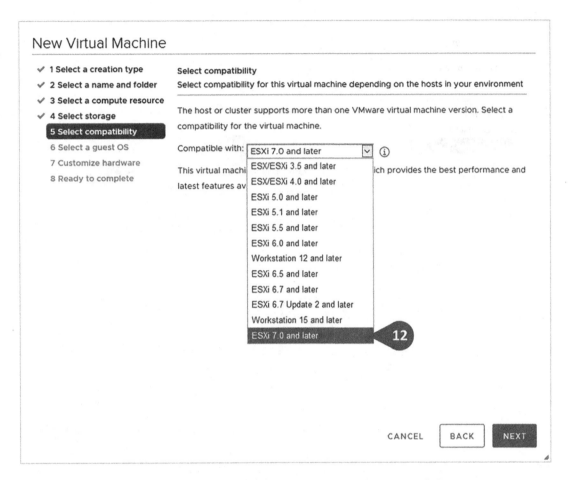

Figure 5-11. *Creating a new virtual machine – Select compatibility*

21.   Click **NEXT** to continue.

22.   You will see the next section for **Select a guest OS**.

23.   In the **Guest OS Family** drop-down menu (13), select the
      operating system for this virtual machine. In this example, select
      the option for **Windows**.

24. Then, in the **Guest OS Version** drop-down menu (14), select the option for the version of the guest OS family. In this example, we are going to select the option for **Microsoft Windows 10 (64-bit)**. This is shown in the following screenshot:

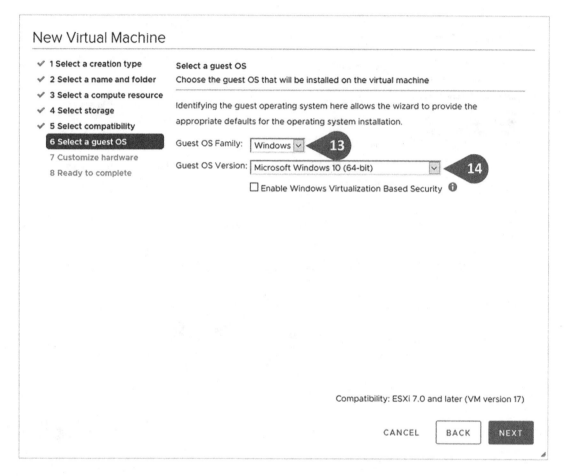

Figure 5-12. Creating a new virtual machine – Select a guest OS

25. You will also see a check box for **Enable Windows Virtualization Based Security**. Check this box if you want to enable hardware virtualization, IOMMU, EFI, and secure boot.

26. Click **NEXT** to continue.

27. You will see the next section for **Customize hardware**.

28. In the customization of hardware page, we are going to configure
     the hardware as per the configuration we discussed earlier in this
     chapter. The CPU and memory will be already set appropriate to the
     guest OS chosen. So, in this example, as we have chosen Windows
     10 64-bit, then the virtual machine will be configured with two
     CPUs and 4 GB memory as shown in the following screenshot:

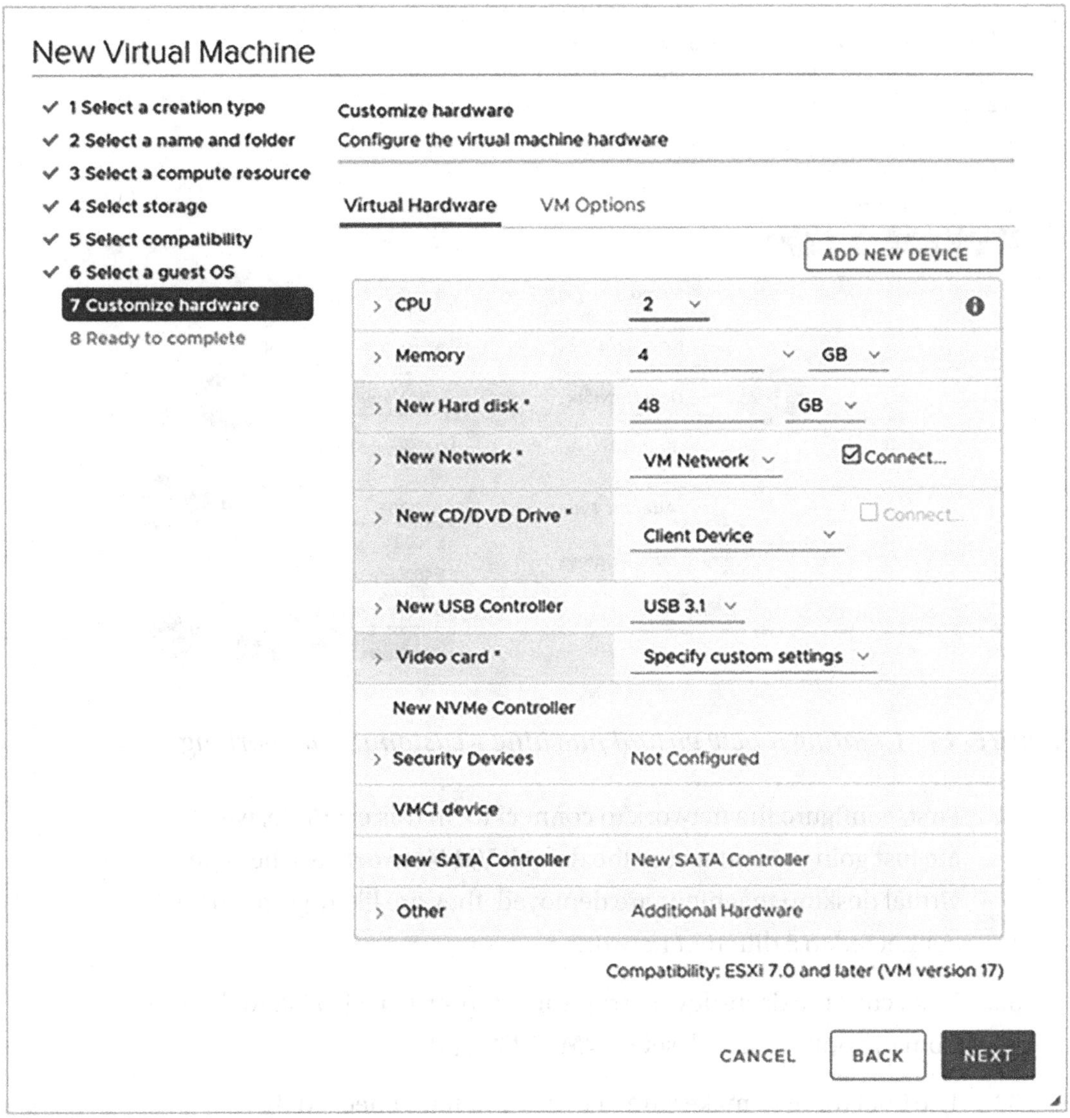

Figure 5-13. *Creating a new virtual machine – Customize hardware*

29. The first thing to configure is the networking, so click the drop-down arrow next to **New Network*** (15) to expand the networking section.

30. This is shown in the following screenshot:

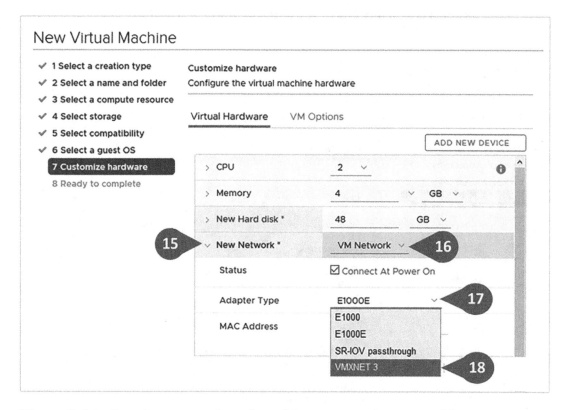

Figure 5-14. *Creating a new virtual machine – customize networking*

31. First, configure the network to connect to. In this example, we are just going to connect to the default **VM Network** as when the virtual desktop machines are deployed, they are likely going to be connected to a different network.

32. Next, click the drop-down arrow for **Adapter Type** (17), and then from the options listed, select **VMXNET 3** (18).

33. The final thing to make sure of is that you have checked the **Connect At Power On** box so that the virtual machine is connected to the network when you power it on.

34.   The next step is to attach the installation media. In this example, we are going to connect to an ISO image of the OS that is stored on a datastore on the ESXi host server.

35.   In the New CD/DVD Drive* section, click the drop-down arrow next to Client Device, and from the options listed, select the option for Datastore ISO File as shown in the following screenshot:

Figure 5-15.   *Creating a new virtual machine – customize CD Drive*

36.   You will then see the Select File window open as shown in the following screenshot:

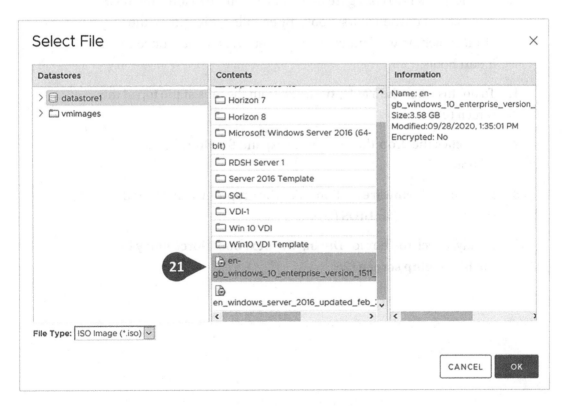

Figure 5-16.   *Creating a new virtual machine – selecting a Windows ISO*

37. Navigate to the OS ISO image. In this example, the ISO image has been saved to the root directory of **datastore1**. Click to select the ISO image. In this example, the Windows 10 ISO (21), and then click **OK**.

38. You will return to the customization screen as shown in the following screenshot:

Figure 5-17. *Creating a new virtual machine – connect CD drive*

39. Ensure that you check the **Connect...** box (22) to ensure the ISO image is mounted when the virtual machine is powered on and so that the virtual machine then boots from the ISO image.

40. The next task is to configure the virtual machine to force the BIOS screen to load when it first boots. By enabling this option, the virtual machine will launch the BIOS setup screen just once when it next boots.

41. To do this, click the **VM Options** tab from the tabs at the top of the screen (23).

42. Then click the drop-down arrow to expand the **Boot Options** section.

43. Now, in the **Firmware** section, click the drop-down arrow and select the option for **BIOS** (25).

44. Finally, check the box for **During the next boot, force entry into the BIOS setup screen** (26).

45.   This is shown in the following screenshot:

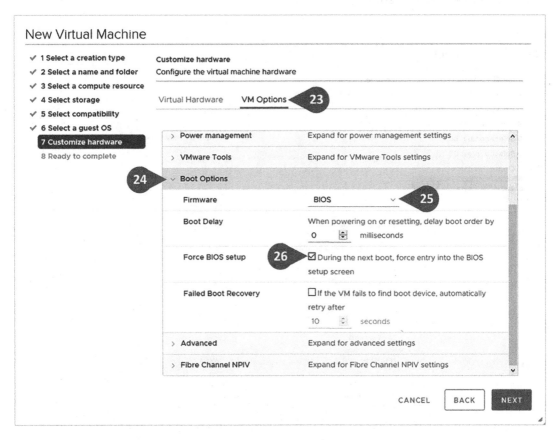

Figure 5-18. *Creating a new virtual machine – BIOS configuration*

46.   Once configured, click the **NEXT** button.

47. You will now see the Ready to complete screen as shown in the following screenshot:

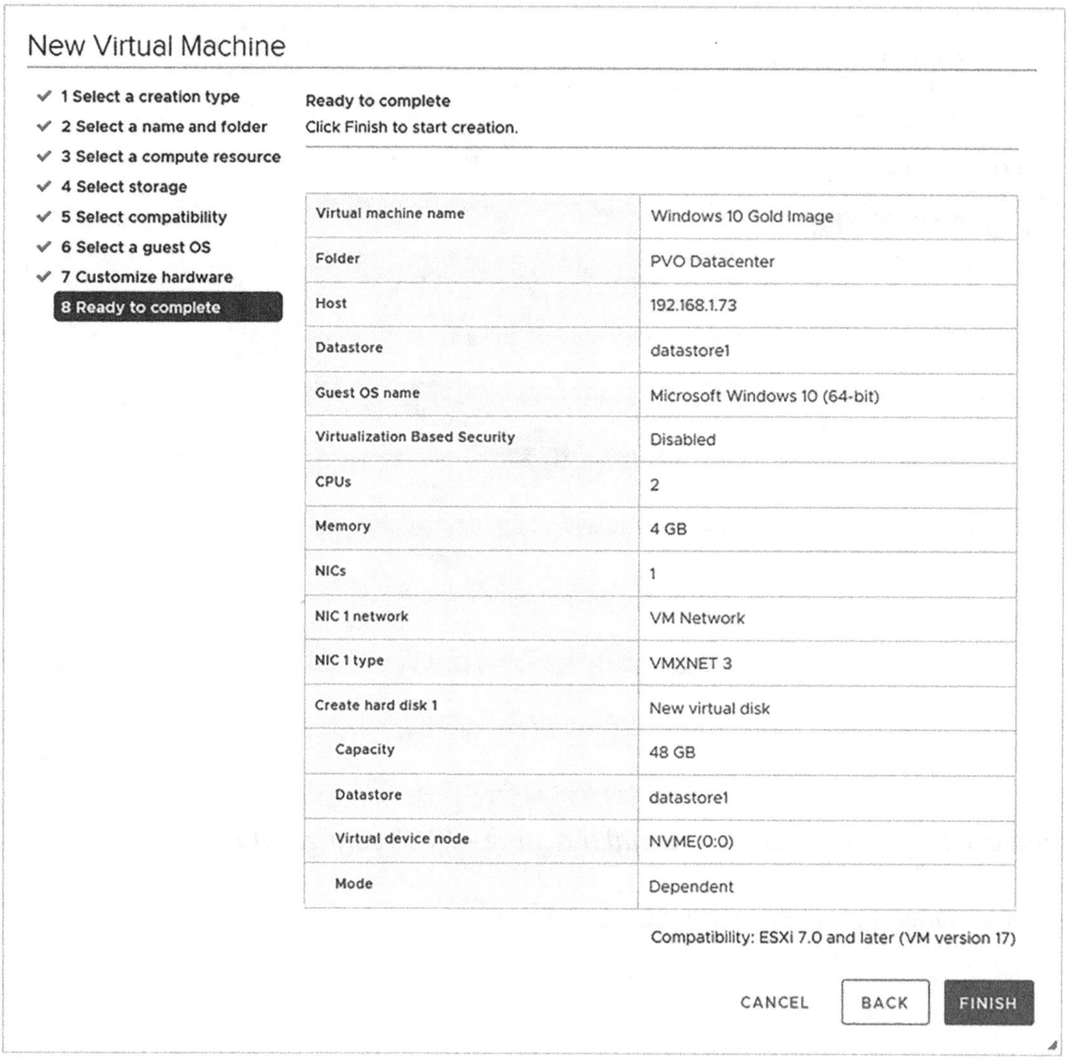

New Virtual Machine

✔ 1 Select a creation type	**Ready to complete**
✔ 2 Select a name and folder	Click Finish to start creation.
✔ 3 Select a compute resource	
✔ 4 Select storage	
✔ 5 Select compatibility	
✔ 6 Select a guest OS	
✔ 7 Customize hardware	
8 Ready to complete	

Virtual machine name	Windows 10 Gold Image
Folder	PVO Datacenter
Host	192.168.1.73
Datastore	datastore1
Guest OS name	Microsoft Windows 10 (64-bit)
Virtualization Based Security	Disabled
CPUs	2
Memory	4 GB
NICs	1
NIC 1 network	VM Network
NIC 1 type	VMXNET 3
Create hard disk 1	New virtual disk
Capacity	48 GB
Datastore	datastore1
Virtual device node	NVME(0:0)
Mode	Dependent

Compatibility: ESXi 7.0 and later (VM version 17)

CANCEL   BACK   FINISH

Figure 5-19. Creating a new virtual machine – Ready to complete

48. Check the details of the configuration settings you have entered, and then click **FINISH** to complete the new virtual machine configuration.

49.   You will see the virtual machine being created as shown:

Figure 5-20. *New machine creation task successfully completed*

Now that the virtual machine has been created, you can now power it on and start the first part of the configuration – the BIOS configuration settings.

50.   Click the power on button (27) as shown in the following screenshot:

Figure 5-21. *Power on the new virtual machine*

With the virtual machine now powered on, you now need to open a console to it so you can configure the BIOS settings required.

Configuring the Virtual Desktop BIOS

The next step of the virtual machine build process is to configure the BIOS settings required for the virtual desktop machine.

In this example, we are going to use the web console to connect to the virtual machine; however, you could also use the VMRC Remote Console application which you will need to download.

1. Click the **LAUNCH WEB CONSOLE** button in the vSphere Client to launch a web-based console in a new browser tab.

2. You will now see the BIOS Setup Utility screen as shown in the following screenshot:

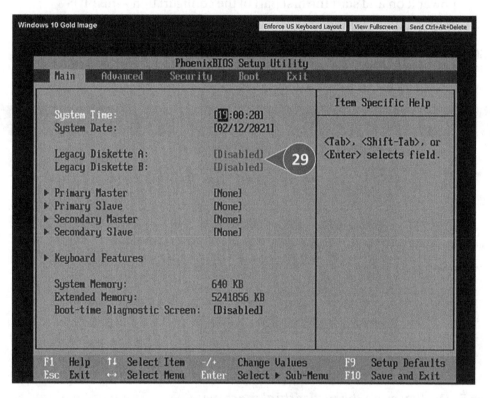

Figure 5-22. *Main BIOS screen displayed in the web console*

3. On the Main BIOS screen, ensure that **Legacy Diskette A:** and **Legacy Diskette B:** are set to disabled.

4. Now, using the cursor keys, press the right cursor key to select the **Advanced** menu.

5. Now, in the Advanced menu, use the down cursor key to move
    down the list until you highlight the option for **I/O Device
    Configuration**. This is shown in the following screenshot:

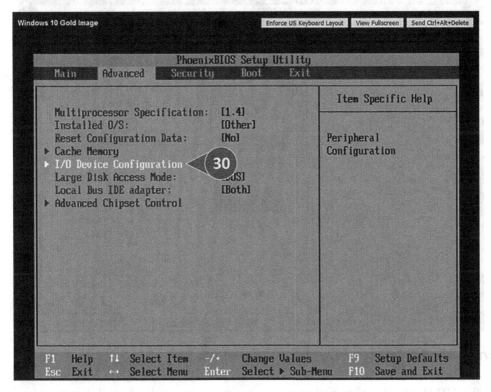

Figure 5-23. *BIOS screen Advanced menu*

6. Once you have selected the I/O Device Configuration menu, press
    Enter to open the next level menu.

7. This is shown in the following screenshot:

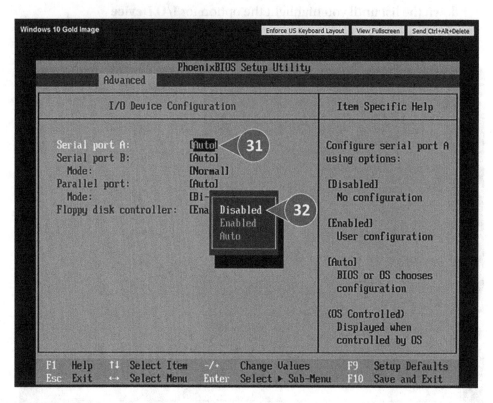

Figure 5-24. *BIOS screen I/O configuration menu*

In the **I/O Device Configuration** menu, we are going to disable all those devices that are listed. So, we will disable serial ports A and B, the parallel port, and finally the floppy disk controller. These are all devices that are not present on the virtual desktop machine, and so the best practice is to disable them – especially the floppy disk controller.

The reason we call out the floppy disk controller is that it checks to see if disks have been inserted. This takes CPU cycles checking a device that does not exist. Disabling the device means it does not check. To disable the devices, follow the steps described:

1. Highlight **Serial Port A:** first, by using the cursor keys.

2. Now press **Enter**.

3. You will see a pop-up box displaying the options for that device. Again, using the down arrow cursor key, highlight **Disabled** and then press Enter.

4. The device is now disabled.

5. Repeat the process for each of the list devices until you have disabled each one of them.

6. Once all devices have been disabled, you will see the following screenshot:

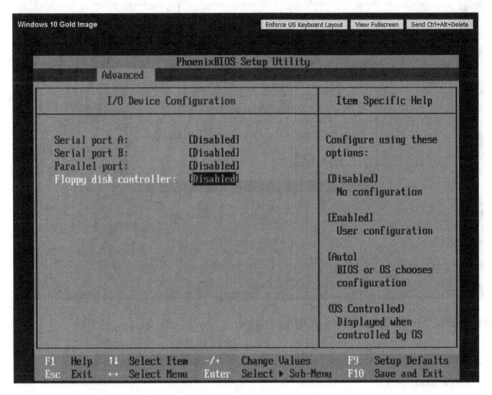

Figure 5-25. *Serial ports, parallel port, and floppy disk controller disabled*

Now that all devices have been disabled, you can save the configuration settings and exit the BIOS Setup Utility. To do this, follow the steps described:

1. Press the **F10** function key on your keyboard.

2. You will see the **Setup Confirmation** pop-up box as shown in the following screenshot:

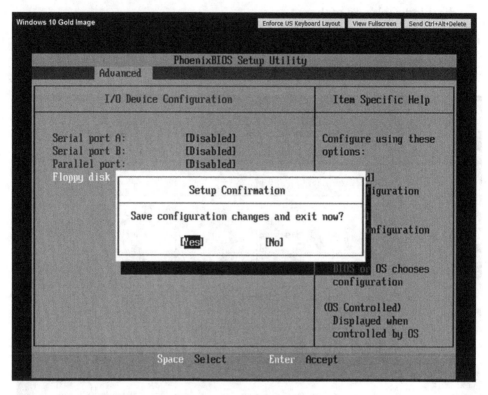

Figure 5-26. *Saving the BIOS configuration*

3. Using the cursor keys, highlight **Yes** and then press enter to accept the changes.

4. The BIOS settings are then saved, and the virtual machine will reboot.

You have now successfully configured the required BIOS settings for the virtual machine. The next step is to install the OS.

Installing the OS on the Virtual Desktop Machine

During the initial hardware configuration of the virtual machine, you configured the virtual machine to boot from the Windows 10 ISO image stored on the datastore of the host server.

The machine will now boot and launch the Windows Setup screen which you will see in the following screenshot:

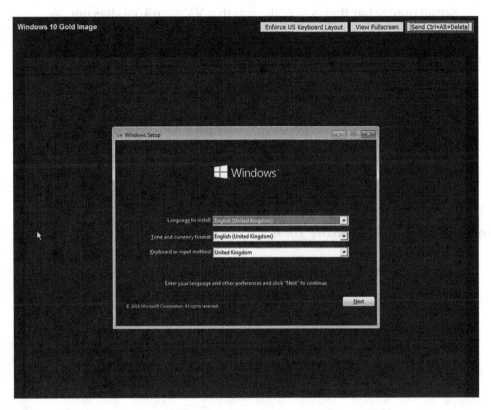

Figure 5-27. *Windows 10 booting to Windows Setup*

We are not going to run through the entire setup of the Windows 10 OS, so work through this as you would normally with your settings and configuration.

Once the OS is built, we will continue with the next step which is to install VMware Tools.

Installing VMware Tools

With the desktop OS now installed and running, the next step of the process is to install VMware Tools to ensure the correct VMware drivers are installed.

To install VMware Tools, follow the steps as described:

1. In the vCenter Client, select the Windows 10 Gold Image. You will see an orange bar that is warning you that VMware Tools has not yet been installed.

2. Now click **Install VMware Tools...** as shown in the following screenshot:

Figure 5-28. *Installing VMware Tools*

3. You will now see the **Install VMware Tools** dialog box as shown in the following screenshot:

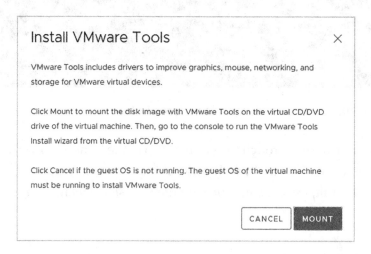

Figure 5-29. *Mount the VMware Tools disk image*

4. Click the **MOUNT** button. This will mount a virtual CD drive that contains the VMware Tools disk image on the new virtual desktop machine.

5. Now switch back to the web console of the new virtual desktop machine. You will see the following screenshot:

Figure 5-30. *VMware Tools DVD Drive*

6. Click the **DVD Drive (D:) VMware Tools** box to choose what happens with the mounted image.

7. You will now see the **DVD Drive (D:) VMware Tools** dialog box as shown in the following screenshot:

Figure 5-31. *Run the VMware Tools setup*

8. Click **Run setup64.exe** to launch the VMware Tools installer.

9. You will now see a **User Account Control** warning box pop up as shown in the following screenshot:

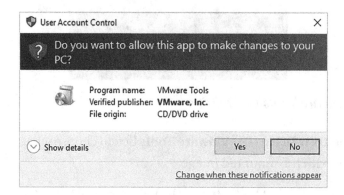

Figure 5-32. *User Account Control (UAC) warning message*

10. Click **Yes** to allow the installation to continue.

11. You will see the VMware Product Installation box pop up in the bottom right-hand side of the screen as VMware Tools prepares to be installed. This is shown in the following screenshot:

Figure 5-33. *VMware Tools preparing for installation*

12. You will now see the **Welcome to the installation wizard for VMware Tools** as shown in the following screenshot:

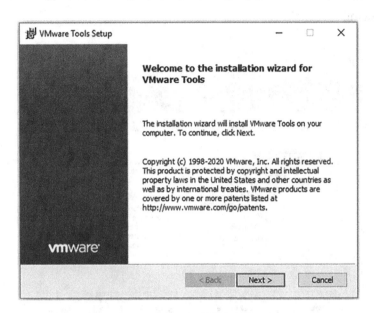

Figure 5-34. *Welcome to the VMware Tools installation wizard screen*

13. Click **Next ➤** to continue. You will see the **Choose Setup Type** screen as shown in the following screenshot:

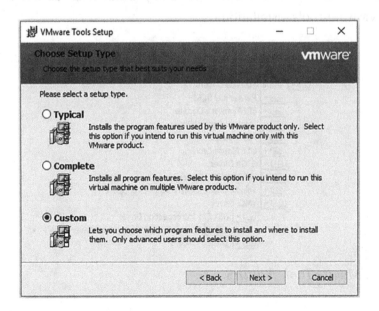

Figure 5-35. *VMware Tools Choose Setup Type*

14. Click the radio button for **Custom** and then click **Next ➤**.

15. You will now see the **Custom Setup** screen as shown in the following screenshot:

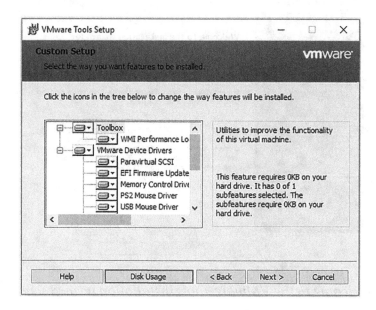

Figure 5-36. *VMware Tools Custom Setup*

16. You will now see a list of the features that you can install as part of the VMware Tools installation.

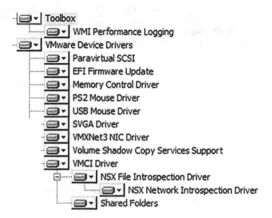

Figure 5-37. *VMware Tools features*

We are going to describe each of the features that you can install as part of VMware Tools as follows:

- **Toolbox – WMI Performance Logging**

- **VMware Device Drivers**

  - **Paravirtual SCSI**: This is for PVSCSI adapters to enhance the performance of virtualized applications.

  - **EFI Firmware Update:** This enables the firmware of the virtual machine to be updated.

  - **Memory Control Driver**: This allows advanced memory management of the virtual desktop machine.

  - **PS2 Mouse Driver**: This enables a virtual mouse driver to improve the performance of a PS2 mouse in a virtual desktop machine.

  - **USB Mouse Driver**: This enables a virtual mouse driver to improve the performance of a USB mouse in a virtual desktop machine.

  - **SVGA Driver**: This enables 32-bit displays, high resolution, and faster graphics performance. It installs a virtual SVGA driver that replaces the standard VGA driver. On Windows Vista and later versions, the VMware SVGA 3D (Microsoft – WDDM) driver is also installed, adding support for Windows Aero.

  - **VMXNET3 NIC Driver**: This improves network performance and is recommended for virtual desktop machines (ndis5/ndis6).

  - **Volume Shadow Copy Services**: This allows you to take backup copies or snapshots of the virtual desktop machine using VSS.

  - **VMCI Driver**: This enables communication with the hypervisor to enable faster communication between virtual machines.

- **NSX Network Introspection Driver**: This installs the agent so that introspective scanning support is added.

- **Shared Folders**: This feature allows folders to be shared between the virtual desktop machine and your host machine.

17. Select the feature you want to install and also make sure you disable any that you will not use, and then click **Next ➤** to continue.

18. You will see the **Ready to install VMware Tools** screen as shown in the following screenshot:

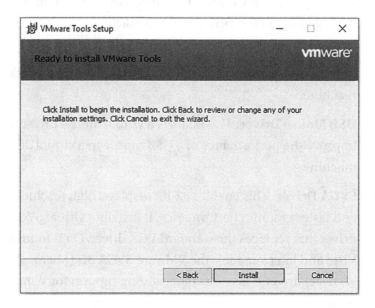

Figure 5-38. *Ready to install VMware Tools*

19. Click the **Install** button. You will see the **Installing VMware Tools** screen as shown:

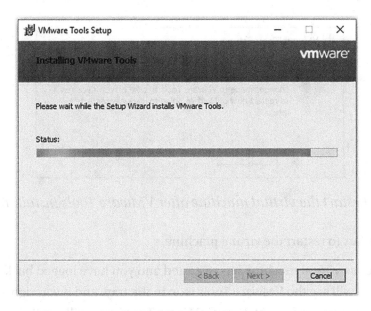

Figure 5-39. *Installing VMware Tools status/progress*

20. Once the installation has completed, you will see the **Completed the VMware Tools Setup Wizard** screen as shown in the following screenshot:

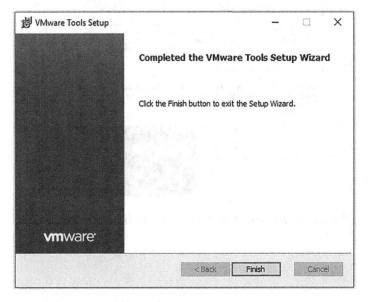

Figure 5-40. *Completed the VMware Tools installation*

21. You will now be prompted to restart the virtual machine as shown in the following screenshot:

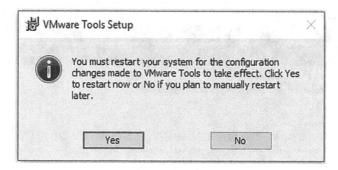

Figure 5-41. *Restart the virtual machine after VMware Tools installation*

22. Click **Yes** to restart the virtual machine.

23. Once the virtual machine has restarted and you have logged back in, you will see the VMware Tools icon in the tray, and if you right-click the icon and select **About VMware Tools,** you will see the following:

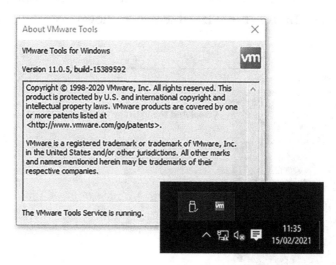

Figure 5-42. *VMware Tools running on the new virtual machine*

24. You will also see in the vCenter Client that the Windows 10 Gold
    Image virtual desktop machine is running, and VMware Tools has
    been installed as shown in the following screenshot:

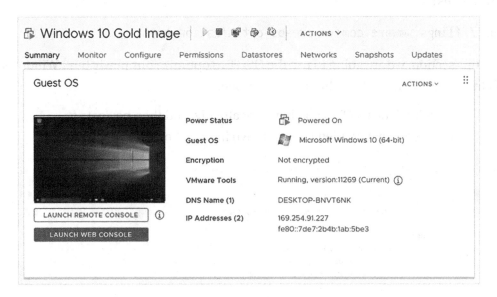

Figure 5-43. *vCenter Client view of the new virtual machine*

Now that the Windows 10 Gold Image virtual machine has been built, the OS
installed, and VMware Tools installed, the next step we are going to complete is the
customization and optimization.

Customize and Optimize the Virtual Desktop OS

The customization and optimization are critical to the performance of the virtual
desktop machine. As this is a virtual desktop machine, then we need to turn off as many
physical-based features or features of the Windows OS that will have a negative impact
on end-user performance.

For example, we are talking about things like screen savers and power management.
Screen savers will take up unnecessary resource, and power management is not
applicable now that the machine is running as a virtual desktop machine.

You can do this manually using scripts, or VMware has a solution for making this task much easier and more automated. This solution is the **VMware OS Optimization Tool** (OSOT). OSOT can be downloaded for free from the VMware Flings website using the following link:

https://flings.vmware.com/vmware-os-optimization-tool

In this section, we are going to use the OSOT to optimize our newly built Windows 10 Gold Image. To do this, follow the steps described:

1. Download the OSOT if you have not already, and then navigate to where you downloaded it to as shown in the following:

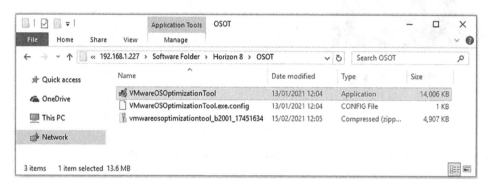

Figure 5-44. *VMware OS optimization tool*

2. If you see the **Open File - Security Warning** dialog box pop up, then click **Run** to continue.

3. You will now see the OSOT main screen as shown in the following screenshot:

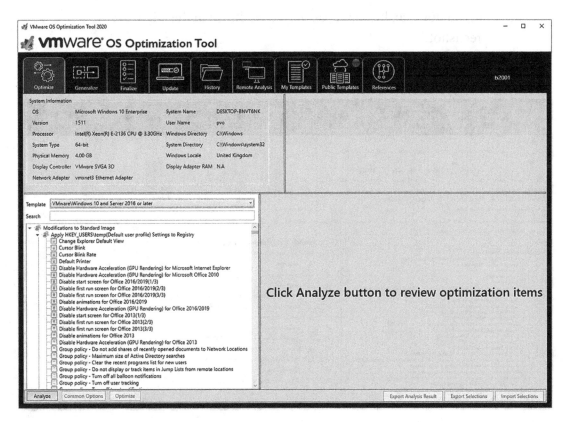

Figure 5-45. *VMware OSOT – main screen*

This main screen is split into four separate panes. As we have not yet performed an analysis, then only two sections are populated:

- **System Information**: This shows the details of the virtual desktop machine that you are analyzing. It shows the hardware configuration, OS details, and system details.

- **Template**: Under the system information pane, you can select the template you wish to use as your baseline analysis. In this example, we have selected Windows 10. Under the template selection, you will see all the recommended modifications that will be implemented on the Windows 10 Gold Image. You can individually select which ones will and will not be implemented.

4. Once you are happy with the modifications that will be made, click the **Analyze** button.

5. You will now see the results displayed as shown in the following screenshot:

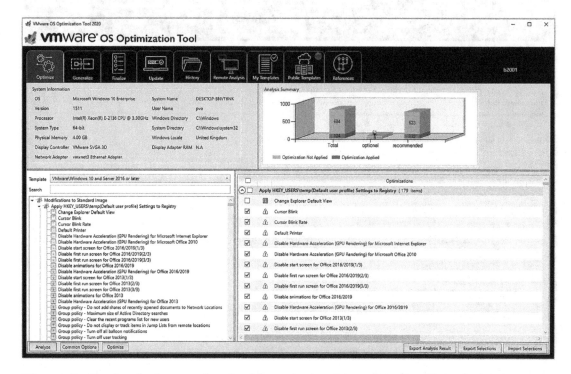

Figure 5-46. *Analysis completed with optimization recommendations*

6. You will now see the remaining two of the four panes populated with information:

- **Analysis Summary**: This pane shows a graph of the number of items analyzed with a breakdown of those that are recommended and those that are optional.

- **Optimizations**: This shows a list of all the optimizations that will be implemented. You can deselect any of them by unchecking the box next to the optimization.

- As well as these optimizations, the OSOT also allows you to make other changes that are required for creating your gold image. To configure these other options, follow the steps described:

7. Click the **Common Options** button on the bottom of the main page. You will now see the **Select Option** screen and the Overview tab as shown in the following screenshot:

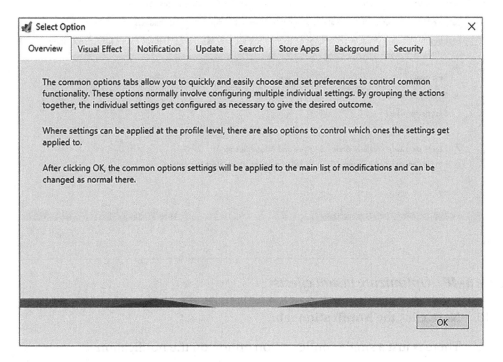

Figure 5-47. Select Option screen

8. Click the **Visual Effect** tab.

9. You will now see the **Prioritize the visual effect optimization** screen.

    The first option on this screen is to select between **Best quality**, **Balanced**, and **Best Performance**. Click the radio button to select the option best suited for this image and its use case.

    The final option on this screen is to **Disable hardware acceleration for IE, Office, and Adobe Acrobat**. This will ensure that additional resources are not consumed with accelerating graphics that are not necessary. The recommendation is to check this box to disable this feature, unless you are going to have hardware-based graphics configured for this image.

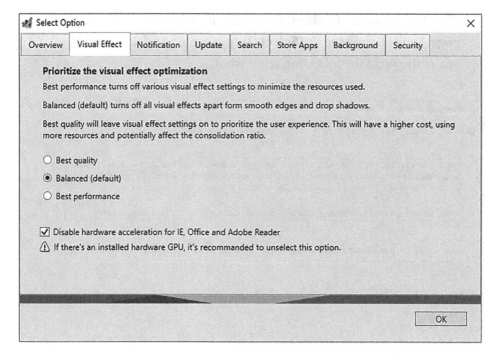

Figure 5-48. *Optimizing visual effects*

10.   Next, click the **Notification** tab.

There is just a single configuration option on the notification
screen and that is to **Disable notifications** by checking the box.

This screen is shown in the following screenshot:

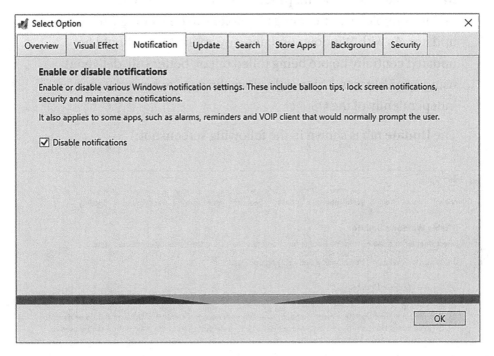

Figure 5-49. *Notification configuration screen*

The next tab is for **Update**.

On this screen, you can disable the Windows update process. This is the recommended best practice as you want the gold image to remain constant, and not effectively have different versions for different users based on different updates. The image should be maintained by the IT admin teams, and any updates should be managed centrally so that they can be tested and deployed to all end users using your chosen cloning method.

Another thing to consider is that with non-persistent virtual desktop machines, they are deleted when the end user logs out. You do not want these to be updating every time a new machine is created. It would download huge amounts of data each time, overloading the network, and then when the end user logs out, all those updates will be lost.

The other option on this screen is for **Disable Office Click-To-Run** updates. Click-to-Run products such as Microsoft Office, in this example, use streaming technology to deliver the Office updates. As with Windows updates, any applications should be updated centrally before being rolled out or, better still, delivered using App Volumes. This would allow the apps to be updated independently of the OS.

The **Update** tab is shown in the following screenshot:

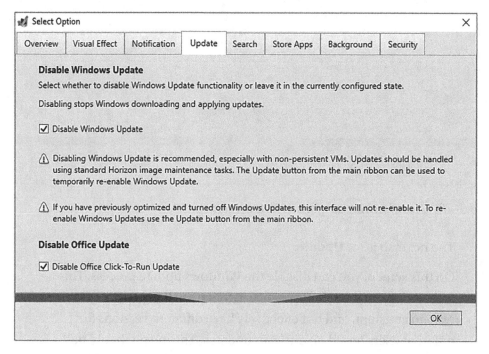

Figure 5-50. *Update configuration screen*

11. Now click the **Search** tab.

On the Search tab, you can configure the Windows search settings for the search box and Cortana. By default, both settings have been disabled, meaning that they will not be available to the end user. If you want to enable Cortana, then check the **Keep Cortana search** box, and if you want to show the search box, then check the **Show Search box as an icon on the taskbar** box.

This is shown in the following screenshot:

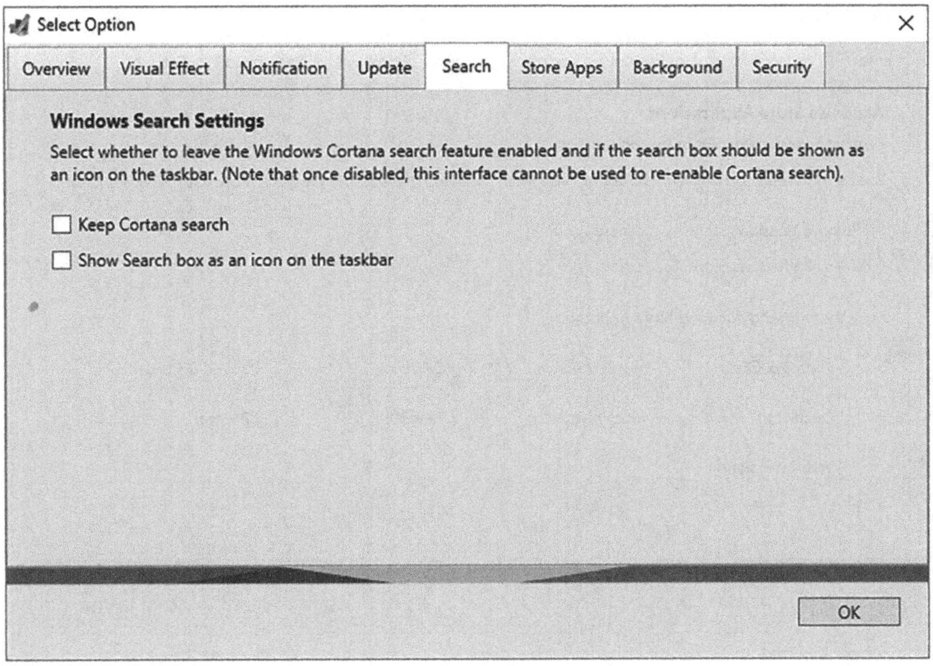

Figure 5-51. *Configuring Windows search settings*

12. Next, click the tab for **Store Apps**.

     With the Windows Store Applications configuration screen, you
     can choose which applications you want to keep. By default, the
     Remove Windows Store Applications button is selected which
     means all Windows Store apps will be removed.

     The second radio button is to **Keep all Windows Store
     Applications** which means no applications will be removed by the
     OSOT during optimization.

     Finally, the last option allows you to select which individual
     applications you want to keep. Simply check the box next to the
     application that you want to be made available to the end user.

The Store Apps screen is shown in the following screenshot:

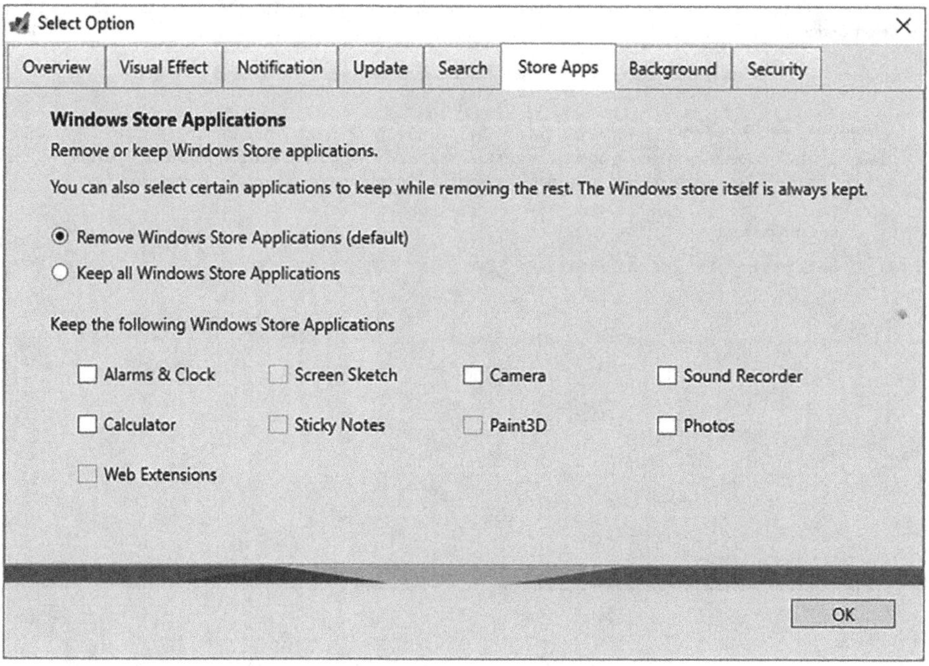

Figure 5-52. *Configuring Windows Store Apps settings*

13. Now click the **Background** tab.

On the background settings configuration screen, you have two options. The first option is Set default background to solid color. This enables you to set the background of the virtual desktop machine to be a solid color, which you can then choose from the colors displayed. This removes the desktop wallpaper.

The second option is for Allow users to change background, which means the end users have the ability to change the background color of their virtual desktop machine. However, if they have a non-persistent desktop, the desktop will be deleted when they log off, and when they log in to a new desktop, the background color will revert to the default.

This is where a user environment management solution will come into play as it can save any customization or personalization settings that the end user makes.

The background configuration screen is shown in the following screenshot:

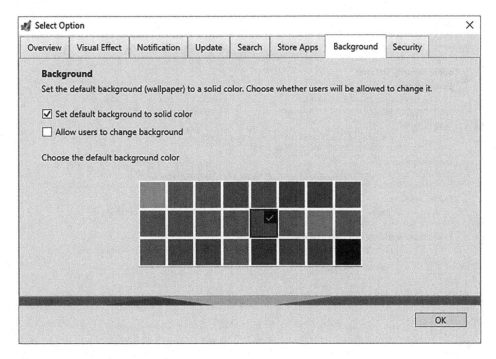

Figure 5-53. *Configuring background settings*

14. Now click the final tab. This is for **Security**.

    On the security configuration screen, you can choose which security options you want to enable or disable. By default, all the options listed are disabled.

    If you want to enable a particular feature, then simply check the box next to that feature.

The security configuration settings are shown in the following screenshot:

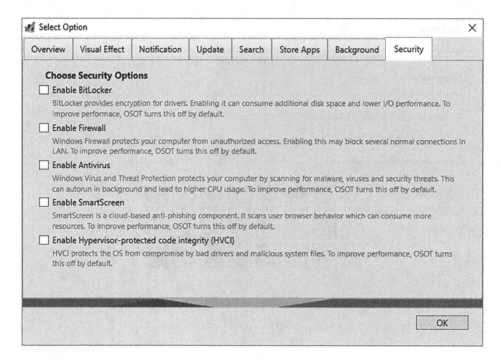

Figure 5-54. *Security settings*

15.   Now click **OK**. You will return to the OSOT main screen.

Before we start the optimization process, there are a number of other configuration options we are going to run through. You will see these options as icons across the top of the screen. We are going to start with the generalization options.

16.   Click the **Generalize** tab.

The generalization settings allow you to remove information that is specific to the computer so that you deploy a clean image each time a new virtual desktop machine is created and the end user logs in. In order to use this feature, the virtual machine needs to be in audit mode. To do this on Windows 10, on the desktop, press Ctrl+Alt+F3.

You have the options configuring the time zone, localization information, and the administrator account and whether you want to auto login as the local administrator on boot. The final options are for copying the profile which copies the built-in administrator profile to the default user profile. This is then used as a template for creating new end-user profiles.

The generalization screen is shown in the following screenshot:

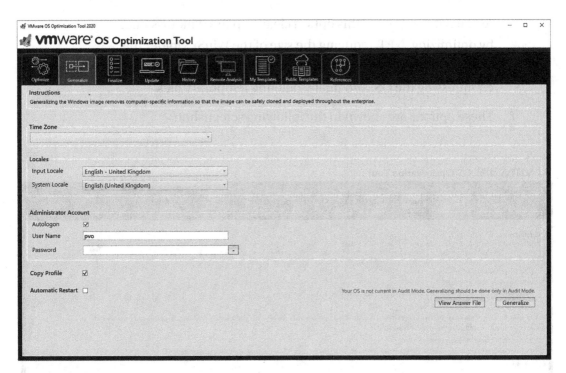

Figure 5-55. *Generalization settings*

17. Now click the **Generalize** button to make the configured changes to the image.

Running the Generalize task will run Sysprep with the out-of-box experience (OOBE) and Generalize options. It will use the unattended answer file which you can view by clicking the View Answer File button. Once optimized and generalized, you will need to reboot the virtual machine to complete the process.

Next, we are going to look at the finalize tab and configuration options.

18. Next, click the **Finalize** tab.

The finalize configuration settings are used to clean up the image and make it ready for deployment. There are a number of settings, categorized under the headings of **Choose system cleanup jobs** and **Choose information to clear**.

We are going to look at the first set of options for **Choose system cleanup jobs**.

As the name suggests, this option cleans up the Windows image by optimizing .NET, reducing the size of the WinSxS folder that contains different versions of files stored together side by side, compressing the OS, and finally deleting temporary files.

These options are shown in the following screenshot:

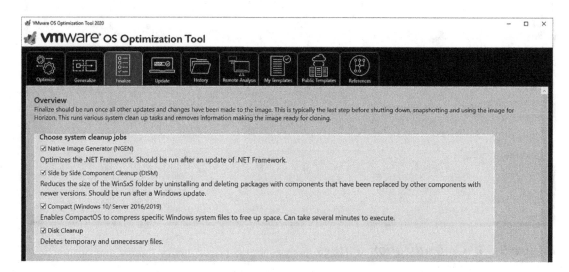

Figure 5-56. *Selecting the system cleanup jobs configuration screen*

The second set of options are for clearing information.

One of the key things on this screen, which you need to ensure is configured, is the option for **Release IP address**. This means that when the image is cloned and built for each new end user, it receives a new IP address and new DHCP lease.

These options are shown in the following screenshot:

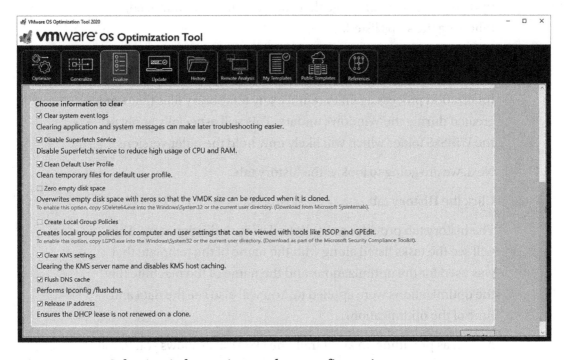

Figure 5-57. *Selecting information to clear configuration screen*

19. Now click the next tab. This is the **Update** tab as shown in the following screenshot:

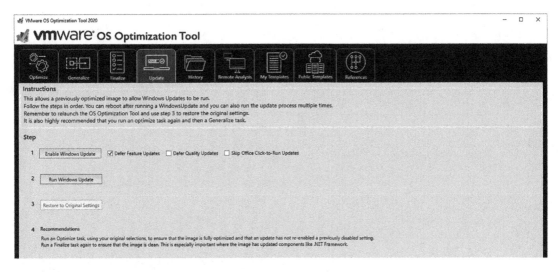

Figure 5-58. *Update configuration screen*

On the update configuration screen, you can run the Windows update process on an image that you have already optimized, by following the steps listed.

It is worth noting that you should also rerun the optimization tasks that you ran on the previous image as well as running the finalization process again to remove any temporary files that were created during the Windows update. This will especially apply to the WinSxS folder which will likely now hold the older versions.

Next, we are going to look at the history tab.

20.   Click the **History** tab.

The history tab provides an audit trail of optimization tasks. You will see the tasks listed along with the name of the template that was used for the optimizations and the name of the machine that the optimizations were applied to. You will also see the data and time of the optimization.

As well as providing an audit trail, the OSOT also allows you to roll back or undo an optimization, reverting to a pre-optimized image. This is a useful feature just in case your optimization disables or stops something from working.

The history screen is shown in the following screenshot:

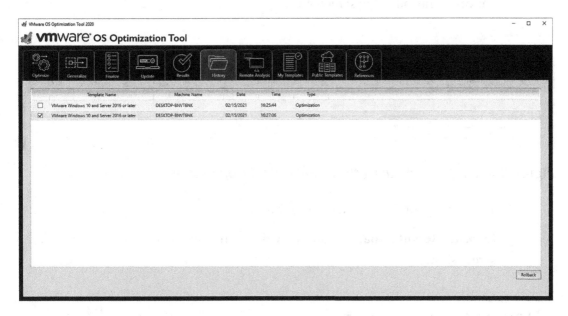

Figure 5-59. *Optimization history*

To roll back to a previous image state, follow the steps described:

1. Check the box next to the optimization you want to undo.

2. Click the **Rollback** button. You will see the following:

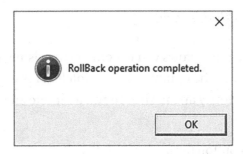

Figure 5-60. *Optimization rollback completed successfully*

3. Once completed, the rollback task will appear in the history as shown in the following screenshot:

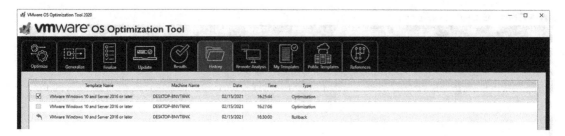

Figure 5-61. *History showing the recent rollback operation*

The next option is to run a remote analysis.

4. Click the **Remote Analysis** tab. You will see the following screenshot:

Figure 5-62. *Remote Analysis screen*

The remote analysis feature allows you to connect to existing virtual desktop machines in Horizon and run the optimization remotely. This is useful for IT admins to update existing images remotely and in situ. To run a remote analysis, follow the steps described:

1. Click the **Login** button (33).

2. You will now see a **Login** box appear. This is a login box to enable you to log in to the Connection Server and access the virtual desktop machines that it is managing. The login box is shown in the following screenshot:

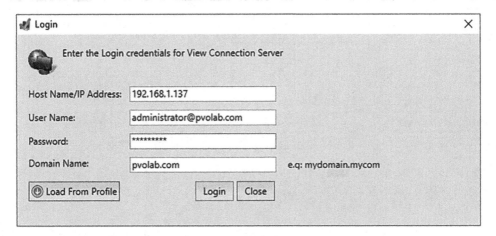

Figure 5-63. *Log in to the Horizon Connection Server for remote analysis*

3. Enter the details for the hostname of the Connection Server, username, password, and then the domain.

4. Now click the **Login** button.

5. You will see a list of the virtual desktop machines managed by the Connection Server. Select the virtual desktop that you want to optimize and then run through the optimization process as you normally would.

6. If you have multiple Connection Servers, you can create a profile for each login by using the Load From Profile feature.

   The next option and tab is for My Templates.

7. Click the **My Templates** tab.

8. You will see the following screenshot:

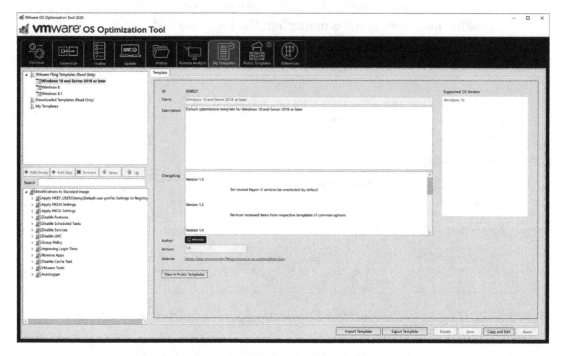

Figure 5-64. *My Templates screen*

The **My Templates** screen shows you a list of the VMware pre-created templates plus a list of any that you have either created yourself or have downloaded. The OSOT allows you to build your own custom templates, so you can choose the optimizations you want to apply based on the use case.

The final option is for Public Templates.

9. Click the **Public Templates** tab.

10.   You will see the following screenshot:

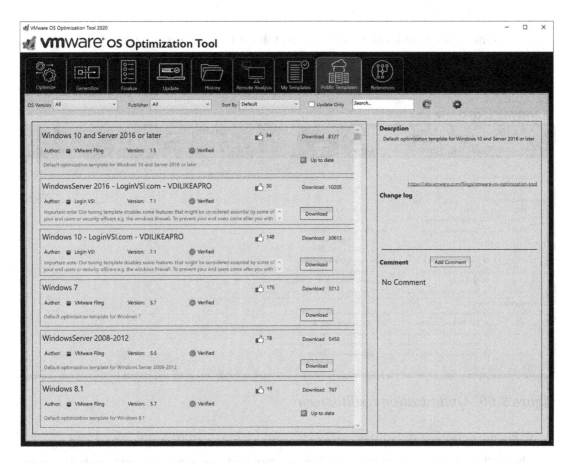

Figure 5-65. *Public Templates screen*

As well as using the pre-built templates and any templates that you create, you can also download templates created by others in the community.

Scroll through the templates, and if you want to make use of one, then click the **Download** button. The template will then be available for use.

There is one other tab, which we are not going to cover in any detail, and that is the **References** tab. This is just links to the online manual and guides.

Having now covered the configuration options, we are now going to optimize the image. To do this, follow the steps described:

1.   Return to the main screen by clicking the **Optimize** tab.

2.   Now click the **Analyze** button.

3. The optimization task will run, and all the selected optimizations will be applied to the image.

4. Once completed, you will see a new tab for **Results** as shown in the following screenshot:

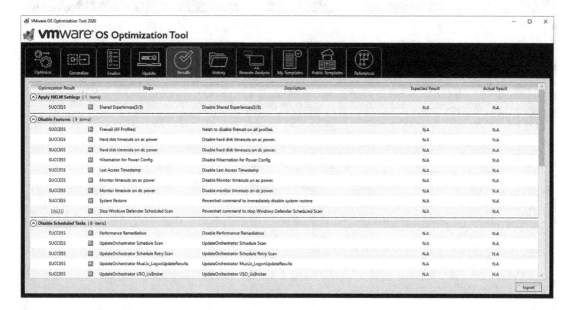

Figure 5-66. *Optimization result screen*

You will see that all the optimizations have been successfully applied to the image.

The optimization process has now been completed, and you can move on to the next task in building a desktop image which is to install any additional applications.

Installing Gold Image Applications

The next step is to install any applications that you want to include in the base image. These are typically apps that all users will use and that will not need updating very often. Do not forget if you need to update an app that is part of the gold image, then you will need to create a new gold image.

This is where VMware App Volumes would be a good solution as applications can be managed and delivered independently.

Once you have installed any gold image applications, then you can move on to the final step of the virtual desktop image build. The final step is to install the Horizon Agent to allow the virtual desktop machine to be managed by the Connection Server and to install the VMware drivers to enable remote delivery to end users.

Install the Horizon Agent

In this section, we are going to install the Horizon Agent.

The reason the Horizon Agent gets installed after the image has been optimized is to ensure that the optimization process does not switch off or disable a key feature that is required by the Connection Server to manage the virtual desktop, or any of the remote experience drivers.

You also need to ensure that the version of the Horizon Agent is supported on your virtual desktop OS.

As we are installing the Horizon 8, 2006 version or later, then the following versions of Windows 10 are supported:

- Windows 10 20H2 SAC (Pro, Education, and Enterprise)

- Windows 10 2004 SAC (Pro, Education, and Enterprise)

- Windows 10 1909 SAC (Pro, Education, and Enterprise)

- Windows 10 LTSC 2019 (Enterprise)

- Windows 10 1607 LTSB (Enterprise)

To install the Horizon Agent, follow the steps described:

1. Navigate to where you have saved the Horizon installation
    software as shown in the following example:

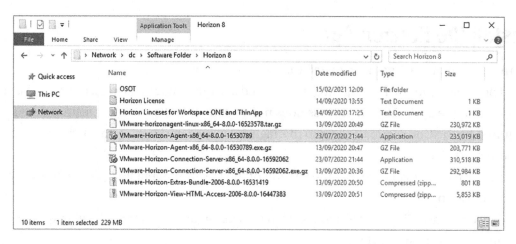

Figure 5-67. *Horizon Agent installer*

2. Double-click the **VMware-Horizon-Agent-x86_64-8.0.0** file to
    launch the installer. In this example, we are installing the 64-bit
    version of the Horizon Agent.

3. You will now see the UAC message as shown in the following
    screenshot:

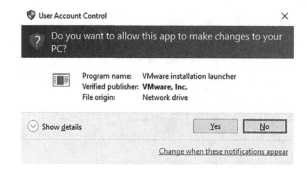

Figure 5-68. *User Account Control warning message*

4. Click **Yes** to continue.

5. The Horizon Agent installer will now launch, and you will see the following screenshot:

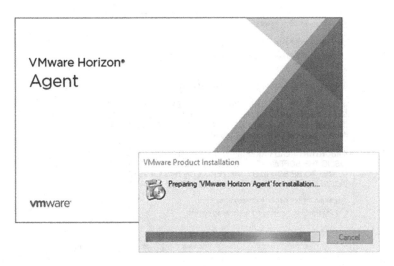

Figure 5-69. *Horizon Agent loading screen*

6. Once loaded, you will see the **Welcome to the Installation Wizard for VMware Horizon Agent** as shown in the following screenshot:

Figure 5-70. *Welcome to the installation wizard*

7. Click **Next ➤** to continue.

8. You will see the **License Agreement** screen as shown in the following screenshot:

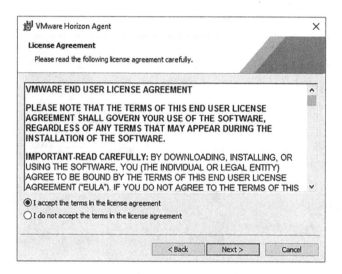

Figure 5-71. *Accepting the license agreement*

9. Click the radio button for **I accept the terms in the license agreement**, and then click the **Next ➤** button.

10. You will now see the **Network protocol configuration** screen as shown in the following screenshot:

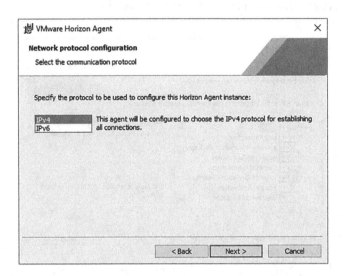

Figure 5-72. *Configure the network protocol*

11. Select the IP protocol version from the list, either IPv4 or IPv6.

Do not forget you will need to choose the same version of IP that you chose when you configured the Connection Server. You cannot mix and match IP versions between Horizon components.

---

12. In this example, we are going to select IPv4 as the Connection Server is using this version.

13. Click the **Next ➤** button to continue.

14. You will now see the **Custom Setup** screen. Here, you can configure which features you want to install as part of the Horizon Agent. This is shown in the following screenshot:

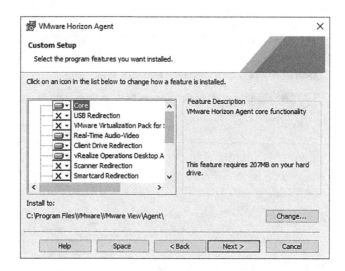

Figure 5-73. *Custom feature setup*

15. The list of the features that you can install as part of the Horizon Agent is detailed as follows:

Figure 5-74. *Custom feature details*

We are going to describe each of the features that you can install as part of the Horizon Agent as follows:

- **Core**: Installs the core Horizon Agent requirements.

- **USB Redirection**: Enables USB devices to be redirected from the end user's end point to the virtual desktop machine.

- **VMware Virtualization Pack for Skype for Business**: Installs the optimizations required to run Skype for Business on a virtual desktop machine.

- **Real-Time Audio-Video**: Enables the redirection of audio and video devices from the end point to the virtual desktop machine.

- **VMware Instant Clone Agent**: Enables the virtual desktop machine to be delivered using Instant Clones. You will need vSphere 6.0/2015 U1 or later to be able to support Instant Clones. If you install this feature, then ensure that you DO NOT install the Horizon View Composer Agent.

- **VMware Horizon View Composer Agent**: Enables the virtual desktop machine to be delivered using Linked Clones.

- **Client Drive Redirection**: Enables the end user's end point device to share local drives with the virtual desktop machine.

- **vRealize Operations Desktop Agent**: Enables the virtual desktop machine to be managed with vRealize Operations Manager. The agent collects metrics and performance data and sends them to the Horizon Adapter.

- **Scanner Redirection**: Enables scanners to be connected to the end user's end point device and redirected to the virtual desktop machine.

- **Smartcard Redirection**: Enables smartcard readers to be connected to the end user's end point device and redirected to the virtual desktop machine.

- **Serial Port Redirection**: Enables serial port devices to be connected to the end user's end point device and redirected to the virtual desktop machine.

- **VMware Audio**: Enables audio on the virtual desktop machine that is played back via the end user's end point device.

- **SDO Sensor Redirection**: Enables Simple Device Orientation Sensor redirection that reports back any orientation changes on the end user's end point, such as switching from landscape to portrait.

- **Geolocation Redirection**: Enables the location information from the end user's end point device to be sent to the virtual desktop machine. Useful for end users that travel so that their location information is reflected on their desktop given the virtual desktop machine remains static in a data center.

- **Horizon Performance Tracker**: Monitors the performance of the display protocol and system resource usage of the virtual desktop machine.

- **VMware Integrated Printing**: Enables printer redirection.

- **Help Desk Plugin for Horizon Agent**: Enables the virtual desktop to be monitored using the Horizon Help Desk Tool that is integrated into the Horizon Console.

16. Having now covered each of the features you can install as part of the Horizon Agent, and selected the ones you need, click **Next ➤** to continue.

17. The next screen you will see is the **Remote Desktop Protocol Configuration** screen as shown in the following screenshot:

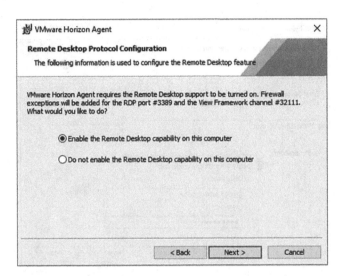

Figure 5-75. *Configuring the remote desktop protocol*

18. Click the radio button for **Enable the Remote Desktop capability on this computer**. This is a required configuration to allow end users to access a virtual desktop machine.

19. Click **Next ➤** to continue.

20. The next screen is the **Register with Horizon Connection Server** as shown in the following screenshot:

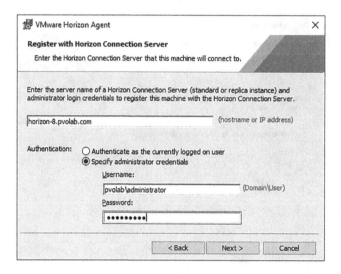

Figure 5-76. *Registering the virtual machine with the Connection Server*

21. On this configuration screen, you need to enter the details of the Connection Server that will manage this virtual desktop machine. This in turn will replicate the information across the Replica Servers in your environment, if you have any configured. In this example, in the hostname or IP address field, type in the name of the Connection Server. In this example, it is called horizon-8. pvolab.com.

22. In the **Authentication** field, click the radio button for **Specify administrator credentials**.

23. In the **Username** field, type in the user's name using the format Domain/User. In this example, we are using **pvolab\ administrator** as the username.

24. Finally, in the **Password** field, type in the password for the account you entered. In this example, the password is for the administrator account we entered previously.

25. Click the **Next ➤** button to continue.

26. You will now see the **Ready to Install the Program** screen as shown in the following screenshot:

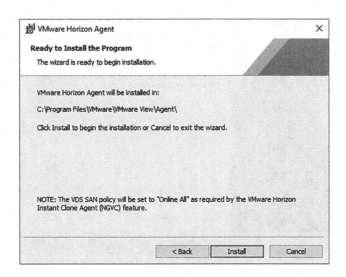

Figure 5-77. *Ready to install the Horizon Agent*

27. Click the **Install** button. You will see the installation process start and the status of the progress as shown in the following screenshot:

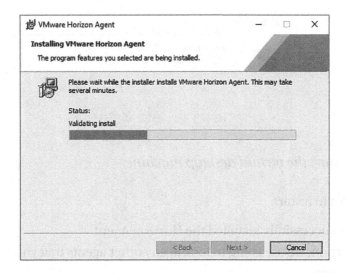

Figure 5-78. *Installation status and progress*

305

28. Once the installation has finished, you will see the **Installer Completed** screen as shown in the following:

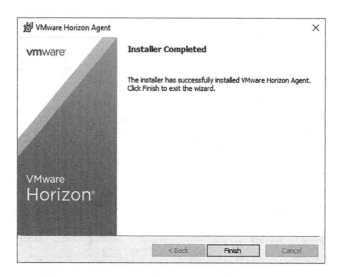

Figure 5-79. *Installation successfully completed*

29. Click the **Finish** button to complete the installation.

30. You will be prompted to restart the machine as shown in the following screenshot:

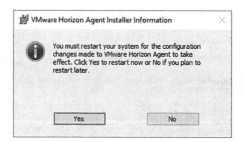

Figure 5-80. *Restart the virtual desktop machine*

31. Click **Yes** to restart.

You have now successfully installed the Horizon Agent.

In the next section, we are going to look at any other agents that you might need to install in the gold image.

Additional Agents

As well as the Horizon Agent, there are a couple of other agents that you may want to install based on other components of the Horizon suite that you plan on deploying.

These agents would be the final part of building the gold image and should be installed now.

So, if you are planning on using either VMware App Volumes or VMware Dynamic Environment Manager, then the agents for each of these solutions should be installed now.

Once you have installed them, then you might want to double-check that no temporary files have been left or installers copied onto the gold image.

You have now successfully built a Windows 10 gold image ready for deployment. In the next section, we are going to look at the additional steps you would need in the build process if you were going to be using hardware accelerated graphics.

Configuring for Hardware-Enabled Graphics

In this section, we are going to look at the steps for configuring a virtual desktop image that will use hardware accelerated graphics.

We are not going to cover the entire build process again as most of the steps are the same as we have already covered, but instead we are going to highlight the different steps that are relevant to adding the hardware accelerated graphics capability.

To do this, follow the steps described:

1. Follow the process for creating a new Windows 10 virtual desktop machine image using the vCenter Client until you reach step **7**
   Customize hardware.

2. Expand the **Memory** section and check the box for **Reserve all guest memory (All locked)** as shown in the following screenshot:

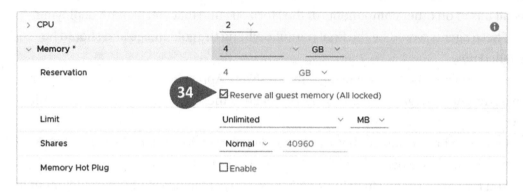

***Figure 5-81.** Configuring reserved memory*

You need to configure the memory reservation; otherwise, the virtual desktop machine will fail to power on, as it cannot guarantee that the memory will be available.

3. Next, click the **ADD NEW DEVICE** button.

4. From the list of devices, select the option for **PCI Device (35)** as shown in the following screenshot:

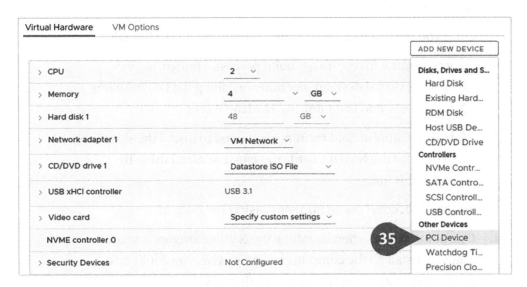

Figure 5-82. *Adding a new PCI device*

5. You will now see the following screenshot:

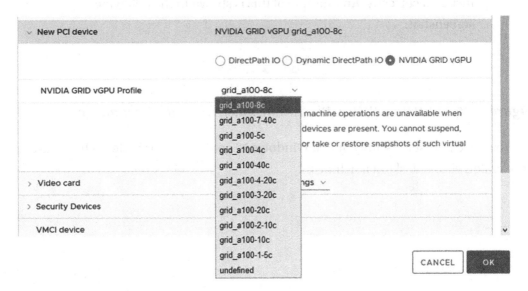

Figure 5-83. *Configuring the NVIDIA GRID vGPU card*

6. ˙ Click the radio button for **NVIDIA GRID vGPU**.

7. Then from the drop-down arrow next to **NVIDIA GRID vGPU Profile**, click and select the profile you want to use from the list of those displayed.

8. Once you have finished the hardware configuration, click **OK**.

9. Now continue with the image build process, configuring the BIOS of the virtual desktop machine, installing the OS, installing VMware Tools, and installing the Horizon Agent.

10. With the OS now up and running, you need to install the standard OS drivers for the NVIDIA card. You can download these by following this link:

    `www.nvidia.com/Download/index.aspx?lang=en-us`

11. One point to note when installing the NVIDIA drivers is to ensure that you install all the components; otherwise, you could miss some of the core virtual desktop functionality.

12. Once the drivers have been installed, open the device manager on the virtual desktop machine and check that the drivers have been installed correctly. An example of this is shown in the following screenshot:

Figure 5-84. *NVIDIA GRID vGPU card installed in the device manager*

You have now successfully built a Windows 10 gold image for building hardware accelerated virtual desktop machines.

Summary

We have given you a comprehensive overview of how to build and create a virtual desktop machine gold image. This gold image will be used to create all end-user virtual desktop machines. We followed a defined process to build the virtual machine, installed the operating system, optimized it to run as a virtual desktop machine, and then installed all the VMware Tools and agents required.

In the next chapter, we are going to take this newly built virtual desktop gold image and create a number of desktop pools which in turn will be used to deliver a virtual desktop machine to end users.

CHAPTER 6

Building and Configuring Desktop Pools

In this chapter, we will start to bring together the two elements that have been discussed and worked through so far. That is, bringing together the virtual desktop machine gold image, the Connection Server, and other infrastructure components, so that virtual desktop machines can be delivered to end users.

To deliver virtual desktop machines to end users, Horizon uses a process called desktop pools, which will be covered in the next section.

What Is a Desktop Pool?

A Horizon desktop pool consists of several virtual desktop machines that all have the same configuration attributes that form part of a group. The group is the desktop pool. This means that all the virtual desktop machines that are part of a desktop pool will all have the same configuration.

For example, they may all be running the same operating system version and the same applications, along with the same CPU and memory requirements. They could also have different hardware requirements, such as having a desktop pool that contains virtual desktop machines, which have access to a physical GPU card in the host server.

The pool configuration could also be based on a departmental basis, to cater for different use cases within your organization that require a different specification or configuration of virtual desktop machine.

The following graphics show example desktop pools, where sales have a virtual desktop machine configured with a single CPU, the development desktop pool is configured with two CPUs, and the engineering team has access to hardware accelerated graphics using an NVIDIA graphics card.

313

© Peter von Oven 2022
P. von Oven, *Mastering VMware Horizon 8*, https://doi.org/10.1007/978-1-4842-7261-9_6

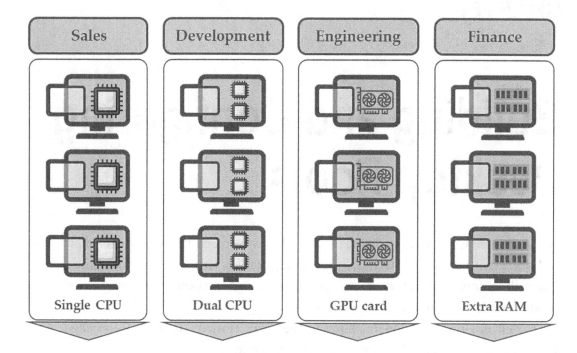

Figure 6-1. *Example desktop pool configurations*

Now that we have covered the different use case perspective of creating desktop pools, the next section will look at the different types of desktop pools that you can configure in Horizon.

Desktop Pool Types

We have already defined desktop pools as the grouping together of virtual desktop machines that are built using the same configuration. However, there are different types of desktop pools. These are described in the following sections.

Automated Desktop Pools

Automated desktop pools are automatically created from either a snapshot or a template of your virtual desktop gold image. Being an automated pool, virtual desktop machines within an automated desktop pool are created on demand, or they can be built up front, meaning they are ready for end users when required.

Deploying automated pools are the most widely used, given the greater flexibility and ease of management that they offer. It also means you can take advantage of a more dynamic environment with Instant Clones, for example.

Manual Desktop Pools

A manual desktop pool allows you to create a desktop pool that contains desktop machines that are already built. These desktops can be either physical desktops or virtual desktop machines that are managed using vCenter but are not built using either Instant Clones or Full Clones. The desktops just need to be running the Horizon Agent to enable them to be delivered to end users by the Connection Server.

This type of pool would be used for more niche use cases, as there is a greater management overhead and none of the flexibility of the automated desktop pool model.

As an example, an end user needs access to a rack mounted workstation, where a physical workstation is in the data center and the end user needs access to it, but also requires a more advanced display protocol than standard RDP.

RDS Desktop Pools

As the name suggests, RDS desktop pools allow IT administrators to create desktop pools for delivering session-based desktops or published applications.

Desktop Pool User Assignments

As discussed, there are different types of desktop pools that you can create, which are based on the use case. In addition to the type of desktop pool, you can also configure how that desktop pool is assigned to the end user.

There are two types of desktop pool end-user assignment, which will now be discussed in the following sections.

Floating

This is sometimes referred to as a non-persistent desktop; end users with this type of assignment do not own their own desktop. Instead, they are allocated a new and maybe different desktop machine from the pool each time they log in.

With a floating assignment, you would need to add VMware DEM to deliver the end-user profile and personalization, to make the desktop look and feel like their own personal desktop, rather than a vanilla new desktop where they would need to configure it each time.

For applications, you would look to deliver these on demand using VMware App Volumes. This means that the applications delivered would be based on the end user, rather than having to install all applications on the base image.

Dedicated

With a dedicated, or persistent desktop, the end user effectively owns their own desktop. This means that they will connect to the same machine each time they log in.

You can still deliver applications dynamically as this will help manage the applications independently, and you can still manage the end-user profile.

Virtual Desktop Creation Options

Along with the consideration as to whether the desktop pools will be floating or dedicated, you also need to decide on how the virtual desktop machines are going to be built. By this we mean what mechanism vCenter is going to use to create the virtual desktop machines.

There are now two options: Instant Clones or Full Clones. Previously, there was also the option of Linked Clones, but that feature no longer exists in the latest versions of Horizon.

Instant Clones

We have already discussed how Instant Clones work, but in this context, you get to choose whether to use Instant Clones to build your virtual desktop machines in the desktop pool.

This would be the recommended approach given the ease of management and the lower overhead on storage infrastructure.

The other option would be to use Full Clone virtual desktop machines.

Full Clones

Full Clone virtual desktop machines are, as the name suggests, a Full Clone of the virtual desktop machine gold image.

As they are Full Clones, then they will take up far more disk storage space, so should only be used if the use case dictates.

It is worth pointing out that assignments and how the virtual desktop machines are built are different. For example, floating desktops could be built using Full Clones or Instant Clones. The reason for highlighting this is that I have often heard customers say that Instant Clones can only be used for floating virtual desktop machines. However, this is not the case as we will see in the following sections.

Having now described the different desktop pool options, the next stage is to move into the practical steps and build the first desktop pool example.

Creating Automated Desktop Pools

The following section will switch to the practical side of desktop pools, working through the process of how to create different types of pools and the differing ways of building those pools.

We are going to build the following example desktop pools, all using the Windows 10 virtual desktop machine gold image we created previously:

- Instant Clone Dedicated Pool

- Instant Clone Floating Pool

- Full Clone Dedicated Pool

- Full Clone Floating Pool

We are going to start with the Instant Clone desktop pools.

Before you start creating your desktop pools, there are a couple of things you need to already have in place:

- A folder in vSphere in which to store the virtual desktop machines. In this example, we have created a folder called **Horizon Desktops**.

- A configured vSphere cluster.

- A configured vSphere resource pool.

317

Creating Instant Clone Desktop Pools

Before starting the actual desktop pool configuration, firstly we need to ensure we have a snapshot of the Windows 10 virtual desktop machine gold image.

To do this, follow the steps described:

1. Open a browser and navigate to the address of the vCenter Server.

2. Log in to the vSphere Client using your administrator credentials as shown in the following screenshot:

Figure 6-2. *Log in to the vSphere Client*

3. Click the **LOGIN** button.

4. You will see the following screenshot:

5. Expand the vCenter Server vcsa.pvolab.com, expand the **PVO Data center**, then navigate to the host server on which the **Windows 10 Gold Image** virtual desktop machine resides.

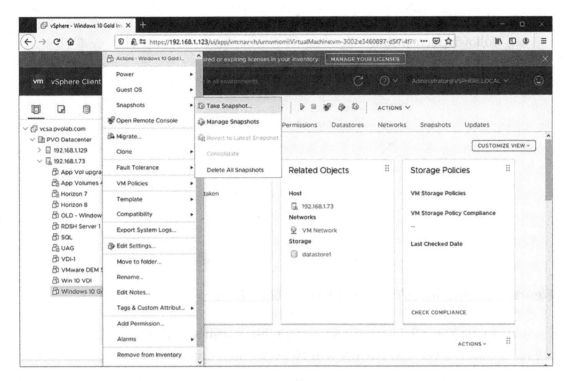

Figure 6-3. *Navigate to the Windows 10 virtual desktop gold image*

6. Click to highlight the virtual desktop machine, right-click, then from the contextual menu, move your cursor onto the entry for **Snapshots**.

7. You will see the snapshot options expand, so from the list of menu options, click **Take Snapshot…**.

8. You will now see the **Take Snapshot** screen as shown in the following screenshot:

Figure 6-4. *Take snapshot of Windows 10 Gold Image*

9. In the **Name** field, type in a name for this snapshot. In this example, we have called it **Win 10 Gold Image Snapshot**.

10. Then, optionally, in the **Description** box, type in a description. In this example, we have given the snapshot the description Gold image of Windows 10.

11. Click **OK** to create the snapshot.

12. Once created, you will see from the inventory and the **Summary** menu the details of the snapshot as shown in the following screenshot:

Figure 6-5. *Snapshot successfully created*

You have now successfully created a snapshot of the Windows 10 Gold Image virtual desktop machine.

In the next section, we are going to create the desktop pool using this newly created snapshot, starting with a dedicated Instant Clone desktop pool.

Instant Clone Dedicated Pools

In this section, we are going to work through, step by step, the tasks for creating an Instant Clone virtual desktop pool with a dedicated assignment.

To do this, follow the steps described:

1. Open a browser and navigate to the Connection Server by entering its address in the address bar.

   In this example, we are doing this directly from the Connection Server, so the address is https://localhost/admin/#/login.

   As we are doing this directly on the Connection Server, you could also double-click the Horizon icon from the desktop.

2. You will see the following screenshot:

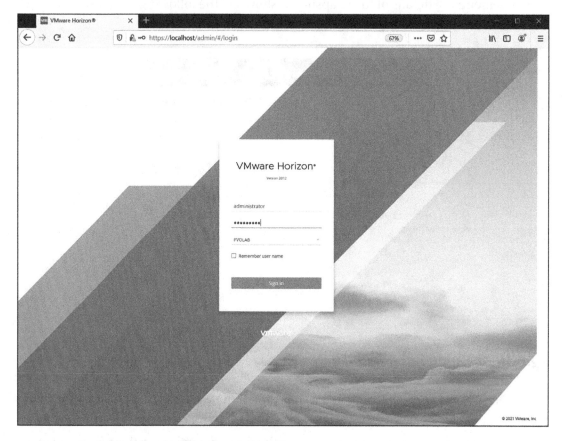

Figure 6-6. *Log in to the Horizon Console*

3. Enter your Horizon administrator username and password.

4. Then, from the drop-down menu, select the domain for these credentials. In this example, we are using the **PVOLAB** domain.

5. Now click the **Sign in** button.

6. From the left-hand navigation pane, expand the option for **Inventory**, then click **Desktops**, as shown in the following screenshot:

Figure 6-7. *Select the Desktop option from the Horizon Console*

7. Now click the **Add** button.

8. You will see the **Add Pool** screen and the first step for configuring the **Type** of pool you want to create and configure, as shown in the following screenshot:

Figure 6-8. *Selecting the desktop pool type*

9. Click the radio button for **Automated Desktop Pool**.

10. Click **Next** to continue.

11.   You will now see step 2 for **vCenter Server,** as shown in the following screenshot:

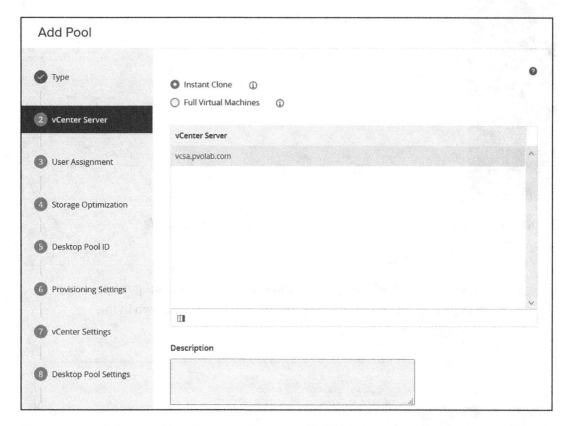

Figure 6-9. *Selecting how Instant Clones are built*

12.   The first part of this configuration screen is to select how the virtual desktop machine will be built. In this example, click the radio button for **Instant Clone**.

13.   Then in the **vCenter Server** section, click to highlight the vCenter Server that will manage and deliver these Instant Clone desktops. In this example, this is vcsa.pvolab.com.

14.   Optionally, in the **Description** box, you can enter a description for this configuration.

15.   Click **Next** to continue.

16. The next step is for **User Assignment,** as shown in the following screenshot:

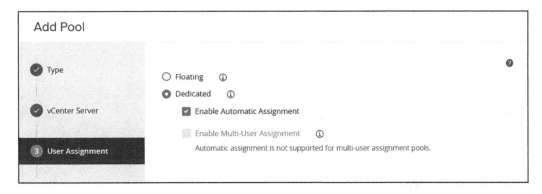

Figure 6-10. *Selecting the user assignment*

17. Click the radio button for **Dedicated**.

18. You then have a check box for **Enable Automatic Assignment**. If you enable this feature, when the end user connects to Horizon, and they do not have a virtual desktop machine, they will be automatically assigned one from the desktop pool they have been entitled to. This virtual desktop may be an existing machine, or if one does not exist, then it will be created for them. If you do not enable automatic assignment, then you will need to manually assign end users to virtual desktop machines.

19. The last option on this configuration screen is for **Enable Multi-User Assignment**. Enabling this feature allows multiple end users to be assigned to a single virtual desktop machine within the pool. This feature cannot be used with the automatic assignment feature. It is also worth noting that if one of the assigned end users already has an active session, whether that is connected or disconnected, then a different user will not be able to access the virtual desktop machine, even though they are entitled. This feature would be useful in an environment that has shift-based workers that perform the same tasks, but do not overlap on when they would require the desktop.

20. Click **Next** to continue.

21.   You will now see step 4 for **Storage Optimization,** as shown in the following screenshot:

Figure 6-11. *Selecting the storage management policy*

22.   Click the radio button to select whether to use a Virtual SAN datastore. In the example lab, there is no VSAN configured.

23.   The next option is the check box for **Use Separate Datastores for Replica and OS Disks**. If you check this box, then you can use different datastores for storing the replica and OS disks. This will be configured in step 7.

24.   Click **Next** to continue.

25.   You will now see step 5 for **Desktop Pool ID**.

26.   In the **ID** box, type in the ID you want to use to identify this desktop pool. In this example, we have given the desktop pool the ID of **IC-Dedicated**.

27.   Next, in the **Display Name** box, you can give the desktop pool a friendly name. This needs to be a more friendly name as is displayed to the end users when they connect. It is worth noting that if you do not enter anything in this box, then the ID will be used as the display name. In this example, we have used **Instant Clone Dedicated** for the display name.

28. In the **Access Group** drop-down menu, select the access group, if you have any configured. In this example, we have selected the access group called **Test-Group**. Access groups enable you to manage desktop pools and delegate different permission levels for administration tasks.

29. Finally, in the **Description** box, type in a description that describes what this desktop pool is used for.

30. The configuration is shown in the following screenshot:

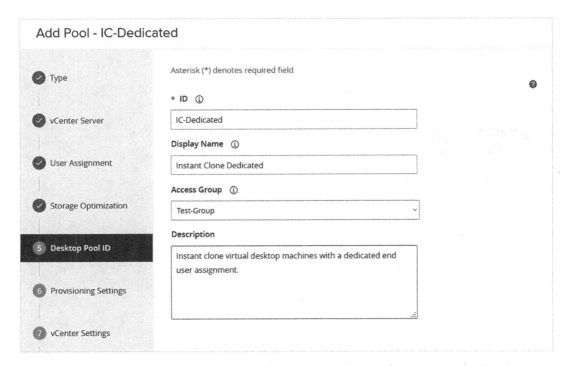

Figure 6-12. *Configuring the desktop pool ID*

31. Click **Next** to continue.

32. You will now see the **Provisioning Settings** screen. There are a few different headings on this screen, so we will start with the **Basic** settings.

33. The provisioning configuration screen is shown in the following screenshot:

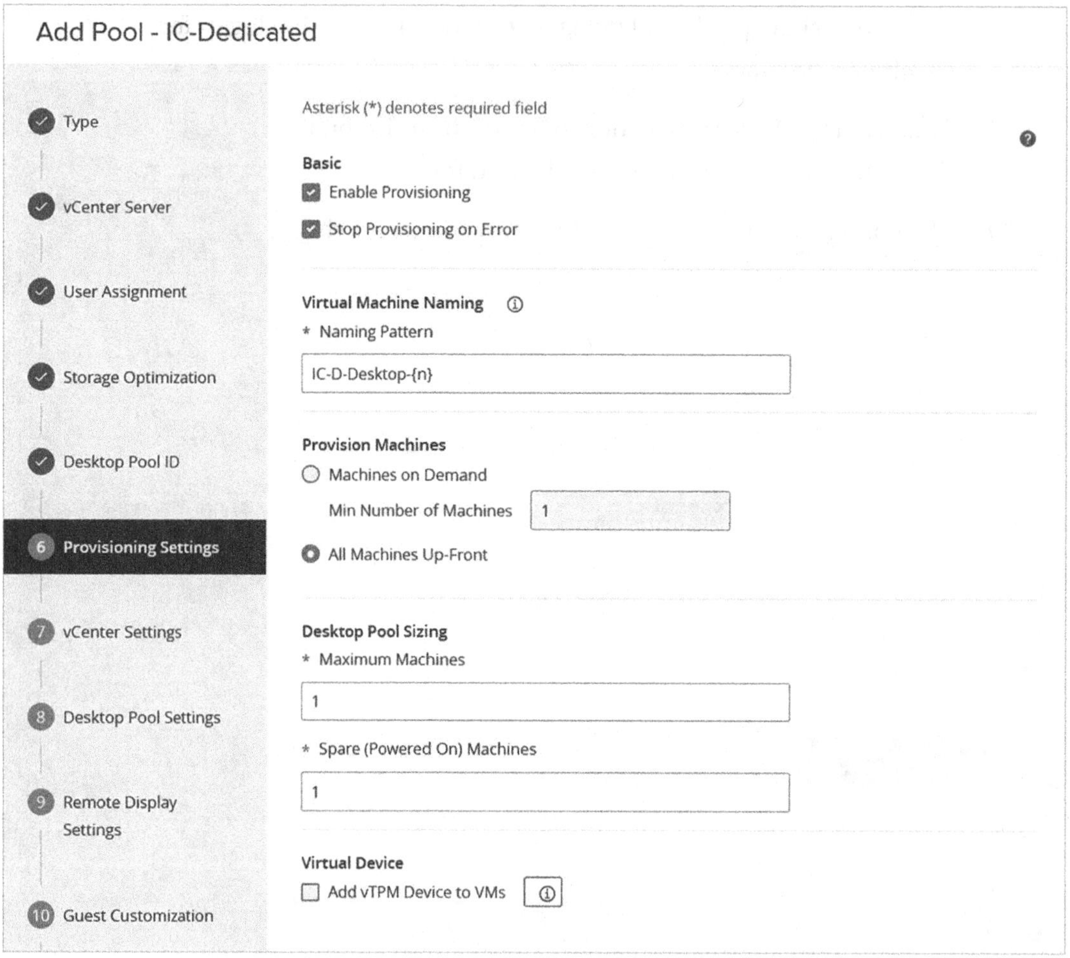

Figure 6-13. *Provisioning settings configuration screen*

34. Check the **Enable Provisioning** box to allow the virtual desktop machines to be provisioned.

This means that the virtual desktop machines will be built and provisioned once you have finished the desktop pool configuration.

35. The other check box is for **Stop Provisioning on Error**. If this setting is enabled, and Horizon detects an error while the virtual desktop machines are being provisioned, then provisioning will stop. This is an important feature when provisioning large numbers of virtual desktop machines. You would want provisioning to stop rather than continue to provision hundreds of potentially faulty virtual desktop machines. In this example, we have checked this box.

36. The next section of the provisioning configuration is for **Virtual Machine Naming**.

37. In the **Naming Pattern** box, type in the names you would like to call the newly created virtual desktop machines. By default, the name you type in here will be appended by a unique number, generated automatically by Horizon as it provisions the virtual desktop machine. In the example, we have configured a naming pattern called **IC-D-Desktop-{n}**. The {n} can be used anywhere within the name to place the number wherever you choose.

38. Next is the **Provision Machines** section.

39. If you want virtual desktop machines to be provisioned on demand, then click the radio button for **Machines on Demand**; then in the **Min Number of Machines** box, you can type in the minimum you want to provision.

40. If you click the radio button for **All machines Up-Front**, then all virtual desktop machines will be provisioned immediately. The number that is provisioned is configured in the next section for **Desktop Pool Sizing**.

41. In the **Desktop Pool Sizing** and the **Maximum Machines** box, type in the maximum number of virtual desktop machines you want in this desktop pool. If you selected to provision all machines up front, then this is the number of machines that will be provisioned.

42. Then, in the **Spare (Powered On) Machines** box, you can enter the number of virtual desktop machines that you want to be powered on immediately and always have ready for end users.

43. The final setting on the configuration screen is for **Virtual Device**. If you want to configure a vTPM (virtual Trusted Platform Module), then check the box.

44. Click **Next** to continue.

45. You will now see step 7 for **vCenter Settings**. This configuration screen is broken into three steps to configure the **Default Image**, the **Virtual Machine Location**, and then the **Resource Settings**, as shown in the following screenshot:

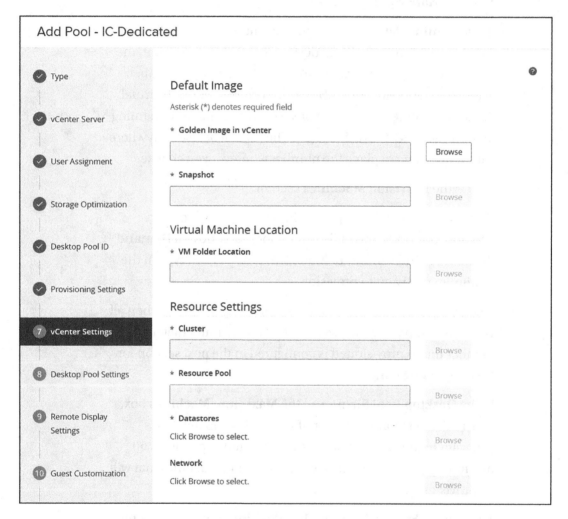

Figure 6-14. *vCenter resource configuration screen*

46. Under the **Default Image** heading and the **Golden Image in vCenter** section, click the **Browse** button.

47. You will see the **Select Golden Image** screen, as shown in the following screenshot:

Figure 6-15. *vCenter resource configuration screen*

48. You will see all the virtual machine images that can be selected. You also have the option to filter the operating system. From the drop-down menu, you can select either Windows or Linux, and then you are able to add a search option in the Filter box. For example, you could enter Windows 10 to search specifically for Windows 10 images.

49. Click to highlight the image, **Windows 10 Gold Image** in this example.

50. Click **Submit**.

51. You will return to the vCenter Settings screen where you will see the gold image has been added as shown:

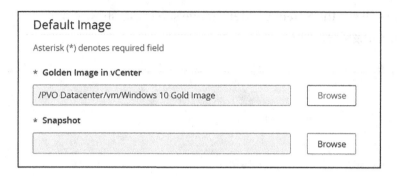

Figure 6-16. *Golden image successfully added*

52. Now in the **Snapshot** box, click **Browse**.

53. You will see the snapshots for the selected image displayed, as shown in the following screenshot:

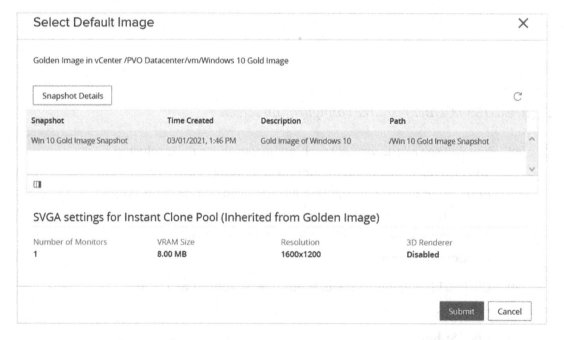

Figure 6-17. *Selecting the snapshot*

54. Click to highlight the snapshot you want to use. In this example, there is just one snapshot, **Windows 10 Gold Image Snapshot,** to select from; click to highlight.

55. Now click **Submit**.

56. You will see that the snapshot details have been successfully added, as shown in the following:

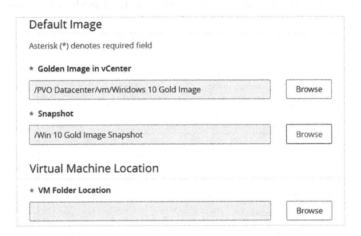

Figure 6-18. *Snapshot successfully added*

57. The next section heading is for the **Virtual Machine Location**. This is the folder in vSphere, where the virtual desktop machines are going to be stored.

58. In the **VM Folder Location** box, click the **Browse** button.

59. You will see the data center folders listed as shown:

Figure 6-19. *Selecting the VM folder location*

60.   In this example, we have a folder already created called **Horizon Desktops**. Click to select the folder, then click the **Submit** button.

61.   You will return to the vCenter Settings screen where you will see that the snapshot details have been successfully added, as shown in the following:

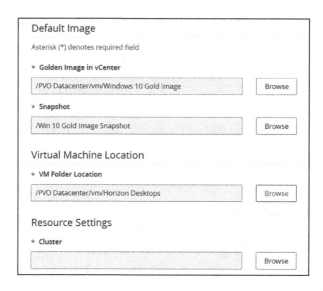

Figure 6-20. *VM folder location successfully configured*

62.   The next settings are for **Resource Settings**.

63.   In the **Cluster** box, click the **Browse** button. You will see the Select Cluster screen, as shown in the following:

Figure 6-21. *Configuring the cluster to run the virtual desktops*

64.   Check the **Show All Cluster** box, if you want to view all available clusters or expand the data center. Then click to select the cluster you want to use for running the virtual desktop machines. In this example, we have a cluster configured called **Horizon Cluster**.

65.   Click the **Submit** button.

66.   You will return to the vCenter Settings screen, where you will see that the cluster details have been successfully added, as shown in the following:

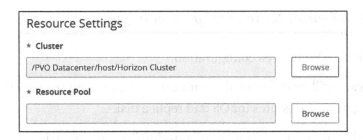

Figure 6-22. *Cluster successfully configured*

67.   Next is the **Resource Pool** configuration.

68.   Click the **Browse** button next to the **Resource Pool** box. You will see the following configuration screen:

Figure 6-23. *Configuring the resource pool settings*

69.   From the list shown, select the resource pool that will run the virtual desktop machines. In this example, we are going to use the root resource pool, which is the cluster called **Horizon Cluster**.

70.   Click to select **Horizon Cluster**, then click **Submit**.

71. You will return to the vCenter Settings screen where you will see
     that the resource pool details have been successfully added, as
     shown in the following:

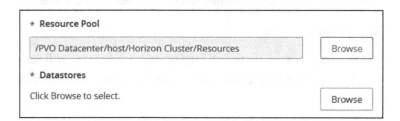

Figure 6-24. *Configuring the resource pool settings*

72. Next is the **Datastores** configuration.

73. This view will be different, depending on whether you selected to
     use separate datastores for OS and replica disks.

     We will look at the standard configuration first, as shown in the
     previous screenshot, and then look at the configuration options
     for when you separate the OS and replica disks.

74. Click the **Browse** button in the **Datastores** box.

75. You will see the **Select Instant Clone Datastores** configuration
     screen.

76. Check the **Show all datastores** box to view all available datastores,
     including those datastores that are local to the ESXi hosts.

77. You will see a list of available datastores along with information
     about the capacity, free space, type of drive, and the storage
     overcommit status.

78.   This is shown in the following screenshot:

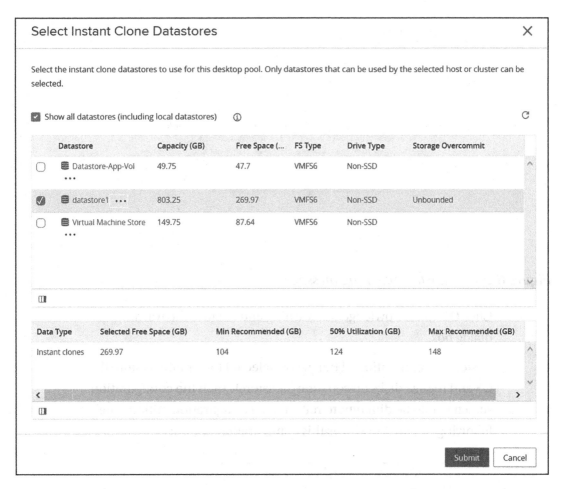

Figure 6-25.   *Configuring the datastores*

79.   Click the check box next to the datastore or datastores that you want to use, and then click the **Submit** button.

80.   In this example lab, we are using local datastores, so you will now see a warning message, highlighting a couple of points to note. The key one in this instance is to ensure that the two ESXi host servers are clustered and that you select the local datastore from each of the hosts.

81.   The warning message is shown in the following screenshot:

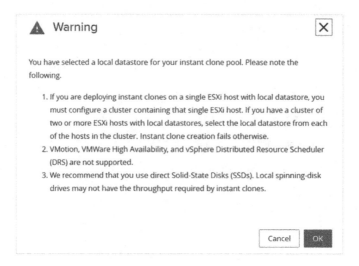

Figure 6-26. *Datastore warning message*

82.   Click **OK** to acknowledge the warning and to close the warning
dialog box.

In step 78, we mentioned that if you selected the option to store the
OS and replica disks on separate datastores, then the configuration
screen would be different to reflect that configuration option. The
following screenshot shows this configuration option:

Figure 6-27. *Configuring separate datastores*

Instead of having the single datastore configuration option, you now
have two configuration options. One for **Instant Clone Datastores**
which is the OS, and another for the **Replica Disk Datastores**. These
are again configured by clicking the **Browse** button for each one,
then selecting the appropriate datastore.

83. Once configured, you will return to the vCenter Settings screen, where you will see that the Instant Clone and replica datastores have been successfully configured, as shown in the following screenshot:

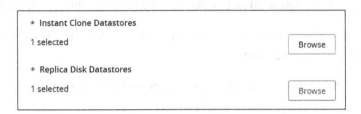

Figure 6-28. *Configuring separate datastores*

84. The final configuration option is for **Network,** as shown in the following screenshot:

Figure 6-29. *Configuring networks*

85. Click the **Browse** button.

86. You will see the **Select Networks** configuration screen:

Figure 6-30. *Select networks configuration screen*

87. On the network configuration screen, you can select to use the same network that was configured with the gold image, or you can select another network to use. To change the network, first uncheck the box for **Use network from current golden image**.

88. Now check the **Show all networks** box; you will see the networks listed.

89. To select a network, check the box next to the network you want to select, then click **Submit**.

90. You will now see the completed **vCenter Settings** screen:

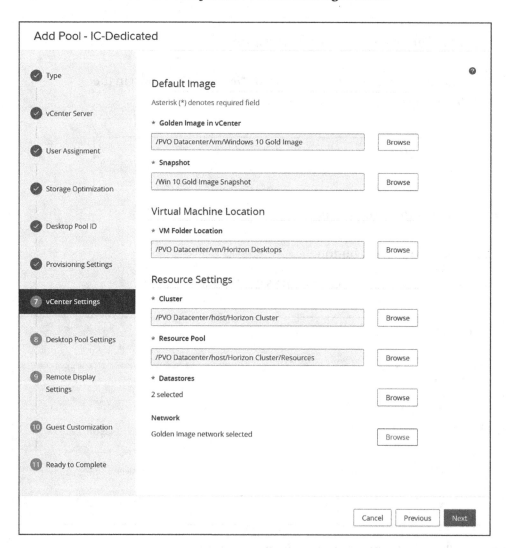

Figure 6-31. *Completed vCenter Settings configuration screen*

91.   Now click the **Next** button for the next configuration step, **Desktop Pool Settings,** as shown in the following screenshot:

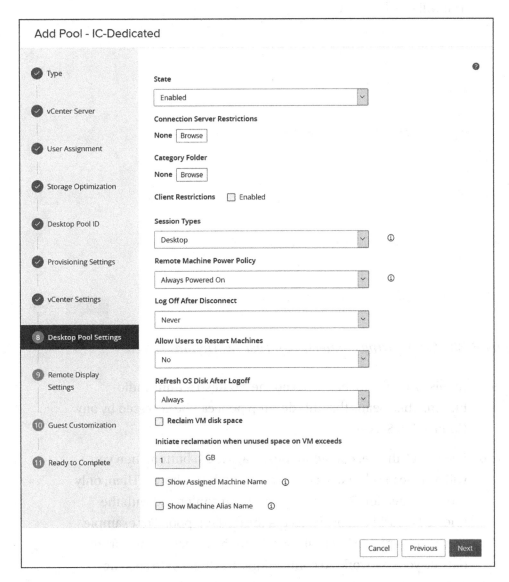

Figure 6-32. Desktop Pool Settings configuration screen

92.   The first option is to configure the **State** of the desktop pool. From the drop-down menu, select **Enabled** or **Disabled**. Disabling an existing desktop pool means that end users who may be entitled to the desktop pool will not be able to connect. In this example, the pool is enabled.

93.   In the next section, you can configure **Connection Server Restrictions**. To configure a restriction, click the **Browse** button. You will see the following.

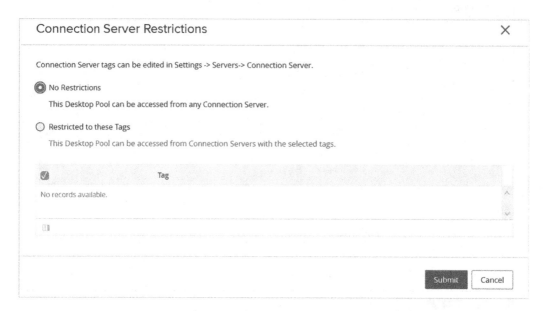

Figure 6-33. *Configuring connection server restrictions screen*

94.   In this example, we have clicked the **No Restrictions** radio button. This means that this desktop pool can be accessed by any Connection Server.

95.   If you click the **Restricted to these Tags** radio button, then you will be able to select a tag from the list of those shown. Then, only those Connection Servers that have been configured with the selected tag will be able to access the desktop pool. For example, you could separate internal users from those that connect from outside your network, so connections are directed to specific Connection Servers.

96.   Click the **Submit** button once you have configured the Connection Server Restrictions.

97.   Next, you have the option to configure a **Category Folder**. This allows you to add a folder or a shortcut that points directly to this desktop pool.

98.   Click the **Browse** button next, under the **Category Folder** option.
       You will see the Category Folder configuration screen as shown:

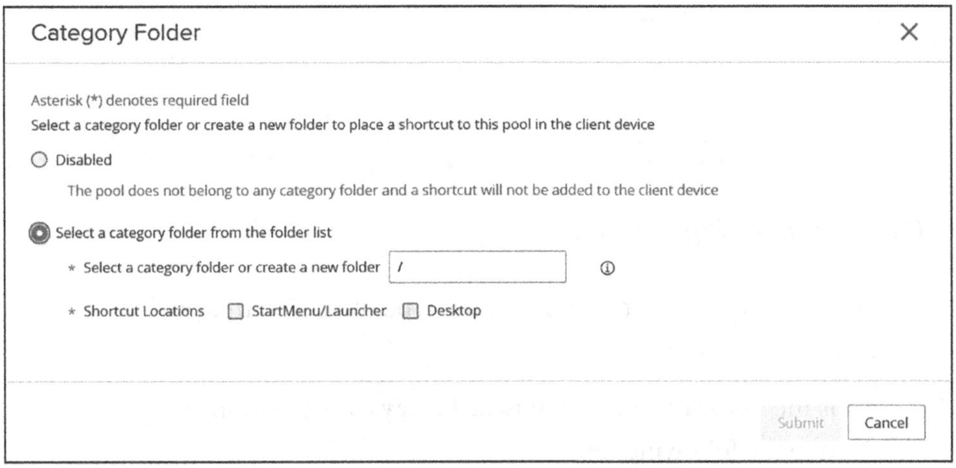

Figure 6-34. *Configuring category folders*

99.   To enable this feature, click the radio button for **Select a category folder from the folder list**.

100.   Then, in the **Select a category folder or create a new folder** box, type in the folder name. The folder name supports up to 64 characters and up to four sub-folders by using the \ to separate them.

101.   You then also have check boxes for **Shortcut Locations,** enabling you to place the shortcut to the desktop pool in the **StartMenu/Launcher** or **Desktop** of the client's device.

102.   Once configured, click the **Submit** button.

103.   Next is the check box for **Client Restrictions**.

104.   If you check the box to enable this setting, then you can prevent end users from connecting to desktops in this pool if they are using specific client devices. You will also need to add the computer names that you want to allow into an Active Directory security group. This group will then need to be selected when you create your desktop pool entitlements.

105. The next option is for **Session Types,** as shown in the following screenshot:

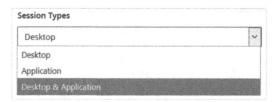

Figure 6-35. *Configuring session types*

106. From the drop-down menu, select the type of session this pool is going to connect to.

107. Next is the **Remote Machine Power Policy** configuration, as shown in the following screenshot:

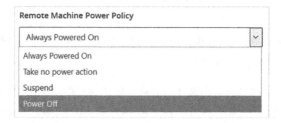

Figure 6-36. *Configuring power policy options*

Select from the following options:

- **Always Powered On**: Virtual desktop machines in the desktop pool will always be restored to a powered on status, after being shut down by an end user. This is monitored by the Connection Server.

- **Take no power action**: Virtual desktop machines will remain in the same power state that they were left in. For example, if the virtual desktop machine was left powered on, then it will stay powered on.

- **Suspend**: Virtual desktop machines will be suspended when a user logs off. The suspend feature is not available if the virtual desktop machine is configured to use vGPU-enabled virtual desktop machines.

- **Power Off**: Virtual desktop machines will be powered off when an end user logs off.

108.   Next is the **Log Off After Disconnect** setting, as shown in the following screenshot:

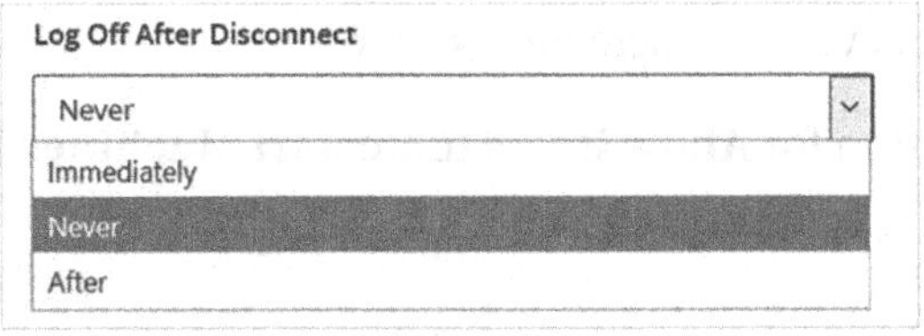

Figure 6-37. *Configuring logoff after disconnect*

This option allows you to configure how or when an end user is logged off from their session when they just disconnect.

Select from the following options:

- **Immediately**: When the end user disconnects from their virtual desktop machine, they are logged off immediately. This means that they will need to log back in again when they reconnect; this could result in them being allocated a new virtual desktop machine.

- **Never**: When the end user disconnects from their virtual desktop machine, they are never logged out, meaning they can return to the same session at any time.

- **After**: Selecting this option allows you to configure a time period for when the end user will be logged off after they disconnect. This means you can allow the end user time to reconnect, should they have been accidentally disconnected or may disconnect from one client and need to connect via a different client. For example, going to a meeting and connecting to your virtual desktop from the meeting room PC or client that is connected to a projector. This is shown in the following screenshot:

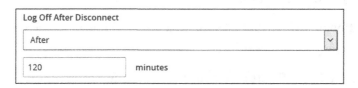

***Figure 6-38.** Configuring the logoff time after disconnect*

109. In this example, we have selected **Never**.

110. Next is the option for **Allow Users to Restart Machines**, as shown in the following screenshot:

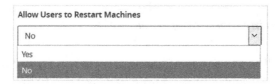

***Figure 6-39.** Allow end users to restart their machines*

111. From the drop-down menu, simply select **Yes** or **No**. Allowing end users to restart their machines is useful when troubleshooting and changes have been made that require a restart.

112. In this example, we have selected **No** to allowing the end users to restart their machines.

113. The next option is to **Refresh OS Disk After Logoff,** as shown in the following screenshot:

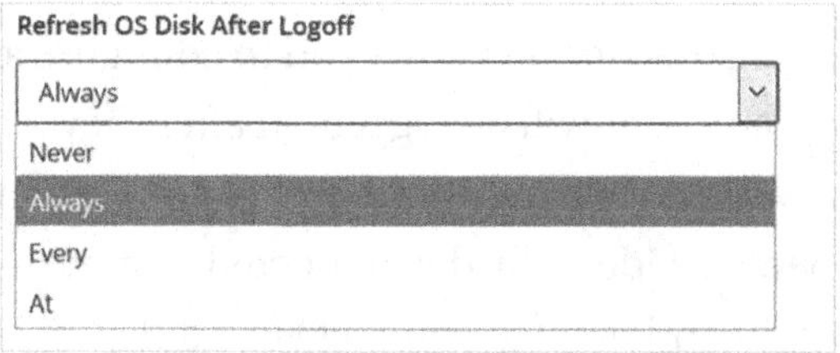

***Figure 6-40.** Refresh the OS disk when end users log off*

114. This setting appears when you configure a dedicated user assignment, where the end user has the same desktop each time they log on. The best practice is to set this configuration option to **Always**. This means that the OS disk is refreshed and essentially reset. This prevents the delta disk from growing. If you had configured a floating end-user assignment for this desktop pool, then the refresh would be automatic as we are using Instant Clones in this example.

115. Next is the **Reclaim disk space** setting, as shown in the following screenshot:

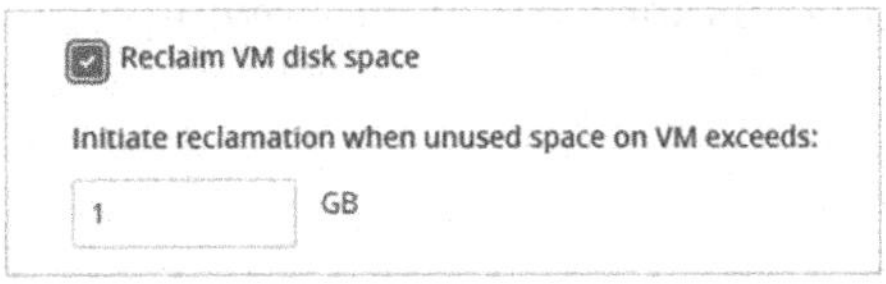

Figure 6-41. *Reclaim disk space configuration*

116. If you check the box to enable this feature, then you will be presented with the **Initiate reclamation when unused space on VM exceeds:** box, in which to enter a value. In this box, type in the size in GB of when you want the reclamation to start. In this example, the reclamation will only start when the unused space on the virtual desktop exceeds 1 GB.

117. The next two options are used for displaying the **Assigned Machine Name** and the **Machine Alias Name,** as shown in the following screenshot:

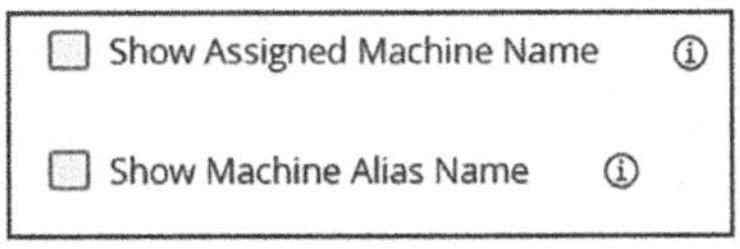

Figure 6-42. *Show machine name options*

118. With the **Show Assigned Machine Name** option enabled, then the Horizon Client will show the hostname of the virtual desktop machine name that is assigned to the end user, instead of showing the desktop pool name.

119. Similarly, when you enable the **Show Machine Alias Name** option, the alias name of the assigned virtual desktop machine is displayed in the Horizon Client.

120. In this example, we have not selected either of these two options, which means that the desktop pool name will be displayed.

121. Click **Next** to continue to the **Remote Display Settings** configuration screen, as shown in the following screenshot:

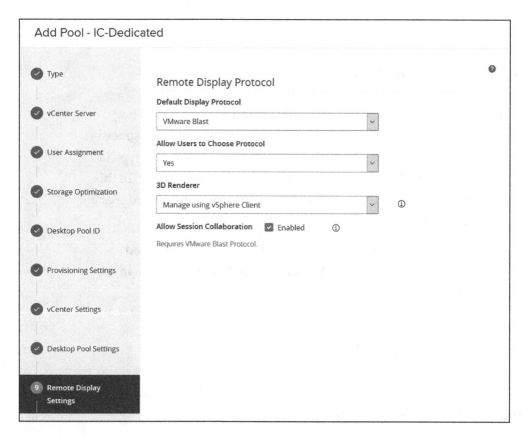

Figure 6-43. *Remote Display Settings configuration screen*

122.   In the **Default Display Protocol** box, from the drop-down menu, select the protocol you want the end users to connect to their virtual desktops with. In this example, we are going to use **Blast**. You can choose from PCoIP, RDP, and Blast.

123.   Next is the **Allow Users to choose Protocol** box. From the drop-down menu, select either **Yes** or **No**. Selecting yes allows the end users to switch from the default protocol to another protocol. An example of why you would do this is when using the PCoIP externally. In some instances, the port PCoIP uses (port 4172) could be blocked. This would mean that although the end user would connect without an issue, they would, however, see a black screen displayed on their client as the pixels sent to their end point device and client are being blocked. Allowing them to change protocols means they can log out and log back in using a different protocol and a different port – one that is not blocked.

124.   You can then choose in the **3D Renderer** box how you want to handle 3D rendering. This setting is managed on the ESXi host servers, and the configuration of the virtual desktop machine gold image using the vSphere Client, and is not managed directly by Horizon. You need to have the Enable 3D Support box checked to use this feature.

125.   The following screenshot is an example from the vSphere Client that shows the video card settings for the Windows 10 Gold Image virtual desktop machine:

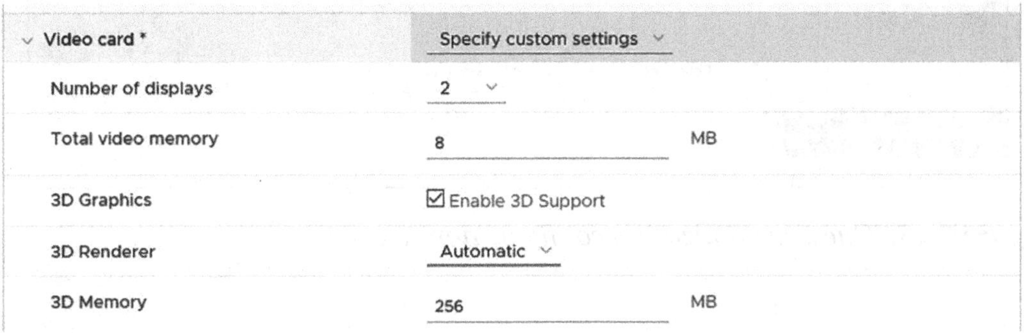

Figure 6-44. *Configuring 3D graphics settings in the vSphere Client*

126.   Finally, there is the **Allow Session Collaboration** box. If you
        enable this feature by checking the box which only works with the
        Blast protocol, you can then shadow an end user's session. This is
        useful for troubleshooting when IT admins need to view the end
        user's desktop.

127.   Click **Next** to continue to the **Guest Customization** configuration
        screen, as shown in the following screenshot:

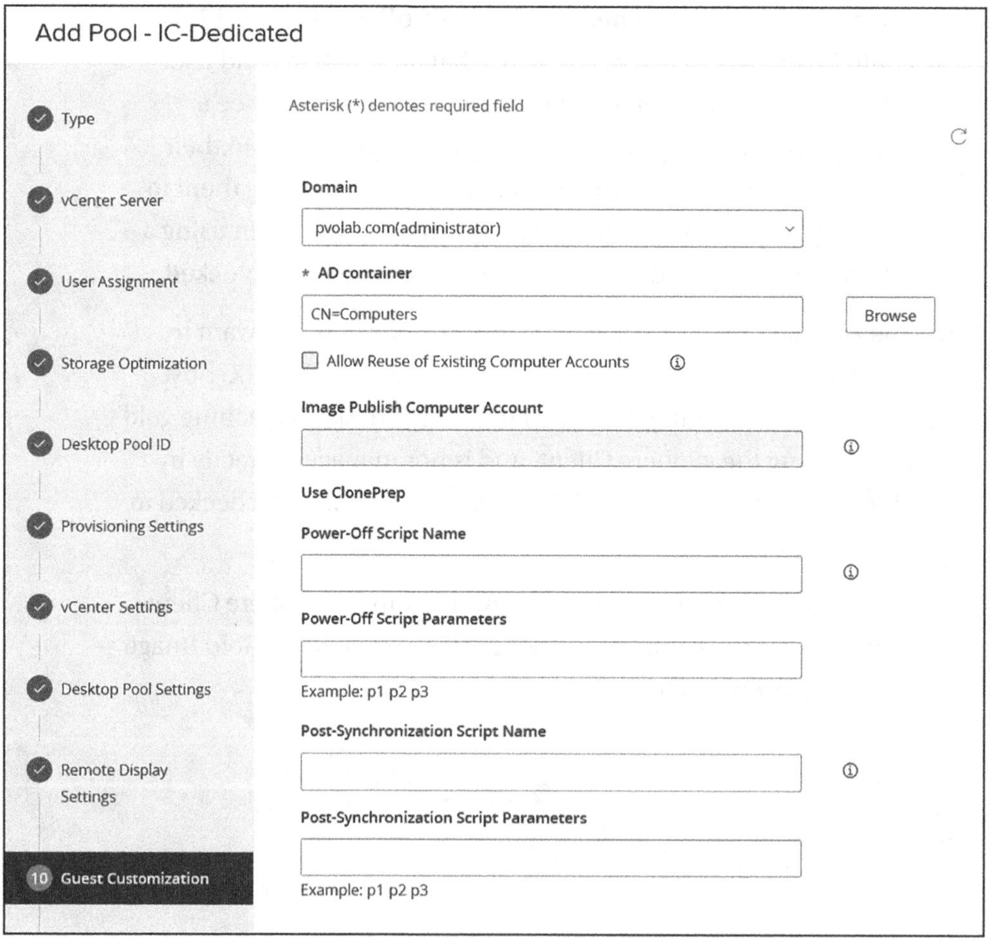

Figure 6-45. *Guest customization configuration screen*

128.   In the **Domain** box, click the drop-down menu and select the domain in which these virtual desktop machines are going to be created. In this example, we are using the pvolab.com domain.

129.   Next, in the **AD container** box, enter the details of the OU in which the virtual desktop machines are going to reside. You can either type directly into the box or click the **Browse** button.

If you click the **Browse** button, then you will see the **AD container** configuration screen as shown:

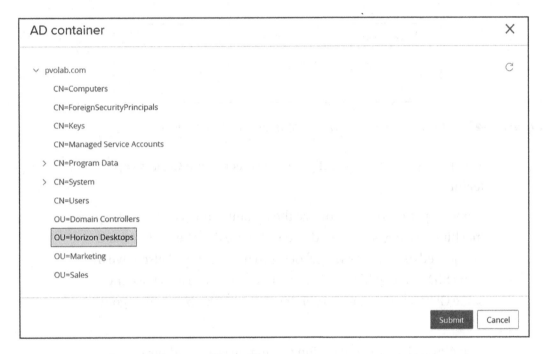

Figure 6-46. *AD container configuration screen*

130.   Navigate to the container in which you want the virtual desktop machines to reside. In this example, we have an OU called **Horizon Desktops**, so select this from the list.

131.   Now click **Submit**.

132.   You will return to the **Guest Customization** screen, where you will see that the details of the AD container have now been configured.

133. The next option is the check box for **Allow Reuse of Existing Computer Accounts**. This option is for Instant Clones, as Instant Clones require an additional computer account that is in the same AD as the Instant Clone desktops themselves. Computer accounts are usually created automatically; however, you can use pre-created accounts and the additional computer account we just mentioned. If you enable this option, then you add this computer account in the **Image Publish Computer Account** box, as shown in the following screenshot:

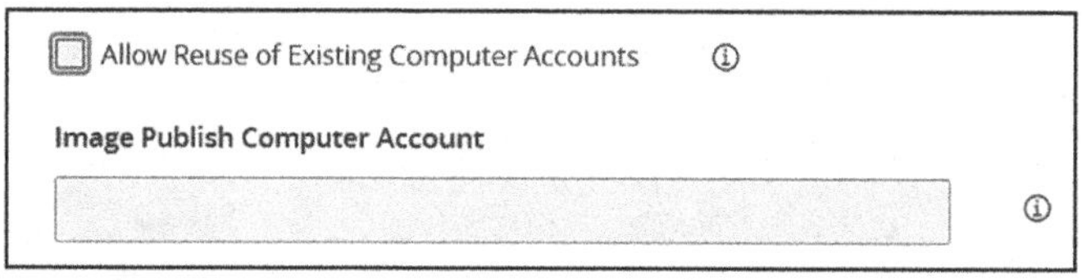

Figure 6-47. Allow reuse of existing accounts configuration

The final option of this configuration screen is the **ClonePrep** feature.

ClonePrep is used to customize the Instant Clone virtual desktop machines as they are created and to ensure that the desktops are also joined to AD. New virtual desktop machines will also have the same SID as the gold image, and applications will also have the same GUID, as they are part of the virtual desktop machine gold image.

ClonePrep gives you the option to run power-off and post-synchronization scripts. Both script options allow you to specify additional parameters.

ClonePrep scripts use the Windows CreateProcess API in order to run the scripts. As such, this means the scripts are able to invoke any of the processes that are created with the CreateProcess API. Meaning scripts that are created with cmd, vbscript, exe, and batch files are all supported with the CreateProcess API.

When you add a ClonePrep script to the desktop pool configuration, you need to ensure that the script is part of the virtual desktop machine gold image, as it will run locally on the virtual desktop as it gets created. You cannot use a network share or UNC path to configure the path to the scripts.

It is also worth noting that any ClonePrep scripts you run will use by default the Instant Clone Agent local account, which potentially may not have the appropriate level of privileges to run certain commands within the scripts.

The privileges that **cannot** be used by the ClonePrep script are listed:

- SeCreateTokenPrivilege

- SeTakeOwnershipPrivilege

- SeSecurityPrivilege

- SeSystemEnvironmentPrivilege

- SeLoadDriverPrivilege

- SeSystemtimePrivilege

- SeUndockPrivilege

- SeManageVolumePrivilege

- SeLockMemoryPrivilege

- SeIncreaseBasePriorityPrivilege

- SeCreatePermanentPrivilege

- SeDebugPrivilege

- SeAuditPrivilege

134. Click **Next**. You will now see the **Ready to Complete** screen, as shown in the following screenshot:

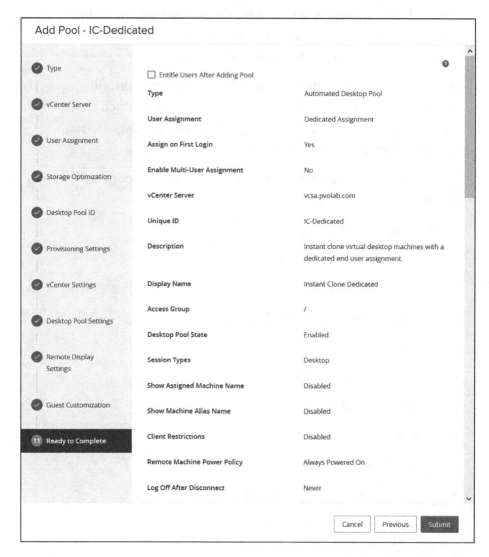

Figure 6-48. *Ready to complete screen*

135. Check the configuration details; if the configuration needs changing, navigate to the section you want to edit.

136. Once you are happy with the desktop pool configuration, click the **Submit** button. One thing to note is that on the Ready to Complete screen, at the top of the screen, you can check the box for **Entitle Users After Adding Pool**. If you check this box, then you will be taken directly to the user entitle configuration screen once the pool has been created. In this example, we are going to leave the box unchecked and will configure user entitlement later in this chapter.

137. You will now return to the **Desktop Pools** screen, as shown in the following screenshot:

Figure 6-49. *Desktop pool successfully created*

138. You will see the pool ID, the display name, the type of desktop pool, and the source of the desktop pool.

139. With the desktop pool now created, you have the options to edit the desktop pool, duplicate the desktop pool, or delete it. You can also configure end-user entitlements, change the status (enable and disable the pool and provisioning), change or add a new access group, and view any unentitled machines or policies.

That leaves the question of what has been created now that the desktop pool has been created and configured.

The easiest way to answer that question is to switch to the vSphere Client, where you will see the following folders have now been created, as shown in the following screenshot:

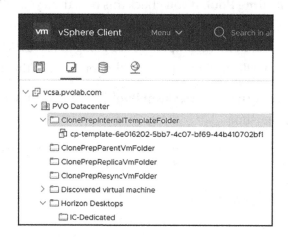

Figure 6-50. *vSphere Client view of Instant Clones*

You will see folders for the parent, replica, and template, as well as the IC-Dedicated folder that has been created in the Horizon Desktops folder. This folder will contain the actual virtual desktop machines, as specified by the desktop pool provisioning settings.

You have now successfully built and configured an automated, Instant Clone, dedicated desktop pool.

In the next section, we are going to create another automated, Instant Clone desktop pool, but this time with a floating end-user assignment.

Virtual Instant Clone Floating Pools

In this section, we are going to create a second automated Instant Clone desktop pool, but this time we are going to configure a floating end-user assignment.

We are going to use the same snapshot as we used in the previous section, from which to create this desktop pool.

As several of the tasks we are going to complete are the same as we configured for the dedicated pool, then we will not cover these again in detail; instead, the focus will be on the screenshots that contain configuration options that we have not yet covered.

To create a floating desktop pool, follow the steps described:

1. Open a browser and navigate to the Connection Server.

2. Enter your Horizon administrator username and password, then click the **Sign in** button.

3. From the left-hand navigation pane, expand the option for **Inventory**, then click **Desktops**.

4. Now click the **Add** button.

5. You will see the **Add Pool** screen. Click the radio button for **Automated Desktop Pool**.

6. Click **Next** to continue.

7. You will now see step 2 for **vCenter Server**.

8. Click the radio button for **Instant Clone**.

9. Then, in the **vCenter Server** section, click to highlight the vCenter Server that will manage and deliver these Instant Clone desktops. In this example, this is vcsa.pvolab.com.

10. Optionally, in the **Description** box, you can enter a description for this configuration.

11. Click **Next** to continue.

12. The next step is for **User Assignment,** as shown in the following screenshot:

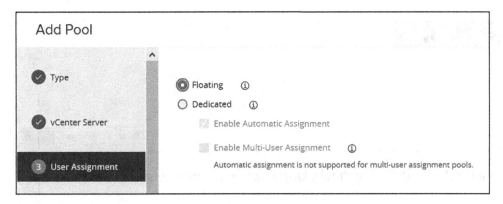

Figure 6-51. *Adding a floating end-user assignment*

13. In this example, we are creating a floating or non-persistent assignment, so click the radio button for **Floating,** then click **Next** to continue.

14. You will now see step 4 for **Storage Optimization**.

15. Click the radio button to select whether to use a Virtual SAN datastore. In the example lab, there is no VSAN configured.

16. The next option is the check box for **Use Separate Datastores for Replica and OS Disks**. If you check this box, you can use different datastores for storing the replica and OS disks. This will be configured in step 7.

17. Click **Next** to continue.

18. You will now see step 5 for **Desktop Pool ID,** as shown in the following screenshot:

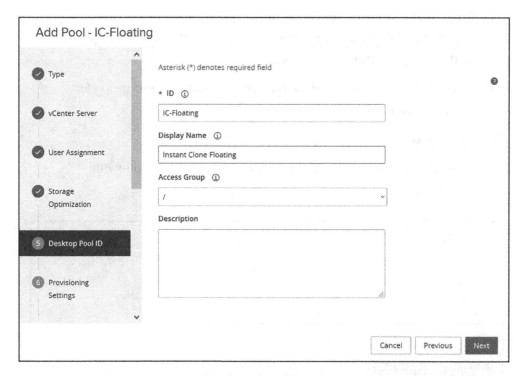

Figure 6-52. *Configuring the desktop pool for floating end-user assignments*

19. In the **ID** box, type in the ID you want to use to identify this desktop pool. In this example, we have given the desktop pool the ID of **IC-Floating**.

20. Next, in the **Display Name** box, you can give the desktop pool a friendly name. This needs to be a more friendly name, as this is displayed to the end users when they connect. It is worth noting that if you do not enter anything in this box, then the ID will be used as the display name. In this example, we have used **Instant Clone Floating** for the display name.

21. In the **Access Group** drop-down menu, select the access group if you have any configured.

22. Finally, in the **Description** box, type in a description that describes what this desktop pool is used for.

23. Click **Next** to continue.

24. You will now see the **Provisioning Settings** screen. There are different headings on this screen, so we will start with the **Basic** settings.

25. Check the **Enable Provisioning** box to allow the virtual desktop machines to be provisioned.

26. Check the box for **Stop Provisioning on Error**.

27. The next section of the provisioning configuration is for **Virtual Machine Naming**.

28. In the Naming Pattern box, type in the names you would like to call the newly created virtual desktop machines. In this example, we have configured a naming pattern called **IC-F-{n}-Desktop**.

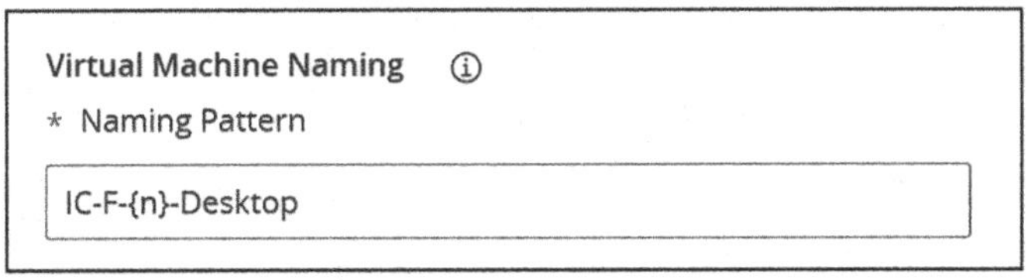

Figure 6-53. Configuring the desktop pool for floating end-user assignments

29. Next is the **Provision Machines** section.

30. If you want virtual desktop machines to be provisioned on demand, then click the radio button for **Machines on Demand;** then in the **Min Number of Machines** box, you can type in the minimum you want to provision.

31. If you click the radio button for **All machines Up-Front**, then all virtual desktop machines will be provisioned immediately. The number that is provisioned is configured in the next section for Desktop Pool Sizing.

32. In the **Desktop Pool Sizing** and the **Maximum Machines** box, type in the maximum number of virtual desktop machines you want in this desktop pool.

33. Then, in the **Spare (Powered On) Machines** box, you can enter the number of virtual desktop machines that you want to be powered on immediately and always have ready for end users.

34. The final setting on the configuration screen is for **Virtual Device**. If you want to configure a vTPM (virtual Trusted Platform Module), then check the box.

35. Click **Next** to continue.

36. You will now see step 7 for **vCenter Settings**. This configuration screen is broken into three steps to configure the **Default Image**, the **Virtual Machine Location**, then the **Resource Settings**.

37. In this example, we are going to use the same Windows 10 Gold Image virtual desktop machine; however, we are going to use a different snapshot that now has the 3D Renderer enabled.

38. In the **Snapshot** field, click the **Browse** button.

39. This is shown in the following screenshot:

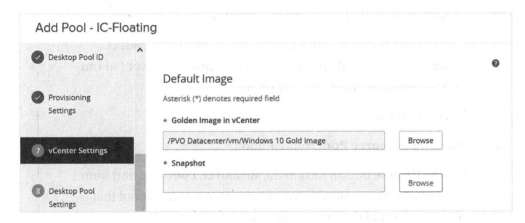

Figure 6-54. *Configuring the snapshot*

40. You will see the **Select Default Image** screen as shown:

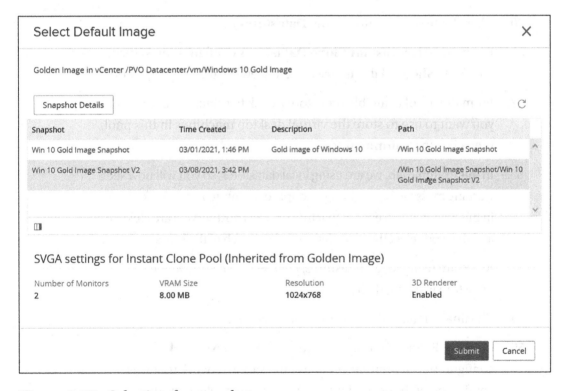

Figure 6-55. *Selecting the snapshot*

41. In this example, we are going to select **Win 10 Gold Image
     Snapshot V2**. This has the 3D renderer enabled.

42. Click to select the snapshot and click **Submit**.

43. The next settings are for **Resource Settings**.

44. In the **Cluster** box, click the **Browse** button, and in the **Select Cluster** screen that is displayed, select the cluster you want to run the virtual desktop machines in this pool.

45. Click the **Submit** button.

46. Next is the **Resource Pool** configuration.

47. Click the **Browse** button next to the **Resource Pool** box, and from the list of resource pools displayed, select the resource pool that will run the virtual desktop machines.

48. Click the **Submit button**.

49. Next is the **Datastores** configuration.

50. Click the **Browse** button in the **Datastores** box.

51. From the **Select Instant Clone Datastores** configuration screen, check the **Show all datastores** box to view all available datastores.

52. From the list of available datastores, click to select the datastore you want to use to store the virtual desktop machines in this pool, then click the **Submit** button.

53. In this example lab, we are using local datastores, so you will now see a warning message highlighting a couple of points to note. The key one in this instance is to ensure that the two ESXi host servers are clustered and that you select the local datastore from each of the hosts.

54. As we are using local datastores, click **OK** to acknowledge the datastore warning dialog box.

55. The final configuration option is for **Network**.

56. Click the **Browse** button, and from the **Select Networks** configuration screen, select to use the same network that was configured with the gold image. You can also select another network to use. To change the network, first uncheck the box for **Use network from current golden image.**

57. Now check the **Show all networks** box; you will see the networks listed.

58. To select a network, check the box next to the network you want to select, then click **Submit**.

59. You have now completed the **vCenter Settings**.

60. Click Next for step 8 **Desktop Pool Settings**.

61. There are a few differences between the pool settings for the floating assignment–based desktop pool. The first is the **Allow Separate Desktop Sessions from Different Client Devices** option, as shown in the following screenshot:

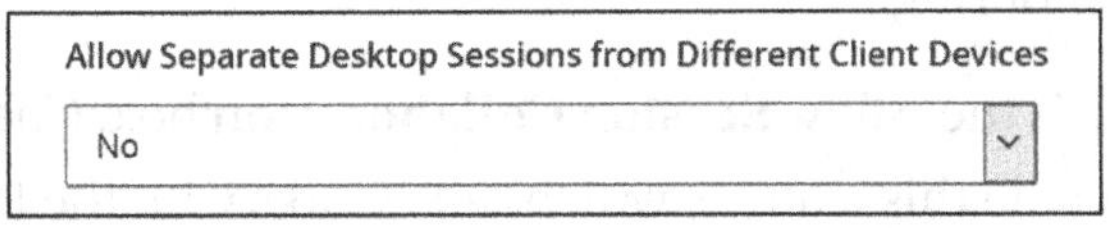

Allow Separate Desktop Sessions from Different Client Devices

No

Figure 6-56. *Allow separate desktop session configuration option*

62. This option, which is either a **Yes** or **No** configuration when enabled, means that should an end user connect to the same desktop pool using a different client device, it will result in them being connected to a different desktop session. It means that they can reconnect to the same session if they use the same end point from which they first connected.

63. The other differences between this pool configuration and the dedicated configuration are that the following options are not available, as they do not apply to a floating virtual desktop machine assignment:

•   Remote Machine Power Policy

•   Refresh OS disk

•   Reclaim disk space

- Show assigned machine name

- Show assigned alias name

64. Click **Next** to continue to step 9, for the **Remote Display Settings** configuration screen.

65. In the **Default Display Protocol** box, from the drop-down menu, select the protocol you want the end users to connect to their virtual desktops with.

66. Next is the **Allow Users to choose Protocol** box. From the drop-down menu, select either **Yes** or **No**.

67. You can then choose in the **3D Renderer** box how you want to handle 3D rendering.

68. Finally, there is the **Allow Session Collaboration** box. Check the box to enable this feature, which only works with the Blast protocol.

69. Click **Next** to continue to the **Guest Customization** configuration screen.

70. In the **Domain** box, click the drop-down menu, and select the domain in which these virtual desktop machines are going to be created.

71. Next, in the **AD container** box, enter the details of the OU in which the virtual desktop machines are going to reside. You can either type directly into the box or click the Browse button. If you click the **Browse** button, then you will see the **AD container** configuration screen, where you can navigate to the container in which you want the virtual desktop machines to reside.

72. Now click **Submit**.

73. The next option is the check box for **Allow Reuse of Existing Computer Accounts**. This option is for Instant Clones, as Instant Clones require an additional computer account that is in the same AD as the Instant Clone desktops themselves. If you enable this

option, then you add this computer account in the **Image Publish Computer Account** box.

74. The final option of this configuration screen is the **ClonePrep** feature, for customizing the Instant Clone virtual desktop machines as they are created and for ensuring that the desktops are also joined to AD.

75. Once you have configured the Guest Customization section, click **Next**. You will now see the **Ready to Complete** screen. Check the configuration options, and if you need to, go back and make any edits to the configuration.

76. You will also see a check box for **Entitle Users After Adding Pool**. Checking this box would mean that after completing the desktop pool configuration, you will be taken directly to the entitlement screen that would allow you to give end-user access to the virtual desktop machines in the pool. We will complete the entitlement task later in this chapter, so for now we will leave the box unchecked.

77. Click **Submit**. You will now see that the **IC-Floating** desktop pool has been successfully created as shown:

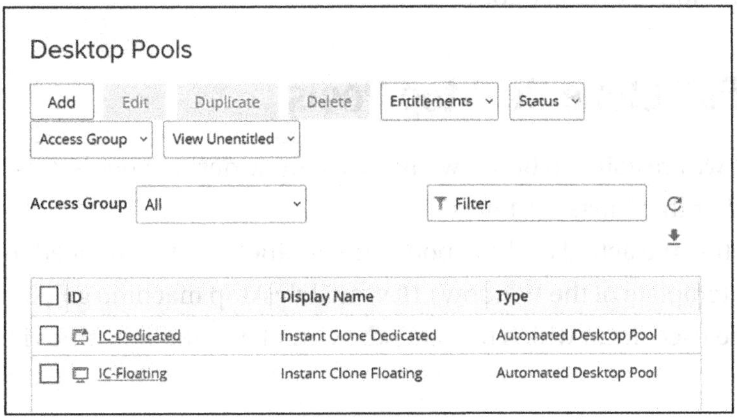

Figure 6-57. Desktop pool successfully created

78.   The vSphere Client will show the following:

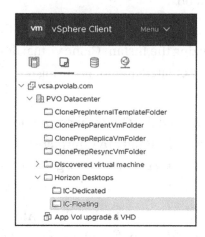

Figure 6-58.   *vSphere Client view: desktop pool successfully created*

You will see folders for the parent, replica, and template, as well as the **IC-Floating** folder that has been created in the **Horizon Desktops** folder. This folder will contain the actual virtual desktop machines, as specified by the desktop pool provisioning settings.

You have now successfully built and configured an automated, Instant Clone, floating desktop pool.

In the next section, we are going to create another desktop pool. This time for automated Full Clone desktop pools.

Creating Full Clone Desktop Pools

In this section, we are going to build two more example desktop pools, this time using Full Clones rather than Instant Clones.

Before starting the actual desktop pool configuration, firstly, we need to ensure we have created a template of the Windows 10 virtual desktop machine gold image. This template will be used, from which to create the virtual desktop machines in the desktop pool.

To do this, follow the steps described:

1.   Open a browser and navigate to the address of the vCenter Server.

2.   Log in to the vSphere Client, as shown in the following:

Figure 6-59. *Log in to the vSphere Client*

3.   Click the **LOGIN** button.

4.   Expand the vCenter Server vcsa.pvolab.com, expand the **PVO Data center,** then navigate to the host server on which the **Windows 10 Gold Image** virtual desktop machine resides.

5.   Click to highlight the **Windows 10 Gold Image** virtual desktop machine, then right-click.

6.   From the contextual menu that appears, click **Clone**, and then select the option for **Clone to Template...** as shown in the following screenshot:

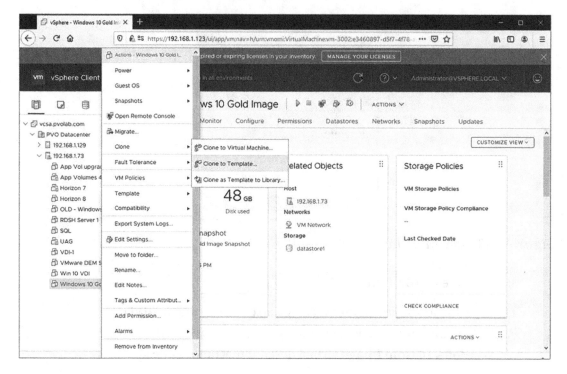

Figure 6-60. *Creating a template of the gold image*

7. You will now see the **Windows 10 Gold Image - Clone Virtual Machine to Template** configuration screen, and step 1 to **Select a name and folder,** as shown in the following screenshot:

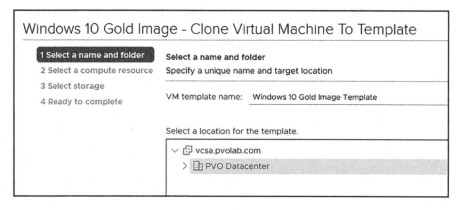

Figure 6-61. *Configure the template name and folder*

8. In the **VM template name** field, type in a name for this virtual machine template. In this example, we have called the template **Windows 10 Gold Image Template**.

9. Next, in the **Select a location for the template** box, expand the vCenter Server entry, then select the data center where this template is going to live. In this example, this is the **PVO Data center**.

10. Click **NEXT** to continue.

11. You will now see the **Select a compute resource** screen, as shown in the following screenshot:

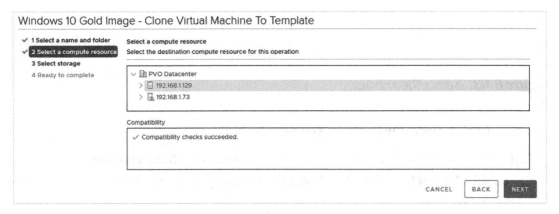

Figure 6-62. *Select a compute resource*

12. Click to select the compute resource of where this template will be created. You will then see the selected resource, validated in the **Compatibility** box with the message **Compatibility checks succeeded**.

13. Click **NEXT** to continue.

14. The next configuration screen is for **Select storage,** as shown in the following screenshot:

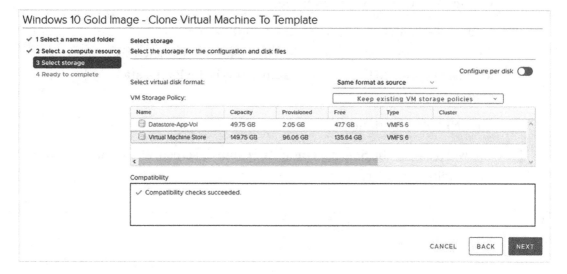

Figure 6-63. *Select the storage*

15. Click to select the datastore you want to use.

16. Once selected, you can then select the format in the **Select virtual disk format** box. From the drop-down menu, you can select the options for

    - Same format as source

    - Thick Provision Lazy Zeroed

    - Thick Provision Eager Zeroed

    - Thin Provision

17. The selected resource is validated in the **Compatibility** box, with the message **Compatibility checks succeeded**.

18. Click **NEXT** to continue.

19. You will now see the **Ready to complete** screen, as shown in the following screenshot:

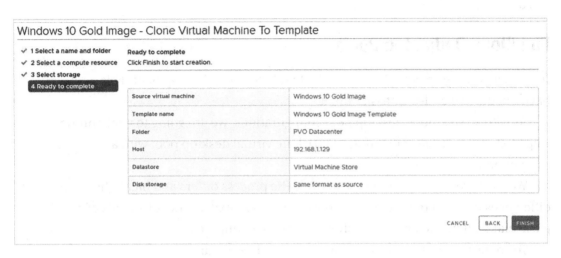

Figure 6-64. Ready to complete screen

20. Review the configuration, then click **FINISH**.

21. You will now see the following in the vSphere Client:

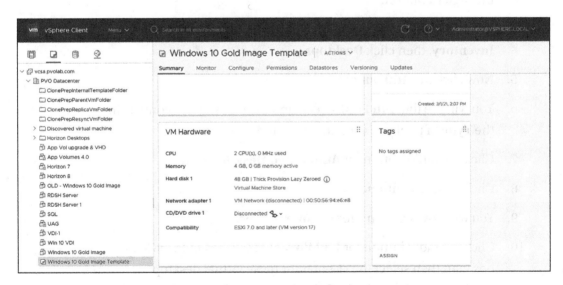

Figure 6-65. Template successfully created

Now that you have a template to create a virtual desktop machine from, we can now continue to the desktop pool configuration, starting with a Full Clone, dedicated desktop pool.

Full Clone Dedicated Pools

In this section, we are going to create the first Full Clone desktop pool. This pool will have a dedicated end-user assignment.

As with the previous desktop pool configurations, we are going to work through, step by step, the tasks for creating a Full Clone virtual desktop pool with a dedicated assignment.

We will focus on the screenshots where the process differs and highlight those differences. You can refer to the first pool that we created for the full details of a particular feature and any screenshots on how to configure it.

To create this desktop pool, follow the steps described:

1. Open a browser and navigate to the Connection Server.

2. You will see the login screen.

3. Enter your Horizon administrator username and password; click the **Sign in** button.

4. From the left-hand navigation pane, expand the option for **Inventory**, then click **Desktops**.

5. Now click the **Add** button.

6. You will see the **Add Pool** screen and the first step for configuring the **Type** of pool you want to create and configure.

7. Click the radio button for **Automated Desktop Pool**.

8. Click **Next** to continue.

9. You will now see step 2 for **vCenter Server**.

10. Click the radio button for **Full Virtual Machines** in the vCenter box, and then select the vCenter for these virtual desktop machines, as shown in the following screenshot:

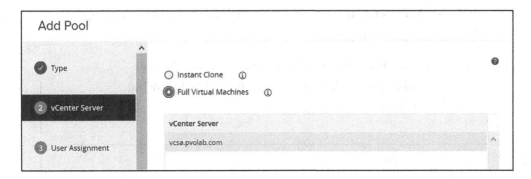

Figure 6-66. *Selecting the full virtual machine pool option*

11. Click **NEXT** to continue.

12. You will now see step 3, the **User Assignment** screen.

13. Click the radio button for **Dedicated**, then check the box for **Enable Automatic Assignment**.

14. Click **NEXT** to continue.

15. You will now see step 4 for **Storage Optimization**.

16. Click the radio button to select whether to use a Virtual SAN datastore. In the example lab, there is no VSAN configured.

17. As we are now creating a Full Clone desktop pool, you will note that the **Use Separate Datastores for Replica and OS Disks** option is not available. This is because the Full Clone is just a single virtual hard disk file.

18. Click **Next** to continue.

19. You will now see step 5 for the **Desktop Pool ID** screen.

20. In the **ID** box, type in the ID you want to use to identify this desktop pool. In this example, we have given the desktop pool the ID of **FC-Dedicated**.

21. Next, in the **Display Name** box, give the desktop pool a friendly name. In this example, we have used **Full Clone Dedicated** for the display name.

22. IDIn the **Access Group** drop-down menu, select the access group if you have any configured.

23. Finally, in the **Description** box, type in a description that describes what this desktop pool is used for. The following screenshot shows the configuration:

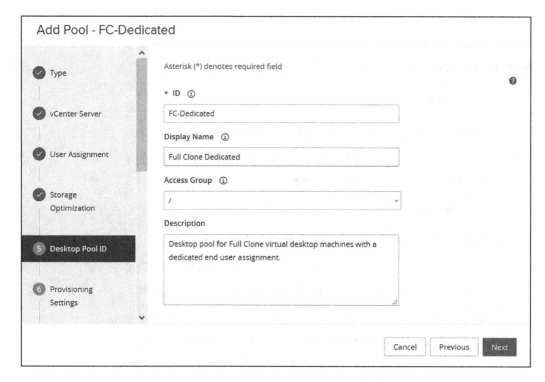

Figure 6-67. *Configuring the desktop pool ID*

24. Click **Next** to continue.

25. You will now see the **Provisioning Settings** screen.

26. Check the **Enable Provisioning** box to allow the virtual desktop machines to be provisioned.

27. Check the box for **Stop Provisioning on Error**.

28. The next section of the provisioning configuration is for **Virtual Machine Naming**. With Full Clone desktop pools, there is another option for virtual machine naming, and that is the ability to **Specify Names Manually**.

29.   Click the radio button for **Specify Names Manually**.

30.   You will see the following screenshot:

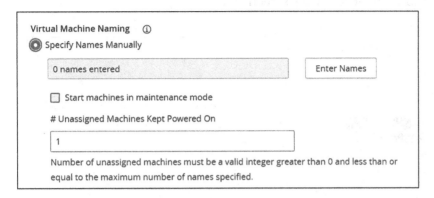

Figure 6-68. Virtual machine naming – specify names manually

31.   Next to the **0 names entered** box, click the **Enter Names** button to start manually entering your machine names.

32.   You will see the **Enter Machine Names** screen:

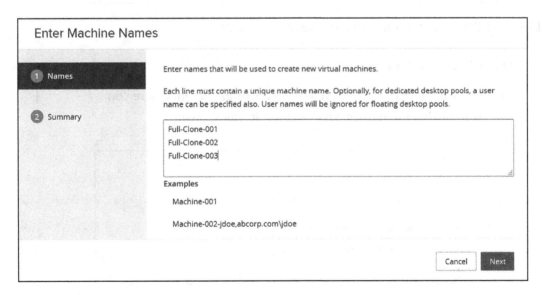

Figure 6-69. Adding manual machine names

33.   In the box, type in the machine name you want to use. In this example, we have added three machines with the naming convention of **Full-Clone-001**, **Full-Clone-002**, and **Full-Clone-003**.

34. Click **Next** to continue.

35. You will see the **Summary** screen showing the machine names, as shown in the following screenshot:

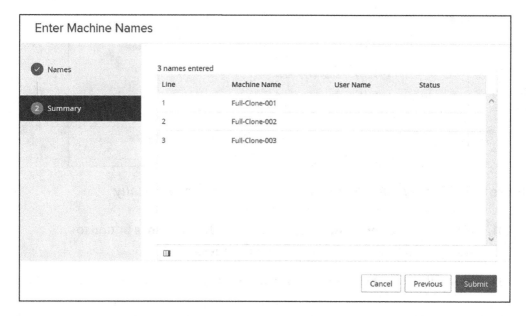

Figure 6-70. *Manual machine names to be added*

36. Click the **Submit** button.

37. You will return to the **Provisioning Settings** screen, where you will see that the names have been added as shown:

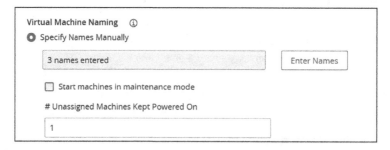

Figure 6-71. *Manual machine names successfully configured*

38. You then have the option to start machines in maintenance mode, by checking the **Start machines in maintenance mode** box.

39. The final option is to configure the number of machines that are not assigned to end users in a powered on state. This means that when you do entitle an end user to a virtual desktop in the pool, then there are virtual desktops already powered on to be used. To configure this, in the **# Unassigned Machines Kept Powered On** box, type in the number of machines you want to be kept powered on. The number of machines you configure to be kept powered on must be greater than zero and less than or equal to the maximum number of machine names you have configured. For example, we have configured three names, so we can only have up to three unassigned machines kept powered on.

40. Alternatively, you can choose to use the naming pattern option that will automatically assign machine names. To do this, follow the next steps.

41. In the **Naming Pattern** box, type in the names you would like to call the newly created virtual desktop machines. In this example, we have configured a naming pattern called **IC-F-{n}-Desktop**.

```
Virtual Machine Naming    ⓘ
 *  Naming Pattern

  IC-F-{n}-Desktop
```

Figure 6-72. *Configuring the desktop pool for floating end-user assignments*

42. You then have the option of selecting whether to provision **Machines on Demand** or to provision **All Machines Up-Front**.

43. In the **Desktop Pool Sizing** section, configure the number of **Maximum Machines** and the number of **Spare (Powered On) Machines**.

44. Finally, select whether to **Add vTPM Device to VMs** by checking the box.

45. In this example, we are going to follow the manual naming of virtual desktop machines option.

46.   Click **Next** to continue.

47.   You will see step 7 for configuring the **vCenter Settings,** as shown in the following screenshot:

Figure 6-73. *Configuring vCenter setting for Full Clones*

The key difference on this configuration screen from the Instant Clone configuration screen is that you now choose a template rather than a snapshot.

48.   In the **Template** box, click **Browse**.

49.   You will see the Select template screen.

50. From the list of templates shown, click to select the template you want to use. In this example, we are going to choose the **Windows 10 Gold Image Template** we created at the start of this section.

51. This is shown in the following screenshot:

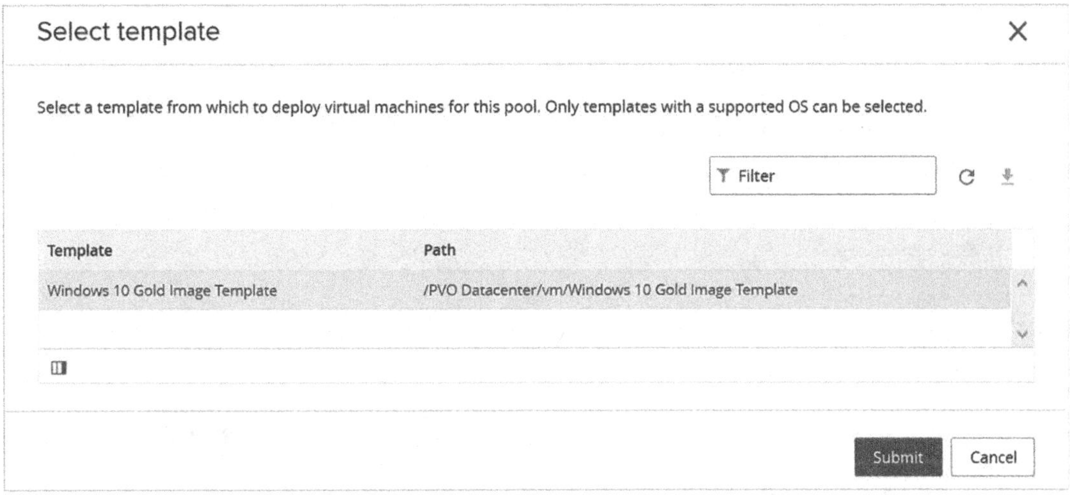

Figure 6-74. *Selecting the template*

52. Click **Submit**.

    You can now complete the remaining sections of this configuration screen for VM Folder Location, Host or Cluster, Resource Pool, and Datastore. You will also notice that the network configuration is not available in this configuration.

    When it comes to the datastore configuration, you will see a different configuration screen. As we are creating a Full Clone of the virtual desktop gold image template, then we will be creating a single virtual disk file that can be stored on an individual datastore. The configuration screen represents that option.

53. From the **Select the Datastore Type** box, click the drop-down menu and select either **Individual Datastore** or **Storage DRS**. In this example, we are going to select the individual datastore option.

54. Then check the box next to the datastore that you want to use to select it, as shown in the following screenshot:

Figure 6-75. *Selecting the datastore*

55. Click **Submit**.

56. With the vCenter Settings configuration completed, click the **Next** button.

57. You will now see step 8 for **Desktop Pool Settings**.

58. The first option is to configure the **State** of the desktop pool. From the drop-down menu, select **Enabled to enable this desktop pool**.

59. Next, configure **Connection Server Restrictions**. To configure a restriction, click the **Browse** button and configure the appropriate restrictions based on Connection Server tags. Click **Submit** once you have configured any Connection Server restrictions.

60. With the next setting, the **Category Folder** setting, you can add a folder or a shortcut to the end user's device that points directly to this particular desktop pool. To configure this, click the **Browse**

button next to the **Category Folder** option, select the category folder, or select to add a shortcut location, a start menu entry, or a desktop icon.

61. Once configured, click the **Submit** button.

62. Next is the check box for **Client Restrictions**. Check the box to enable this setting, then you can prevent end users from connecting to desktops in this pool if they are using specific client devices.

63. The next option is for **Session Types**. Select from **Desktop**, **Application**, or **Desktop & Application**. As this pool is delivering virtual desktop machines, select the Desktop option from the drop-down menu.

64. Next is the **Remote Machine Power Policy** configuration. From the drop-down menu, select from the following options:

    - **Always Powered On**

    - **Take no power action**

    - **Suspend**

    - **Power Off**

65. In the **Log Off After Disconnect** setting, from the drop-down menu select whether an end user is logged off when they disconnect. Select from the following options:

    - **Immediately**

    - **Never**

    - **After**

66. Next is the option for **Allow Users to Restart Machines**. From the drop-down menu, simply select **Yes** or **No**.

67. The final two options are used for displaying the **Assigned Machine Name** and the **Machine Alias Name**.

68. Check the boxes next to each option to enable that feature.

69. Once you have completed the configuration of the Desktop Pool Settings, click **Next** to continue.

70. You will now see step 9 for the **Remote Display Settings** configuration screen, as shown in the following screenshot:

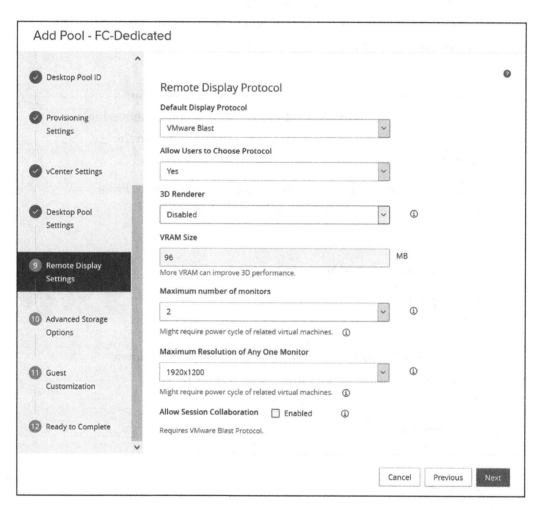

Figure 6-76. Remote display protocol configuration screen

71. In the **Default Display Protocol** box, from the drop-down menu, select the protocol you want the end users to connect to their virtual desktops with. In this example, we are going to use **Blast**.

72. Next is the **Allow Users to choose Protocol** box. From the drop-down menu, select either **Yes** or **No, depending on whether you want end users to choose their protocol**.

73. You can then choose in the **3D Renderer** box how you want to handle 3D rendering. If you click the drop-down menu, you will see the following options, as shown in the screenshot:

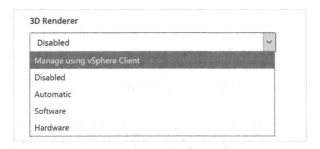

Figure 6-77. *3D renderer configuration options*

74. **Manage using vSphere Client**: Allows you to configure Automatic, Software, or Hardware options in the vSphere Client when editing the settings of the virtual machine. Although configured in the vSphere Client, these options deliver the same result as configuring them in the desktop pool configuration screen, in the Horizon Administrator Console. This setting is used to configure vDGA, vSGA, and AMD MxGPU.

75. When you configure the 3D renderer to use the vSphere Client settings, you cannot change the configuration for video memory, the maximum number of monitors and the maximum resolution of the monitors.

   • **Disabled**: 3D Renderer is switched off.

   • **Automatic**: 3D rendering is enabled and controlled by the ESXi host server. GPU resources are allocated on a first-come, first-served basis, as end users connect and log in to virtual machines that have access to the GPU hardware. If an end user connects to a GPU-enabled virtual desktop and there are no resources available, that is, all GPU resources have been allocated already, then the software renderer will be used instead. You can configure video memory to the virtual machine by configuring the 3D Memory field, as shown in the following:

∨ Video card *	Specify custom settings ∨	
Number of displays	2 ∨	
Total video memory	8	MB
3D Graphics	☑ Enable 3D Support	
3D Renderer	Automatic ∨	
3D Memory	256	MB

Figure 6-78. *3D Memory configuration options*

- **Software**: If you select the software 3D rendering option, then the ESXi host server will use software 3D graphics rendering even if the ESXi host server has a physical GPU card installed.

- **Hardware**: If you select the hardware option for 3D rendering, then the ESXi host server will reserve GPU resources on a first-come, first-served basis as end users connect and log in to virtual machines that have access to the GPU hardware. With this setting, it will only ever use GPU hardware; therefore, you should be aware of a couple of scenarios where the virtual desktop machine may not be able to power on. These scenarios are listed as follows:

  - If all the GPU resources are already allocated, as the virtual desktop machine does not meet the requirements, then it will not power on.

  - If you move the virtual desktop machine to another ESXi host that does not have a GPU card, then the hardware requirements cannot be met, so the virtual desktop machine will not power on.

- **NVIDIA GRID vGPU**: This setting enables 3D rendering when using vGPU. ESXi host servers will reserve GPU resources on a first-come, first-served basis, as end users connect and log in to virtual machines that have access to the GPU hardware. There are also several limitations to be aware of which are listed as follows:

- The Remote Machine Power Policy is not available to be configured, as vGPU-enabled virtual desktop machines cannot be suspended or resumed.

- If you vMotion a virtual desktop machine to an ESXi host server without GPU hardware, then the virtual desktop machine will not power on.

- Live vMotion is not available.

- ESXi host servers in the cluster must be on ESXi 6.0 or later; virtual desktop machines must be configured to use hardware version 11 or later.

- If the cluster contains one ESXi host server with vGPU enabled and another ESXi host server that does not have a vGPU enabled, then in the Horizon Console dashboard you will see a yellow warning status.

76. Next is the **VRAM Size** box, where you can configure the amount of video memory. This option is only available with the Hardware, Software, and Automatic 3D Renderer setting.

77. In the **Maximum number of monitors** box from the drop-down menu, select the number of screens the end user will be using on their endpoint device to display the virtual desktop machine. You have the following options:

- With the 3D Renderer disabled, you can choose from one, two, three, or four monitors.

- With the Manage using vSphere Client, you cannot configure this option.

- With the Hardware, Software, and Automatic 3D Renderer settings, you can choose from one or two monitors.

78. Next, you have the **Maximum Resolution of Any One Monitor** option. This is only available with 3D Renderer disabled. You can choose from the following resolutions, as shown in the following screenshot:

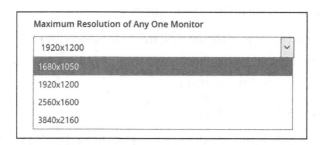

Figure 6-79. Maximum resolution configuration options

79. The final option on the **Remote Display Settings** configuration screen is for **Allow Session Collaboration**. If you check the box to enable this feature, then end users can invite other users, such as support teams, to their session. This feature only works with the Blast protocol.

80. Click **Next** to continue.

81. You will now see step 10 for **Advanced Storage Options**.

82. The first option is to enable **the View Storage Accelerator**. As we discussed in a previous chapter, the View Storage Accelerator allows you to enable desktop pools to use the ESXi host servers to cache virtual machine disk data, using the Content-Based Read Cache (CBRC) feature of the ESXi host server. Using the View Storage Accelerator can reduce the disk IOPS and so improves the performance.

83. To enable this feature, check the **Use View Storage Accelerator**
     box, as shown in the following screenshot:

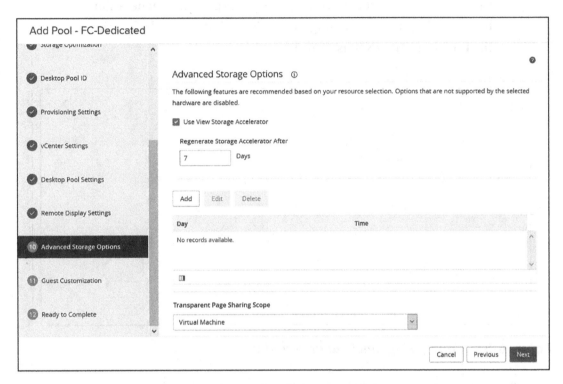

Figure 6-80. Advanced storage configuration screen

84. Then, in the **Regenerate Storage Accelerator After** box, you can
     configure the time in days of when you want to regenerate the
     cached data. This will clear the cache and rebuild or regenerate it.
     The default setting, if you enable this feature, is set to regenerate
     every seven days.

85. You can then configure when the cache regenerates or, more
     importantly, when it should regenerate. Regeneration could have
     a performance impact as the cached blocks are being read while
     they are regenerating. To stop this, you can configure blackout
     times. To do this, click the **Add** button under the regenerate
     storage accelerator box.

86.   You will see the **Set Blackout Days** configuration screen that allows you to select when the regeneration process *should not* run.

87.   Check the boxes next to the days you want to prevent regeneration from running, and then configure the time window for blackout in the **From** and **To** boxes as shown:

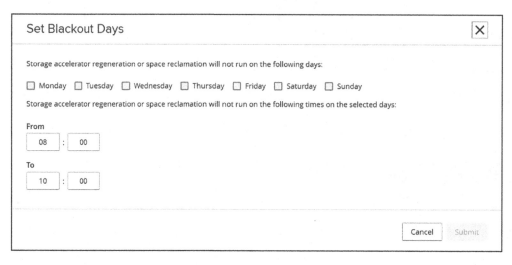

Figure 6-81. *Configuring blackout days and times*

88.   Once configured, click the **Submit** button.

89.   The final setting on the Advanced Storage Options screen is for configuring the **Transparent Page Sharing Scope,** as shown in the following screenshot:

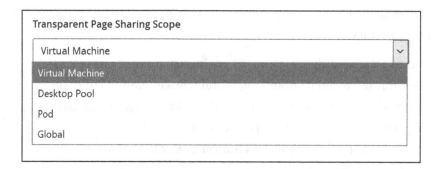

Figure 6-82. *Configuring transparent page sharing*

Transparent Page Sharing is a virtualization-based memory management technology. When deployed with virtual desktop machines, by the nature of the type of machine, desktops in this case, they will be running hundreds, if not thousands, of copies of the same operating system and applications. These OSs and apps will not only be consuming memory resource, but this memory resource will be holding the same memory pages. Deploying TPS in this environment will reduce the number of duplicate memory pages in the virtual machines at a host server level, reducing the multiple copies of the same memory pages down to a single memory page.

ESXi looks for duplicate pages; when it identifies identical memory pages across multiple virtual desktop machines that are running on the same ESXi host server, then it removes the duplicate pages and shares just a single page across the virtual desktop machines. Where pages are no longer part of the virtual desktop machine, memory pointers are put in place to refer to the shared page, hence the term transparent, as the virtual desktop machines have no idea that they are referring to a shared page hosted elsewhere.

The result is a more efficient way of managing memory, potentially creating further free resources for adding more virtual desktop machines.

In the desktop pool configuration screen, you have the option to configure how the pages are shared, either at the **Virtual Machine** level, at the **Desktop Pool** level, at the **Pod** level, or at a **Global** level.

90. Once configured, click the **Next** button.

91. You will now see step 11 for **Guest Customization**.

Figure 6-83. *Guest customization configuration screen*

On the Guest Customization screen, you can configure how the virtual desktop machines are going to be customized as they are deployed. You can choose the option for **None – Customization will be done manually,** which means that the virtual desktop machine will be the same as the template from which it was created.

You then have a check box for **Do not Power on Virtual Machine After Creation**. This, as the name suggests, means that once the virtual desktop machines have been created, they remain powered off. With the manual customization, this option would allow you to power on each machine manually, then perform any customization locally on each virtual desktop machine, therefore preventing any conflicts between machines.

If you click the radio button for **Use this customization specification**, then you will see a list of the configured VM Customization Specifications from the vSphere Client. In this example, we have created a customization specification called **Windows 10 Customization,** as shown in the following screenshot:

○ Use this customization specification

☐ Allow Reuse of Existing Computer Accounts   ⓘ

Name	Guest OS	Description
Windows 10 Customization	Windows	

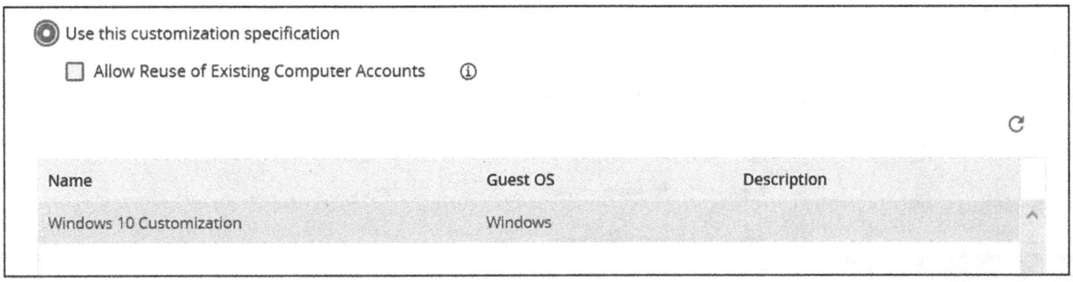

Figure 6-84. *Selecting a customization specification option*

92. Click to select the customization you want to use. You also have the option to enable, by checking the box, the **Allow Reuse of Existing Computer Accounts** setting.

93. Click **Submit**.

94. You return to the Guest Customization screen.

95. Click **Next** to continue.

96. You will now see the **Ready to Complete** screen, where you will see a summary of all the options that you have configured, as shown in the following screenshot:

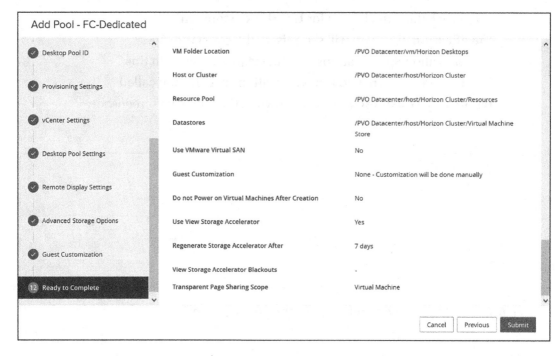

Figure 6-85. *Selecting a customization specification option*

97. Once you have reviewed the configuration settings and options, click **Submit**.

98. You will now see that the desktop pool has been created, as shown in the following screenshot:

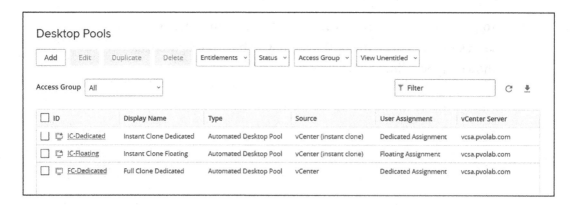

Figure 6-86. *Desktop pool successfully created*

99.   If you switch to the vSphere Client and the task view, you will see
      that the Full Clones have been created as per the settings in the
      provisioning configuration as shown:

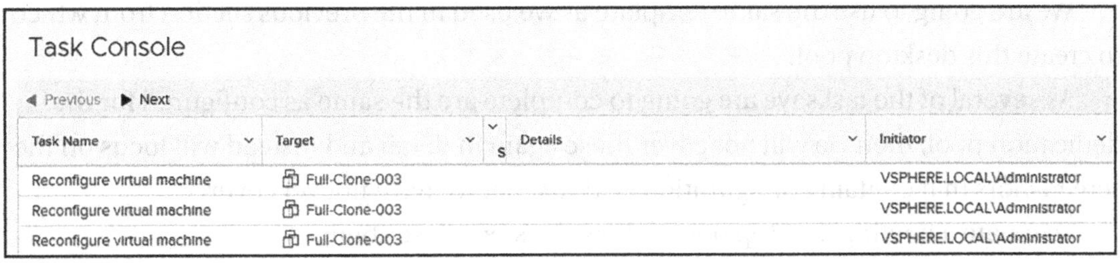

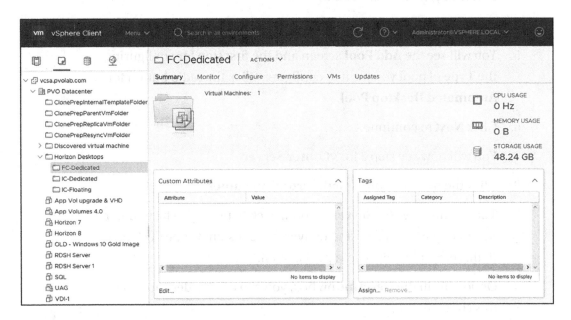

Figure 6-87.   *Desktop pool creation task running*

100.   You will then see that the FC-Dedicated folder has been created
       and currently contains a virtual desktop machine ready for use, as
       shown in the following screenshot:

Figure 6-88.   *Desktop pool folder in the vSphere Client*

You have now successfully built and configured an automated, Full Clone Dedicated
desktop pool.

In the next section, we are going to create a final desktop pool. This time for
automated Full Clone Floating desktop pools.

Full Clone Floating Pools

In this section, we are going to create one final automated Full Clone desktop pool, but this time we are going to configure a floating end-user assignment.

We are going to use the same template as we used in the previous section from which to create this desktop pool.

As several of the tasks we are going to complete are the same as configured for the dedication pool, then we will not cover these again in detail and instead will focus on the screenshots that contain configuration options that we have not yet covered.

To create a floating desktop pool, follow the steps described:

1. Open a browser and navigate to the Connection Server.

2. Enter your Horizon administrator username and password, then click the **Sign in** button.

3. From the left-hand navigation pane, expand the option for **Inventory**, then click **Desktops**.

4. Now click the **Add** button.

5. You will see the **Add Pool** screen and the first step for configuring the **Type** of pool you want to configure. Click the radio button for **Automated Desktop Pool**.

6. Click **Next** to continue.

7. You will now see step 2 for **vCenter Server**.

8. Click the radio button for **Full Virtual Machines**.

9. Then in the **vCenter Server** section, click to highlight the vCenter Server that will manage and deliver these Instant Clone desktops. In this example, this is vcsa.pvolab.com.

10. Optionally in the **Description** box, you can enter a description for this configuration.

11. Click **Next** to continue.

12. The next step is for **User Assignment,** as shown in the following screenshot:

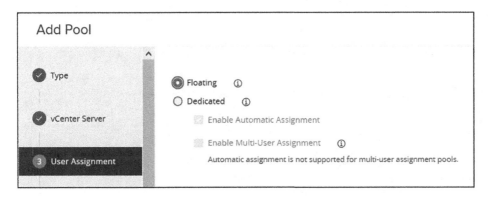

Figure 6-89. *Adding a Full Clone floating end-user assignment*

13. In this example, we are creating a floating or non-persistent assignment, so click the radio button for **Floating**, then click **Next** to continue.

14. You will now see step 4 for **Storage Optimization**.

15. Click the radio button to select whether to use a Virtual SAN datastore. In the example lab, there is no VSAN configured.

16. Click Next to move to step 5 for **Desktop Pool ID**.

17. In the **ID** box, type in the ID you want to use to identify this desktop pool. In this example, we have given the desktop pool the ID of **FC-Floating**.

18. Next, in the **Display Name** box, give the desktop pool a friendly name. In this example, we have used **Full Clone Floating** for the display name.

19. In the **Access Group** drop-down menu, select the access group if you have any configured.

20. Finally, in the **Description** box, type in a description that describes what this desktop pool is used for.

21.   The following screenshot shows the configuration:

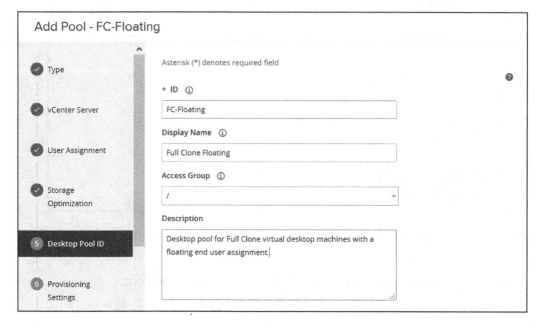

Figure 6-90. *Configuring the desktop pool ID*

22.   Click **Next** to continue.

23.   You will now see the **Provisioning Settings** screen.

24.   Check the **Enable Provisioning** box to allow the virtual desktop
       machines to be provisioned.

25.   Check the box for **Stop Provisioning on Error**.

26.   The next section of the provisioning configuration is for **Virtual
       Machine Naming**. As discussed in the previous section, Full Clone
       desktop pools have the option to **Specify Names Manually**.

27.   Click the radio button for **Specify Names Manually**.

28.   Next to the **0 names entered** box, click the **Enter Names** button to
       start manually entering your machine names.

29.   You will see the **Enter Machine Names** screen.

30.   In the box, type in the machine name to use. In this example,
       we have added three machines with the naming convention of
       Full-Clone-F-01, **Full-Clone-F-02**, and **Full-Clone-F-03**.

31. Note there is a 15-character limit on the names.

32. Click **Next** to continue.

33. You will see the **Summary** screen showing the machine names that you entered.

34. Click the **Submit** button.

35. You will return to the **Provisioning Settings** screen where you will see that the names have been added.

36. You then have the option to start machines in maintenance mode, by checking the **Start machines in maintenance mode** box.

37. Finally, in the **# Unassigned Machines Kept Powered On** box, type in the number of machines you want to be kept powered on.

38. Alternatively, you can choose to use the naming pattern option that will automatically assign machine names. To do this, click the radio button for **Use a Naming Pattern**, then in the **Naming Pattern** box, type in the names you would like to call the newly created virtual desktop machines.

39. Next is the Provision Machines section, you will see that the **All Machines Up-Front** option is automatically selected.

40. In the **Desktop Pool Sizing** section, configure the number of **Maximum Machines** and the number of **Spare (Powered On) Machines**.

41. Finally, select whether to **Add vTPM Device to VMs** by checking the box.

42. In this example, we are going to follow the manual naming of virtual desktop machines option.

43. Click **Next** to continue.

44. You will now move on to step 7 for configuring the **vCenter Settings**.

45. In the **Template** box, click **Browse**.

46. You will see the **Select template** screen.

47. From the list of templates shown, click to select the template you want to use. In this example, we are going to choose the **Windows 10 Gold Image Template** we created at the start of this section.

48. Click **Submit**.

49. Now complete the remaining sections of this configuration screen for VM Folder Location, Host or Cluster, Resource Pool, and Datastore.

50. With the vCenter Settings configuration completed, click the **Next** button.

51. You will now see step 8 for **Desktop Pool Settings**.

52. The first option is to configure the **State** of the desktop pool. From the drop-down menu, select **Enabled to enable this desktop pool**.

53. Next, configure **Connection Server Restrictions**. To configure a restriction, click the **Browse** button and configure the appropriate restrictions based on Connection Server tags. Click **Submit once** you have configured any Connection Server restrictions.

54. With the next setting, the **Category Folder** setting, you can add a folder or a shortcut to the end user's device that points directly to this desktop pool. To configure this, click the **Browse** button next to the **Category Folder** option, then select the category folder, or select to add a shortcut location, a start menu entry, or a desktop icon.

55. Once configured, click the **Submit** button.

56. Next is the check box for **Client Restrictions**. Check the box to enable this setting, then you can prevent end users from connecting to desktops in this pool if they are using specific client devices.

57. The next option is for **Session Types**. Select from **Desktop**, **Application**, or **Desktop & Application**. As this pool is delivering virtual desktop machines, select the Desktop option from the drop-down menu.

58. Next is the **Remote Machine Power Policy** configuration. From the drop-down menu, select from **Always Powered On, Take no power action, Suspend, and Power Off**.

59. In the **Log Off After Disconnect** setting, from the drop-down menu select whether an end user is logged off when they disconnect. Select from **Immediately, Never, and After**.

60. Next is the option for **Allow Users to Restart Machines**. From the drop-down menu, simply select **Yes** or **No**.

61. The final option is to configure the **Allow Separate Desktop Sessions from Different Client Devices** setting; simply select **Yes** or **No**.

62. With the **Desktop Pool Settings** configuration completed, click the **Next** button.

63. You will now see step 9 for the **Remote Display Settings** configuration screen.

64. In the **Default Display Protocol** box, from the drop-down menu, select the protocol you want the end users to connect to their virtual desktops with. In this example, we are going to use **Blast**.

65. Next is the **Allow Users to choose Protocol** box. From the drop-down menu, select either **Yes** or **No, depending on whether you want end users to choose their protocol**.

66. You can then choose, in the **3D Renderer** box, how you want to handle 3D rendering. Click the drop-down menu and select **Manage using vSphere Client, Disabled, Automatic, Software, Hardware, or NVIDIA GRID vGPU**.

67. Next is the **VRAM Size** box where you can configure the amount of video memory. This option is only available with the **Hardware**, **Software,** and **Automatic** 3D Renderer setting.

68. In the **Maximum number of monitors** box, from the drop-down menu, select the number of screens the end user will be using on their endpoint device to display the virtual desktop machine.

69. Next, you have the **Maximum Resolution of Any One Monitor** option. This is only available with 3D Renderer disabled and allows you to select the resolution of an individual monitor.

70. The final option on the **Remote Display Settings** configuration screen is for **Allow Session Collaboration**. If you check the box to enable this feature, then end users can invite other users, such as support teams, to their session. This feature only works with the Blast protocol.

71. Click **Next** to continue.

72. You will now see step 10 for **Advanced Storage Options**.

73. The first option is to enable **the View Storage Accelerator**. To enable this feature, check the **Use View Storage Accelerator** box.

74. Then in the **Regenerate Storage Accelerator After** box, you can configure the time, in days, of when you want to regenerate the cached data.

75. You can then configure **Set Blackout Days** by clicking the **Add** button.

76. Check the boxes next to the days you want to prevent regeneration from running, then configure the time window for blackout in the **From** and **To** boxes, and click **Submit**.

77. The final setting is for configuring the **Transparent Page Sharing Scope**.

78. Configure how the pages are shared, either at the **Virtual Machine** level, **Desktop Pool** level, **Pod** level, or at a **Global** level.

79. Click **Next** to continue.

80. You will now see step 11 for **Guest Customization**.

81. Choose the option for **None – Customization will be done manually,** which means that the virtual desktop machine will be exactly the same as the template from which it was created, then check box for **Do not Power on Virtual Machine After Creation,** if you want to leave the machine powered off.

82. Or click the radio button for **Use this customization
     specification**, and then from the list of the available VM
     Customization Specifications, select the one you want to use.
     You also have the option to enable the Allow Reuse of Existing
     Computer Accounts.

83. Click **Next** to continue.

84. You will now see the **Ready to Complete** screen, where you will
     see a summary of all the options that are configured.

85. To confirm the chosen configuration options, click the **Submit**
     button.

86. You will now see that the desktop pool has been successfully
     created, configured, and added as shown:

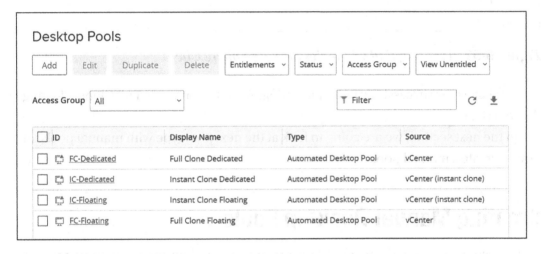

Figure 6-91. Floating Full Clone desktop pool created

87. If you switch to the vSphere Client, you will see that the
     FC-Floating folder has been created as a sub-folder in the
     Horizon Desktops folder, and that the virtual desktop machines
     have been provisioned as we configured them, to be provisioned
     up front.

88.   This is shown in the following screenshot:

Figure 6-92. *Floating Full Clone desktop in vSphere Client*

You have now successfully built and configured an automated, Full Clone, Floating desktop pool.

In the next section, we are going to look at the next pool type with manual pools and how to create a manual pool.

Creating Manual Desktop Pools

In this section, we are going to look at the process for building and configuring manual desktop pools. Manual desktop pools are used for creating a desktop pool made up of existing resources. By this, we mean that the desktops are already built, rather than created through Instant Clones or Full Clones.

That means that they can be either virtual or physical. All they need is to be running the Horizon Agent to enable them to communicate with the Connection Server.

In the next section, we are going to work through the process for creating a manual pool using virtual desktop machines.

Using vCenter Virtual Desktop Machines

In this section, we are going to create two manual desktop pools, one with a dedicated end-user assignment and another with a floating end-user assignment. We are going to start with the dedicated manual desktop pool.

Dedicated

To create a dedicated manual desktop pool, follow the steps described:

1. Open a browser and navigate to the Connection Server.

2. Enter your Horizon administrator username and password, then click the **Sign in** button.

3. From the left-hand navigation pane, expand the option for **Inventory**, then click **Desktops**.

4. Now click the **Add** button.

5. You will see the **Add Pool** screen and the first step for configuring the **Type** of pool you wish to configure. Click the radio button for **Manual Desktop Pool**, as shown in the following screenshot:

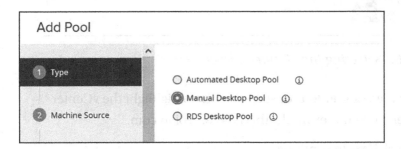

Figure 6-93. *Adding a manual desktop pool*

6. Click **Next** to continue.

7. You will see step 2 for selecting the **Machine Source**.

8. Click the radio button for **vCenter virtual machines**, as shown in the following screenshot:

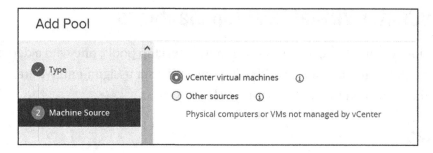

Figure 6-94. *Selecting the machine source*

9.   Click **Next** to continue.

10.   You will now see step 3 for **vCenter Server,** as shown in the
       following screenshot:

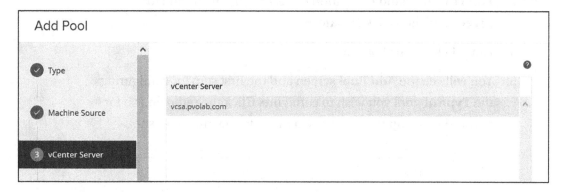

Figure 6-95. *Selecting the vCenter Server*

11.   In the **vCenter Server** section, click to highlight the vCenter
       Server. In this example, this is vcsa.pvolab.com.

12.   Click **Next** to continue.

13.   You will now see step 4 for the User Assignment.

14.   In this example, we are going to create a manual desktop pool with
       a dedicated assignment, so click the radio button for **Dedicated**.
       You can also check the **Enable Automatic Assignment** box if
       you want to automatically assign end users to virtual desktop
       machines.

15.   This is shown in the following screenshot:

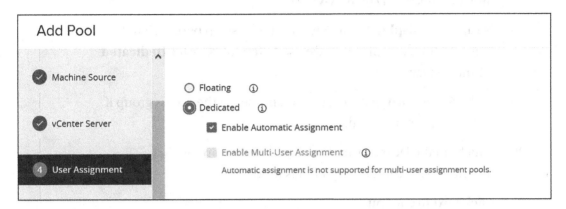

Figure 6-96. *Selecting the end-user assignment type*

16.   Click Next to move to step 5 for **Desktop Pool ID,** as shown in the
following screenshot:

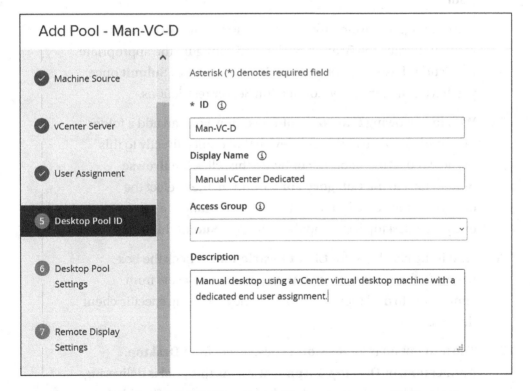

Figure 6-97. *Configuring the desktop pool ID*

17. In the **ID** box, type in the ID. In this example, we have given the desktop pool the ID of **Man-VC-D**.

18. Next, in the **Display Name** box, give the desktop pool a friendly name. In this example, we have used **Manual vCenter Dedicated** for the display name.

19. In the **Access Group** drop-down menu, select the access group if you have any configured.

20. Finally, in the **Description** box, type in a description that describes what this desktop pool is used for.

21. Click **Next** to continue.

22. You will now see step 6 for **Desktop Pool Settings**.

23. The first option is to configure the **State** of the desktop pool. From the drop-down menu, select **Enabled to enable this desktop pool**.

24. Next, configure **Connection Server Restrictions**. To configure a restriction, click the **Browse** button and configure the appropriate restrictions based on Connection Server tags. Click **Submit** once you have configured any Connection Server restrictions.

25. With the following **Category Folder** setting, you can add a folder or a shortcut to the end user's device that points directly to this particular desktop pool. To configure this, click the **Browse** button, next to the **Category Folder** option, then select the category folder, or select to add a shortcut location, a start menu entry, or a desktop icon, and then click the **Submit** button.

26. Next is the check box for **Client Restrictions**. Check the box to enable this setting, then you can prevent end users from connecting to desktops in this pool if they are using specific client devices.

27. The next option is for **Session Types**. Select from **Desktop, Application,** or **Desktop & Application**. As this pool is delivering virtual desktop machines, select the Desktop option from the drop-down menu.

28. Next is the **Remote Machine Power Policy** configuration. From the drop-down menu, select from **Always Powered On, Take no power action, Suspend, and Power Off**.

29. In the **Log Off After Disconnect** setting from the drop-down menu, select whether an end user is logged off when they disconnect. Select from **Immediately, Never, and After**.

30. Next is the option for **Allow Users to Restart Machines**. From the drop-down menu, simply select **Yes** or **No**.

31. With the **Desktop Pool Settings** configuration completed, click the **Next** button.

32. You will now see step 9 for the **Remote Display Settings** configuration screen.

33. In the **Default Display Protocol** box, from the drop-down menu, select the protocol you want the end users to connect to their virtual desktops with. In this example, we are using **Blast**.

34. Next is the **Allow Users to choose Protocol** box. From the drop-down menu, select either **Yes** or **No**, depending on whether you want end users to choose their protocol.

35. The final two options, when enabled, will **Show Assigned Machine Name** and **Show Machine Alias Name**.

36. Click **Next** to continue. You will see step 7 for **Remote Display Settings**.

37. In the **Default Display Protocol** box from the drop-down menu, select the protocol you want the end users to connect to their virtual desktops with. In this example, we are going to use **Blast**.

38. Next is the **Allow Users to choose Protocol** box. From the drop-down menu, select either **Yes** or **No, depending on whether you want end users to choose their protocol.**

39. You can then choose in the **3D Renderer** box how you want to handle 3D rendering. Click the drop-down menu and select **Manage using vSphere Client, Disabled, Automatic, Software, Hardware,** or **NVIDIA GRID vGPU**.

40. Next is the **VRAM Size** box, where you can configure the amount of video memory. This option is only available with the **Hardware**, **Software,** and **Automatic** 3D Renderer setting.

41. In the **Maximum number of monitors** box from the drop-down menu, select the number of screens the end user will use on their endpoint device to display the virtual desktop.

42. Next, you have the **Maximum Resolution of Any One Monitor** option. This is only available with 3D Renderer disabled. From the drop-down menu, choose the resolution.

43. The final option is for **Allow Session Collaboration**. Check the box to enable this feature.

44. Click **Next** to continue to step 8 for **Virtual Machine**. You will see the **Add vCenter Virtual Machines** screen:

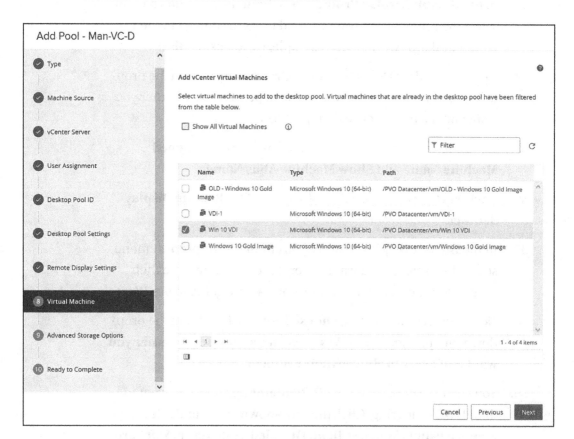

Figure 6-98. *Adding the virtual desktop machines*

45. Check the box next to the virtual desktop machine you want to add to this desktop pool. In this example, we have a virtual desktop machine called **Win 10 VDI**, so click to select this virtual desktop machine.

46. Click **Next** to continue to step 9 for **Advanced Storage Options**.

47. The first option is to enable **the View Storage Accelerator**. To enable this feature, check the **Use View Storage Accelerator** box.

48. Then in the **Regenerate Storage Accelerator After** box, you can configure the time, in days, of when you want to regenerate the cached data.

49. You can then configure **Set Blackout Days** by clicking the **Add** button.

50. Check the boxes next to the days you want to prevent regeneration from running, then configure the time window for blackout in the **From** and **To** boxes, and click **Submit**.

51. The final setting is for configuring the **Transparent Page Sharing Scope**.

52. Configure how the pages are shared, either at the **Virtual Machine** level, at the **Desktop Pool** level, at the **Pod** level, or at a **Global** level.

53. Click **Next** to continue.

54. You will now see the **Ready to Complete** screen, where you will see a summary of all the options that you have configured.

55. Once happy with the chosen configuration options, click the **Submit** button.

56. You will now see that the desktop pool has been successfully created, configured, and added as shown:

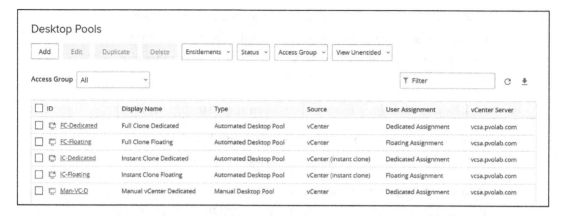

Figure 6-99. *Manual desktop pool successfully created*

As the manual pool is using an existing virtual desktop machine, then nothing will be created in the vSphere Client.

You have now successfully created a manual desktop pool, using an existing vCenter virtual desktop machine with a dedicated end-user assignment. In the next section, we are going to touch on the process for building the same manual desktop pool, but with a floating assignment instead.

Floating

To create a manual desktop pool using a vCenter virtual desktop as the source machine, the process is the same as described in the previous section, with one key difference, other than the different desktop pool ID and desktop pool name that you would give to the pool.

When configuring a floating desktop pool, in step 4 for **User Assignment**, click the radio button for **Floating**.

In the next section, we are going to look at the process for creating manual desktop pools using non-vCenter virtual desktop machines.

Creating Desktop Pools from Other Sources

The final manual desktop pool we are going to build is going to use a non-vCenter virtual machine. In this example, we are going to use a physical desktop machine that is running the Horizon Agent to enable the Connection Broker to connect this to the end user's client.

The use case for this is if you have rack mounted workstations located in a data center that you will need to connect to remotely.

To create this desktop pool, follow the steps described:

1. Open a browser and navigate to the Connection Server.

2. Enter your Horizon administrator username and password and click the **Sign in** button.

3. From the left-hand navigation pane, expand the option for **Inventory**, then click **Desktops**.

4. Now click the **Add** button.

5. You will see the **Add Pool** screen and the first step for configuring the **Type** of pool you want to configure. Click the radio button for **Manual Desktop Pool**.

6. Click **Next** to continue.

7. You will see step 2 for selecting the **Machine Source**.

8. Click the radio button for **Other sources,** as shown in the following screenshot:

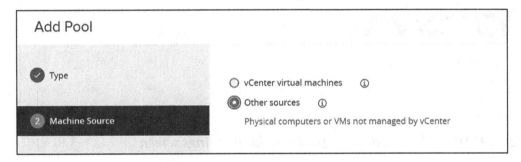

Figure 6-100. *Manual desktop pool using other sources*

9. Click **Next** to continue.

10. You will now see step 3 for **User assignment**. Click the radio button to choose either **Dedicated** or **Floating**.

11. Click **Next** to continue.

12. You will see step 4 for **Desktop Pool ID**.

13. In the **ID** box, type in the ID for this desktop pool, then enter a **Display Name**, select the **Access Group,** and then finally type in a **Description**.

14. In this example, we have given the desktop pool the ID of **Physical-Desktops** and similar display name and description details.

15. Click **Next** to continue.

16. You will now see step 5 for **Desktop Pool Settings,** as shown in the following screenshot:

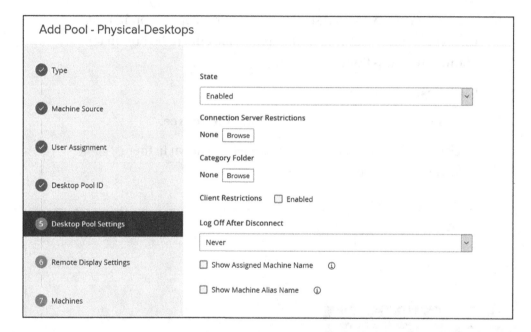

Figure 6-101. *Manual desktop pool – desktop settings screen*

17. The first option is to configure the **State** of the desktop pool. From the drop-down menu, select **Enabled** to enable this desktop pool.

18. Next, configure any **Connection Server Restrictions**, the **Category Folder,** and any **Client Restrictions**.

19. You then have the option to configure the **Log Off After Disconnect** option and finally the options for **Show Assigned Machine Name** and **Show Machine Alias Name**.

20. Click **Next** to continue.

21. You will see step 6 for configuring the **Remote Display Protocol**.

22. On this screen, there are only three options to select from: the **Default Display Protocol**, **Allow Users to Choose Protocol**, and **Allow Session Collaboration** options.

23. Click **Next** to continue.

24. You will now see step 7 for **Machines**.

25. On this configuration screen, you can add the desktop machines that you wish to add to this desktop pool.

26. In this example, we have a physical desktop called **desktop-3081ktl** that has the Horizon Agent installed on it.

27. Check the box next to the machine, as shown in the following screenshot:

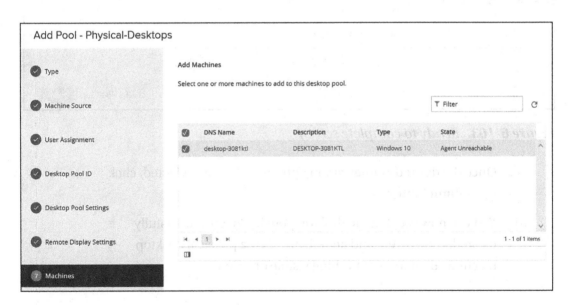

Figure 6-102. *Selecting the non-vCenter machine*

28. Click **Next** to continue.

29. You will now see the **Ready to Complete** screen, as shown in the following screenshot:

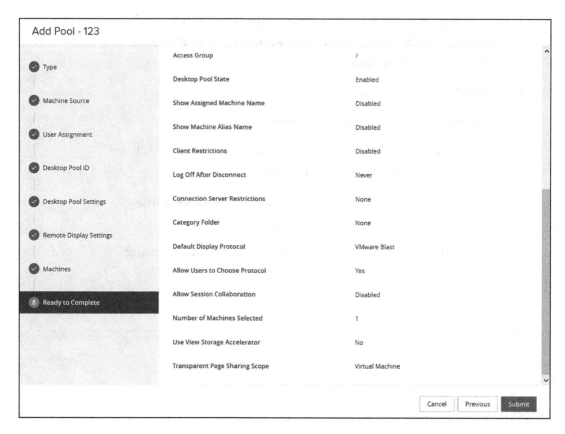

Figure 6-103. *Ready to complete screen*

30. Once the desired configuration options have been selected, click the **Submit** button.

31. You will now see that the desktop pool has been successfully created, configured, and added. As this is a physical desktop machine, then there is nothing visible on vCenter.

32. The configured desktop pool is shown in the following screenshot:

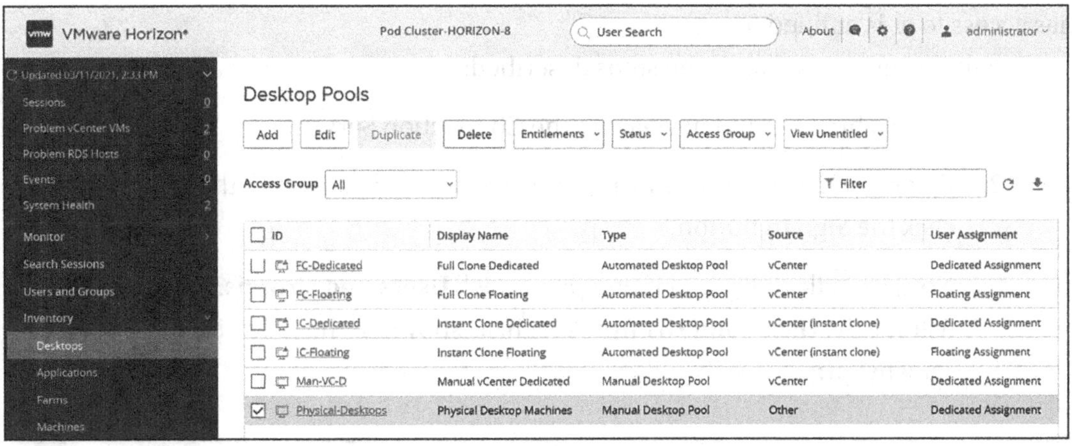

Figure 6-104. *Manual non-vCenter desktop pool*

You have now successfully configured a desktop pool using other sources or, in other words, non-vCenter virtual desktop machines. In this example, we added a physical desktop machine to the pool.

The final desktop pool is the RDS desktop pool.

Creating RDS Desktop Pools

The final type of desktop pool you can create is an RDS desktop pool.

This is used to deliver published desktop sessions rather than full virtual desktop machines, enabling the Connection Server to broker session from a Microsoft RDSH host server.

This will be covered in more detail in Chapter 12, where we are going to focus on session-based desktops and how to configure them.

In the final section of this chapter, we will look at how to entitle end users to be able to access their desktop pools, plus the virtual or physical desktop machines that are part of those desktop pools.

Desktop Pool End-User Entitlements

In this section, we are going to entitle or enable end users to have access to the desktop pools and so the desktops within those desktop pools.

When an end user connects via the Horizon Client or browser, they are shown several icons within the client. These icons represent the desktop pools that the end user has access to or is entitled to.

To entitle end users, follow the steps described:

1. Open a browser and navigate to the Connection Server.

2. Enter your Horizon administrator username and password, then click the **Sign in** button.

3. Now, from the left-hand menu pane, click **Users and Groups**. You will see the **Users and Groups** screen, as shown in the following screenshot:

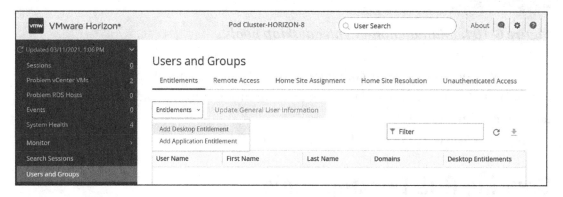

Figure 6-105. *Entitling end users to desktop pools*

4. From the top menu, click **Entitlements**, then click the **Entitlements** drop-down menu below.

5. From the list of options, select **Add Desktop Entitlement**.

6. You will now see the **Add Desktop Entitlement** screen.

7. The first option in the **Type** section is to choose either the **Users** or **Groups** that you want to entitle to a desktop pool.

8. In the **Domain** box from the drop-down menu, select the domain in which you wish to perform the search. In this example, this is our pvolab.com test lab domain.

9. In the **Name/Username** box, you can type in the name or part of the name you want to search for. First, select the filter for the search. You have the option of **Contains**, **Starts with**, or **Is exactly**. In this example, we have selected Contains.

10. Then, in the box next to the filter option, enter what name or part of the name you are searching for. In the example, we are searching for a name or username that contains **pvo**.

11. You can also search based on **Description,** using the same filter process to find the description and entering the description text you want to search for.

12. Now click the **Find** button.

13. The results are then displayed in the box below the Find button, as shown in the following screenshot:

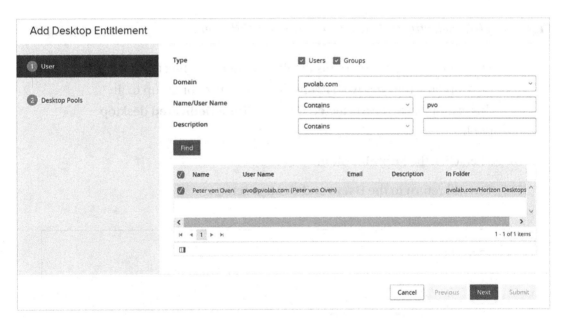

Figure 6-106. *Adding a user or group*

14. Check the box next to the name from the results list to select it. In this example, we have the user **Peter von Oven**.

15. Click the **Next** button to continue.

16.   You will now see the second step for **Desktop Pools** and **Select the desktop pools to entitle** as shown:

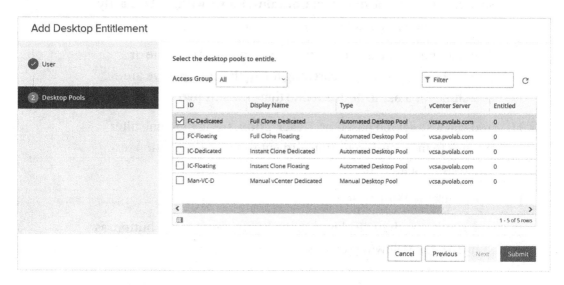

Figure 6-107.   *Selecting the desktop pool for entitlement*

17.   From the list of desktop pools displayed, check the box for the desktop pool that you wish to entitle the end user or group to. In this example, we have selected the **Full Clone Dedicated** desktop pool.

18.   Then click the **Submit** button.

19.   You will return to the **Users and Groups** screen:

Figure 6-108.   *End user successfully entitled to a desktop pool*

20. You will now see from the screenshot that the username has been added and an end user has been entitled to a desktop pool – in this case, the Full Clone Dedicated desktop pool.

You have now successfully entitled a desktop pool to an end user. In the next section, we are going to look at how to create global entitlements for the Cloud Pod Architecture.

Global Entitlements with CPA

In this section, we are going to look at how to configure a global entitlement.

To do this, follow the steps described:

1. From the Horizon Console dashboard, expand the option for **Inventory**, then click **Global Entitlements**. You will see the **Global Entitlements** screen as shown:

Figure 6-109. *Global entitlements configuration screen*

2. Click the **Add** button.

3. You will see the **Add Global Entitlement** screen and the first step to complete for the **Type** of entitlement.

4. Click the radio button for **Desktop Entitlement,** as we are going to create an entitlement for a virtual desktop.

5. This is shown in the following screenshot:

Figure 6-110. *Adding a global entitlement configuration screen*

6. Click **Next** to continue.

7. You will now see step 2 for **Name and Policies** as shown:

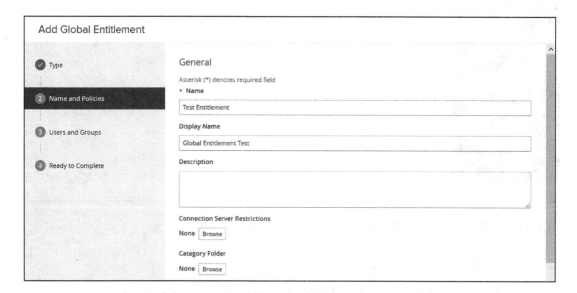

Figure 6-111. *Global entitlement names and policies configuration – General*

8. We will start with the **General** settings.

9. In the **Name** box, type in a name for this entitlement.

10. Next, in the **Display Name** box, type in a name for this entitlement; then in the **Description** box, you can optionally add a description.

11. You then have the option of configuring **Connection Server Restrictions and** adding a **Category Folder** to the end user's endpoint.

12. Scroll down to the **Policies** settings section, as shown:

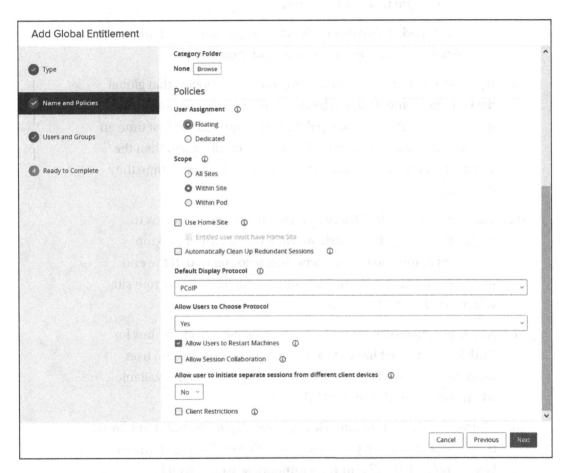

Figure 6-112. *Global entitlement names and policies configuration – Policies*

13. The first option is to configure either a **Floating** or **Dedicated** assignment, by clicking the radio button next to the option you want.

421

14. Next is the **Scope** option. This configuration option specifies where to look for desktops, when an end user with a global entitlement wants to connect to a virtual desktop machine. You can select from the following options:

    - **All Sites**: This will look for virtual desktop machines across any pod that is configured as part of the pod federation.

    - **Within Site**: This will look for virtual desktop machines across pods that are within the same site.

    - **Within Pod**: This will look for virtual desktop machines only in the pod that the user is currently connected to.

15. It is worth noting, when configuring the scope policy, that global desktop entitlements use a desktop pool with a dedicated end-user assignment. The scope policy is only applied the first time an end user connects to a virtual desktop. Once allocated, then the end user will connect to the same virtual desktop each time they connect.

16. The next option is for **Use Home Site**. If you check the box to enable this policy, then Horizon will look for virtual desktop machines in the end user's Home Site, if configured. If the end user does not have a Home Site configured, then the current site will be used as the home site.

17. As a sub-option of the Use Home Site, you can check the box for **Entitled user must have Home Site**. This means the end user must have a Home Site configured. This option is only available when you select All Sites and Within Site.

18. The next option for **Automatically Clean Up Redundant Sessions** is only available when you select a Floating end-user assignment. When enabled, it will remove redundant sessions, which is particularly useful if end users move around and leave a trail of unused sessions behind them.

19. The next options are all options that we have configured before. These are for selecting the **Default Display Protocol** from the

drop-down menu, **Allow Users to Choose Protocol** either Yes or No, and then the check boxes to enable the **Allow Users to Restart Machines** and the **Allow Session Collaboration** options.

20. Finally, you have the **Allow user to initiate separate sessions from different client devices,** which you select either Yes or No from the drop-down menu, then the check box to enable **Client Restrictions**.

21. If you had chosen a **Dedicated** end-user assignment, then you would have also seen the **options for Show Assigned Machine Name and Show Machine Alias Name**.

22. Click the **Next** button to continue.

23. You will now see the third step for **Users and Groups,** as shown in the following screenshot:

Figure 6-113. *Global entitlement users and groups configuration*

24. Click the **Add** button.

25. You will see the **Find User and Group** screen.

26. The first option, in the **Type** section, is to choose either the **Users** or **Groups** that you want to entitle to a desktop pool.

27. In the **Domain** box, from the drop-down menu, select the domain in which you want to perform the search. In this example, this is our pvolab.com test lab domain.

28. In the **Name/Username** box, you can type in the name or the part
     of the name you want to search for. First, select the filter for the
     search. You have the option of **Contains**, **Starts with**, or **Is exactly**.
     In this example, we have selected **Contains**.

29. Then, in the box next to the filter option, enter what name or
     part of the name you are searching for. In the example, we are
     searching for a name or username that contains **pvo**.

30. You can also search based on **Description,** using the same filter
     process to find the description and entering the description text
     you want to search for.

31. Now click the **Find** button.

32. The results are then displayed in the box below the **Find** button,
     as shown in the following screenshot:

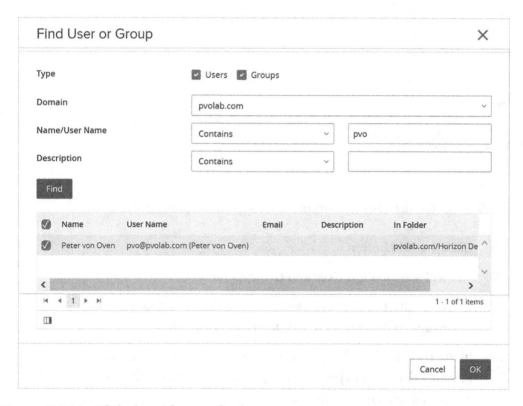

Figure 6-114. *Global entitlement find user and group screen*

33. Check the box next to the name from the results list to select it. In this example, we have the user **Peter von Oven**.

34. Click the **OK** button to continue.

35. You will return to the **Add Global Entitlement** screen, where you will see the user has been added.

36. You can check the box to select the end user; then the **Remove** button is available should you wish to remove them. You can also click the **Add** button if you want to add more end users.

37. This is shown in the following screenshot:

Figure 6-115. *Global entitlement – end user added*

38. Click the **Next** button.

39. You will now see the final step, step 4, and the **Ready to complete** screen.

40. Review your configuration options, as shown in the following screenshot:

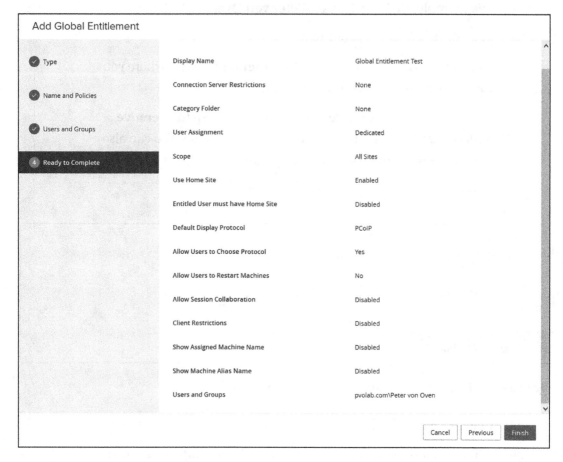

Figure 6-116. *Global entitlement – ready to complete screen*

41. Once you are happy with the configuration, click the **Finish**
button. You will see the **Global Entitlements** screen:

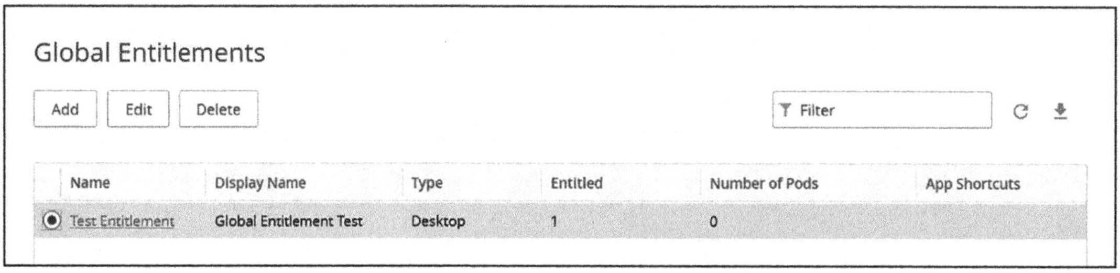

Figure 6-117. *Global entitlement successfully configured*

You have now successfully configured a global entitlement.

In the next section, we are going to look at some of the management tasks available now that we have created several desktop pools to work with.

Managing Desktop Pools

Now that you have created a number of desktop pools, you can then manage them from the Desktop Pools screen, enabling you to perform a few tasks which we will cover in this section.

Adding a Desktop Pool

We have already covered this option a few times throughout this chapter. To add a new desktop pool, simply click the **Add** button, then complete the associated configuration screens.

Editing an Existing Desktop Pool

To edit an existing desktop pool, check the box next to the pool that you want to change or update, then click the **Edit** button.

The pool settings will be displayed, enabling you to click through each configuration section using the tabs across the top in blue, as shown in the following screenshot:

Figure 6-118. *Editing existing desktop pool settings*

It is worth noting that you cannot edit or change the Desktop Pool ID.

Duplicating Desktop Pools

To duplicate an existing desktop pool, check the box next to the pool that you want to change or update, then click the **Duplicate** button, as shown in the following screenshot:

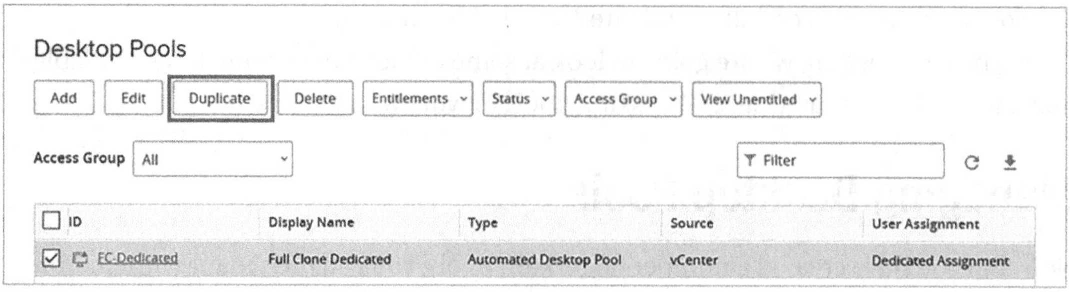

Figure 6-119. *Duplicating an existing desktop pool*

You will then see the Duplicate Pool screen as shown:

Figure 6-120. *Duplicate desktop pool configuration screen*

On this screen, you can step through the configuration and make any changes from the already configured settings. You will need to configure a new desktop pool ID.

Deleting an Existing Desktop Pool

To delete a desktop pool, simply check the box next to the pool that you wish to delete, then click the **Delete** button from the menu.

1. You will then see the **Delete Desktop Pool** warning box, as shown in the following screenshot:

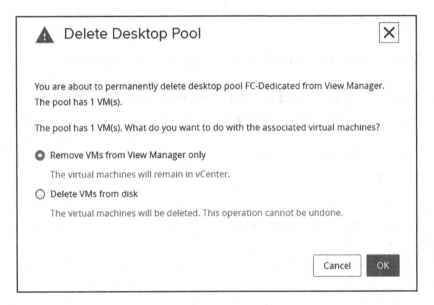

Figure 6-121. *Deleting a desktop pool*

In the warning box, you have two options. The first is to just delete the virtual desktop machines that are part of the desktop pool from the Horizon Console. This means that the virtual desktop machines themselves are not deleted and will still be available in the vSphere Client and in place on the host servers.

The second option will delete the virtual desktop machines completely, deleting them from vCenter and from the ESXi host server. Select which option you want by clicking the corresponding radio button, then click **OK**.

Adding and Removing Entitlements

To add or remove an end-user entitlement to a desktop pool, click the **Entitlement** button from the menu and then select either **Add Entitlements** or **Remove Entitlements** from the drop-down menu as shown:

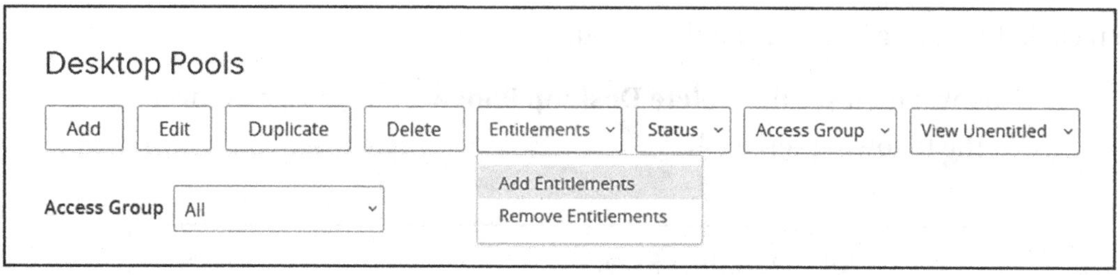

Figure 6-122. *Adding and removing entitlements to a desktop pool*

If you select the option for **Add Entitlements**, then you will see the **Add Entitlements** screen, as shown in the following screenshot:

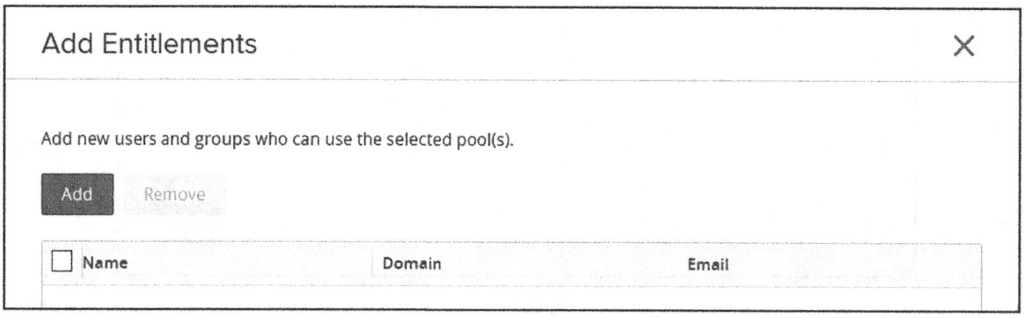

Figure 6-123. *Adding entitlements to a desktop pool*

If you select the option for **Remove Entitlements,** then you will see the **Remove Entitlements** screen, as shown in the following screenshot:

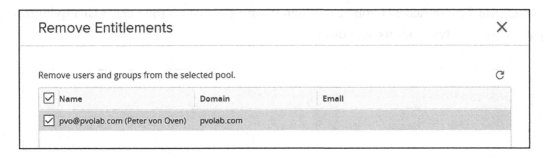

Figure 6-124. Removing entitlements to a desktop pool

Check the box next to the end user you want to remove from having access to this desktop pool, then click **OK.**

Status

The status option allows you to change the desktop pool status. Select a desktop pool; then if you click the **Status** button, you will see the following options:

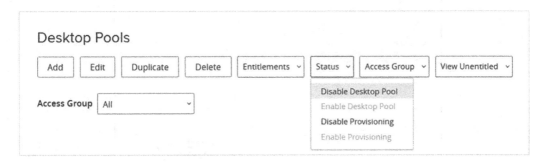

Figure 6-125. Desktop pool status

This allows you to disable and enable desktop pools as well as enabling and disabling the provisioning process. You may wish to suddenly stop desktops being built or to prevent end users from connecting as you are performing other admin tasks on the pools or desktops.

Access Group

This option allows you to create a new Access Group for the selected desktop pool or to change the current Access Group to a different one. If you click the **Access Group** button, you will see the two options as shown:

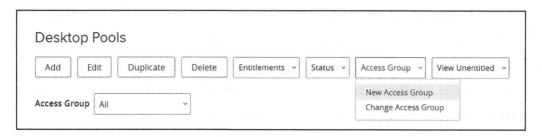

Figure 6-126. *Editing the access groups*

If you select the **New Access Group** option, you will see the **New Access Group** configuration screen, as shown in the following screenshot:

Figure 6-127. *Creating a new access group*

Configure the details for the **Name** and **Description** for this new Access Group, then click the **Submit** button.

If you select the **Change Access Group** option, then you will see the **Change Access Group** configuration screen, as shown in the following screenshot:

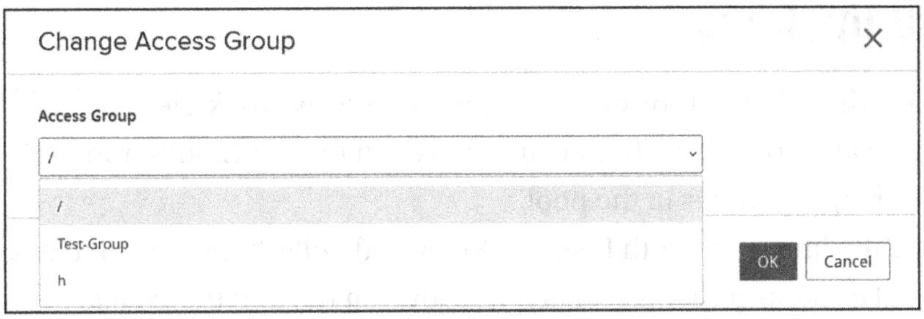

Figure 6-128. *Changing to a different access group*

From the **Access Group** drop-down menu, select the Access Group that you want to change to, then click the **OK** button.

View Unentitled

The final option is to view unentitled machines or unentitled policies. If you click the View Unentitled button, then you have the two options as shown in the following screenshot:

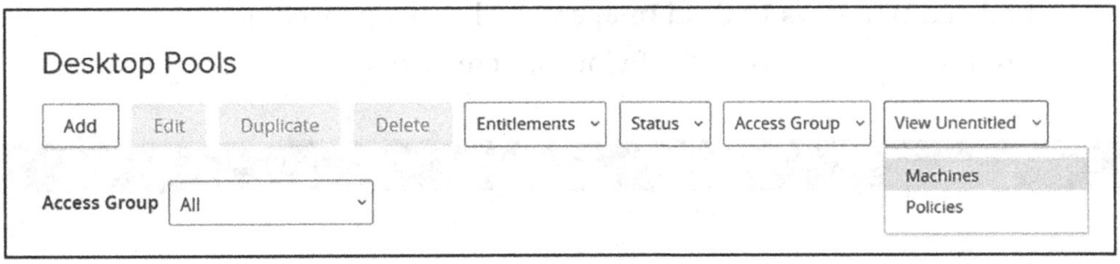

Figure 6-129. *Unentitled machines and policies*

If you select **Machines,** you will see the **View Unentitled Machines** screen where you will see a list of virtual desktop machines that are assigned to end users, but the end users are no longer entitled to the desktop pool. This scenario is only seen with desktop pools that have dedicated end-user assignments.

If you select **Policies,** then you will see the **View Unentitled Policies** screen, where you will see a list of policies that are assigned to end users, but the end users are no longer entitled to the desktop pool.

The final thing we are going to look at is updating the virtual desktop machine image and how to then deploy that within the pools.

Updating the Image

In the example desktop pools discussed in this chapter, we took the virtual desktop machine image and configured both Full Clones and Instant Clones from which to build the virtual desktop machines in the pool.

To update the image, for both Instant Clones and Full Clones, the first task is to take the virtual desktop gold image machine, power it on, and then make the required changes. This may be to update or patch the OS or add a new application to the base image.

With the gold image now updated, you can start the process to update the desktop pool. We will start with the Instant Clone desktop pool.

Updating the Instant Clone Desktop Pool Image

The next task, now that the gold image has been updated, is to take a snapshot of that update. This is done using the vCenter Client following the steps described:

1. Expand the vCenter Server vcsa.pvolab.com, expand the **PVO Data center**, then navigate to the host server on which the updated **Windows 10 Gold Image** virtual desktop machine resides. This is shown in the following screenshot:

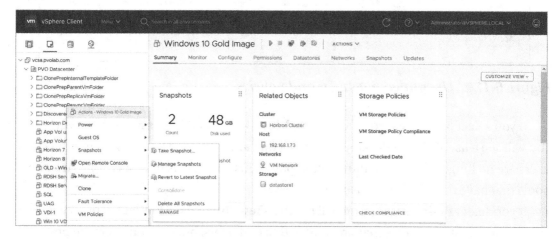

Figure 6-130. *Creating a new snapshot for updating the pool*

2. Click to highlight the virtual desktop machine, right-click, then from the contextual menu, move your cursor onto the entry for **Snapshots**.

3. You will see the snapshot options expand, so from the list of menu options, click **Take Snapshot…**.

4. You will now see the **Take Snapshot** screen as shown:

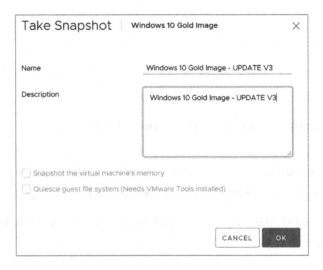

Figure 6-131. *Take snapshot of the updated Windows 10 Gold Image*

5. In the **Name** field, type in a name for this snapshot. In this example, we have called it **Windows 10 Gold Image - UPDATE V3**.

6. Then, optionally, add a description in the **Description** box.

7. Click **OK** to create the snapshot.

You now have a new snapshot of the gold image virtual desktop machine that can be used to update the desktop pool. The next step is to edit the desktop pool.

To do this, complete the steps described:

1. From the Horizon Console, navigate to and expand the **Inventory** option from the left-hand navigation pane, and then click **Desktops**.

2. You will see the following screenshot:

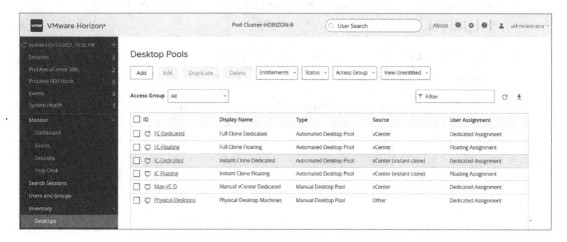

Figure 6-132. *Selecting desktops from the inventory*

3. From the list of desktop pools shown, click the link for the desktop
    pool you want to edit and add the new and updated image to.

    In this example, we are going to click the link to the **IC-Floating**
    desktop pool.

Remember to click the hyperlink to the desktop pool rather than checking the box
next to it.

---

4. You will now see the **IC-Dedicated** desktop pool as shown in the following screenshot:

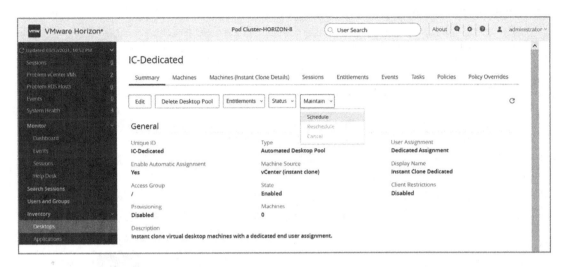

Figure 6-133. *Editing the desktop pool*

5. Click the **Maintain** box, and then from the drop-down menu, select the **Schedule** option as shown in the previous screenshot.

6. You will see the **Schedule Push Image** screen as shown:

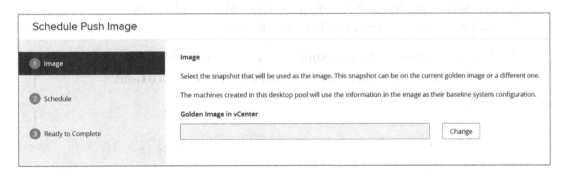

Figure 6-134. *Selecting the new image*

7. The first step is to select the image. In the **Golden Image in vCenter** box, click the **Change** button.

8. You will see the **Select Golden Image** screen as shown:

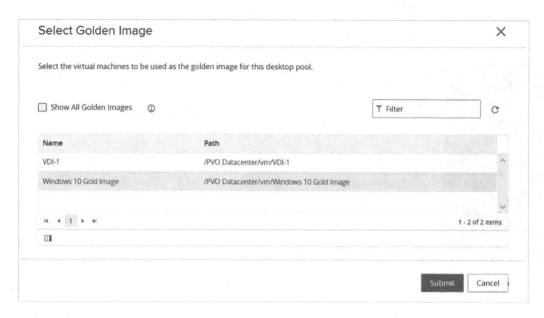

Figure 6-135. *Selecting the image from vCenter*

9. Click to select the image you want to use and then click the
    Submit button.

10. You will return to the main image screen which now lists the
    various different snapshots that are available.

11. Click and highlight the snapshot you want to use. In this example,
    we are going to select the new version called **Windows 10 Gold
    Image - UPDATE V3**.

12. This is shown in the following screenshot:

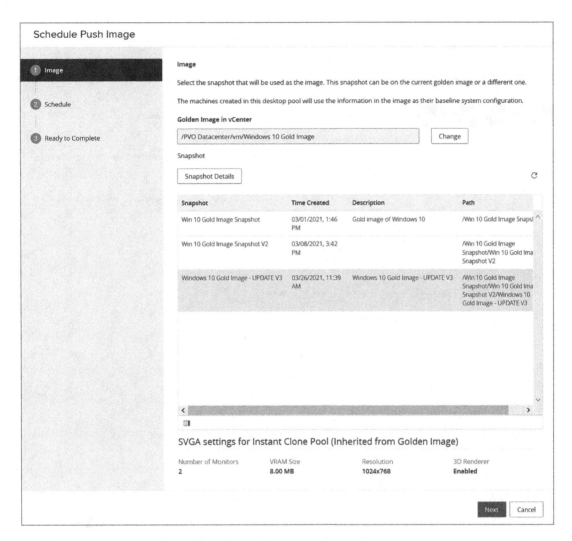

Figure 6-136. *Selecting the snapshot*

13. Click **Next** to continue.

14. You will now see the second configuration step for **Schedule**.

On this configuration screen, you can configure when the update is going to be implemented and how it will affect your end users.

15.   The configuration screen is shown in the following:

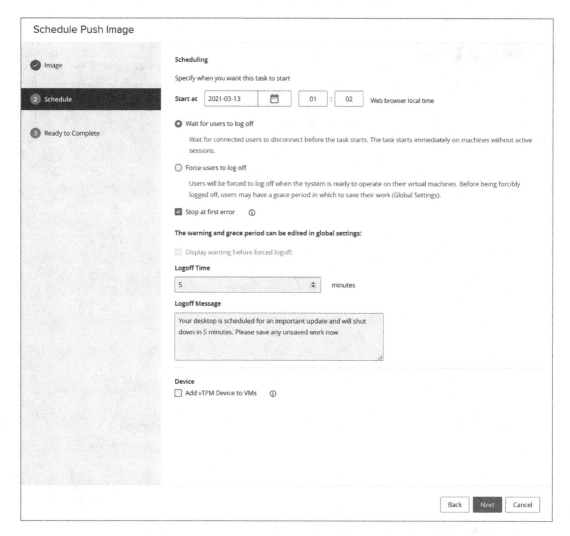

Figure 6-137. *Configuring the update schedule*

16.   The first option is to configure when the update will run, so in
the **Start at** boxes, enter the date and time of when you want to
update the image.

You then have two options to configure what happens to the end
users when the update starts.

The first option, selected by clicking the radio button, is **Wait for users to log off**.

Selecting this option means that the image update will only start when the end user logs off, even if the scheduled time is reached. Any machines that are already built and do not currently have end users connected to them when the scheduled time is reached will update immediately.

The second option is **Force users to log off**. Selecting this option means that end users will forcibly be logged off when the scheduled time is reached. If you have configured a grace period for a forced logoff in the global settings, then this policy still applies.

Next is the **Stop at first error** check box. Enabling this option means that if there is an error when provisioning the new image, then provisioning will stop. You will not be able to change this option if you have already set the Stop provisioning on error setting.

Finally, you can configure the warning message that gets displayed to end users when being forcibly logged off, along with the grace period. As we have this already configured in the global settings, then you would need to edit the settings there.

The last option is to **Add vTPM Device to VMs** to the virtual desktop machines in the pool.

17. Now click the **Next** button once you have configured the options.

18. You will see the **Ready to Complete** screen as shown in the following screenshot:

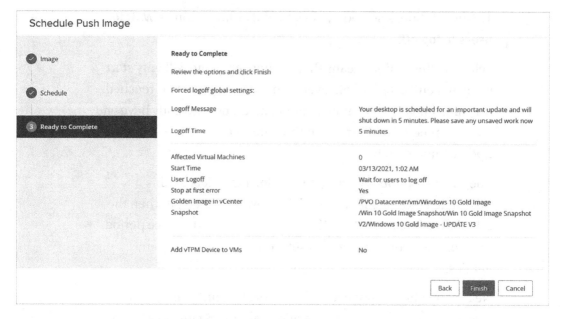

Figure 6-138. *Ready to complete screen*

19.   Once you are happy with the configuration, click **Finish**.

In the next section, we are going to look at how to update the image for a Full Clone desktop pool.

Updating the Full Clone Desktop Pool Image

We start at the same point, and that is the updated virtual desktop machine gold image. However, this time we are going to create a new template of the updated image using the Clone to Template feature in the vSphere Client. You can then edit the desktop pool.

To do this, complete the steps described:

1.   From the Horizon Console, navigate to and expand the **Inventory** option from the left-hand navigation pane, and then click **Desktops**.

2.   You will see the following screenshot:

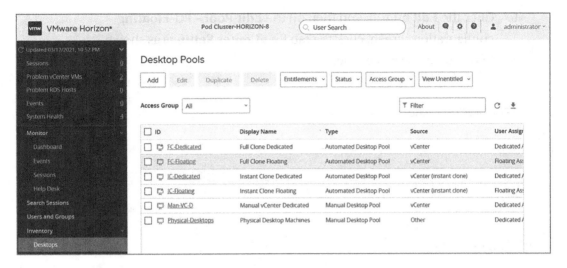

Figure 6-139. *Select the desktop pool to update*

3. From the list of desktop pools shown, click the link for the desktop pool you want to edit and add the new image to.

4. In this example, we are going to click the link to the **FC-Floating** desktop pool.

5. You will now see the **FC-Floating** desktop pool as shown:

Figure 6-140. *Desktop pool configuration screen*

6. Click the **Edit** button, and then on the **Edit Pool – FC-Floating** configuration screen, click the tab for **vCenter Settings** as shown in the following screenshot:

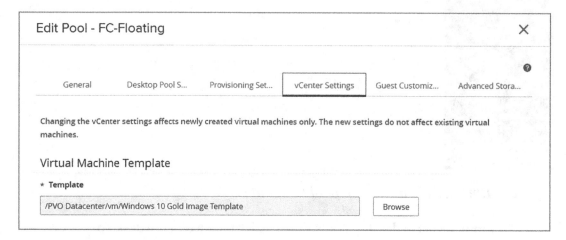

Figure 6-141. *Editing the desktop pool configuration*

7. In the **Template** box, click the **Browse** button. You will see the **Select template** screen as shown:

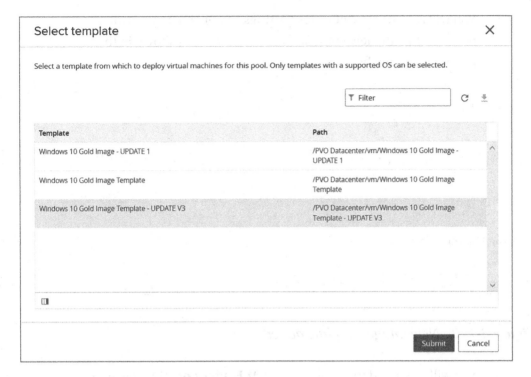

Figure 6-142. *Select the new image template*

8. From the list of templates shown, select the new template you want to use as the updated image. In this example, we created a new template for the updated gold image called **Windows 10 Gold Image Template - UPDATE V3**.

9. Click the **Submit** button.

10. You will return to the **vCenter Settings** screen where you will now see that the new template has been added as shown in the following screenshot:

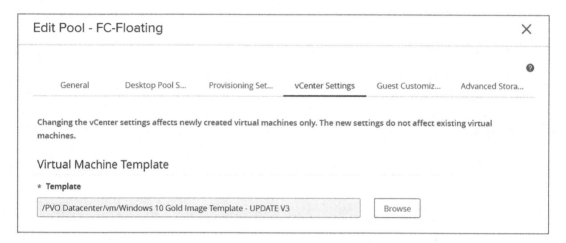

Figure 6-143. *New image template added*

11. You will also need to configure the **VM Folder Location**, **Host or Cluster**, **Resource Pool**, and **Datastores**.

You have now successfully updated the desktop pool to use the new Windows 10 Gold Image template.

Summary

In this chapter, we have given you a comprehensive introduction to desktop pools and how to create and configure them. As a reminder, a desktop pool is a group of several virtual desktop machines that all have the same configuration attributes, such as the same CPU and memory, and share the same gold image build.

We discussed the different types of desktop pools, from automated to manual, and briefly touched on RDS pools. We also discussed how the virtual desktop machines in the desktop pool are created, using either Instant Clones or Full Clones, and how they are assigned to end users, with either a floating (non-persistent) assignment or a dedicated (persistent) assignment.

With each option, we demonstrated, using a test lab environment and actual screenshots, the steps required to build each type of desktop pool.

In the next chapter, we are going to look at how to optimize the end-user experience.

## CHAPTER 7

Managing Horizon with Active Directory GPOs

We have already completed one optimization task, and that was to optimize the desktop operating system running on the virtual desktop machine, configuring the virtual hardware and drivers to enable it to deliver the performance required from a virtual desktop machine.

The next optimization task to complete is to optimize and configure how the end user interacts with their virtual desktop machine. By this we mean configuring the features such as whether or not end users can attach USB devices, cut and paste between their virtual desktop machine and their end point device, and how the display protocol behaves, to name just a few.

These optimization configurations are all managed and deployed using standard Active Directory Group Policy Objects (GPOs), and in this chapter, the first of three chapters covering this subject, we are going to deploy the pre-built templates and then walk through each configuration option and show you how to deliver virtual desktop machines customized for both your environment and your end users. In this particular chapter, we are going to start by configuring the core Active Directory components.

Active Directory Configuration

As we just highlighted in the introduction to this chapter, the features and configurations available to an end user when using their virtual desktop machine are all controlled and managed using standard Active Directory Group Policies.

These policy options, delivered as pre-built ADMX templates, are used to configure features such as controlling how the graphics experience is delivered or whether or not the end user can cut and paste between their end point client device and their virtual desktop machine.

© Peter von Oven 2022
P. von Oven, *Mastering VMware Horizon 8*, https://doi.org/10.1007/978-1-4842-7261-9_7

The pre-built ADMX templates can be downloaded along with the rest of the Horizon software and are compressed into a zip file called **VMware-Horizon-Extras-Bundle-2012-8.1.0-17349995** as shown in the following screenshot:

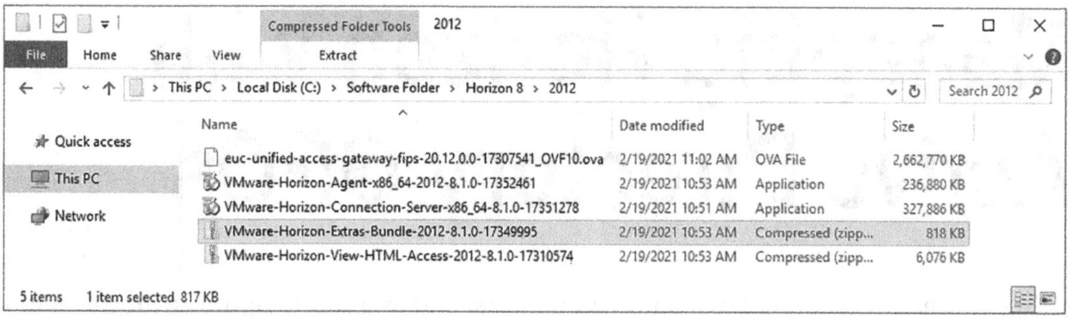

Figure 7-1. *Horizon Extras Bundle ZIP file*

Unzip the Horizon Extras Bundle file into a folder that is accessible by the domain controller. In this example, we have used the Horizon 8 folder in the Software Folder on the file server itself. Once extracted, you will see the 18 Administrative Template (ADMX) files, as shown in the following screenshot:

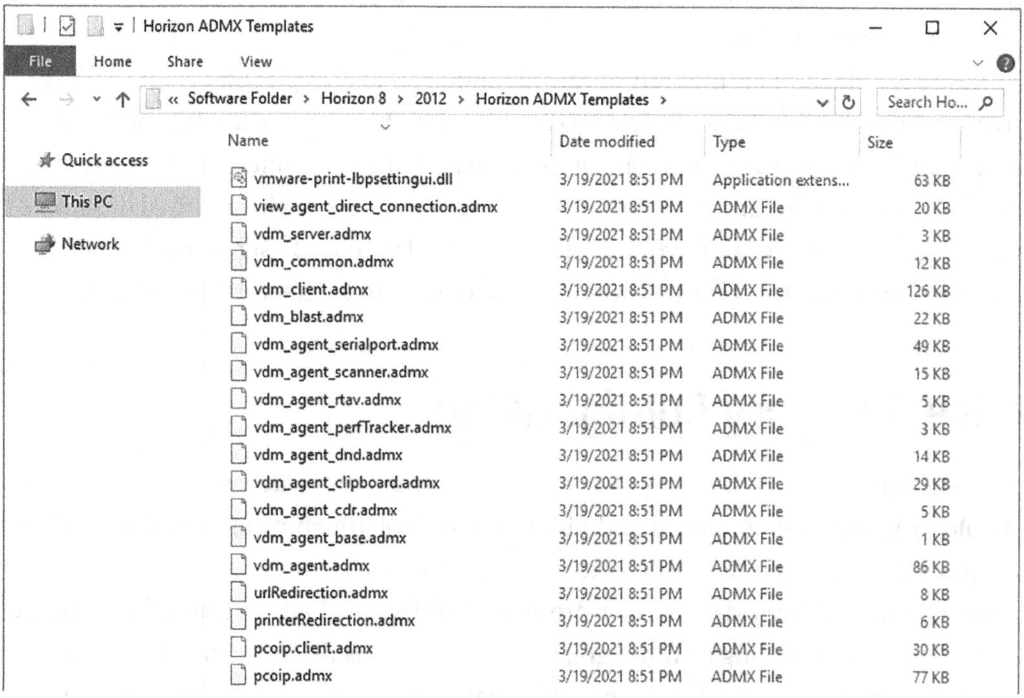

Figure 7-2. *Horizon Extras Bundle ZIP file extracted*

The next step is to add the unzipped files to the relevant folders on the domain controller.

Adding the Horizon ADMX Templates

Adding the pre-built ADMX templates to AD is just a case of copying the template files into the correct location on the domain controller.

There are two types of files to copy, the ADMX file which defines the group policy settings and the ADML which contains the language to be used with the ADMX file. Each file type has its unique folder on the domain controller, and so you need to copy these into the corresponding locations by following the steps described:

1. Open Windows Explorer, and navigate to the location of where you have unzipped the ADMX files.

2. Now open a second Windows Explorer and navigate to the folder **C:\Windows\PolicyDefinitions**.

3. Copy the Horizon ADMX files from their current location into the C:\Windows\PolicyDefinitions folder as shown in the following screenshot:

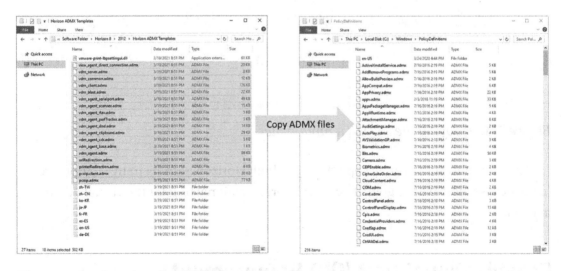

Figure 7-3. *Copying the ADMX template files*

The next step is to copy the ADML files for your chosen language. In this example, we are using **en_US** for the US English language. To copy these files, follow the steps described:

1. Open Windows Explorer, and navigate to the location of where you have unzipped the ADML files. This will be a sub-folder called en-US in the same folder as the ADMX templates.

2. Now open a second Windows Explorer and navigate to the folder **C:\Windows\PolicyDefinitions\en-US**.

3. Copy the Horizon ADML files from their current location into the C:\Windows\PolicyDefinitions\en-US folder as shown in the following screenshot:

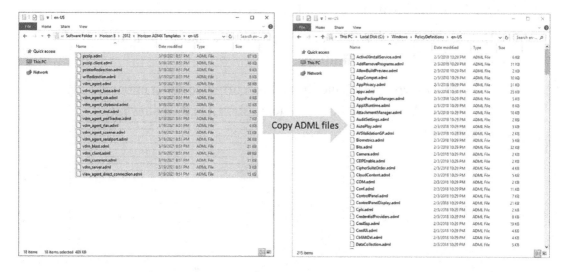

Figure 7-4. *Copying the ADML template files*

You have now successfully copied the pre-built Horizon administrative templates. In the next section, we are going to create an organizational unit for the virtual desktop machines.

Organizational Unit (OU) Requirements

In this section, we are going to create an organizational unit (OU) in which the virtual desktop machines are going to reside.

It's best practice to configure a separate OU for virtual desktop machines. This enables you to manage the virtual desktop machines independently to ensure only policies that relate specifically to virtual desktop machines get applied. Applying physical desktop policies to virtual desktop machines could potentially cause performance issues. The same applies to configuring virtual desktop–based policies on physical desktops.

Depending on how you configure your AD environment, you could create a single OU for all virtual desktop machines, with sub-OUs for different use cases, or you could configure different OUs on a departmental basis. This deployment model could be useful if you have different use cases that required different policies.

For example, if you had a use case where the end users are using high-end graphics, you could create an OU for those users, such as an OU called Engineering. You could then create a policy and apply it to the Engineering OU where that policy is configured to deliver a richer graphical experience rather than a standard user who didn't need that capability.

Another example could be for external end users where the policy would need to be configured specifically to address bandwidth limitations and what to do on slower connections.

In the example lab, we are going to create a single OU and call it Horizon Virtual Desktops, following the steps described:

1. Open a console to the desktop of the domain controller.

2. Click the **Start** menu button and then expand the option for **Windows Administrative Tools**, and then select Active Directory Users and Computers as shown in the following:

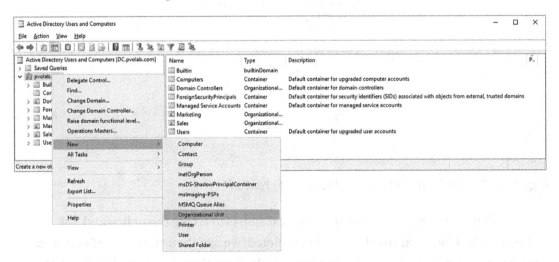

Figure 7-5. *Creating a new OU for Horizon desktops*

3. You will now see the **New Object - Organizational Unit** dialog box
    as shown in the following screenshot:

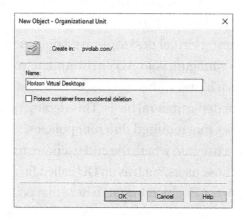

Figure 7-6. *Creating a new OU for Horizon desktops*

4. In the **Name** box, type in the name for this OU. In this example,
    this is **Horizon Virtual Desktops**.

5. Click **OK**. You will now return to the **Active Directory Users and
    Computers** screen showing the new OU.

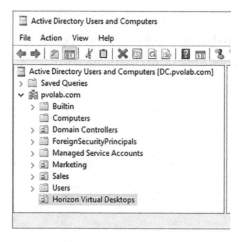

Figure 7-7. *Horizon Virtual Desktops OU created*

Now that the OU has been created, the next step is to create the policy and link it
to the new OU. Once that step has been completed, we can then start to configure and
apply the Horizon-specific policies to virtual desktop machines that reside in the OU.

Configuring Horizon Group Policy Objects (GPOs)

The next step is to create and configure group policy objects and link them to the Horizon Virtual Desktops OU that we created in the previous section.

In this example, we are going to create a group policy object and call it **Horizon Virtual Desktop Policies**. To configure the GPO, follow the steps:

1. Press the **Windows Key** and **R** to launch a **Run** dialog box as shown in the following screenshot:

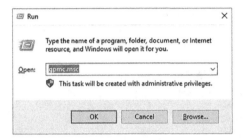

Figure 7-8. *Launching the Group Policy Manager*

2. In the **Open** box, type in **gpmc.msc** and then click **OK**.

3. You will now see the **Group Policy Management** screen as shown in the following screenshot:

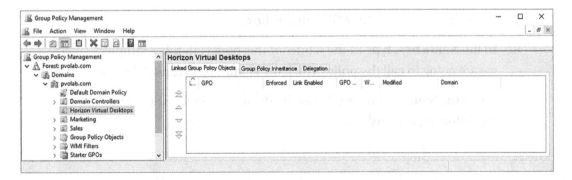

Figure 7-9. *Group Policy Management screen*

4. Expand the **Forest:pvolab.com** entry from the tree view on the left-hand side and then continue expanding the **Domains** and then **pvolab.com**.

453

5. Now click the **Horizon Virtual Desktops** OU that we created previously as we are going to create our policies and apply them to this OU.

6. Right-click, and from the contextual menu, click the option for **Create a GPO in this domain, and Link it here...** as shown in the following screenshot:

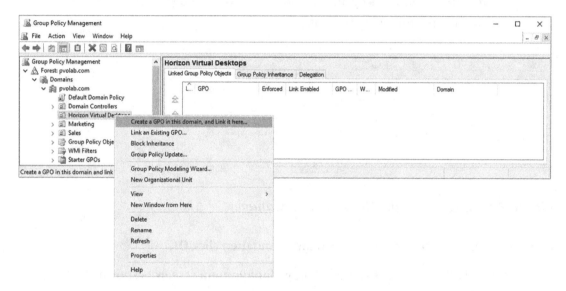

Figure 7-10. *Creating a new GPO for the Horizon Virtual Desktops OU*

7. You will now see the **New GPO** dialog box.

8. In the **Name** box, type in the name for this policy. In this example, we are going to call the policy **Horizon Virtual Desktops Policies**.

9. Leave the **Source Starter GPO** as the default setting as shown in the following screenshot:

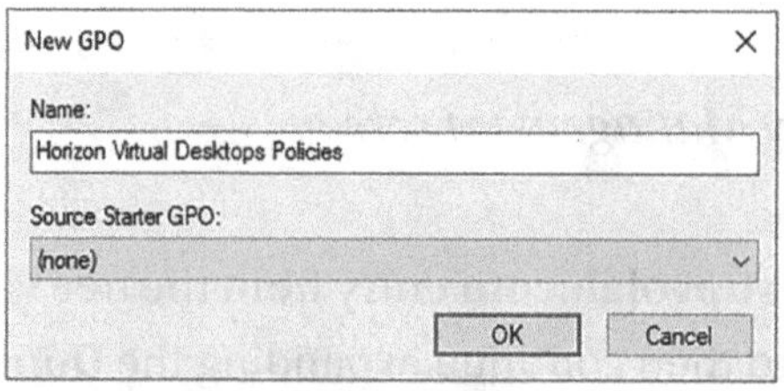

Figure 7-11. *Entering a name for the new GPO*

10. Click **OK**.

11. You will return to the Group Policy Management screen that now shows the policy that you just created, as shown in the following screenshot:

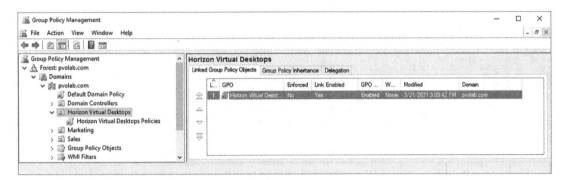

Figure 7-12. *New GPO successfully created*

You have now successfully added a GPO for configuring the virtual desktop machines, for the OU that those machines will be part of. We will configure the policies themselves later in this chapter, but before we do there is one other task we need to complete in setting up policies. That task is to configure the loopback policy.

Configuring the Loopback Policy

When delivering virtual desktop machines with a floating end-user assignment, that is, the scenario where multiple users have access to the same virtual desktop machine, then you will need to configure the loopback policy option.

If an end user makes configuration changes to a virtual desktop machine, as that virtual desktop machine is shared between multiple users, then they will get those changes too.

This is where the loopback processing feature comes in, particularly important if the virtual desktop machines are going to be used in a kiosk environment.

This only really applies to Full Clone virtual desktop machines as with Instant Clones the virtual desktop is deleted at logoff, and the next end user to log in will receive a brand-new machine.

To configure loopback mode, follow the steps described:

1. Press the **Windows Key** and **R** to launch a **Run** dialog box.

2. In the **Open** box, type in **gpmc.msc** and then click **OK**.

3. You will see the **Group Policy Management** screen as shown:

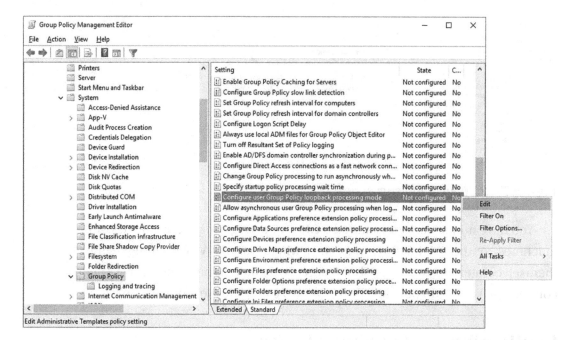

Figure 7-13. *Editing the loopback policy*

4. From the Group Policy Management Editor screen, under the
    Computer Configuration section, expand the folders for **Policies**,
    Administrative Templates: Policy definitions, and then **System**.

5. Highlight **Group Policy**.

6. You will now see the associated policy options listed in the
    right window pane, showing the policy settings and their status,
    whether they are configured or not.

7. Scroll down the page until you see the **Configure user Group
    Policy loopback processing mode** setting.

8. Click to select the setting and then right-click.

9. From the contextual menu, click **Edit**.

10. You will see the **Configure user Group Policy loopback processing mode** configuration screen, as shown in the following screenshot:

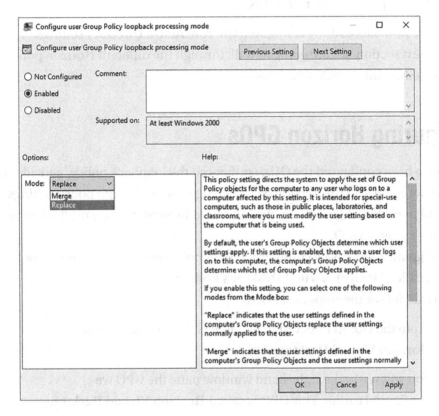

Figure 7-14. *Editing the loopback policy*

11. Click the radio button for **Enabled**.

12. Now select the loopback **Mode**. This configures how the loopback policy will be applied.

13. Click the drop-down menu and select the option for **Replace**. The Replace option means the end-user policy is applied, which is associated with the computer, and any other end user–based policies are ignored.

The other option is for **Merge**. The Merge option means that both the end-user and the computer policies are applied. If there is a conflict in the policies being merged, then the computer policy will be applied.

14. Click **Apply** and then click **OK**.

You have now successfully configured the core Active Directory settings.

In the next section, we are going to walk through the different Horizon policy settings that we added via the ADMX templates.

Configuring Horizon GPOs

Now that we have configured the OUs, configured the loopback policy, and added the ADMX templates, in this section we are going to walk through policy settings and understand how to configure them, the options, and what they are used for, by adding them to our example GPO.

We are going to do this by configuring these policy options in the group policy object we created called **Horizon Virtual Desktops Policies**.

To do this, follow the steps described:

1. From the Group Policy Management screen, click and select the **Horizon Virtual Desktops** OU.

2. You will see in the right-hand window pane the GPO we configured earlier. This GPO is called **Horizon Virtual Desktops Policies**.

3. Right-click the GPO, and from the contextual menu, click **Edit**.

4.   This is shown in the following screenshot:

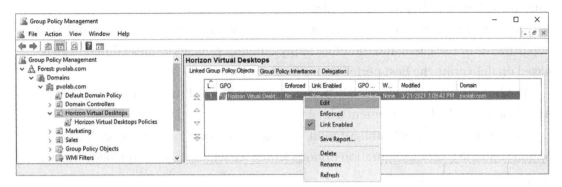

Figure 7-15. *Editing the GPO policy settings*

5.   You will now see the **Group Policy Management Editor**.

6.   Click the **Computer Configuration** section, and expand the folders for **Policies** and then **Administrative Templates** as shown in the following screenshot:

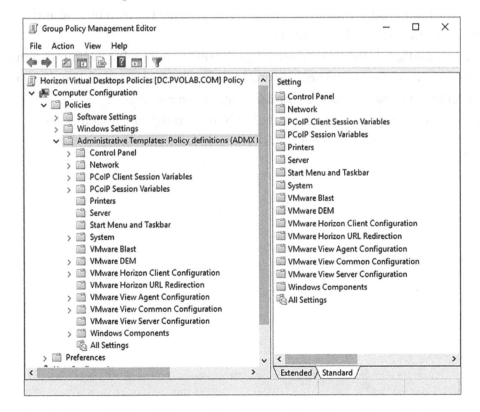

Figure 7-16. *Group Policy Management Editor showing policy settings*

In this example, we are going to add all the available policies to the same GPO to show the different policy settings available.

As we have discussed previously, you could create different OUs to reflect different departments or use cases and therefore apply different policies to these different OUs based on delivering the best performance for that chosen use case.

The best practice is to do exactly that as it will make any future policy troubleshooting and management a lot easier.

As with any other GPO configuration, you have both the Computer Configuration options and the User Configuration options which we will discuss in the following two chapters.

Summary

In this chapter, we have looked at the first stage of configuring Active Directory to manage the end-user experience.

We started the chapter by discussing how to prepare AD with Horizon-specific policies and administrative templates, by downloading the Horizon Bundle and extracting the pre-built ADMX templates.

Next, we configured the OUs for creating the policies to provide the foundation from which to define how the virtual desktop machine's desktop sessions and application sessions behave to deliver the best end-user experience possible.

In the next chapter, we are going to look at how to configure the Computer Configuration policies to manage the end-user environment.

## CHAPTER 8

Horizon Computer GPO Settings

In the previous chapter, we looked at the first stage of setting up the Horizon GPO settings by importing the GPO settings into Active Directory in readiness for creating policies to manage the end-user experience.

The next task to complete is to start configuring how the end user interacts with their virtual desktop machine. By this we mean configuring the features such as whether or not end users can attach USB devices, cut and paste between their virtual desktop machine and their end point device, and how the display protocol behaves, to name just a few.

In this chapter, we are going to take a closer look at the pre-built policy templates, for computer-based configurations, and then walk through each policy configuration setting and show you how to manage virtual desktop machines using these policies.

Computer Configuration GPO Settings

In this section, we are going to walk through the GPO policy settings that are based on the computer configuration. We will start with the PCoIP Client Session Variables policy settings.

461

© Peter von Oven 2022
P. von Oven, *Mastering VMware Horizon 8*, https://doi.org/10.1007/978-1-4842-7261-9_8

PCoIP Client Session Variables

In this section, we are going to look at the first set of GPO policy settings. These are the PCoIP Client Session Variables as shown in the following:

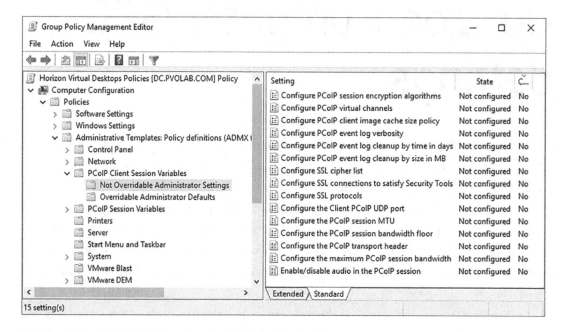

***Figure 8-1.** PCoIP Client Session Variables policies*

These policies are then subdivided into Not Overridable Administrator Settings and Overridable Administrator Settings. We are going to start with the Not Overridable Administrator Settings.

Not Overridable Administrator Settings

The Not Overridable Administrator Settings folder contains settings that specify the default settings for the PCoIP session that the administrator is unable to override. You will find these settings in the registry under the following:

`HKLM\Software\Policies\Teradici\PCoIP\pcoip_admin`

Click the **Not Overridable Administrator Settings** folder, and then in the **Setting** pane, you will see all the different configurable policy settings you can configure for this GPO.

We are now going to take a look at each of these settings in turn.

Configure PCoIP session encryption algorithms

To configure this policy, double-click the **Configure PCoIP session encryption algorithms** policy setting. You will see the following screenshot:

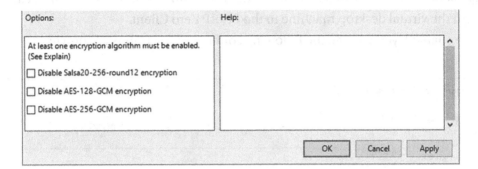

Figure 8-2. *Configure PCoIP session encryption algorithms policy setting*

Click the **Enabled** button to enable the policy and to apply it.

This policy setting, which applies to the Horizon Agent and the Horizon Client, is used to control the encryption algorithms that are advertised by the PCoIP endpoint during session negotiation. Checking one of the three boxes for the different encryption algorithm types listed will disable that encryption algorithm. However, with the policy enabled, you must have at least one encryption algorithm selected which is negotiated with the session.

If you enable FIPS140-2 approved mode, then the option for Disable AES-128-GCM encryption will be overridden if both AES-128-GCM encryption and AES-256-GCM encryption are disabled.

When the Configure SSL Connections policy is either disabled or has not been configured, then both the Salsa20-256-round12 and AES-128-GCM algorithms can be negotiated by the endpoint.

If endpoints are configured to support all of the three listed algorithms in this policy setting, and the connection does not use a Security Gateway, the SALSA20 algorithm will be negotiated and used instead.

However, if the connection uses a Security Gateway, then SALSA20 is automatically disabled, and AES128 will be negotiated and used instead. Finally, if the endpoints or the Security Gateway disables SALSA20 and AES128, then AES256 will be negotiated and used instead.

Configure PCoIP virtual channel

A virtual channel within the PCoIP session is designed to send encrypted data between servers and client endpoints during an active PCoIP session. For example, the Imprivata OneSign solution uses a virtual channel within the PCoIP session to send smart card data from the virtual desktop machine to the PCoIP Zero Client.

Once enabled, you will see the following configuration options as shown:

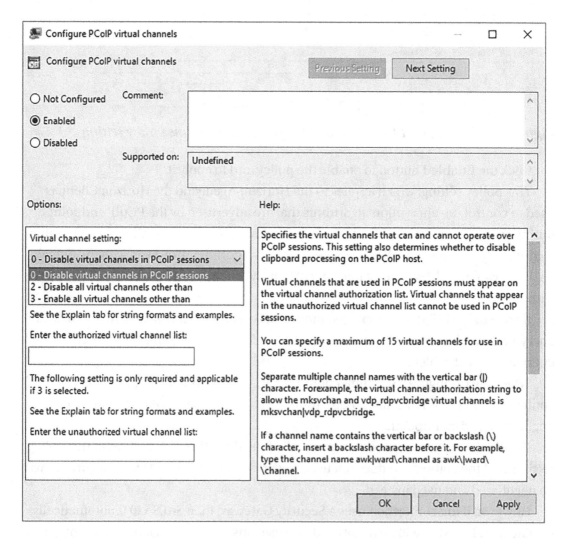

Figure 8-3. *Configure PCoIP virtual channels policy setting*

This policy setting is used to specify which virtual channels can or cannot be used during a PCoIP session. It is also used for determining whether or not clipboard processing is disabled on the PCoIP host. There are three configuration options:

- **0 – Disable virtual channels in PCoIP session**: This disables all virtual channels.

- **2 – Disable all virtual channels other than**: This option disables all virtual channels with the exception of those that you list in the box below.

- **3 – Enable all virtual channels other than**: This option enables all virtual channels with the exception of those that you list in the box below.

Any virtual channels that you want to use during a PCoIP session must appear on the virtual channel authorization list. If a virtual channel is listed in the unauthorized virtual channel list, then that means it cannot be used during the PCoIP session.

In total, you can configure a maximum of 15 virtual channels in any one PCoIP session.

If you need to configure multiple channel names, then they will need to be separated with a vertical bar | character. Should the channel name already contain a vertical bar, or a backslash, then you will need to insert a backslash character before it.

If you enable this policy setting and the authorized virtual channel list doesn't contain any virtual channels, then they are all disallowed. On the flip side, if the unauthorized virtual channel list is empty, then all virtual channels will be allowed.

The virtual channels settings apply to both the Horizon Agent and the Horizon Client, and as such they must be enabled on both the Horizon Agent and the Horizon Client in order for them to be used.

The default policy setting is to allow all virtual channels, including clipboard processing.

Configure PCoIP client image cache size policy

The Configure PCoIP client image cache size policy is used to control the size of the PCoIP client image cache. PCoIP works by caching the images on the client which is used to reduce the amount of data that needs to be retransmitted.

By default, with this policy setting either not configured or disabled, then PCoIP will use a default client image cache of 250 MB.

If you enable this policy setting, you can configure a client image cache size ranging from a minimum size of 50 MB up to a maximum size of 1024 MB.

If you just enable this policy without configuring a value, then it will just configure this policy with the default setting of 250 MB. The policy is shown in the following screenshot:

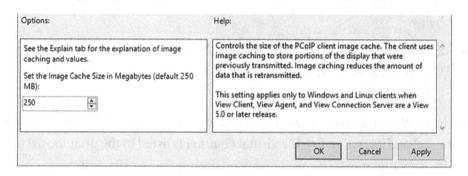

Figure 8-4. *Configure PCoIP client image cache size policy setting*

Configure PCoIP event log verbosity

The Configure PCoIP event log verbosity policy enables how the PCoIP event log verbosity is configured; this is how much detail is captured in the event log.

If you enable this policy and set the value to 0, then this captures the least amount of information in the log file. If you set the policy to 3, then this is the most detailed amount of information that will be captured in the event log.

The default setting is 2 and is the setting that is applied when this policy is either disabled or not configured.

Any setting changes that you make to this policy are applied immediately. The configuration screen is shown in the following screenshot:

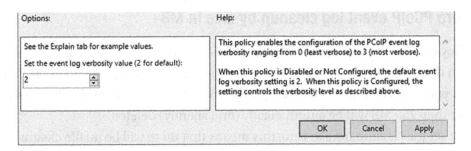

Figure 8-5. Configure PCoIP event log verbosity policy setting

Configure PCoIP event log cleanup by time in days

This policy enables the configuration of the PCoIP event log cleanup.

When this policy is configured, this setting controls the log file cleanup by time in days. For example, with a nonzero setting of ten entered into the configuration box, any log files older than ten days will be automatically (and silently) deleted.

If you set this policy to **Disabled** or **Not Configured**, the default event log cleanup time is set to seven days.

The log file cleanup is performed when the session starts, and any changes you make to the configuration will not get applied until the next session.

You will see the configuration box for Configure PCoIP event log cleanup by time in days in the following screenshot:

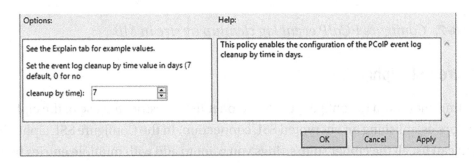

Figure 8-6. Configure PCoIP event log cleanup by time in days

The next policy setting is the **Configure PCoIP event log cleanup by size in MB** policy.

Configure PCoIP event log cleanup by size in MB

This policy enables the configuration of the PCoIP event log cleanup by size.

When this policy is configured, you can set the log file cleanup by size in MB, for example, you could configure this setting to be 250 MB, which means that log files that are larger than 250 MB will be automatically (and silently) deleted.

If you set the cleanup time to zero, this means that there will be no file cleanup taking place. If you leave this policy set to **Disabled** or **Not Configured**, then the default event log cleanup by size in MB is set to the default 100 MB.

As with the cleanup by time setting, the log file cleanup is performed when the session starts, and any changes you make to the policy configuration will not get applied until the next session.

You will see the configuration box for Configure PCoIP event log cleanup by size in the following screenshot:

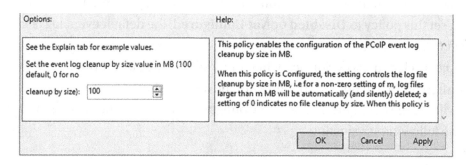

Figure 8-7. *Configure PCoIP event log cleanup by size in MB*

Configure SSL cipher list

This setting allows you to configure the SSL cipher list to restrict the use of the cipher suite before establishing an encrypted SSL connection. In the Configure SSL cipher list box, you can list all the cipher suite strings you want to add with multiple entries being separated by colons. The default value is

```
ECDHE-RSA-AES256-GCM-SHA384:AES256-SHA256:AES256-SHA:ECDHE-RSA-AES128-
GCM-SHA256:AES128-SHA256:AES128-SHA:@STRENGTH
```

When you configure an SSL cipher list, then the check box for **Enforce AES-256 or stronger ciphers for SSL connection negotiation** will be automatically checked on the **Configure SSL connections to satisfy Security Tools** policy settings which we will cover next.

You need to apply this setting to the PCoIP server and the PCoIP client at the same time.

You will see the configuration box for Configure PCoIP event log cleanup by size in the following screenshot:

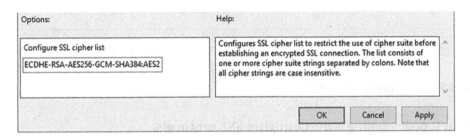

Figure 8-8. *Configure SSL cipher list*

Configure SSL connections to satisfy Security Tools

This policy setting allows you to specify how SSL session negotiation connections are established.

In order to satisfy port scanners, you need to enable this policy setting and configure the following:

1. Store the certificate for the Certificate Authority that signed any Server certificate to be used with PCoIP in the Trusted Root certificate store.

2. Next, configure the agent to load certificates only from the certificate store. If the personal store for the local machine is used, then leave the CA certificate store name unchanged with the value **ROOT**, unless you have configured a different store location in the previous step.

If this policy is set to Disabled or Not Configured, then the endpoint device will use Certification Authority certificates from the machine account's **MY** store and Certification Authority certificates from the **ROOT** store.

This is shown in the following screenshot:

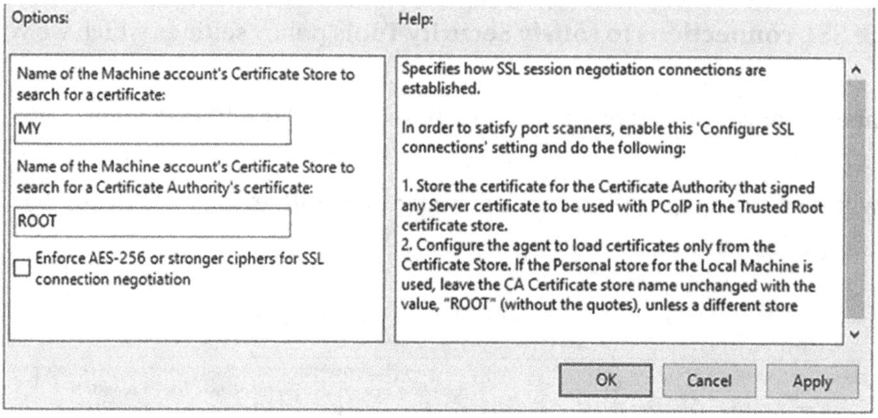

Figure 8-9.   *Configure SSL cipher list*

The next policy setting is the **Configure SSL protocols**.

Configure SSL protocols

This policy allows you to configure the SSL protocol to restrict certain protocols from being used to establish an encrypted SSL connection. To configure this setting, you would enter the protocols in the Configure SSL protocols box, with multiple entries being separated using colons.

By enabling the policy, you will see that the default setting is to restrict the following three protocols: **TLS1.0:TLS1.1:TLS1.2**. This will disable these protocols for both the Horizon Agent and the Horizon Client.

The following screenshot shows the configuration settings for **Configure SSL protocols**:

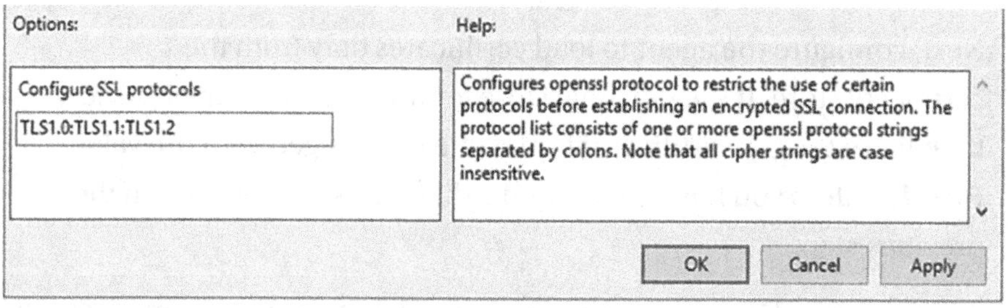

Figure 8-10.   *Configure SSL cipher list*

The next policy setting is the **Configure the Client PCoIP UDP port**.

Configure the Client PCoIP UDP port

Configuring this setting, which applies to the client device, allows you to specify the UDP client port that is used by software-based PCoIP clients. You can configure this manually or automatically which allows the OS on the client to determine the port setting.

To configure this setting manually, click the Enabled button, and then in the Choose a UDP port box, enter a UDP port, and then in the Set the size of the retry port range, enter the range which determines how many additional ports to try if the base port is unavailable. The range can span from the base port to the sum of the base port and port range with the default settings set to 50002 for the base port with a port range of 64.

You also have the option to check the Allow OS to automatically determine UDP port. This means that the OS running on the client will ignore any settings that you have manually entered and instead will choose a UDP port automatically avoiding those that may already be in use.

The following screenshot shows the **Configure the Client PCoIP UDP port** settings:

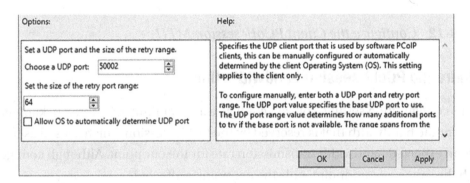

Figure 8-11. *Configure the Client PCoIP UDP port*

Configure the PCoIP session MTU

With this configuration setting, you can specify the Maximum Transmission Unit or MTU size for the UDP packets in a PCoIP session. This setting only applies to UDP, and TCP will use the standard MTU discovery method.

The MTU size also includes the IP and UDP packet headers. You can set a maximum size of 1500 bytes and a minimum size of 500 bytes, with the default setting being 1200 bytes.

In most environments, this setting will not need to be changed; however, if you have a network environment that could cause PCoIP packet fragmentation, then you can configure the MTU size to prevent this.

When you enable this setting, it will apply to both the Connection Server and the Horizon Client; however, if you have different MTU settings between the two, then the lowest setting will be the one that gets applied.

If you configure this setting to be **Disabled**, or set it to **Not Configured**, then the client will use the default value.

The following screenshot shows the **Configure the PCoIP session MTU**:

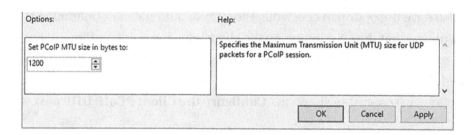

Figure 8-12. *Configure the Client PCoIP session MTU*

Configure the PCoIP session bandwidth floor

With this configuration setting, you can configure a lower limit, measured in kilobits per second, for the bandwidth that is reserved by the PCoIP session which is used as the minimum expected bandwidth transmission rate for the endpoint. Although configured on both the server and endpoint, only the endpoint is affected.

If you use this setting for reserving bandwidth for an endpoint device, then when additional bandwidth becomes available, the session does not need to wait to make use of the improved bandwidth.

When configuring this setting, you need to ensure that you do not oversubscribe the total reserved bandwidth for all endpoints as well as ensuring that the sum of bandwidth floors for all the connections in your configuration does not exceed the network capability.

By default, the session bandwidth floor has no minimum reserved and is set to zero. If you set this to **Disabled** or **Not Configured**, then no minimum bandwidth will be reserved with any changes you make taking effect straight away, even when an active session is running.

The following shows the **Configure the PCoIP session bandwidth floor**:

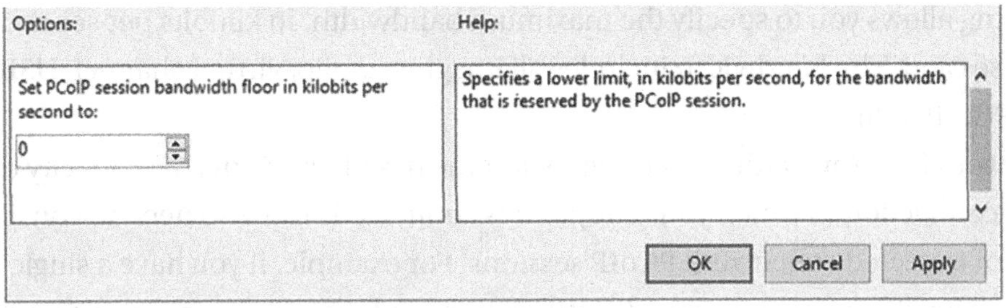

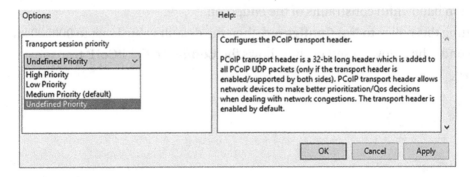

Figure 8-13. *Configure the Client PCoIP session MTU*

Configure the PCoIP transport header

The PCoIP transport header is a 32-bit long header which gets added to all PCoIP UDP packets if the transport header is enabled and is supported by both the Horizon Agent and the Horizon Client. Its job is to allow network devices to make better prioritization or quality of service (QoS) decisions when the network becomes congested.

The transport session priority determines the PCoIP session priority that gets reported in the PCoIP Transport Header. That allows devices to make better prioritization or QoS decisions based on the specified transport session priority. The transport session priority value is negotiated by the PCoIP agent and client. If the agent has specified a transport session priority value, which can be configured as either high, medium, or low, then the session uses the session priority that the agent specifies.

If only the client has specified a transport session priority, then the session will use that. If you don't specify a transport session priority, then the session will use the medium session priority as the configured setting.

The following screenshot shows the **Configure the PCoIP transport header**:

Figure 8-14. *Configure the PCoIP transport header*

Configure the maximum PCoIP session bandwidth

This setting allows you to specify the maximum bandwidth, in kilobits per second, for a PCoIP session. The bandwidth includes all imaging, audio, virtual channel, USB, and control PCoIP traffic.

You would use this setting to configure a value based on the overall capacity of the network connection to which your endpoint is connected. You also need to consider the number of expected concurrent PCoIP sessions. For example, if you have a single VDI user which would count as a single PCoIP session, and that session connects over a 10 Mbit/s Internet connection, then you would set this value to 10 Mbit. You should also consider setting this to 10% lower than the actual value in order to leave some headroom for other network traffic.

If you are going to be using multiple concurrent PCoIP sessions that share a link, such as multiple VDI users or an RDSH published sessions, then you would adjust this setting accordingly, but you need to bear in mind that this will restrict the maximum bandwidth for each of the active sessions.

By configuring this policy, it stops the agent from attempting to transmit at a higher rate than the capacity of the link. If you tried to exceed this capacity, then the result would be excessive packet loss which would ultimately lead to a poor end-user experience.

This value is symmetric. That means that it forces both the client and the agent to use the lower of the two values set. For example, if you set a 10 Mbit/s maximum bandwidth, then this will force the agent to transmit at a lower rate, even though you have configured the setting on the client. If the two endpoints have different settings, then it is the lower value that is used.

If you set the policy to **Disabled**, then there will be no bandwidth restraints placed on the endpoint. If you set the policy to **Enabled**, then you have the option to enter the maximum bandwidth constraints of the endpoint.

Setting this policy to **Not Configured**, then the default value is set to 900000 kilobits per second. The following screenshot shows the **Configure the PCoIP transport header**:

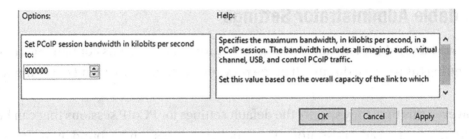

Figure 8-15. *Configure the maximum PCoIP session bandwidth*

The final PCoIP Client Session policy setting is the **Enable/disable audio in the PCoIP session** setting.

Enable/disable audio in the PCoIP session

The **Enable/disable audio in the PCoIP session setting** allows you to configure whether or not audio is enabled during the PCoIP session. For this to work, then both endpoints must have audio enabled.

This setting is simply enabled or disabled, so when set to **Enabled**, then PCoIP audio is allowed. When set to **Disabled**, the PCoIP audio is disabled. If you set the policy to Not Configured, then audio is enabled by default.

The following screenshot shows the **Enable/disable audio in the PCoIP session** setting:

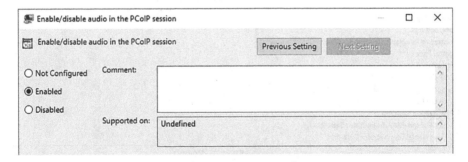

Figure 8-16. *Configure the enable/disable audio in the PCoIP session*

In the next section, we are going to touch on the PCoIP Client Session Variables that are able to be overridden by administrator settings.

Overridable Administrator Settings

The **Overridable Administrator Settings** for PCoIP Client Sessions contain the same policy settings as we have discussed in the previous section, so we won't cover them again.

However, this time they specify the default settings for PCoIP sessions that can be overridden by system administrators. These policy settings can be found in the following registry location:

HKLM\Software\Policies\Teradici\PCoIP\pcoip_admin_defaults

In the next section, we are going to look at the PCoIP Session Variables policy settings.

PCoIP Session Variables

In this section, we are going to look at the next set of GPO policy settings. These policy settings are for configuring the **PCoIP Session Variables** and are shown in the following screenshot:

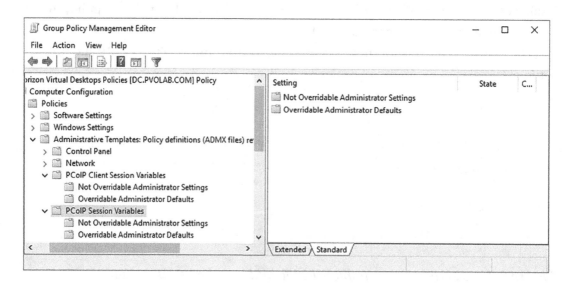

Figure 8-17. *Configuring PCoIP Session Variables*

As with the PCoIP Client Session Variables, these policies are subdivided into **Not Overridable Administrator Settings** and **Overridable Administrator Settings**. We are going to start with the Not Overridable Administrator Settings.

Not Overridable Administrator Settings

To configure the **Not Overridable Administrator Settings** for the PCoIP Session Variables, click the **PCoIP Session Variables** folder to expand it.

Now click the **Not Overridable Administrator Settings** folder.

In the **Setting** pane on the right-hand side, you will now see all the different configurable policy settings you can configure for this GPO.

You will see that a number of these policy settings are exactly the same as those that we have already described in the previous section for PCoIP Client Session Variables, so we won't cover those again, and you can refer back to these for the details. Instead, we will just detail those policy settings that are different.

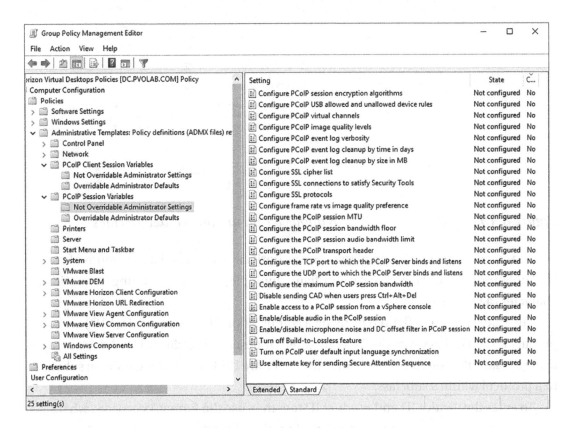

Figure 8-18. *Configuring Not Overridable Admin Settings*

We will start with the **Configure PCoIP USB allowed and unallowed device rules** setting.

Configure PCoIP USB allowed and unallowed device rules

This policy setting allows you to specify which USB devices are authorized and which are not authorized for PCoIP sessions that use a zero client running Teradici firmware. The default setting is that all devices are allowed and none are disallowed.

Any USB devices that are used during a PCoIP session need to appear in the USB authorization table, and any USB devices that appear in the USB unauthorization table cannot be used during a PCoIP session.

The configuration settings are shown in the following screenshot:

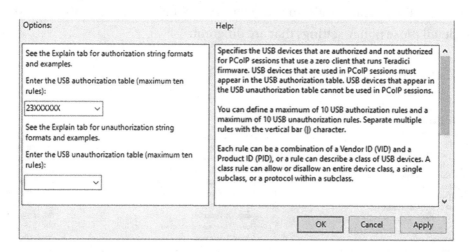

Figure 8-19. *Configure PCoIP USB allowed and unallowed device rules*

You can define a maximum of ten USB authorization rules and a maximum of ten USB unauthorization rules. You can configure multiple rules by separating them with a | character (a vertical bar).

The rules can be configured by using a combination of the vendor ID (VID) and a product ID (PID). They can also be configured by describing a class of USB devices. By using a class rule, you can allow or disallow an entire USB device class, a single subclass, or a protocol within a subclass.

To enter the vendor ID and product ID together, use the format 1xxxxyyyy, where xxxx is the VID in hexadecimal and yyyy is the PID in hexadecimal. For example, the rule to authorize or block a device with VID 0x1a2b and PID 0x3c4d is 11a2b3c4d.

For class rules, use one of the following formats:

- Allow all USB devices – Format: 23XXXXXX

- Allow USB device with a specific class ID – Format: 22classXXXX

- Allow a specific subclass – Format: 21class-subclassXX

- Allow a specific protocol – Format: 20class-subclass-protocol

For example, the USB authorization string to allow USB HID devices such as a mouse or keyboard (class ID 0x03) and webcams (class ID 0x0e) is 2203XXXX|220eXXXX. The USB unauthorization string to disallow USB Mass Storage devices (class ID 0x08) is 2208XXXX.

If you leave the authorization string empty, then no USB devices are authorized. Similarly, leaving the unauthorized string empty means that no USB devices are banned.

Settings only apply to the server and only when the server is in a session with a zero client that is running Teradici firmware. The device use is negotiated between the endpoints.

Configure PCoIP image quality levels

This setting allows you to control how PCoIP renders images when the network is congested. There are a number of settings for this particular policy.

The **Set the Minimum Image Quality value** setting can be used to balance the image quality and frame rate when you have limited bandwidth.

You can specify a value between 30 and 100, with the default value setting being 40. Setting a lower value allows for higher frame rates, but the trade-off will be a lower-quality display. A higher value will deliver a higher image quality, but the trade-off this time will be lower frame rates. When network bandwidth is not constrained, then PCoIP maintains maximum quality regardless of what values you configure for this setting.

The **Set the Maximum Initial Image Quality value** setting can be used to reduce the network bandwidth peaks that are required by PCoIP, by limiting the initial quality of the changed regions of the displayed image. You can specify a value between 30 and 100, with the default value being set to 80.

Configuring a lower value will reduce the image quality of any content changes and therefore decreases peak bandwidth requirements. If you set a higher value, then that increases the image quality of any content changes and also increases peak bandwidth requirements.

Unchanged regions of the image displayed will progressively build to a lossless quality, or perfect quality, regardless of what you set this value to. Configuring this to a value of 80 or less will deliver the best bandwidth utilization. The Minimum Image Quality value cannot exceed the Maximum Initial Image Quality value. The settings are shown in the following screenshot:

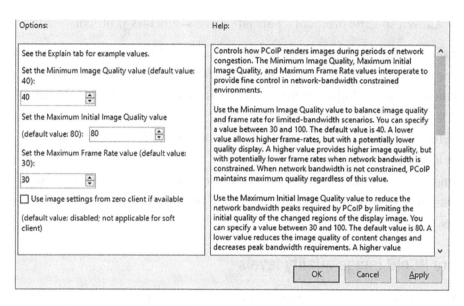

Figure 8-20. *Configure PCoIP image quality levels*

The **Set the Maximum Frame Rate value** is used to manage the average bandwidth consumed by each end user. It does this by limiting the number of screen updates per second. You can configure a value between 1 and 120 frames per second, with the default setting being 30 frames per second. A higher value can be set which will use more bandwidth but will provide less jitter and allow smoother transitions in changing images such as a video. A lower value, although consuming less bandwidth, will result in more jitter.

The next setting is the **Use image settings from zero client if available** when you want to use the Minimum Image Quality, Maximum Initial Image Quality, Maximum Frame Rate, and Disable Build to Lossless values from the client instead of the host. These settings only apply to the client and to Zero Client Firmware 3.5 and above.

You need to bear in mind that any image quality values apply to only the soft host and have no effect on a soft client.

If you set this configuration to **Disabled** or **Not Configured,** then this policy setting will use the default values, and any settings you change during a session would take effect immediately.

The next policy setting is the **Configure frame rate vs. image quality preference** setting.

Configure frame rate vs image quality preference

This setting allows you to configure the frame rate and image quality preference on a sliding scale between having a better frame rate and better image quality. You can choose the setting appropriate to your environment. The following shows the Configure frame rate vs. image quality preference setting:

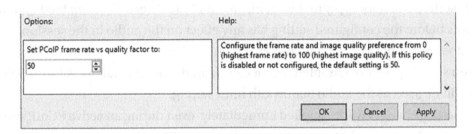

Figure 8-21. *Configure frame rate vs. image quality preference*

Enabling this policy allows you to configure the highest frame rate, which would mean setting the value to 0, and for the highest image quality, you would set the value to 100.

If this policy is **Disabled** or **Not Configured**, then the default setting is set in the middle and the value will be 50, balanced halfway between frame rate and image quality.

This setting will be applied immediately and during an active session.

The next policy setting is the **Configure the PCoIP session audio bandwidth limit** setting.

Configure the PCoIP session audio bandwidth limit

An audio compression algorithm is used to deliver the best audio experience possible based on the state of the current network bandwidth and utilization. If you set a bandwidth limit, using this policy setting, then this reduces the audio quality by changing the compression algorithm until the bandwidth limit you set is reached.

If the minimum audio quality cannot be delivered within the bandwidth limit that you set, then audio for the session is disabled.

Depending on what you configure for this setting, it will determine the quality of audio delivered. For example, if you configure this policy to be Enabled, you can configure the following example values:

- **1600 kbit/s or more**: Uncompressed high-quality stereo audio

- **450 kbit/s and higher**: Stereo, high-quality, compressed audio

- **50 kbit/s to 450 kbit/s**: Somewhere between FM radio and phone call quality

- **50 kbit/s and below**: Poor or no audio playback

This setting will only apply to the agent, and audio will need to be enabled on both endpoints before the configured setting has any effect on the audio in the session. This setting does not apply to audio that is delivered using USB.

If you set this policy to Disabled or Not Configured, then the default value of 500 kbits/s will be used as the audio bandwidth limit setting.

Any setting changes will be applied immediately, even during an active PCoIP session.

The following screenshot shows the **Configure the PCoIP session audio bandwidth limit** setting:

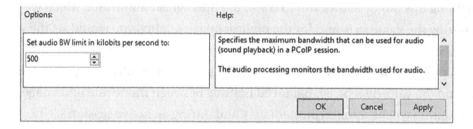

Figure 8-22. *Configure frame rate vs. image quality preference*

Configure the TCP port to which the PCoIP Server binds and listens

This policy allows you to configure the TCP agent port that is bound to by software-based PCoIP hosts.

The TCP port value you configure in the **Choose a TCP port to listen and bind to** box, when this policy is enabled, allows you to choose the base TCP port that the agent will attempt to bind to.

Then, in the **Set the size of the return port range** box, you can enter a range value that determines how many additional ports to try should the base port be unavailable. The port range setting must be between 0 and 10. So if you use the base port of 4172, the default PCoIP port, and the port range is set to 10, then the TCP port range is set between 4172 and 4182. This setting only applies to the agent.

The following screenshot shows the **Configure the TCP port to which the PCoIP Server binds and listens** setting:

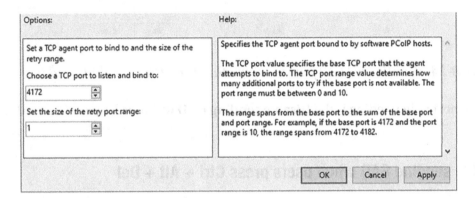

Figure 8-23. *Configure TCP port to which the PCoIP Server binds and listens*

Configure the UDP port to which the PCoIP Server binds and listens

Similar to the previous policy that configured the TCP port for PCoIP, this policy configures the same settings but now for the UDP port that is bound to by software-based PCoIP hosts.

The UDP port value you configure in the **Choose a UDP port to listen and bind to** box, when this policy is enabled, allows you to choose the base UDP port that the agent will attempt to bind to.

Then, in the **Set the size of the return port range** box, you can enter a range value that determines how many additional ports to try should the base port be unavailable. The port range setting must be between 0 and 10. So if you use the base port of 4172, the default PCoIP port, and the port range is set to 10, then the UDP port range is set between 4172 and 4182. This setting only applies to the agent.

The following screenshot shows the **Configure the UDP port to which the PCoIP Server binds and listens** setting:

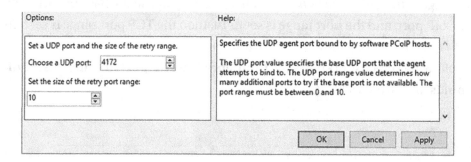

Figure 8-24. *Configure UDP port to which the PCoIP Server binds and listens*

The next policy setting is the **Disable sending CAD when users press Ctrl+Alt+Del** setting.

Disable sending CAD when users press Ctrl + Alt + Del

Enabling this policy means that end users will need to press Ctrl+Alt+Insert instead of pressing Ctrl+Alt+Del to send a Secure Attention Sequence (SAS) to the virtual desktop during a PCoIP session so that they can log in, log off, or lock their current session.

This setting is useful if end users become confused when they press Ctrl+Alt+Del to lock their endpoint device, and an SAS is sent to both the endpoint device and the virtual desktop machine.

This setting is for the agent only and has no effect on a client, and when the policy is either Disabled or Not Configured, the end user can press either Ctrl+Alt+Del or Ctrl+Alt+Insert to send an SAS to the desktop.

The following screenshot shows the **Disable sending CAD when users press Ctrl+Alt+Del** setting:

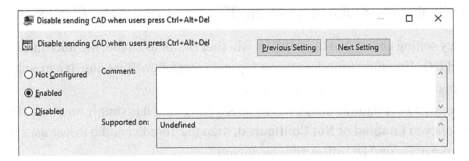

Figure 8-25. *Disable sending CAD when users press Ctrl+Alt+Del*

Enable access to a PCoIP session from a vSphere console

This policy allows you to configure whether or not to allow a vSphere Client console to display an active PCoIP session and send input to the desktop.

By default, when a client is attached using PCoIP, the vSphere Client console screen will be blank and the console cannot send any input. This setting is deliberate and is used as a security feature so that a rogue administrator has no access to the end user's desktop to view the screen or to provide input all the time the end user has an active session running.

If you configure this setting to be Disabled or Not Configured, then console access is denied. If you set this policy to Enabled, then the console has the ability to view the PCoIP session and console input is allowed.

The following screenshot shows the **Enable access to a PCoIP session from a vSphere console** setting:

The next policy setting is the **Enable/disable microphone noise and DC offset filter in PCoIP session** setting.

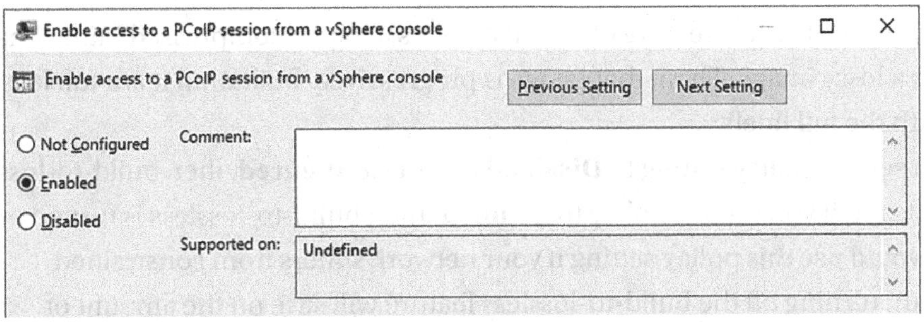

Figure 8-26. *Enable access to a PCoIP session from a vSphere console*

Enable/disable microphone noise an DC offset filter in PCoIP session

This policy setting allows you to configure whether or not to enable the microphone noise and DC offset filter for microphone input during a PCoIP session. It can only be applied to the agent and Teradici audio driver.

There are no configuration options for this setting, and it is simply on or off. If you set this policy to **Enabled** or **Not Configured,** then the Teradici audio driver uses the microphone noise and DC offset filter by default.

The following screenshot shows the **Enable/disable microphone noise and DC offset filter in PCoIP session** setting:

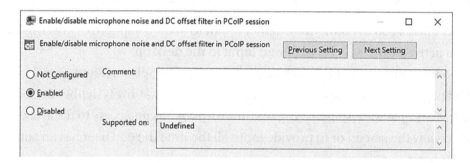

Figure 8-27. *Enable/disable microphone noise and DC offset filter in PCoIP session*

The next policy setting is the **Turn off Build-to-Lossless feature** setting.

Turn off Build-to-Lossless feature

This policy setting allows you to configure whether or not to turn the PCoIP build-to-lossless feature on or off. By default, build-to-lossless is enabled.

The build-to-lossless feature of PCoIP delivers a highly compressed initial image known as a lossy image. Then, that image is progressively built until it is a full lossless image with the full fidelity.

If you set this policy setting to **Disabled** or **Not Configured**, then build-to-lossless is turned off, and if you set this policy to **Enabled**, then build-to-lossless is turned on.

You would use this policy setting if your network suffers from constrained bandwidth; turning off the build-to-lossless feature will save on the amount of bandwidth required as the desktop image won't be built at full fidelity. Any setting changes you make to this policy will be applied immediately.

The following shows the **Turn off Build-to-Lossless feature** setting:

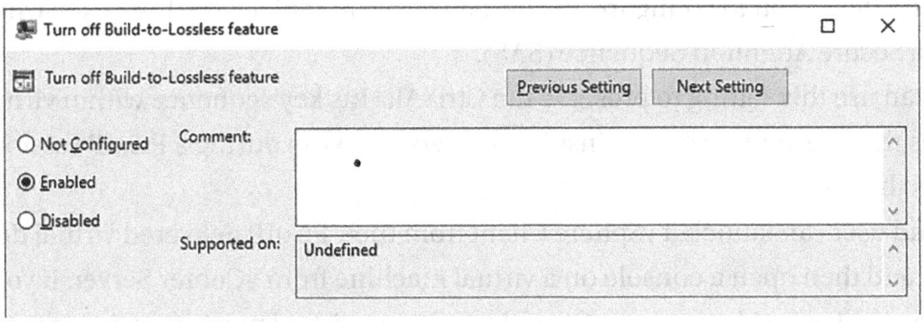

Figure 8-28. *Turn off Build-to-Lossless feature*

The next policy setting is the **Turn on PCoIP user default input language synchronization** setting.

Turn on PCoIP user default input language synchronization

This policy allows you to configure whether or not the default input language for the end user in the PCoIP session is synchronized with the default input language of the PCoIP client endpoint, and this only applies to the agent.

There are no configuration options for this setting, it is simply on or off. If set to **Enabled,** then synchronization is allowed, and if the policy is set to **Disabled** or **Not Configured**, synchronization is not allowed.

The following screenshot shows the **Turn on PCoIP user default input language synchronization** setting:

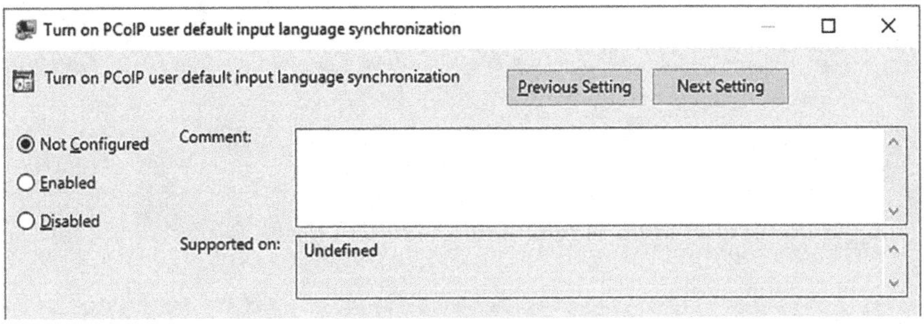

Figure 8-29. *Turn on PCoIP user default input language synchronization*

The final policy setting in this section is the **Use alternate key for sending Secure Attention Sequence** setting.

Use alternate key for sending Secure Attention Sequence

This policy allows you to configure an alternative key to replace the Insert key when sending a Secure Attention Sequence (SAS).

You can use this setting to preserve the Ctrl+Alt+Ins key sequence within virtual machines that are launched from inside a Horizon desktop during a PCoIP session. So how does that work?

An end user can launch a vSphere Client from their PCoIP delivered virtual desktop machine and then open a console on a virtual machine from vCenter Server. If you then press Ctrl+Alt+Ins inside the guest OS of that vCenter virtual machine, what is actually sent is Ctrl+Alt+Del. This setting allows you to configure Ctrl+Alt+X, where X is the alternate key press and the key you want to configure.

By enabling this setting, which applies only to the agent, you will then need to select what that alternate key press is from the list shown on the Sequence (SAS) drop-down menu. If you enable this setting, then you will have to select the alternative key press, and you cannot leave it blank.

If you set this policy to Disabled or Not Configured, then Ctrl+Alt+Ins will continue to be used.

The following screenshot shows the **Use alternate key for sending Secure Attention Sequence** setting:

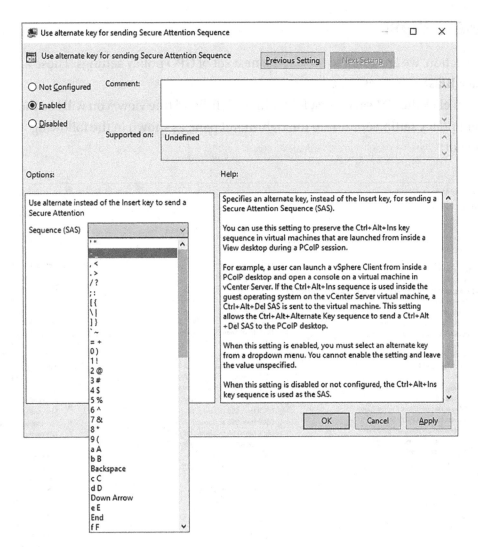

Figure 8-30. *Use alternate key for sending Secure Attention Sequence*

In the next section, we are going to look at the GPO policy settings that you can configure for the Blast protocol.

VMware Blast

In this section, we are going to look at the next set of GPO policy settings. These are the **VMware Blast** policy settings.

If you click the **VMware Blast** folder in the left-hand tree view, you will see the different policy setting options in the right-hand pane as shown in the following screenshot:

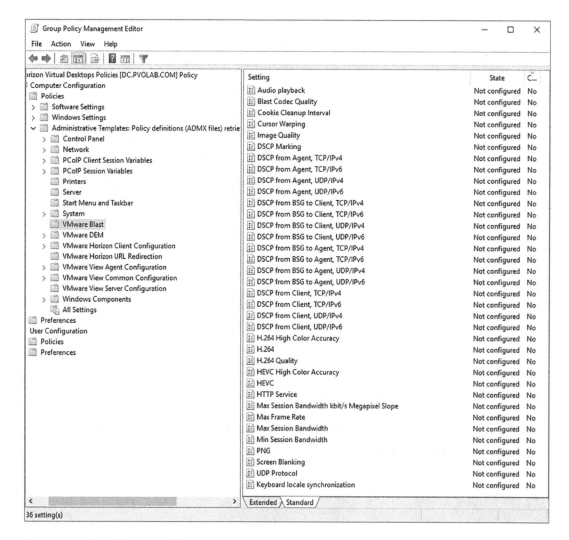

Figure 8-31. *VMware Blast policy settings*

Audio playback

This first policy allows you to configure audio playback.

There are no configuration options for this setting, and it is simply on or off. If you set this policy to **Enabled,** then audio playback is switched on, which is also the default setting.

The following screenshot shows the **Audio playback** setting:

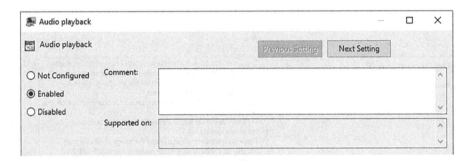

Figure 8-32. *Audio playback setting*

Blast Codec Quality

The **Blast Codec Quality** settings are used to control the quality of the image that gets displayed on the client device and is delivered by using Blast Codec compression. The settings are controlled by setting the Quantization Parameter or QP which in turn controls how much the resulting image is compressed. Note that these settings only apply to images and have no effect on text.

You can configure this using the following two settings. The first of these settings is the **Blast Codec Maximum QP** setting. This allows you to set the lower bound for quantization which will result in the best image quality.

The other setting is the **Blast Codec Minimum QP** setting. This allows you to set the upper bound for quantization which will result in the lowest image quality.

These QP settings occupy the range [1, 8] and map to a JPEG quality value in the range of [20, 88]. If you set either of these two settings to 0, then this will cause the setting to be overridden by the default behavior which is configured by the Low and High JPEG quality configuration settings.

The following screenshot shows the **Blast Codec Quality** setting:

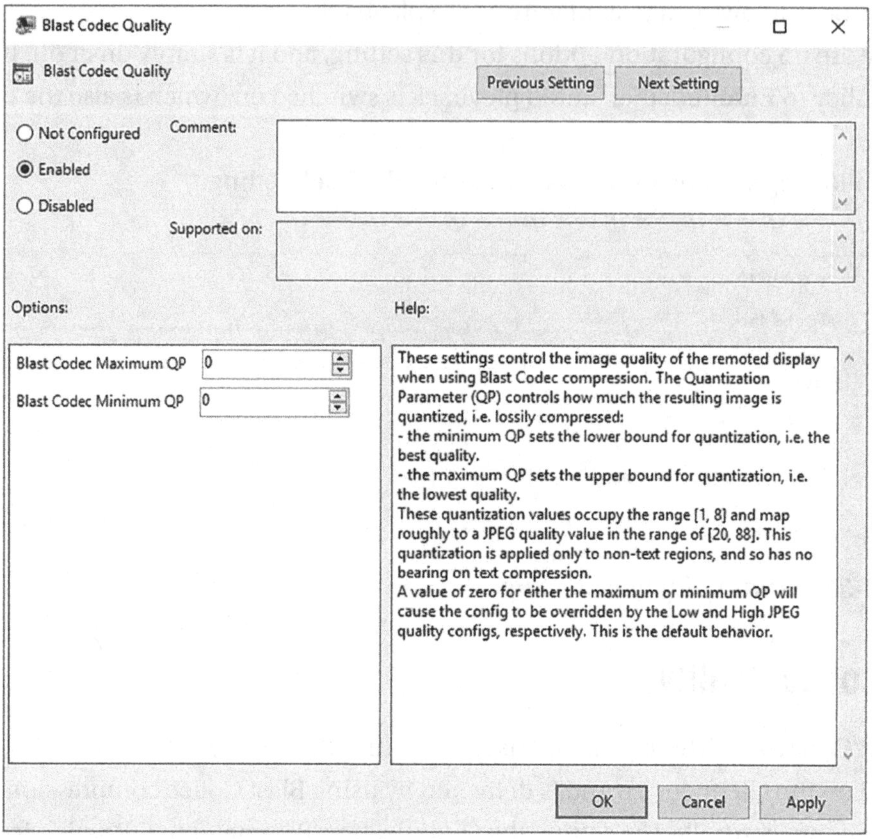

Figure 8-33. *Blast Codec Quality setting*

The next policy setting is the **Cookie Cleanup Interval** setting.

Cookie Cleanup Interval

This setting configures how often the cookie that is associated with a session is cleaned up in order to delete inactive sessions. The inactive session is cleaned up by removing its cookie.

To enable this policy, click the **Enabled** button, and then in the **Interval (ms)** box, enter the time interval in milliseconds for how often you want any inactive sessions to be cleaned up.

The following screenshot shows the **Cookie Cleanup Interval** setting:

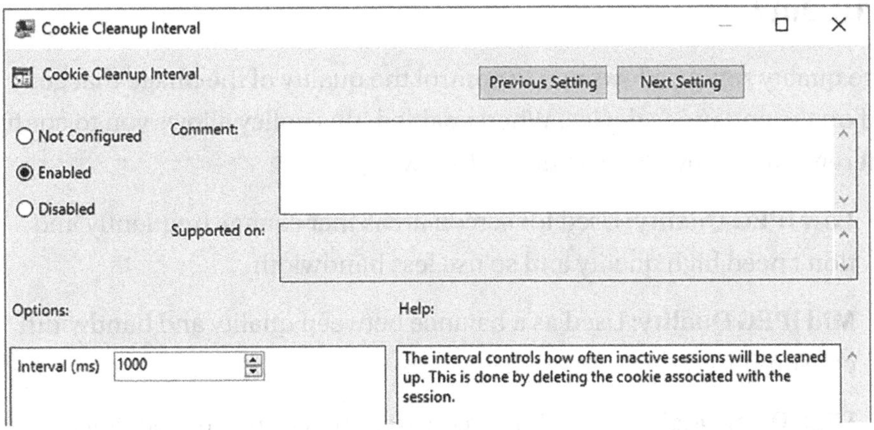

Figure 8-34. *Cookie Cleanup Interval setting*

The next policy setting is the **Cursor Warping** setting.

Cursor Warping

This setting configures the cursor warping feature. If you set this policy to Enabled, then this switches the mouse into absolute mode. This means that if the end user makes sudden quick mouse movements, then these movements will be detected on the virtual machine by the agent that will then reflect those movements on the client device by moving the cursor.

If this setting is Disabled or Not Configured, then any sudden movements of the mouse will be ignored by the client. This is also the default setting, to ignore the sudden movements.

The following screenshot shows the **Cursor Warping** setting:

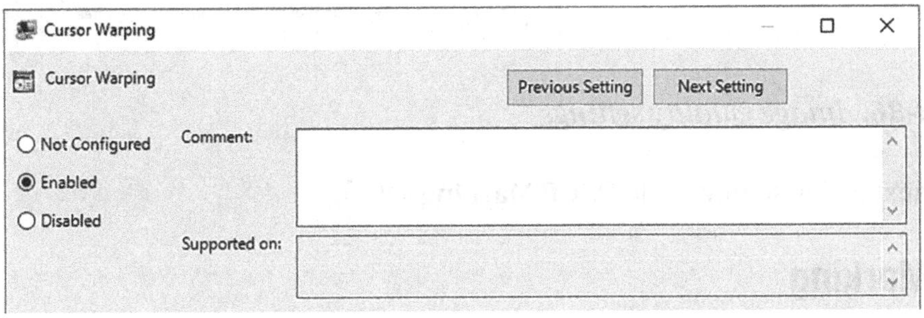

Figure 8-35. *Cursor Warping*

The next policy setting is the **Image Quality** setting.

Image Quality

The image quality setting allows you to control the quality of the image that gets displayed on the end user's device. When enabled, this policy allows you to configure three different profiles by configuring the following:

- **Low JPEG Quality**: Used for screen areas that change frequently and don't need high quality and so use less bandwidth

- **Mid JPEG Quality**: Used as a balance between quality and bandwidth consumption

- **High JPEG Quality**: Used for screen areas that don't change much, delivering higher quality but using more bandwidth

These settings are shown in the following screenshot:

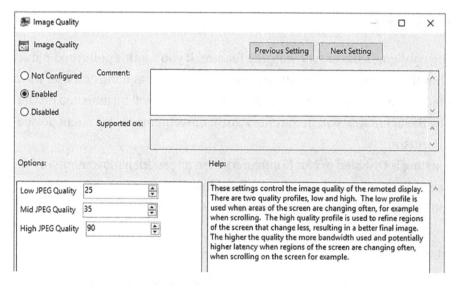

Figure 8-36. *Image Quality settings*

The next policy setting is the **DSCP Marking** setting.

DSCP Marking

Differentiated Services Code Point, or DSCP, enables you to classify and manage network traffic to deliver a quality of service, or QoS, across your network.

It works by using the 6-bit Differentiated Services, the DS field, in the IP header. This allows the packet to have a classification.

Differentiated Services is a networking architecture that specifies a simple and scalable way of classifying and managing network traffic to deliver QoS on the network.

The following table shows some of the configurable values:

	ToS Value (decimal)	DSCP Value (decimal)	TOS Byte (IPv4) / Traffic Class (IPv6)									
			DSCP						Flow Control			
			IP Precedence									
			b7	b6	b5	b4	b3	b2	b1	b0	PHB	Drop Probability
Best Effort	0	0	0	0	0	0	0	0	0	0	Default	
Class Selector (Backward Compatibility with IP Precedence)	32	8	0	0	0	0	0	0	0	0	CS1	
	64	16	0	1	1	0	0	0	0	0	CS2	
	96	24	0	1	0	0	0	0	0	0	CS3	
	128	32	1	0	1	0	0	0	0	0	CS4	
	160	40	1	0	0	0	0	0	0	0	CS5	
	192	48	1	1	1	0	0	0	0	0	CS6	
	224	56	1	1	0	0	0	0	0	0	CS7	
Assured Forwarding	40	10	0	0	1	0	1	0	0	0	AF11	Low
	48	12	0	0	1	1	0	0	0	0	AF12	Medium
	56	14	0	0	1	1	1	0	0	0	AF13	High
	72	18	0	1	0	0	1	0	0	0	AF21	Low
	80	20	0	1	0	1	0	0	0	0	AF22	Medium
	88	22	0	1	0	1	1	0	0	0	AF23	High
	104	26	0	1	1	0	1	0	0	0	AF31	Low
	112	28	0	1	1	1	0	0	0	0	AF32	Medium
	120	30	0	1	1	1	1	0	0	0	AF33	High
	136	34	1	0	0	0	1	0	0	0	AF41	Low
	144	36	1	0	0	1	0	0	0	0	AF42	Medium
	152	38	1	0	0	1	1	0	0	0	AF43	High
Expedited Forwarding	184	46	1	0	1	1	1	0	0	0	EF	

Figure 8-37. Differentiated Services Code Point values

To take advantage of this feature, you first switch it on by clicking the Enabled button as shown in the following screenshot:

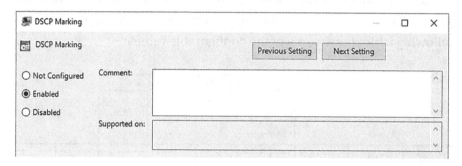

Figure 8-38. *DSCP Marking setting*

Once enabled, you can then configure the next set of policies to specify the DSCP values for network traffic sent by the Blast agent, the client, and the secure gateway.

If you set this policy to **Disabled** or **Not Configured**, then now DSCP marking will be used.

The next set of configuration settings allow you to configure the DSCP Markings for different scenarios, such as from the gateway to the client, or either TCP or UDP. We will start with the agent and using TCP over IPv4.

DSCP from Agent, TCP/IPv4

This setting, when enabled, allows you to configure a DSCP value for network traffic that is sent by the Blast Agent, using TCP over an IPv4 network.

The following screenshot shows the **DSCP from Agent, TCP/IPv4** setting:

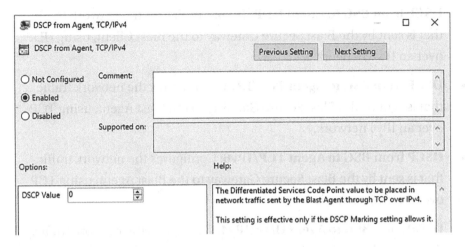

Figure 8-39. DSCP from Agent, TCP/IPv4

The remainder of the DSCP settings all have the same configuration option in that you configure the DSCP value on the settings screen, once you have enabled the policy.

Rather than show the same screenshot over again, we are going to list the different DSCP configuration scenarios and combinations:

- **DSCP from Agent, TCP/IPv6**: As with the previous policy setting, this configures the network traffic that is sent by the Blast Agent, using TCP over an IPv6 network.

- **DSCP from Agent, UDP/IPv4**: Configures the network traffic that is sent by the Blast Agent, using UDP over an IPv4 network.

- **DSCP from Agent, UDP/IPv6**: Configures the network traffic that is sent by the Blast Agent, using UDP over an IPv6 network.

- **DSCP from BSG to Client TCP/IPv4**: Configures the network traffic that is sent by the Blast Secure Gateway to the Blast Client, using TCP over an IPv4 network.

- **DSCP from BSG to Client TCP/IPv6**: Configures the network traffic that is sent by the Blast Secure Gateway to the Blast Client, using TCP over an IPv6 network.

- **DSCP from BSG to Client UDP/IPv4**: Configures the network traffic that is sent by the Blast Secure Gateway to the Blast Client, using UDP over an IPv4 network.

- **DSCP from BSG to Client UDP/IPv6**: Configures the network traffic that is sent by the Blast Secure Gateway to the Blast Client, using UDP over an IPv6 network.

- **DSCP from BSG to Agent TCP/IPv4**: Configures the network traffic that is sent by the Blast Secure Gateway to the Blast Agent, using TCP over an IPv4 network.

- **DSCP from BSG to Agent TCP/IPv6**: Configures the network traffic that is sent by the Blast Secure Gateway to the Blast Agent, using TCP over an IPv6 network.

- **DSCP from BSG to Agent UDP/IPv4**: Configures the network traffic that is sent by the Blast Secure Gateway to the Blast Agent, using UDP over an IPv4 network.

- **DSCP from BSG to Agent UDP/IPv6**: Configures the network traffic that is sent by the Blast Secure Gateway to the Blast Agent, using UDP over an IPv6 network.

- **DSCP from Client TCP/IPv4**: Configures the network traffic that is sent by the Blast Client using TCP over an IPv4 network.

- **DSCP from Client TCP/IPv6**: Configures the network traffic that is sent by the Blast Client using TCP over an IPv6 network.

- **DSCP from Client UDP/IPv4**: Configures the network traffic that is sent by the Blast Client using UDP over an IPv4 network.

- **DSCP from Client UDP/IPv6**: Configures the network traffic that is sent by the Blast Client using UDP over an IPv6 network.

The next policy setting is for H.264 High Color Accuracy.

H.264 High Color Accuracy

This policy enables you to increase the color accuracy by using the YUV 4:4:4 colorspace instead of the standard YUV 4:2:0 setting. Bear in mind that increasing the color accuracy could result in a drop in performance, especially when using high resolutions or multiple screens.

The policy setting is a simple on and off setting, and to switch on the feature, click the **Enabled** radio button as shown in the following screenshot:

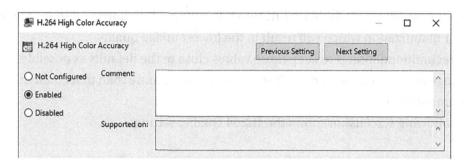

Figure 8-40. *High Color Accuracy*

H.264

The H.264 setting allows you to use H.264 encoding when set to **Enabled** or when set to **Not Configured**. If you set this policy to **Disabled,** then JPEG/PNG will be used for encoding. The following screenshot shows the **H.264** setting:

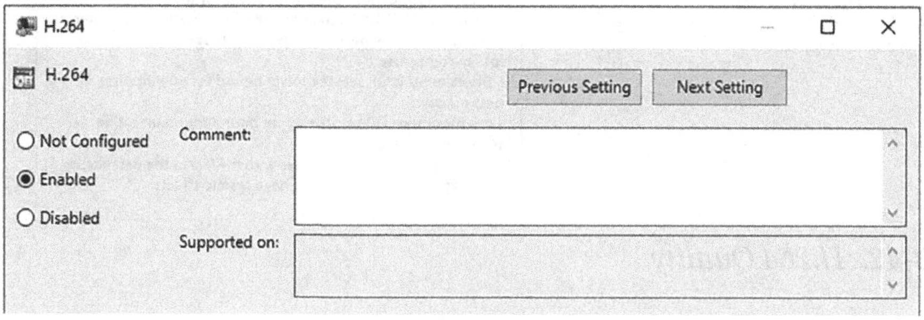

Figure 8-41. *H.264*

H.264 Quality

This setting allows you to control the quality of the image displayed on the client end point when using H.264 compression.

As with the Blast Codec Quality, these settings are controlled by setting the Quantization Parameter or QP which in turn controls how much the resulting image is compressed. Note that these settings only apply to images and have no effect on text.

You can configure this using the following two settings. The first of these settings is the **H.264 Maximum QP** setting. This allows you to set the lower bound for quantization which will result in the best image quality.

The other setting is the **H.264 Minimum QP** setting. This allows you to set the upper bound for quantization which will result in the lowest image quality.

The recommendation is to keep these values close to the defaults as possible and with a range of + or –5 of those default settings. Anything more than that could have a more dramatic effect.

The following screenshot shows the **H.264** Quality setting:

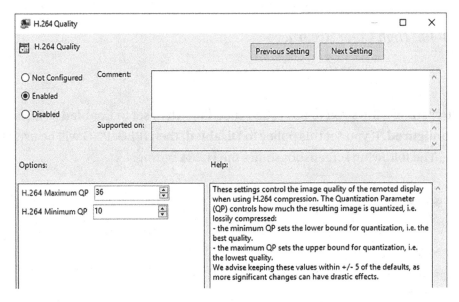

Figure 8-42. *H.264 Quality*

HEVC High Color Accuracy

This policy enables you to increase the color accuracy by using the YUV 4:4:4 colorspace instead of the standard YUV 4:2:0 setting when using High Efficiency Video Coding or HEVC. You will also need client hardware acceleration of HEVC 4:4:4 for this policy to work.

The policy setting is a simple on and off setting, and to switch on the feature, click the **Enabled** radio button as shown in the following screenshot.

The following screenshot shows the **HEVC High Color Accuracy** setting:

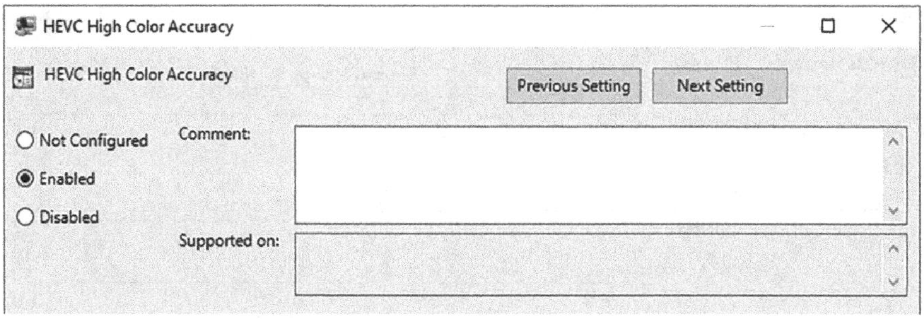

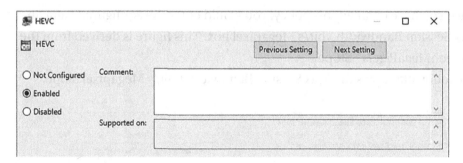

Figure 8-43. *HEVC High Color Accuracy*

HEVC

This setting simply enables HEVC encoding. By clicking **Enabled** or **Not Configured,** then you will switch this feature on, and HEVC encoding will be allowed for the remote desktop.

If this policy is **Disabled,** then JPEG/PNG will be used for encoding. The following screenshot shows the **HEVC** setting:

Figure 8-44. *HEVC policy setting*

HTTP Service

The **HTTP Service**, when set to **Enabled**, allows you to control the Blast HTTP service by configuring the port number that is used. You can enter the port in the Secured (HTTPS) port box. Remember that the port number needs to match the port configured on the firewall.

The following screenshot shows the **HTTP Service** setting:

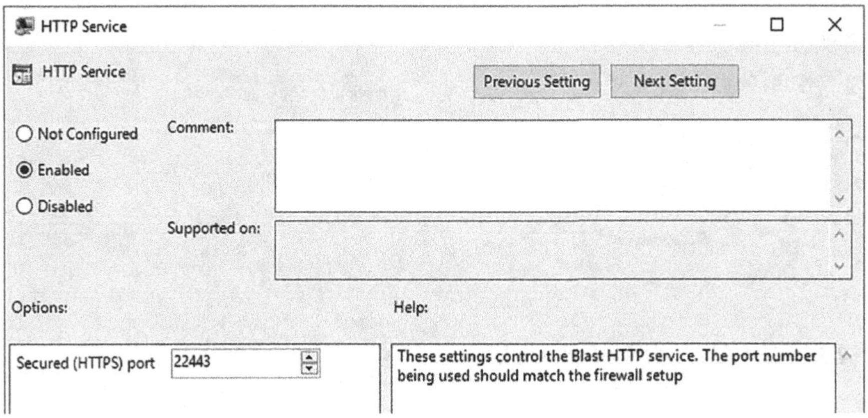

Figure 8-45. *HTTP Service*

The next setting is for **Max Session Bandwidth kbit/s Megapixel Slope**.

Max Session Bandwidth kbit/s Megapixel Slope

This setting allows you to specify the slope of the kbps per megapixel of the resolution of the remote screen.

Once you have enabled this policy, you would enter the configured value in the Max Session Bandwidth kbit/s Megapixel box. This figure is derived from the TotalScreenMegaPixels * Slope.

The following shows the Max Session Bandwidth kbit/s Megapixel Slope:

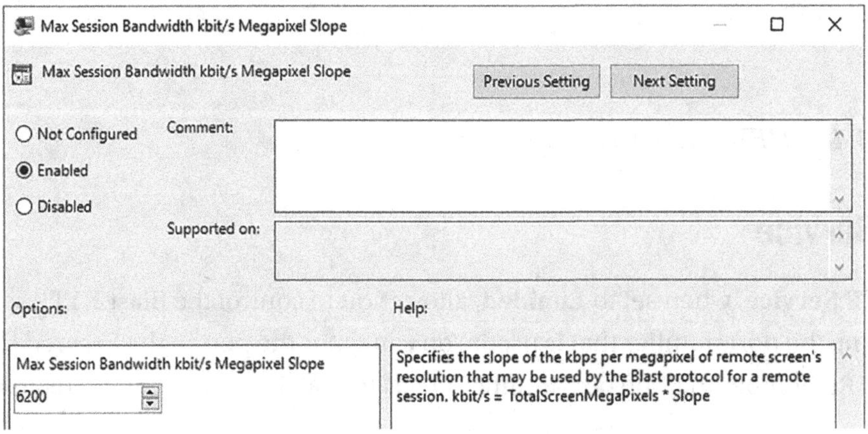

Figure 8-46. *Max Session Bandwidth kbit/s Megapixel Slope*

Max Frame Rate

The **Max Frame Rate** or frames per second setting is used to configure and manage the average bandwidth. This is done by enabling the policy and then in the Max Frame Rate box entering the value you want to set.

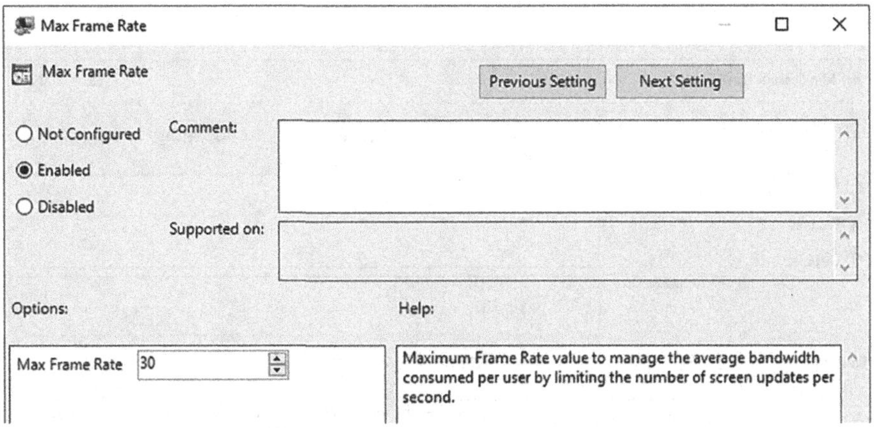

Figure 8-47. *Max Frame Rate*

Max Session Bandwidth

The **Max Session Bandwidth** setting is used to set the bandwidth for a Blast session. Note that bandwidth configured also includes anything else included in that session such as audio, USB, and any additional virtual channels that you may have configured.

Enter the new value in kbps in the **Max Session Bandwidth** box as shown:

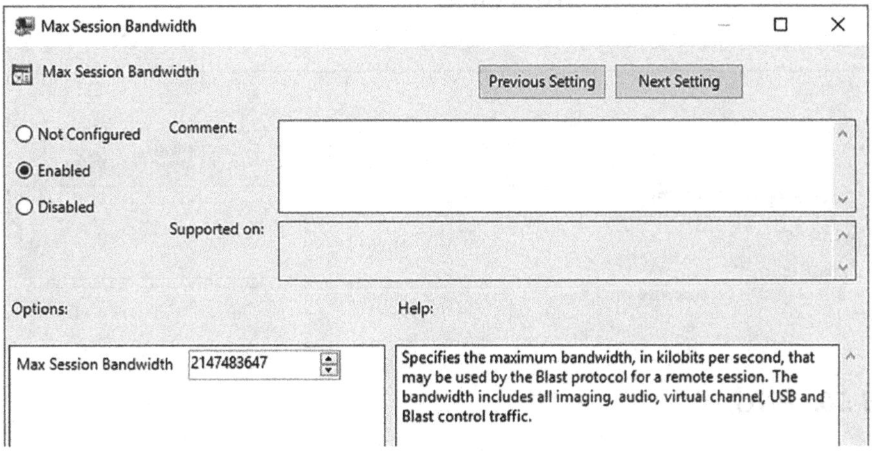

Figure 8-48. *Max Session Bandwidth*

Min Session Bandwidth

This is the opposite to the previous setting and allows you to set a minimum session bandwidth. By enabling this setting, you can configure the minimum reserved bandwidth for the session.

Enter the new value in kbps in the **Min Session Bandwidth** box as shown:

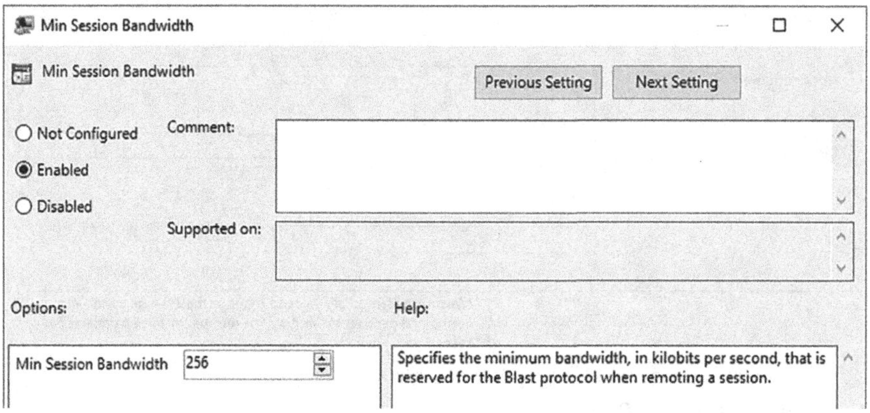

Figure 8-49. *Min Session Bandwidth*

PNG

If you set this policy, which does not apply if you enabled the H.264 encoder, to **Enabled** or **Not Configured,** then this means that PNG encoding will be used for any sessions.

Setting this policy to **Disabled** means that JPEG will be used for encoding. The following screenshot shows the **PNG** setting:

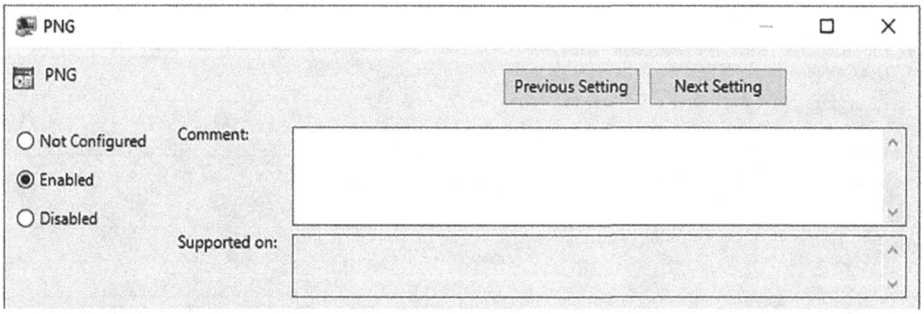

Figure 8-50. *PNG*

Screen Blanking

This policy allows you to configure a blank screen on the virtual desktop machine when it is in use by an end user so that it is not visible in the console.

If you click the radio button for Enabled or Not Configured, then this will show a blank screen in the console, and if you set this to Disabled, then the desktop of the virtual desktop machine will be visible in the console.

The following screenshot shows the **Screen Blanking** setting:

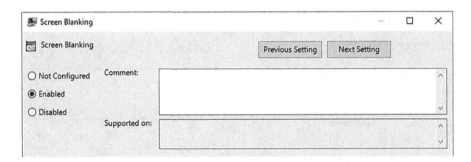

Figure 8-51. *Screen Blanking*

UDP Protocol

This setting enables you to switch on and off the UDP protocol.

If this setting is set to **Enabled** or **Not Configured,** then UDP is used as the protocol. Setting this to **Disabled** means that TCP will be used as the protocol.

This is shown in the following screenshot:

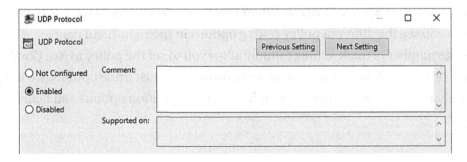

Figure 8-52. *UDP Protocol*

Keyboard locale synchronization

This setting, which only applies to the agent, is used to determine whether or not the keyboard locale list and the default locale of the current end user's session are synchronized with the data on the client's endpoint.

Clicking the **Enabled** button means synchronization will take place, and clicking either **Disabled** or **Not Configured** means that synchronization will not happen. This setting is shown in the following screenshot:

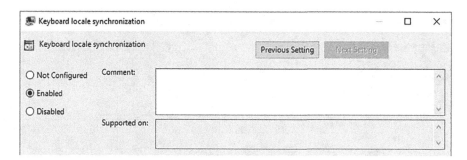

Figure 8-53. *Keyboard locale synchronization*

In the next section, we are going to look at the GPO policy settings that you can configure for the VMware Horizon Client Configuration.

VMware Horizon Client Configuration

The next set of GPO policy settings define the behavior and the configuration of the Horizon Client.

If you click the **VMware Horizon Client Configuration** folder in the left-hand tree view, you will see the different policy setting options in the right-hand pane.

A large number of these settings simply allow you to set the policy to Not Configured, Enabled, or Disabled. Rather than show screenshots with just these options, we will just show the screenshots where there are additional configuration options and fields to complete.

You will also see that there are a number of sub-folders within the client policy settings as shown in the following screenshot:

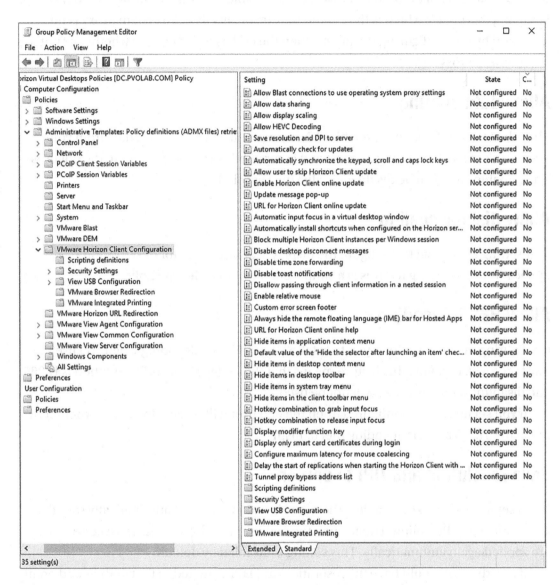

Figure 8-54. *VMware Horizon Client Configuration settings*

We will work through the policy settings starting with **Allow Blast connections to use operating system proxy** settings.

Allow Blast connections to use operating system proxy settings

If you enable this policy, then it allows Blast to be able to connect through a proxy server. Disabling this policy, which is the default setting, means that the system proxy is not used, and by not configuring the policy, then the end user can choose whether or not to use a system proxy.

Allow data sharing

The Allow data sharing policy enables VMware to collect anonymous data from your client devices used for aiding support and compatibility issues. By default, the policy is set to Enabled and can be disabled by clicking Disabled.

Allow display scaling

This setting allows you to configure the display scaling feature for desktop and application sessions. Again, this is a simple enable or disable type policy.

Allow HEVC Decoding

Configuring this policy allows you to set the HEVC (H.265) decoding when you use the Blast protocol. Enabling this feature means that the preferred decoding method is H.265, and disabling it means H.265 will not be used.

If you set this to not configured, then the end user will be able to choose whether or not to use H.265 as their decoding mechanism.

Save resolution and DPI to server

If you set this policy to be enabled, then the Horizon Client will automatically save the resolution and DPI scaling. Then, when the end user next logs in, these saved settings are applied again automatically. This setting is disabled by default.

If not, the user would have the resolution and DPI matched to that of their end point device.

Automatically check for updates

Enabling this policy means that the Horizon Client will automatically check for any new updates. It only applies to the Horizon Client version 8.1 and later.

Automatically synchronize the keypad, scroll and caps lock keys

This policy allows you to configure whether the state of the keypad, scroll lock, and caps lock is synchronized between the virtual desktop machine and the physical end point device.

If this policy is not enabled, then those keys will only be updated manually when the end user presses them.

Allow user to skip Horizon Client update

Enabling this policy means that an end user has the option to skip the Horizon Client update. If they skip the update, then they won't be prompted again until there is a new update. It only applies to the Horizon Client v8.1 and later.

Enable Horizon Client online update

This policy allows you to configure whether or not the Horizon Client can be updated using the online update feature. This is supported from Horizon Client version v4.6.

Update message pop-up

The update message pop-up policy allows you to configure a message that will pop up on the end user's device telling them that there is a new version of the Horizon Client available. By default, this setting is disabled and is supported with the version 8.1 of the Horizon Client or later.

URL for Horizon Client online update

This policy allows you to specify the URL from where to download the Horizon Client updates. Type the address in the **URL for Horizon Client online update** box as shown in the following screenshot:

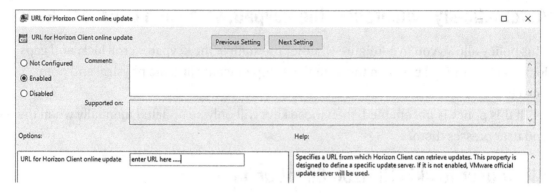

Figure 8-55. *URL for Horizon Client online update*

If you leave this policy setting disabled, then the VMware update server will be used.

Automatic input focus in a virtual desktop window

This policy, when enabled, brings the virtual desktop window displayed in the Horizon Client to the forefront, meaning that the end user will be able to use the virtual desktop immediately without first having to click the window to change the focus.

Automatically install shortcuts when configured on the Horizon server

This policy configures shortcuts and whether they should be automatically installed on the Horizon Client when they have been configured on the Server.

If you enable this policy, then the end user is not prompted and shortcuts are installed automatically, and if you set this policy to **Disabled**, then shortcuts will not be installed.

Finally, if you set this policy to **Not Configured**, then the end user will be prompted whether or not they want to install shortcuts.

Block multiple Horizon Client instances per Windows sessions

If you want to only allow one session per end user, then enabling this policy will prevent end users from launching more than one session by only allowing them to launch a single instance of the Horizon Client. Disabling this policy means that end users can launch more than one session of the Horizon Client and therefore have multiple sessions. By default, this policy is set to disabled.

Disable desktop disconnect messages

This policy specifies whether or not disconnection messages that are shown by default are disabled when the disconnection is not initiated by the end user, for example, when the administrator forcibly logs end users off when performing maintenance tasks.

Disable time zone forwarding

When enabled, this policy allows the time zone synchronization between the Horizon Client and the virtual desktop machine. It will only apply if the Disable Time Zone Synchronization is enabled on the Horizon Agent running on the virtual desktop machines or servers. By default, this policy is disabled.

Disable toast notifications

This policy setting allows you to disable toast notifications from the Horizon Client so that end users won't see them.

A toast notification is an animated Windows 10 notification message that appears by sliding in and out of the screen on an end user's desktop. By default, this setting is disabled, and so end users will see the notifications.

Disallow passing through client information in a nested session

This policy allows you to configure whether the Horizon Client can pass through client information during a nested session. Enabling this policy means that if the Horizon Client is running inside a Horizon session, then it will send the physical end point information instead of the information relating to the VM.

The information that is passed during a nested session is the device name, domain name, type of client, IP, and MAC address, and this policy is disabled by default which means the passing through of the client information is allowed in a nested session.

Enable relative mouse

Relative mouse mode will improve the mouse performance, particularly when running graphical based apps, for PCoIP sessions using the Horizon Client. Therefore, enabling this feature on supported remote desktops will result in a better end-user experience. By default, this policy is disabled.

Custom error screen footer

Enabling this policy allows you to specify a specific text file containing a custom message that will then be displayed at the bottom of the screen with any error messages.

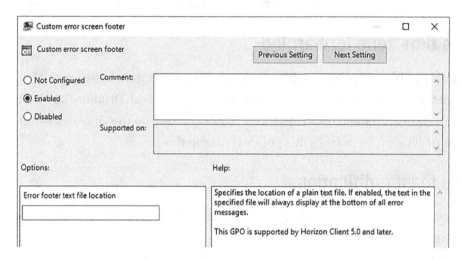

Figure 8-56. *Custom error screen footer*

For example, the custom message could display the number and email address of the help desk, so the end user sees both the error message and the help desk details.

Always hide the remote floating language bar for hosted apps

This policy is used to force the floating language bar to be switched off when running application sessions. This means that enabling this policy, the language bar will never be visible to the end user during that application session regardless of whether or not the Input Method Editor (IME) feature is enabled.

If you set this policy to disabled, then the floating language bar will only be shown if the local IME feature is disabled. Disabled is the default setting for this policy.

URL for Horizon Client online help

With the URL for Horizon Client online help setting, you can specify a different URL for the Horizon Client help pages. This would be used to point to internal documentation or when there is no Internet connection.

To configure the policy, type the new URL into the URL for Horizon Client online help box once you have enabled the policy as shown in the following:

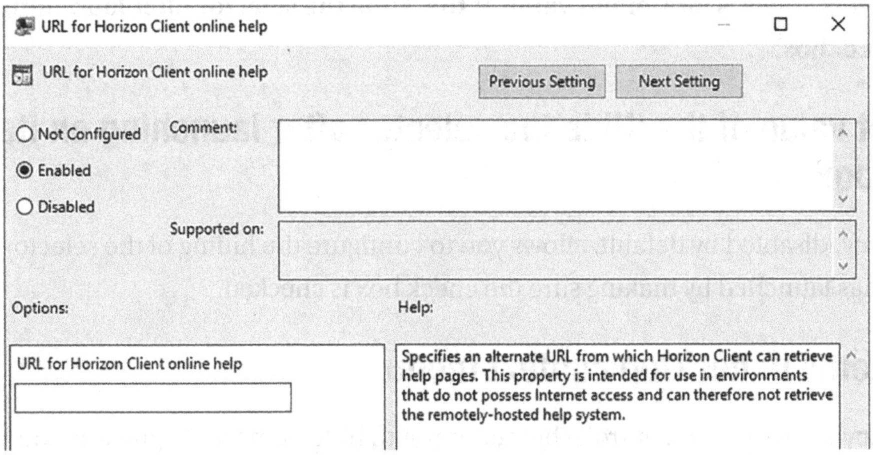

Figure 8-57. *URL for Horizon Client online help*

Hide items in application context menu

This policy allows you to hide contextual menu items when you right-click the Horizon Client launcher page. By default, this policy is disabled, and so all the configuration options shown in this policy can be set by the end user.

The configuration options are configured by simply clicking the drop-down menu next to each one and selecting either **Yes** or **No**. You have the following configurable options. These are shown in the following screenshot:

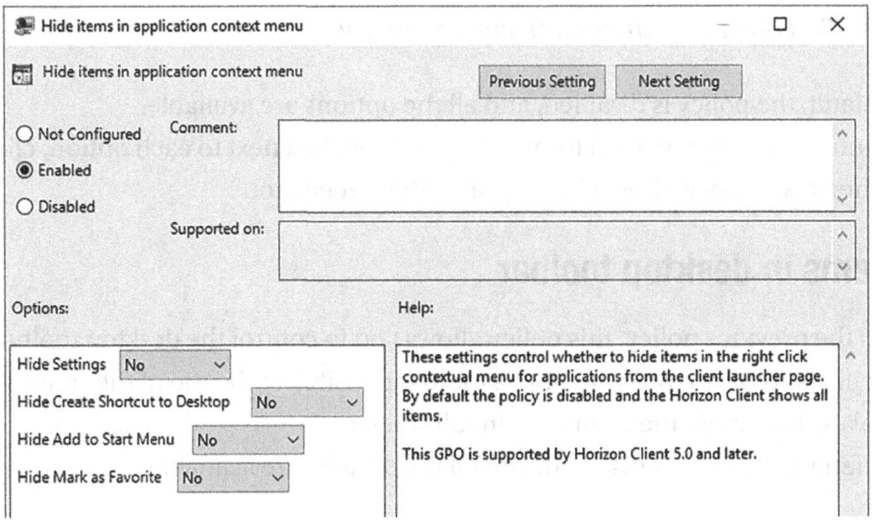

Figure 8-58. *URL for Horizon Client online help*

The next policy is for **Default value of the 'Hide the selector after launching an item' checkbox**.

Default value of the 'Hide the selector after launching an item' checkbox

This policy, disabled by default, allows you to configure the hiding of the selector once a session has launched by making sure the check box is checked.

Hide items in desktop context menu

This policy allows you to control whether or not to hide items that appear in the contextual menu that appears when you right-click the client launcher page.

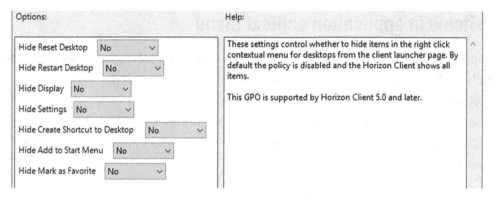

Figure 8-59. *Hide items in desktop context menu*

By default, the policy is disabled, and all the options are available.

To configure an option, then from the drop-down box next to each option, click and select either **Yes** or **No** as shown in the preceding screenshot.

Hide items in desktop toolbar

Similar to the previous policy, this policy allows you to control the desktop toolbar and to hide specific items from the toolbar. The toolbar is visible at the top of the screen when the virtual desktop machine is running in full screen.

By default, the policy is disabled, and all the options are available.

To configure an option, then from the drop-down box next to each option, click and select either **Yes** or **No** as shown in the following screenshot:

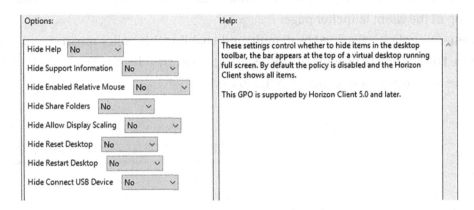

Figure 8-60. *Hide items in desktop toolbar*

Hide items in system tray menu

This policy enables you to hide items in the system tray on the local Windows screen. It is disabled by default, meaning all system tray items are shown.

If you enable this policy, then you can configure **Hide Sharing** or **Hide Settings** by selecting **Yes** or **No** from the respective drop-down box as shown:

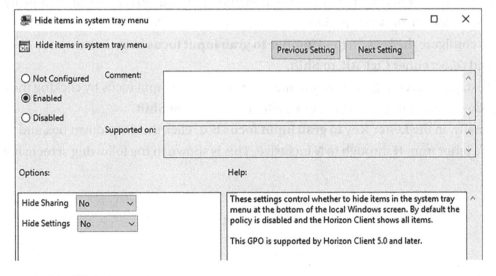

Figure 8-61. *Hide items in system tray menu*

Hide items in the client toolbar menu

Similar to the previous policy setting, this policy allows you to hide items in the toolbar on the top of the client launcher page.

Again, this policy is disabled by default, and enabling this policy means you can then configure **Hide Favorites Toggle** or **Hide Settings Gear** by selecting **Yes** or **No** from the respective drop-down box as shown in the following:

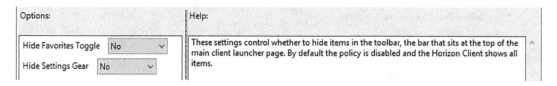

Figure 8-62. *Hide items in the client toolbar menu*

Hotkey combination to grab input focus

In this policy, you can configure a hotkey combination that enables you to grab the input focus for the last used session.

The hotkey combination is made up of one or two configurable modifier keys followed by a letter key to complete the sequence. When this policy is enabled, then the keys configured, when pressed, will grab the input focus to the session.

If this policy is disabled or not configured, then the focus to the session is done by clicking inside the desktop window.

To configure the keys, in the **Modifier to grab input focus** box, click the drop-down box and select either **Ctrl**, **Alt**, or **Shift**.

Next, you can configure a second modifier key to grab input focus by clicking the drop-down box and selecting either **Disabled**, **Ctrl**, **Alt**, or **Shift**.

Finally, in the **Letter Key to grab input focus** box, click the drop-down box and select a letter from **H** through to **N** inclusive. This is shown in the following screenshot:

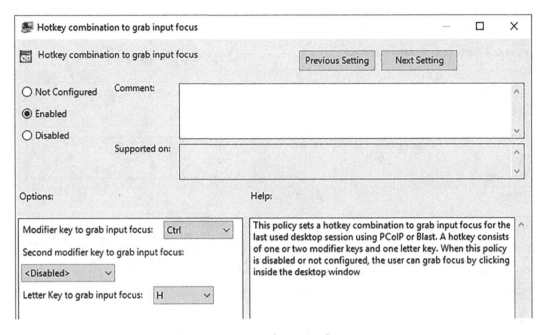

Figure 8-63. *Hotkey combination to grab input focus*

Hotkey combination to release input focus

Similar to the previous policy, with this policy you can configure a hotkey combination
that enables you to release the input focus for the last used session.

If this policy is disabled or not configured, then to release the focus from the desktop
windows, the end user would press **Ctrl+Alt**.

To configure the keys, in the **Modifier to release input focus** box, click the drop-
down box and select either **Ctrl**, **Alt**, or **Shift**.

Next, you can configure a second modifier key to release input focus by clicking the
drop-down box and selecting either **Disabled**, **Ctrl**, **Alt**, or **Shift**.

Finally, in the **Function Key to release input focus** box, click the drop-down box
and select a function key from **F5** through to **F8** inclusive as shown:

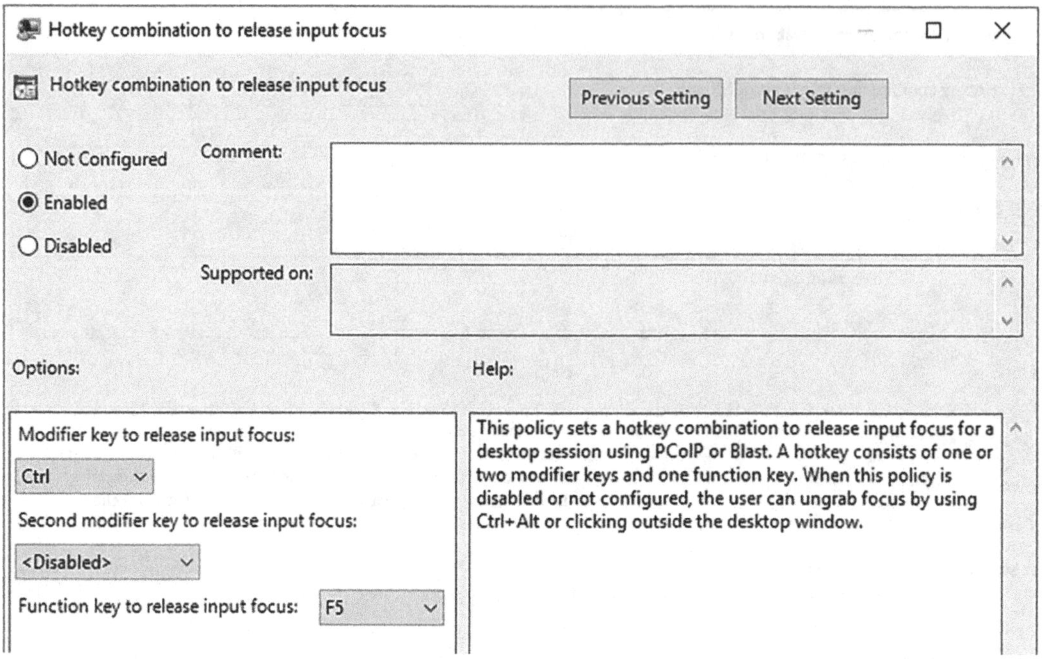

Figure 8-64. *Hotkey combination to release input focus*

The next policy is for **Display modifier function key**.

Display modifier function key

With this policy setting, you can configure a key press combination that allows you to change the configuration of the display on the client device.

If you don't configure this policy, then the end user first needs to release the focus from the session window to the client by pressing **Ctrl+Alt.** Then they would need to change the display configuration on the client in the normal way by pressing the Windows key and P.

To configure the keys, in the **Display Switch Modifier Key** box, click the drop-down box and select either **Disabled**, **Ctrl**, **Alt**, or **Shift**.

Then, in the **Display Switch Function Key** box, click the drop-down box and select a function key from **F1** through to **F9** inclusive as shown:

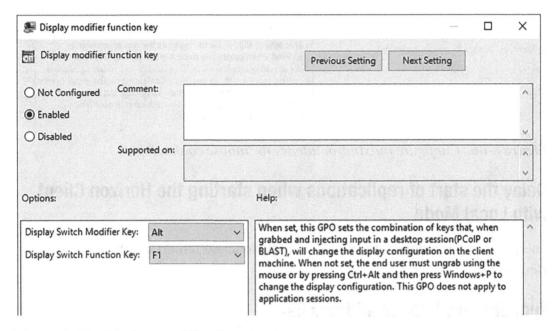

Figure 8-65. *Display modifier function key*

Display only smart card certificates during login

This policy allows you to either show all certificates from the end user and system stores or to only show certificates of smart cards.

If you enable this policy, then the certificate selection dialog box only shows certificates for smart cards. If the policy is disabled, then all types of certificates will be displayed in the dialog box. Disabled is the default policy setting.

Configure maximum latency for mouse coalescing

This configuration setting allows you to configure the maximum latency when coalescing mouse movements. Coalescing mouse movements can reduce the bandwidth between the client and the agent. Configuring the setting to a value of zero will disable the coalescing, which is also the default policy setting as shown:

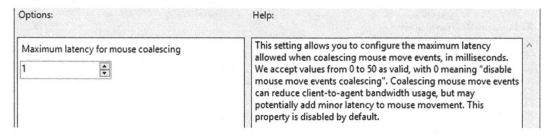

Figure 8-66. Configure maximum latency for mouse coalescing

Delay the start of replications when starting the Horizon Client with Local Mode

This policy is now redundant as the View Local Mode was removed with the release of Horizon 6.0.

Tunnel proxy bypass address list

With this policy, you can specify a list of proxy servers that will not be used for tunneled connections, by specifying the first part of the string.

In the Tunnel proxy bypass address list, type in a list of the addresses with multiple addresses being separated by a semicolon as shown:

The next set of policy settings sit within a sub-folder. This sub-folder contains the **Scripting definitions** policy settings.

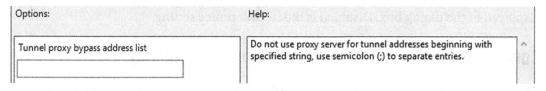

Figure 8-67. Tunnel proxy bypass address list

Scripting Definitions

In this section, we are going to look at the scripting definitions policy settings as shown in the following screenshot:

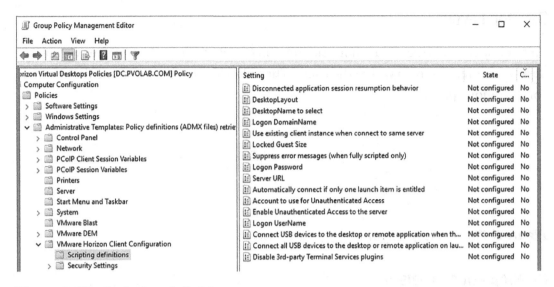

Figure 8-68. *Scripting definitions*

Disconnected application session resumption behavior setting

This policy setting defines what happens with the automatic app session resumption feature and is disabled by default which means the end user chooses what happens when resuming applications. The configuration options are shown in the following:

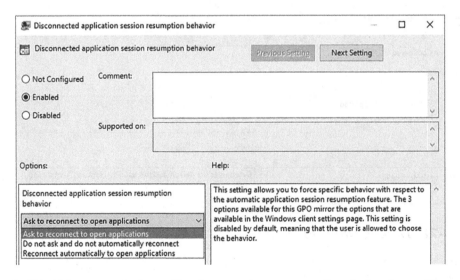

Figure 8-69. *Disconnected application session resumption behavior setting*

Desktop Layout

This policy is used to configure how the Horizon Client window displays your virtual desktop machines screen within the client. The following screenshot shows the configuration options:

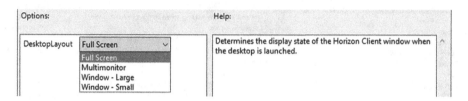

Figure 8-70. *Desktop Layout*

DesktopName to select

This policy allows you to configure the default desktop used by the Horizon Client when the end user logs in.

When enabled, type in the name of the desktop in the **DesktopName to select** box as shown in the following screenshot:

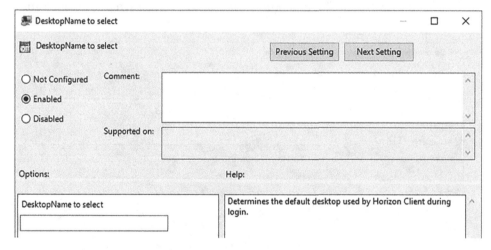

Figure 8-71. *DesktopName to select*

Logon DomainName

This policy allows you to specify the name of the domain name, using its NETBIOS name, to log on to using the Horizon Client. The configuration screen is shown in the following screenshot:

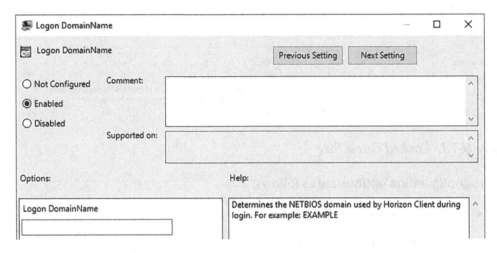

Figure 8-72. *Logon DomainName*

When enabled, type in the name of the domain in the **Logon DomainName** box.

Use existing client instance when connect to same server

This policy is either enabled or disabled and controls whether or not a connection is added to the existing Horizon Client which the end user has already used to connect to the same server. It is disabled by default and when not configured.

Locked Guest Size

With this policy, you can set the resolution of the remote desktop, and once enabled you cannot use the autofit feature. You can set the width and the height of the desktop as shown in the following screenshot:

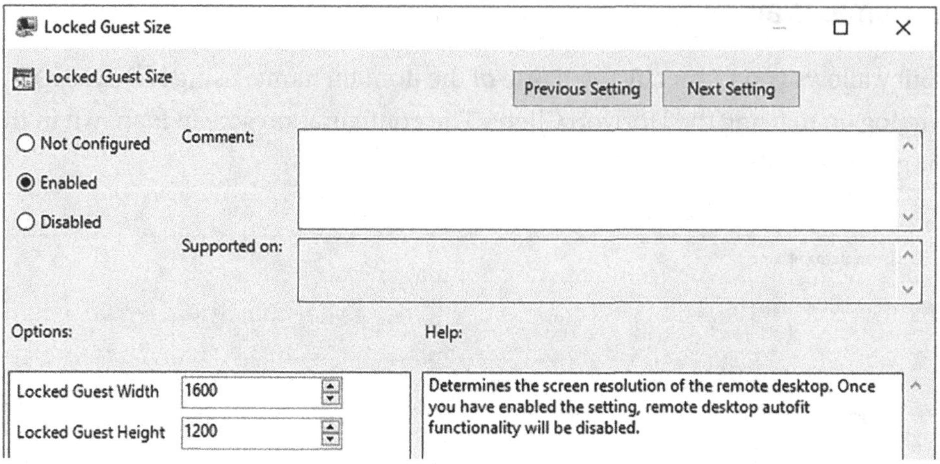

Figure 8-73. *Locked Guest Size*

The configuration options are as follows:

- Max screen size = 4096 x 4096

- Min screen size = 640 x 480

Note: This policy does not apply to sessions delivered by RDP.

Suppress error messages (when fully scripted only)

With this policy option, you can configure whether or not any error messages are displayed when an end user logs in. It is simply a case of enabling or disabling the policy.

Logon Password

This policy allows you to enter the password that is used by the Horizon Client to log in. Once enabled, type in the password in the **Logon Password** box noting that the password is stored in plain text! This is shown in the following screenshot:

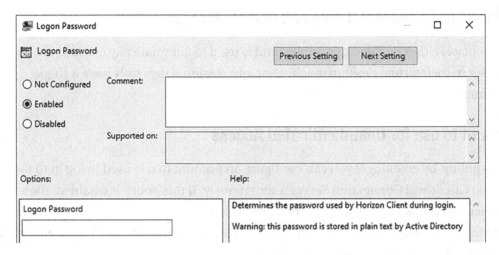

Figure 8-74. *Logon Password*

Server URL

The Server URL policy allows you to enter the URL to the Connection Server.

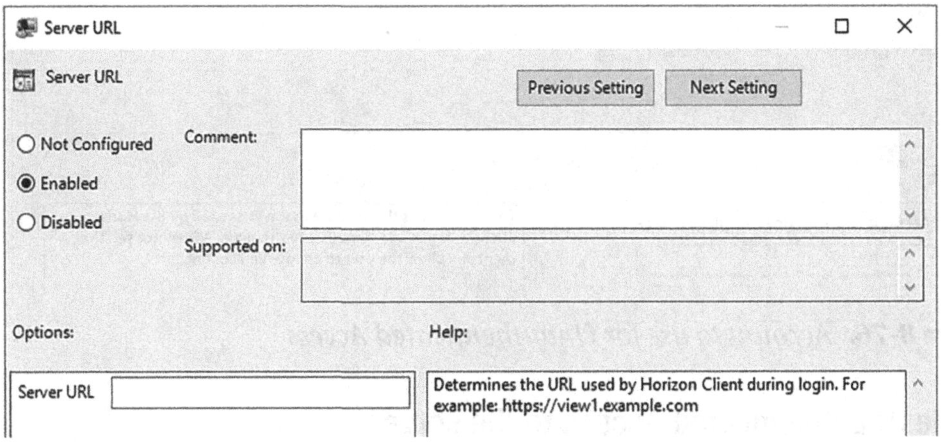

Figure 8-75. *Server URL*

Once enabled, type in the URL in the **Server URL** box.

Automatically connect if only one launch item is entitled

This policy is either enabled or disabled and is used to automatically connect an end user to their virtual desktop machine or app session if they only have a single entitlement.

Account to use for Unauthenticated Access

In this policy, by enabling it you can configure an account that is used to log in to the Horizon Client and Connection Server anonymously. If this policy is disabled, then the end user can choose which account they use to log in with.

Once enabled, type in the account name in the Account to use for Unauthenticated Access box as shown in the following screenshot:

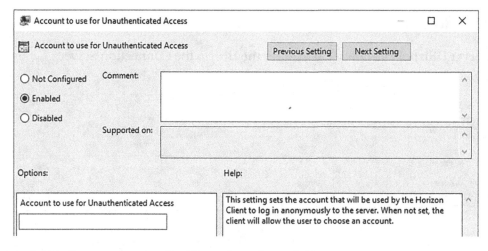

Figure 8-76. *Account to use for Unauthenticated Access*

Enable Unauthenticated Access to the server

This policy is enabled or disabled. Enabling this policy configures whether or not an end user needs to enter their credentials to access apps using the Horizon Client. It means that Unauthenticated Access is always requested from the server.

If the policy is disabled, then end users will always need to enter their credentials to log in.

Logon UserName

This policy allows you to configure the username that is used by the Horizon Client to log in with.

Once enabled, in the Logon UserName box, enter the username to use for logging in with as shown in the following screenshot:

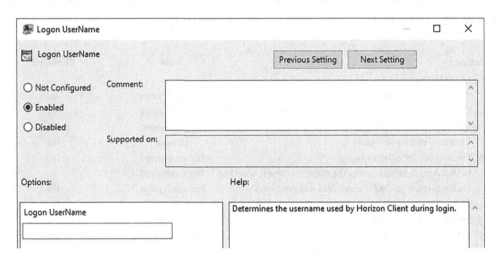

Figure 8-77. *Logon UserName*

Connect USB devices to the desktop or remote application when they are plugged in

Either enabled or disabled, this policy allows USB devices to be automatically connected to the remote session when the end user plugs them into their end point.

Connect all USB devices to the desktop or remote application on launch

Either enabled or disabled, this policy enables you to configure whether or not all USB devices attached to the end point are made available on the remote session.

Disable 3rd-party Terminal Services plugins

If you enable this policy, then no checking will take place for third-party terminal services plug-ins that are installed as normal RDP plug-ins. Horizon-specific plug-ins such as USB redirection are not affected.

Next is the second sub-folder that is listed under the VMware Horizon Client Configuration policy. These policy settings are for **Security Settings**.

Security Settings

The Security Settings section allows you to configure the Horizon Client security settings. This set of policy settings also has its own sub-folder. The policy settings are shown in the following screenshot:

Setting	State	Comment
NTLM Settings		
Allow command line credentials	Not configured	No
Configures the SSL Proxy certificate checking behavior of th...	Not configured	No
Servers Trusted For Delegation	Not configured	No
Certificate verification mode	Enabled	No
Enable jump list integration	Not configured	No
Unlock remote sessions when the client machine is unlocked	Not configured	No
Enable Single Sign-On for smart card authentication	Not configured	No
Enable SSL encrypted framework channel	Enabled	No
Ignore certificate revocation problems	Not configured	No
Default value of the 'Log in as current user' checkbox	Not configured	No
Display option to Log in as current user	Not configured	No
Configures SSL protocols and cryptographic algorithms	Not configured	No

Figure 8-78. *Security Settings*

We will start security settings policies by looking at the **Allow command line credentials** setting.

Allow command line credentials

This policy setting is either enabled or disabled and allows credentials to be entered using the command line. It is enabled by default.

Configures the SSL Proxy certificate checking behavior of the Horizon Client

With this policy setting, you can enable end users to connect through an SSL proxy. By default, the Horizon Client is set to block SSL proxy connections for tunneled connections using Blast.

Servers Trusted for Delegation

Enabling this policy allows you to configure a list of Connection Servers that allow delegated credentials to use with the "Log in as current user" feature. Server names must be entered using their SPN. The configuration screen is shown in the following screenshot:

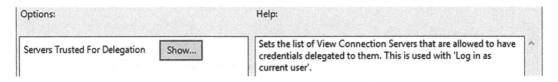

Figure 8-79. Servers Trusted for Delegation

Once the policy settings have been enabled, click the **Show...** button. You will see the **Show Content** box as shown in the following screenshot:

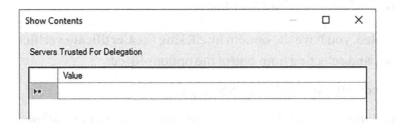

Figure 8-80. Show Contents for Servers Trusted For Delegation

In the **Value** field, enter the names of the servers. All servers are trusted by default.

Certificate verification mode

With this policy setting, you can configure how the Horizon Client checks certificates as shown in the following screenshot:

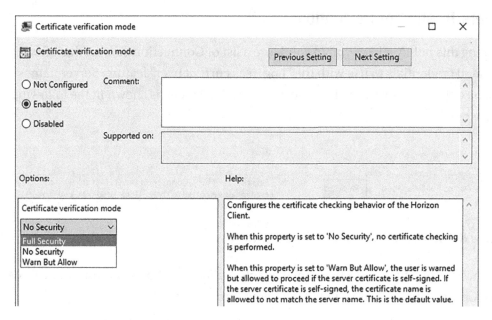

Figure 8-81.   *Certificate verification mode*

When enabled, you have the option, by clicking the **Certificate verification mode** drop-down box and selecting from one of the options listed:

- **No Security**: No certificate checking takes place.

- **Full Security**: All certificate errors are reported and the end user cannot connect.

- **Warn But Allow**: The end user receives a warning but can continue to connect. This is the default configuration.

Enable jump list integration

This policy allows you to add a jump list to the Horizon Client icon displayed on the Windows taskbar. The jump list displays a list of the recent connections and is enabled by default.

Unlock remote sessions when the client machine is unlocked

This policy, enabled by default, enables you to control the recursive unlock feature which allows you to unlock all remote sessions after the client machine has been unlocked. It only works when the end user is logged in using the login as current user.

Enable Single-Sign-On for smart card authentication

Either enabled or disabled, this policy allows you to enable single sign-on for smart card authentication. When enabled, the Horizon Client will temporarily store the encrypted smart card pin before sending to the Connection Server.

Enable SSL encrypted framework channel

This policy allows you to configure the SSL encrypted framework channel with the following options as shown in the following screenshot:

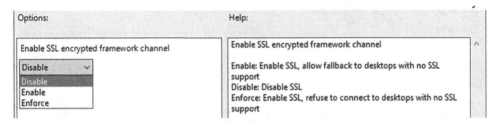

Figure 8-82. *Enable SSL encrypted framework channel*

The next policy is for **Ignore certificate revocation problems**.

Ignore certificate revocation problems

Either enabled or disabled, this policy allows you to configure what happens with revoked server certificate errors. The default setting for this policy is disabled. Enabling this policy means that revoked certificates will be ignored.

Default value of the 'Log in as current user' checkbox

Either enabled or disabled, this policy allows you to configure the Log in as current user check box and whether or not it is checked. By default, this policy setting is disabled.

Display option to log in as current user

This policy configures whether the Log in as current user check box is visible in the Horizon Client. This setting is enabled by default.

Configures SSL protocols and cryptographic algorithms

With this policy, you can configure a cipher list to restrict certain types of cryptographic algorithms and protocols before an encrypted SSL connection is established as shown in the following screenshot:

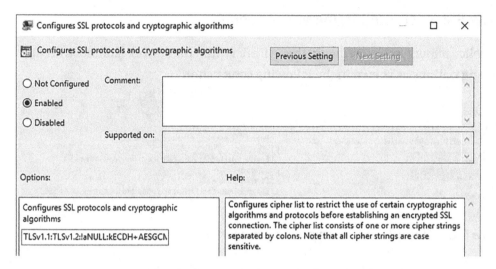

Figure 8-83. *Configures SSL protocols and cryptographic algorithms*

If you enable this policy, then the default value as shown in the screenshot is set. This means that TLS v1.1 and c1.2 are enabled.

The final setting in the **Security Settings** folder is a sub-folder for **NTLM Settings** which we will cover next.

NTLM Settings

The final configuration settings that fall under security settings are for NTLM settings. There are just two policy options within this sub-folder as shown in the following screenshot:

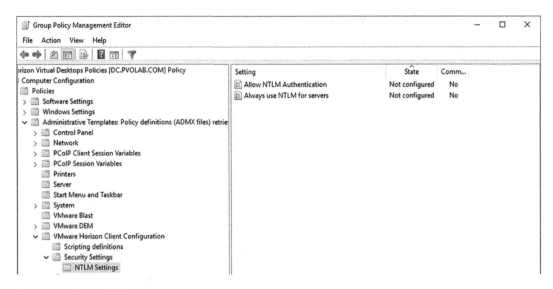

Figure 8-84. *NTLM settings*

The first setting is to **Allow NTLM Authentication** as shown:

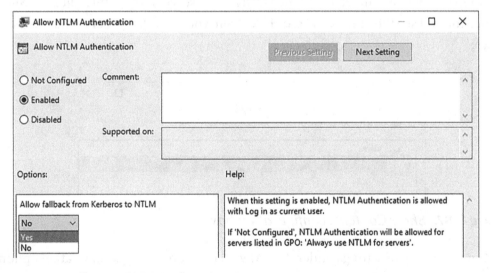

Figure 8-85. *Allow NTLM Authentication*

Enabling this policy then allows you to configure the **Allow fallback from Kerberos to NTLM** setting. Click the drop-down menu and select either **Yes** or **No**.

Finally, you have the **Always use NTLM for servers** setting as shown:

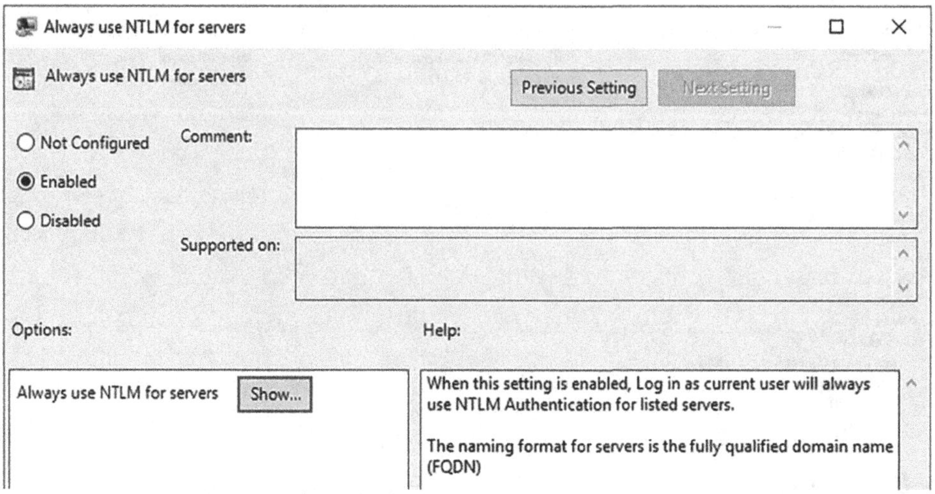

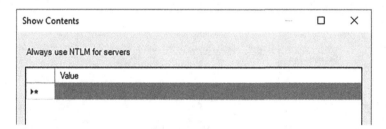

Figure 8-86. *Always use NTLM for servers*

When enabled, you need to add the FQDN of the servers. To do this, click the **Show...** button. You will see the **Show Contents** box where you can add the server names as shown:

Figure 8-87. *Show Contents configuration box*

The next group of settings under the VMware Horizon Client Configuration options heading are for **View USB Configuration**.

View USB Configuration

In the **View USB Configuration** policy settings folder, there are a number of policy settings and some additional settings that can be found in the **Settings not configurable by Agent** sub-folder as shown in the following screenshot:

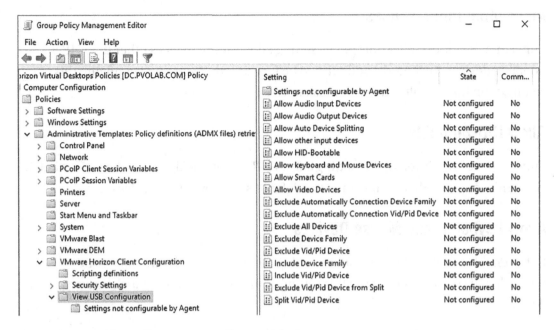

Figure 8-88. Show Contents configuration box

Most of these settings are simply enabled or disabled with no additional configuration settings required. That being the case, we haven't shown a screenshot of each individual setting as they pretty much look the same. Any screenshots shown will be those that require additional configuration settings.

We will start the View USB Configuration policies by looking at the **Allow Audio Input Devices** setting.

Allow Audio Input Devices

Either enabled or disabled, this setting allows audio input devices to be forwarded.

Allow Audio Output Devices

Either enabled or disabled, this setting allows audio output devices to be forwarded.

Allow Auto Device Splitting

Either enabled or disabled, this policy setting allows you to exclude the component devices that make up a composite device and stop it from being treated as a separate device.

Allow other input devices

Either enabled or disabled, this policy setting allows input devices other than HID-bootable devices, keyboards, and mice to be forwarded. If you don't configure this setting, then the default is to allow these devices.

Allow HID-Bootable

Either enabled or disabled, this setting allows HID-bootable devices to be forwarded. If you don't configure this setting, then the default is to allow these devices.

Allow keyboard and Mouse Devices

Either enabled or disabled, this policy setting allows keyboards and mice to be forwarded. If you don't configure this setting, then the default is to block these types of devices.

Allow Smart Cards

This policy simply allows you to configure whether or not smart card devices such as smart card readers are forwarded. If you don't configure this setting, then the default is to block these types of devices.

Allow Video Devices

This setting allows you to configure whether or not video devices are forwarded. If you don't configure this setting, then the default is to allow forwarding.

Exclude Automatically Connection Device Family

This policy allows you to configure a set of USB devices that are prevented from being automatically forwarded to the client.

Enter the name of the device family you want to exclude in the **Exclude Automatically Connection Device Family** box once the policy has been enabled. This is shown in the following screenshot:

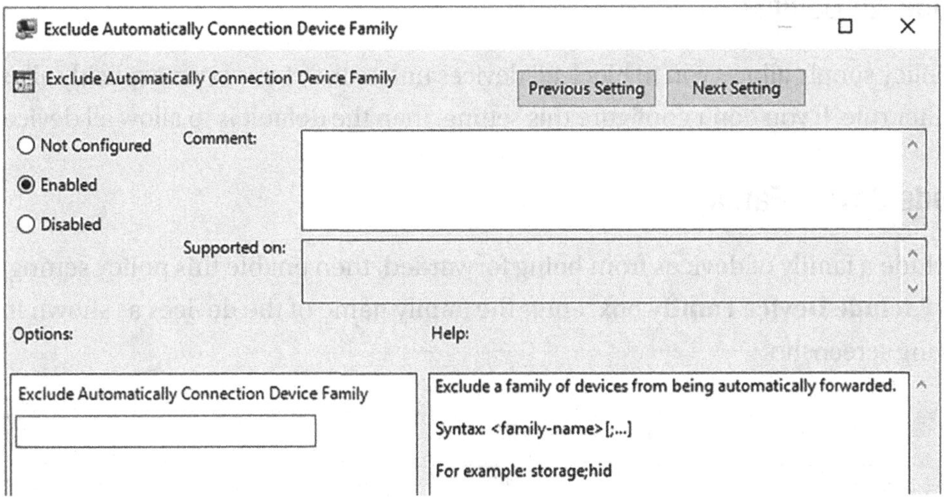

Figure 8-89. Exclude Automatically Connection Device Family

Exclude Automatically Connection Vid/Pid Device

This policy allows you to configure a set of USB devices that are prevented from being automatically forwarded to the client by specifying their vendor ID and product ID as shown in the following screenshot:

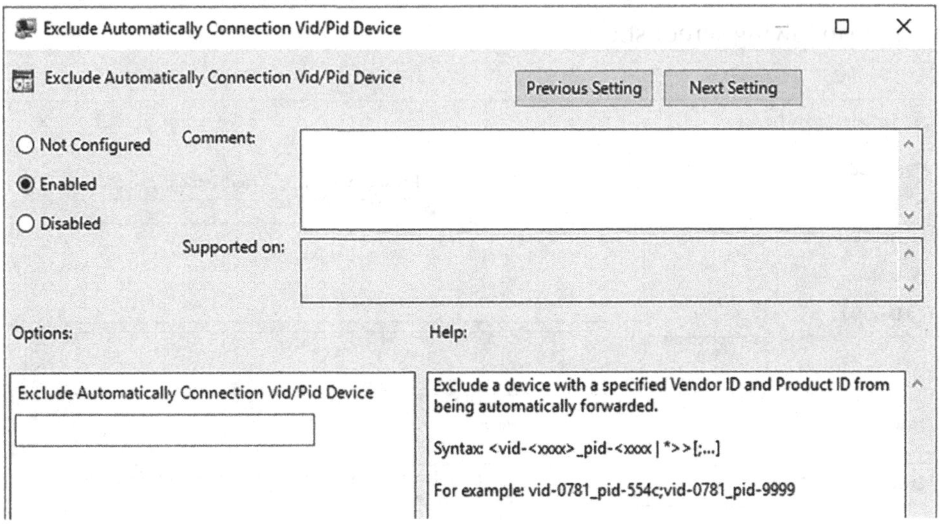

Figure 8-90. Exclude Automatically Connection Vid/Pid Device

Exclude All Devices

This policy simply allows you to block all devices unless they have been explicitly allowed via a filter rule. If you don't configure this setting, then the default is to allow all devices.

Exclude Device Family

To exclude a family of devices from being forwarded, then enable this policy setting, and in the **Exclude Device Family** box, enter the family name of the devices as shown in the following screenshot:

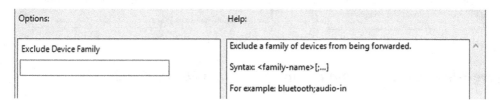

Figure 8-91. Exclude Device Family

Exclude Vid/Pid Device

To exclude a specific device based on the vendor ID and product ID, then enable this policy setting, and in the **Exclude Vid/Pid Device** box, enter the details of the device as shown in the following screenshot:

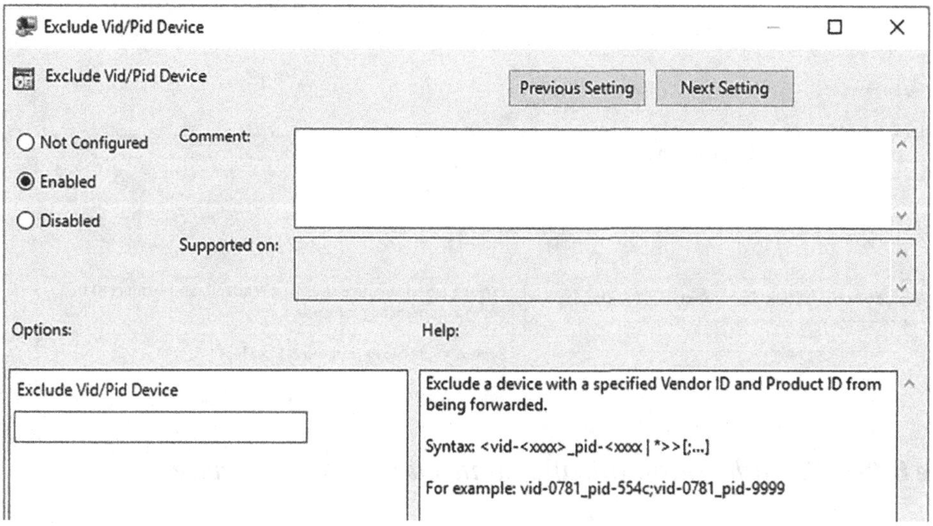

Figure 8-92. Exclude Vid/Pid Device

Include Device Family

This policy, when enabled, allows you to include a USB device family as shown in the following screenshot:

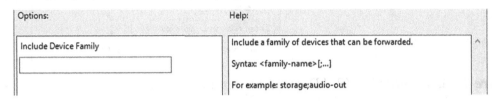

Figure 8-93. *Include Device Family*

In the **Include Device Family** box, type in the family name of the devices you want to be forwarded to the remote desktop.

Include Vid/Pid Device

This policy, when enabled, allows you to include a USB device based on its vendor ID and product ID as shown in the following screenshot:

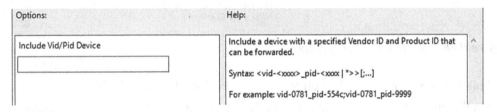

Figure 8-94. *Include Vid/Pid Device*

In the **Exclude Vid/Pid Device** box, enter the details of the device using its vendor ID and product ID.

Exclude Vid/Pid Device from Split

This next policy allows you to exclude component devices when using a composite USB device based on its vendor ID and product ID. Enabling this policy means that the device is prevented from being treated as a separate device.

This is shown in the following screenshot:

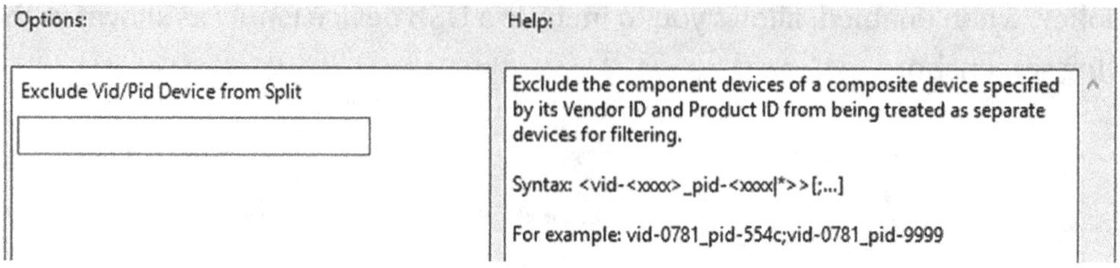

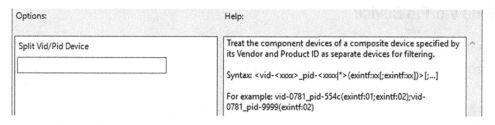

Figure 8-95. *Exclude Vid/Pid Device from Split*

Split Vid/Pid Device

This policy setting, when enabled, treats the component devices of a composite device as separate devices configured as shown in the following screenshot:

Figure 8-96. *Split Vid/Pid Device*

This is filtered based on the vendor ID and product ID of the device.

Finally, in the View USB Configuration folder within a sub-folder called **Settings not configurable by Agent,** you will see four additional policy settings as shown in the following screenshot:

Setting	State	Comment
Allow Device Descriptor Failsafe behavior	Not configured	No
Disable Remote Configuration	Not configured	No
Exclude Path	Not configured	No
Include Path	Not configured	No

Figure 8-97. *Settings not configurable by Agent*

We will now look at these policy settings in more detail.

Allow Device Descriptor Failsafe behavior

This policy allows you to enable whether devices are blocked if the system fails to fetch the descriptor. Enabling it means that devices won't be blocked.

Disable Remote Configuration

When enabled, this policy setting simply disabled downloads for the remote configuration.

Exclude Path

If you enable this policy setting, then you can exclude a specific device that uses a specific hub or port path from being forwarded to the remote session.

Enter the path in the **Exclude Path** box as shown in the following:

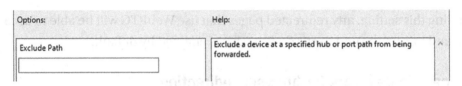

Figure 8-98. *Exclude Path*

Include Path

This policy is the opposite of the previous policy and, when enabled, allows you to include the specific hub or port path to be forwarded as shown:

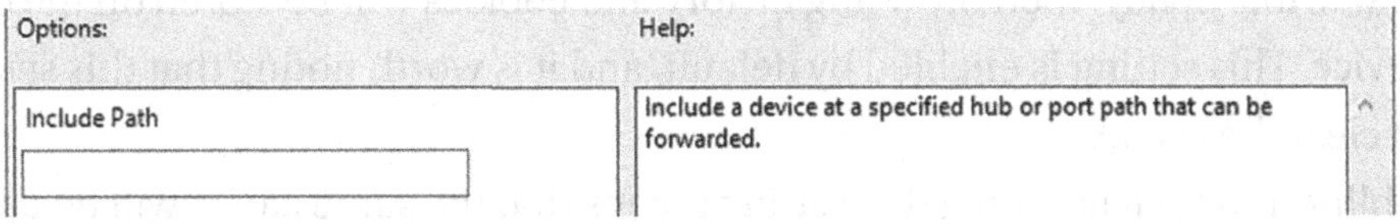

Figure 8-99. *Include Path*

Enter the path in the **Include Path** box as shown.

The next sub-folder under the VMware Horizon Client Configuration policy settings is for **Browser Redirection**.

VMware Browser Redirection

The VMware Browser Redirection policy setting allows you to configure browser-specific settings and is made up of the three individual policy settings as shown in the following screenshot:

Setting	State	Comm...
Enable WebRTC camera and microphone access...	Not configured	No
Ignore certificate errors for browser redirection	Not configured	No
Enable cache for browser redirection	Not configured	No

Figure 8-100. *VMware Browser Redirection configuration settings*

The first policy is for configuring webcam and microphone access.

Enable WebRTC camera and microphone access for browser redirection

By enabling this setting, any redirected pages that use WebRTC will be able to access the camera and mic on the end user's device. This is enabled by default.

Ignore certificate errors for browser redirection

When enabled, this setting allows end users to continue browsing should a certificate error occur on the redirected page.

This policy is disabled by default.

Enable cache for browser redirection

If you enable this policy, then browsing history and cookies will be stored on the end user's device. This setting is enabled by default, and it is worth noting that this setting does not clear the cache.

Disabling and then enabling this setting means that the same cache will be used.

The final group of policy settings under the VMware Horizon Client Configuration settings is for **VMware Integrated Printing**.

VMware Integrated Printing

The VMware Integrated Printing policy setting allows you to manage printer redirection and is made up of two policy settings as shown in the following screenshot:

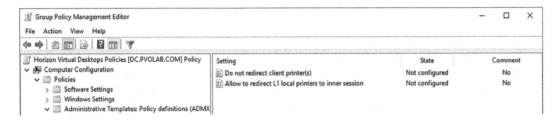

Figure 8-101. *VMware Integrated Printing configuration settings*

The first policy setting is to not redirect the client printer.

Do not redirect client printer(s)

The first setting, when enabled, means that no client printers will be redirected. If you set this to disabled, then all client printers will be directed. By default, this setting is not configured.

Allow to redirect L1 local printers to inner session

The other setting configures whether local printers are redirected to a nested session and by default is not configured.

With nested mode, there are three layers as listed:

- **L0**: End point device

- **L1**: Remote desktop (when enabled, this is where the printer is redirected from to the L2 session)

- **L2**: Remote desktop/application running in the L1 remote desktop

The next group of policy settings are for **VMware Horizon URL Redirection**.

VMware Horizon URL Redirection

The policy settings in this section allow you to control and manage URL redirection and are shown in the following screenshot:

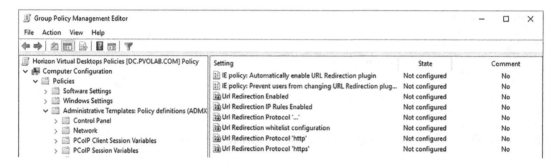

Figure 8-102. *VMware Horizon URL Redirection*

The first policy is to automatically enable URL redirection for IE.

IE policy: Automatically enable URL Redirection plugin

Enabling this policy allows newly installed IE plug-ins to be activated automatically.

IE policy: Prevent users from changing URL Redirection plugin loading behavior

Enabling this policy allows end users to disable URL content redirection.

Url Redirection Enabled

This setting simply enables the URL redirection setting and is not configured by default.

Url Redirection IP Rules Enabled

Enabling this setting configures whether IP rules are switched on or off.

When enabled, the IP specified supports DNS Resolve, meaning that you can add an IP range in the client rules or agent rules configuration, and if the URL entered does not match, then the URL rules will resolve to the IP address that does match.

Url Redirection Protocol '...'

This policy allows URLs that use this protocol to be redirected as shown and described in the following screenshot:

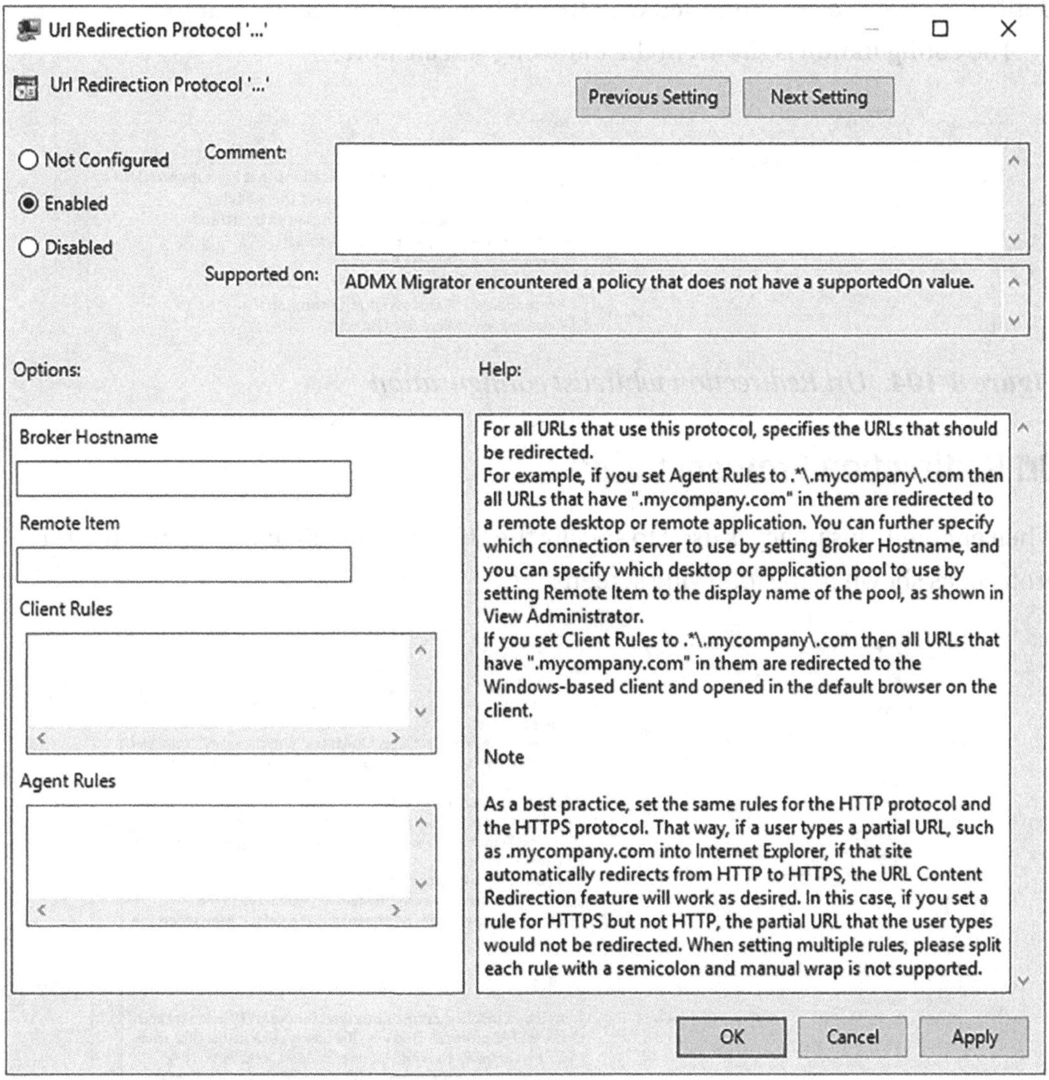

Figure 8-103. *Url Redirection Protocol '...'*

Url Redirection whitelist configuration

With this policy, you can configure the apps that are supported for the protocol in the URL.

This means that any apps that are added to the Whitelist are the only ones that will support the URL content redirection feature. It's worth noting that only Chrome, Outlook, and Skype are supported with the URL content redirection feature.

The configuration is shown in the following screenshot:

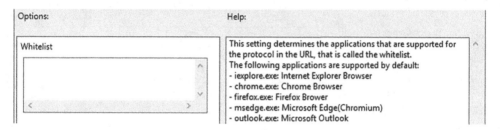

Figure 8-104. *Url Redirection whitelist configuration*

Url Redirection Protocol 'http'

When enabled, this policy is used to specify the URLs to be redirected that use the HTTP protocol as shown in the following screenshot:

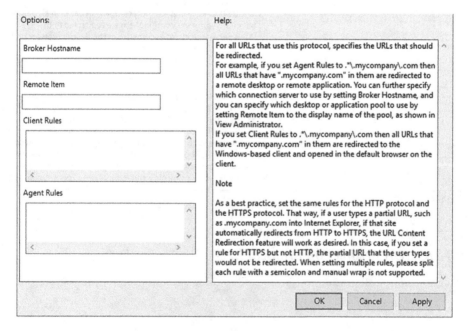

Figure 8-105. *Url Redirection Protocol 'http'*

Url Redirection Protocol 'https'

When enabled, this policy is used to specify the URLs to be redirected that use the HTTPS protocol.

When enabled, the configuration settings are identical to those for configuring the HTTP protocol, so refer to Figure 8-105 for these configuration options.

The next set of policy settings relate to the **VMware View Agent Configuration**, which we will discuss in the next section.

VMware View Agent Configuration

The **VMware View Agent Configuration** policies consist of all the policies that relate to the Horizon Agent that is running on the virtual desktop machine and the configuration of the agent.

Click the folder to show the available policy options. You will see that these options are contained within sub-folders that relate to a specific agent setting as shown in the following screenshot:

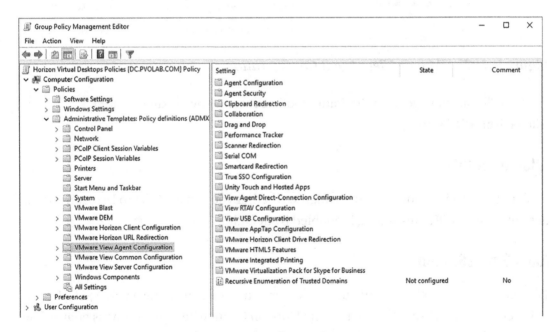

Figure 8-106. *VMware View Agent Configuration*

We will start by looking at the policy settings in the **Agent Configuration** folder.

547

Agent Configuration

Click the **Agent Configuration** folder. This folder contains the policy settings as shown in the following screenshot:

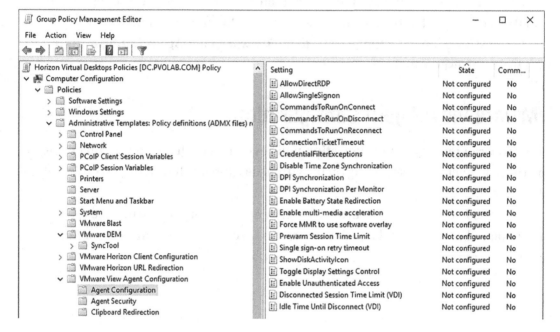

Figure 8-107. *VMware View Agent Configuration*

We will start the Agent Configuration policies section by looking at the **AllowDirectRDP** setting.

AllowDirectRDP

Enabling this policy allows you to configure whether you can connect to Horizon virtual desktops using RDP. This setting is enabled by default.

AllowSingleSignon

This policy, when enabled, configures whether end users can connect using SSO. Users only need to enter their credentials in the Horizon Client when this setting is enabled. It is enabled by default.

CommandsToRunOnConnect

With this policy enabled, you can add a list of commands that you want to run when a session connects for the first time. When enabled, you will see the following:

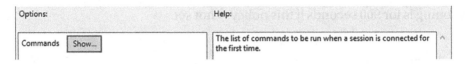

Figure 8-108. *CommandsToRunOnConnect settings*

Click the **Show...** button to add the commands in the **Show Contents** box and the Value field as shown in the following screenshot:

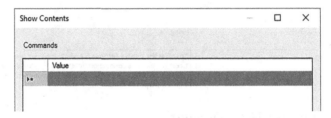

Figure 8-109. *CommandsToRunOnConnect settings*

CommandsToRunOnDisconnect

As with the previous setting, this one, when enabled, allows you to configure a command to run when a session is disconnected. You configure it in exactly the same way as the previous setting.

CommandsToRunOnReconnect

Again, as with the previous two settings, when enabled, this setting allows you to configure a command to run when an end user reconnects to a session. As with the previous settings, the configuration is exactly the same.

ConnectionTicketTimeout

This policy setting, when enabled, allows you to configure a time for how long the connection ticket is valid. This is used by clients when connecting to the agent for verification and SSO. The ticket is valid for the time period that you configure. The default setting is for 900 seconds if this policy is not set.

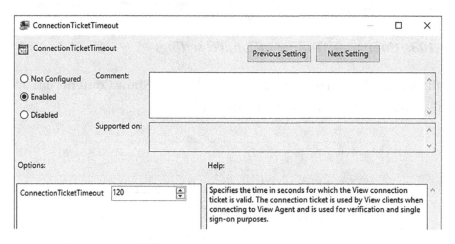

Figure 8-110. *ConnectionTicketTimeout*

CredentialFilterExceptions

This allows you to configure a list of executable files that are not able to load the agent CredentialFilter as shown in the following screenshot:

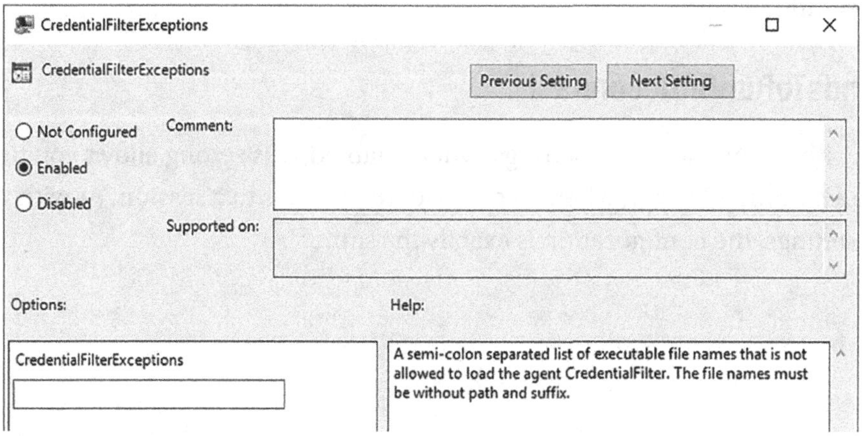

Figure 8-111. *CredentialFilterExceptions*

Disable Time Zone Synchronization

This policy setting, when enabled, synchronizes the time zone between the virtual desktop and the end user's device. It is disabled by default.

DPI Synchronization

This adjusts the system-wide DPI setting for the remote session. When this setting is enabled or not configured, the system-wide DPI setting for the remote session is set to match the corresponding DPI setting on the client operating system. When this setting is disabled, the system-wide DPI setting for the remote session is never changed.

This setting is enabled by default.

DPI Synchronization Per Monitor

This setting allows you to adjust the DPI setting when using multiple screens. When set to enabled or not configured, then the DPI setting on all screens matches the OS setting of the client device while running a remote session.

Enable Battery State Redirection

This policy setting configures whether battery state redirection is enabled. This feature is supported with both Windows and Linux client systems and is enabled by default.

When enabled, information about the client system's battery is redirected to a Windows remote desktop.

Enable multi-media acceleration

This policy setting allows you to configure the multimedia redirection (MMR) on the remote desktop. This setting is enabled by default.

Force MMR to use software overlay

MMR will use the hardware overlay for video playback to deliver better performance. With multiple screens, the hardware overlay exists on only one of the screens. This is the primary screen or the screen where WMP was started.

If WMP is dragged to another screen, video will appear as a black rectangle. Enable this policy to force MMR to use a software overlay that will work on all screens.

Prewarm Session Time Limit

This policy setting specifies the amount of time after which a prewarm session will automatically log off. This setting is not configured by default and is shown in the following screenshot:

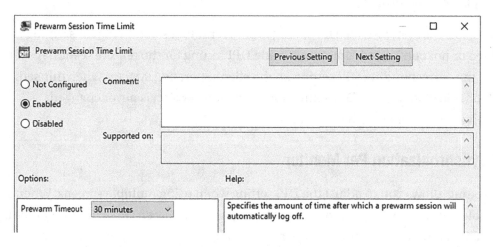

Figure 8-112. *Prewarm Session Time Limit*

Single sign-on retry timeout

This policy setting configures the time, in milliseconds, after which SSO is retried. Set the value to 0 to disable SSO retry. The default value is 5000 ms.

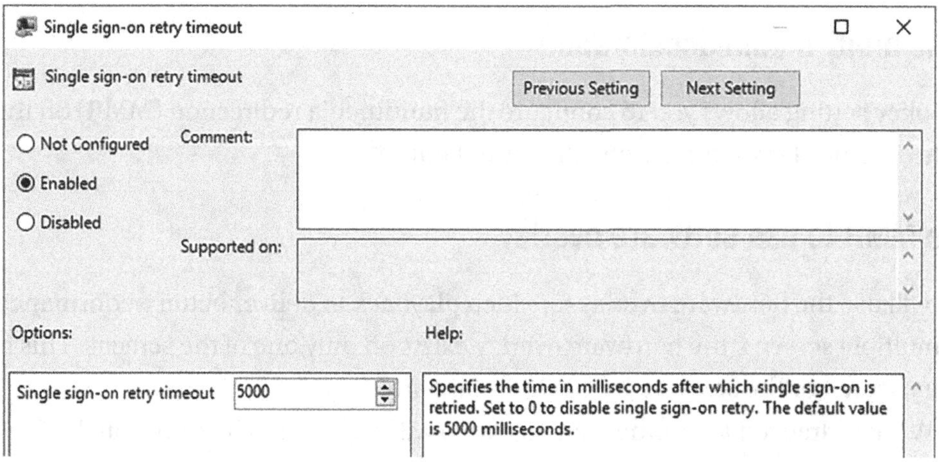

Figure 8-113. *Single sign-on retry timeout*

ShowDiskActivityIcon

This policy enables you to configure the disk activity icon on the system tray. By default, this is enabled.

Toggle Display Settings Control

Enabling this policy configures whether you disable the settings page on the display control panel page when a session is running. By default, this policy is set to enabled and only applies to the PCoIP session.

Enable Unauthenticated Access

This policy setting allows you to enable the Unauthenticated Access feature and is enabled by default. If you make any changes to this setting, then you will need to reboot.

Disconnected Session Time Limit (VDI)

Enabling this policy allows you to configure the time after which a session that becomes disconnected is logged off. This setting is similar to the desktop pool setting of automatically log off after disconnect; however, if both are configured, then this setting will override the pool setting.

If you click to enable this policy setting and then click the **Disconnect Timeout** drop-down menu, you will see the following options as shown in the following screenshot:

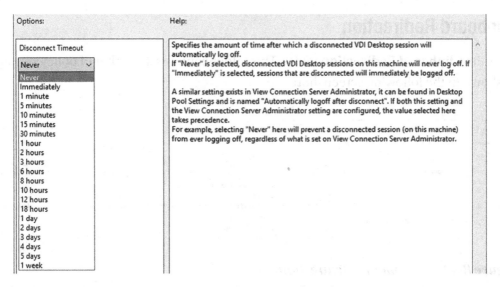

Figure 8-114. *Disconnected Session Time Limit (VDI)*

Idle Time Until Disconnect (VDI)

Similar to the previous policy setting, enabling this policy allows you to configure the time after which a session that is idle is disconnected.

If disabled or not configured, then the session will never be disconnected, which is the same outcome as setting this policy to **Never**.

By clicking enable, you can then click the **Idle Timeout** drop-down menu where you will see the timing options which are the same as with the previous policy shown in Figure 8-114.

Agent Security

Click the **Agent Security** folder. This folder contains just a single policy for **Accept SSL encrypted framework channel**. This is shown in the following screenshot, along with the settings options in the drop-down menu.

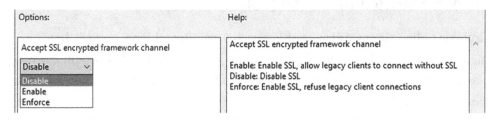

Figure 8-115. *Accept SSL encrypted framework channel*

Clipboard Redirection

Click the **Clipboard Redirection** folder. This folder contains a number of policy settings as shown in the following screenshot:

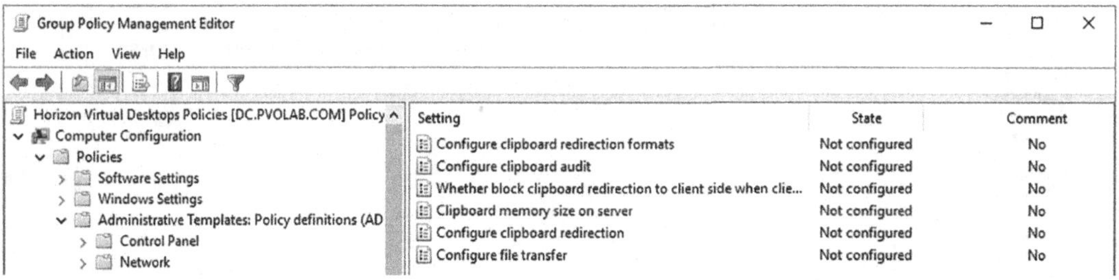

Figure 8-116. *Clipboard Redirection*

We will walk through the Clipboard Redirection policies starting with the **Configure clipboard redirection formats** setting.

Configure clipboard redirection formats

This setting allows you to configure clipboard redirection for the listed apps:

Figure 8-117.   *Configure clipboard redirection formats*

Configure clipboard audit

The clipboard audit setting allows you to configure which direction the clipboard audit is allowed and by default is set to disabled for both directions. The setting and configuration options are shown in the following screenshot:

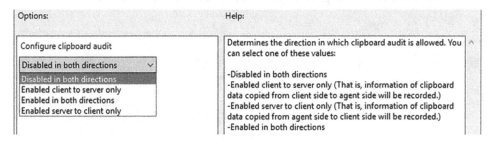

Figure 8-118. *Configure clipboard audit*

Whether block clipboard redirection to client side when client doesn't support audit

This setting enables configuration of blocking clipboard redirection if the client does not support the audit feature.

Note that this setting only works if you enable the audit feature in the previous policy setting.

The configuration options are shown in the following screenshot:

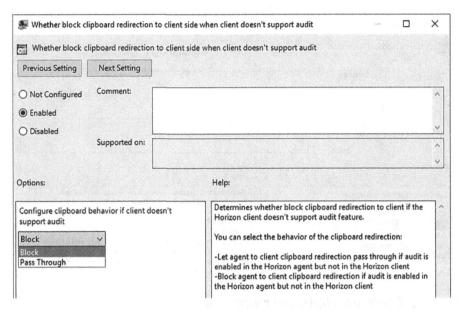

Figure 8-119. *Block clipboard redirection to client side*

Clipboard memory size on server

Enabling this setting allows you to configure the size of the memory used for the clipboard on the server in either kilobytes or bytes as shown in the following:

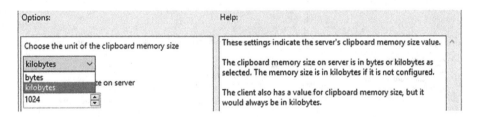

Figure 8-120. *Clipboard memory size on server*

Configure clipboard redirection

Enabling the clipboard redirection setting allows you to configure in which direction clipboard redirection is allowed. This is shown in the following:

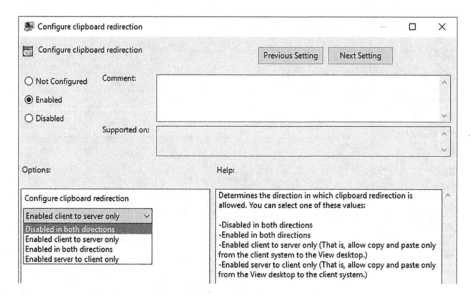

Figure 8-121. *Configure clipboard redirection*

Configure file transfer

This policy allows you to enable file transfer between the agent and HTML access and configures whether upload, download, or both is allowed. The configuration options are shown in the following screenshot:

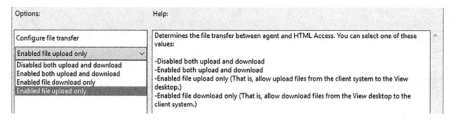

Figure 8-122. *Configure file transfer*

Collaboration

Click the **Collaboration** folder. This folder contains a number of policy settings as shown in the following screenshot:

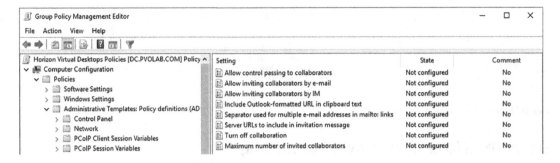

Figure 8-123. *Collaboration*

We will walk through the Collaboration policies starting with the **Allow control passing to collaborators** setting.

Allow control passing to collaborators

Enabling this setting allows end users to pass input control to other end users when using the collaboration feature. This is enabled by default.

Allow inviting collaborators by e-mail

By enabling this setting, you can allow end users to send collaboration invites to other end users via email. This is enabled by default.

Allow inviting collaborators by IM

By enabling this setting, you can allow end users to send collaboration invites to other end users via an instant messaging app. This is enabled by default.

Include Outlook-formatted URL in clipboard text

This policy setting, when enabled, allows end users to send an Outlook invitation URL so that they can paste the invitation text into an email. This is disabled by default.

Separator used for multiple e-mail addresses in mailto: links

With this setting, you can configure the separator that is used to separate multiple email addresses in a list of emails on a mailto link. The default is to use a semicolon. The configuration screen is shown in the following:

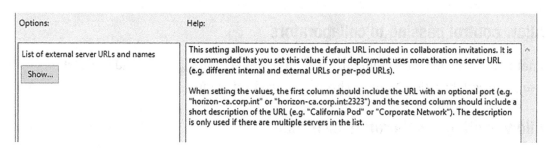

Figure 8-124. Collaboration

Server URLs to include in invitation message

Enabling this policy means that you can override the default URL that is included in the collaboration invites. You should use this setting if you have more than one server. You will see the following screenshot:

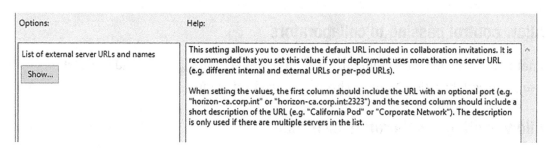

Figure 8-125. Collaboration

Click the **Show...** button. You will see the **Show Content** box where you can add the server URLs you want to include in this setting. Enter the server URL in the first column and a description in the second.

Turn off collaboration

Either enabled or disabled, this setting simply turns the collaboration feature on or off. If you set this to disabled or not configured, then this setting will be controlled by the desktop pool.

Maximum number of invited collaborators

Enabling this policy allows you to set the maximum number of end users that can collaborate on a session. The configuration is shown in the following screenshot:

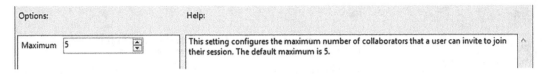

Figure 8-126. *Collaboration*

Drag and Drop

Click the **Drag and Drop** folder. This folder contains a number of policy settings as shown in the following screenshot:

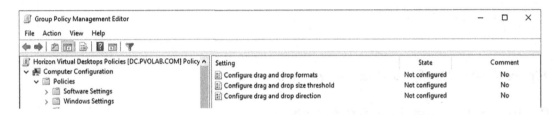

Figure 8-127. *Drag and Drop*

We will start with the **Configure drag and drop formats** setting.

Configure drag and drop formats

When enabled, this setting allows you to set and control the direction of dragging and dropping different file formats.

The following screenshot shows the configuration options that can be configured for each one:

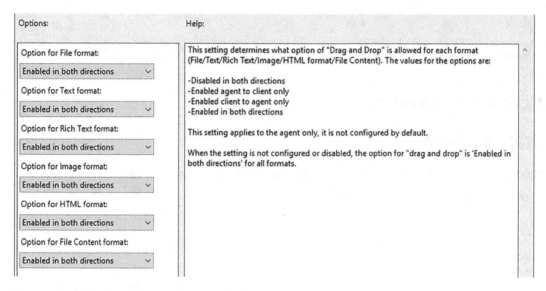

Figure 8-128. *Configure drag and drop formats*

Configure drag and drop size threshold

This setting allows you to configure a size limit (bytes, kilobytes, and megabytes) for the data that is dragged and dropped as shown in the following screenshot:

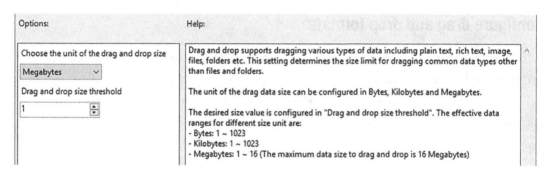

Figure 8-129. *Configure drag and drop size threshold*

If you set this to disabled or not configured, then a 1 MB limit is set, which applies only to the Horizon Agent.

Configure drag and drop direction

This policy allows you to configure the direction of drag and drop between the agent and the client. The following screenshot shows the configuration options:

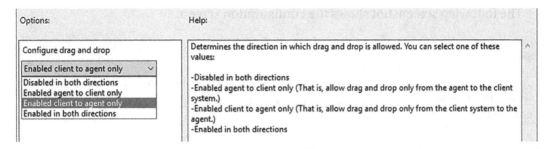

Figure 8-130. *Configure drag and drop direction*

Performance Tracker

Click the **Performance Tracker** folder. This folder contains a number of policy settings as shown in the following screenshot:

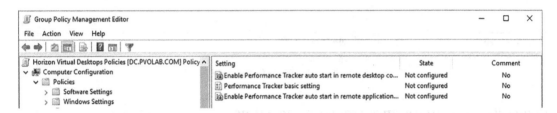

Figure 8-131. *Performance Tracker settings*

We will walk through the Performance Tracker policies starting with the **Enable Performance Tracker auto start in remote desktop connection** setting.

Enable Performance Tracker auto start in remote desktop connection

Enabling this setting means that the performance tracker will automatically start when an end user connects and logs in to a session. When enabled, you can enter the performance tracker installation path. By default, the path is as shown:

```
C:\Program Files\VMware\VMware View\Agent\Horizon Performance Tracker\VMware.Horizon.PerformanceTracker.exe
```

The following screenshot shows the configuration screen:

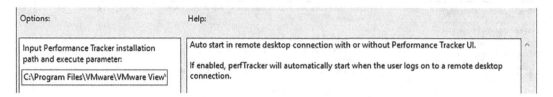

Figure 8-132. *Enable Performance Tracker auto start in remote desktop*

Performance Tracker basic setting

With this policy setting, you can configure the rate at which the performance tracker updates the data as shown in the following screenshot:

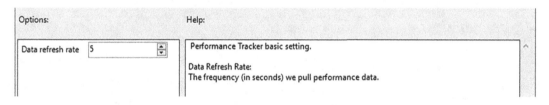

Figure 8-133. *Performance Tracker basic setting*

Enable Performance Tracker auto start in remote application session

By enabling this setting, the performance tracker will automatically start in a remote app session when an end user logs in. As with the remote desktop version of this setting, you can specify the installation path of the performance tracker.

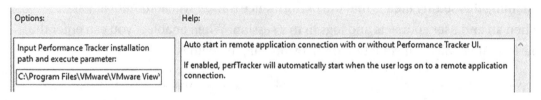

Figure 8-134. *Enable Performance Tracker auto start in app sessions*

The next set of configuration settings are for **Scanner Redirection** policy settings.

Scanner Redirection

Click the **Scanner Redirection** folder. This folder contains a number of policy settings as shown in the following screenshot:

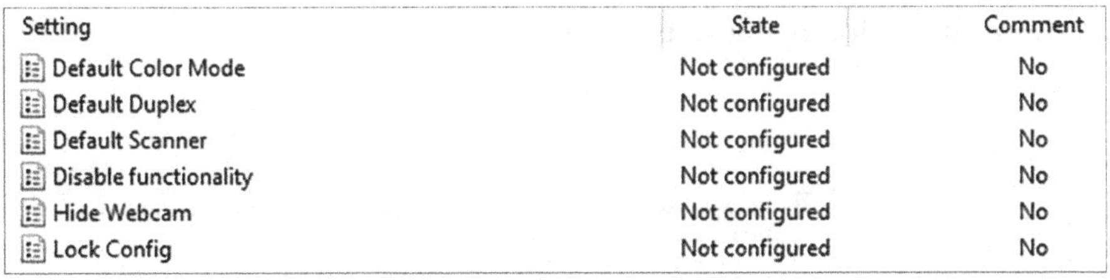

Setting	State	Comment
Default Color Mode	Not configured	No
Default Duplex	Not configured	No
Default Scanner	Not configured	No
Disable functionality	Not configured	No
Hide Webcam	Not configured	No
Lock Config	Not configured	No

Figure 8-135. *Scanner Redirection settings*

We will walk through the Scanner Redirection policies starting with the **Default Color Mode** setting.

Default Color Mode

This policy allows you to override the scanner color mode as shown in the following screenshot:

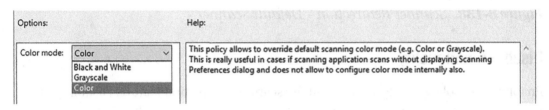

Figure 8-136. *Scanner Redirection – Default Color Mode*

Default Duplex

Enabling this policy allows you to override the duplex mode as shown in the following screenshot:

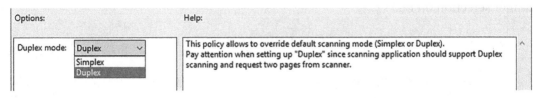

Figure 8-137. *Scanner Redirection – Default Duplex*

Default Scanner

This policy allows you to centrally manage the scanner auto selection by clicking the drop-down menu for either TWAIN scanners or WIA scanners and selecting **Autoselect**, **Last used**, or **Specified**. With specified, you can then enter the name of the scanner in the box as shown in the following screenshot:

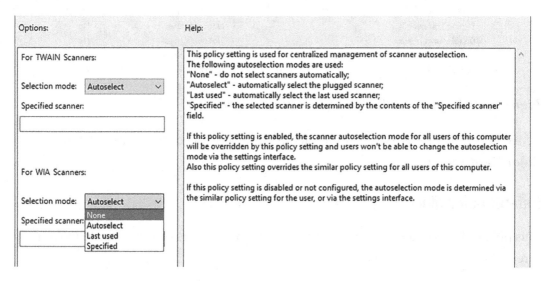

Figure 8-138. *Scanner Redirection – Default Scanner*

Disable functionality

Enabling this policy simply switches off the scanner redirection feature. Disabling or setting this policy to not configured means that scanners will be redirected.

Hide Webcam

Enabling this policy will hide the webcam so that it cannot be used as a scanner. This means that the webcam will not appear in the scanner selection menu. Disabling or setting this policy to not configured means that webcams will be available from the scanner selection menu.

Lock Config

This policy, when enabled, locks the settings UI of the program. This means that an end user cannot change tray menu settings.

The next set of configuration options are for **Serial COM** policy settings.

Serial COM

Click the **Serial COM** folder. This folder contains a number of policy settings as shown in the following screenshot:

Setting	State	Comment
PortSettings		
Bandwidth limit	Not configured	No
Disable functionality	Not configured	No
Local settings priority	Not configured	No
Lock configuration	Not configured	No
COM Port Isolation Mode	Not configured	No
Connect all ports automatically	Not configured	No

Figure 8-139. *Serial COM settings*

There is also a sub-folder for **PortSettings** which we will discuss at the end of this section.

We will start this section by taking a walk-through of the Serial COM policies starting with the **Bandwidth limit** setting.

Bandwidth limit

This policy, when enabled, allows you to configure a bandwidth limit between the agent and the client as shown in the following screenshot:

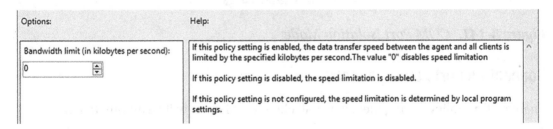

Options:	Help:
Bandwidth limit (in kilobytes per second): 0	If this policy setting is enabled, the data transfer speed between the agent and all clients is limited by the specified kilobytes per second. The value "0" disables speed limitation If this policy setting is disabled, the speed limitation is disabled. If this policy setting is not configured, the speed limitation is determined by local program settings.

Figure 8-140. *Bandwidth limit*

Disable functionality

This policy simply enables or disables the setting. When enabled, there will be no client connection, ports are not redirected, and the tray menu icon is not shown.

Local settings priority

If you enable this policy, then any local program settings will take priority over the settings configured in the policy. When set to disabled or not configured, then the policy settings will take priority.

Lock configuration

This policy setting, when enabled, locks the UI that has the program settings so that an end user cannot change any of the settings in the system tray menu. If this policy is set at the computer level, it takes priority over the user policy.

COM Port Isolation Mode

Enabling this policy allows you to configure the COM port isolation mode. In full isolation mode, end users will be able to see and access COM ports within just their session. If you select isolation disabled from the drop-down menu, then COM ports are visible globally as shown in the following screenshot:

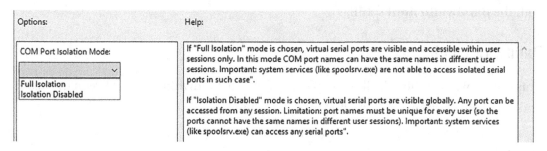

Figure 8-141. *COM Port Isolation Mode*

Connect all ports automatically

Enabling this policy setting means that all client COM ports will be automatically connected.

Finally, under this set of policy settings, there is the **PortSettings** folder. This contains five different port settings that allow you to configure the properties for each port.

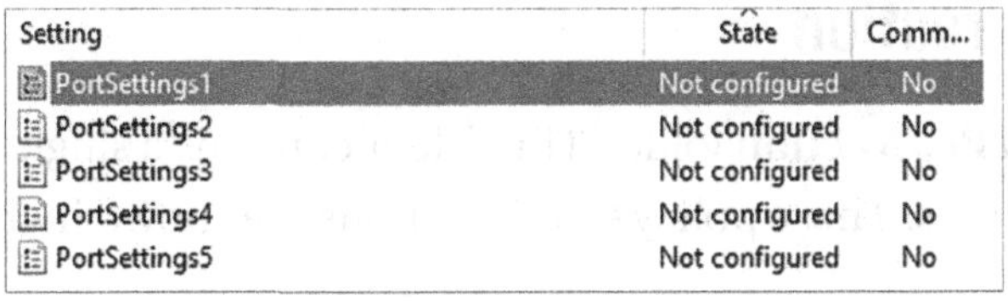

Setting	State	Comm...
PortSettings1	Not configured	No
PortSettings2	Not configured	No
PortSettings3	Not configured	No
PortSettings4	Not configured	No
PortSettings5	Not configured	No

Figure 8-142. *Port Settings*

You have the following configuration options:

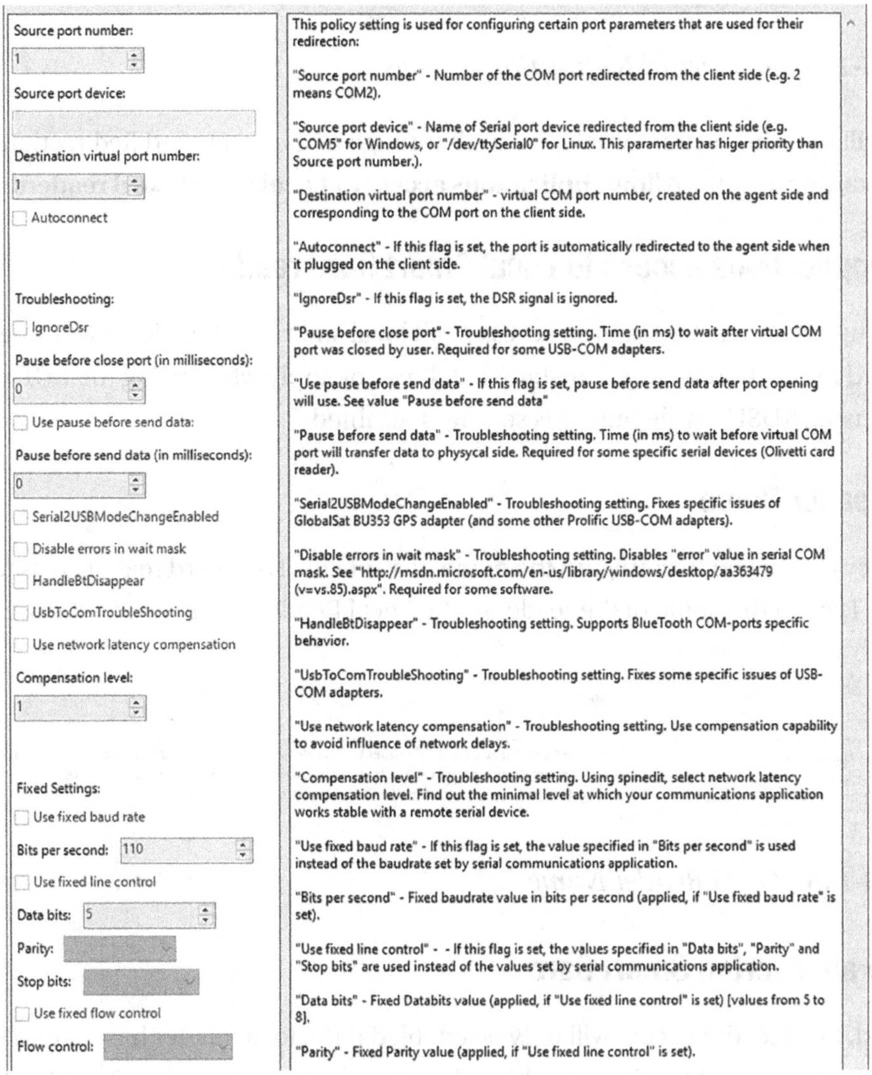

Figure 8-143. *Port Settings configuration*

Smartcard Redirection

Click the **Smartcard Redirection** folder. This folder contains a single sub-folder for **Local Reader Access**. These policy setting options are shown in the following screenshot:

Setting	State	Comment
Allow applications access to Local Smart Card readers	Not configured	No
Local Reader Name	Not configured	No
Require an inserted Smart Card	Not configured	No

Figure 8-144. *Smartcard Redirection settings*

We will start this section by taking a walk-through of the Smartcard Redirection policies starting with the **Allow applications access to Local Smart Card readers** setting.

Allow applications access to Local Smart Card readers

This setting, when enabled, allows access to all local smart card readers even when the smart card redirection feature is installed. It does not apply when using the RDP protocol or when using RDSH. By default, this setting is disabled.

Local Reader Name

This policy allows you to configure the name of a specific local card reader so as to allow it access. Type in the name of the reader in the Local Reader Name box as shown:

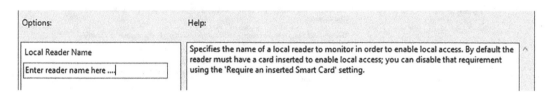

Options:	Help:
Local Reader Name Enter reader name here	Specifies the name of a local reader to monitor in order to enable local access. By default the reader must have a card inserted to enable local access; you can disable that requirement using the 'Require an inserted Smart Card' setting.

Figure 8-145. *Local Reader Name*

Require an inserted Smart Card

If enabled, local reader access will only be enabled if the local reader has a smart card inserted. By default, this policy is enabled. The next folder contains the **True SSO Configuration** policy settings.

True SSO Configuration

Click the **True SSO Configuration** folder. These policy setting options are shown in the following screenshot:

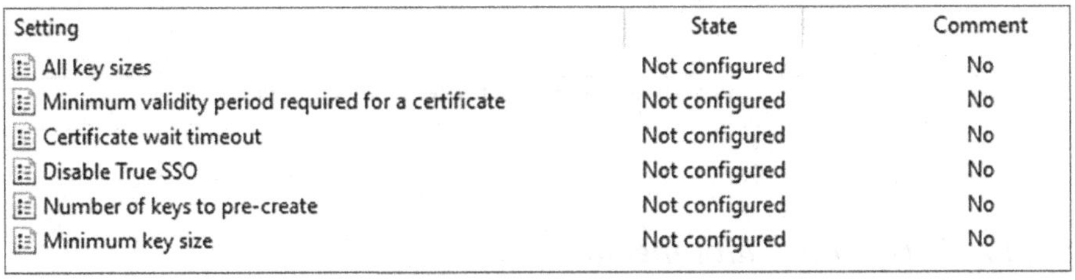

Setting	State	Comment
All key sizes	Not configured	No
Minimum validity period required for a certificate	Not configured	No
Certificate wait timeout	Not configured	No
Disable True SSO	Not configured	No
Number of keys to pre-create	Not configured	No
Minimum key size	Not configured	No

Figure 8-146. *True SSO Configuration*

We will start with the **All key sizes** setting.

All key sizes

This policy, when enabled, allows you to configure the key sizes that can be used. You can specify a maximum of five as shown in the following:

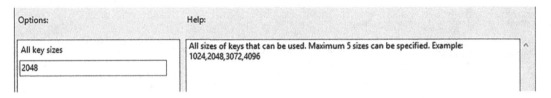

Options:	Help:
All key sizes 2048	All sizes of keys that can be used. Maximum 5 sizes can be specified. Example: 1024,2048,3072,4096

Figure 8-147. *All key sizes*

Minimum validity period required for a certificate

This policy allows you to configure the minimum validity period for a certificate that is being reused when an end user reconnects.

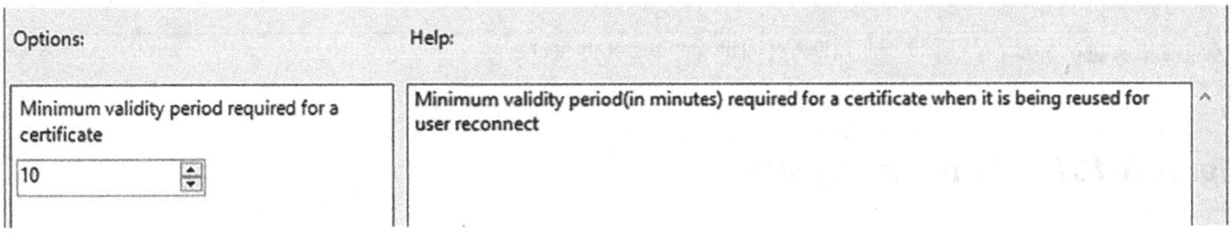

Options:	Help:
Minimum validity period required for a certificate 10	Minimum validity period(in minutes) required for a certificate when it is being reused for user reconnect

Figure 8-148. *Minimum validity period required for a certificate*

Certificate wait timeout

With this policy setting, you can specify a certificate timeout period as shown in the following screenshot:

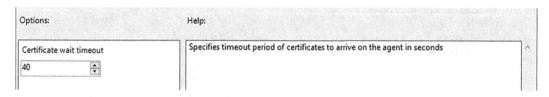

Figure 8-149. *Certificate wait timeout*

Disable True SSO

Enabling this policy allows you to disable the True SSO feature on the Agent.

Number of keys to pre-create

With this policy, you can configure the number of keys that can be pre-created for using RDSH as shown in the following screenshot:

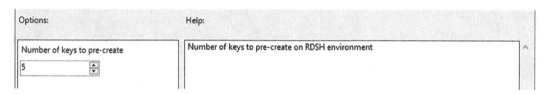

Figure 8-150. *Number of keys to pre-create*

Minimum key size

This policy allows you to configure a minimum size for keys as shown:

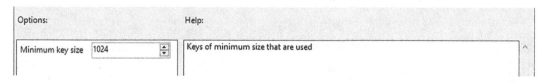

Figure 8-151. *Minimum key size*

The next folder contains the **Unity Touch and Hosted Apps** policy settings.

Unity Touch and Hosted Apps

Click the Unity Touch and Hosted Apps folder. The policy setting options are shown in the following screenshot:

Setting	State	Comment
Send updates for empty or offscreen windows	Not configured	No
Enable UWP support on RDSH platforms	Not configured	No
Enable Unity Touch	Not configured	No
Enable system tray redirection for Hosted Apps	Not configured	No
Enable user profile customization for Hosted Apps	Not configured	No
Only launch new instances of Hosted Apps if arguments are...	Not configured	No
Limit usage of Windows hooks	Not configured	No
Unity Filter rule list	Not configured	No

Figure 8-152. *Unity Touch and Hosted Apps*

We will start this section with the **Send updates for empty or offscreen windows** setting.

Send updates for empty or offscreen windows

Enabling this policy setting configures whether the client should receive updates about empty or off-screen windows. With this policy disabled, windows smaller than 2x2 pixels or not currently shown on screen will not be sent to the client.

Enable UWP support on RDSH platforms

This policy, when enabled, configures whether Universal Windows Platform (UWP) apps can be scanned and launched using RDSH Servers that support UWP. Note this is for server OSs and not for virtual desktop machines.

Enable Unity Touch

With this policy, you can simply enable the unity touch feature as shown:

Options:	Help:
☑ Enable Universal Windows Platform(UWP) app support for Unity Touch on Windows 10.	This policy specifies whether the Unity Touch functionality is enabled on the View Agent. The default for this setting is that Unity Touch is enabled.

Figure 8-153. *Enable Unity Touch*

Once enabled, you can select whether you want to enable UWP apps for unity touch on Windows 10.

The next few policy settings are simply enabled or disabled and have no other settings that can be configured.

Enable system tray redirection for Hosted Apps

This policy configures whether system tray redirection should be enabled when using hosted apps. By default, this setting is enabled.

Enable user profile customization for Hosted Apps

This policy allows you to configure whether end-user profile customization is enabled when an end user is using hosted apps.

Only launch new instances of Hosted Apps if arguments are different

With this policy, by enabling it you can control what happens if the end user launches a hosted app and there is already an instance of that hosted app still running but in a disconnected session.

Setting this policy to disabled means that the existing session will be used rather than a new one. The default setting is disabled.

Limit usage of Windows hooks

You can configure this policy to switch off hooks when using hosted apps or Unity Touch. This can be used for compatibility or performance issues when OS hooks are set. This setting disables things like Windows accessibility and in-process hooks and is disabled by default, meaning all preferred hooks can be used.

Unity Filter rule list

Enabling this policy allows you to configure filter rules when using hosted apps. The filter rules are used by the agent so that custom apps can be supported and would be used if you experience display problems.

To create a filter rule list, first enable the policy, and then click the **Show...** button as shown in the following screenshot:

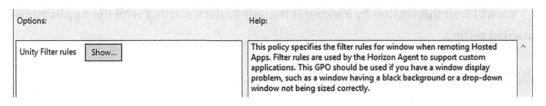

Options:	Help:
Unity Filter rules Show...	This policy specifies the filter rules for window when remoting Hosted Apps. Filter rules are used by the Horizon Agent to support custom applications. This GPO should be used if you have a window display problem, such as a window having a black background or a drop-down window not being sized correctly.

Figure 8-154. *Unity Filter rules*

Then, in the **Show Contents** box, enter the details for the rule, starting with the characteristics as shown in the following:

```
1. Window classname, identified in a custom rule as classname=XYZ
2. Product company, identified as company=XYZ
3. Product name, identified as product=XYZ
4. Product major version, identified as major=XYZ
5. Product minor version, identified as minor=XYZ
6. Product build number, identified as build=XYZ
7. Product revision number, identified as revision=XYZ
```

Figure 8-155. *Unity Filter rules – characteristics*

Then, you need to configure an action. This can be either **action=block** or **action=map**. Block stops the agent from remoting the windows to the client, while map will also need the type to map the windows to, such as a toolbar or desktop.

View Agent Direct-Connection Configuration

Click the **View Agent Direct-Connection Configuration** folder. These policy setting options are shown in the following screenshot and also include a number of sub-folders:

Setting	State	Comment
Authentication		
Protocol and Network Settings		
Applications Enabled	Not configured	No
Client Config Name Value Pairs	Not configured	No
Client Session Timeout	Not configured	No
Client setting: AlwaysConnect	Not configured	No
Client setting: AutoConnect	Not configured	No
Client setting: ScreenSize	Not configured	No
Multimedia redirection (MMR) Enabled	Not configured	No
Reset Enabled	Not configured	No
Session Timeout	Not configured	No
USB AutoConnect	Not configured	No
USB Enabled	Not configured	No
User Idle Timeout	Not configured	No

Figure 8-156. *View Agent Direct-Connection Configuration*

We will start this section by looking at the sub-folders, starting with the **Applications Enabled** setting.

Application Enabled

This policy simply enables apps to be launched from an RDSH Server and is enabled by default.

Client Config Name Value Pairs

This policy allows you to configure a list of values that can be passed to the client as shown:

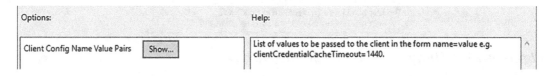

Figure 8-157. *Client Config Name Value Pairs*

To configure a list of values, click the **Show...** button, and then in the **Show Contents** box, enter the values you want to configure.

Client Session Timeout

With this policy, when enabled, you can configure the maximum length of time that a session will remain active for as shown in the following:

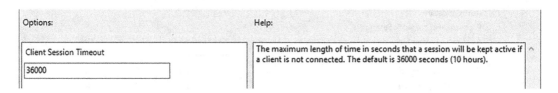

Figure 8-158. *Client Session Timeout*

Client setting: AlwaysConnect

Either enabled or disabled, this setting allows you to configure whether the client is set to always connect.

Client setting: AutoConnect

Either enabled or disabled, this setting allows you to configure whether the client is set to auto connect.

Client setting: ScreenSize

This policy setting allows you to configure the screen size that is sent to the client.

Multimedia redirection (MMR) Enabled

With this policy, you can configure whether to use MMR or not. By default, this setting is disabled.

Reset Enabled

Enabling this policy allows an authenticated end user to reboot the OS.

Session Timeout

This policy allows you to configure how long an end user can keep their session open once they have logged in. The default setting is 600 minutes and is shown in the following screenshot:

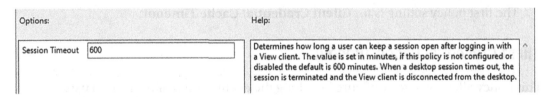

Figure 8-159. *Session Timeout*

USB AutoConnect

This allows you to configure whether USB devices are automatically connected when they are plugged in.

USB Enabled

This policy simply switches on or off the USB feature and if USB can be used.

User Idle Timeout

When enabled, this policy configures the maximum amount of time an end user can remain idle for as shown in the following screenshot:

Options:	Help:
User Idle Timeout	The maximum length of time in seconds that a user can be idle before the service takes measures to protect the session. A value of -1 indicates that the session will never be considered idle. The default is 900 seconds (15 minutes).

Figure 8-160. *User Idle Timeout*

The first of the sub-folders in this folder is for the **Authentication** settings. The Authentication folder contains the following policy settings:

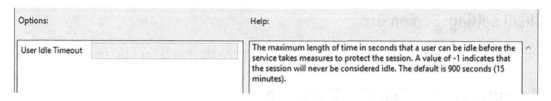

Setting	State	Comment
Log On As Current User		
Client Credential Cache Timeout	Not configured	No
Disclaimer Enabled	Not configured	No
Disclaimer Text	Not configured	No
X509 Certificate Authentication	Not configured	No
X509 SSL Certificate Authentication Enabled	Not configured	No

Figure 8-161. *Authentication configuration settings*

The first policy setting is for **Client Credential Cache Timeout**.

Client Credential Cache Timeout

This policy allows you to configure how long the client should allow an end user's password to be saved for as shown in the following screenshot:

Options:	Help:
Client Credential Cache Timeout 0	How long in minutes a View client should allow a user to use a saved password for. 0 means never, -1 means forever. View clients will offer users the option of saving their passwords if this is set to a valid value. The default is 0 (never).

Figure 8-162. *Client Credential Cache Timeout*

Disclaimer Enabled

This policy allows you to enable a text message disclaimer when an end user logs in. By default, this setting is disabled. The message displayed can be configured in the next setting.

Disclaimer Text

When enabled and the disclaimer policy is enabled, this screen allows you to type in the text that gets displayed in the disclaimer as shown:

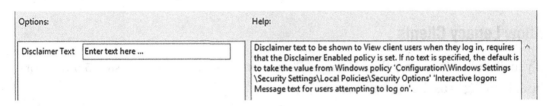

Figure 8-163. *Disclaimer text*

X509 Certificate Authentication

With this policy, you can configure whether smart card X.509 certification is required or not. The following screenshot shows the configurable options:

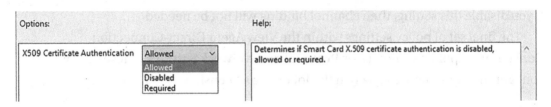

Figure 8-164. *X509 Certificate Authentication*

X509 SSL Certificate Authentication Enabled

With this policy, you can configure whether a smart card X.509 certificate is enabled when connecting from a client using a direct SSL connection.

Finally, there is another sub-folder in the Authentication section for **Log On As Current User**. This folder contains the following policy configuration options as shown:

Setting	State	Comment
Allow Legacy Clients	Not configured	No
Allow NTLM fallback	Not configured	No
Require Channel Bindings	Not configured	No

Figure 8-165. *Log On As Current User configuration settings*

We will start with the **Allow Legacy Clients** policy settings.

Allow Legacy Clients

If you disable this setting, then Horizon Client versions earlier than version 5.5 will not be able to log in as the current user.

Allow NTLM fallback

By enabling this policy, you allow fallback from Kerberos to NTLM authentication should the client not be able to contact a domain controller.

Require Channel Binding

If you disable this setting, then channel binding will not be needed.

The final set of policy settings within the View Agent Direct-Connection Configuration policy section is for **Protocol and Network Settings**. These policy configuration options are shown in the following screenshot:

Setting	State	Comment
Default Protocol	Not configured	No
External Blast Port	Not configured	No
External Framework Channel Port	Not configured	No
External IP Address	Not configured	No
External PCoIP Port	Not configured	No
External RDP Port	Not configured	No
HTTPS Port Number	Not configured	No

Figure 8-166. *Protocol and Network configuration settings*

The first policy setting in this folder is for **Default Protocol**.

Default Protocol

This policy setting allows you to configure the default display protocol that is used by the client to connect to the desktop. The default setting is BLAST as shown:

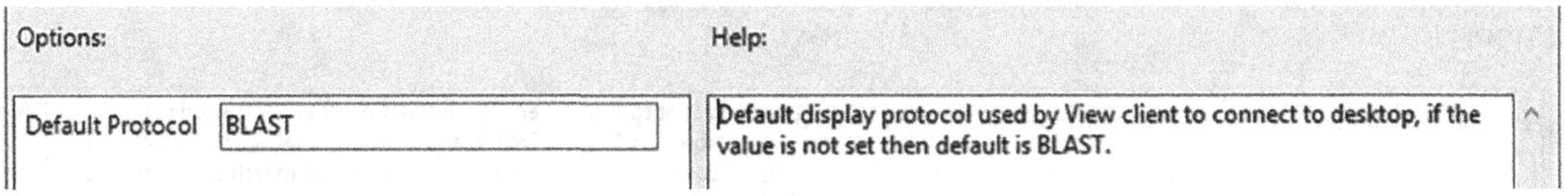

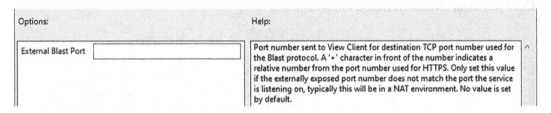

Figure 8-167. *Default Protocol*

External Blast Port

This policy enables you to configure the port number for Blast that is sent to the client as shown in the following:

Figure 8-168. *External Blast Port*

External Framework Channel Port

This policy enables you to configure the port number for Blast that is sent to the client used for the Framework Channel as shown in the following:

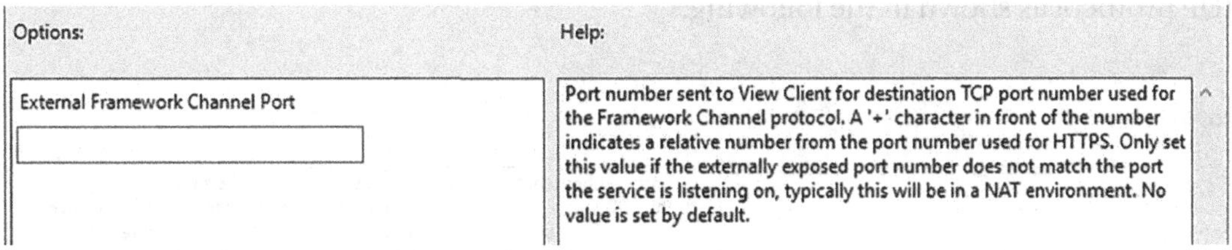

Figure 8-169. *External Framework Channel Port*

External IP Address

This policy allows you to configure an IPv4 address to send to the client as shown in the following:

Options:
Help:
External IP Address
IP v4 address sent to View Client for destination IP address used for secondary protocols (RDP, PCoIP, Framework channel, Blast ...). Only set this value if the externally exposed address does not match the address of the desktop machine, typically this will be in a NAT environment. No value is set by default.

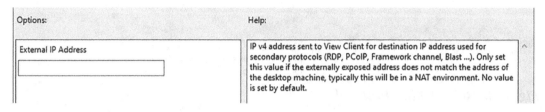

Figure 8-170. *External IP Address*

External PCoIP Port

This policy enables you to configure the port number sent to the client when using the PCoIP protocol as shown in the following:

Options:
Help:
External PCoIP Port
Port number sent to View Client for destination TCP/UDP port number used for the PCoIP protocol. A '+' character in front of the number indicates a relative number from the port number used for HTTPS. Only set this value if the externally exposed port number does not match the port the service is listening on, typically this will be in a NAT environment. No value is set by default.

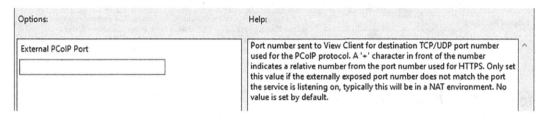

Figure 8-171. *External PCoIP Port*

External RDP Port

This policy enables you to configure the port number sent to the client when using the RDP protocol as shown in the following:

Options:
Help:
External RDP Port
Port number sent to View Client for destination TCP port number used for the RDP protocol. A '+' character in front of the number indicates a relative number from the port number used for HTTPS. Only set this value if the externally exposed port number does not match the port the service is listening on, typically this will be in a NAT environment. No value is set by default.

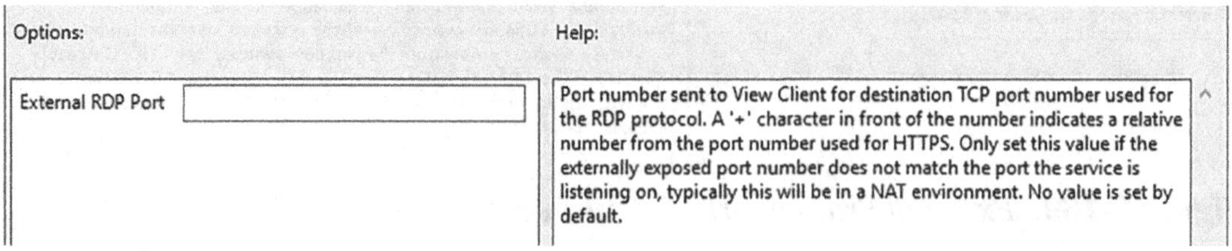

Figure 8-172. *External RDP Port*

HTTPS Port Number

This policy, when enabled, configures the TCP port which the agent listens on for incoming client HTTPS connections. The default port is 443. If you change the port number, then you may also need to update the firewall port to reflect the change.

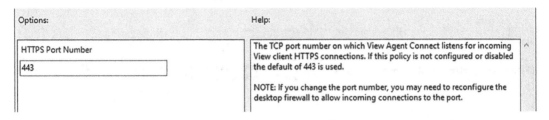

Options:	Help:
HTTPS Port Number 443	The TCP port number on which View Agent Connect listens for incoming View client HTTPS connections. If this policy is not configured or disabled the default of 443 is used. NOTE: If you change the port number, you may need to reconfigure the desktop firewall to allow incoming connections to the port.

Figure 8-173. *HTTPS Port Number*

The next folder contains the **View RTAV Configuration** policy settings.

View RTAV Configuration

Click the **View RTAV Configuration** folder. You will see that there is a single policy setting and a sub-folder for webcam settings as shown in the following:

Setting	State	Comment
View RTAV Webcam Settings		
Disable RTAV	Not configured	No

Figure 8-174. *View RTAV Configuration*

The only policy setting is for **Disable RTAV**, which when enabled turns off the Real Time Audio Video feature.

Next, you have the sub-folder for **View RTAV Webcam Settings**. Double-click to open the folder where you will see the policy settings as shown:

Setting	State	Comment
Resolution - Default image resolution height in pixels	Not configured	No
Resolution - Default image resolution width in pixels	Not configured	No
Max frames per second	Not configured	No
Resolution - Max image height in pixels	Not configured	No
Resolution - Max image width in pixels	Not configured	No

Figure 8-175. *View RTAV Webcam Settings*

583

The first policy setting in the View RTAV Webcam Settings folder is for **Resolution – Default image resolution height in pixels**.

Resolution – Default image resolution height in pixels

This setting, when enabled, allows you to set the image height in pixels as shown:

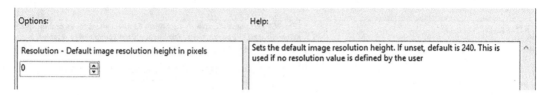

Figure 8-176. *Resolution – Default image resolution height in pixels*

Resolution – Default image resolution width in pixels

This setting, when enabled, allows you to set the image width in pixels as shown:

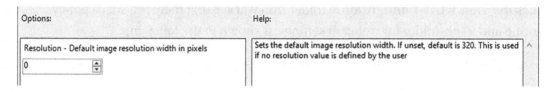

Figure 8-177. *Resolution – Default image resolution width in pixels*

Max frames per second

This policy allows you to configure the max frame rate for the webcam as shown:

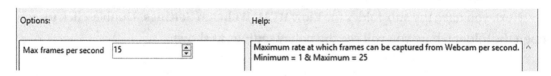

Figure 8-178. *Max frames per second*

Resolution – Max image height in pixels

This setting, when enabled, allows you to set the max image height in pixels:

Figure 8-179. *Max image height in pixels*

Resolution – Max image width in pixels

This setting, when enabled, allows you to set the max image width in pixels:

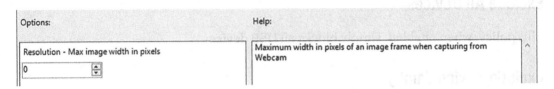

Figure 8-180. *Max image width in pixels*

The next folder contains the **View USB Configuration** policy settings.

View USB Configuration

Click the **View USB Configuration** folder. You will see that there are a number of policy settings and a sub-folder for Client Downloadable only settings as shown in the following screenshot:

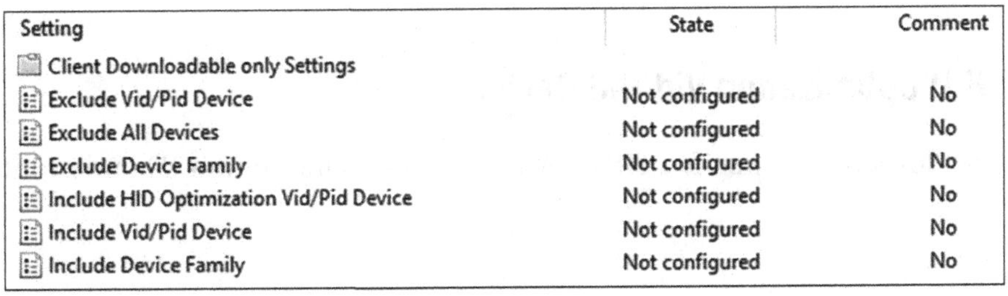

Setting	State	Comment
Client Downloadable only Settings		
Exclude Vid/Pid Device	Not configured	No
Exclude All Devices	Not configured	No
Exclude Device Family	Not configured	No
Include HID Optimization Vid/Pid Device	Not configured	No
Include Vid/Pid Device	Not configured	No
Include Device Family	Not configured	No

Figure 8-181. *View USB Configuration settings*

The first policy setting is for **Exclude Vid/Pid Device**.

Exclude Vid/Pid Device

With this policy, you can configure a specific USB device by vendor ID and product ID from being forwarded.

Use the syntax **{m|o}:<vid-<xxxx>_pid<xxxx>**, where **m** means the client setting is merged with the agent setting, and **o** means the agent overrides the client setting.

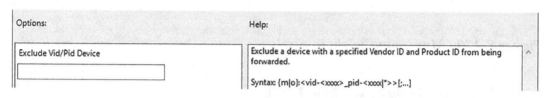

Figure 8-182. *Exclude Vid/Pid Device*

Exclude All Devices

This policy, when enabled, simply blocks all USB devices.

Exclude Device Family

This policy allows you to configure a specific family of devices that are prevented from being forwarded.

Use the syntax **{m|o}:<family-name>[....]**.

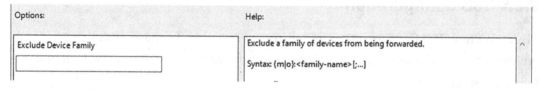

Figure 8-183. *Exclude Device Family*

Include HID Optimization Vid/Pid Device

This policy allows you to specify a HID device with a specific vendor ID and product ID.

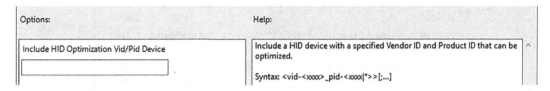

Figure 8-184. *Include HID Optimization Vid/Pid Device*

Include Vid/Pid Device

This policy allows you to specify a device by vendor ID and product ID that can be forwarded.

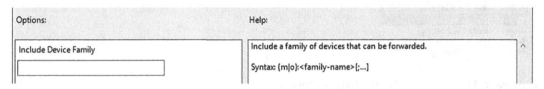

Figure 8-185. *Include Vid/Pid Device*

Include Device Family

This policy allows you to configure a specific family of devices that are able to be forwarded.

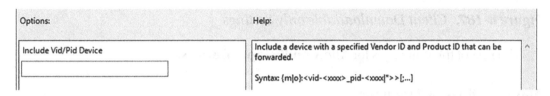

Figure 8-186. *Include Device Family*

Finally, there is the **Client Downloadable only Settings** sub-folder as shown in the following screenshot:

Setting	State	Comm...
Allow Audio Input Devices	Not configured	No
Allow Audio Output Devices	Not configured	No
Allow Auto Device Splitting	Not configured	No
Allow HID-Bootable	Not configured	No
Allow Smart Cards	Not configured	No
Allow Video Devices	Not configured	No
Allow keyboard and Mouse Devices	Not configured	No
Allow other input devices	Not configured	No
Exclude Automatically Connection Vid/Pid Device	Not configured	No
Exclude Vid/Pid Device from Split	Not configured	No
Exclude Automatically Connection Device Family	Not configured	No
Split Vid/Pid Device	Not configured	No

Figure 8-187. *Client Downloadable only Settings*

The first of the policies is for **Allow Audio Input Devices**.

Allow Audio Input Devices

This policy, when enabled, allows you to forward audio input devices as shown in the following screenshot:

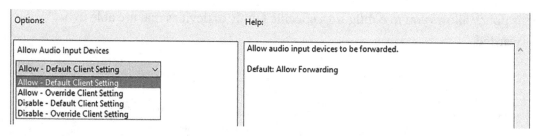

Figure 8-188. *Allow Audio Input Devices*

Allow Audio Output Devices

Similar to the previous policy, when enabled this setting allows you to forward audio output devices and has the same configuration options as shown in the previous settings screen.

Allow Auto Device Splitting

This setting allows you to exclude components when using composite devices from being automatically treated as separate devices and again has the same configuration options as shown in the previous settings screen.

Allow HID-Bootable

This policy setting enables bootable input devices to be forwarded. By default, forwarding is enabled. The settings are exactly the same as the previous policies.

Allow Smart Cards

This policy, simply enabled or disabled, enables smart card devices to be forwarded. By default, forwarding is disabled. The settings are exactly the same as the previous policies.

Allow Video Devices

This policy, simply enabled or disabled, enables video devices to be forwarded. By default, forwarding is enabled. The settings are exactly the same as the previous policies.

Allow keyboard and Mouse Devices

This policy, simply enabled or disabled, enables keyboards and mice to be forwarded. By default, forwarding is disabled. The settings are exactly the same as the previous policies.

Allow other input devices

The setting that shares exactly the same setting as the previous policies is to allow other types of input devices to be forwarded.

Again, it is a simple enabled or disabled policy, which enables devices other than those devices explicitly specified in the previous policy settings to be forwarded. By default, forwarding is enabled.

Exclude Automatically Connection Vid/Pid Device

This policy setting, when enabled, allows you to automatically exclude a device with the vendor ID and product ID that you specify from being forwarded.

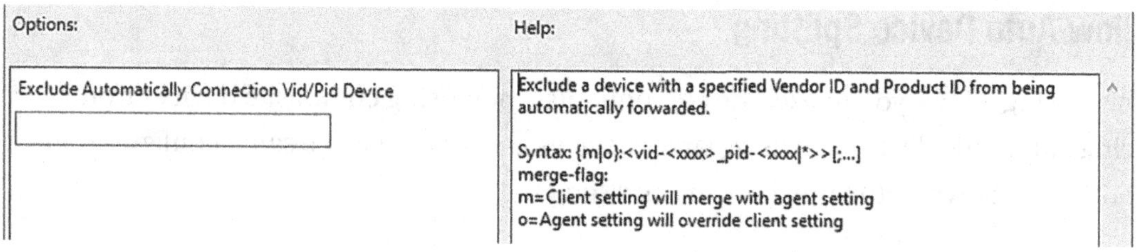

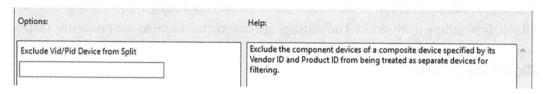

Figure 8-189. *Exclude Automatically Connection Vid/Pid Device*

Exclude Vid/Pid Device from split

This policy enables you to exclude component devices of a composite device that is specified by using its vendor ID and product ID as shown in the following:

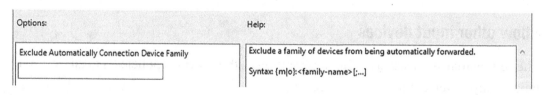

Figure 8-190. *Exclude Vid/Pid Device from split*

Exclude Automatically Connection Device Family

This policy setting, when enabled, allows you to exclude a device family from being automatically forwarded.

Figure 8-191. *Exclude Automatically Connection Device Family*

Split Vid/Pid Device

This policy enables you to treat component devices of a composite device using its vendor ID and product ID as shown in the following:

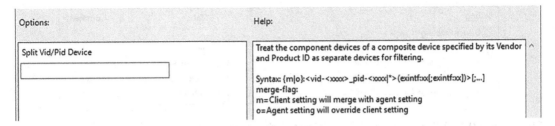

Figure 8-192. *Split Vid/Pid Device*

The next folder contains the **VMware App Tap Configuration** policy setting.

VMware App Tap Configuration

Click the **VMware App Tap Configuration** folder. You will see that there is just a single policy setting for Processes to ignore when detecting empty application sessions as shown in the following screenshot:

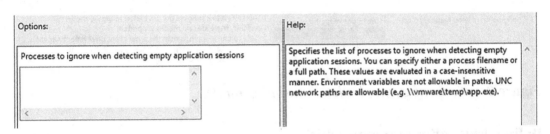

Figure 8-193. *VMware App Tap Configuration settings*

The next folder contains the **VMware Horizon Client Drive Redirection** policy setting.

VMware Horizon Client Drive Redirection

Click the **VMware Horizon Client Drive Redirection** folder. You will see that there are a number of policy settings and also a sub-folder for **Device Filtering** as shown in the following screenshot:

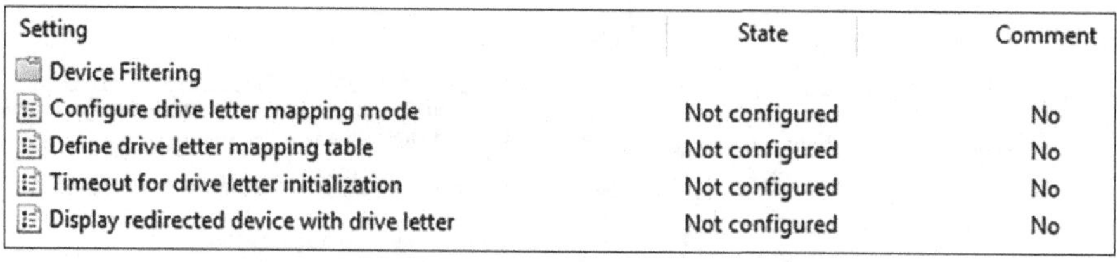

Setting	State	Comment
Device Filtering		
Configure drive letter mapping mode	Not configured	No
Define drive letter mapping table	Not configured	No
Timeout for drive letter initialization	Not configured	No
Display redirected device with drive letter	Not configured	No

Figure 8-194. *VMware Horizon Client Drive Redirection*

The first of the policies is for **Configure drive letter mapping mode**.

Configure drive letter mapping mode

This policy setting is used to configure drive letter mapping mode, choosing from one of the modes shown on the configuration screen as shown in the following:

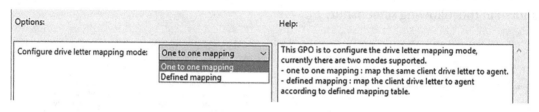

Figure 8-195. *Configure drive letter mapping mode*

Define drive letter mapping table

This policy allows you to define drive letter mapping between the client and the agent as shown in the following screenshot:

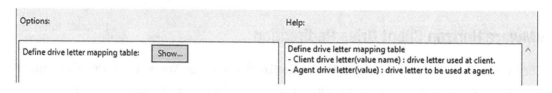

Figure 8-196. *Configure drive letter mapping mode*

Click the **Show...** button to see the **Show Contents** screen where you can enter a value name and a value.

Timeout for drive letter initialization

By setting this policy, you can configure a timeout for how long Windows Explorer waits to process the drive mapping as shown in the following screenshot:

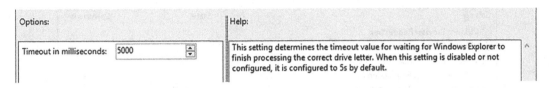

Figure 8-197. *Configure Timeout for drive letter initialization*

Display redirected device with drive letter

This policy allows you to configure whether the Client Drive Redirection feature has a drive letter enabled. By default, this setting is enabled.

Finally, in the **VMware Horizon Client Drive Redirection** settings folder, there is the **Device Filtering** sub-folder as shown in the following screenshot:

Figure 8-198. *Device Filtering configuration settings*

Exclude Vid/Pid Device

When enabled, this policy allows you to exclude a device by entering its vendor ID and product ID.

Include Vid/Pid Device

When enabled, this policy allows you to include a device by entering its vendor ID and product ID.

The next folder contains the **VMware HTML5 Features** policy settings.

VMware HTML5 Features

Click the **VMware HTML5 Features** folder. You will see that there are two policy settings and also a number of sub-folders as shown in the following screenshot:

Setting	State	Comment
VMware Browser Redirection		
VMware Geolocation Redirection		
VMware HTML5 Multimedia Redirection		
VMware WebRTC Redirection Features		
Enable VMware HTML5 Features	Not configured	No
Disable Automatically Detect Intranet	Not configured	No

Figure 8-199. *VMware HTML5 Features*

The first of the two policies is for **Enable VMware HTML5 Features**.

Enable VMware HTML5 Features

This policy simply allows you to switch on the HTML5 features. It is required for HTML5 multimedia, geolocation, and browser redirection features.

Disable Automatically Detect Intranet

With this policy enabled, the intranet setting to **Include all local intranet sites not listed in other zones** and Include all sites that bypass the proxy server will be disabled at the next login.

You then have a number of sub-folders for **VMware Browser Redirection**, which contains the following policy settings:

Setting	State	Comm...
Enable automatic fallback after a whitelist violation	Not configured	No
Enable Navigation URL list for VMware Browser Redirection	Not configured	No
Show a page with error information before automatic fallback	Not configured	No
Enable URL list for VMware Browser Redirection	Not configured	No
Enable VMware Browser Redirection	Not configured	No

Figure 8-200. *VMware Browser Redirection*

Let's take a closer look at those policy settings individually.

Enable automatic fallback after a whitelist violation

Enabling this policy means that navigating a tab to a URL, by either entering it in the address bar or navigating to it from a URL in either whitelists, that is not in either of the lists will stop the redirection for that tab. It will instead fetch and display the URL on the agent.

Enable Navigation URL list for VMware Browser Redirection

This policy allows you to specify URLs that a user can navigate to by entering it in the address bar or navigating to it from a URL in another list as shown:

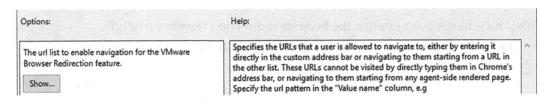

Figure 8-201. *Enable Navigation URL list for VMware Browser Redirection*

Click the **Show...** button to see the **Show Contents** screen where you can enter a value name and a value.

Show a page with error information before automatic fallback

This setting is used only when the Enable automatic fallback after a whitelist violation is enabled. With this enabled, a page will be displayed showing a five-second countdown timer. Once the time has elapsed, the tab will automatically fall back to fetching and rendering the URL which caused the violation.

If set to disabled, then the tab will fall back to the agent rendering and no countdown timer will be displayed.

Enable URL list for VMware Browser Redirection

This policy allows you to specify all the URLS used in the browser redirection policy as shown in the following screenshot:

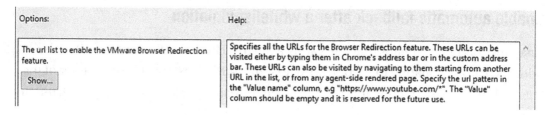

Figure 8-202. *Enable URL list for VMware Browser Redirection*

Click the **Show...** button to see the **Show Contents** screen where you can enter a value name and a value to create the URL list.

Enable VMware Browser Redirection

This policy allows you to switch the browser redirection feature on or off.

The next sub-folder is for **VMware Geolocation Redirection** as shown:

Setting	State	Comm...
Enable VMware Geolocation Redirection	Not configured	No
Set the minimum distance for which to report location upda...	Not configured	No
Enable URL list for VMware Geolocation Redirection.	Not configured	No

Figure 8-203. *Enable VMware Browser Redirection*

Enable VMware Geolocation Redirection

This policy allows you to switch the geolocation redirection feature on or off.

Set the minimum distance for which to report location updates

Enabling this policy allows you to configure the minimum distance between a location update in the client and the last update to the agent as shown:

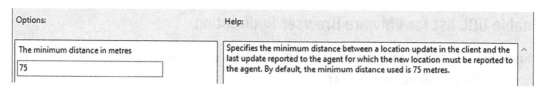

Figure 8-204. *Set the minimum distance for which to report location updates*

Enable URL list for VMware Geolocation Redirection

This allows you to specify the URL list for geolocation redirection as shown:

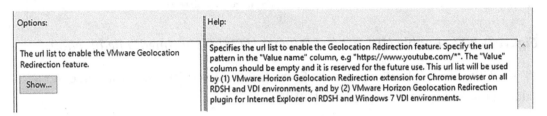

Figure 8-205. *Enable URL list for VMware Geolocation Redirection*

Click the **Show...** button to see the **Show Contents** screen where you can enter a value name and a value to create the URL list.

The next sub-folder is for **VMware HTML5 Multimedia Redirection** and contains the following policy options as shown in the following screenshot:

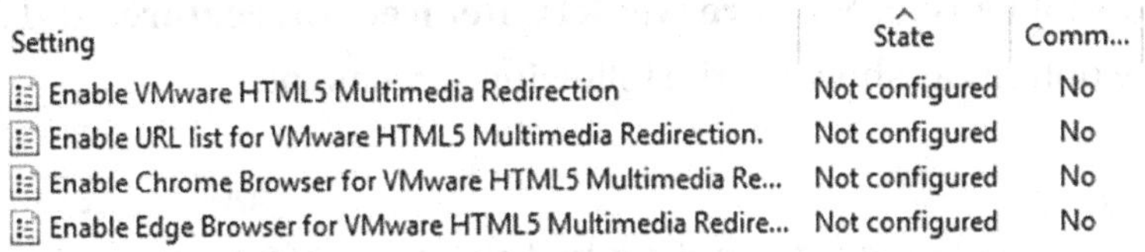

Setting	State	Comm...
Enable VMware HTML5 Multimedia Redirection	Not configured	No
Enable URL list for VMware HTML5 Multimedia Redirection.	Not configured	No
Enable Chrome Browser for VMware HTML5 Multimedia Re...	Not configured	No
Enable Edge Browser for VMware HTML5 Multimedia Redire...	Not configured	No

Figure 8-206. *VMware HTML5 Multimedia Redirection configuration settings*

Let's take a closer look at those policy settings individually.

Enable VMware HTML5 Multimedia Redirection

This policy allows you to switch the HTML5 MMR redirection feature on or off.

Enable URL list for VMware HTML5 Multimedia Redirection

This policy allows you to specify the URL list to enable the HTML5 MMR as shown:

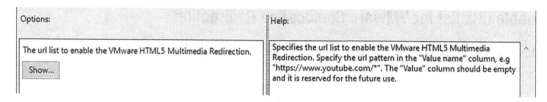

Figure 8-207. Enable URL list for VMware HTML5 Multimedia Redirection

Click the **Show…** button to see the **Show Contents** screen where you can enter a value name and a value to create the URL list.

Enable Chrome Browser for VMware HTML5 Multimedia Redirection

This policy is enabled to allow the Chrome browser to use the HTML5 MMR features.

Enable Edge Browser for VMware HTML5 Multimedia Redirection

This policy is enabled to allow the Edge browser to use the HTML5 MMR features.

The final sub-folder is for **VMware WebRTC Redirection Features** and contains the following policy options as shown in the following screenshot:

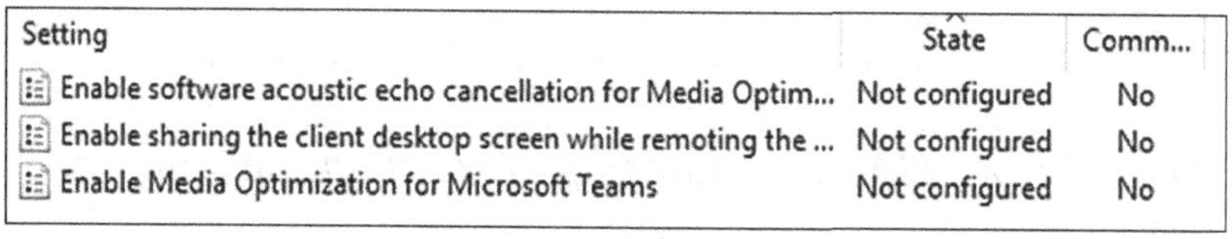

Setting	State	Comm...
Enable software acoustic echo cancellation for Media Optim...	Not configured	No
Enable sharing the client desktop screen while remoting the ...	Not configured	No
Enable Media Optimization for Microsoft Teams	Not configured	No

Figure 8-208. VMware WebRTC Redirection Features

Let's take a closer look at those policy settings individually.

Enable software acoustic echo cancellation for Media Optimization for MS Teams

This policy allows you to enable the acoustic echo cancellation feature for Media Optimization when using MS Teams.

Enable sharing the client desktop screen while remoting the MS Teams app in app sharing mode

This policy setting enables the client screen to be shared rather than the remote session screen, when running MS Teams.

Enable Media Optimization for Microsoft Teams

To the optimization features for MS Teams, you need to enable this policy.

The next folder contains the **VMware Integrated Printing** policy settings.

VMware Integrated Printing

Click the **VMware Integrated Printing** folder. You will see that there are a number of settings as shown in the following screenshot:

Setting	State	Comment
Do not change default printer	Not configured	No
Disable LBP	Not configured	No
Do not redirect client printer(s)	Enabled	No
Disable printer redirection for non-desktop client	Not configured	No
Disable Printer Property Persistence	Not configured	No
Print Preview Setting	Not configured	No
Printer Driver Selection	Not configured	No
Printer Name Schema	Not configured	No
Specify a filter in redirecting client printers	Not configured	No

Figure 8-209. *VMware WebRTC Redirection Features*

Let's start with the **Do not change default printer** policy setting.

Do not change default printer

This policy allows you to configure whether integrated printing can change the default printer in a remote session. Enabling this setting means that the default printer will not be changed, and by default this is set to not configured.

Disable LBP

This setting allows you to switch location-based printing on or off. By default, this is set to not configured.

Do not redirect client printer(s)

Enabling this policy means that no client printers will be redirected. By default, this is set to not configured.

Disable printer redirection for non-desktop client

Enabling this policy means that the integrated printing feature is not supported for non-desktop devices. By default, this is set to not configured.

Disable Printer Property Persistence

This policy allows you to configure whether the printer properties setting is kept. When enabled, if the end user changes any printing properties, they will not be kept when they log off. By default, this is set to not configured.

Print Preview Setting

This policy allows you to select from the two print preview settings:

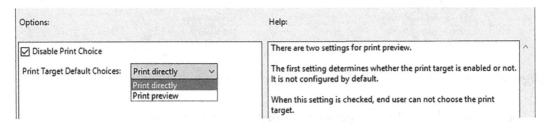

Figure 8-210. *Print Preview Setting*

Printer Driver Selection

This policy, when enabled, allows you to select the printer driver selection and the printer creation choices as shown in the following screenshot:

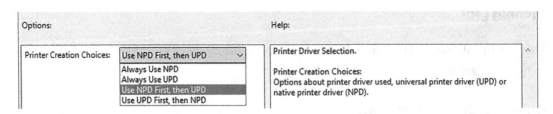

Figure 8-211. *Printer Driver Selection*

Printer Name Schema

With this setting, you can configure the printer name schema as shown:

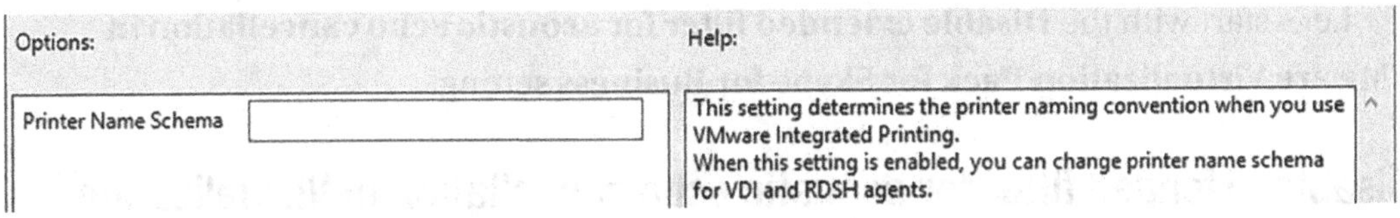

Figure 8-212. *Printer Name Schema*

The printer name schema should use the following syntax: **%P(xxxxxx)**, where **xxxxxx** is where you configure the name you want to use. You can also use **%S** to enter a session ID or **%C** to enter the machine name of a client. By default, this setting is not configured.

Specify a filter in redirecting client printers

This policy enables you to create a filter on the client printers when redirecting as shown:

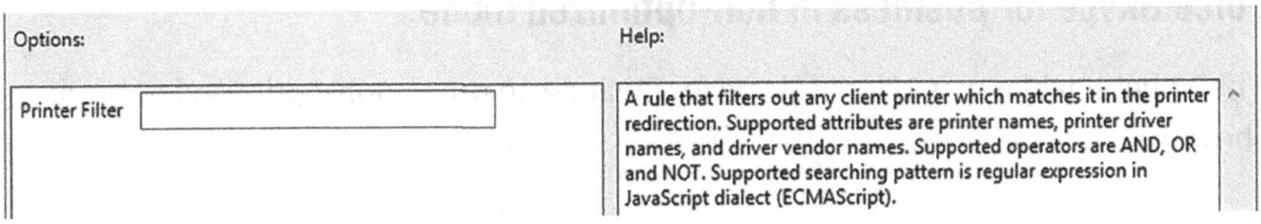

Figure 8-213. *Specify a filter in redirecting client printers*

The final folder is the **VMware Virtualization Pack for Skype for Business** policy settings.

VMware Virtualization Pack for Skype for Business

Click the **VMware Virtualization Pack for Skype for Business** folder. You will see that there are a number of policy settings as shown in the following:

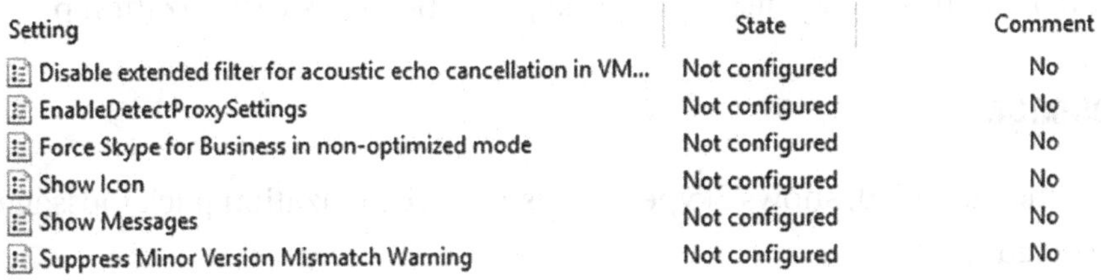

Figure 8-214. *VMware Virtualization Pack for Skype for Business*

Let's start with the **Disable extended filter for acoustic echo cancellation in VMware Virtualization Pack for Skype for Business** setting.

Disable extended filter for acoustic echo cancellation in Virtualization Pack for Skype for Business

When this policy is enabled, the Skype for Business virtualization pack will not use extended filter for acoustic echo cancellation. By default, this is enabled.

Enable Detect Proxy Settings

This policy, when enabled, allows the Skype for Business virtualization pack to detect any proxy settings on the client and use those settings for the media traffic. If no proxy settings are detected, a direct connection will be used.

Force Skype for Business in non-optimized mode

This policy enables you to force Skype for Business to run in non-optimized mode as shown:

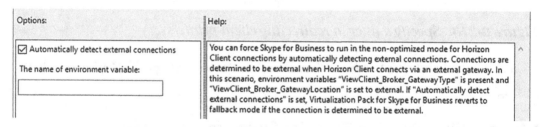

Figure 8-215.   Force Skype for Business in non-optimized mode

Show Icon

Enabled by default, this policy displays the Skype for Business virtualization pack icon.

Show Messages

This policy, when enabled, shows Skype for Business virtualization pack messages and is enabled by default.

Suppress Minor Version Mismatch Warning

Enabling this policy will suppress the error message that would pop up if the Skype for Business virtualization pack does not have the same minor API version on the client and the agent.

The next set of policy settings are the **VMware View Common Configuration** policy settings.

VMware View Common Configuration

Click the **VMware View Common Configuration** folder. You will see that there are a number of policy settings and three sub-folders as shown in the following:

Setting	State	Comment
Log Configuration		
Performance Alarms		
Security Configuration		
Enable extended logging	Not configured	No
Configure dump creation on program error	Enabled	No
Disk threshold for log and events in Megabytes	Enabled	No
Override the default View Windows event generation	Not configured	No

Figure 8-216. *VMware View Common Configuration settings*

Let's start with the **Enable extended logging** policy setting.

Enable extended logging

Enabling this policy means that trace and debug events will be captured in the log files.

Configure dump creation on program error

This policy allows you to configure the number of dumps that get created as shown:

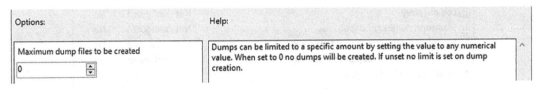

Options:	Help:
Maximum dump files to be created	Dumps can be limited to a specific amount by setting the value to any numerical value. When set to 0 no dumps will be created. If unset no limit is set on dump creation.
0	

Figure 8-217. *Configure dump creation on program error*

Disk threshold for log and events in Megabytes

This policy, when enabled, allows you to configure a threshold for the minimum amount of remaining disk space when creating logs and events. 200 is the default setting as shown:

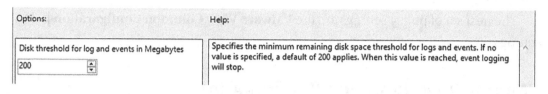

Figure 8-218. *Disk threshold for log and events in Megabytes*

Override the default View Windows event generation

This policy allows you to override the generation of Windows events as shown:

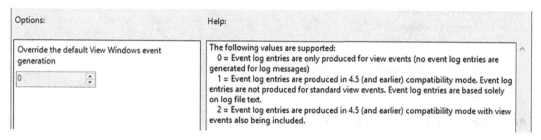

Figure 8-219. *Override the default View Windows event generation*

The first sub-folder in the **VMware View Common Configuration** folder contains the policy settings for **Log Configuration.**

Log Configuration

The next set of policy settings are for the **Log Configuration** as shown:

Setting	State	Comm...
Log directory	Not configured	No
Maximum number of debug logs	Not configured	No
Maximum debug log size in Megabytes	Not configured	No
Number of days to keep production logs	Not configured	No
Send logs to a Syslog server	Not configured	No

Figure 8-220. *Log configuration settings*

Let's start with the **Log directory** policy setting.

Log directory

This policy allows you to add a directory for saving log files.

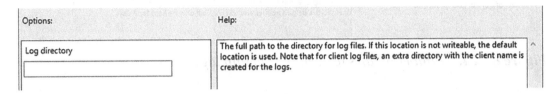

Figure 8-221. Log directory

Maximum number of debug logs

This policy allows you to configure the maximum number of debug logs to be kept.

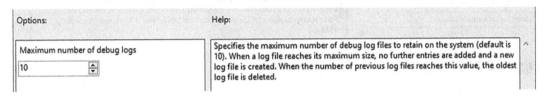

Figure 8-222. Maximum number of debug logs

Maximum debug log size in Megabytes

This policy allows you to configure the maximum size that debug logs can grow to before a new one is created. This is shown in the following screenshot:

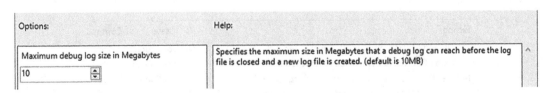

Figure 8-223. Maximum debug log size in Megabytes

Number of days to keep production logs

This policy allows you to specify the length of time production logs are kept.

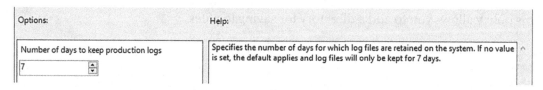

Figure 8-224. Number of days to keep production logs

Send logs to a Syslog server

This policy allows you to configure a Syslog server to send log files to as shown:

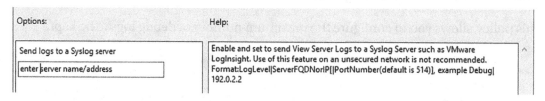

Figure 8-225. Send logs to a Syslog server

The next sub-folder in the **VMware View Common Configuration** section is for **Performance Alarms**.

Performance Alarms

The next set of policy settings are for **Performance Alarms** and are shown in the following screenshot:

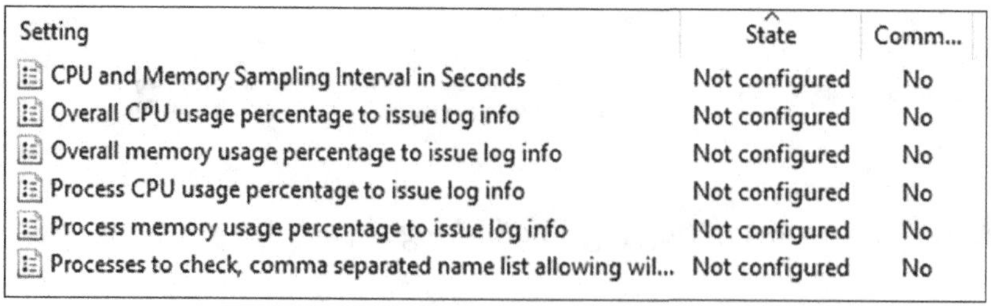

Setting	State	Comm...
CPU and Memory Sampling Interval in Seconds	Not configured	No
Overall CPU usage percentage to issue log info	Not configured	No
Overall memory usage percentage to issue log info	Not configured	No
Process CPU usage percentage to issue log info	Not configured	No
Process memory usage percentage to issue log info	Not configured	No
Processes to check, comma separated name list allowing wil...	Not configured	No

Figure 8-226. Performance Alarms configuration settings

The first policy setting in this section is for **CPU and Memory Sampling Interval in Seconds**.

CPU and Memory Sampling Interval in Seconds

This policy, when enabled, allows you to configure the CPU and memory sampling times as shown:

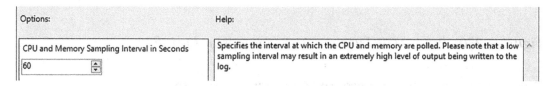

Figure 8-227. *CPU and Memory Sampling Interval in Seconds*

Overall CPU usage percentage to issue log info

This policy, when enabled, allows you to configure the threshold at where CPU usage is logged.

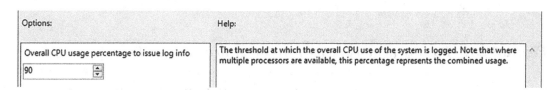

Figure 8-228. *Overall CPU usage percentage to issue log info*

Overall memory usage percentage to issue log info

This policy, when enabled, allows you to configure the threshold, as a percentage, of where memory usage is logged.

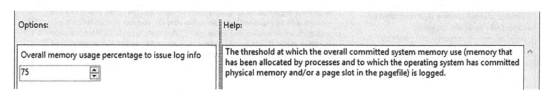

Figure 8-229. *Overall memory usage percentage to issue log info*

Process CPU usage percentage to issue log info

This policy enables you to configure CPU usage, as a percentage, to be logged for an individual process.

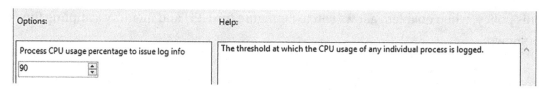

Figure 8-230. *Process CPU usage percentage to issue log info*

Process memory usage percentage to issue log info

This policy enables you to configure the percentage threshold of when memory usage is logged.

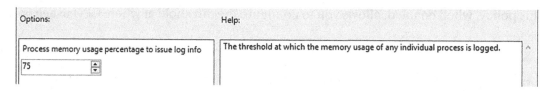

Figure 8-231. *Process memory usage percentage to issue log info*

Processes to check comma separated name list allowing wild card and exclusions

This setting allows you to configure a list of processes that you want to examine as shown in the following screenshot:

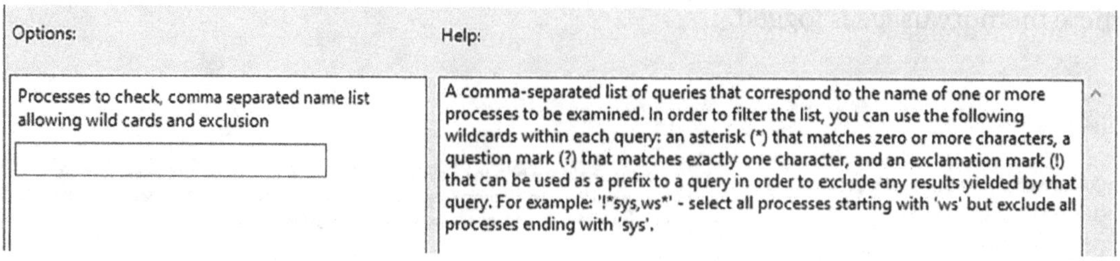

Figure 8-232. *Processes to check comma separated name list allowing wild card and exclusions*

The final sub-folder in this section is for **Security Configuration**.

Security Configuration

The next set of policy settings are for the **Security Configuration** and are shown in the following screenshot:

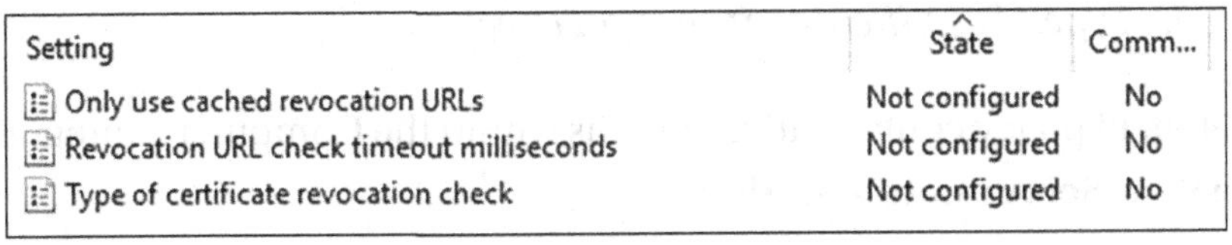

Setting	State	Comm...
Only use cached revocation URLs	Not configured	No
Revocation URL check timeout milliseconds	Not configured	No
Type of certificate revocation check	Not configured	No

Figure 8-233. *Security Configuration policy settings*

The first policy setting is for **Only use cached revocation URLs**.

Only use cached revocation URLs

Enabling this policy means that certificate revocation checking will only access URLs that have been cached. By default, this is disabled.

Revocation URL check timeout in milliseconds

This policy configures the timeout for URL revocation as shown:

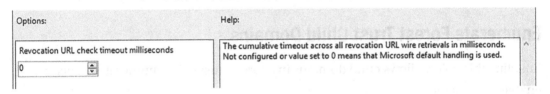

Options:	Help:
Revocation URL check timeout milliseconds	The cumulative timeout across all revocation URL wire retrievals in milliseconds. Not configured or value set to 0 means that Microsoft default handling is used.
0	

Figure 8-234. *Revocation URL check timeout in milliseconds*

Type of certificate revocation check

Following on from the previous policy, this setting allows you to configure the type of revocation check as shown in the following:

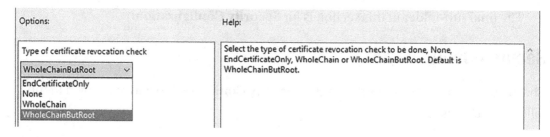

Figure 8-235.   *Type of certificate revocation check*

The final set of policy configuration options within the Computer Configuration is for **VMware View Server Configuration**.

VMware View Server Configuration

This final set of policy settings applies to the **VMware View Server Configuration** and is shown in the following screenshot:

Setting	State	Comment
Enumerate Forest Trust Child Domains	Not configured	No
Recursive Enumeration of Trusted Domains	Not configured	No
Windows Password Authentication Mode	Not configured	No

Figure 8-236.   *VMware View Server Configuration settings*

Let's start with the **Enumerate Forest Trust Child Domains** policy setting.

Enumerate Forest Trust Child Domains

Enabling this policy allows child domains in a forest trust to be enumerated. This is enabled by default.

Recursive Enumeration of Trusted Domains

When enabled, this policy enables you to configure whether every domain that is trusted by the domain in which Horizon lives gets enumerated. By default, this is set to enabled.

Windows Password Authentication Mode

Enabling this policy setting allows you to configure the password authentication mode for Windows. You have the following options as shown:

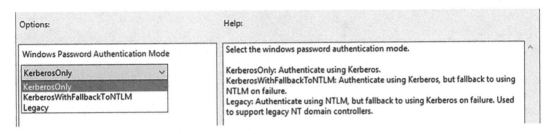

Figure 8-237. *Windows Password Authentication Mode*

We have now covered the **Computer Configuration** GPO policy settings. In the next chapter, we are going to look at the policy settings that are focused on the end users.

Summary

In this chapter, we have taken a deep dive into the computer configuration policy settings, walking through each policy setting option, what it is used for and how to configure it.

In the next chapter, we are going to take a closer look at the user configuration policy settings.

CHAPTER 9

Horizon User GPO Settings

In the previous chapter, we looked at the computer-based policy configuration settings included within the Horizon Bundles.

In this chapter, we are going to take a closer look at the pre-built policy templates, for user-based configurations, and then walk through each policy configuration setting and show you how to manage virtual desktop machines using these policies.

User Configuration GPO Settings

In this section, we are going to walk through the GPO policy settings that are based on the end-user configuration.

We will start with the **VMware Blast** policy settings.

VMware Blast

To access the user configuration settings, click and expand the **User Configuration section**, then click **Policies**, and then finally click to expand the **Administrative Templates: Policy definitions** section.

Now click the **VMware Blast** folder.

You will see that the individual policy settings listed here are identical to those that we covered in the **Computer Configuration** section for **VMware Blast**. However, in this section, they apply to the end user who is currently logged in rather than the computer they are using.

To understand the configuration settings in more detail, you can refer to that previous section for the detailed configuration settings.

The next set of policy options are for **VMware Horizon Client Configuration**.

613

© Peter von Oven 2022
P. von Oven, *Mastering VMware Horizon 8*, https://doi.org/10.1007/978-1-4842-7261-9_9

VMware Horizon Client Configuration

The next set of policy configuration settings are for the **VMware Horizon Client Configuration**. There are also a number of sub-folders within the client policy settings as shown in the following screenshot:

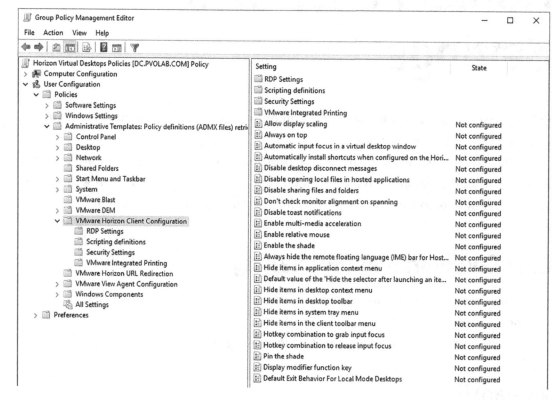

Figure 9-1. *VMware Horizon Client Configuration settings*

Let's start with the **Allow display scaling** policy setting.

Allow display scaling

This setting allows you to configure the display scaling feature for desktop and application sessions. Again, this is a simple enable or disable type policy.

Always on top

This policy allows you to configure whether the Horizon Client window is always on top. By default, this is disabled.

Automatic input focus in a virtual desktop window

This policy, when enabled, brings the virtual desktop window displayed in the Horizon Client to the forefront, meaning that the end user will be able to use the virtual desktop immediately without first having to click the window to change the focus.

Automatically install shortcuts when configured on the Horizon Server

This policy configures shortcuts and whether they should be automatically installed on the Horizon Client when they have been configured on the Server.

If you enable this policy, then the end user is not prompted, and shortcuts are installed automatically, and if you set this policy to **Disabled,** then shortcuts will not be installed. Finally, if you set this policy to **Not Configured,** then the end user will be prompted whether or not they want to install shortcuts.

Disable desktop disconnect messages

This policy specifies whether or not disconnection messages that are shown by default are disabled when the disconnection is not initiated by the end user, for example, when the administrator forcibly logs end users off.

Disable opening local files in hosted applications

Enabling this policy allows you to configure whether the client registers local handlers for file extensions that are supported by hosted apps.

Disable sharing files and folders

Enabling this policy switches off file and folder sharing between the client and remote session. This is disabled by default.

Don't check monitor alignment on spanning

Enabling this policy allows the client desktop to span multiple screens even if they don't form an exact rectangle.

Disable toast notifications

This policy, when enabled, disables toast notifications.

Enable multi-media acceleration

This policy allows you to enable or disable multimedia acceleration on the client.

Enable relative mouse

Relative mouse mode will improve the mouse performance, particularly when running graphical based apps, for PCoIP sessions using the Horizon Client. Therefore, enabling this feature on supported remote desktops will result in a better end-user experience. By default, this policy is disabled.

Enable the shade

This policy enables you to switch the menu bar at the top of the client window on or off. By default, this is enabled.

Always hide the remote floating language (IME) bar for Hosted Apps

This policy is used to force the floating language bar to be switched off when running application sessions. This means that enabling this policy the language bar will never be visible to the end user during that application session regardless of whether or not the Input Method Editor (IME) feature is enabled.

If you set this policy to disabled, then the floating language bar will only be shown if the local IME feature is disabled. Disabled is the default setting for this policy.

Hide items in application context menu

This policy allows you to hide contextual menu items for applications when you right-click the Horizon Client launcher page. By default, this policy is disabled, and so all the configuration options shown in this policy can be set by the end user.

The configuration options are configured by simply clicking the drop-down menu next to each one and selecting either **Yes** or **No**. You have the following configurable options. These are shown in the following screenshot:

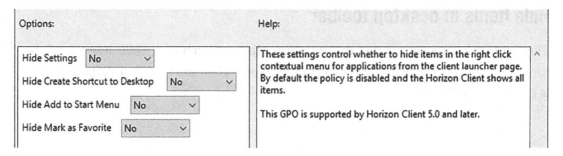

Figure 9-2. *Hide items in application context menu*

Default value of 'Hide selector after launching an item' checkbox

This policy, disabled by default, allows you to configure the hiding of the selector once a session has launched by making sure the check box is checked.

Hide items in desktop context menu

This policy allows you to hide contextual menu items for desktops when you right-click the Horizon Client launcher page. By default, this policy is disabled, and so all the configuration options shown in this policy can be set by the end user.

The configuration options are configured by simply clicking the drop-down menu next to each one and selecting either **Yes** or **No**. You have the following configurable options. These are shown in the following screenshot:

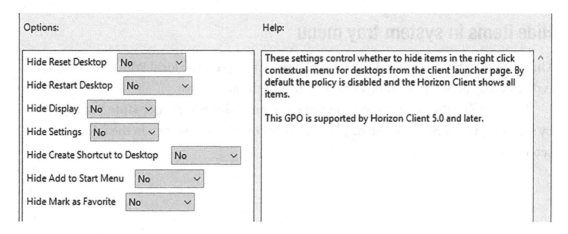

Figure 9-3. *Hide items in desktop context menu*

Hide items in desktop toolbar

This policy allows you to control the desktop toolbar and to hide specific items from the toolbar. The toolbar is visible at the top of the screen when the virtual desktop machine is running in full screen.

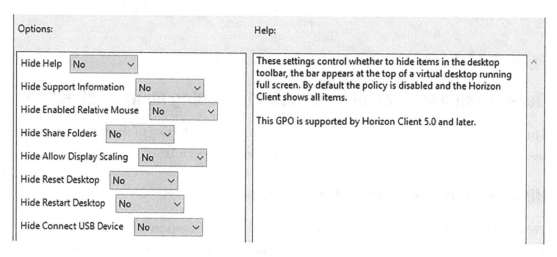

Figure 9-4. *Hide items in desktop toolbar*

By default, the policy is disabled, and all the options are available.

To configure an option, then from the drop-down box next to each option, click and select either **Yes** or **No** as shown in the screenshot.

Hide items in system tray menu

This policy enables you to hide items in the system tray on the local Windows screen. It is disabled by default, meaning all system tray items are shown.

If you enable this policy, then you can configure **Hide Sharing** or **Hide Settings** by selecting **Yes** or **No** from the respective drop-down box as shown in the following screenshot:

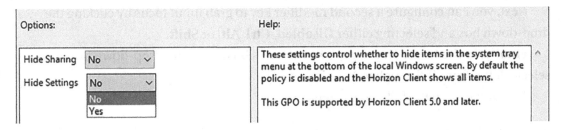

Figure 9-5. *Hide items in system tray menu*

Hide items in the client toolbar menu

Similar to the previous policy setting, this policy allows you to hide items in the toolbar on the top of the client launcher page.

Again, this policy is disabled by default, and enabling this policy means you can then configure **Hide Favorites Toggle** or **Hide Settings Gear** by selecting **Yes** or **No** from the respective drop-down box as shown in the following:

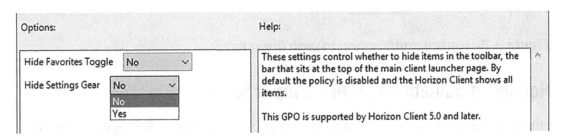

Figure 9-6. *Hide items in the client toolbar menu*

Hotkey combination to grab input focus

In this policy, you can configure a hotkey combination that enables you to grab the input focus for the last used session.

The hotkey combination is made up of one or two configurable modifier keys followed by a letter key to complete the sequence. When this policy is enabled, then the keys configured, when pressed, will grab the input focus to the session.

If this policy is disabled or not configured, then the focus to the session is done by clicking inside the desktop window.

To configure the keys, in the **Modifier to grab input focus** box, click the drop-down box and select either **Ctrl**, **Alt**, or **Shift**.

Next, you can configure a second modifier key to grab input focus by clicking the drop-down box and selecting either **Disabled**, **Ctrl**, **Alt**, or **Shift.**

Finally, in the Letter Key to grab input focus box, click the drop-down box and select a letter from **H** through to **N** inclusive.

This is shown in the following screenshot:

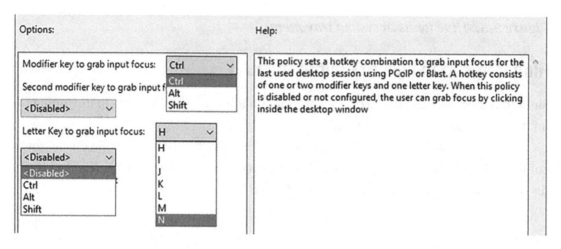

Figure 9-7.   *Hotkey combination to grab input focus*

Hotkey combination to release input focus

Similar to the previous policy, with this policy you can configure a hotkey combination that enables you to release the input focus for the last used session.

If this policy is disabled or not configured, then to release the focus from the desktop windows, the end user would press **Ctrl+Alt**.

To configure the keys, in the **Modifier to release input focus** box, click the drop-down box and select either **Ctrl**, **Alt**, or **Shift**.

Next, you can configure a second modifier key to release input focus by clicking the drop-down box and selecting either **Disabled**, **Ctrl**, **Alt**, or **Shift.**

Finally, in the Function Key to release input focus box, click the drop-down box and select a function key from **F5** through to **F8** inclusive.

This is shown in the following screenshot:

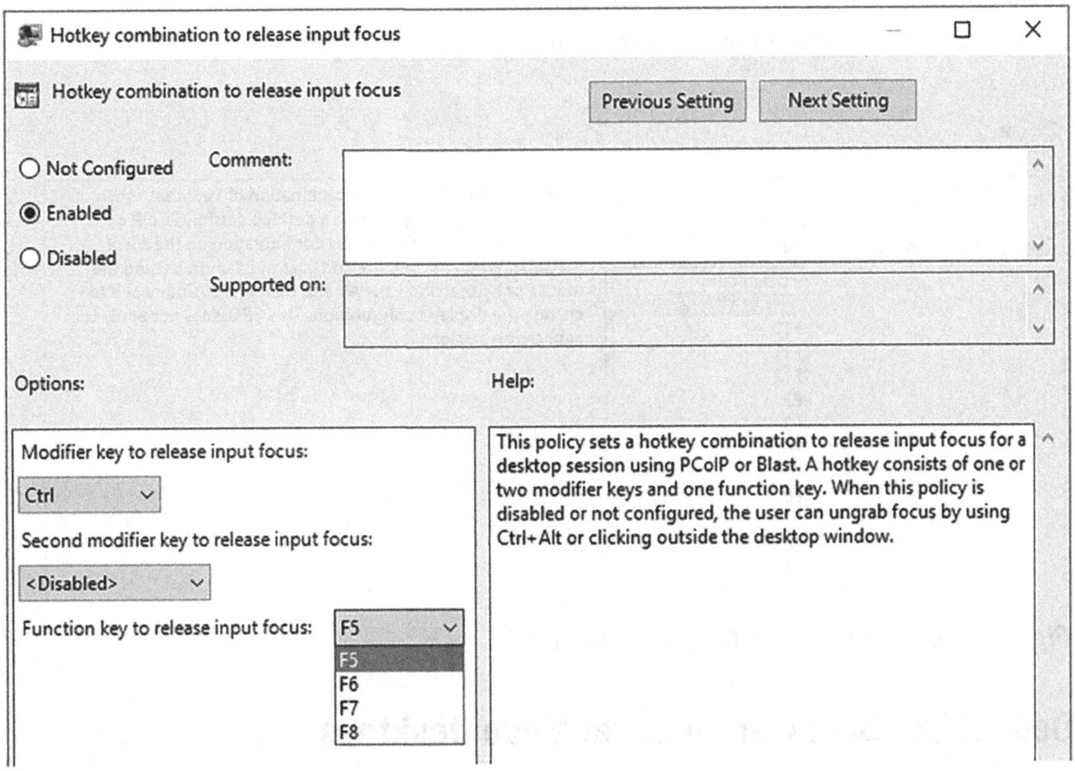

Figure 9-8. *Hotkey combination to release input focus*

Pin the shade

This policy enables you to configure whether the pin on the top of the client window is enabled. By default, this is enabled.

Display modifier function key

With this policy setting, you can configure a keypress combination that allows you to change the configuration of the display on the client device.

If you don't configure this policy, then the end user first needs to release the focus from the session window to the client by pressing **Ctrl+Alt**. Then they would need to change the display configuration on the client in the normal way by pressing the Windows key and P.

To configure the keys, in the **Display Switch Modifier Key** box, click the drop-down box and select either **Disabled**, **Ctrl**, **Alt**, or **Shift**.

621

Then, in the Display Switch Function Key box, click the drop-down box and select a function key from **F1** through to **F9** inclusive.

This is shown in the following screenshot:

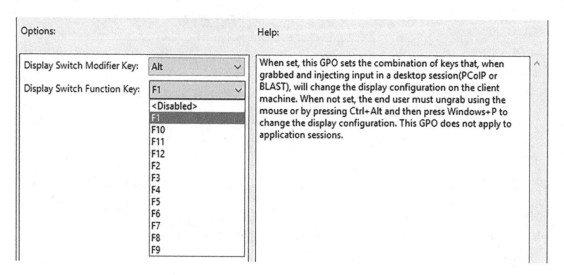

Figure 9-9. *Display modifier function key*

Default Exit Behavior for Local Mode Desktops

This feature is no longer available in the latest versions of Horizon.

In the next section, we are going to look at **RDP Settings**.

RDP Settings

The first sub-folder contains the policy settings for **RDP Settings** as shown in the following screenshot:

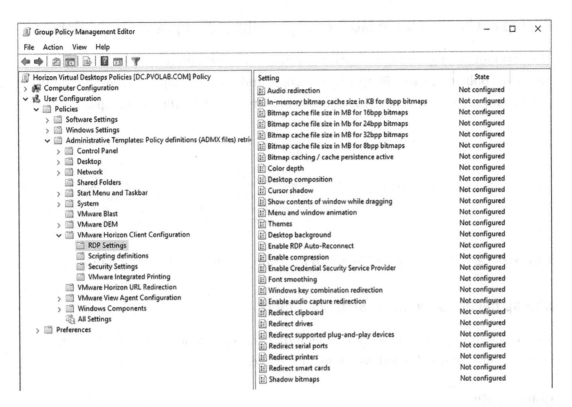

Figure 9-10. *RDP Settings*

Let's start with the **Audio redirection** policy setting.

Audio redirection

This policy allows you to configure how audio redirection is channeled as shown:

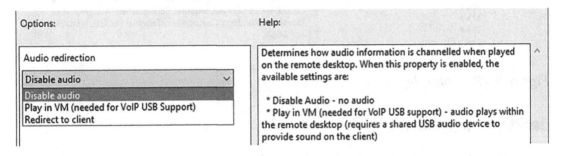

Figure 9-11. *Audio redirection*

Bitmap cache file size in MB for 16bpp, 24bpp, 32bpp, and 8bpp bitmaps

The next four settings configure the bitmap cache file size, entered in MB. The four individual policies are for 16bpp, 24bpp, 32bpp, and 8bpp bitmaps and have the same configuration screen as shown in the following screenshot for 16bpp bitmaps:

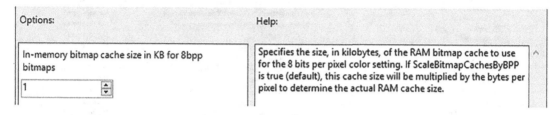

Figure 9-12. *Bitmap cache file in MB for 16bpp, 24bpp, 32bpp, 8bpp bitmaps*

Bitmap caching/cache persistence active

This policy configures whether persistent bitmap caching should be used. This can improve performance but will use more disk space.

Color depth

This policy setting allows you to configure the depth of color on the remote desktop.

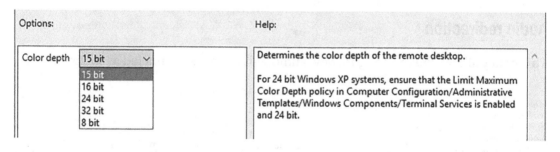

Figure 9-13. *Color depth*

Desktop composition

This policy when enabled prevents individual windows from drawing directly to the screen or primary display. Drawing will now be redirected off-screen to video memory which is then rendered into a desktop image and presented on the display.

Cursor shadow

This policy setting configures the cursor with a shadow that appears underneath it on the remote desktop.

Show contents of window while dragging

This policy configures whether or not folder contents get displayed when the folder is dragged to a new location.

Menu and windows animation

This policy configures the animation and how menus and windows behave when clients connect to remote sessions.

Themes

This policy configures if themes are displayed when clients connect to remote desktops.

Desktop background

This policy configures whether the desktop background is displayed when clients connect to remote desktops.

Enable RDP Auto-Reconnect

By enabling this setting, you can configure whether the RDP client can reconnect to a desktop if the connection drops out. By default, this is disabled.

Enable compression

Enabling this policy switches on RDP data compression, and this is enabled by default.

Enable Credential Security Service Provider

With this policy, you can configure whether the desktop connection uses Network Level Authentication (NLA). This is required if the virtual desktop uses NLA, and if it is not enabled, then the client will not be able to connect.

Font smoothing

This is used to configure whether anti-aliasing is applied to remote desktop fonts.

Windows key combination redirection

This policy configures where key combinations are sent as shown in the following:

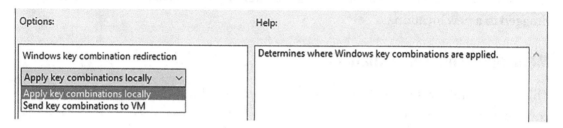

Figure 9-14. *Windows key combination redirection*

Enable audio capture redirection

This policy enables you to redirect the default audio device. By default, this is disabled.

Redirect clipboard

This policy enables you to configure automatic redirection of the clipboard when an end user is connected to a remote desktop.

Redirect drives

This policy enables you to configure automatic redirection of the local drives when an end user is connected to a remote desktop.

Redirect supported plug-and-play devices

This policy enables you to configure automatic redirection of plug and play devices when an end user connects to a remote desktop. Note this is different to the USB redirection settings.

Redirect serial ports

This policy enables you to configure automatic redirection of local COM when an end user is connected to a remote desktop.

Redirect printers

This policy enables you to configure automatic redirection of the local printers when an end user is connected to a remote desktop.

Redirect smart cards

This policy enables you to configure automatic redirection of the local smart cards when an end user is connected to a remote desktop.

Shadow bitmaps

Enabling this policy means that shadow bitmaps can be used.

Next, we are going to look at the policies in the second sub-folder. These are for the **Scripting Definitions**.

Scripting Definitions

The second sub-folder contains the policy settings for Scripting definitions as shown in the following screenshot:

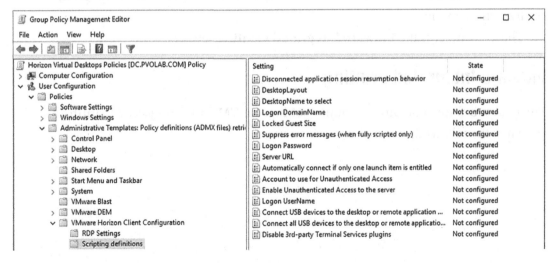

Figure 9-15. *Scripting definitions configuration settings*

The configuration settings within this folder are identical to those in the Scripting definitions folder that we looked at in the **Computer Configuration** policies.

Rather than cover the same policy settings again, refer to the Computer Configuration settings for details on the Scripting definitions policy settings.

Next, we are going to look at the policies in the third sub-folder. These are for the **Security Settings**.

Security Settings

The third sub-folder contains the policy settings for **Security settings** as shown in the following screenshot:

Setting	State
Unlock remote sessions when the client machine is unlocked	Not configured
Enable SSL encrypted framework channel	Not configured
Ignore certificate revocation problems	Not configured
Default value of the 'Log in as current user' checkbox	Not configured
Display option to Log in as current user	Not configured
Configures SSL protocols and cryptographic algorithms	Not configured

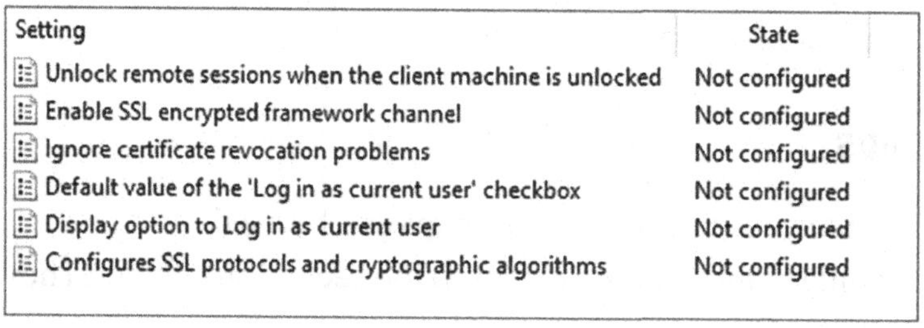

Figure 9-16. *Security settings configurations*

Again, the configuration settings within this folder are identical to those in the Security settings folder that we looked at in the **Computer Configuration** policies. You can refer to the Computer Configuration settings for details on the Security settings configuration options.

The final folder is the **VMware Integrated Printing** settings.

VMware Integrated Printing

The final sub-folder contains the policy settings for **VMware Integrated Printing** as shown in the following screenshot:

Setting	State
▤ Do not redirect client printer(s)	Not configured
▤ Allow to redirect L1 local printers to inner session	Not configured

Figure 9-17. *VMware Integrated Printing*

Let's start with the **Do not redirect client printer(s)** setting.

Do not redirect client printer(s)

Enabling this policy means that no client printers will be redirected. By default, this is set to not configured.

Allow to redirect L1 local printers to inner session

The other setting configures whether local printers are redirected to a nested session and by default is not configured.

With nested mode, there are three layers as listed:

- **L0**: End point device

- **L1**: Remote desktop (when enabled, this is where the printer is redirected from to the L2 session)

- **L2**: Remote desktop/application running in the L1 remote desktop

The next policy option is for configuring the VMware Horizon URL Redirection feature.

VMware Horizon URL Redirection

If you click the **VMware Horizon URL Redirection** folder in the left-hand tree view, you will see there is just a single policy setting to **Install the Chrome extension that is required in the URL content redirection feature**.

Enabling this policy means that the Chrome extension that URL content redirection needs will be installed automatically and silently. By default, this policy is set to not configured.

The final policies are the **VMware View Agent Configuration** policies.

VMware View Agent Configuration

If you click the **VMware View Agent Configuration** folder in the left-hand tree view, you will see that there are a number of sub-folders as shown in the following screenshot:

Figure 9-18. *VMware View Agent Configuration*

As you can see, there are no settings in the root of this folder. Instead, there are seven sub-folders for each subset of policy options.

Let's start with the sub-folder for the **Agent Configuration** settings.

Agent Configuration

In the **Agent Configuration** sub-folder, you will find the policy settings for Agent Configuration as shown in the following screenshot:

Setting	State
Disable Time Zone Synchronization	Not configured
DPI Synchronization Per Monitor	Not configured
DPI Synchronization	Not configured

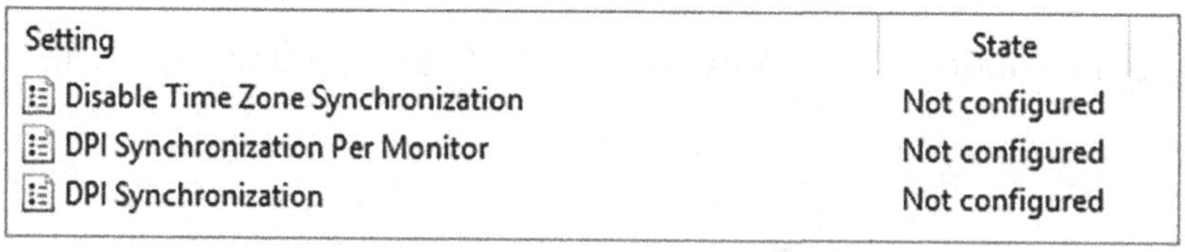

Figure 9-19. *Agent Configuration*

Let's take a closer look at those policy settings individually starting with the **Disable Time Zone Synchronization** policy setting.

Disable Time Zone Synchronization

This policy setting, when enabled, synchronizes the time zone between the virtual desktop and the end user's device. It is disabled by default.

DPI Synchronization Per Monitor

This setting allows you to adjust the DPI setting when using multiple screens. When set to enabled or not configured, then the DPI setting on all screens matches the OS setting of the client device while running a remote session.

DPI Synchronization

This adjusts the system-wide DPI setting for the remote session. When this setting is enabled or not configured, the system-wide DPI setting for the remote session is set to match the corresponding DPI setting on the client operating system.

When this setting is disabled, the system-wide DPI setting for the remote session is never changed. This setting is enabled by default.

The next set of policy options are for Agent Security.

Agent Security

The next set of policy options are for the **Agent Security** settings. There is a single policy setting in the root of the folder and then a sub-folder for **Unity Touch and Hosted Apps** as shown in the following screenshot:

Setting	State	Comment
Unity Touch and Hosted Apps		
Accept SSL encrypted framework channel	Not configured	No

Figure 9-20. Agent Security configuration settings

Let's start with the setting for **Accept SSL encrypted framework channel**.

Accept SSL encrypted framework channel

This policy setting allows you to accept SSL encrypted connections or to disable them as shown in the following screenshot:

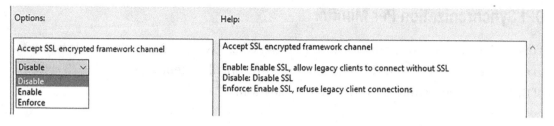

Figure 9-21. *Accept SSL encrypted framework channel*

Next is the **Unity Touch and Hosted Apps** sub-folder which contains just two additional policy settings as shown in the following screenshot:

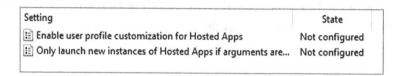

Figure 9-22. *Unity Touch and Hosted Apps configuration settings*

Let's take a closer look at the two policy settings, starting with **Enable user profile customization for Hosted Apps**.

Enable user profile customization for Hosted Apps

This policy allows you to configure whether end-user profile customization is enabled when an end user is using hosted apps.

Only launch new instances of Hosted Apps if arguments are different

With this policy, by enabling it you can control what happens if the end user launches a hosted app and there is already an instance of that hosted app still running but in a disconnected session.

Setting this policy to disabled means that the existing session will be used rather than a new one. The default setting is disabled.

The next set of policy settings are for **Clipboard Redirection**.

Clipboard Redirection

If you click the **Clipboard Redirection** folder in the left-hand tree view, you will see the policy settings as shown in the following screenshot:

Setting	State	Comment
▤ Configure clipboard redirection formats	Not configured	No
▤ Configure clipboard audit	Not configured	No
▤ Whether block clipboard redirection to client side when clie...	Not configured	No
▤ Clipboard memory size on server	Not configured	No
▤ Configure clipboard redirection	Not configured	No

Figure 9-23. *Clipboard Redirection configuration settings*

The configuration settings within this folder are identical to those in the Clipboard Redirection folder that we looked at in the **Computer Configuration** policies.

Rather than cover the same policy settings again, refer to the Computer Configuration settings for details on the Clipboard Redirection policy settings.

Scanner Redirection

If you click the **Scanner Redirection** folder in the left-hand tree view, you will see the policy settings as shown in the following screenshot:

Setting	State	Comment
▤ BandwidthLimit	Not configured	No
▤ Compression	Not configured	No
▤ Default Color Mode	Not configured	No
▤ Default Duplex	Not configured	No
▤ Default Scanner	Not configured	No
▤ Force the TWAIN Scanning Properties dialog	Not configured	No
▤ Hide Webcam	Not configured	No
▤ TWAIN Scanner Properties dialog location	Not configured	No

Figure 9-24. *Scanner Redirection configuration settings*

Four of these settings, namely, **Default Color Mode**, **Default Duplex**, **Default Scanner**, and **Hide Webcam,** are identical to the settings covered in the Computer Configuration, so refer to that section for details of these settings.

Let's now start with the **Bandwidth Limit** settings.

Bandwidth Limit

This policy, when enabled, allows you to configure a bandwidth limit for sending scanned data to the remote session as shown in the following screenshot:

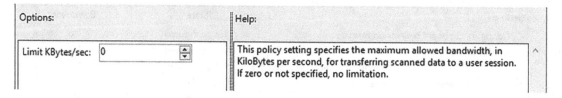

Figure 9-25. Scanner Redirection – Bandwidth Limit

Compression

Enabling this policy allows you to configure the image compression rate during transfer as shown in the following screenshot:

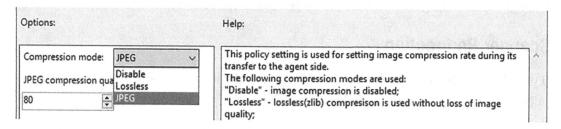

Figure 9-26. Scanner Redirection – Compression

Force the TWAIN Scanning Properties dialog

Enabling this policy forces the displaying of the TWAIN scanning properties dialog box.

TWAIN Scanner Properties dialog location

Enabling this policy configures where the TWAIN scanning properties dialog box will be displayed. You can configure either an agent or a client as shown:

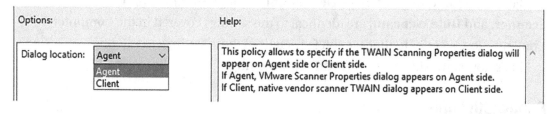

Figure 9-27. Scanner Redirection – TWAIN Scanner Properties dialog location

The next set of policy settings are for **Serial COM**.

Serial COM

If you click the **Serial COM** folder in the left-hand tree view, you will see the policy settings and a sub-folder as shown in the following:

Setting	State	Comment
PortSettings		
Local settings priority	Not configured	No
Lock configuration	Not configured	No

Figure 9-28. *Serial COM configuration settings*

The configuration settings within this folder are identical to those in the **Serial COM** folder that we looked at in the **Computer Configuration** policies.

Rather than cover the same policy settings again, refer to the Computer Configuration settings for details on the **Serial COM** policy settings.

The next set of policy settings are for **VMware Integrated Printing**.

VMware Integrated Printing

The configuration settings within this folder are identical to those in the **VMware Integrated Printing** folder that we looked at in the **Computer Configuration** policies.

Rather than cover the same policy settings again, refer to the Computer Configuration settings for details on the **VMware Integrated Printing** policy settings.

The final policy setting is to configure the **Watermark** feature.

Watermark

If you click the **Watermark** folder in the left-hand tree view, you will see the single policy setting for **Watermark Configuration**.

Watermark Configuration

Enabling the Watermark setting allows you to configure a watermark that appears on the screen of the virtual desktop machine. In the **Text** box shown in the following screenshot, you can enter what you want to be displayed, with a limit of 256 characters, as the watermark:

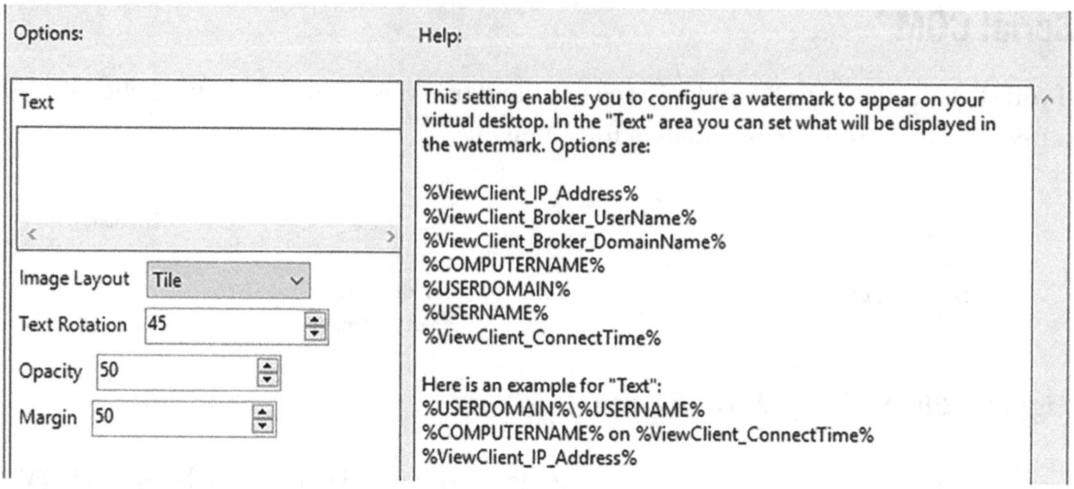

Figure 9-29. *Watermark Configuration*

With the **Image Layout** configuration, you can choose **Tile**, **Center**, or **Multiple**. Multiple means the watermark text is displayed in the middle of the screen and in each corner.

Summary

In this chapter, we have given you a comprehensive introduction and overview of the different policy options that ship with the Horizon GPO bundle for configuring user-based policies to control and manage your Horizon environment.

To do this, we took a guided tour of each of the individual policy settings and how to configure them and what they are used for.

In the next chapter, we are going to look at how to manage the end-user environment from a user profile perspective.

CHAPTER 10

Managing the End-User Environment

Although not specifically a virtual desktop solution, in desktop computing, managing the end-user environment is paramount to delivering a great end-user experience. A great user experience equals happy end users.

End users require their applications, data, personal files, and settings delivered to them no matter where they log in from. That is also a given whether they use physical desktops or virtual desktops. Upon login, they expect to see all the correct icons on the desktop for the applications they use, their favorite printer is connected (or the most convenient one to the desk location), and, above all else, access to their documents, data, and files. Fulfillment of all these parameters means the end users tend be more productive, with fewer calls logged to the help desk for simple issues.

When it comes to the IT teams supporting and managing end-user desktops, having a solution that allows them to centrally manage the end user and desktop estate frees them up to work on more strategic projects. Changes can simply be made centrally that will be propagated to all the end users that are targeted for the changes. IT can centrally manage end-user settings and access to applications, which printer users can access along with any other policy- and security-based settings. It also means that they can ensure desktops are running up-to-date policies and security settings to ensure a safe working environment.

What we have described are user profiles.

As part of delivering a fully stateless, non-persistent virtual desktop environment, end-user profiles should be abstracted from the underlying OS, essentially anonymizing the OS, and then delivered back to the virtual desktop on demand as an end user logs in.

In VMware solution terms, this is the functionality that VMware Dynamic Environment Manager is designed to deliver, but before we talk specifically about that solution, we are going to discuss user profiles in more detail.

© Peter von Oven 2022
P. von Oven, *Mastering VMware Horizon 8*, https://doi.org/10.1007/978-1-4842-7261-9_10

What Is a User Profile?

The purpose of a user profile is to save an individual end user's configuration information to a secure location, from where it will be available to the end user each time they log on to a desktop machine.

This configuration information, or user profile, includes the Windows desktop settings and icon placement, mapped network drives, network printer connections, personal program groups, and program items within the personal program groups.

It can also store less important configuration information such as screen colors, screen savers, mouse settings, window size, and position. When an end user logs on to their desktop, Windows loads that end user's profile and configures the Windows environment according to the settings for that user. It basically adds the personalization to the desktop to make it theirs.

From a historical perspective, if you go back in time as far as the Windows 95 and Windows 98 operating systems, long before VDI, desktops did not have any form of profile management features. This was primarily due to these versions; the Windows operating systems then were not multi-user enabled. Instead, they were designed for a single user working on a static desktop or using the same desktop every day.

If the desktop was operated by other users, then any documents and settings were all shared regardless of who was using the desktop. So, for example, if one user changed the screensaver, background colors, or any of the desktop icons, then the next user with the same desktop would see those changes too.

There was no way of having a personalized desktop for each user. Likewise, if that second user changed anything, it would also remain for whoever used the machine next. All settings were shared. There was, however, a feature in the control panel that when activated provided basic profile management, although it was rarely used.

It was not until Windows NT came along that profiles really came into being. Windows NT had its own profile folder in the form of C:\WINNT\Profiles. This was later updated in Windows 2000 to the Documents and Settings folders we have in operating systems such as Windows 10.

An example of the end-user folder structure is shown in the following screenshot:

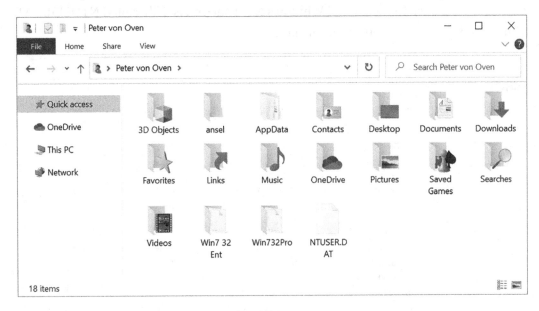

Figure 10-1. *Windows 10 user profile folders*

You will also see with the folders a folder called **AppData**, as shown in the following screenshot:

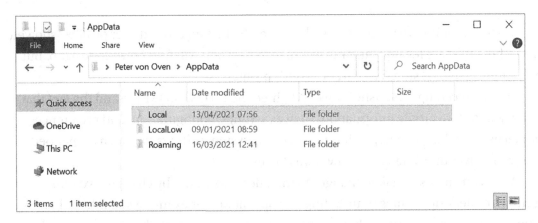

Figure 10-2. *Windows 10 AppData folder with profile folders*

In the AppData folder, you will find the details of the different profile types. We will discuss the different profile types later in this chapter.

If you go back to the user folder, you will see another link back to the past and user profiles pointing back to the days of Windows NT. That link is a file called NTUSER.DAT, which is used to store the settings information.

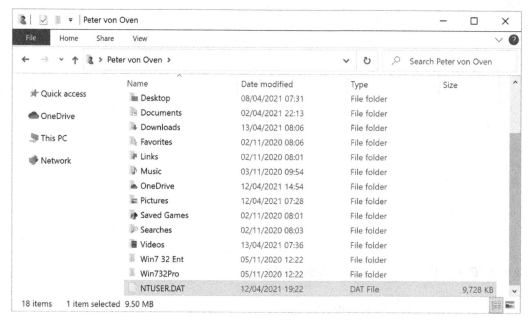

Figure 10-3. *NTUSER.DAT file*

Up to this point, we have discussed some of the history around user profiles, showed you where they are located, and the example folders you will find on your desktop. But what information is stored as part of a user's profile?

In the preceding screenshot, we highlighted the NTUSER.DAT file and the fact that it is used to store profile information, such as settings, configuration, and preferences for all users of the machine, including operating system settings too, such as mapped network drives or printers. But how is this file used?

When an end user makes changes to their desktop, either by changing system settings or desktop themes or installing an application, for example, the information is stored in the local registry of that machine. These configuration changes made by the user on their desktop are saved in the NTUSER.DAT file when they log out.

When the end user next logs in to their desktop machine, or they log in to a different desktop machine on the network, the NTUSER.DAT file is now loaded into the memory of that desktop machine, thereby loading all the preferences and settings for that specific end user, along with all the corresponding registry settings.

If the NTUSER.DAT file gets deleted, then all the end user–specific settings are lost, resulting in the desktop machine returning to the default profile. This means that the end user will need to reconfigure their desktop environment from the beginning. However, when an end user makes configuration changes to their desktop environment, Windows will create a log of this and keep the previous settings as a backup.

But it is not just the NTUSER.DAT file that controls the end-user settings. As we have mentioned, settings also are loaded from and to the registry on the end user's desktop machine, as shown in the following example screenshot:

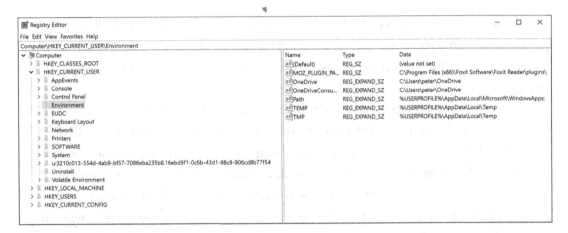

Figure 10-4. *Example of the HKEY_CURRENT_USER registry hive*

The registry component consists of a registry hive and a group of folders and files that contain the end user's settings and data. When an end user logs on, Windows loads the registry hive into the HKEY_CURRENT_USER and merges NTUSER.DAT. The hive, and any subtrees to that hive, contains the registry-based settings and preferences for the end user's environment. The registry then keeps track of the end user and saves any settings changes and maintains the multi-profile structure.

How Are End-User Profiles Created?

When an end user logs on to a desktop for the first time, a folder is created under **Documents and Settings**. This folder will be named the same as the username that was used to log in with.

If a folder already exists for that username, then the profile creation process will create a new folder. This new folder will be named username.computername. If the machine is part of a domain, then it will use the format username.domainname for the folder name.

The following shows an example of the username folder that gets created:

Figure 10-5. *Example of the profile folder naming*

One thing to note is that once this folder has been created, the folder will keep the same name, even if you update the username. It will also contain the NTUSER.DAT file that is created for every new end user, containing their specific user environment configuration.

New profiles are created from a default template, using a special profile called the Default User profile. As this is the starting point for all new profiles that are created, then the Default User profile can be modified to deliver a customized and personalized environment for all new profiles that are created. It can serve as a custom template.

However, if you are going to modify the Default User profile, then plan to do this before you create any new user profiles. So, when the end user logs in to their desktop machine for the first time, you ensure they get the new customized Default User profile. If the end user has already logged in to a desktop machine and been using it, then the Default User profile will not be applied, and as a result they will not have any of these changes applied to their profile.

Now that the end-user profile and associated folders and files have been created, a question that is often asked concerns the size of the profile and how much disk space it will take up. The question is asked mainly due to the potential impact on the network that occurs when profiles are being synchronized. The actual size of the profile file depends on the amount of personal data and settings the user adds to their profile.

For example, if an end user saves files to their local Documents folder that are particularly large, then the profile will equally be as large, meaning they could take a lot longer to load and result in slower login times. However, there are ways of managing this, particularly when it comes to stateless virtual desktop machines, which are built on demand at every login and therefore would copy the user profile each time. The solution to this problem is with App Volumes and storing the user profile on a separate virtual hard disk. We will discuss this later in this chapter.

User Profile Types

Now that we have outlined the basics of what a user profile is and how it is used, in this section we are going to look at the different types of profile and what they are used for:

- **Local profile**: A local profile is created when an end user logs on to a new desktop for the first time. This profile is created and stored locally on the hard drive of the desktop that the end user logs in to. If they make any changes to the desktop, such as change settings, create shortcuts, create files, etc., then these changes will only apply to that particular end user and to the machine they are logged in to at the time. If they log on to a new or different desktop, then the profile they created will not be available, and likewise if a different end user logs on to the same desktop as the original user, they will have a new profile created if they have not logged on to this desktop previously.

- **Roaming profiles**: Roaming profiles are copies of the local profile that are taken from the local machine and copied to some form of centralized shared folder on a file server. Then, when an end user logs in to a desktop machine on the network that has access to that central profile store, a copy of that end user's profile is downloaded to the desktop. Should they make any changes to their desktop, then these changes are saved and synchronized with the centralized profile located on the file server. The synchronization process is not continuous and only executes when the end user logs out of their desktop. Then, when they log in to a different desktop, the central profile is again downloaded so that they have the same settings even though they potentially have a different desktop machine.

- **Mandatory profiles**: A mandatory profile is used by the desktop admin team to specify mandatory settings that end users will have applied to them. These settings are typically based on corporate policy and could be used to enforce security-based policies or other policies that all end users must have. Any changes to this type of profile can only be made by the desktop admins. Any changes made by end users will not be saved when the end user logs off, and when they log in again, the mandatory profile will again be applied.

- **Temporary profiles**: There may be instances of an end user's profile failing to load when they log in. This could be either a corrupt profile or issues with network connectivity. So as this does not prevent the end user from logging in, a temporary profile is created. They can at least log in even though they will not have their personal settings available to them. When the end user logs out of the machine with the temporary profile, it gets deleted along with any changes they may have made.

As well as the different types of user profile, there are also different versions. As newer OS versions become available, so do profile versions. The issue here is that some profile versions do not work with some OSs, and therefore the profile will need to be migrated as part of any OS migration.

The following profile versions are listed along with which operating system version they apply to:

- **Version 1 profiles**

  - Windows NT

  - Windows 2000

  - Windows XP

  - Windows Server 2003

- **Version 2 profiles**

  - Windows Vista

  - Windows Server 2008

  - Windows 7

  - Windows Server 2008 R2

- **Version 3 profiles**

  - Windows 8

  - Windows Server 2012

- **Version 4 profiles**

  - Windows 8.1

  - Windows Server 2012 R2

- **Version 5 profiles**

  - Windows 10 RTM

  - Windows 10 1511

  - Windows Server 2016 Tech preview

- **Version 6 profiles**

  - Windows 10 1607

  - Windows Server 2016 RTM

  - Windows Server 2019

Profile Management for Horizon Desktops

End-user profiles are used to manage the end user's desktop machine, in any desktop environment whether it is physical or virtual. However, with virtual desktop environments, this becomes a key consideration in enabling fully stateless virtual desktop machines.

In the next sections, we are going to look at how to deliver user profiles for virtual desktop machines.

User Environment Management (UEM)

The first thing to clarify is what we mean when we say UEM as there are other similar solutions using the same acronym. In this context, we are talking about **User Environment Manager** and the ability to manage the end-user desktop experience. We are *not* talking about Unified Endpoint Management, which is used to manage physical end points.

The question that often gets asked is how UEM is different to user profiles and Active Directory Group Policy. The user profile contains all the end user's relevant configuration settings and data, whereas UEM is the delivery mechanism to applying these user profiles to end users, based on context such as end-user location or the type of device. Basically, UEM offers a far more comprehensive set of features and functionality and a much simpler way to manage the policies.

Group policies can become complex and difficult to manage and over time also become bloated. They stay bloated as most desktop administrators do not want to delete a policy just in case it deletes something that the end user really needs. As profiles become big and bloated, they will end up having a negative effect on end users, such as increasing the login times as the profile is so large it takes much longer to process.

UEM enables the desktop administrator to manage the end-user profiles in a much more simplified way and at a more granular level. As we mentioned previously, this could be to add context to where and how the end user is logging in. You can apply filters or conditions to the policies that get delivered.

For example, if an end user is connected to the internal network, then a specific policy is applied to deliver settings relevant to being connected internally. But if the same end user then connects from a location outside the network, such as the Internet, then a different policy is applied – one where maybe additional security steps are required in authenticating to reflect the fact that they are coming in via an untrusted connection.

What Is UEM?

So, what is UEM and how does it work?

UEM is a software-based solution that enables organizations to manage the end-user environment via policies. It is used to abstract user-specific data, such as configuration information, and settings for each end user. This makes up everything that is unique and personal to the end user, for example, saving their wallpaper background, icon layout, and accessibility features. All of these settings are stored centrally on a domain controller, file server, or other centralized storage that is accessible by the end users.

With the end-user profile abstracted from the OS, it can now be delivered on demand to any virtual desktop machine that the end user logs in to. The ability to deliver profiles just in time and on demand allows an organization to deploy fully stateless virtual desktops, safe in the knowledge that each brand-new desktop is automatically customized to provide the end user's personal experience, making it look like their own desktop.

Why UEM?

The old static desktop model has evolved into a more dynamic model and as a result is now referred to as the modern workspace. Organizations now manage end-user access to desktops and applications based on the role that the user has within the organization.

Instead of every user having every application, setting, and configuration regardless of the role they perform, settings and configurations are delivered on a more personal level and on a per-user basis, delivering the tools, apps, and data that the end user requires to perform their role. This means that you are managing the end user's profile rather than devices and delivering the right end-user experience no matter where the end user logs in from.

This is where UEM solutions come into play. UEM has been designed to manage the end-user personalization within these new and more dynamic, on-demand, just-in-time environments. These types of environments did not exist previously when user profiles first came into being.

How Does UEM Work?

UEM takes standard policies from Active Directory Group Policy and takes them to the next level delivering enhancements, by allowing a more granular way of delivering policies back to end users, while adding context around what gets applied.

UEM integrates into your current Active Directory architecture, so there is no need to rip and replace. It will sit beside and above your current solutions, providing a more user-friendly interface where IT admins can build an experience at the end-user level and appropriate to their working environment. In the same way as AD Group Policy, UEM profiles are stored centrally and essentially become portable, applying to whichever desktop the end user logs in to.

Building upon standard group policy, UEM also adds some more advanced features, such as elevation rights management, which can allow users to install certain apps without needing an admin password to do so, or context aware triggers, whereby a policy only gets applied when certain criteria are met. It also allows management of Outlook folders and cache and a lot more besides.

Another useful feature of UEM is its ability to migrate between profile versions. As seen earlier in this chapter, there are several profile versions for Windows operating systems. Partly, these differences are related to how the profiles are stored. Some have been registry based, some have been held in a database, while others have been a hybrid of both.

With UEM, these different profile versions can be translated or migrated to the newer profile versions. This is particularly useful if you migrate from physical to virtual desktops and update the OS at the same time. UEM can also take care of migrating application settings, ensuring any application settings are maintained as end users log in to different virtual desktop machines.

The Composite Desktop Model

Throughout this chapter, a common word that has been used is the word abstraction. It is the word that describes the core VMware solutions when virtualization became mainstream.

Abstraction in this case was used to describe the separation of the operating system from the underlying hardware, with that separation being delivered by the hypervisor.

In the context of virtual desktop infrastructure, we are again abstracting the operating system, in this case, a desktop operating system, from the underlying hardware. The hypervisor is then used to deliver multiple instances of the desktop OS. But in a virtual desktop environment, the abstraction does not stop at the OS.

Let me introduce you to the composite desktop model.

As we discussed previously in this chapter, the ideal model to deliver a virtual desktop machine is to deliver a completely stateless virtual desktop machine. A stateless desktop is a virtual desktop machine that starts life being completely vanilla. It has no end-user ownership or personalization, contains a vanilla build of the OS, and has no applications installed other than the core OS-based apps that are then delivered to the end user on demand when they log in and request a virtual desktop machine to connect to.

Before that point, the virtual desktop did not exist. I use the analogy of going to a DIY store and having a custom paint color made up. The store has loads of paint cans on the shelf, all ready and waiting, but all using the same base color. You come along, take a can, then the store adds the different color mixes to make the color you requested.

In this example, the paint cans with the base color are the virtual desktop machines waiting for end users to log in, and then the custom colors added to make the color you want represent the apps, profiles, data, and settings, all designed to deliver the end user's requirements to enable them to perform their specific role.

The virtual desktop machine can be broken down into three different specific components: the operating system, applications, and the user's profile. These components come together to make up the end user's complete desktop environment, as shown in the following graphic:

Figure 10-6. *The composite desktop model*

In the following sections, we are going to look at the components that make up the composite desktop.

The Operating System

The first component to be delivered on demand as the end user logs in is the operating system, delivered using Instant Clones.

The OS in this case is a completely new and vanilla version of the OS and is therefore delivered with no user personalization settings or apps.

As well as the operating system and its components, any core apps that you want to deliver to every user should also be included as part of the operating system. These are typically those applications that cannot be delivered using application layering or application virtualization technologies.

Delivering Applications

As part of your Horizon deployment, you need to have an application delivery strategy to manage the delivery of apps when deploying stateless desktops.

App Volumes Delivered Applications

Similar to how user profiles work and are delivered in a stateless virtual desktop environment, applications will have been abstracted from the core OS image. It is then deciding the best way of delivering these to end users. With VMware, the solution for this is App Volumes.

We will cover this in more detail in Chapter 14, but suffice to say, App Volumes enables applications to be captured as independent layers (stored as virtual hard disks) which are then attached to the OS on demand, based on the end-user entitlement.

This approach enables applications to be managed independently of the OS layer and also to be delivered based on end-user profile and entitlement.

App Volumes ships as standard with Horizon Enterprise and Horizon Apps Advanced editions.

App Volumes Writable Volumes

The next question, if you are deploying stateless virtual desktop machines, is can end users install applications? The answer is, of course, they can. If they install applications onto a stateless virtual desktop machine, when they log out and the virtual desktop is destroyed, the next time the end user logs in, then they will not have access to that application, unless they install it again. They would have to do this each time.

In a previous version of Horizon, you could configure a persistent disk; however, that feature no longer exists. This is where App Volumes can solve the issue, with Writable Volumes.

A Writable Volume is a blank virtual hard disk that is assigned and owned by individual end users and is used to capture and store user-installed applications. Each time they log in, this virtual hard disk will be attached, and their applications made available, along with those delivered by the desktop admins as part of the standard build.

If you cast your mind back to earlier in this chapter, we talked about large profiles and the potential for those to cause slow login times, given the time they would take to copy from the central location to the desktop. Although in VDI this is better because the data only has to traverse the network backbone, you can improve it further still by using a Writable Volume to store the user profile. When an end user logs in, rather than having to copy the profile, it simply gets attached to the virtual desktop machine as a virtual hard disk.

Bringing all these component parts together, OS, profiles, apps, and data, delivers the complete desktop experience.

In the next section, we are going to focus on the VMware solution for managing end-user environments, VMware Dynamic Environment Manager.

VMware Dynamic Environment Manager (DEM)

VMware Dynamic Environment Manager, previously known as VMware User Environment Manager, was added to the Horizon portfolio of EUC solutions when VMware acquired a Dutch company called Immidio back in February 2015.

Immidio started as a software company that created a set of tools designed to assist their consultants working out in the field in managing end-user environments. It was productized and soon became a product rather than an internally developed consultancy tool.

Availability comes in two versions, Standard and Advanced. Standard ships with Horizon Standard and Horizon Advanced, while DEM Enterprise ships with Horizon Enterprise, Horizon Apps Standard, and Horizon Apps Advanced.

DEM provides advanced features and functionality; one of the key differences between it and standard Active Directory Group Policy management is that it is managed via a central management console rather than using the standard group policy editor and having to create and manage policies in a manual way.

One point to note is that DEM not only works across virtual desktop machines but also works with physical PCs, as well as cloud-based Windows desktop environments or DaaS. It is all about managing the end user's environment rather than where or how the operating system runs. To enable DEM to manage the end-user profile, you just install the DEM agent onto the desktop operating system that you want to manage the end-user environment on. This can be simply installed as part of the standard gold image OS build.

In the next section, we are going to look at how DEM works and its architecture.

How Does DEM Work?

To begin, let us take a quick look at the high-level overview of how DEM works and the different components, such as the help desk support tool and the application profiler.

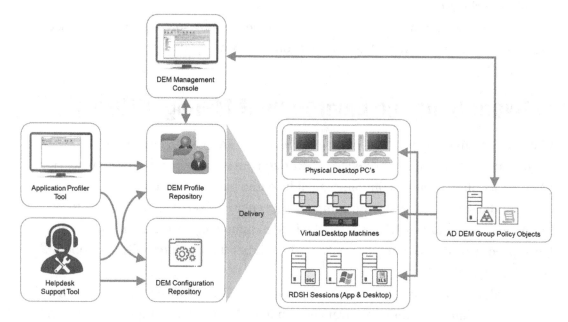

Figure 10-7. *VMware Dynamic Environment Manager high-level architecture*

As we have highlighted previously, DEM is far more advanced than standard group policy and has been designed to provide a solution covering the following:

- **Application configuration management**: Allows the specific configuration of an app's initial settings rather than deploying the default settings.

- **User environment settings**: Allows you to centrally manage user environment settings such as the following:

  - Application blocking

  - Application shortcuts and file type associations

  - Drive and printer mappings

- Environment variables

- Files, folders, and registry settings

- Folder redirection

- **Personalization**: Abstracts user-specific desktop and app settings from the underlying OS and then makes these settings available across multiple devices, Windows versions, and apps. It also supports OS migration.

- **Application migration**: Allows an end user to roam app and personalization settings so that they can move between different OS versions and keep their app settings.

- **Dynamic desktop configuration**: This uses condition sets to enable you to configure certain conditions that are based on variables such as user, location, and device, to dynamically deliver content and appearance. For example, if location were set as a condition, then the content that gets delivered to the end user could be different, depending on where they log in from. If it were a public location outside the network, then certain datasets could be unavailable.

In addition to the core use cases, DEM also has several configuration options designed specifically to customize a Horizon virtual desktop environment. We will look at these in the next section.

Horizon Smart Policies

The SmartPolicies feature of DEM delivers a set of policies that are specific to Horizon virtual desktop machines, in that the policies delivered contain settings that only apply to Horizon virtual desktop features.

SmartPolicies work with Horizon version 7.2 or later and DEM version 9.2.

By deploying SmartPolicies, virtual desktop admins have a more granular level of control over a virtual desktop machine. Horizon features can be dynamically enabled, disabled, or controlled based on the end user, as well as other variables such as client device type, IP address, and desktop pool name. For example, you can configure the following Horizon settings:

- USB redirection

- Printing

- Clipboard behavior

- Client drive redirection

- HTML access file transfer

- Bandwidth profile

If you deploy DEM v9.1 or later and the Horizon Agent v7.0.1 or later, you can use SmartPolicies when delivering virtual desktops with either the Blast Extreme or PCoIP display protocol.

Summary

We have given you an introduction to the composite desktop model and how virtual desktops are built and delivered with the different elements being abstracted, then delivered back to the end user on demand as they log in. One of those components that we discussed was the end-user profile or the end-user environment, the component that tailors and personalizes the desktop specific to the end user that is using it.

We then covered a high-level overview of the VMware solution for managing the end-user environment and end-user profiles, VMware Dynamic Environment Manager. As part of the overview, we discussed the advanced features that DEM delivers in order to manage the end-user environment, along with some of the Horizon-specific features.

In the next chapter, we are going to discuss how Horizon delivers just the applications using the Horizon Apps solution.

CHAPTER 11

Horizon Apps

So far in this book, we have discussed the delivery of a full-blown virtual desktop machine to your end users. However, as we discussed at the start of this book, that model may not be appropriate.

Maybe you have a group of end users that typically just use a single application. In this case, why would you want or need to provide them with a full virtual desktop machine that requires both resource and management?

In this use case, it may be prudent to just deliver that single app to their end point device and do that by publishing it using a Microsoft RDS solution, but allowing Horizon to broker the connection to the application via the Connection Server.

The end-user experience is therefore simplified, as they will have both applications and desktops available using the same client.

In this chapter, we are going to discuss the Horizon Apps solution for delivering published applications, starting with an overview of the architecture.

Horizon Apps High-Level Architecture

In terms of infrastructure, delivering apps with Horizon Apps means no real change to the back-end Horizon infrastructure requirements. The only addition to the infrastructure is the Microsoft RDSH Server, on which the applications will be installed.

As the Microsoft RDSH Server now effectively becomes the resource that is being delivered to the end users, that is, it is delivering the applications, it means that the Horizon Agent is installed on the RDSH Server rather than on a virtual desktop machine.

With the Horizon Agent installed on the RDSH Server, the Connection Server can now communicate with it, enabling you to create an RDS Farm and then, from the farm, create an application pool. The application pool like the desktop pool shows the end user the applications that they are entitled to run.

© Peter von Oven 2022
P. von Oven, *Mastering VMware Horizon 8*, https://doi.org/10.1007/978-1-4842-7261-9_11

Double-click the application icon; the published application is delivered via the Connection Server using the display protocol. This is shown in the following screenshot:

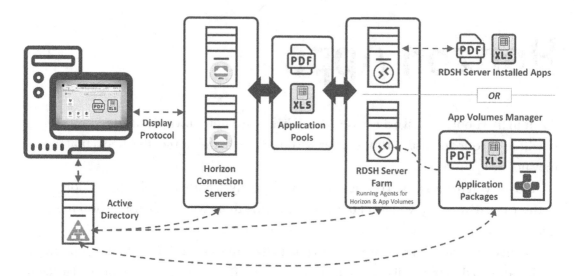

Figure 11-1. *Horizon Apps architecture*

The preceding example also demonstrates the two methods for installing or delivering the apps to the RDSH Servers in the farm.

First, you can simply install the apps using the same process that you would use for any other RDSH app install, installing them directly onto the server. However, this is a fairly static model, and a far better option would be to layer the apps using App Volumes. This would enable you to build a stateless RDSH Server farm and easily scale and manage the lifecycle of apps.

We will talk more about App Volumes in Chapter 14 when we discuss the additional solutions that come as part of the Horizon Enterprise license. You can also read the *Delivering Applications with VMware App Volumes 4* book by Apress at www.apress.com/gb/book/9781484266885.

Design Considerations

As detailed in the previous diagram, Horizon uses the concept of farms to group together RDSH host servers that provide a common set of applications for the end users. Farms could contain several host servers to provide the resources to run the applications.

These farms will then be used to create specific application pools, from where the end users select their apps.

When architecting virtual RDSH host servers, it is important to ensure that you do not overcommit the ratio of virtual CPUs to physical CPUs.

When architecting virtual desktop machines, higher consolidation levels can be achieved when you over-allocate virtual CPUs to physical cores. Whereas with RDSH host servers, you can achieve higher consolidation levels by over-allocating end users to physical or virtual cores.

If you over-allocate virtual CPUs to physical CPUs in this environment, then it could potentially result in poor performance for your end users.

This is illustrated in the following diagram:

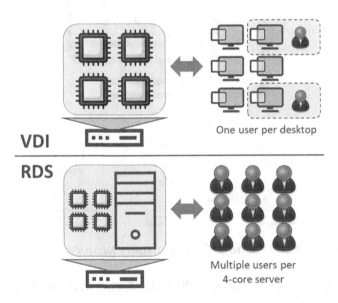

Figure 11-2. *VDI and RDS comparison*

When creating your design, you should not include memory over-allocation as part of the design.

As Horizon Apps is using an RDS back-end infrastructure to deliver your apps, you need to consider the design when it comes to where the applications will be deployed. By this we mean: Will all your apps be installed on a single server farm? Or will they be installed across separate server farms?

This will mean you need to consider your CPU, memory, and disk resources, depending on the workload requirements of the different apps.

When it comes to resources, you need to consider more than just standard CPU and memory requirements needed to run the apps. You also need to think about how many PCoIP or Blast Extreme connections are going to be required to connect to the various sessions.

An example of this is shown in the following diagram:

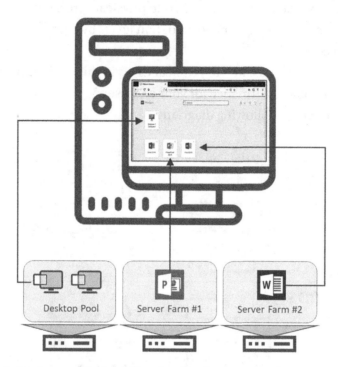

Figure 11-3. *Multiple connections for the display protocol*

The diagram illustrates the Horizon Client displaying to the end user the different resources that are available to them. Each one of these would be classed as a separate session.

This means that the end user could connect to their virtual desktop machine and launch the app being delivered by server farm #1 and also the app being delivered by server farm #2.

In this example, the end user will be using three connections or sessions. When sizing your environment, you will need to ensure you understand the maximum number of connections available from the Connection Server. In the example scenario, if all users were accessing apps and virtual desktop machines in this way, then you have essentially divided the number of supported end users by a third, as each individual end user is consuming three sessions.

In this configuration, the Connection Server can support a maximum of 150 sessions, based on a server configured with 4 CPUs and 64 GB of memory.

In the next section, we are going to install a Horizon Apps environment, starting with setting up and configuring the RDS role.

Installing and Configuring Horizon Apps

In this section, we are going to build an example environment, setting up a Horizon Apps environment to deliver published apps to the end users.

We are going to follow the process depicted in the following diagram:

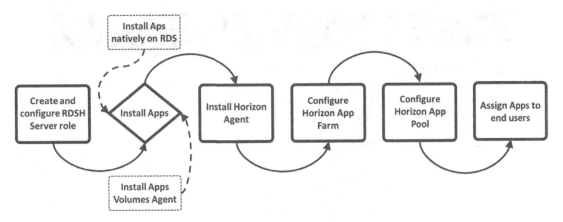

Figure 11-4. *Horizon Apps install and configuration process*

When it comes to the app install, you will note we have two options here. The first is to install them directly onto the RDSH Server.

The second option, which is a better way of managing the apps and aids scalability, is to create a stateless server farm (no apps installed). Apps are then attached or layered using VMware App Volumes. This being the case, it is at this stage you would install the App Volumes Agent onto the RDSH Server, so that it can communicate with the App Volumes Manager to assign application packages.

In the next section, we are going to configure the RDS role.

Building and Configuring an RDSH Environment

In this section, we are going to install and configure the RDSH role onto an example server that we have already built. The hostname of this server is **rdsh-apps.pvolab.com**.

To set up the RDSH role, follow the steps as described:

1. Open a console to the rdsh-apps.pvolab.com server, the server we are going to add the RDSH role to.

2. From the **Server Manager** console and the **Dashboard** page, click **(2) Add roles and features**, as shown in the following screenshot:

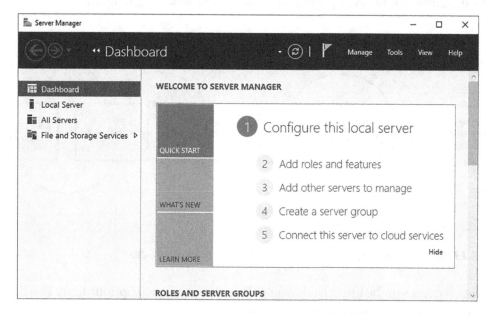

Figure 11-5. *Launch the Server Manager console*

3. The **Add Roles and Features Wizard** will now launch, and the first screen you will see is the **Before you begin** screen, as shown in the following screenshot:

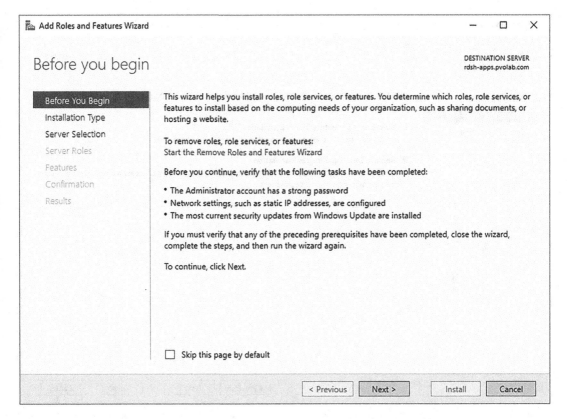

Figure 11-6. Add Roles and Features Wizard – Before you begin screen

4. You can opt to skip this page in the future by checking the **Skip this page by default** box.

5. Click **Next ➤** to continue.

6. You will see the **Select installation type** screen, as shown in the following screenshot:

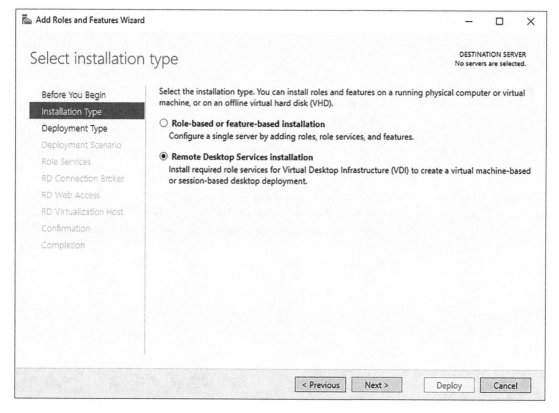

Figure 11-7. *Selecting the installation type screen*

7. Click the **Remote Desktop Services installation** radio button, then click **Next ➤** to continue.

8. You will now see the **Select deployment type** screen, as shown in the following:

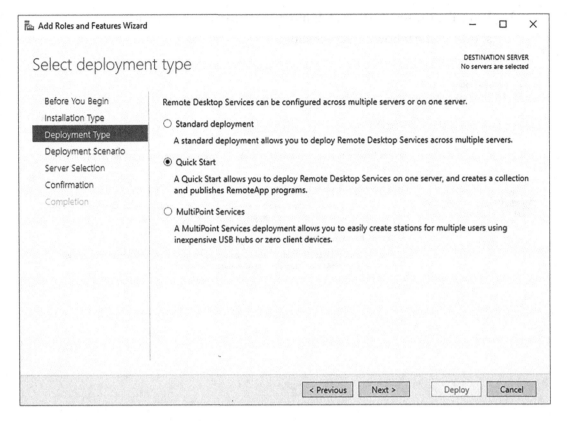

Figure 11-8. *Selecting the deployment type screen*

9. Click the **Quick Start** radio button. Quick start allows you to
    quickly and simply set up the RDSH role on a single server and
    automatically set up several applications that are already installed
    as part of the OS, namely, WordPad, Calculator, and Paint. This
    helps with testing before adding the App Volumes applications
    and demonstrates that the RDSH Server is functioning correctly. It
    also aids troubleshooting when the App Volumes apps are added.

10. Click **Next ➤** to continue.

11. You will now see the **Select deployment scenario** screen, as shown in the following screenshot:

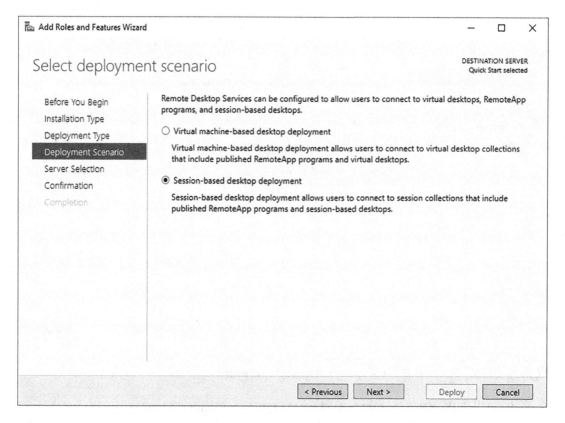

Figure 11-9. *Selecting the deployment scenario screen*

12. Click the **Session-based desktop deployment** radio button. This enables end users to connect to session collections (collections of available applications) that are published using the RDSH Server and the RemoteApp feature. We will use RemoteApp to test the applications are available and launch correctly before replacing that with Horizon Apps as the broker in a future chapter.

13. Click **Next ➤** to continue.

14. You will now see the **Select a server** screen.

15. Select the server you are going to use for capturing the App Volumes applications. Select the server's name by clicking to highlight it, from the list shown in the Server Pool box. In the test lab example, this is the server called **rdsh-apps.pvolab.com**.

16. Click the right arrow next to the box to add the server to the Selected box, as shown in the following screenshot:

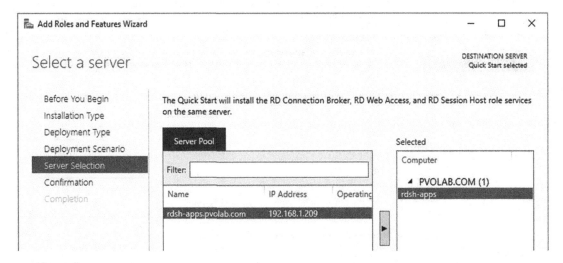

Figure 11-10. *Select a server to install the RDSH role to*

17. Click **Next ➤** to continue.

18. You will now see the **Confirm selections** screen. On this screen, you will see a summary of what is going to be installed on the server. This will be the RD Connection Broker, RD Web Access, and RD Session Host. You will also see a warning message highlighted by the yellow triangle, which states that the server will be restarted once the installation of the role services has been completed.

19. Check the **Restart the destination server automatically if required** box. This means as the server will need to be restarted as part of the installation, then it will be done automatically.

20.   This is shown in the following screenshot:

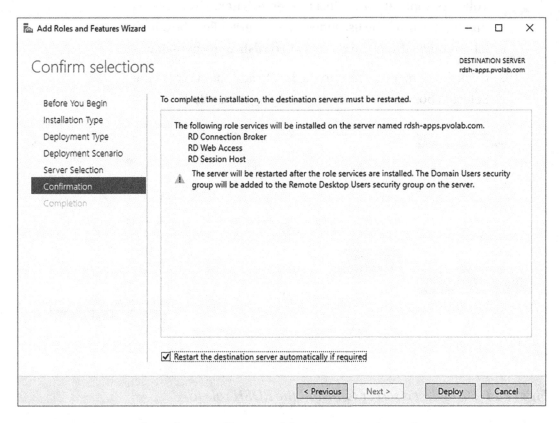

Figure 11-11. Confirm the installation of the RDSH Server roles

21.   Click the **Deploy** button.

22.   You will now see the **View progress** screen that shows the
       progress of each of the individual tasks and features. As we are
       installing the RDSH role, the installation will include the Remote
       Desktop Service role services, the Session collection, and the
       RemoteApp programs that get added by default when the quick
       start option is selected.

23.   This screen is shown in the following screenshot:

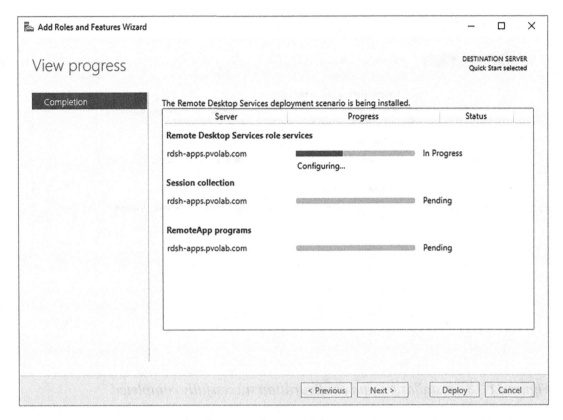

Figure 11-12. *Progress of the RDS deployment*

24.   The server will restart during the installation process, and once
       successfully completed, you will see **Succeeded** against each task,
       as shown in the following screenshot:

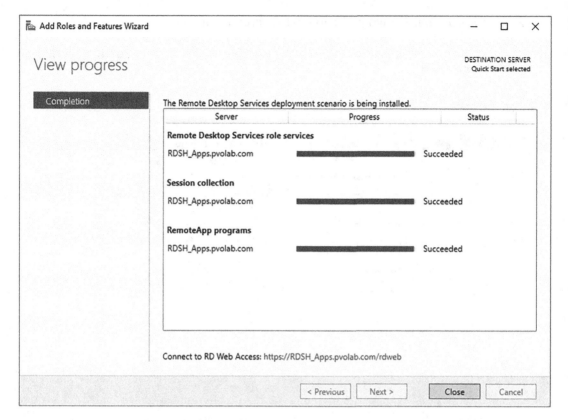

Figure 11-13. *Installation and configuration successfully completed*

25.   Finally, you will return to the **Server Manager Dashboard** where you will see that the **Remote Desktop Services** role has been successfully deployed, as shown in the following screenshot:

Figure 11-14. *Remote Desktop Services installed and running*

Now that you have completed the installation of the Remote Desktop Services role and it is up and running, you will need to ensure you have the appropriate licensing in place, as shown in the following message box that will appear:

Figure 11-15. *Remote Desktop licensing mode not configured warning*

The next thing to complete before we start to use the server to capture an application is to ensure that an end user can connect and launch the applications that were published as part of the quick start application collection.

This approach ensures that the RDSH and RemoteApp elements are running correctly before capturing App Volumes applications. It can help with future troubleshooting, as to whether the issue is RDSH related or App Volumes related. If you know that RDSH and RemoteApp are functioning as expected, then any issue would therefore point toward them being related to the captured application in App Volumes.

Testing RemoteApp Functionality

To test RDSH and RemoteApp, we are going to connect as a test by using the following steps as described:

1. From a desktop machine, open a browser and first type in the address of the RDSH Server. In the test lab example, this is the rdsh-apps server. You will also need to add /RDWeb to the end of the server's name. This is to connect to the RemoteApp website. In the test lab example, you would type the following: **https://rdsh-apps/RDWeb**.

2. You will see the login box, as shown in the following:

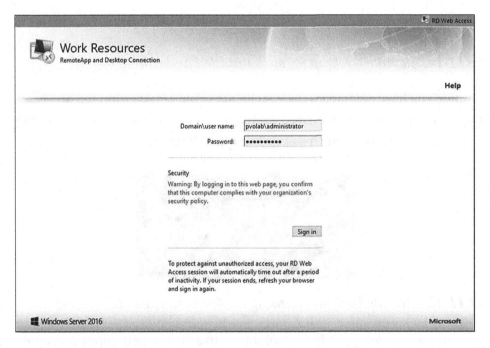

Figure 11-16. *Logging in to the RemoteApp website*

3. In the **Domain\username** box, type the username in the format specified; in this example, we are going to log in as the administrator, so in the box, type **pvolab\administrator**.

4. Then in the **Password** box, type in the password for the account you used in the previous step.

5. Click **Sign in**.

6. You will see the RemoteApp screen showing the available apps. In this example, we have WordPad, Calculator, and Paint available as the published apps, as shown in the following screenshot:

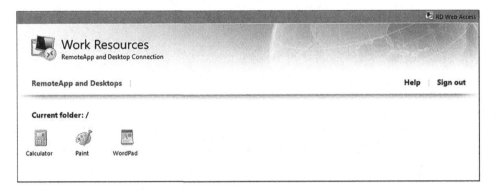

Figure 11-17. *RemoteApp applications*

7. Test that an application launches, and the end user can connect and run it, by double-clicking one of the app icons – in this example, Calculator.

8. You will see the RemoteApp pop-up box showing that the end user is being connected to the application, as shown in the following screenshot:

Figure 11-18. *Calculator launching via RemoteApp*

9. Once connected and the app has launched, the end user will see the following:

Figure 11-19. Calculator running as a published app via RemoteApp

10. Close the Calculator app.

You have now successfully installed and tested the RDSH role on your server that is going to be used to publish applications for Horizon Apps.

The next step is to install the actual apps that you want to deliver. As we mentioned previously, there are two methods for installing apps. You can either install the apps natively and directly onto the RDSH host server or deliver them using App Volumes app packages.

Installing Applications for Horizon Apps Delivery

In the previous section, we looked at the standard apps that are an integrated part of the server operating system; however, you will want to install the apps that are required by your organization and your end users.

With that in mind, this section will look at how to install additional apps: firstly how to install them natively onto the RDSH host server and secondly how to deliver them using App Volumes app packages.

Installing Apps Natively on RDSH

Installing apps on an RDSH Server is a different process to that of installing applications as you would do normally on an individual end user's desktop.

On an RDSH Server, any applications need to be installed via the **Install Application on Remote Desktop** option. This is to enable apps to run in a multi-user environment. To start the installation, follow the steps described:

1. Open a console to the RDSH Server being used for capture, and launch the **Control Panel**, as shown in the following:

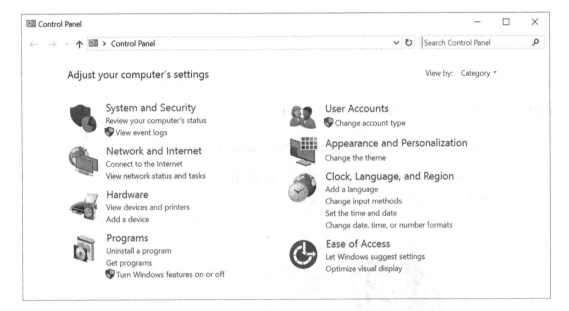

Figure 11-20. *Launching the Control Panel on the RDSH Server*

2. Click **Programs** in the bottom left-hand corner of the Control Panel main screen.

3. You will now see the **Programs** screen of the Control Panel, as shown in the following screenshot:

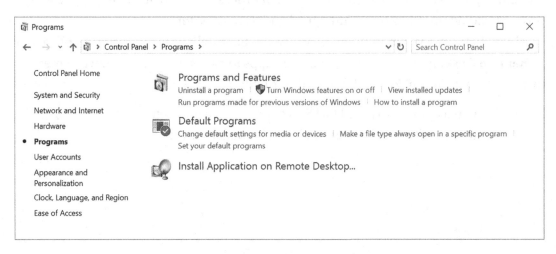

Figure 11-21. *Programs section of the Control Panel*

4. Now click **Install Application on Remote Desktop...**.

5. You will see the **Install Program From Floppy Disk or CD-ROM** as shown in the following screenshot:

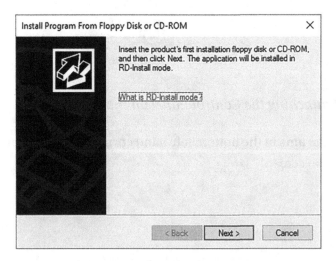

Figure 11-22. *Installing a program using RD-Install mode*

Before we get started with the actual application installation, we mentioned at the start of this section that the installation process for applications running on RDSH is different to a normal installation. That is where the **RD-Install** option comes in.

Clicking the **Install Application on Remote Desktop...** automatically switches the server into the RD-Install mode.

Once the applications have been installed on the RDSH Server, the RDSH Server can then be switched back into execution mode or **RD-Execute**. This mode is for normal operation and allows end users to connect and launch their applications hosted on the RDSH Server.

Although RD-Install mode can be automatically enabled by using the **Install Application on Remote Desktop...** option in the Control Panel, you can also initiate this from the command line by using the following commands:

```
change user /install
change user /execute
```

To check which mode the RDSH Server is currently using, you can use the following command:

```
change user /query
```

In this example, we are going to continue using the automated method that is initiated from the Control Panel. To do this, follow the steps as described:

6. On the **Install Program From Floppy Disk or CD-ROM** dialog box, click **Next** to start the application installation.

7. You will see the **Run Installation Program** dialog box, as shown in the following screenshot:

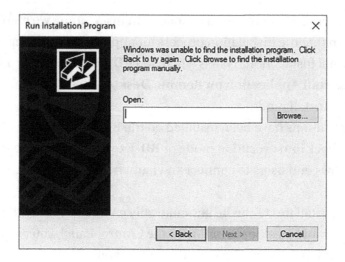

Figure 11-23. *Run Installation Program dialog box*

8. Click the **Browse...** button.

9. You will see a Windows Explorer open from where you can navigate to the application installer for the required application. In this example, we are going to install VLC Media Player as the application we are going to publish, as shown in the following screenshot:

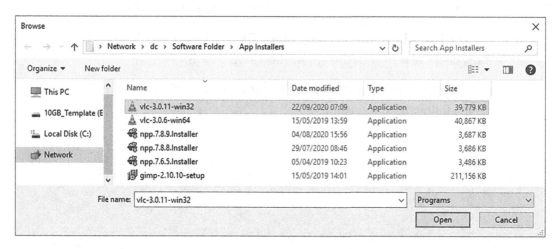

Figure 11-24. *Browse and navigate to the application installer*

10. Click and highlight the installer, in this example the **vlc-3.0.11-win32** file, then click **Open**.

11. The selected installer will now be added to the **Open** box in the **Run Installation Program** dialog box, as shown in the following screenshot:

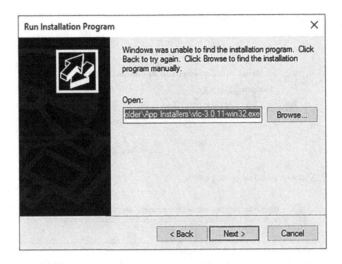

Figure 11-25. *Application installer added*

12. Now click the **Next ➤** button.

13. You will see the **Finish Admin Install** dialog box appear, which will be grayed out for the time being. This will be used once the installation has been completed, shown in the following screenshot:

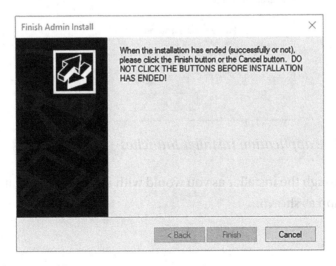

Figure 11-26. *The Finish Admin Install dialog box*

14. At the same time, the application installer will also have launched, as you will see with the **Open File – Security Warning** dialog box, shown in the following screenshot:

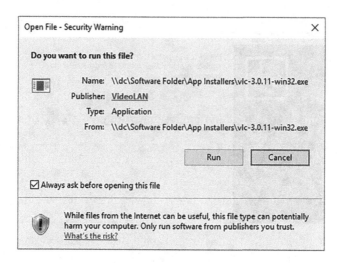

Figure 11-27. *Open File – Security Warning for the app installer*

15. Click the **Run** button.

16. You will now see the first installation screen for VLC Media Player, as shown in the following screenshot:

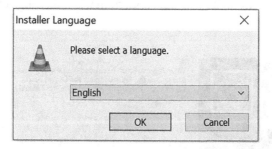

Figure 11-28. *The application installer launches*

17. Run through the installer as you would with any other installation of the app as shown:

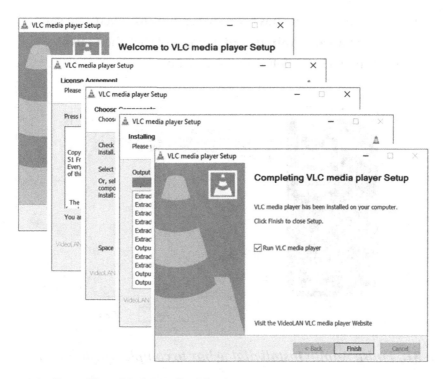

Figure 11-29. *Installing VLC Media Player*

18.   Once installed, launch the app and test that it runs correctly, as
well as making any settings or configuration changes, as shown in
the following screenshot:

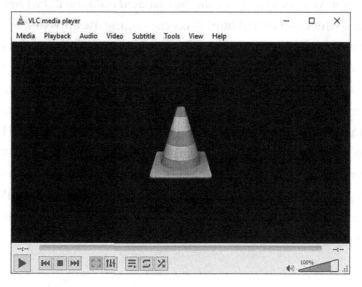

Figure 11-30. *VLC Media Player running*

19. Now that the application has been successfully installed, you can return to the **Finish Admin Install** dialog and click the **Finish** button, as shown in the following screenshot:

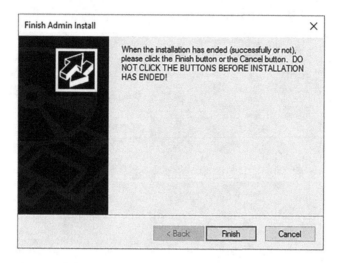

Figure 11-31. *Finish Admin Install dialog box to complete installation*

App Volumes Delivered Apps

With App Volumes, the apps are not installed directly onto the OS of the RDSH Server as we discussed in the previous section.

Instead, the App Volumes Agent would be installed onto the RDSH Server and then the app packages, which are virtual hard disks containing the apps that are attached to the RDSH Server. The App Volumes Agent then makes the apps appear as if they were natively installed, and therefore they can then be published.

To learn more about App Volumes and how to create app packages, you can read the book entitled *Delivering Applications with VMware App Volumes 4* by Apress.

The important point to note when creating the app packages for RDSH is that you follow the same multi-user installation process as we described in the previous section. This ensures that the apps are captured in multi-user mode and so will work with RDSH.

The next step after the apps or the App Volumes Agent has been installed is to install the Horizon Agent. This enables the Horizon Connection Server to communicate with the RDSH Server to enable it to broker sessions to the end users.

Installing the Horizon Agent for RDSH

As with any other Horizon Agent installation, the purpose of the agent is so the Horizon Connection Server can communicate with the resource you are delivering.

With the case of Horizon Apps, the agent enables you to configure the server farms and the application pools in the Horizon Console. We will complete this task later in the chapter.

In this example, the resource being delivered is a published application that is hosted on the RDSH Server.

To install the Horizon Agent, follow the steps as described:

1. From the console of the RDSH Server you are using to publish the app from, navigate to the VMware Horizon Agent installer, as shown in the following screenshot:

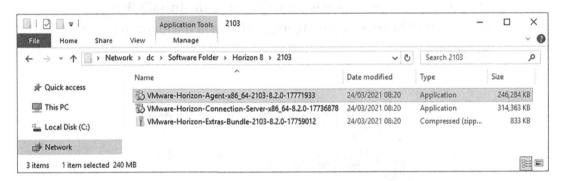

Figure 11-32. *Launch the Horizon Agent installer*

2. Double-click to launch the VMware-Horizon-Agent-x86_64-8.2.0-17771933 agent installer.

3. You will see the installer launch and the splash screen, as shown in the following screenshot:

Figure 11-33. *VMware Horizon Agent installer splash screen*

4. The next screen you will see is the **Welcome to the Installation Wizard for VMware Horizon Agent**, as shown in the following screenshot:

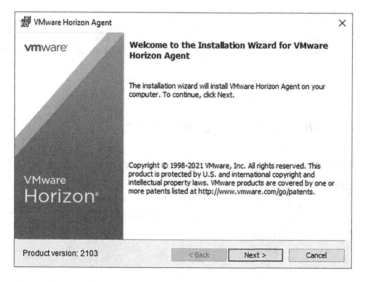

Figure 11-34. *Installer welcome screen*

5. Click **Next ➤** to continue.

6. You will see the **License Agreement** screen as shown:

Figure 11-35. *License Agreement screen*

7. Click the radio button for **I accept the terms in the license agreement**.

8. Click **Next ➤** to continue.

9. You will now see the **Network protocol configuration** screen where you can choose the IP version you want to use. As the Connection Server in our example environment is using IPv4, we will need to also choose IPv4, as you are unable to mix different versions within Horizon, as shown in the following screenshot:

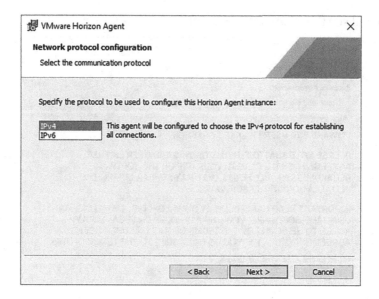

Figure 11-36. *Network protocol configuration screen*

10.   Click to select **IPv4**.

11.   Click **Next ➤** to continue.

The next screen is the **Custom Setup** screen.

Here, you can configure the different features of the Horizon Agent, as shown in the following screenshot:

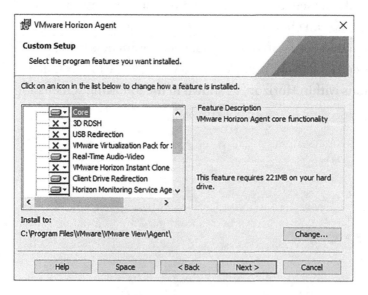

Figure 11-37. *Custom Setup configuration screen*

12. The list of the features that you can install as part of the Horizon
     Agent is detailed as follows:

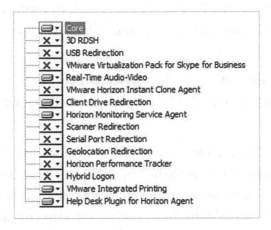

Figure 11-38. *Horizon Agent features*

We are going to describe each of the features you can install as part of the Horizon
Agent as follows:

- **Core**: Installs the core Horizon Agent requirements.

- **3D RDSH**: Installs the 3D graphics features for RDSH.

- **USB Redirection**: Enables USB devices to be redirected from the end
  user's end point to the app session.

- **VMware Virtualization Pack for Skype for Business**: Installs the
  optimizations required to run Skype for Business on a virtual desktop
  machine.

- **Real-Time Audio-Video**: Enables the redirection of audio and video
  devices from the end point to the virtual desktop machine.

- **VMware Instant Clone Agent**: Enables the virtual desktop machine
  to be delivered using Instant Clones. You will need vSphere 6.0/2015
  U1 or later to be able to support Instant Clones. If you install this
  feature, ensure that you DO NOT install the Horizon View Composer
  Agent.

- **Client Drive Redirection**: Enables the end user's end point device to
  share local drives with the virtual desktop machine.

- **Horizon Monitoring Service Agent**: Monitors the performance of the Horizon environment.

- **Scanner Redirection**: Enables scanners to be connected to the end user's end point device and redirected to the virtual desktop machine.

- **Serial Port Redirection**: Enables serial port devices to be connected to the end user's end point device and redirected to the virtual desktop machine.

- **Geolocation Redirection**: Enables the location information from the end user's end point device to be sent to the virtual desktop machine. Useful for end users **who** travel so their location information is reflected on their desktop, given the virtual desktop machine remains static in a data center.

- **Horizon Performance Tracker**: Monitors the performance of the display protocol and system resource usage of the virtual desktop machine.

- **Hybrid Logon**: Enables unauthenticated user access to network resources without the need for user credentials.

- **VMware Integrated Printing**: Enables printer redirection.

- **Help Desk Plugin for Horizon Agent**: Enables the virtual desktop to be monitored using the Horizon Help Desk Tool that is integrated into the Horizon Console.

13. Having now covered each of the features you can install as part of the Horizon Agent and selected the ones you need, click **Next ➤** to continue.

14. The next configuration screen is for **Register with Horizon Connection Server**, as shown in the following screenshot:

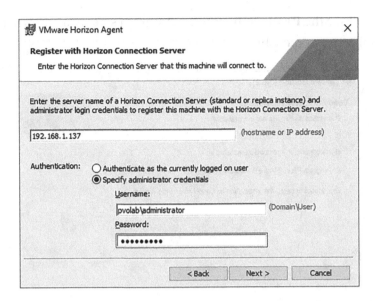

Figure 11-39. Registering the Horizon Agent with the Connection Server

15. In the **hostname or IP address** box, enter the address details of the Connection Server you want the agent to register with. In this example, we have entered **192.168.1.137** as the IP address of the Connection Server.

16. Then in the **Authentication** section, click the radio button for **Specify administrator credentials**. This is the account that can register the agent with the Connection Server. In this example, we are using the administrator account.

17. In the **Username** box, type in the account details using the Domain\User format. In this example, we are going to type **pvolab\administrator**.

18. In the **Password** box, type in the password for the administrator account you entered.

19. Now click the **Next ➤** button.

20. You will see the **Ready to Install the Program** screen, as shown in the following screenshot:

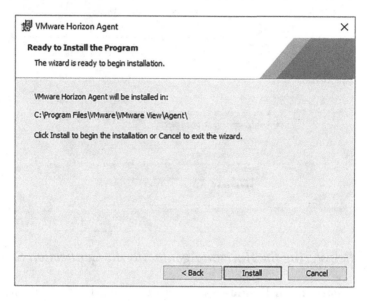

***Figure 11-40.** Ready to install the Horizon Agent*

21. Click the **Install** button to start the installation. You will see the **Installing VMware Horizon Agent** screen, as shown in the following screenshot:

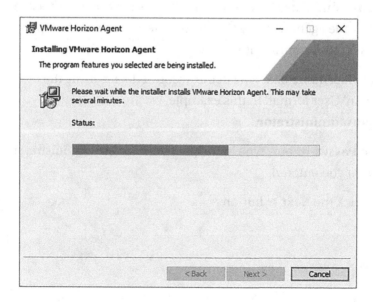

***Figure 11-41.** Horizon Agent installation status*

22.   Once the installation has completed, you will see the **Installer
       Completed** screen, as shown in the following:

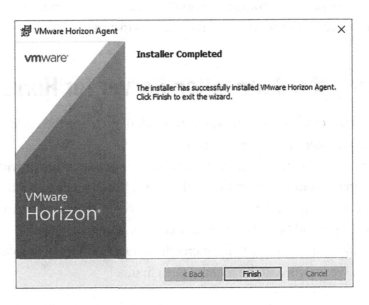

Figure 11-42. Installation completed

23.   Click the **Finish** button.

24.   You will be prompted to reboot the machine, as shown by the
       following message:

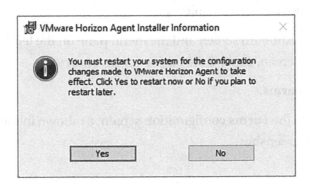

Figure 11-43. Restart the RDSH Server

25.   Click the **Yes** button to reboot the RDSH Server.

The RDSH Server will now reboot and load the Horizon Agent components to enable sessions to be brokered by the Connection Server.

In the next section, we are going to complete the first task in enabling the Connection Server to broker sessions, and the task is to create a farm.

Configuring the Connection Server for Horizon Apps

The next steps of the configuration process are carried out using the Horizon Console, and the first of those steps is to create a farm.

A server farm in this context is a group of servers or a cluster that provides the combined resources required to run the applications. When an end user logs in and launches an app, they will not know which actual server is delivering that app. That is decided based on the load balancing of resources at the time of login.

In Horizon, there are two methods for creating a farm: a manual farm and an automated farm. We will look at the manual farm first.

Creating a Manual Farm

In this section, we are going to build and configure a manual farm for delivering published apps using Horizon.

To do this, follow the steps described:

1. Log in to the Horizon Console.

2. From the dashboard screen and the menu pane on the left-hand side of the screen, expand the option for **Inventory**.

3. Now click **Farms**.

4. You will see the **Farms** configuration screen, as shown in the following screenshot:

Figure 11-44. *Farms configuration screen*

5. Click the **Add** button.

6. You will see the **Add Farm** configuration screen, as shown in the following screenshot:

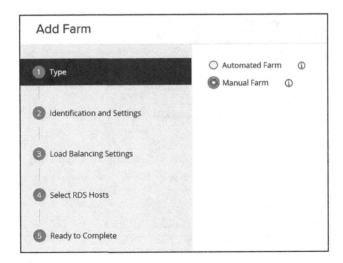

Figure 11-45. *Configuring the farm type*

7. The first section of this configuration screen is for **Type**. This is whether you want to create an automated farm or a manual farm.

    In this example, click the radio button for **Manual Farm**. We have already built and configured an RDSH Server to use this for the farm configuration.

8. Click the **Next** button to continue to the **Identification and Settings** screen, as shown in the following screenshot:

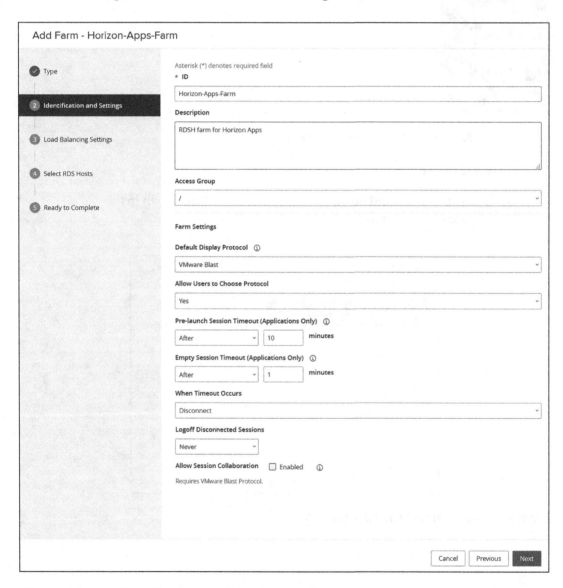

Figure 11-46. *Identification and Settings configuration screen*

9. In the **ID** box, type in the ID you want to use to identify this farm. In this example, we have given the desktop pool the ID of **Horizon-Apps-Farm**.

10. Next, in the **Description** box, you can optionally give the farm a better description as to its use case. In this example, we have used **RDSH farm for Horizon Apps** for the description.

11. In the **Access Group** drop-down menu, select the access group if you have any configured. In this example, we have selected the default access group. The access group enables you to manage desktop pools and delegate different permission levels for administration tasks.

12. Next are the **Farm Settings** and the first setting for configuring the **Default Display Protocol**.

13. In the **Default Display Protocol** box from the drop-down menu, select the protocol you want the end users to connect their virtual desktops with. In this example, we are going to use **Blast**. You can choose from PCoIP, RDP, and Blast.

14. Next is the **Allow Users to choose Protocol** box. From the drop-down menu, select either **Yes** or **No**. Selecting yes allows the end users to switch from the default protocol to another protocol.

15. In the **Pre-Launch Session Timeout** configuration, you can specify a timeout period to disconnect an app session, should a pre-launched app not be launched during the specified timeout period. From the drop-down menu, you can select either **Never** or **After**. When selecting the **After** option, you can then specify a time in minutes for when to disconnect the app session.

16. If an end user closes the apps that are running in the session, then that session gets marked as being empty. This means the apps are not being used, but the end user is still connected to the RDSH Server. The **Empty Session Timeout** setting allows you to specify a time to wait before actioning the **When Timeout Occurs** setting, which we will look at next.

17. When the Empty Session Timeout configured time has elapsed, the **When Timeout Occurs** setting will either **Disconnect** the end user or perform a **Log Off**. Select one of these options from the drop-down menu.

18. Next is the **Logoff Disconnected Sessions** setting. With this setting, you can choose what to do with sessions that get disconnected.

    These are sessions where the connection between the end user and the app session drops rather than the end user logging out. This could be down to an unstable network connection or the user being mobile.

    From the drop-down menu, you can select from the following options:

    a. **Never:** Even though disconnected, the end user's session stays active.

    b. **After:** Allows you to specify a time in minutes to wait before the end user then gets logged out.

    c. **Immediate:** The end user will be logged out at the same time as they disconnect.

19. The final setting is for **Allow Session Collaboration**. Check the box to enable this setting, which means end users can invite others to the same session.

20. Click the **Next** button to continue to the **Load Balancing Settings** screen.

21. The first option on this configuration screen is for **Use Custom Script**. This allows you to use your own script to calculate resources. We will look at this in more detail in the "Load Balancing with Custom Scripts" section of this chapter.

22. The next option is for Include Session Count. Enabling this feature, by checking the box, means that load balancing will be performed on the number of active sessions for each server. This means that the next end user to log in will be directed to the server that is running the lower number of sessions.

However, you need to be aware that even though a particular server in the farm has fewer active sessions running on it, the session count does not consider the amount of resources being consumed. It may be that the server has 95% resource usage, even though it has far fewer active sessions than other servers. This is the default load balancing method if no other metrics or custom scripts are selected.

The Load Balancing Settings are shown in the following:

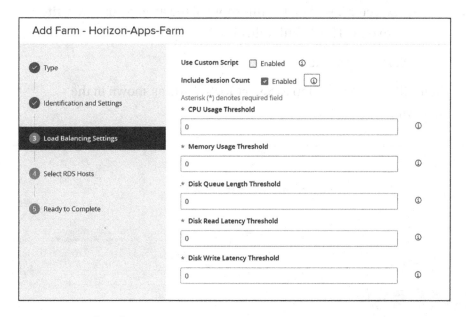

Figure 11-47. *Load Balancing Settings*

23. The next group of settings allow you to configure specific thresholds for CPU, memory, and disk:

- **CPU Usage Threshold**: Used to calculate the CPU load index factor as a percentage. 90% is the recommended setting with the default value being 0.

- **Memory Usage Threshold**: Used to calculate the memory load index factor as a percentage. 90% is the recommended setting with the default value being 0.

- **Disk Queue Length Threshold**: Used to calculate the disk load index factor. It sets the threshold of the average number of reads and writes that were queued during the sample interval with the default value being 0.

- **Disk Read Latency Threshold**: Used to calculate the disk load index factor based on the threshold of the average time to read data from disk. The default value is 0.

- **Disk Write Latency Threshold**: Used to calculate the disk load index factor based on the threshold of the average time to write data to disk. The default value is 0.

24. Click **Next** to continue.

25. You will see the next step to **Select RDS Hosts** as shown in the following screenshot:

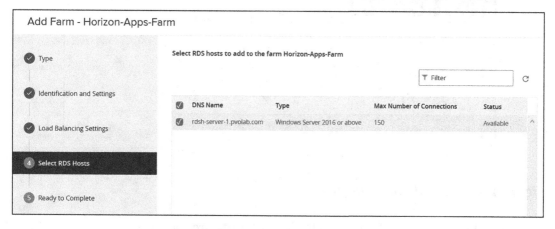

Figure 11-48. *Selecting the RDS hosts for the farm*

26. Check the box to select the RDS host servers that you want to add to this farm. In this example, we have a single server with the hostname of **rdsh-sever-1.pvolab.com** server.

    You will also see that the type of server is listed along with the maximum number of connections that this server can provide.

27. Click **Next** to continue.

28. You will now see the final screen, the **Ready to Complete** screen, as shown in the following screenshot:

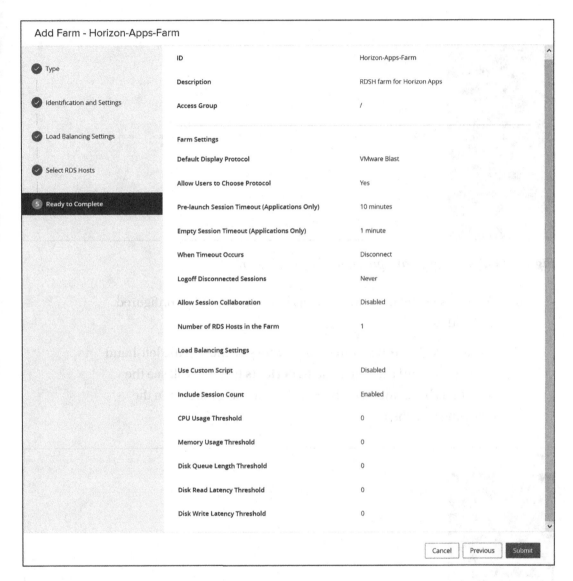

Figure 11-49. *Ready to Complete screen*

29. Review the configuration options, and once you are happy with them, click the **Submit** button.

30. You will now return to the main **Farms** configuration screen as shown in the following screenshot:

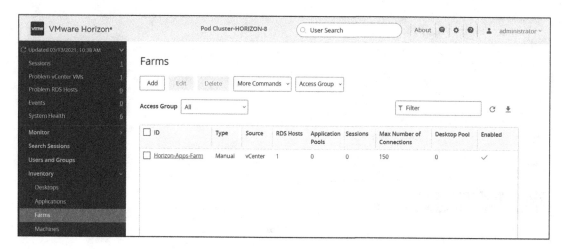

Figure 11-50. *Newly configured and added farm*

31. You will see that the new farm has been successfully configured and added.

32. If you click **Machines** from the **Inventory** section in the left-hand menu pane, and then click the **RDS Hosts** tab, you will see the server has been added to the RDS Server list, as shown in the following screenshot:

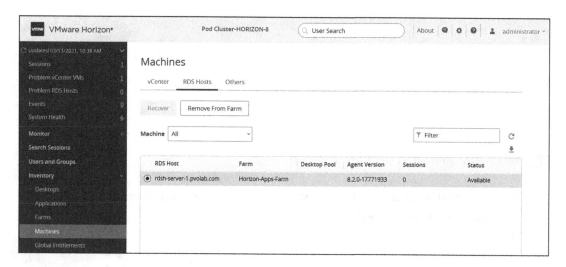

Figure 11-51. *RDS Host added*

You have now successfully created and configured a farm, ready to deliver the app sessions to end users.

The next step, which will be discussed in the following section, is to create an application pool to select which apps to publish to the end users.

Creating an Application Pool

In this section, we are going to create an application pool. In Horizon terms, an application pool is a group of apps that are running on an RDSH Server. In this example, we are going to create an application pool using the apps and resources of the RDSH Server we used to create the farm in the previous section of this chapter.

Application pools can be created manually or automatically by selecting the apps you want to add to the pool from the list of apps available on the servers in the farm. We will start with the automatic method.

Creating an Application Pool from Installed Applications

In this section, we are going to create an application pool using the list of installed apps from the RDSH Servers in the farm. To do this, follow the steps described:

1. From the left-hand menu pane, expand the option for **Inventory**, then click **Applications** as shown:

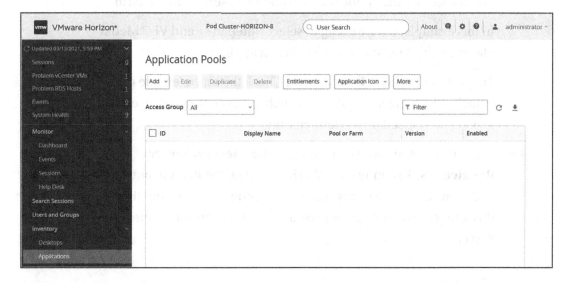

Figure 11-52. *Application Pools configuration screen*

2. From the **Application Pools** screen, click the **Add** drop-down
    button, as shown in the following screenshot:

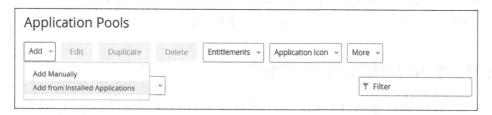

Figure 11-53. *Adding an application pool from installed applications*

3. Select the **Add from Installed Applications** option.

4. You will now see the **Add Application Pool** screen.

5. The first configuration task is to **Select Applications**, and the first
    setting is to select the **Application Pool Type**.

6. Click the radio button for **RDS Farm**.

7. Then from the drop-down menu, select the farm you want to use
    to select the applications from. In this example, we are going to
    use the **Horizon-Apps-Farm** that we configured previously.

8. Once you have selected the farm, then the applications list will be
    populated with the applications installed on servers in the farm.

    In this example, we are going to select Notepad++ and VLC Media
    Player by checking the box next to each application.

9. The next option is for **Pre-Launch**. Check the box to enable pre-
    launch, which means apps will launch in advance of end users
    logging in to speed up the launch time.

10. In the next section, you can configure **Connection Server
    Restrictions**. To configure a restriction, click the **Browse** button
    and then select which tags you want to configure to ensure that
    this application pool can only be accessed via certain Connection
    Servers.

11. Next, you have the option to configure a **Category Folder**. This allows you to add a folder or a shortcut that points directly to this desktop pool.

12. Click the **Browse** button next, under the **Category Folder** option. You will see the Category Folder configuration screen as shown:

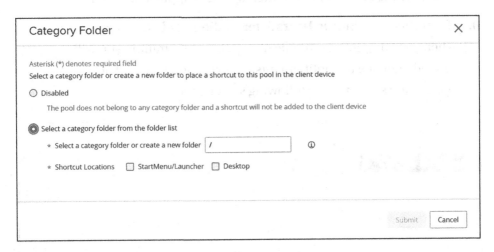

Figure 11-54. *Configuring the category folder*

13. To enable this feature, click the radio button for **Select a category folder from the folder list**.

14. Then in the **Select a category folder or create a new folder** box, type in the folder name. The folder name supports up to 64 characters and up to four sub-folders by using the \ to separate them.

15. You then also have check boxes for **Shortcut Locations**, enabling you to place the shortcut to the desktop pool in the **StartMenu/ Launcher** or **Desktop** of the client's device.

16. Once configured, click the **Submit** button.

17. You will return to the Select Applications configuration screen.

18. Next is the check box for **Client Restrictions**.

19. If you check the box to enable this setting, then you can prevent end users from connecting to the applications in this pool if they are using specific client devices. You will also need to add the computer names that you want to allow into an Active Directory security group. This group will then need to be selected when you configure the end-user entitlements for this application pool.

20. If you check the **Entitle Users After Adding Pool** box, then when you complete the application pool configuration, you will immediately see the entitlements configuration screen. These options are shown in the following screenshot:

Figure 11-55. *Selecting the applications for the pool*

21. The final setting is for **Multi-Session Mode**. If you click the drop-down menu, you will see that you have a number of configuration options, as shown in the following screenshot:

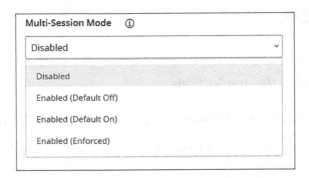

Figure 11-56. *Multi-session configuration options*

Apps that are launched in multi-session mode do not support app reconnect, should a user try and connect from a different client device. Also, the pre-launch feature is not supported when using multi-session apps.

You have the following configuration options:

- **Disabled**: Multi-session support is disabled.

- **Enabled (Default Off)**: Multi-session support is enabled, and the app is launched in single-session mode.

- **Enabled (Default On)**: Multi-session support is enabled, and the app is launched in multi-session mode.

- **Enabled (Enforced)**: Multi-session support is enabled, and the app can only be launched in multi-session mode.

22. Now click **Next** to continue.

23. The next configuration task is to **Edit Applications**.

24. On this configuration screen, you will see the **ID** and the **Display Name** for each of the applications that you selected, as shown in the following screenshot:

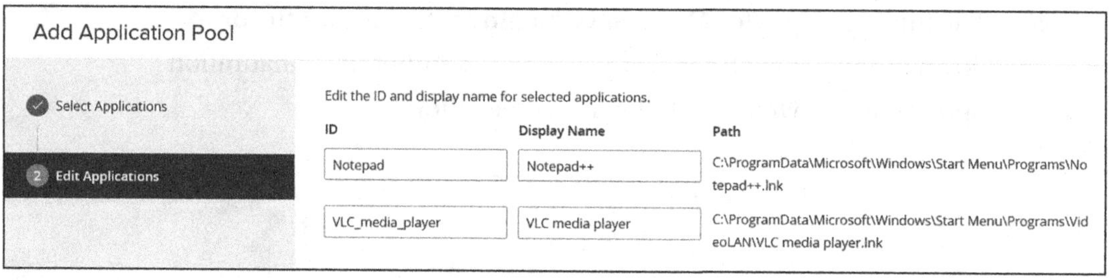

ID	Display Name	Path
Notepad	Notepad++	C:\ProgramData\Microsoft\Windows\Start Menu\Programs\Notepad++.lnk
VLC_media_player	VLC media player	C:\ProgramData\Microsoft\Windows\Start Menu\Programs\VideoLAN\VLC media player.lnk

Figure 11-57. Editing the applications

25.   Edit the ID and Display Names if required, then click **Submit**.

26.   You have now successfully created and configured an application pool.

As we checked the box for Entitle Users After Adding Pool, then you will be taken straight to the **Add Entitlements** screen. We will configure the entitlements in the next section.

End-User Entitlements

In this section, we are going to entitle an end user to the newly created application pool.

We will pick up where we left off in the previous section with the **Add Entitlements** screen, as shown in the following screenshot:

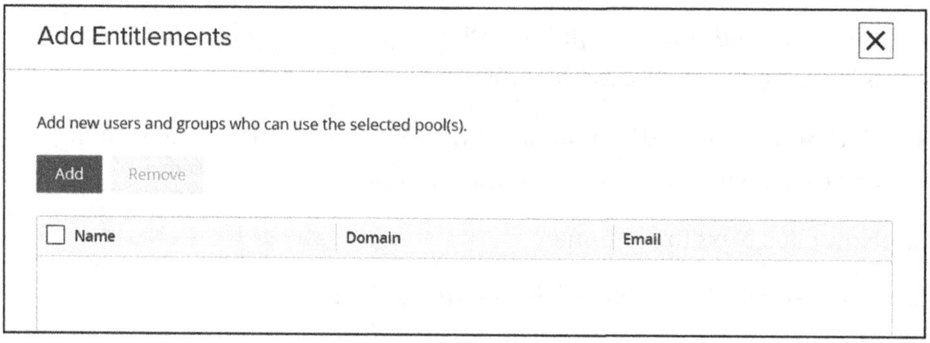

Figure 11-58. Adding an end-user entitlement

To add an end-user entitlement, follow the steps described:

1.   On the **Add Entitlements** screen, click the Add button.

2.   You will see the **Find User or Group** screen.

3. In the **Type** section, check the box or boxes to select what you are going to search for. You can choose **User**, **Group**, or **Unauthenticated Users**.

4. In the **Domain** box from the drop-down menu, select the domain in which you want to search. In this example, we are using the pvolab.com domain.

5. Next, you have a couple of filters to help refine the search.

6. In the **Name/Username** box, you can type in the name or part of the name you want to search for. First, select the filter for the search. You have the option of **Contains**, **Starts with**, or **Is exactly**. In this example, we have selected Contains.

7. Then, in the box next to the filter option, enter what name or part of the name you are searching for. In this example, we are searching for a name or username that contains **bob**.

8. You can also search based on **Description**, using the same filter process to find the description and entering the description text you want to search for.

9. Now click the **Find** button.

10. The following screenshot shows the options and results:

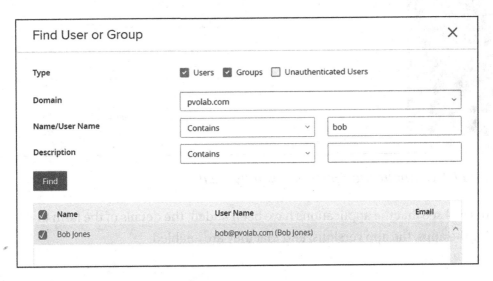

Figure 11-59. *Finding a user or group to entitle*

11. From the results box, check the box for the user you want to select. In this example, the user is Bob Jones.

12. Click the **Next** button to continue.

13. You will see the following screenshot:

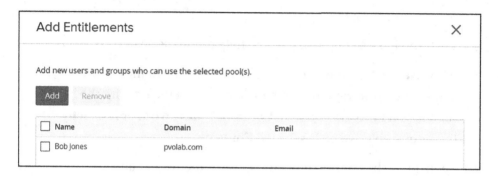

Figure 11-60. *Adding the end user*

14. Click **OK** to add the user to the application pool.

15. You will now return to the **Application Pools** screen, as shown in the following screenshot:

Figure 11-61. *Application pool successfully created*

You will see that the applications have been added, the details of the farm that is hosting the apps, the app versions, and that they are enabled.

With the farm created and configured, the application pool configured, and an end user entitled to use the applications, the next step is to log in and check that the apps are available to launch.

To do this, follow the steps described:

1. Launch the Horizon Client and add the Connection Server if you have not already done so. We will cover this in more detail in Chapter 13. The screenshot shows the Connection Server **Horizon-8.pvolab.com** added.

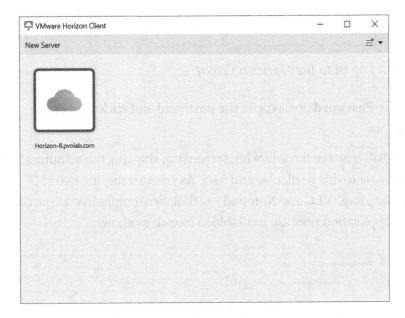

Figure 11-62. *Launching the Horizon Client*

2. Double-click the icon for Horizon-8.pvolab.com.

3. You will now see the **Login** box.

4. The **Server** information will have already been added, so in the **User Name** box, type in the name of the user that has been entitled to use this application pool.

In this example, this is the user called Bob Jones, as shown in the following screenshot:

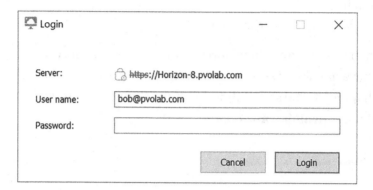

Figure 11-63. *Log in to the Horizon Client*

5.   In the **Password** box, type in the password and click the **Login** button.

6.   You will now see the following screenshot showing the resources available to this particular end user. As you can see, the two applications, **VLC** and **Notepad++**, that were configured as part of the application pool are available to launch as shown:

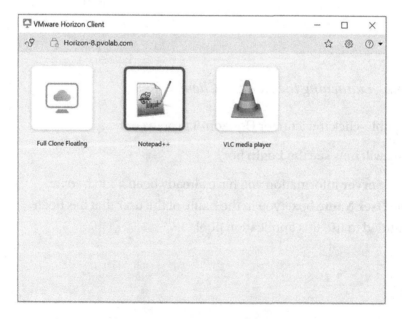

Figure 11-64. *Horizon Client showing entitled resources*

7. Double-click one of the apps to check that it launches. In this example, we have launched a VLC Media Player session, as shown in the following screenshot:

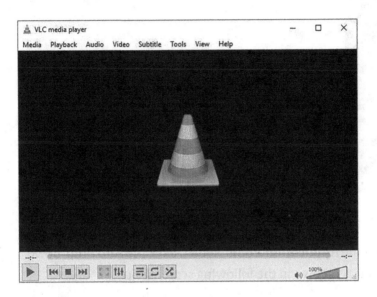

Figure 11-65. Application successfully launched and running

You have now successfully tested that the application pool works and that the end user can launch an app session – in this example, VLC Media Player.

In the next section, we are going to look at how to create the application pool manually.

Creating an Application Pool Manually

In the previous section, we worked through the process of creating an application pool by using the list of applications that were installed on the RDSH Server.

You also have the option to create the application manually, whereby you will need to manually enter all the details of the apps that you want to add to the application pool.

To do this, follow the steps described:

1. From the left-hand menu pane, expand the option for **Inventory** and then click **Applications** as shown:

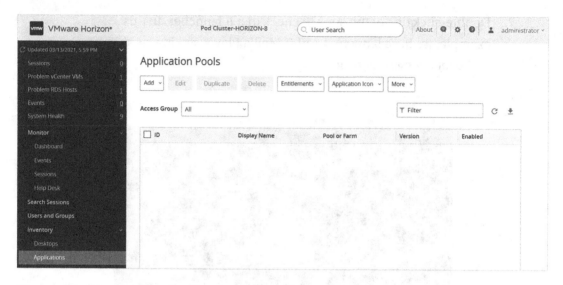

Figure 11-66. *Application Pools configuration screen*

2. From the **Application Pools** screen, click the **Add** drop-down
    button, as shown in the following screenshot:

Figure 11-67. *Adding a manual application pool*

3. Select the **Add Manually** option.

4. You will now see the **Add Application Pool** screen.

5. The first thing you need to enter is the ID information. This is so
    Horizon can identify this application. In this example, as we are
    configuring VLC, we have entered the ID of **VLC_media_player**.

6. In the **Display Name** field, type in the display name that you want
    end users to see from their Horizon Client. In this example, we
    have used the Display Name **VLC media player**.

7. Next, you can configure the **Access Group**, so you can specify a particular group of administrators to be able to manage this pool.

8. In the **Version** field, you can type in a version number for this application; then in the **Publisher** field, you can type in the name of the software vendor who delivers this application.

9. Next is the **Path** field. In this box, you need to type in the path of the application so it can be launched. In this example, we have shown the link to the Start menu; however, if the app is not on the Start menu, then you will need to enter the path to it. In the **Start Folder**, you can enter the details of the folder in which you want to start the application.

10. If you want to add any parameters to the application, then you can add them in the **Parameters** box. For example, if you wanted to launch VLC using a particular setting, then you would add that setting here.

11. The **Anti-Affinity Patterns** setting allows you to ensure that this application only runs on an RDSH Server that has enough resources to run it, and not to run it on resource-constrained servers.

    To configure this option, you can type in a list of patterns that will be used to match against other applications running on the servers. If there is a match with one of the listed patterns, then this adds to the **Anti-Affinity Count** (configured in the next field). When this count number is exceeded, then that RDSH Server is missed out when an end user launches a new session of that application.

    You can use wildcards in the pattern text with an * representing zero or more characters and a ? representing any one character.

12. Once you have configured the patterns, then the next field is to configure the **Anti-Affinity Count** setting. This is the number of pattern matches before this RDSH Server gets missed out the next time the end user launches a new application session.

13. In the **Description** field, you can type in a description for this application pool.

14. The next option is for **Pre-Launch**. Check the box to enable pre-launch, which means apps will launch in advance of end users logging in, so as to speed up the launch time.

15. In the next section, you can configure **Connection Server Restrictions**. To configure a restriction, click the **Browse** button, then select which tags you want to configure to ensure that this application pool can only be accessed via certain Connection Servers.

16. Next, you have the option to configure a **Category Folder**. This allows you to add a folder or a shortcut that points directly to this desktop pool.

17. Click the **Browse** button next, under the **Category Folder** option, to configure this option.

18. Next is the check box for **Client Restrictions**.

19. If you check the box to enable this setting, then you can prevent end users from connecting to the applications in this pool if they are using specific client devices. You will also need to add the computer names that you want to allow into an Active Directory security group. This group will then need to be selected when you configure the end-user entitlements for this application pool.

20. The final setting is for **Multi-Session Mode**. If you click the drop-down menu, you will see that you have several configuration options:

    • **Disabled**: Multi-session support is disabled.

    • **Enabled (Default Off)**: Multi-session support is enabled, and the app is launched in single-session mode.

    • **Enabled (Default On)**: Multi-session support is enabled, and the app is launched in multi-session mode.

    • **Enabled (Enforced)**: Multi-session support is enabled, and the app can only be launched in multi-session mode.

21. The **Add Application Pool** screen for the manual pool is shown in the following screenshot:

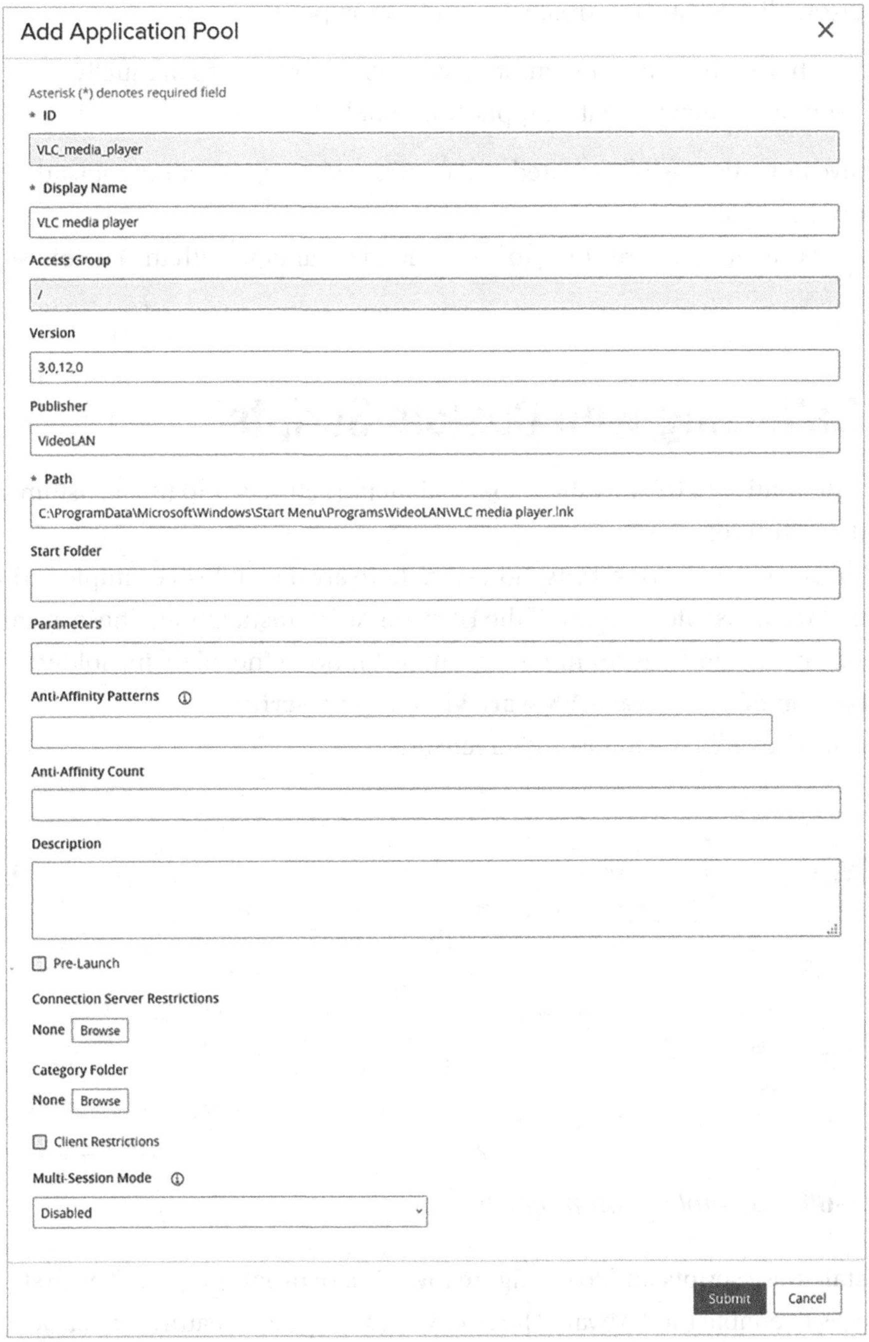

Add Application Pool   ✕

Asterisk (*) denotes required field

* ID

VLC_media_player

* Display Name

VLC media player

Access Group

/

Version

3,0,12,0

Publisher

VideoLAN

* Path

C:\ProgramData\Microsoft\Windows\Start Menu\Programs\VideoLAN\VLC media player.lnk

Start Folder

Parameters

Anti-Affinity Patterns   ⓘ

Anti-Affinity Count

Description

☐ Pre-Launch

Connection Server Restrictions

None   Browse

Category Folder

None   Browse

☐ Client Restrictions

Multi-Session Mode   ⓘ

Disabled

Submit   Cancel

Figure 11-68. *Adding a manual application configuration screen*

22.   Now click **Submit** to create the application pool.

23.   As this is a manual configuration, you will now need to manually entitle this newly created application pool.

You have now successfully created and configured an application pool, adding the applications manually.

In the next section, we are going to look at load balancing with the custom script option.

Load Balancing with Custom Scripts

The other alternative to the threshold load balancing settings is to use a custom script to monitor the utilization.

You can create your own scripts; however, there are a couple of example scripts you will find that were installed as part of the Horizon Agent installation. These example scripts, one for CPU and one for memory, can be found in the following folder:

C:\Program Files\VMware\VMware View\Agent\scripts

These are shown in the following screenshot:

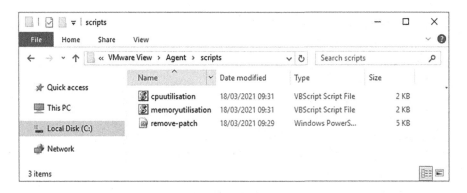

Figure 11-69. *Example custom scripts*

To install these scripts and to configure them is a two-part process. The first part of the service is to enable the VMware Horizon View Script Host feature, which you will find as one of the VMware Horizon services that are installed and disabled as part of the Horizon Agent installation.

In the next section, we are going to enable that service on the RDSH host server that is part of the Horizon-Apps-Farm.

Enable Script Host Service

In order to run the scripts that are going to be used as part of the utilization monitoring for load balancing custom scripts, the first task is to enable the VMware Horizon View Script Host service.

To do this, follow the steps described:

1. Open a console or log on to the RDSH Server and launch a Run dialog box by pressing the Windows Key and R. You will see the following screenshot:

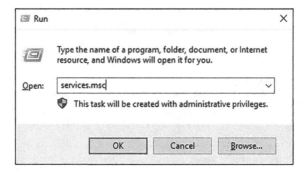

Figure 11-70. *Launching the Services manager*

2. In the **Open** box, type **services.msc** and click the OK button.

3. The Services screen will launch, as shown in the following screenshot:

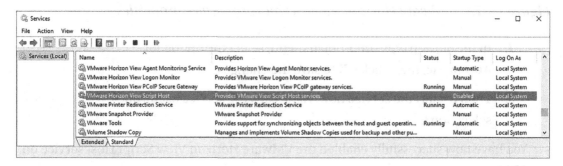

Figure 11-71. *Services manager*

4. Navigate to the **VMware Horizon View Script Host** service, then click to select it, as highlighted in the preceding screenshot.

5. Now right-click and select **Properties**.

6. You will now see the **VMware Horizon View Script Host Properties (Local Computer)** configuration screen, as shown in the following screenshot:

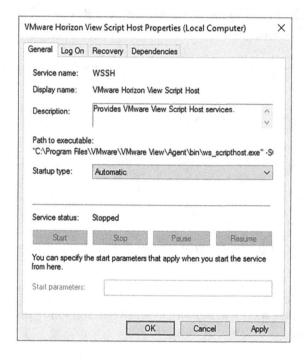

Figure 11-72. *VMware Horizon View Script Host service properties*

7. In the Startup type drop-down menu, select the option for **Automatic**, then click **OK** to save the changes.

8. Then to start the service now, right-click the service again, and select **Start**.

You have now successfully enabled the VMware Horizon View Script Host service on the RDSH Server.

In the next section, we are going to add one of the example scripts to the configuration to be used as a custom script.

Configure the Script to Run

In this section, we are going to configure one of the example scripts to run on the RDS host server. For this example, we are going to use the CPU utilization script.

To do this, follow the steps described:

1. If you do not have the console open from the previous section, then open a console or log on to the RDSH.

2. From the desktop of the RDSH Server, launch the Registry Editor. To do this, first press the Windows Key and R. You will see the following screenshot:

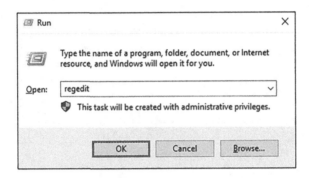

Figure 11-73. *Launching the Registry Editor*

3. In the **Open** box, type **regedit** and click the **OK** button.

4. The Registry Editor will launch.

5. In the Registry Editor, navigate to the following location:

HKEY_LOCAL_MACHINE\SOFTWARE\VMware, Inc.\VMware VDM\ScriptEvents

6. Then click the **RdshLoad** key. You will see in the right-hand pane that there is already a key string, as shown in the following screenshot:

Figure 11-74. *Registry Editor*

7. Next, we are going to enter a new string value for adding the
    custom script. To enable this, in the right-hand pane, right-click
    somewhere on the blank area of the screen. But do not right-click
    the existing string, as this will edit this string.

8. From the contextual menu that pops up, move the mouse to highlight **New ➤**, then from the expanded menu options, select the option for **String Value**, as shown in the following screenshot:

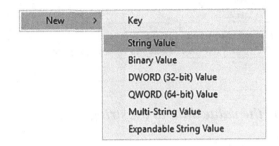

Figure 11-75. *Adding a new string value*

9. The new string will be created, and you will be prompted to enter a name. In this example, we have called this new string **CPU_ Utilization** to reflect the fact that this script will be used to measure the CPU utilization, as shown in the following screenshot:

Name	Type	Data
ab] (Default)	REG_SZ	(value not set)
ab] CPU_Utilization	REG_SZ	

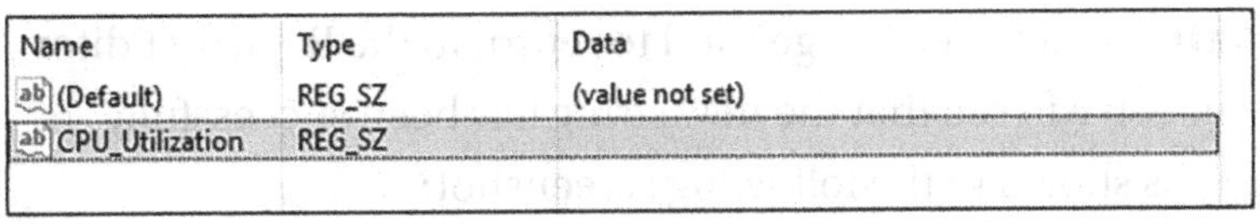

Figure 11-76. *Naming the new string value*

10. Now right-click the new **CPU_Utilization** string; from the contextual menu, select the option for **Modify...** as shown in the following screenshot:

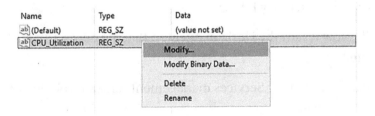

Figure 11-77. *Modifying the new string*

You will see the Edit String box as shown in the following screenshot:

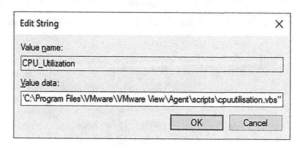

Figure 11-78. Adding the value data to the string

11. In the **Value data** box, enter the command to invoke the script and the path to the script. In this example, the VBS script is located in the Horizon Agent folder, so to run the script, we would enter the following:

```
cscript.exe "C:\Program Files\VMware\VMware View\Agent\scripts\
cpuutilisation.vbs"
```

12. Click **OK** to save the changes and to return to the Registry Editor screen. You will see that the new string has been successfully added, as shown in the following screenshot:

Name	Type	Data
(Default)	REG_SZ	(value not set)
CPU_Utilization	REG_SZ	"C:\Program Files\VMware\VMware View\Agent\s...

Figure 11-79. String successfully configured

13. Now close the Registry Editor.

14. Finally, now restart the Horizon Agent so that the new script is executed.

15. To do this, launch the Services management screen if you do not still have it open.

16. Scroll down until you find the entry for **VMware Horizon View Agent** and click to select it.

17. Now right-click the **VMware Horizon View Agent** service, and
     from the contextual menu, click **Restart**, as shown in the following
     screenshot:

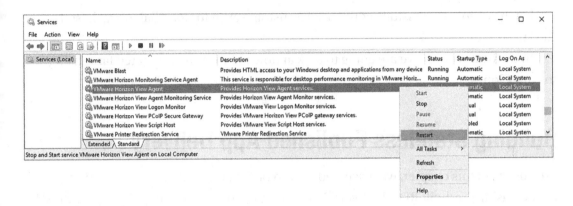

Figure 11-80. *Restarting the Horizon Agent*

The final step is to edit the farm settings and to update the load balancing settings to
reflect the new custom script option.

To do this, follow the steps described:

1. Log in to the Horizon Console as an administrator.

2. From the left-hand navigation pane, expand the option for
    Inventory, and then click **Farms**.

3. Click the link to the **Horizon-Apps-Farm**, and then on the
    Summary screen, click the **Edit** button.

4. Finally, click the **Load Balancing Settings** tab as shown:

Edit Farm - Horizon-Apps-Farm	✕
Farm Settings	Load Balancing Settings
Use Custom Script ☑ Enabled ⓘ	
Include Session Count ☐ Enabled ⓘ	

Figure 11-81. *Editing the farm settings*

5. To enable the custom script feature, check the **Use Custom Script** box.

6. Click **OK** to save the changes and close the Horizon Console.

You have now successfully configured a custom script for load balancing based on CPU utilization.

In the next section, we are going to look at how to build an automated farm using Instant Clones.

Building Stateless Published App Delivery

Previously, in this chapter, we discussed how to build a manual farm – a farm that is created using pre-built RDSH Servers. However, a feature of Horizon is to deliver RDSH Servers in the same way as you would with non-persistent virtual desktop machines. That is to build the host servers using cloning technology, in this case, Instant Clones.

As with any other Instant Clone, you would build the server OS image and configure the RDSH role on the server. This would become your gold image from which to deploy servers.

Obviously, with an RDSH Server that is delivering application sessions, you need to install the applications onto the server. However, as we also discussed previously, there is another option to make this solution truly stateless, and that is to deliver the applications using App Volumes.

Instead of installing the applications directly onto the RDSH Server, you would install the App Volumes Agent and attach the required application packages (virtual disk files) using a machine-based entitlement. You would also need to capture the applications using a Windows OS running the RDSH role, so that you capture the applications in multi-user mode.

Then, as you create and build additional RDSH host servers using Instant Clones, as they boot, the applications are automatically attached and are available immediately. It also means that farms can be quickly and easily scaled as you do not need to install the apps onto the server.

To set up automated RDSH Servers in Horizon, follow the steps described:

1. Log in to the Horizon Console using an administrator account.

2. From the left-hand menu pane, expand the option for **Inventory** and then click **Farms**, as shown in the following screenshot:

Figure 11-82. *Farms configuration screen*

3. Click the **Add** button.

4. You will see the **Add Farm** configuration screen and the first section for **Type**, as shown in the following screenshot:

Figure 11-83. *Adding an automated farm*

5. Click the radio button for **Automated Farm**.

6. Now click the **Next** button to continue to the next configuration section for **vCenter Server**, as shown in the following screenshot:

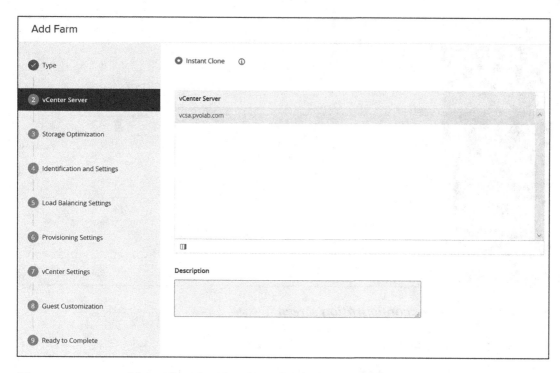

Figure 11-84. *Adding the vCenter to the configuration*

7. Select the vCenter Server from the list of those shown. This is the vCenter which is managing the build of the Instant Clone RDSH Servers in the farm.

8. Click the **Next** button to continue to the next configuration section for **Storage Optimization**, as shown in the following:

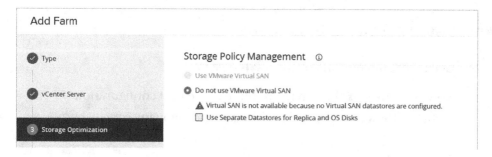

Figure 11-85. *Storage Optimization configuration screen*

9. Click the radio button to select whether you are using VSAN. In this example, there is no VSAN, so the **Do not use VMware Virtual SAN** option has been selected. You also have the option by checking the box to select different datastores for replica and OS disks.

10. Click the **Next** button to continue to the **Identification and Settings** configuration as shown:

Figure 11-86. *Identification and Settings screen*

11.   In the **ID** box, type in the ID you want to use to identify this desktop pool. In this example, we have given the desktop pool the ID of **Automated-Farm**.

12.   In the **Description** box, type in a description that represents what this farm is used for.

13.   In the **Access Group** drop-down menu, select the access group if you have any configured. Access groups enable you to manage farms and delegate different permission levels for administration tasks.

14.   In the **Default Display Protocol** box, from the drop-down menu, select the protocol you want the end users to connect to their virtual desktops with. In this example, we are going to use **Blast**. You can choose from PCoIP, RDP, and Blast.

15.   Next is the **Allow Users to choose Protocol** box. From the drop-down menu, select either **Yes** or **No**. Selecting yes allows the end users to switch from the default protocol to another protocol.

16.   You can then choose in the **3D Renderer** box how you want to handle 3D rendering. This setting is managed by the ESXi host servers and is configured by editing the configuration of the RDSH Server using the vSphere Client. This is not configured from within Horizon. You can only use the 3D option with RDSH Servers and the Windows Server OS if you have vGPU enabled.

17.   In the **Pre-Launch Session Timeout** configuration, you can specify a timeout period to disconnect an app session, should a pre-launched app not be launched during the specified timeout period. From the drop-down menu, you can select either **Never** or **After**. When selecting the **After** option, you can then specify a time in minutes for when to disconnect the app session.

18.   If an end user closes the apps that are running in the session, then that session gets marked as being empty. This means the apps are not being used, but the end user is still connected to the RDSH Server. The **Empty Session Timeout** setting allows you to specify a time to wait before actioning the **When Timeout Occurs** setting, which we will look at next.

19. When the **Empty Session Timeout** configured time has elapsed, the **When Timeout Occurs** setting will either **Disconnect** the end user or perform a **Log Off**. Select one of these options from the drop-down menu.

20. Next is the **Logoff Disconnected Sessions** setting. With this setting, you can choose what to do with sessions that get disconnected.

   These are sessions where the connection between the end user and the app session drops rather than the end user logging out. This could be down to an unstable network connection or the user being mobile.

   From the drop-down menu, you can select from the following options:

   - **Never**: Even though disconnected, the end user's session stays active.

   - **After**: Allows you to specify a time in minutes to wait before the end user then gets logged out.

   - **Immediate**: The end user will be logged out at the same time as they disconnect.

21. The penultimate setting is for **Allow Session Collaboration**. Check the box to enable this setting, which means end users can invite others to the same session.

22. Finally, you can configure the **Max Sessions per RDS Host** setting to define the maximum number of sessions this host server will deliver. The default setting is 150 sessions.

23. Once configured, click the **Next** button to continue.

24. You will now see the **Load Balancing Settings** configuration screen.

25. The first option on this configuration screen is for **Use Custom Script**. This allows you to use your own script to calculate resources.

26.   The next option is for Include Session Count. Enabling this feature, by checking the box, means that load balancing will be performed on the number of active sessions for each server. This means that the next end user to log in will be directed to the server that is running the lower number of sessions.

27.   The Load Balancing Settings are shown in the following:

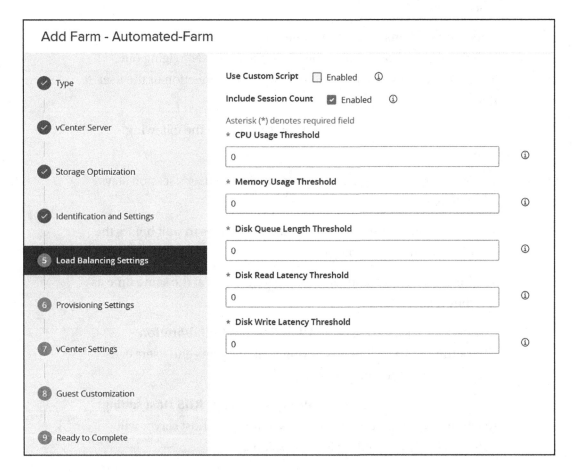

Figure 11-87. *Load Balancing Settings configuration screen*

28.   The next group of settings allow you to configure specific thresholds for CPU, memory, and disk:

- CPU Usage Threshold

- Memory Usage Threshold

- Disk Queue Length Threshold

- Disk Read Latency Threshold

- Disk Write Latency Threshold

29. Click **Next** to continue.

30. You will now see the next step for **Provisioning Settings**, as shown in the following screenshot:

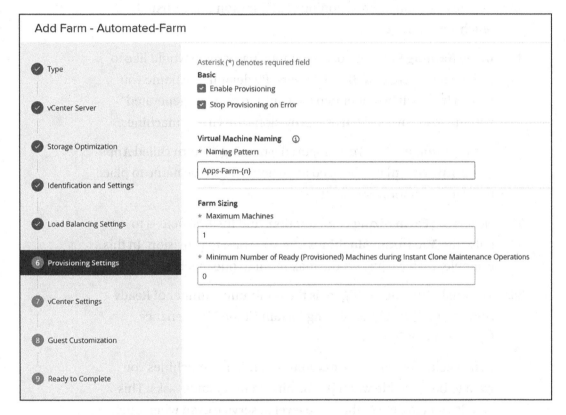

Figure 11-88. *Provisioning Settings*

31. Check the **Enable Provisioning** box to allow the RDSH Servers to be provisioned. This means that the virtual RDSH Server machines will be built and provisioned once you have finished the farm configuration.

32. The other check box is for **Stop Provisioning on Error**. If this
    setting is enabled and Horizon detects an error while the virtual
    RDSH Servers are being provisioned, then provisioning will stop.

    This is an important feature when provisioning large numbers
    of virtual server machines. You would want provisioning to stop
    rather than continue to provision hundreds of potentially faulty
    servers. In this example, we have checked this box.

33. The next section of provisioning configuration is for **Virtual
    Machine Naming**.

34. In the **Naming Pattern** box, type in the names you would like to
    call the newly created RDSH Servers. By default, the name you
    type in here will be appended by a unique number generated
    automatically by Horizon as it provisions the virtual machines.

    In the example, we have configured a naming pattern called **Apps-
    Farm-{n}**. The {n} can be used anywhere within the name to place
    the number wherever you choose.

35. Next is the **Farm Sizing** configuration, and the first field is to
    enter the **Maximum Machines** that you want to provision. In this
    example, we have just set the maximum to one machine.

36. The final setting to configure is the Minimum Number of Ready
    (Provisioned) Machines during Instant Clone Maintenance
    Operations setting.

    In this field, you enter the minimum number of machines you
    want to be available when performing maintenance tasks. This
    enables you to deliver the same level of service even when other
    machines are effectively offline.

37. Click the **Next** button to continue.

38. You will now see step 7 for **vCenter Settings**. This configuration
    screen is broken into three steps to configure the **Default Image**,
    the **Virtual Machine Location**, and then the **Resource Settings**,
    as shown in the following screenshot:

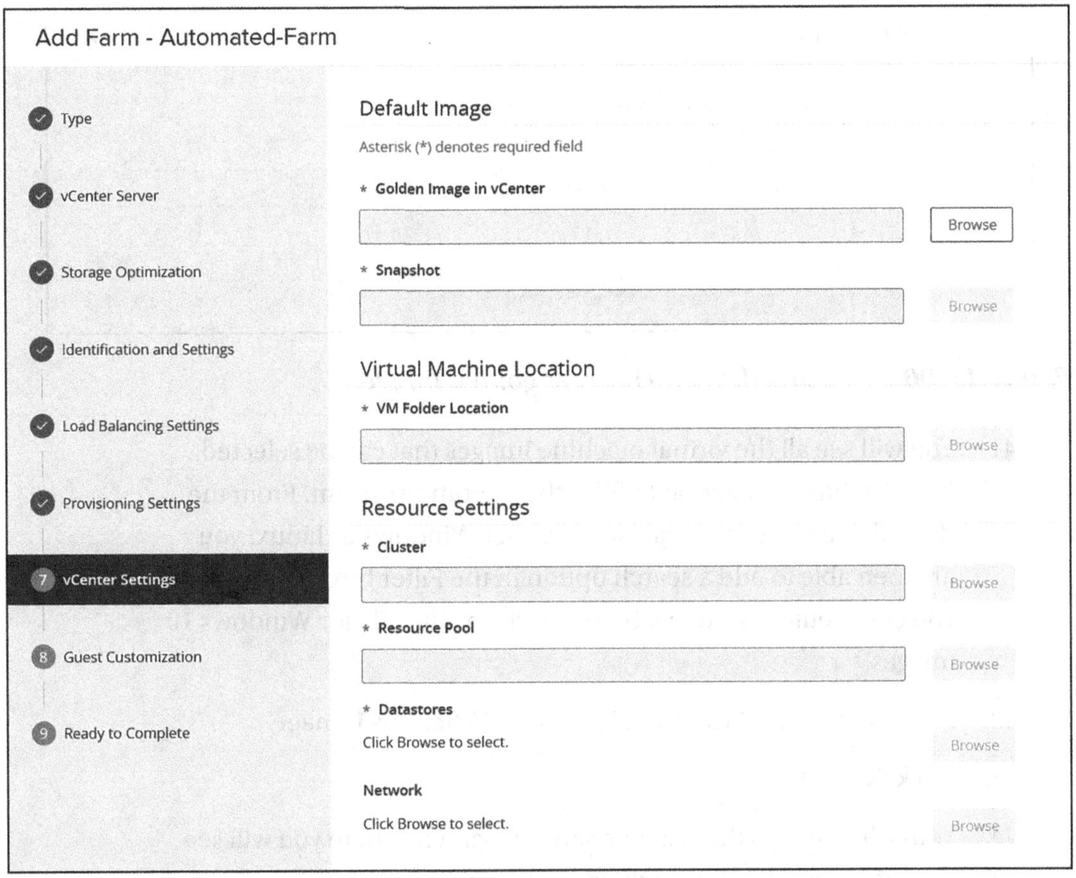

Figure 11-89.   *vCenter Settings*

39. Under the **Default Image** heading and the **Golden Image in vCenter** section, click the **Browse** button.

40. You will see the **Select Golden Image** screen, as shown in the following screenshot:

Select Golden Image   ✕

Select the virtual machines to be used as the golden image for this Automated Farm.

☐ Show All Golden Images   ⓘ   **Operating System** | All   ⌄ | | ▼ Filter | ⟳

Name	Path
RDSH Server 1	/PVO Datacenter/vm/RDSH Server 1

Figure 11-90. *Selecting the RDSH Server golden image*

41. You will see all the virtual machine images that can be selected.
     You also have the option to filter the operating system. From the
     drop-down menu, you can select either Windows or Linux; you
     are then able to add a search option in the Filter box. For example,
     you could enter Windows 10 to search specifically for Windows 10
     images.

42. In this example, click to select the **RDSH-Server-1** image.

43. Click **Submit**.

44. You will return to the vCenter Settings screen, where you will see
     the gold image has been added as shown:

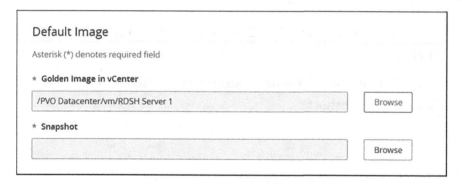

Default Image

Asterisk (*) denotes required field

★ Golden Image in vCenter

| /PVO Datacenter/vm/RDSH Server 1 | Browse

★ Snapshot

| | Browse

Figure 11-91. *Configuring the golden image snapshot*

45. The next box is to configure the **Snapshot**, as shown in the
     preceding screenshot.

46. In the **Snapshot** field, click the **Browse** button.

47. You will now see the **Select Default Image** screen, as shown in the following screenshot:

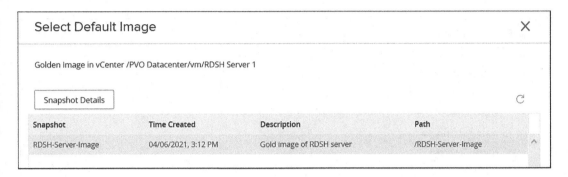

Figure 11-92. *Selecting the snapshot to use*

48. Click to highlight the snapshot you want to use. In this example, there is just one snapshot, **RDSH-Server-Image**, to select from.

49. Now click **Submit**.

50. You will see that the snapshot details have been added, as shown in the following:

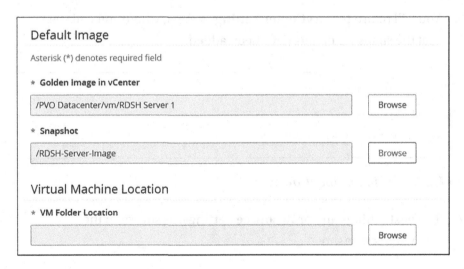

Figure 11-93. *Configuring the VM folder location*

51. The next section heading is for the **Virtual Machine Location**. This is the folder in vSphere where the virtual desktop machines are going to be stored.

52. In the **VM Folder Location** box, click the **Browse** button.

53. You will see the folders listed as shown:

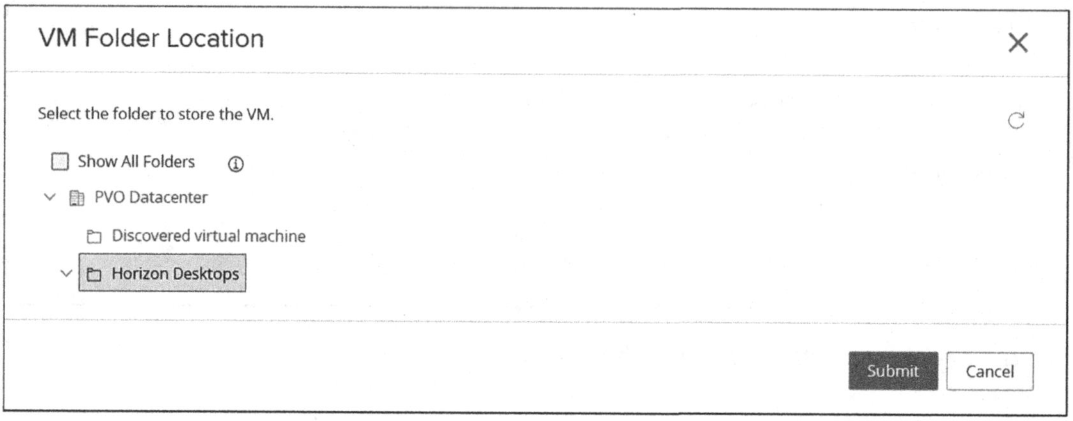

VM Folder Location   ✕

Select the folder to store the VM.   ↻

☐ Show All Folders   ⓘ

∨ ▤ PVO Datacenter

    ▭ Discovered virtual machine

∨ ▭ Horizon Desktops

                                                      Submit   Cancel

Figure 11-94. Selecting the VM folder location

54. In this example, we are going to select the **Horizon Desktops** folder, so click this option to select it.

55. Now Click the **Submit** button.

56. You will return to the **vCenter Settings** screen, where you will see that the snapshot details have been added.

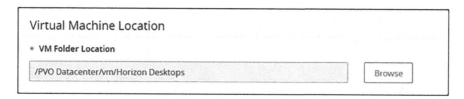

Virtual Machine Location

∗ VM Folder Location

/PVO Datacenter/vm/Horizon Desktops   Browse

Figure 11-95. VM folder location added

57. The next settings are for **Resource Settings**, as shown in the following screenshot:

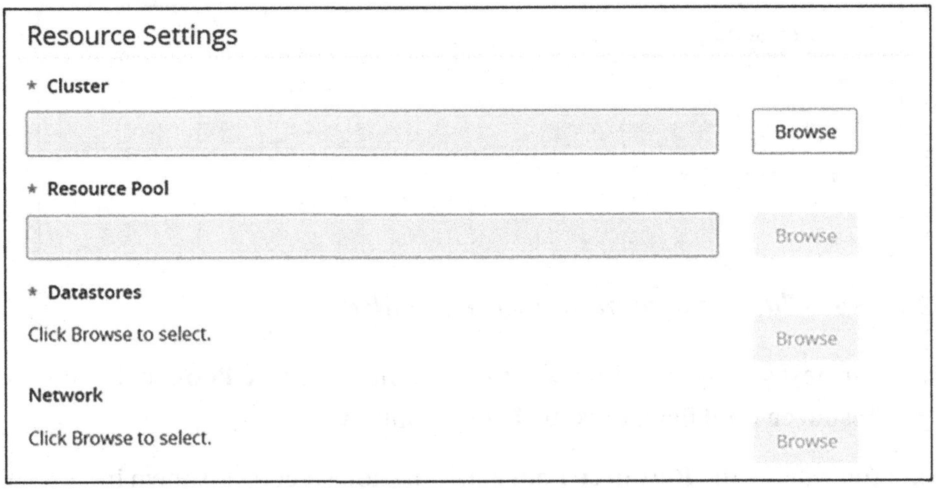

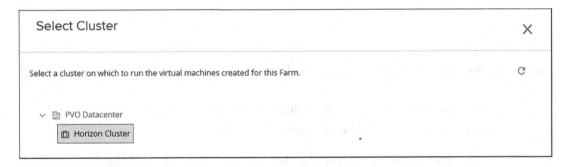

Resource Settings

* Cluster

[Browse]

* Resource Pool

[Browse]

* Datastores

Click Browse to select.   Browse

Network

Click Browse to select.   Browse

Figure 11-96. *Resource Settings*

58. In the **Cluster** box, click the **Browse** button. You will see the Select Cluster screen, as shown in the following:

Select Cluster   ✕

Select a cluster on which to run the virtual machines created for this Farm.   ↻

∨ 🗋 PVO Datacenter

    🗋 Horizon Cluster

Figure 11-97. *Selecting the cluster*

59. Select the cluster that you want to provide the resources to run the RDSH Servers, in this example the **Horizon Cluster**, and then click the **Submit** button.

60. You will return to the **vCenter Settings** screen, where you will see that the cluster details have been added.

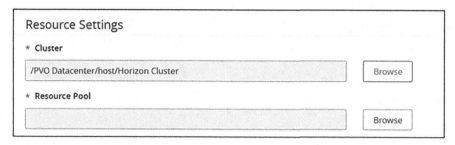

Figure 11-98. *Cluster configuration settings added*

61. The next setting to configure is to select the **Resource Pool**. In the **Resource Pool** field, click the **Browse** button.

62. You will see the **Resource Pool** configuration screen, as shown in the following screenshot:

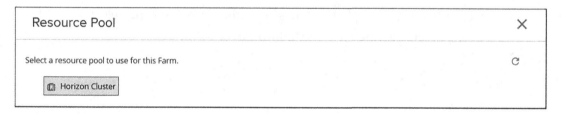

Figure 11-99. *Selecting the resource pool*

63. Select the cluster you want to deliver the resources to this RDSH Server from, and then click the **Submit** button.

64. You will return to the **vCenter Settings** screen where you will see that the resource pool details have been added, as shown in the following screenshot:

Resource Settings

* **Cluster**

/PVO Datacenter/host/Horizon Cluster   Browse

* **Resource Pool**

/PVO Datacenter/host/Horizon Cluster/Resources   Browse

* **Datastores**

Click Browse to select.   Browse

Figure 11-100. *Resource pool added*

65.   The next configuration option is for **Datastores**.

66.   In the **Datastores** field, click the **Browse** button.

67.   You will see the **Select Instant Clone Datastores** configuration
      screen, as shown in the following:

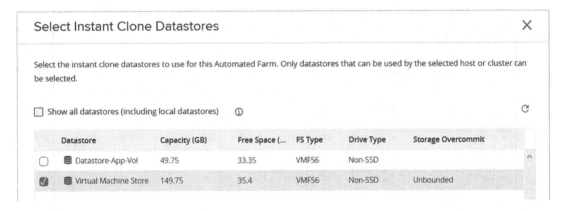

Select Instant Clone Datastores   ✕

Select the instant clone datastores to use for this Automated Farm. Only datastores that can be used by the selected host or cluster can
be selected.

☐ Show all datastores (including local datastores)   ⓘ   ↻

	Datastore	Capacity (GB)	Free Space (...	FS Type	Drive Type	Storage Overcommit
☐	Datastore-App-Vol	49.75	33.35	VMFS6	Non-SSD	
☑	Virtual Machine Store	149.75	35.4	VMFS6	Non-SSD	Unbounded

Figure 11-101. *Selecting the datastore*

68.   Select the datastore that you want to use, then click the **Submit**
      button.

69. You will return to the **vCenter Settings** screen, where you will see that the datastore has been selected, as shown in the following screenshot:

Figure 11-102. *Datastore selected*

70. The final setting is for **Network**.

71. In the **Network** field, click the **Browse** button.

72. You will see the **Select Networks** screen, as shown in the following screenshot:

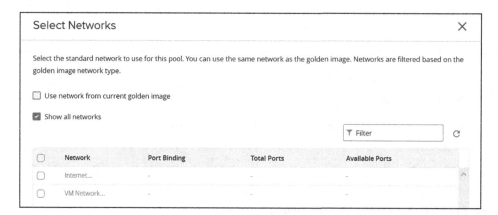

Figure 11-103. *Selecting the network*

73. On the network configuration screen, you can select to use the same network that was configured with the gold image, or you can select another network to use. To change the network, first uncheck the box for **Use network from current golden image**.

74. If you check the **Show all networks** box, you will see all available networks listed.

75. To select a network, check the box next to the network you want to select, then click **Submit**.

76. You will now see the completed **vCenter Settings** screen:

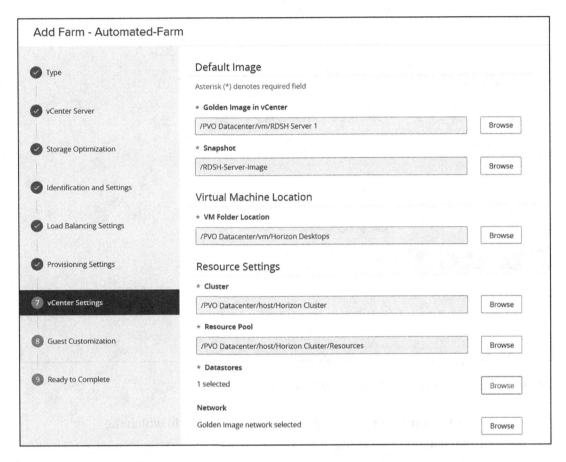

Figure 11-104. *vCenter Settings screen*

77. Click the **Next** button.

78. You will now move on to the next step of the configuration for **Guest Customization**.

79. In the **Domain** box, click the drop-down menu and select the domain in which these virtual desktop machines are going to be created. In this example, we are using the pvolab.com domain.

80. This is shown in the following screenshot:

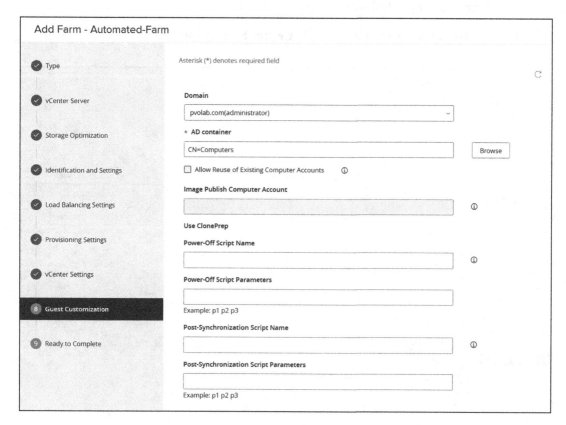

Figure 11-105. *Guest Customization screen*

81. In the **AD container** box, enter the details of the OU in which the virtual machines are going to reside.

82. You can either type directly into the box or click the **Browse** button to navigate to the desired OU.

83. The next option is the check box for **Allow Reuse of Existing Computer Accounts**. This option requires an additional computer account that resides in the same AD as the Instant Clone desktops themselves.

Computer accounts are usually created automatically; however, you can use pre-created accounts and the additional computer account we just mentioned.

If you enable this option, then you add this computer account in the **Image Publish Computer Account** box.

84. The final option of this configuration screen is the **Use ClonePrep** feature.

85. ClonePrep is used to customize the Instant Clone virtual machines as they are created and to ensure that the virtual machines are joined to the domain. New virtual machines will have the same SID as the gold image, and applications will also have the same GUID, as they are part of the gold image.

    ClonePrep gives you the option to run power-off and post-synchronization scripts. Both script options allow you to specify additional parameters. These script names and parameters can be entered in their respective fields.

86. Once you have configured the guest customization features, click the Next button to continue to the final section.

87. You will now see the **Ready to Complete** screen, as shown in the following screenshot:

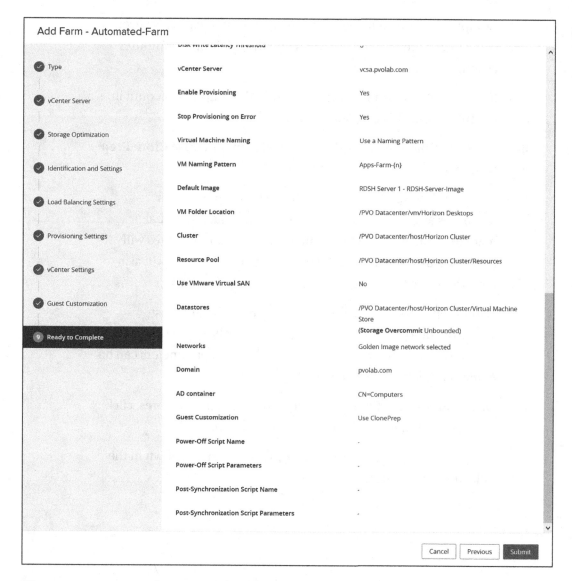

Figure 11-106. *Ready to Complete screen*

88. Once you are satisfied with the configuration, click the **Submit** button to complete the configuration.

89. You will now return to the main **Farms** screen, where you will see that the newly created farm has been added, as shown in the following screenshot:

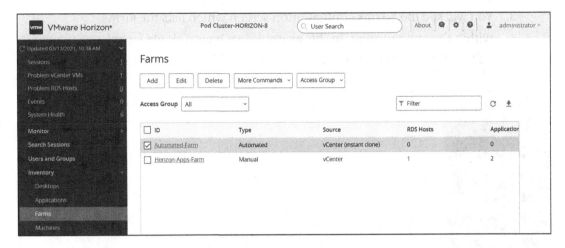

Figure 11-107. *Automated farm successfully configured and added*

You have now successfully created an automated farm that is built using Instant Clones.

In the next section of this chapter, we are going to look at some of the management tasks for existing farms and application pools.

Managing Farms and Application Pools

So far in this chapter, we have looked at how to build farms consisting of RDSH Servers and how to configure application pools, so that we can create groups of applications ready to deliver to end users.

In this section, we are going to look at the tasks you can perform on these existing farms and application pools to provide ongoing management and updates.

We are going to start by looking at managing existing farms.

Managing Existing Farms

In this section, we are going to look at the tasks you can perform on existing farms. To do this, follow the steps described:

1. First, log in to the Horizon Console.

2. Now, by navigating using the options from the left-hand menu pane, expand the option for **Inventory**, then click **Farms**.

3. You will see the **Farms** configuration screen which lists the farms within the environment. In this example, we have a single farm called Horizon-Apps-Farm, as shown in the following screenshot:

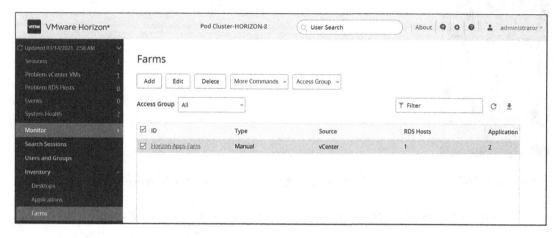

Figure 11-108. *Farms configuration screen*

4. Select the farm you want to manage by checking the box next to the farm name. You will now have access to the icon boxes across the top of the screen. These boxes or buttons provide the following tasks:

- **Add**: Clicking this enables you to add a new farm.

- **Edit**: Opens the edit screen, where you can change the farm settings and load balancing settings.

- **Delete**: Clicking this button will delete the selected farm.

- **More Commands**: If you click this button, you will see several menu options from the drop-down list. These allow you to **Disable Farm** (no users can access the apps it delivers), **Enable Farm** (enable users to access the apps), **Disable Provisioning** (for automated farms), and finally **Enable Provisioning** (for automated farms). These options are shown in the following:

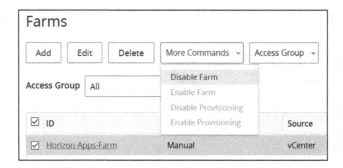

Figure 11-109. *Farms configuration screen with More Commands options*

5. The final button is for **Access Group**, as shown in the following screenshot:

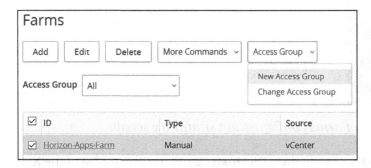

Figure 11-110. *Farms configuring the access group*

6. If you click the **Access Group** button, you will see two options. You can create a **New Access Group**, or you can **Change Access Group**.

7. You will have also noticed on the Farms configuration screen that the name or ID of the configured farms in the list appears as links.

8. If you click the **Horizon-Apps-Farm** link, you will see the Summary screen showing the details of the farm configuration, as shown in the following screenshot:

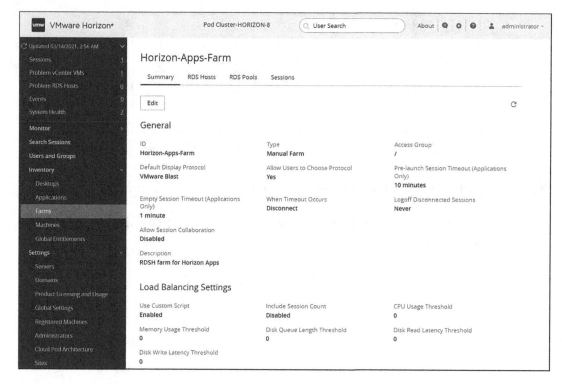

Figure 11-111. *Farms configuration summary screen*

9. If you now click the **RDS Hosts** tab, you will see a list of the RDS
    host servers that are part of this farm. In this example, it is the
    rdsh-server-1 server, as shown in the following screenshot:

Figure 11-112. *RDS Host servers in the farm*

10. You will also see that it details the type of server OS, the maximum
     number of connections the server can support, the Horizon Agent
     version, and whether the server is enabled.

11. If you check the box to select the RDS host server, you can then perform the following actions using the buttons as described:

- **Add**: Adds another RDS host server to the farm.

- **Edit**: Enables you to edit the server details.

- **Remove**: Removes this host server from the farm.

- **More Commands**: If you click this button, you will see two options from the drop-down list. These allow you to **Enable** or **Disable** the selected host server. These options are shown in the following:

Figure 11-113. *RDS Host server's More Commands option*

12. The next tab is for RDS Pools.

13. If you click the **RDS Pools** tab, you will see all the application pools assigned to this farm, as shown in the following:

Figure 11-114. *Application pools*

If you want to manage the app pools from here, then simply click the app link. We will look at managing the app pools in the next section.

14. Finally on this Farm configuration screen, you have the **Sessions**
tab as shown in the following screenshot:

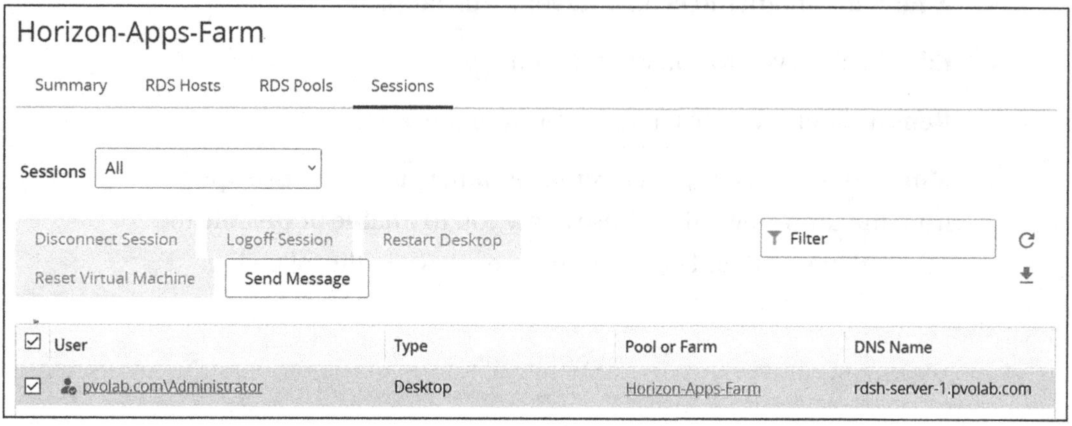

Horizon-Apps-Farm

Summary   RDS Hosts   RDS Pools   Sessions

Sessions | All   ⌄ |

| Disconnect Session   Logoff Session   Restart Desktop | ⊤ Filter | C |
| Reset Virtual Machine   Send Message | | ↓ |

| ☑ User | Type | Pool or Farm | DNS Name |
| ☑ 👤 pvolab.com\Administrator | Desktop | Horizon-Apps-Farm | rdsh-server-1.pvolab.com |

Figure 11-115. Sessions screen

15. On this screen, you can see current sessions. In this example, the
administrator is currently logged on to a desktop, or in this case
the administrator has a console open to the RDS server.

16. If you click a user under the **User** column, this will take you to the
Users and Groups screen for this user; if you click the link under
the **Pool or Farm** column, in this case Horizon-Apps-Farm, then
you will be taken to the farm summary screen for the farm you
clicked the link for.

17. Now click that link for **Horizon-Apps-Farm**, and you will see the
Summary screen for the farm you clicked:

Horizon-Apps-Farm

Summary   RDS Hosts   RDS Pools   Sessions

| Edit | C

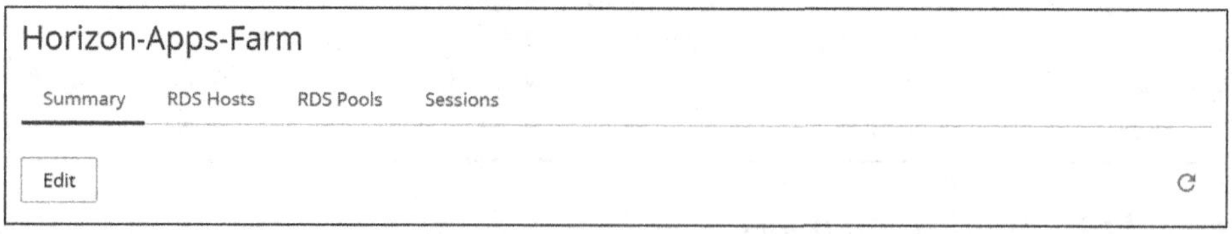

Figure 11-116. Editing the farm configuration

748

18. Now click the **Edit** button, as shown in the following:

Edit Farm - Horizon-Apps-Farm	☒
Farm Settings	Load Balancing Settings

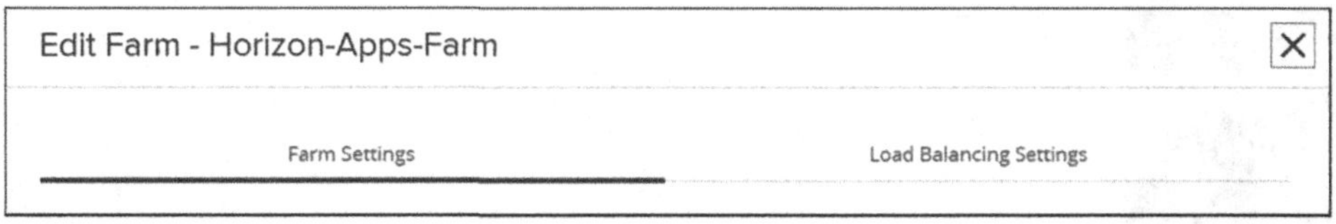

Figure 11-117. *Editing the farm settings and load balancing*

19. From here, you can edit the **Farm Settings** and the **Load Balancing Settings**.

We have now looked at the various tasks you can perform on existing farms. In the next section, we are going to look at the tasks that you can perform on your existing application pools.

Application Pool Management

In this section, we are going to look at the tasks that you can perform on existing application pools.

1. First, log in to the Horizon Console.

2. Now by navigating (using the options from the left-hand menu pane), expand the option for **Inventory**, then click **Applications**.

3. You will see the **Application Pools** configuration screen, which shows the ID, Display Name, Pool or Farm, the Version, and whether or not the application pool is enabled.

    In this example, we have two applications, Notepad++ and VLC Media Player, as you can see from those listed under the **ID** column.

    You will also see the **Display Name**, which **Pool or Farm** the application is part of, the **Version** of the application, and finally whether it is **Enabled**, as shown in the following screenshot:

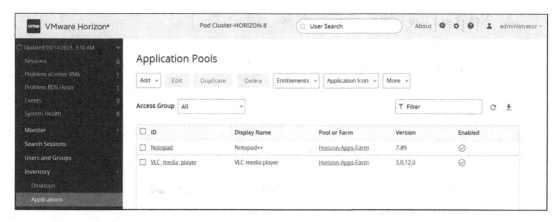

Figure 11-118. *Application Pools screen*

4. From the list of applications on this screen, check the box next to the application you want to perform the task on.

5. You will now see the buttons across the top are now available, each one with a different task that you can perform on the selected application.

6. In this example, we have selected **Notepad++**, as shown in the following screenshot:

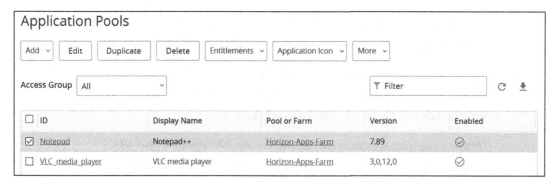

Figure 11-119. *Performing tasks on the selected application*

7. You can then perform the following actions using the buttons as described:

- **Add**: Adds another application pool either manually or from a list of installed applications.

- **Edit**: Opens the **Edit Application Pool** configuration screen, allowing you to change the settings for the selected application, as shown in the following screenshot:

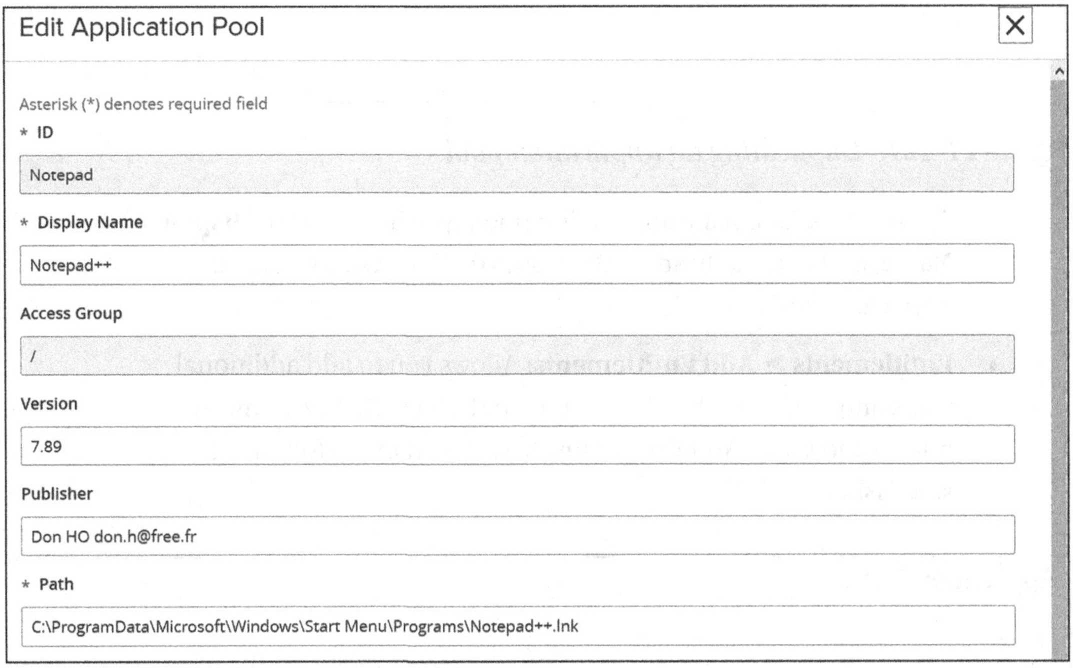

Figure 11-120. Editing the application pool

- **Duplicate**: Creates a duplicate copy of the selected application pool. By clicking, you will see the **Duplicate Application Pool** screen as shown in the following:

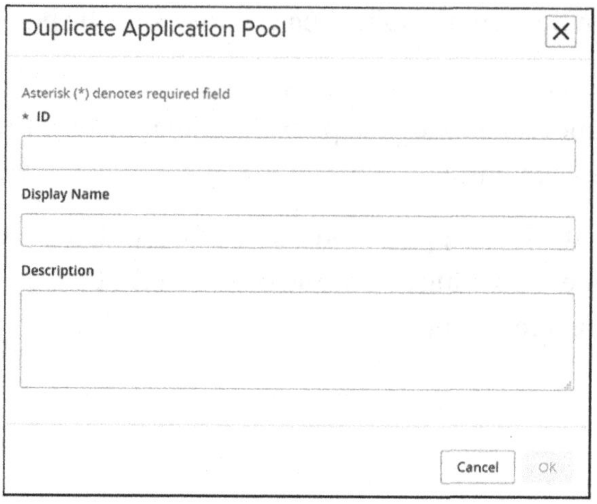

Duplicate Application Pool   ☒

Asterisk (*) denotes required field
* ID

Display Name

Description

                                            Cancel   OK

Figure 11-121. *Duplicating an application pool*

To create the duplicate application pool, type in a new **ID**, **Display Name**, and optionally add a **Description**. Click **OK** to create the duplicated pool.

- **Entitlements ➤ Add Entitlements**: Allows you to add additional users and groups to the application pool. Click the **Entitlements** button and select **Add Entitlement**, as shown in the following screenshot:

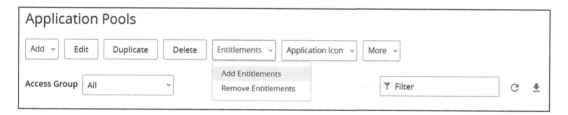

Figure 11-122. *Adding an entitlement to an application pool*

You will see the **Add Entitlements** screen, as shown:

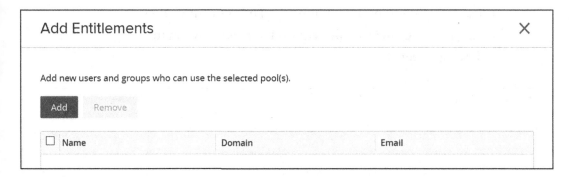

Figure 11-123. *Add Entitlements configuration screen*

Simply click the **Add** button. This will launch the **Find User or Group** configuration screen, from where you can select the individual user or group of users entitled to the application pool.

- **Entitlements ➤ Remove Entitlements**: Allows you to remove users and groups from the application pool. Click the **Entitlements** button and select **Remove Entitlement**. You will see the **Remove Entitlements** screen, as shown in the following screenshot:

Figure 11-124. *Remove Entitlements configuration screen*

To remove an individual user or a group of users, check the box next to the entry you want to remove and click **OK**.

- **Application Icon ➤ Associate Application Icon**: Allows you to configure an icon for the selected application.

Click the **Application Icon** button, and from the drop-down menu, select **Associate Application Icon**, as shown in the following screenshot:

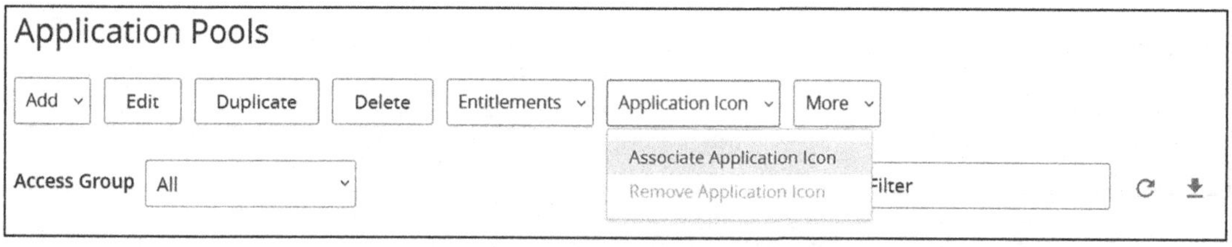

Figure 11-125. *Associate an icon to an application*

You will now see the **Associate Application Icon** configuration screen, as shown in the following screenshot:

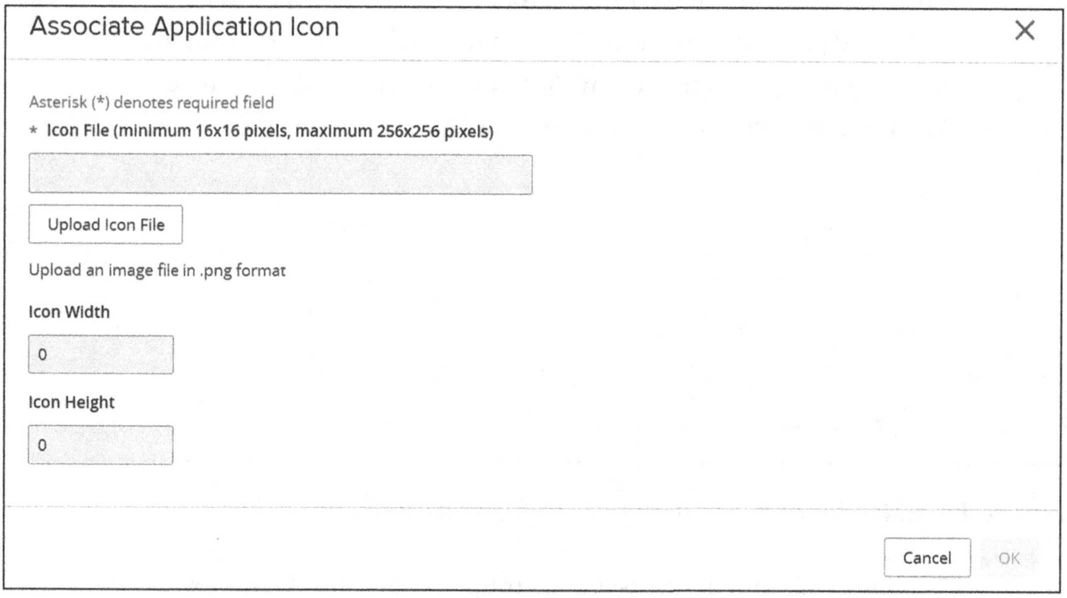

Figure 11-126. *Associate Application Icon configuration screen*

- In the **Icon File** field, click the **Upload Icon File** button to upload an icon file in a PNG file format. A Windows Explorer window will open to enable you to navigate to the required file.

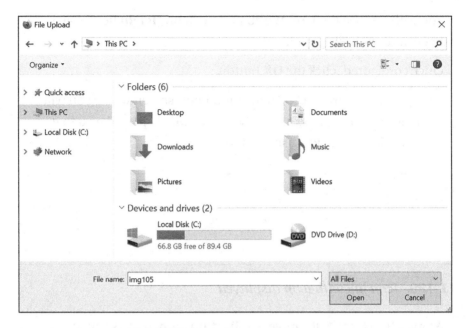

Figure 11-127. *Select an icon file*

Select the PNG file you want to use as the icon file and click **Open**.
You will see the icon file has been uploaded, as shown in the
following screenshot:

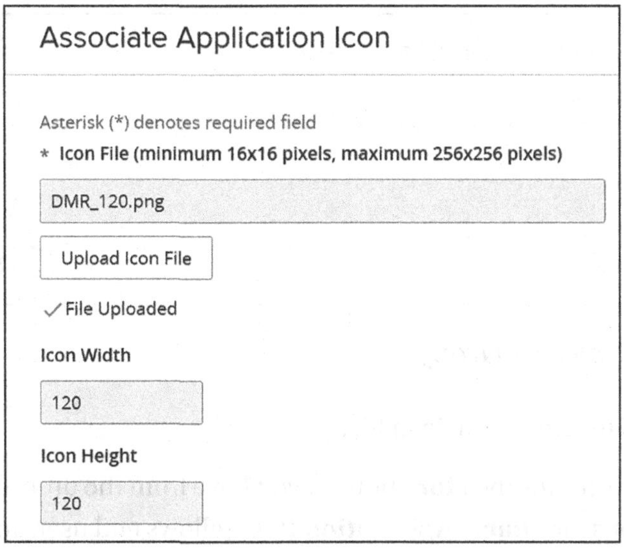

Associate Application Icon

Asterisk (*) denotes required field
* **Icon File (minimum 16x16 pixels, maximum 256x256 pixels)**

> DMR_120.png

> Upload Icon File

✓ File Uploaded

Icon Width

> 120

Icon Height

> 120

Figure 11-128. *Icon file uploaded*

You will then see the **Icon Width** and the **Icon Height** fields have been automatically populated.

Once configured, click the **OK** button.

Now you will return to the Application Pools screen where you will see that Notepad++ now has the selected icon displayed next to it, as shown in the following screenshot:

☐ ID	Display Name	Pool or Farm
☐ Notepad	▦ Notepad++	Horizon-Apps-Farm
☐ VLC_media_player	VLC media player	Horizon-Apps-Farm

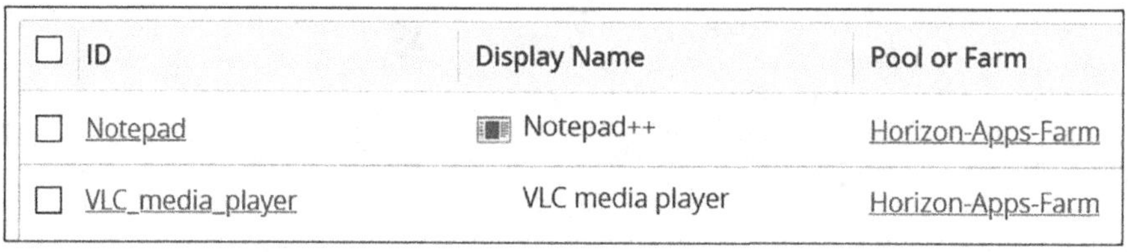

Figure 11-129. *Icon file with icon displayed*

- **Application Icon ➤ Remove Application Icon**: Allows you to remove an icon for the selected application.

  Click the **Application Icon** button, and from the drop-down menu, select **Remove Application Icon**. You will see the following screenshot:

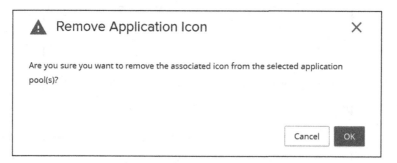

Figure 11-130. *Remove an icon file*

  Click **OK** to remove the icon file.

- **More**: If you click the **More** button, you have from the drop-down the options for **Enable Application Pool** (allows end users to launch application sessions) or **Disable Application Pool** (prevents end users from launching application sessions), as shown:

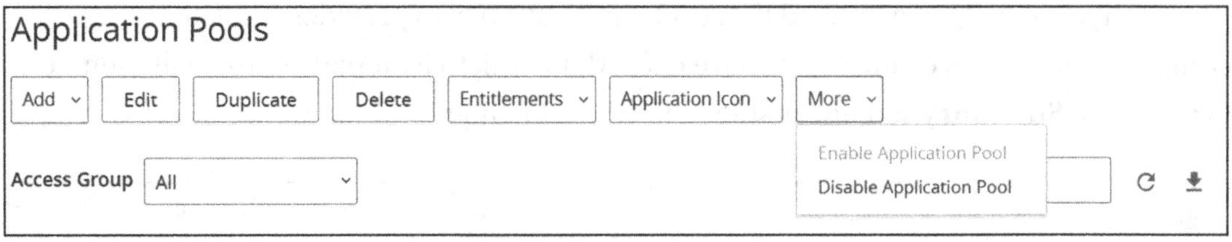

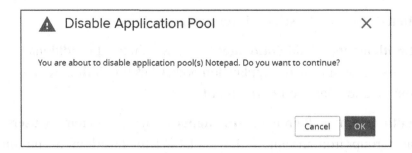

Application Pools

| Add ⌄ | Edit | Duplicate | Delete | Entitlements ⌄ | Application Icon ⌄ | More ⌄ |

Enable Application Pool
Disable Application Pool

Access Group | All ⌄ | C ⬇

Figure 11-131. *More command for enabling and disabling the pool*

If you select the **Enable Application Pool** option, then you will see the following screenshot:

⚠ Enable Application Pool   ✕

You are about to enable application pool(s) Notepad. Do you want to continue?

Cancel   OK

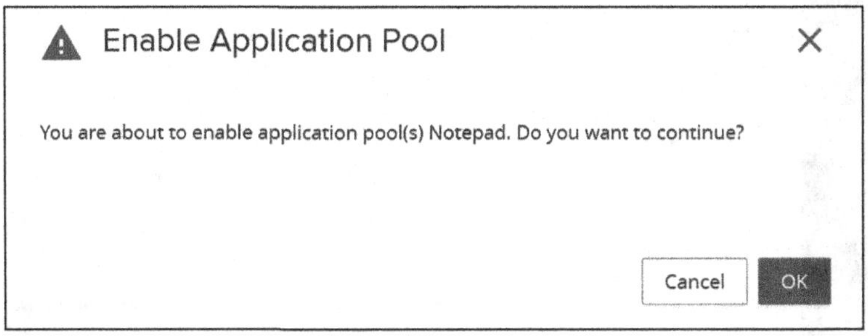

Figure 11-132. *Enabling an application pool*

Click **OK** to enable the application pool.

If you select the **Disable Application Pool** option, you will see the following screenshot:

⚠ Disable Application Pool   ✕

You are about to disable application pool(s) Notepad. Do you want to continue?

Cancel   OK

Figure 11-133. *Disabling an application pool*

Click **OK** to disable the application pool.

Finally, you will have noticed that each application also provides a link to its configuration. In this example, we have clicked the link to Notepad++. You will then be taken to the **Summary** screen, as shown in the following:

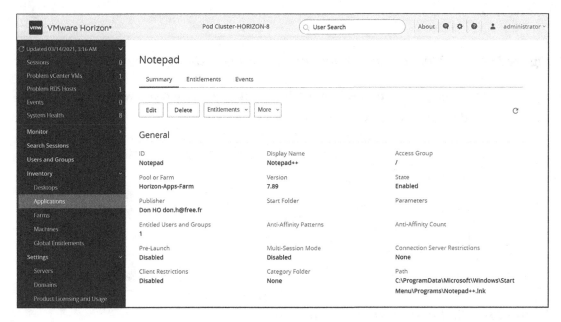

Figure 11-134. *Application summary screen*

Firstly, you will again see that you have several buttons across the top that represent a few tasks. These are as follows:

- **Edit**: Edits the selected application pool.

- **Delete**: Deletes the selected application pool.

- **Entitlements ➤ Add Entitlements**: Allows you to add additional users and groups to the application pool. Click the **Entitlements** button and select **Add Entitlement**.

- **Entitlements ➤ Remove Entitlements**: Allows you to remove users and groups from the application pool. Click the **Entitlements** button and select **Remove Entitlement**.

- **More**: If you click the **More** button, you have from the drop-down the options for **Enable Application Pool** (allows end users to launch application sessions) or **Disable Application Pool** (prevents end users from launching application sessions).

You will also see a few tabs next to the **Summary** tab. The first of these is for **Entitlements**, as shown in the following:

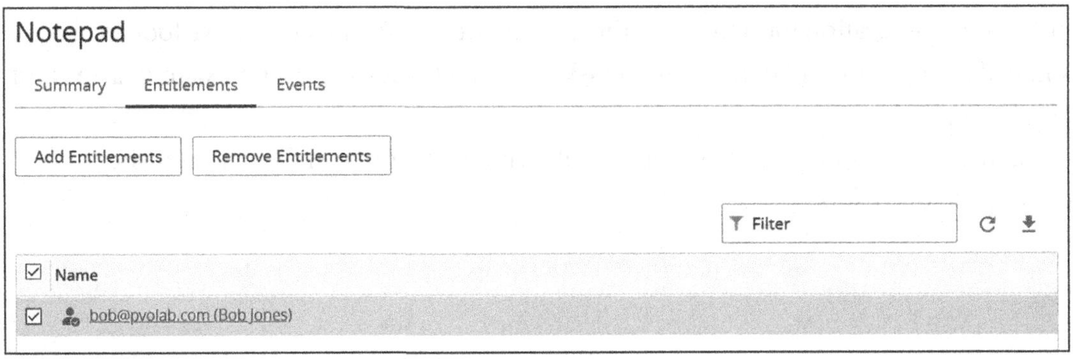

Figure 11-135. *Entitlements tab*

On this screen, you will see that there is a user entitled to use this application pool. You can, from this screen, add another entitlement, or you can remove an entitlement by selecting the user or group to remove, then clicking the **Remove Entitlement** button.

The final tab is for **Events**. Any listed events that are presented here are stored in the Horizon events database.

You can select a time period to search events, as well as being able to check the box to Retrieve Legacy Data.

This is shown in the following screenshot:

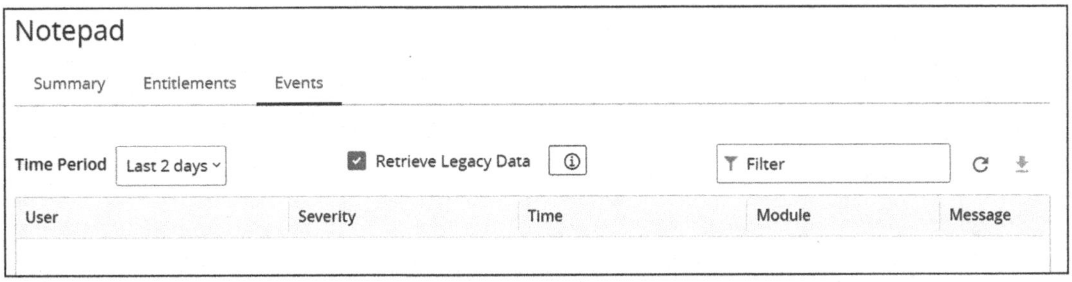

Figure 11-136. *Events tab*

Summary

In this chapter, we have taken a deep dive into Horizon Apps and how to configure Horizon to broker and deliver published apps. We started the chapter by looking at the design and architecture of the solution and some of the considerations around sizing. From there, we installed and configured the RDSH Server role and prepared the infrastructure for delivering apps. The next steps were to configure the Horizon elements of the solution and configure the farms and application pools and load balancing options in preparation for delivering the apps to the end users. Finally, we looked at some of the options and management tasks that can be performed on existing farms and application pools.

In the next chapter, we are going to look at how Horizon can deliver published desktops to end users.

## CHAPTER 12

Horizon Published Desktops

In the previous chapter, we discussed how Horizon can deliver applications by taking advantage of RDSH technology to deliver published applications to end users with the Horizon Apps solution. Now we are going to look at how to deliver published desktop sessions.

If you refer back to Chapter 1, we discussed the differences between VDI and SBC, how delivering a full desktop machine may not be the correct solution, as the end user does not need access to a full-blown desktop.

In this use case, it may be prudent to just deliver a desktop environment by publishing it using Microsoft RDS and enabling Horizon to broker the connection to the desktop session via the Horizon Connection Server.

The end-user experience is therefore simplified, as is the management of delivery. It also means that you potentially need less infrastructure to deliver the solution.

In this chapter, we are going to discuss how to configure Horizon for delivering published desktops, rather than full virtual desktop machines. We will start by looking at an overview of the architecture.

Horizon Architecture for Desktop Sessions

In terms of infrastructure, delivering published desktop sessions with Horizon means no real change to the back-end Horizon infrastructure requirements. The only addition to the infrastructure is the Microsoft RDSH Server, which will be used to deliver the desktop sessions from.

As the Microsoft RDSH Server now effectively becomes the resource that is being delivered to the end users, that is, it is delivering the desktop sessions, this means that the Horizon Agent is now installed on the RDSH Server rather than on a virtual desktop machine.

© Peter von Oven 2022
P. von Oven, *Mastering VMware Horizon 8*, https://doi.org/10.1007/978-1-4842-7261-9_12

With the Horizon Agent installed on the RDSH Server, the Connection Server can now communicate with it, enabling you to create an RDS Farm and then, from the farm, create a desktop pool. The desktop pool provides the end user with the desktop sessions they are entitled to use, displayed as icons within the Horizon Client.

Double-click the icon, and the published desktop session is initiated and delivered via the Connection Server using the display protocol. This is shown in the following screenshot:

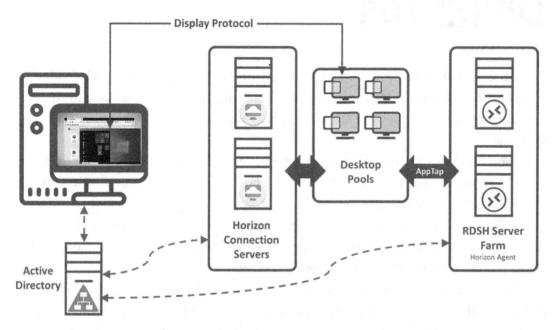

Figure 12-1. *Horizon architecture for delivering published desktops*

In the next section, we are going to look at the design considerations.

Design Considerations

As detailed in the previous diagram, Horizon uses the concept of farms to group together RDSH host servers that provide a common set of resources for delivering desktop sessions to the end users. Farms could contain several host servers to provide the resources.

These farms will then be used to create specific desktop pools, from where the end users select their desktop session.

When architecting virtual RDSH host servers, it is important to ensure that you do not overcommit the ratio of virtual CPUs to physical CPUs.

When architecting virtual desktop machines, higher consolidation levels can be achieved when you over-allocate virtual CPUs to physical cores. Whereas with RDSH host servers, you can achieve higher consolidation levels by over-allocating end users to physical or virtual cores.

If you over-allocate virtual CPUs to physical CPUs in this environment, it could potentially result in poor performance for your end users.

This is illustrated in the following diagram:

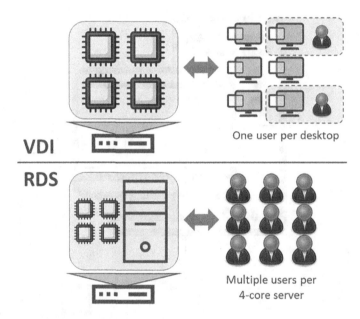

Figure 12-2. *VDI and RDS comparison*

When creating your design, you should not include memory over-allocation as part of the design.

As desktops are being delivered as sessions using an RDS back-end infrastructure, you need to consider the design when it comes to the sizing of the farm. This means that you need to look at the use cases, such as GPU resource requirement, and whether only some servers will have access to GPU cards or all of them.

Typically, you would not enable all servers with GPU due to cost, in which case, then, different farms that have that GPU access and different desktop pools are required to manage an entitlement to those GPU-enabled resources.

You also need to consider your CPU, memory, and disk resources, depending on the workload requirements of the various apps that are going to run within those desktop sessions.

When it comes to resources, you need to consider more than just standard CPU and memory requirements needed to run the apps. Also thinking about how many PCoIP or Blast Extreme connections are going to be required to connect to the multiple sessions. This is particularly important if you also plan to deliver published applications, as well as published desktops, as each one counts as an individual session.

An example of this is shown in the following diagram:

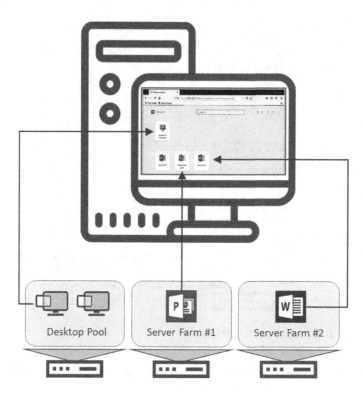

Figure 12-3. *Multiple connections for the display protocol*

The preceding diagram illustrates the Horizon Client displaying to the end user the different resources that they are entitled to. Each one of these would be classed as a separate session.

This means that the end user could connect to their published desktop machine and launch the app being delivered by server farm #1 and also the app being delivered by server farm #2.

In this example, the end user will be using three connections or sessions.

When sizing your environment, you will need to ensure you understand the maximum number of connections available from the Connection Server. In the example scenario, if all users were accessing apps and desktops in this way, then you have essentially divided the number of supported end users by a third, as each individual end user is consuming three sessions.

In this configuration, the Connection Server can support a maximum of 150 sessions, based on a server configured with 4 CPUs and 64 GB of memory.

In the next section, we are going to configure Horizon to deliver published desktop sessions, starting with setting up and configuring the RDS server role.

Configuring Horizon Desktop Sessions

In this section, we are going to build an example environment, setting up an RDSH environment and then configuring Horizon to deliver published desktop sessions to the end users.

We are going to follow the process depicted in the following diagram:

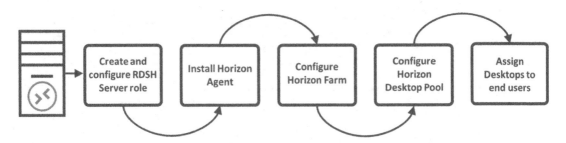

Figure 12-4. *Configuration process for Horizon published desktops*

In the next section, we are going to start the process and configure the RDS role.

Building and Configuring an RDSH Environment

In this section, we are going to install and configure the RDS role onto an example server, running Windows Server 2019, which we have already built. The hostname of this server is **RDS-Server.pvolab.com**.

To set up the RDSH role, follow the steps as described:

1. Open a console to the rdsh-desktops.pvolab.com server.

2. From the **Server Manager** console and the **Dashboard** page, click
   (2) Add roles and features, as shown in the following:

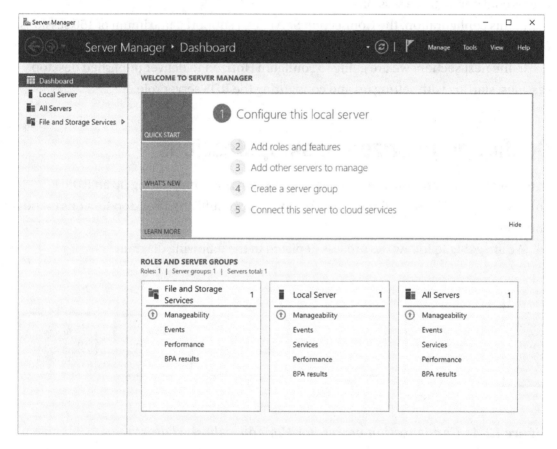

Figure 12-5. *Launching the Server Manager console*

3. The **Add Roles and Features Wizard** will now launch; the first
   screen you will see is the **Before you begin** screen, as shown in
   the following screenshot:

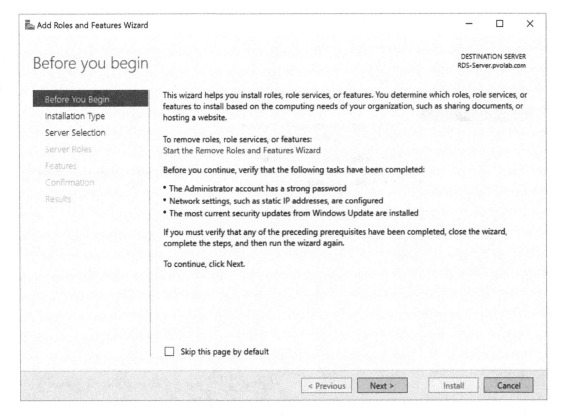

Figure 12-6. *Add Roles and Features Wizard – Before you begin screen*

4. You can opt to skip this page in the future by checking the **Skip this page by default** box.

5. Click **Next ➤** to continue.

6. You will see the **Select installation type** screen, as shown in the following screenshot:

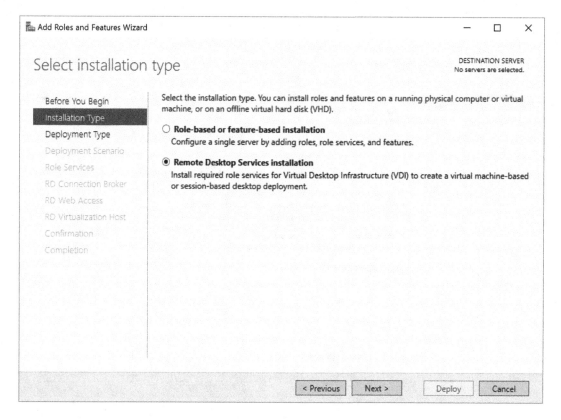

Figure 12-7. Selecting the installation type screen

7. Click the radio button for **Remote Desktop Services installation**.

8. Now click **Next ➤** to continue.

9. The next screen you will see is the **Select deployment type** screen, as shown in the following screenshot:

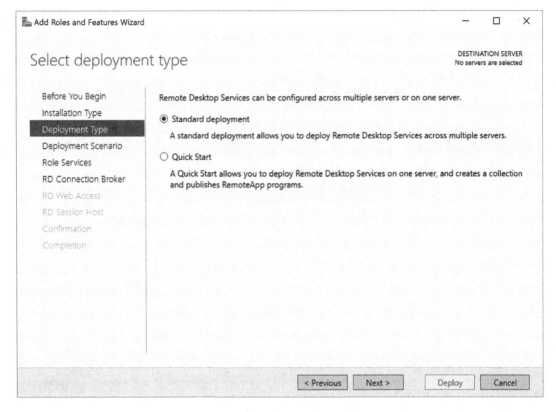

Figure 12-8. *Selecting the deployment type screen*

10. Click the radio button for **Standard deployment**. This option allows you to deploy Remote Desktop Services on this server, as well as across multiple servers if you are creating a farm.

11. Click **Next ➤** to continue.

12. You will now see the **Select deployment scenario** screen, as shown in the following screenshot:

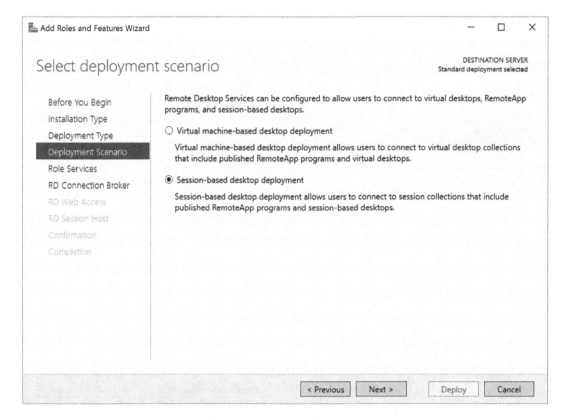

Figure 12-9. *Selecting the deployment scenario screen*

13. Click the **Session-based desktop deployment** radio button. This
enables end users to connect to session-based desktops delivered
by this server and others that are also configured with the RDS
role and are part of the farm.

14. Click **Next ➤** to continue.

15. You will now see the **Role Services** screen.

16. On this screen, you will see the role services that are going to be
installed and configured – in this example, the Remote Desktop
Connection Broker (although this role will actually be performed
by the Horizon Connection Server), the Remote Desktop Web
Access role, and the Remote Desktop Session Host role itself.

These are shown in the following screenshot:

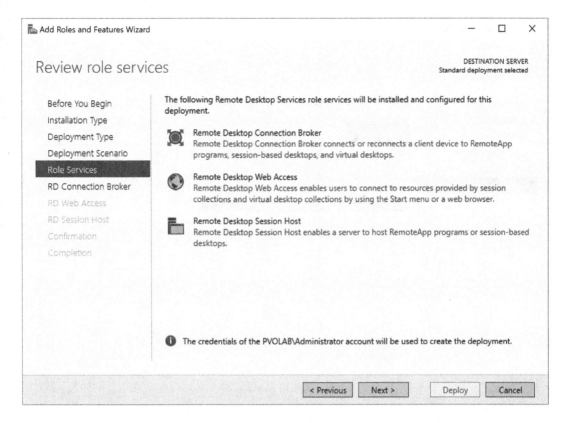

Figure 12-10. *Role Services screen*

17. Click **Next ➤** to continue.

18. You will now see the **RD Connection Broker** screen. On this screen, you need to select the server or servers from the list of those shown that are going to perform the RD Connection Broker role.

19. In this example, as we are installing a single server, select that server from the list. This is the server with the hostname of RDS-Server.pvolab.com, as shown in the following screenshot:

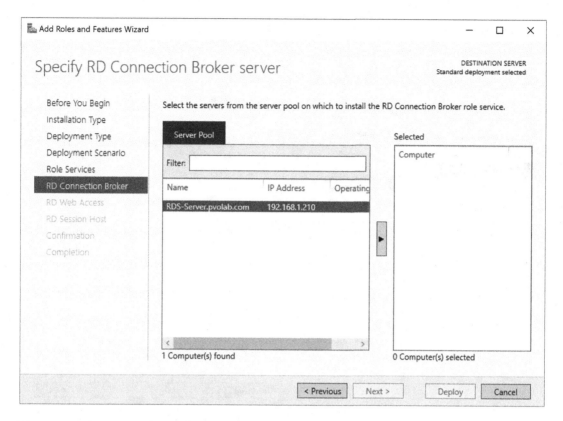

Figure 12-11. *Specifying the server to perform the RDS role*

20. Click the Arrow box in between the Server Pool box and the **Selected** box to add the server to the **Selected** pane, as shown in the following screenshot:

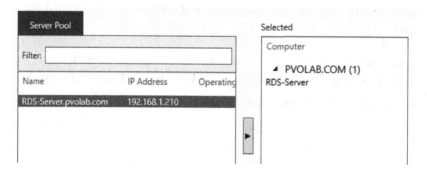

Figure 12-12. *Server successfully selected for the RDS role*

21. Click **Next ➤** to continue.

22. You will now see the **Specify RD Web Access server** screen, as
    shown in the following screenshot:

Figure 12-13. *Specifying the RD Web Access server*

23. Check the box for **Install the RD Web Access role service on the
    RD Connection Broker server**. The server will automatically be
    added to the Selected pane.

24. Now select the server or servers from the list; click the [] button
    to add them to the **Selected** pane, as shown in the following
    screenshot:

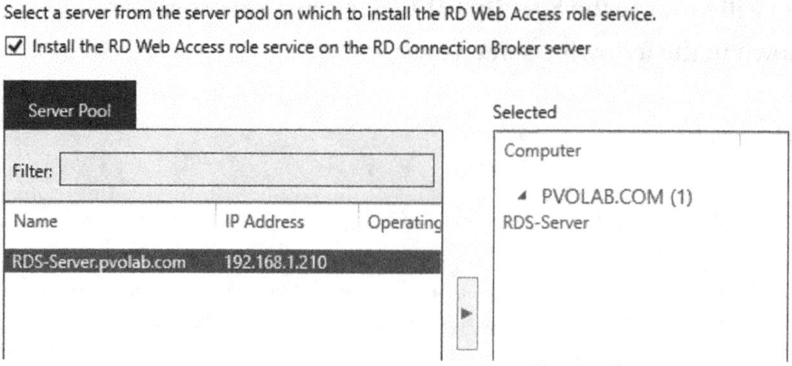

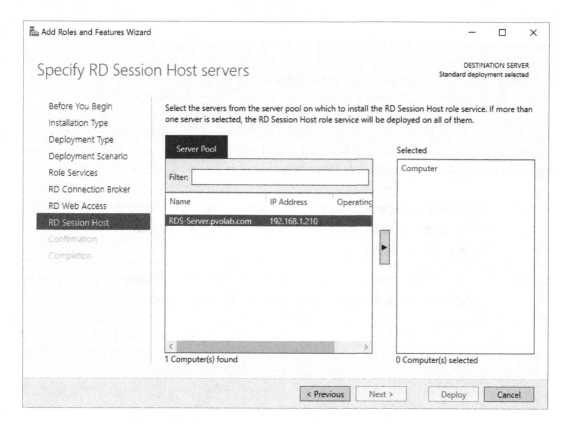

Figure 12-14. *Adding the RD Web Access server*

25. Click **Next ➤** to continue.

26. You will now see the **Specify RD Session Host servers** screen, as shown in the following screenshot:

Figure 12-15. *Adding the RD Session Host server*

27. From the list of servers shown, click the server to add and then
     click the ⬜ button. You will see the server added to the Selected
     pane, as shown in the following screenshot:

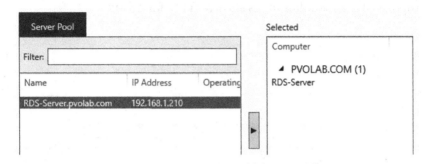

Figure 12-16. *RD Session Host server successfully added*

28. Click **Next ➤** to continue.

29. You will see the **Confirm selections** screen as shown:

Figure 12-17. *Confirm selection screen*

30. Check the Restart the destination server automatically if required box, then click the Deploy button.

31. You will now see the **View progress** screen which shows the progress of the installation, as shown in the following:

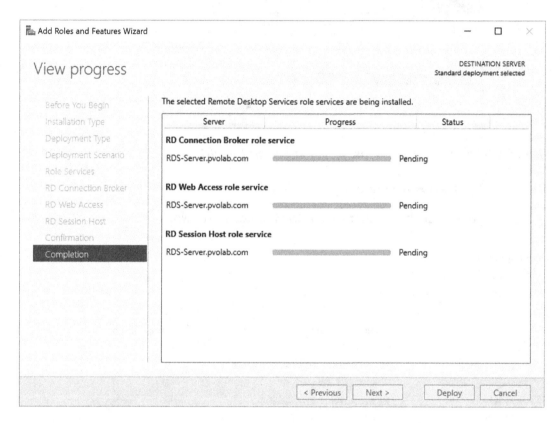

Figure 12-18. *Remote Desktop Services installation progress*

32. During the installation process, the server will reboot and then automatically resume the installation process.

33. Once the installation of the role services has successfully completed, then you will see the following screenshot, stating Succeeded next to each role installed:

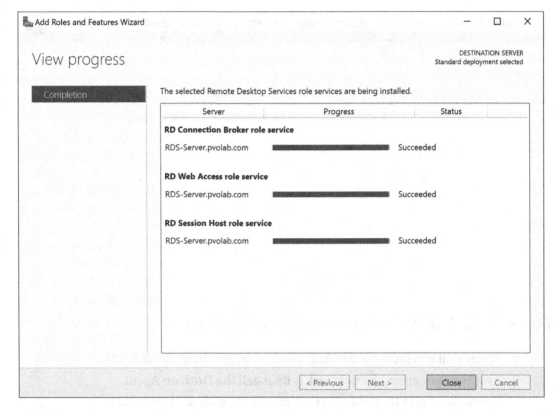

Figure 12-19. *Remote Desktop Services installation succeeded*

34. Click the **Close** button.

35. You will now return to the **Server Manager** screen.

36. If you click the **Remote Desktop Services** entry from the left-hand navigation pane, you will see the Remote Desktop Services Overview screen, as shown in the following screenshot:

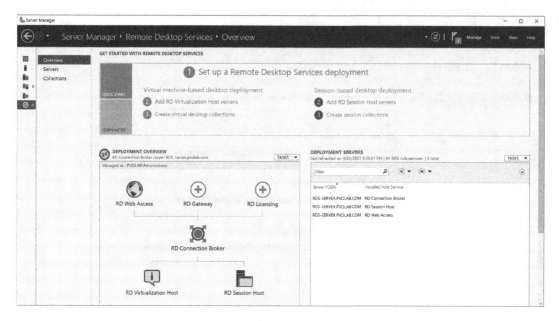

Figure 12-20. *Remote Desktop Services Overview screen*

Now that you have successfully configured and installed the RDS
role on the server, the next task is to install the Horizon Agent
onto the server to enable it to communicate with the Connection
Server.

Installing the Horizon Agent for RDSH

As with any other Horizon Agent installation, the purpose of the agent is so the Horizon
Connection Server can communicate with the resource you are delivering.

With the case of Horizon delivered desktop sessions, the Horizon Agent enables you
to configure the server farms and the RDS desktop pools in the Horizon Console. We will
complete this task later in the chapter.

To install the Horizon Agent, follow the steps as described:

1. From the console of the RDSH Server you are using to deliver the
   desktop sessions, navigate to the VMware Horizon Agent
   installer, as shown in the following screenshot:

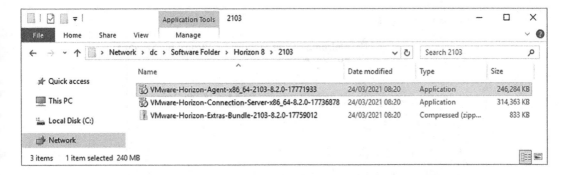

Figure 12-21. *Launching the Horizon Agent installer*

2. Double-click to launch the **VMware-Horizon-Agent-x86_64-2103-8.2.0-17771933** agent installer.

3. You will see the installer launch and the splash screen, as shown in the following screenshot:

Figure 12-22. *VMware Horizon Agent installer splash screen*

4. The next screen you will see is the **Welcome to the Installation Wizard for VMware Horizon Agent**, as shown in the following screenshot:

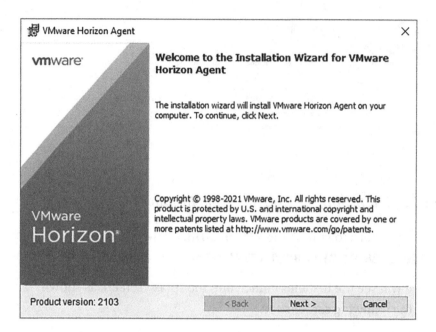

Figure 12-23. *Installer welcome screen*

5. Click **Next ➤** to continue.

6. You will see the **License Agreement** screen as shown:

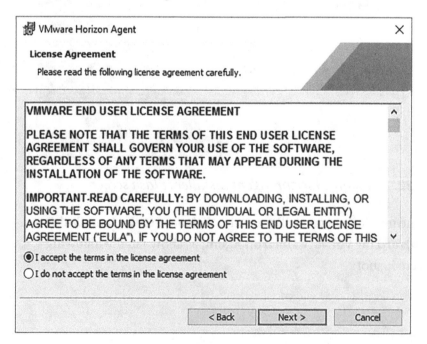

Figure 12-24. *License Agreement screen*

7. Click the radio button for I accept the terms in the license agreement.

8. Click **Next ➤** to continue.

9. You will now see the **Network protocol configuration** screen, where you can choose the IP version you want to use. As the Connection Server in our example environment is using IPv4, we too need to choose IPv4, as you are unable to mix different versions within Horizon, as shown in the following screenshot:

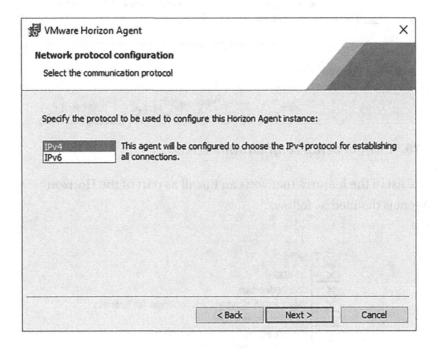

Figure 12-25. Network protocol configuration screen

10. Click to select **IPv4**.

11. Click **Next ➤** to continue.

The next screen is the **Custom Setup** screen**.**

Here, you can configure the different features of the Horizon Agent**,** as shown in the following screenshot:

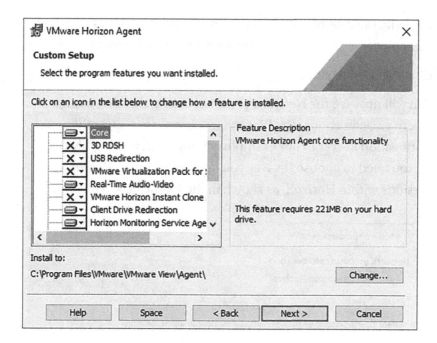

Figure 12-26. *Custom Setup configuration screen*

12.   The list of the features that you can install as part of the Horizon
Agent is detailed as follows:

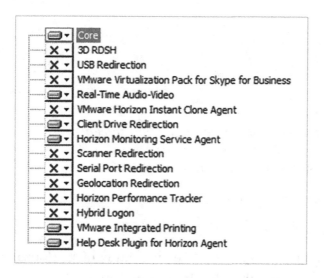

Figure 12-27. *Horizon Agent features*

We are going to describe each of the features you can install as part of the Horizon Agent as follows:

- **Core**: Installs the core Horizon Agent requirements.

- **3D RDSH**: Installs the 3D graphics features for RDSH.

- **USB Redirection**: Enables USB devices to be redirected from the end user's end point to the app session.

- **VMware Virtualization Pack for Skype for Business**: Installs the optimizations required to run Skype for Business on a virtual desktop machine.

- **Real-Time Audio-Video**: Enables the redirection of audio and video devices from the end point to the virtual desktop machine.

- **VMware Instant Clone Agent**: Enables the virtual desktop machine to be delivered using Instant Clones. You will need vSphere 6.0/2015 U1 or later to be able to support Instant Clones. If you install this feature, ensure that you DO NOT install the Horizon View Composer Agent.

- **Client Drive Redirection**: Enables the end user's end point device to share local drives with the virtual desktop machine.

- **Horizon Monitoring Service Agent**: Monitors the performance of the Horizon environment.

- **Scanner Redirection**: Enables scanners to be connected to the end user's end point device and redirected to the virtual desktop machine.

- **Serial Port Redirection**: Enables serial port devices to be connected to the end user's end point device and redirected to the virtual desktop machine.

- **Geolocation Redirection**: Enables the location information from the end user's end point device to be sent to the virtual desktop machine. Useful for end users who travel, so their location information is reflected on their desktop, given the virtual desktop machine remains static in a data center.

- **Horizon Performance Tracker**: Monitors the performance of the display protocol and system resource usage of the virtual desktop machine.

- **Hybrid Logon**: Enables unauthenticated user access to network resources without the need for user credentials.

- **VMware Integrated Printing**: Enables printer redirection.

- **Help Desk Plugin for Horizon Agent**: Enables the virtual desktop to be monitored using the Horizon Help Desk Tool that is integrated into the Horizon Console.

13. Having now covered each of the features you can install as part of the Horizon Agent and selected the ones required, click **Next ➤** to continue.

14. The next configuration screen is for **Register with Horizon Connection Server**, as shown in the following screenshot:

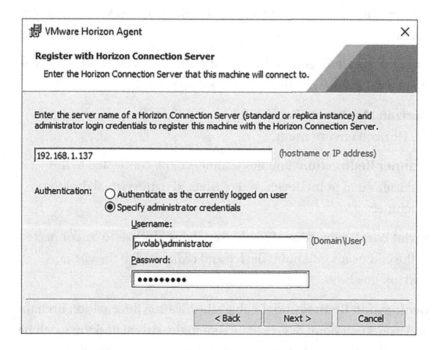

Figure 12-28. Registering the Horizon Agent with the Connection Server

15. In the **hostname or IP address** box, enter the address details of the Connection Server you want the agent to register with. In this example, we have entered **192.168.1.137** as the IP address of the Connection Server.

16. Then in the **Authentication** section, click the radio button for **Specify administrator credentials**. This is the account that can register the agent with the Connection Server. In this example, we are using the administrator account.

17. In the **Username** box, type in the account details using the Domain\User format. In this example, we are going to type **pvolab\administrator**.

18. In the **Password** box, type in the password for the administrator account you entered.

19. Now click the **Next ►** button.

20. You will see the **Ready to Install the Program** screen, as shown in the following screenshot:

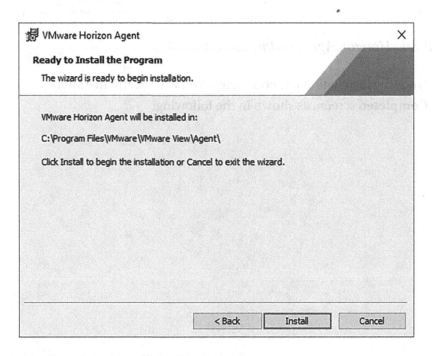

Figure 12-29. Ready to install the Horizon Agent

21. Click the **Install** button to start the installation. You will see the **Installing VMware Horizon Agent** screen, as shown in the following screenshot:

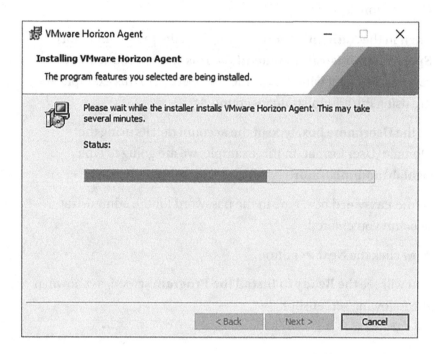

Figure 12-30. *Horizon Agent installation status*

22. Once the installation has completed, you will see the **Installer Completed** screen, as shown in the following:

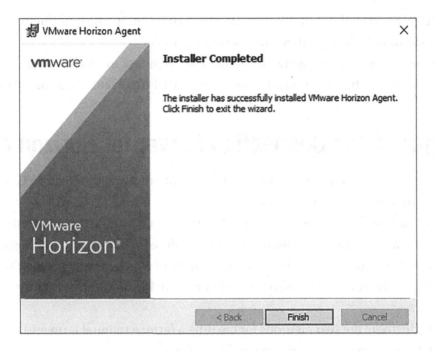

Figure 12-31. *Installation completed*

23. Click the **Finish** button.

24. You will be prompted to reboot the machine, as shown by the following message:

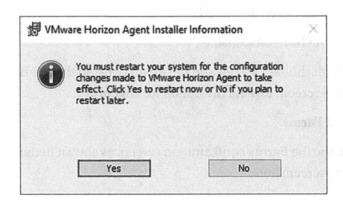

Figure 12-32. *Restart the RDSH Server*

25. Click the **Yes** button to reboot the RDSH Server.

The RDSH Server will now reboot and load the Horizon Agent components to enable desktop sessions to be brokered by the Connection Server.

In the next section, we are going to complete the first task in enabling the Connection Server to broker desktop sessions; the task is to create a farm of RDS servers.

Configuring the Connection Server for Horizon Apps

The next steps of the configuration process are carried out using the Horizon Console, and the first of those steps is to create a farm.

A server farm in this context is a group of servers or a cluster that provides the combined resources required to deliver desktop sessions. When an end user logs in and launches a desktop session, they will be unaware of which server is delivering that session. That decision is made based on the load balancing of resources at the time of login.

In Horizon, there are two methods for creating a farm: a manual farm and an automated farm. We will look at the manual farm first.

Creating a Manual Farm

In this section, we are going to build and configure a manual farm for delivering published apps using Horizon.

To do this, follow the steps described:

1. Log in to the Horizon Console.

2. From the dashboard screen and the menu pane on the left-hand side of the screen, expand the option for **Inventory**.

3. Now click **Farms**.

4. You will see the **Farms** configuration screen, as shown in the following screenshot:

Figure 12-33. *Farms configuration screen*

5. Click the **Add** button.

6. You will see the **Add Farm** configuration screen, as shown in the following screenshot:

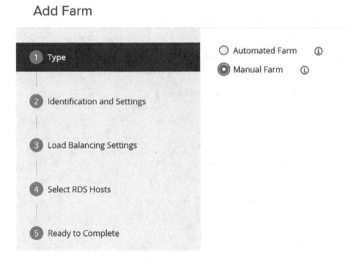

Figure 12-34. *Configuring the farm type*

7. The first section of this configuration screen is for **Type**. This is whether you want to create an automated farm or a manual farm.

   In this example, click the radio button for **Manual Farm**. We have already built and configured an RDSH Server to use this for the farm configuration.

8. Click the **Next** button to continue to the **Identification and Settings** screen, as shown in the following screenshot:

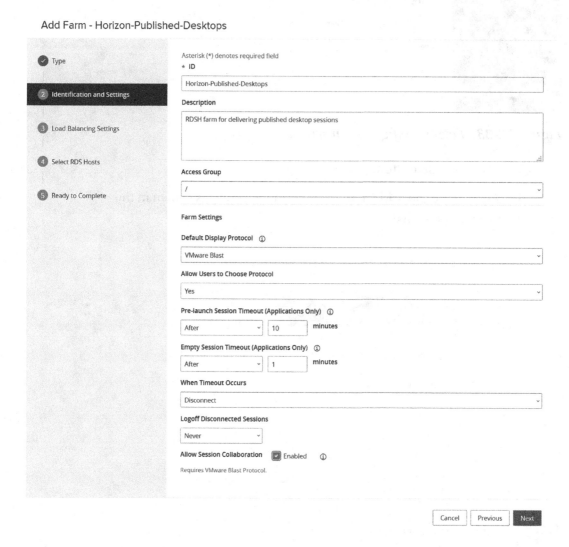

Figure 12-35. *Identification and Settings configuration screen*

9. In the **ID** box, type in the ID you want to use to identify this farm. In this example, we have given the desktop pool the ID of **Horizon-Published-Desktops**.

10. Next, in the **Description** box, you can optionally give the farm a better description as to its use case. In this example, we have used **RDSH farm for delivering published desktop sessions** for the description.

11. In the **Access Group** drop-down menu, select the access group if you have any configured. In this example, we have selected the default access group. The access group enables you to manage desktop pools and delegate different permission levels for administration tasks.

12. Next are the **Farm Settings** and the first setting for configuring the **Default Display Protocol**.

13. In the **Default Display Protocol** box from the drop-down menu, select the protocol you want the end users to connect their virtual desktops with. In this example, we are going to use **Blast**. You can choose from PCoIP, RDP, and Blast.

14. Next is the **Allow Users to choose Protocol** box. From the drop-down menu, select either **Yes** or **No**. Selecting yes allows the end users to switch from the default protocol to another protocol.

15. In the **Pre-Launch Session Timeout** configuration, you can specify a timeout period to disconnect an app session, should a pre-launched app not be launched during the specified timeout period. From the drop-down menu, you can select either **Never** or **After**. When selecting the **After** option, you can then specify a time in minutes for when to disconnect the app session. Note that this option is for delivering applications.

16. If an end user closes the apps that are running in the session, then that session gets marked as being empty. This means the apps are not being used, but the end user is still connected to the RDSH Server. The **Empty Session Timeout** setting allows you to specify a time to wait before actioning the **When Timeout Occurs** setting, which we will look at next.

17. When the Empty Session Timeout configured time has elapsed, the **When Timeout Occurs** setting will either **Disconnect** the end user or perform a **Log Off**. Select one of these options from the drop-down menu. Note that this option is for delivering applications.

18. Next is the **Logoff Disconnected Sessions** setting. With this setting, you can choose what to do with sessions that get disconnected.

    These are sessions where the connection between the end user and the app session drops rather than the end user logging out. This could be down to an unstable network connection or the user being mobile.

    From the drop-down menu, you can select from the following options:

    a. **Never**: Even though disconnected, the end user's session stays active.

    b. **After**: Allows you to specify a time in minutes to wait before the end user then gets logged out.

    c. **Immediate**: The end user will be logged out at the same time as they disconnect.

19. The final setting is for **Allow Session Collaboration**. Check the box to enable this setting, which means end users can invite others to the same session.

20. Click the **Next** button to continue to the **Load Balancing Settings** screen.

21. The first option on this configuration screen is for **Use Custom Script**. This allows you to use your own script to calculate resources. We will look at this in more detail in the "Load Balancing with Custom Scripts" section of this chapter.

22. The next option is for Include Session Count. Enabling this feature, by checking the box, means that load balancing will be performed on the number of active sessions for each server. This means that the next end user to log in will be directed to the server that is running the lower number of sessions.

However, you need to be aware that even though a particular server in the farm has fewer active sessions running on it, the session count does not consider the amount of resources being consumed. It may be that the server has 95% resource usage, even though it has far fewer active sessions than other servers. This is the default load balancing method if no other metrics or custom scripts are selected.

The Load Balancing Settings are shown in the following:

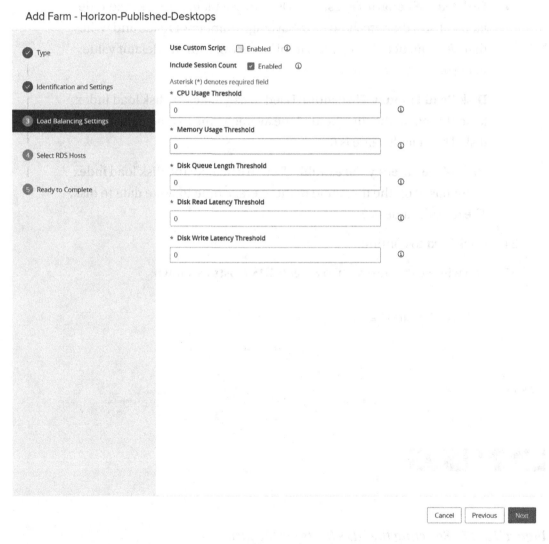

Figure 12-36. *Load Balancing Settings*

23. The next group of settings allow you to configure specific thresholds for CPU, memory, and disk:

- **CPU Usage Threshold**: Used to calculate the CPU load index factor as a percentage. 90% is the recommended setting with the default value being 0.

- **Memory Usage Threshold**: Used to calculate the memory load index factor as a percentage. 90% is the recommended setting with the default value being 0.

- **Disk Queue Length Threshold**: Used to calculate the disk load index factor. It sets the threshold of the average number of reads and writes that were queued during the sample interval, with the default value being 0.

- **Disk Read Latency Threshold**: Used to calculate the disk load index factor based on the threshold of the average time to read data from disk. The default value is 0.

- **Disk Write Latency Threshold**: Used to calculate the disk load index factor based on the threshold of the average time to write data to disk. The default value is 0.

24. Click **Next** to continue.

25. You will see the next step to **Select RDS Hosts** as shown:

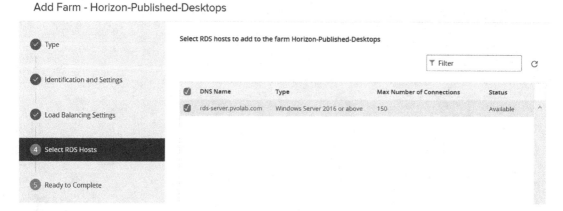

Figure 12-37. *Selecting the RDS hosts for the farm*

26. Check the box to select the RDS host servers that you want to add to this farm. In this example, we have a single server with the hostname of **rds-server.pvolab.com** server.

    You will also see that the type of server is listed, along with the maximum number of connections that this server can deliver.

27. Click **Next** to continue.

28. You will now see the final screen, the **Ready to Complete** screen, as shown in the following screenshot:

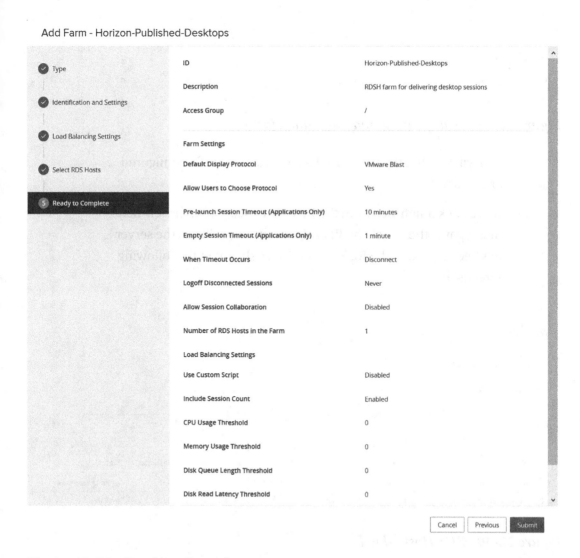

Add Farm - Horizon-Published-Desktops

ID	Horizon-Published-Desktops
Description	RDSH farm for delivering desktop sessions
Access Group	/
Farm Settings	
Default Display Protocol	VMware Blast
Allow Users to Choose Protocol	Yes
Pre-launch Session Timeout (Applications Only)	10 minutes
Empty Session Timeout (Applications Only)	1 minute
When Timeout Occurs	Disconnect
Logoff Disconnected Sessions	Never
Allow Session Collaboration	Disabled
Number of RDS Hosts in the Farm	1
Load Balancing Settings	
Use Custom Script	Disabled
Include Session Count	Enabled
CPU Usage Threshold	0
Memory Usage Threshold	0
Disk Queue Length Threshold	0
Disk Read Latency Threshold	0

Steps: Type · Identification and Settings · Load Balancing Settings · Select RDS Hosts · 5 Ready to Complete

Cancel   Previous   Submit

Figure 12-38. *Ready to Complete screen*

29. Review the configuration options, and if satisfactory, click the **Submit** button.

30. You will now return to the main **Farms** configuration screen, as shown in the following screenshot:

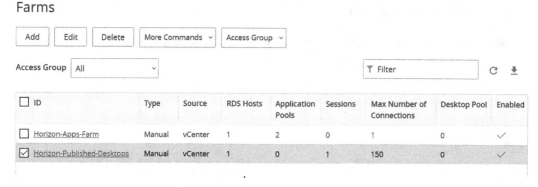

Figure 12-39. *Newly configured and added farm*

31. You will see that the new farm has been successfully configured and added.

32. If you click **Machines** from the **Inventory** section in the left-hand menu pane, then click the **RDS Hosts** tab, you will see the server has been added to the RDS Server list, as shown in the following screenshot:

Figure 12-40. *RDS Host added*

You have now successfully created and configured a farm, ready to deliver the published desktop sessions to end users.

The next step, which will be discussed in the following section, is to create a desktop pool to select which resources to publish to the end users.

Creating a Desktop Pool

In this section, we are going to create a desktop pool. In this case, rather than giving the users access to a full virtual desktop machine, end users are only going to have access to a published desktop session.

In this example, we are going to create a desktop pool configured to use the resources of the RDSH Server we used when the farm was created in the previous section of this chapter. To create an RDS-based desktop pool, follow the steps described:

1. From the left-hand menu pane, expand the option for **Inventory**, then click **Desktops** as shown:

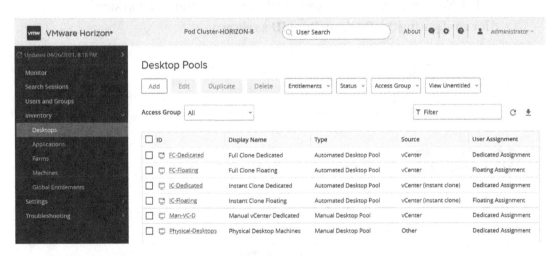

Figure 12-41. *Desktop Pools configuration screen*

2. From the **Desktop Pools** screen, click the **Add** button.

3. You will now see the **Add Pool** configuration screen and the first step to select a **Type**, as shown in the following screenshot:

Add Pool

Figure 12-42. *Adding an RDS Desktop Pool*

4. Click the radio button for **RDS Desktop Pool**.

5. Click **Next** to continue. You will see the second configuration step for configuring the **Desktop Pool ID** as shown:

Add Pool - Horizon-Published-Desktop-Pool

Figure 12-43. *Configuring the Desktop Pool ID*

6. In the **ID** box, type in the ID name that you want to use to identify this RDS desktop pool. In this example, we have called it **Horizon-Published-Desktop-Pool**. You can only use the letters **a–z**, **A–Z**, numbers **0–9**, and a _ or - as characters for the ID name.

7. Next, in the **Display Name** box, you can give the desktop pool a friendly name as this is displayed to the end users when they connect. It is worth noting that if you do not enter anything in this box, then the ID will be used as the display name. In this example, we have used **Published Desktop Sessions** for the display name.

8. Finally, in the **Description** box, type in a description that defines what this desktop pool is used for.

9. Click **Next** to continue.

10. You will now see the third configuration step for **Desktop Pool Settings**, as shown in the following screenshot:

Figure 12-44. *Configuring the Desktop Pool Settings*

11. The first option is to configure the **State** of the desktop pool. From the drop-down menu, select **Enabled** or **Disabled**. Disabling an existing RDS desktop pool means that end users who may be entitled to the desktop pool will not be able to connect. In this example, the pool is enabled.

12. In the next section, you can configure **Connection Server Restrictions**. To configure a restriction, click the **Browse** button.

Connection Server Restrictions   ×

Connection Server tags can be edited in Settings -> Servers-> Connection Server.

◉ No Restrictions
   This Desktop Pool can be accessed from any Connection Server.

○ Restricted to these Tags
   This Desktop Pool can be accessed from Connection Servers with the selected tags.

☑	Tag

No records available.

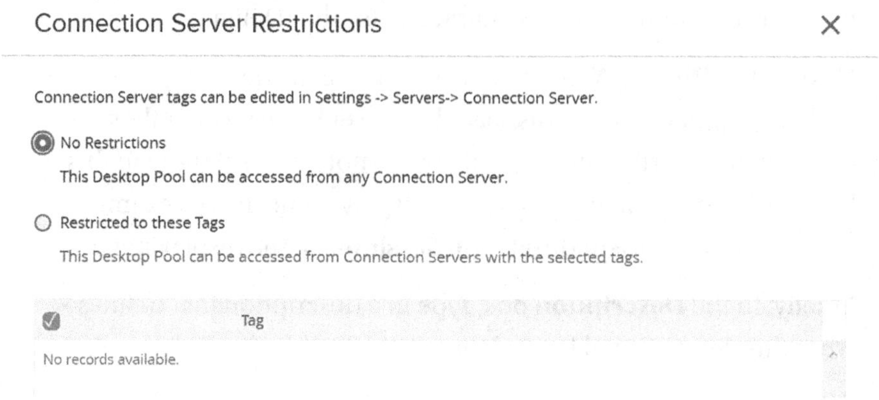

Figure 12-45. *Configuring Connection Server Restrictions*

13. In this example, we have clicked the **No Restrictions** radio button. This means that this desktop pool can be accessed by any Connection Server.

14. If you click the **Restricted to these Tags** radio button, then you are able to select a tag from the list of those shown. Then, only those Connection Servers that have been configured with the selected tag will be able to access the desktop pool. For example, you could separate internal users from those that connect from outside your network, so connections are directed to specific Connection Servers.

15. Click the **Submit** button once you have configured the Connection Server Restrictions.

16. Next, you have the option to configure a **Category Folder**. This allows you to add a folder or a shortcut that points directly to this desktop pool.

17. Click the **Browse** button next, under the **Category Folder** option. You will see the Category Folder configuration screen as shown:

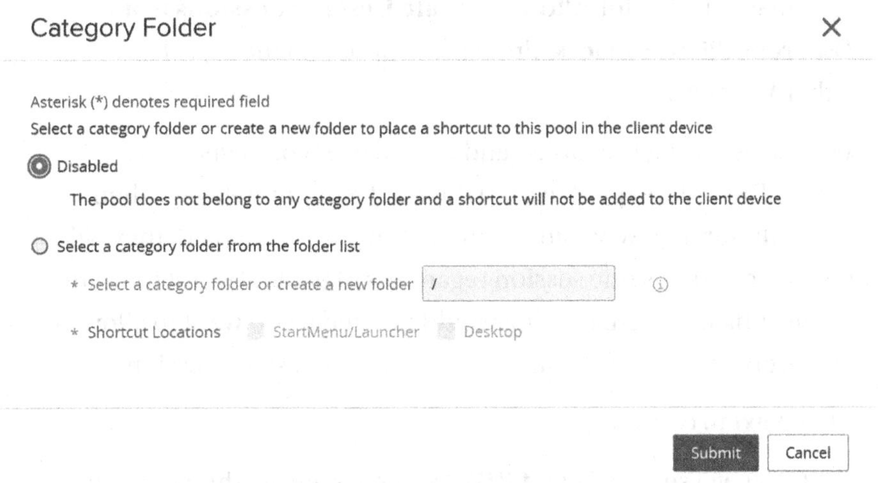

Category Folder   ✕

Asterisk (*) denotes required field
Select a category folder or create a new folder to place a shortcut to this pool in the client device

◉ Disabled

    The pool does not belong to any category folder and a shortcut will not be added to the client device

◯ Select a category folder from the folder list

    * Select a category folder or create a new folder [/   ] ⓘ

    * Shortcut Locations ☐ StartMenu/Launcher ☐ Desktop

[Submit]   [Cancel]

Figure 12-46. *Configuring category folders*

18. To enable this feature, click the radio button for **Select a category folder from the folder list**.

19. Then, in the **Select a category folder or create a new folder** box, type in the folder name. The folder name supports up to 64 characters and up to four sub-folders, by using the \ to separate them.

20. There are also check boxes for **Shortcut Locations**, enabling you to place the shortcut to the desktop pool in the **StartMenu/ Launcher** or **Desktop** of the client's device.

21. Once configured, click the **Submit** button.

22. Next is the check box for **Client Restrictions**.

23. If you check the box to enable this setting, you can prevent end users from connecting to desktops in this pool if they are using specific client devices. You will need to add the computer names that you want to allow into an Active Directory security group. This group will then need to be selected when you create your desktop pool entitlements.

24. The final option is for **Allow Separate Desktop Sessions from Different Client Devices**. From the drop-down menu, select either **Yes** or **No**.

When this setting is enabled and an end user connects to the same RDS desktop pool using a different end point device, then they will start a new session. If this setting is not enabled, they will reconnect to the same session regardless of the end point they are connecting from. This setting would be used if you want to allow end users to have more than one concurrent desktop session.

25. Click **Next** to continue.

26. Next, you will see the **Select RDS Farms** screen, as shown in the following screenshot:

Figure 12-47. *Selecting the RDS farms*

27. Select the farm from the list of those shown. This is the farm that will deliver the resources for the RDS desktop pool. In this example, we are going to select the **Horizon-Published-Desktops** farm by clicking it.

28. Click **Next** to continue.

29. The final screen is the **Ready to Complete** screen.

30. Review the configuration settings. If you need to go back, change, or amend the configuration, use the **Previous** button to do this.

This screen is shown in the following screenshot:

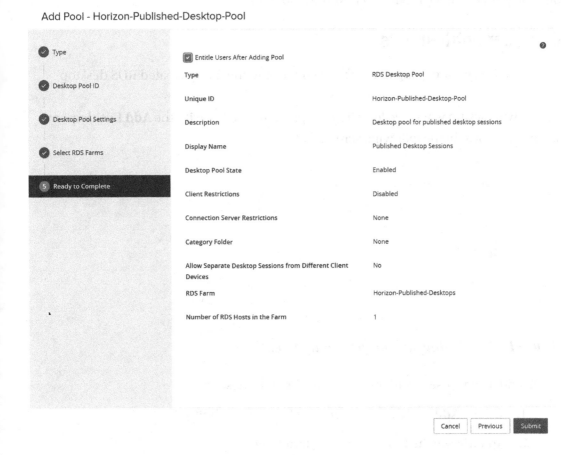

Figure 12-48. *Ready to Complete screen*

31. As we are going to entitle an end user to this newly created RDS desktop pool, ensure that you check the **Entitle Users After Adding Pool** box, as shown in the following screenshot:

☑ Entitle Users After Adding Pool

Figure 12-49. *Entitling end users after a pool is added*

32. Click **Submit** to create the RDS desktop pool.

33. You will now see the Add Entitlements screen.

In the next section, we are going to add an end user to the newly created RDS desktop pool to enable them to access the resources.

End-User Entitlements

In this section, we are going to entitle an end user to the newly created RDS desktop pool.

We will pick up where we left off in the previous section with the **Add Entitlements** screen, as shown in the following screenshot:

Figure 12-50. *Adding an end-user entitlement*

To add an end-user entitlement, follow the steps described:

1. On the **Add Entitlements** screen, click the Add button.

2. You will see the **Find User or Group** screen.

3. In the **Type** section, check the box or boxes to select what you are going to search for. You can choose **User**, **Group**, or **Unauthenticated Users**.

4. In the **Domain** box from the drop-down menu, select the domain in which you want to search. In this example, we are using the pvolab.com domain.

5. Next, you have a couple of filters to help refine the search.

6. In the **Name/Username** box, you can type in the name or part of the name you want to search for. First, select the filter for the search. You have the option of **Contains**, **Starts with**, or **Is exactly**. In this example, we have selected Contains.

7. Then in the box next to the filter option, enter the name or part of the name you are searching for. In this example, we are searching for a name or username that contains **bob**.

8. You can also search based on **Description**, using the same filter process to find the description and entering the description text you want to search for.

9. Now click the **Find** button. The following screenshot shows the options and results:

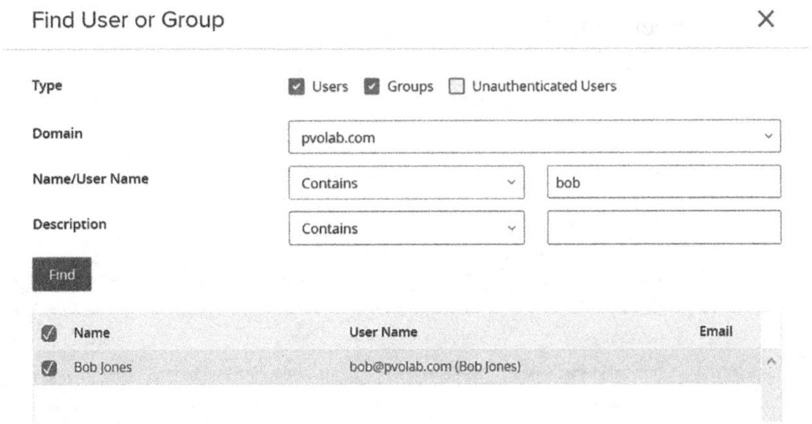

Figure 12-51. *Finding a user or group to entitle*

10. From the results box, check the box for the user you want to select. In this example, the user is Bob Jones.

11. Click the **Next** button to continue. You will see the following screenshot:

Figure 12-52. *Adding the end user*

12.   Click **OK** to add the user to the desktop pool.

13.   You will see a message pop up confirming that the user has been successfully added.

14.   You will now return to the **Desktop Pools** screen, where you will see that the desktop pool has been created, as shown in the following screenshot:

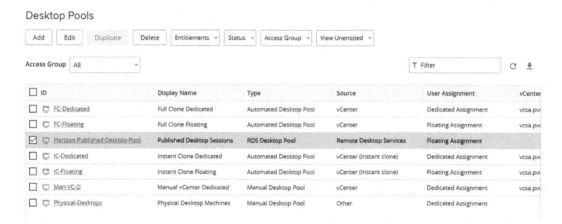

Figure 12-53. *RDS desktop pool successfully created*

With the farm created and configured, the application pool configured, and an end user entitled to use the applications, the next step is to log in and check that the apps are available to launch.

To do this, follow the steps described:

15. Launch the Horizon Client and add the Connection Server if you have not already done so. We will cover this in more detail in Chapter 13 when we explore the client options.

The following screenshot shows the Connection Server **Horizon-8.pvolab.com** added.

Figure 12-54. *Launching the Horizon Client*

16. Double-click the icon for **Horizon-8.pvolab.com**.

17. You will now see the **Login** box.

18. The **Server** information will have already been added, so in the **User Name** box, type in the name of the user that has been entitled to use this desktop pool.

In this example shown, it is the user Bob Jones, as displayed in the following screenshot:

Login		—	□	×
Server:	🔒 https://Horizon-8.pvolab.com			
User name:	bob@pvolab.com			
Password:				
		Cancel	Login	

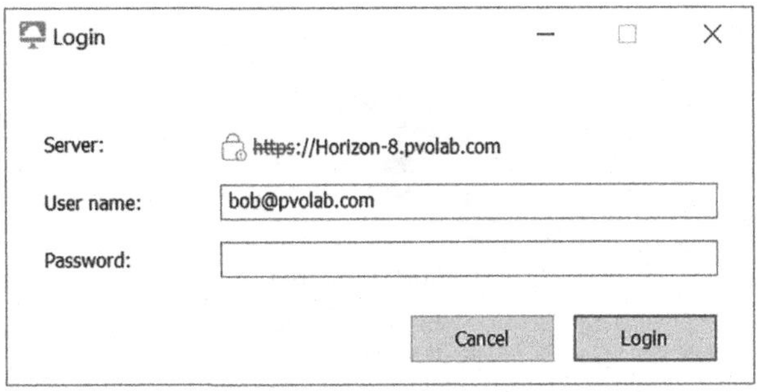

Figure 12-55. *Log in to the Horizon Client*

19. In the **Password** box, type in the password for the end user and click the **Login** button.

You will see the following screenshot, showing the resources available to this particular end user. As you can see, there is a Full Clone floating VDI desktop, VLC Media Player delivered as a published app, and the Published Desktop Session icon as shown:

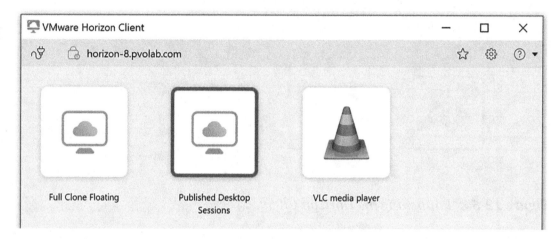

Figure 12-56. Horizon Client showing entitled resources

20. Double-click the **Published Desktop Sessions** icon.

21. You will see the **Loading Desktop...** screen, as shown in the following screenshot:

Figure 12-57. Connecting to a published desktop

22. Once connected, you will see the desktop session displayed, as shown in the following screenshot:

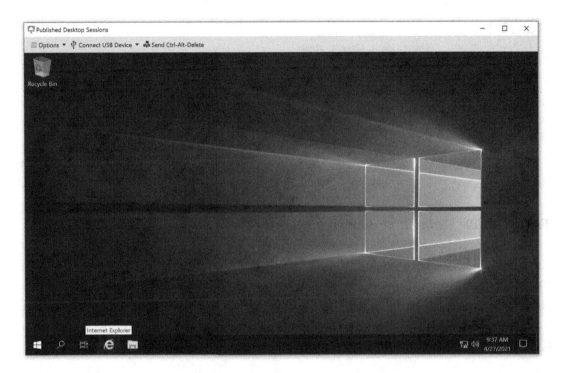

Figure 12-58. *Published desktop session*

You have now successfully tested that the RDS desktop pool works, and the end user can launch a desktop session.

In the next section, we are going to look at how to configure load balancing by using the custom script options.

Load Balancing with Custom Scripts

The other alternative to the threshold load balancing settings is to use a custom script to monitor the utilization.

You can create your own scripts; however, there are a couple of example scripts you will find that were installed as part of the Horizon Agent installation. These example scripts, one for CPU and one for memory, can be found in the following folder:

C:\Program Files\VMware\VMware View\Agent\scripts

These are shown in the following screenshot:

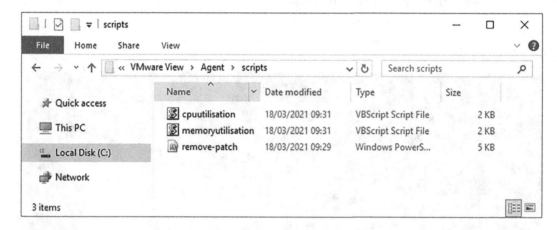

Figure 12-59. *Example custom scripts*

To install these scripts and configure them is a two-part process. The first part is to enable the VMware Horizon View Script Host feature, which is one of the VMware Horizon services that are installed and disabled as part of the Horizon Agent installation.

In the next section, we are going to enable that service on the RDSH host server that is part of the **Horizon-Published-Desktops** farm.

Enable Script Host Service

In order to run the scripts that are going to be used as part of the utilization monitoring for load balancing custom scripts, the first task is to enable the VMware Horizon View Script Host service.

To do this, follow the steps described:

1. Open a console or log on to the RDSH Server, then launch a Run dialog box by pressing the Windows Key and R. You will see the following screenshot:

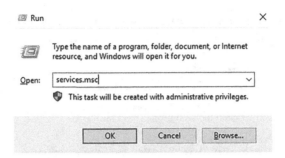

Figure 12-60. *Launching the Services manager*

2. In the **Open** box, type **services.msc** and click the OK button.

3. The Services screen will launch, as shown in the following
    screenshot:

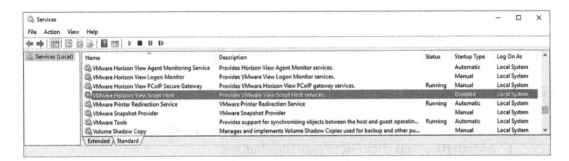

Figure 12-61. *Services managerscreen*

4. Navigate to the **VMware Horizon View Script Host** service, then
    click to select it, as highlighted in the preceding screenshot.

5. Now right-click and select **Properties**.

6. You will see the **VMware Horizon View Script Host Properties
    (Local Computer)** configuration screen, as shown in the
    following screenshot:

Figure 12-62. *VMware Horizon View Script Host service properties*

7. In the Startup type drop-down menu, select the option for **Automatic**, then click **OK** to save the changes.

8. Then to start the service now, right-click the service again and select **Start**.

You have now successfully enabled the VMware Horizon View Script Host service on the RDSH Server.

In the next section, we are going to add one of the example scripts to the configuration to be used as a custom script.

Configure the Script to Run

In this section, we are going to configure one of the example scripts to run on the RDS host server. For this example, we are going to use the CPU utilization script.

To do this, follow the steps described:

1. If you do not have the console open from the previous section, then open a console or log on to the RDSH.

2. From the desktop of the RDSH Server, launch the Registry Editor. To do this, first press the Windows Key and R. You will see the following screenshot:

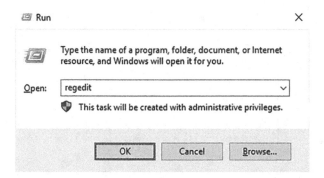

Figure 12-63. *Launching the Registry Editor*

3. In the **Open** box, type **regedit** and click the **OK** button.

4. The Registry Editor will launch.

5. In the Registry Editor, navigate to the following location:

HKEY_LOCAL_MACHINE\SOFTWARE\VMware, Inc.\VMware VDM\ScriptEvents

6. Then click the **RdshLoad** key. You will see in the right-hand pane that there is already a key string, as shown in the following screenshot:

Figure 12-64. *Registry Editor*

7. Next, we are going to enter a new string value for adding the
    custom script. To enable this, in the right-hand pane, right-click
    somewhere on the blank area of the screen. But do not right-click
    the existing string, as this will edit this string.

8. From the contextual menu that pops up, move the mouse to
    highlight **New ➤**, then from the expanded menu options, select
    the option for **String Value**, as shown in the following screenshot:

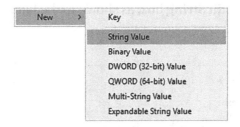

Figure 12-65. *Adding a new string value*

9. The new string will be created, and you will be prompted to enter a name. In this example, we have called this new string **CPU_Utilization** to reflect the fact that this script will be used to measure the CPU utilization, as shown in the following screenshot:

Name	Type	Data
ab (Default)	REG_SZ	(value not set)
ab CPU_Utilization	REG_SZ	

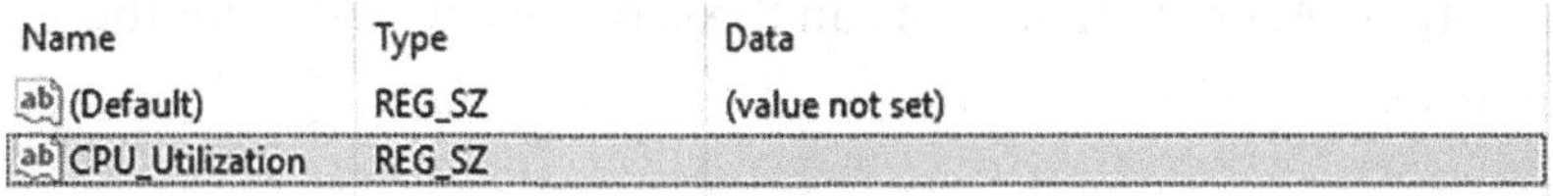

Figure 12-66. *Naming the new string value*

10. Now right-click the new **CPU_Utilization** string; from the contextual menu, select the option for **Modify...** as shown in the following screenshot:

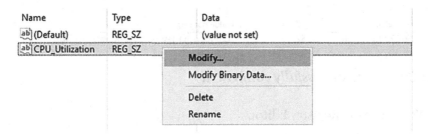

Figure 12-67. *Modifying the new string*

11. You will see the **Edit String** box, as shown in the following screenshot:

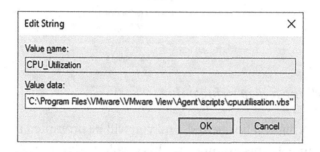

Figure 12-68. *Adding the value data to the string*

12. In the **Value data** box, enter the command to invoke the script and the path to the script. In this example, the VBS script is located in the Horizon Agent folder, so to run the script, we would enter the following:

```
cscript.exe "C:\Program Files\VMware\VMware View\Agent\scripts\
cpuutilisation.vbs"
```

13. Click **OK** to save the changes and to return to the Registry Editor screen. You will see that the new string has been successfully added, as shown in the following screenshot:

Name	Type	Data
(Default)	REG_SZ	(value not set)
CPU_Utilization	REG_SZ	"C:\Program Files\VMware\VMware View\Agent\s...

Figure 12-69. *String successfully configured*

14. Now close the Registry Editor.

15. Finally, now restart the Horizon Agent so the new script is executed.

16. To do this, launch the Services management screen if you do not still have it open.

17. Scroll down until you find the entry for **VMware Horizon View Agent**, and click to select it.

18. Now right-click the **VMware Horizon View Agent** service, and from the contextual menu, click **Restart**, as shown in the following screenshot:

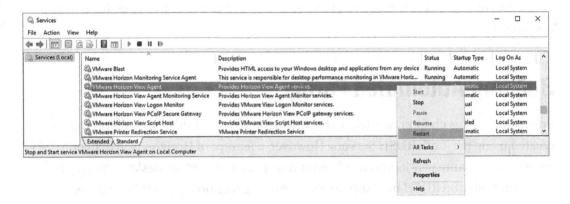

Figure 12-70. *Restarting the Horizon Agent*

The final step is to edit the farm settings and to update the load balancing settings to reflect the new custom script option.

To do this, follow the steps described:

1. Log in to the Horizon Console as an administrator.

2. From the left-hand navigation pane, expand the option for **Inventory**, then click **Farms**.

3. Click the link to the **Horizon-Apps-Farm**, then on the **Summary** screen, click the **Edit** button.

4. Finally, click the **Load Balancing Settings** tab as shown:

Edit Farm - Horizon-Apps-Farm	×
Farm Settings	Load Balancing Settings

Use Custom Script   ☑ Enabled   ⓘ

Include Session Count   ☐ Enabled   ⓘ

Figure 12-71. *Editing the farm settings*

5. To enable the custom script feature, check the **Use Custom Script** box.

6. Click **OK** to save the changes and close the Horizon Console.

You have now successfully configured a custom script for load balancing based on CPU utilization.

In the next section, we are going to look at how to build an automated farm using Instant Clones.

Building Automated Farms

Previously, in this chapter, we discussed how to build a manual farm – a farm that is created using pre-built RDSH Servers. However, a feature of Horizon is to deliver RDSH Servers in the same way as you would with non-persistent virtual desktop machines. That is to build the RDSH host servers using cloning technology, in this case, Instant Clones.

As with any other Instant Clone, you would build the server OS image and configure the RDSH role on the server. This would become your gold image from which to deploy servers.

Then, as you create and build additional RDSH host servers using Instant Clones, as they boot, the RDS role is already installed and configured. It means that farms can be quickly and easily scaled as you do not need to install the OS and then configure the RDS role each time you add a server.

To set up automated RDSH Servers in Horizon, follow the steps described:

1. Log in to the Horizon Console using an administrator account.

2. From the left-hand menu pane, expand the option for **Inventory** and then click **Farms**, as shown in the following screenshot:

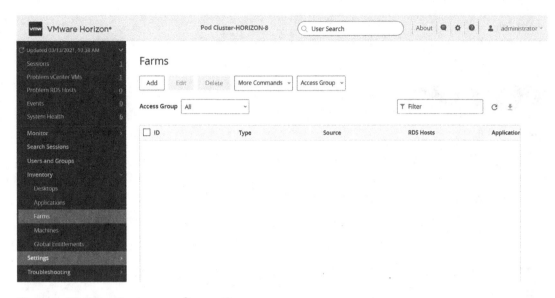

Figure 12-72. *Farms configuration screen*

3. Click the **Add** button.

4. You will see the **Add Farm** configuration screen and the first section for **Type**, as shown in the following screenshot:

Figure 12-73. *Adding an automated farm*

5. Click the radio button for **Automated Farm**.

6. Now click the **Next** button to continue to the next configuration section for **vCenter Server**, as shown in the following screenshot:

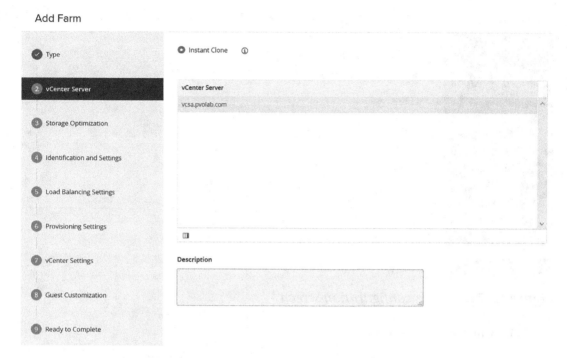

Figure 12-74. *Adding the vCenter to the configuration*

7. Select the vCenter Server from the list of those shown. This is the vCenter which is managing the build of the Instant Clone RDSH Servers in the farm.

8. Click the **Next** button to continue to the next configuration section for **Storage Optimization**, as shown in the following:

Figure 12-75. *Storage Optimization configuration screen*

9. Click the radio button to select whether you want to use VSAN. In this example, there is no VSAN, so the **Do not use VMware Virtual SAN** option has been selected. You also have the option to select different datastores for replica and OS disks.

10. Click the **Next** button to continue to the **Identification and Settings** configuration as shown:

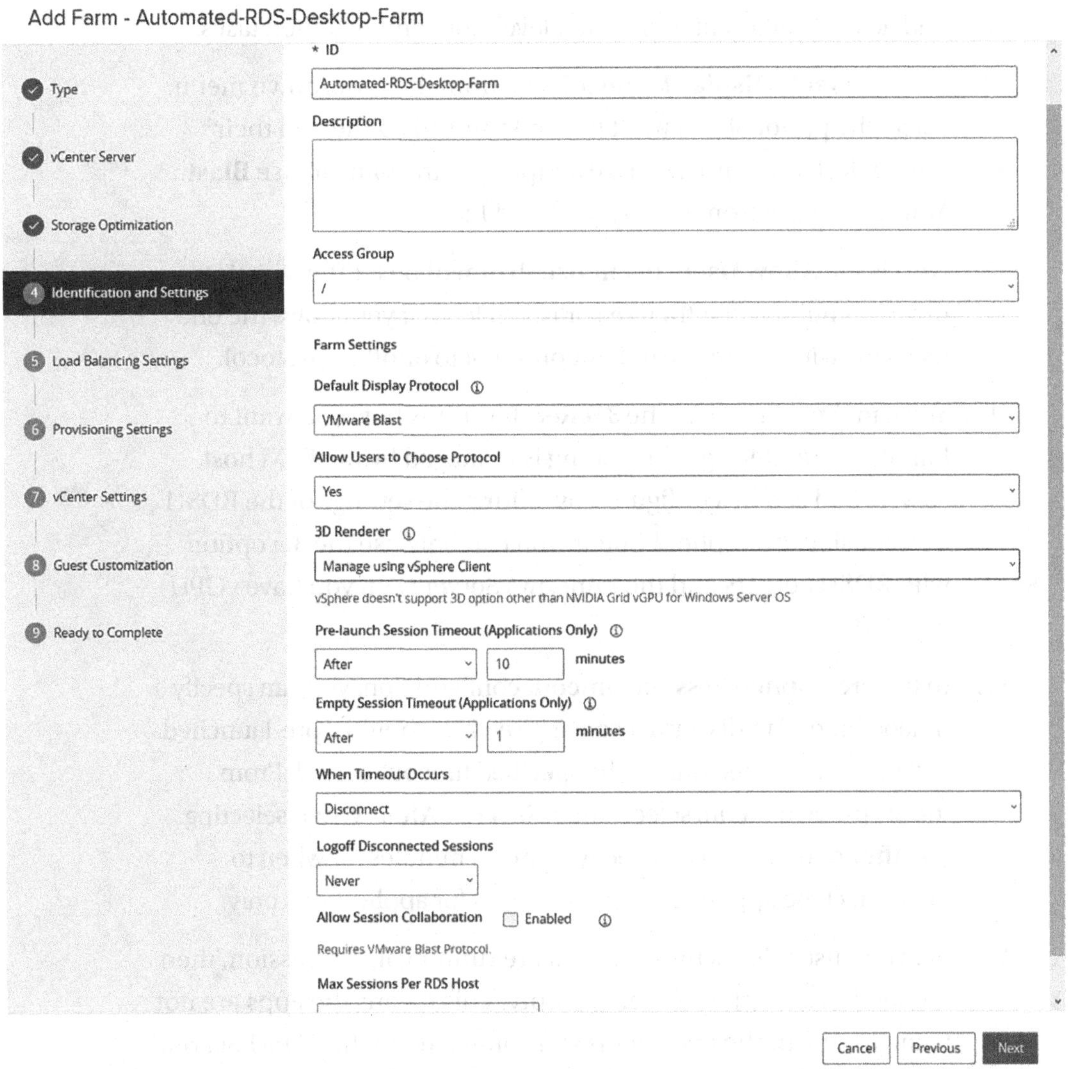

Add Farm - Automated-RDS-Desktop-Farm

Figure 12-76. Identification and Settings screen

11. In the **ID** box, type in the ID you want to use to identify this desktop pool. In this example, we have given the desktop pool the ID of **Automated-RDS-Desktop-Farm**.

12. In the **Description** box, type in a description that represents what this farm is used for.

13. In the **Access Group** drop-down menu, select the access group if you have any configured. Access groups enable you to manage farms and delegate different permission levels for administration tasks.

14. In the **Default Display Protocol** box, from the drop-down menu, select the protocol you want the end users to connect to their virtual desktops with. In this example, we are going to use **Blast**. You can choose from PCoIP, RDP, and Blast.

15. Next is the **Allow Users to choose Protocol** box. From the drop-down menu, select either **Yes** or **No**. Selecting yes allows the end users to switch from the default protocol to another protocol.

16. You can then choose in the **3D Renderer** box how you want to handle 3D rendering. This setting is managed by the ESXi host servers and can be configured by editing the settings of the RDSH Server using the vSphere Client. You can only use the 3D option with RDSH Servers and the Windows Server OS if you have vGPU enabled.

17. In the **Pre-Launch Session Timeout** configuration, you can specify a timeout period to disconnect an app session, should a pre-launched app not be launched during the specified timeout period. From the drop-down menu, select either **Never** or **After**. When selecting the **After** option, you can specify a time in minutes for when to disconnect the app session. This option is for applications only.

18. If an end user closes the apps that are running in the session, then the session is marked as being empty. This means the apps are not being used, but the end user is still connected to the RDSH Server. The **Empty Session Timeout** setting allows you to specify a time to wait before actioning the **When Timeout Occurs** setting, which we will look at next.

19. When the **Empty Session Timeout** configured time has elapsed, the **When Timeout Occurs** setting will either **Disconnect** the end user or perform a **Log Off**. Select one of these options from the drop-down menu. Again, this setting is for applications.

20. Next is the **Logoff Disconnected Sessions** setting. With this setting, you can choose what to do with sessions that get disconnected.

    These are sessions where the connection between the end user and the app session drops rather than the end user logging out. This could be down to an unstable network connection or the user being mobile.

    From the drop-down menu, you can select from the following options:

    - **Never**: Even though disconnected, the end user's session stays active.

    - **After**: Allows you to specify a time in minutes to wait before the end user then gets logged out.

    - **Immediate**: The end user will be logged out at the same time as they disconnect.

21. The penultimate setting is for **Allow Session Collaboration**. Check the box to enable this setting, which means end users can invite others to the same session. This only works when using Blast as the display protocol.

22. Finally, you can configure the **Max Sessions per RDS Host** setting to define the maximum number of sessions this host server will deliver. The default setting is 150 sessions.

23. Once configured, click the **Next** button to continue.

24. You will now see the **Load Balancing Settings** configuration screen.

25. The first option on this configuration screen is for **Use Custom Script**. This allows you to use your own script to calculate resources.

26. The next option is for **Include Session Count**. Enabling this feature, by checking the box, means that load balancing will be performed on the number of active sessions for each server. This means that the next end user to log in will be directed to the server that is running the lower number of sessions.

27. The Load Balancing Settings are shown in the following:

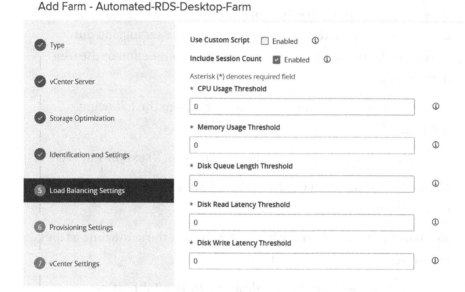

Figure 12-77. *Identification and Settings screen*

28. The next group of settings allow you to configure specific thresholds for CPU, memory, and disk:

- CPU Usage Threshold

- Memory Usage Threshold

- Disk Queue Length Threshold

- Disk Read Latency Threshold

- Disk Write Latency Threshold

29. Click **Next** to continue.

30. You will now see the next step for **Provisioning Settings**, as shown in the following screenshot:

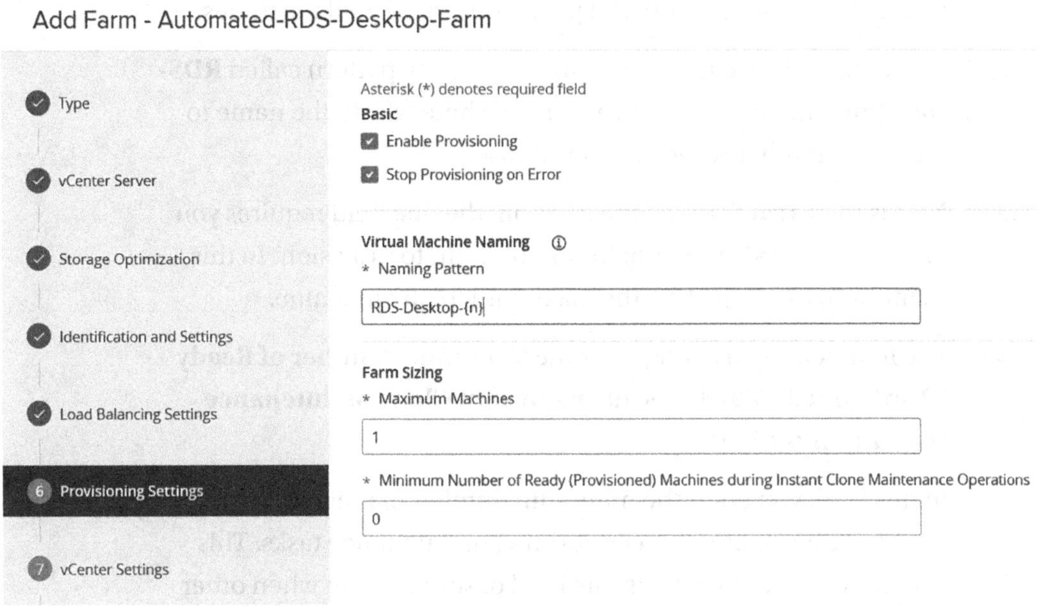

Add Farm - Automated-RDS-Desktop-Farm

Figure 12-78. *Provisioning Settings*

31. Check the **Enable Provisioning** box to allow the RDSH Servers to be provisioned. This means that the virtual RDSH Server machines will be built and provisioned once you have finished the farm configuration.

32. The other check box is for **Stop Provisioning on Error**. If this setting is enabled and Horizon detects an error while the virtual RDSH Servers are being provisioned, then provisioning will stop.

This is an important feature when provisioning large numbers of virtual server machines. You would want provisioning to stop rather than continue to provision hundreds of potentially faulty servers.

In this example, we have checked this box.

33. The next section of provisioning configuration is for **Virtual Machine Naming**.

825

34. In the **Naming Pattern** box, type in the names you would like to call the newly created RDSH Servers. By default, the name you type in here will be appended by a unique number generated automatically by Horizon as it provisions the virtual machines.

   In the example, we have configured a naming pattern called **RDS-Desktop-{n}**. The {n} can be used anywhere within the name to place the number wherever you choose.

35. Next is the **Farm Sizing** configuration; the first field requires you to enter the **Maximum Machines** you want to provision. In this example, we have just set the maximum to one machine.

36. The final setting to configure is the **Minimum Number of Ready (Provisioned) Machines during Instant Clone Maintenance Operations** setting.

   In this field, you enter the minimum number of machines you want to be available when performing maintenance tasks. This enables you to deliver the same level of service even when other machines are effectively offline.

37. Click the **Next** button to continue.

38. You will now see step 7 for **vCenter Settings**.

   This configuration screen is broken into three steps to configure the following elements:

   - Default Image

   - Virtual Machine Location

   - Resource Settings

This is shown in the following screenshot:

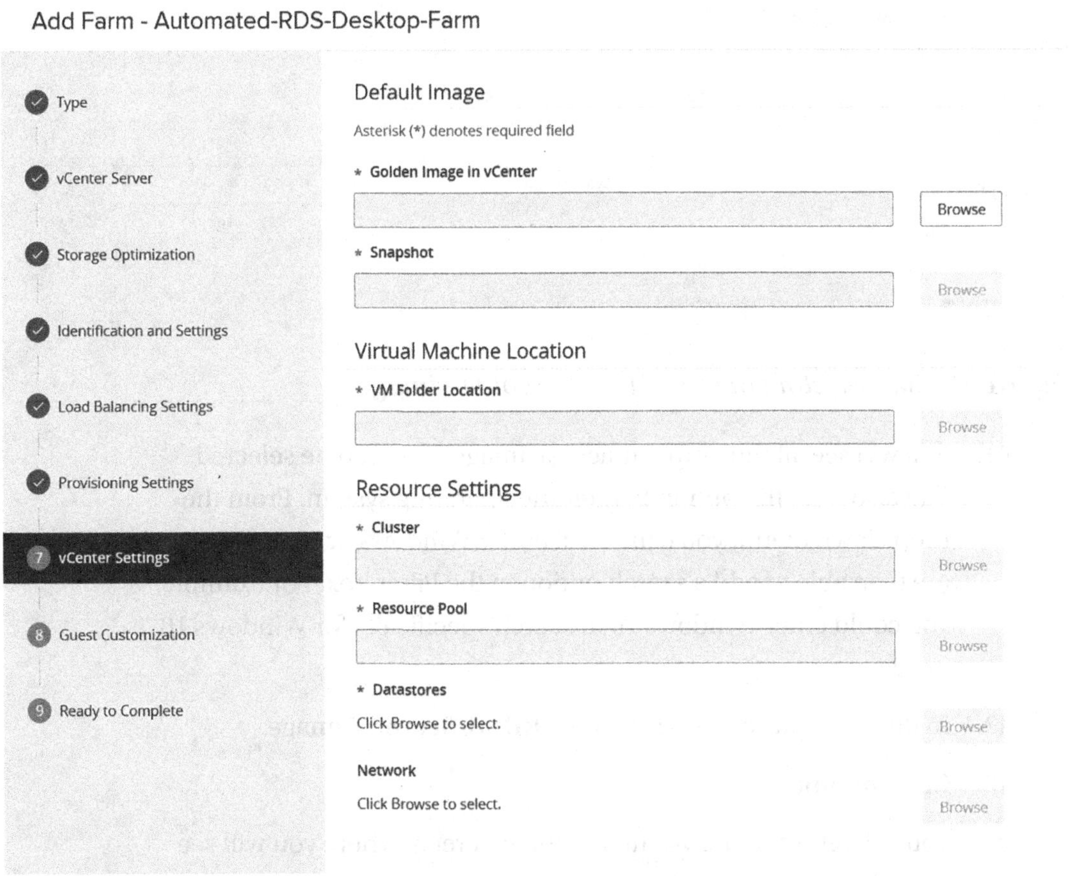

Add Farm - Automated-RDS-Desktop-Farm

Figure 12-79. vCenter Settings

39. Under the **Default Image** heading and the **Golden Image in vCenter** section, click the **Browse** button.

40. You will see the **Select Golden Image** screen, as shown in the following screenshot:

Figure 12-80. *Selecting the RDSH Server golden image*

41.   You will see all the virtual machine images that can be selected. You also have the option to filter the operating system. From the drop-down menu, you can select either Windows or Linux; you are then able to add a search option in the Filter box. For example, you could enter Windows 10 to search specifically for Windows 10 images.

42.   In this example, click to select the **RDSH-Server-1** image.

43.   Click **Submit**.

44.   You will return to the vCenter Settings screen, where you will see the gold image has been added as shown:

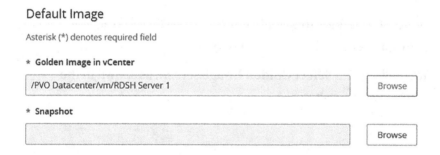

Figure 12-81. *Configuring the golden image snapshot*

45.   The next box is to configure the **Snapshot**, as shown in the preceding screenshot.

46.   In the **Snapshot** field, click the **Browse** button.

47. You will now see the **Select Default Image** screen, as shown in the
     following screenshot:

Figure 12-82. *Selecting the snapshot to use*

48. Click to highlight the snapshot you want to use. In this example,
     there is just one snapshot, **RDSH-Server-Image**, to select from.

49. Now click **Submit**.

50. You will see that the snapshot details have been added, as shown
     in the following:

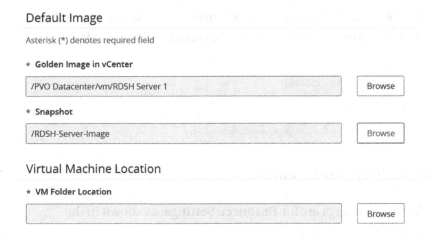

Figure 12-83. *Configuring the VM folder location*

51. The next section heading is for the **Virtual Machine Location**.
     This is the folder in vSphere where the virtual desktop machines
     are going to be stored.

52.   In the **VM Folder Location** box, click the **Browse** button.

53.   You will see the folders listed as shown:

Figure 12-84. *Selecting the VM folder location*

54.   In this example, we are going to expand the **Horizon Desktops** folder, and select the Automated-Farm folder.

55.   Now click the **Submit** button.

56.   You will return to the **vCenter Settings** screen, where you will see that the Virtual Machine Location details have been added:

Figure 12-85. *VM folder location added*

57.   The next settings are for **Resource Settings**, as shown in the following screenshot:

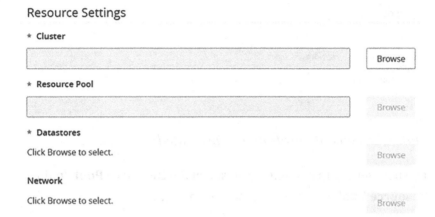

Figure 12-86. *Resource Settings*

58.   In the **Cluster** box, click the **Browse** button. You will see the Select Cluster screen, as shown in the following:

Figure 12-87. *Selecting the cluster*

59.   Select the cluster that you want to provide the resources to run the RDSH Servers, in this example the **Horizon Cluster**, and then click the **Submit** button.

60.   You will return to the **vCenter Settings** screen, where you will see that the cluster details have been added.

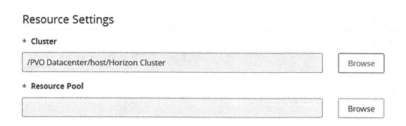

Figure 12-88. *Cluster configuration settings added*

61. The next setting to configure is to select the **Resource Pool**. In the **Resource Pool** field, click the **Browse** button.

62. You will see the **Resource Pool** configuration screen, as shown in the following screenshot:

Figure 12-89. *Selecting the resource pool*

63. Select the cluster you want to deliver the resources to this RDSH Server from, then click the **Submit** button.

64. You will return to the **vCenter Settings** screen where you will see that the resource pool details have been added, as shown in the following screenshot:

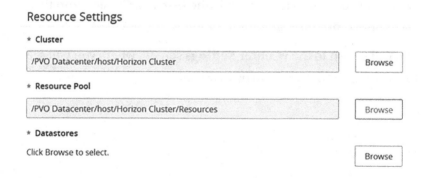

Figure 12-90. *Resource pool added*

65. The next configuration option is for **Datastores**.

66. In the **Datastores** field, click the **Browse** button.

67. You will see the **Select Instant Clone Datastores** configuration screen, as shown in the following:

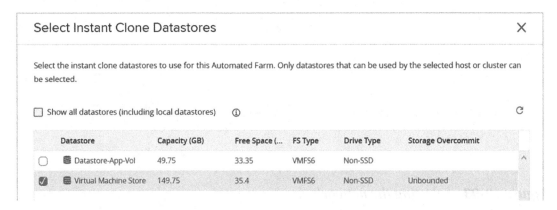

Figure 12-91. *Selecting the datastore*

68. Select the datastore that you want to use, then click the **Submit** button.

69. You will return to the **vCenter Settings** screen, where you will see that the datastore has been selected, as shown in the following screenshot:

Figure 12-92. *Datastore selected*

70. The final setting is for **Network**.

71. In the **Network** field, click the **Browse** button.

72. You will see the **Select Networks** screen, as shown in the following screenshot:

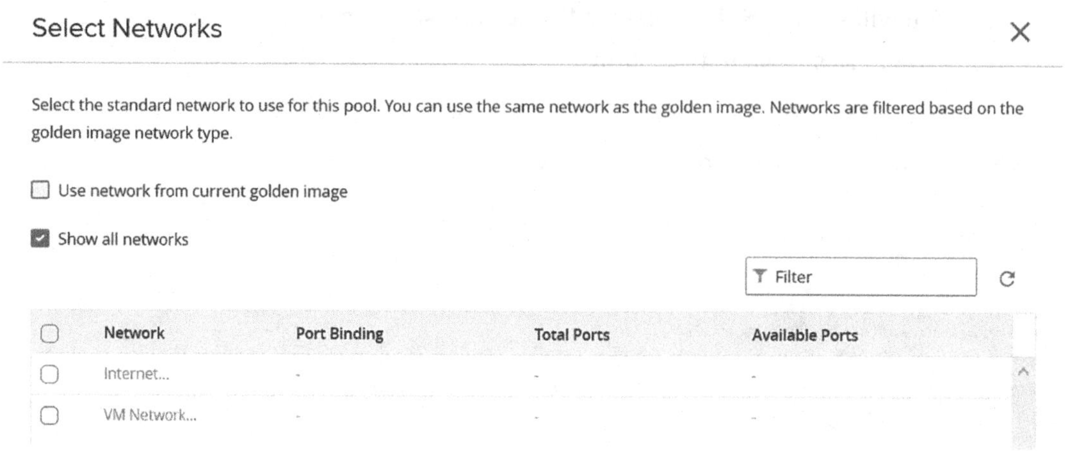

Select Networks   ✕

Select the standard network to use for this pool. You can use the same network as the golden image. Networks are filtered based on the golden image network type.

☐ Use network from current golden image

☑ Show all networks

▼ Filter   ⟳

	Network	Port Binding	Total Ports	Available Ports
☐	Internet...	-	-	-
☐	VM Network...	-	-	-

Figure 12-93. *Selecting the network*

73. On the network configuration screen, you can select to use the same network that was configured with the gold image, or you can select another network to use. To change the network, first uncheck the box for **Use network from current golden image**.

74. If you check the **Show all networks** box, you will see all available networks listed.

75. To select a network, check the box next to the network you want to select, then click **Submit**.

76. You will now see the completed **vCenter Settings** screen:

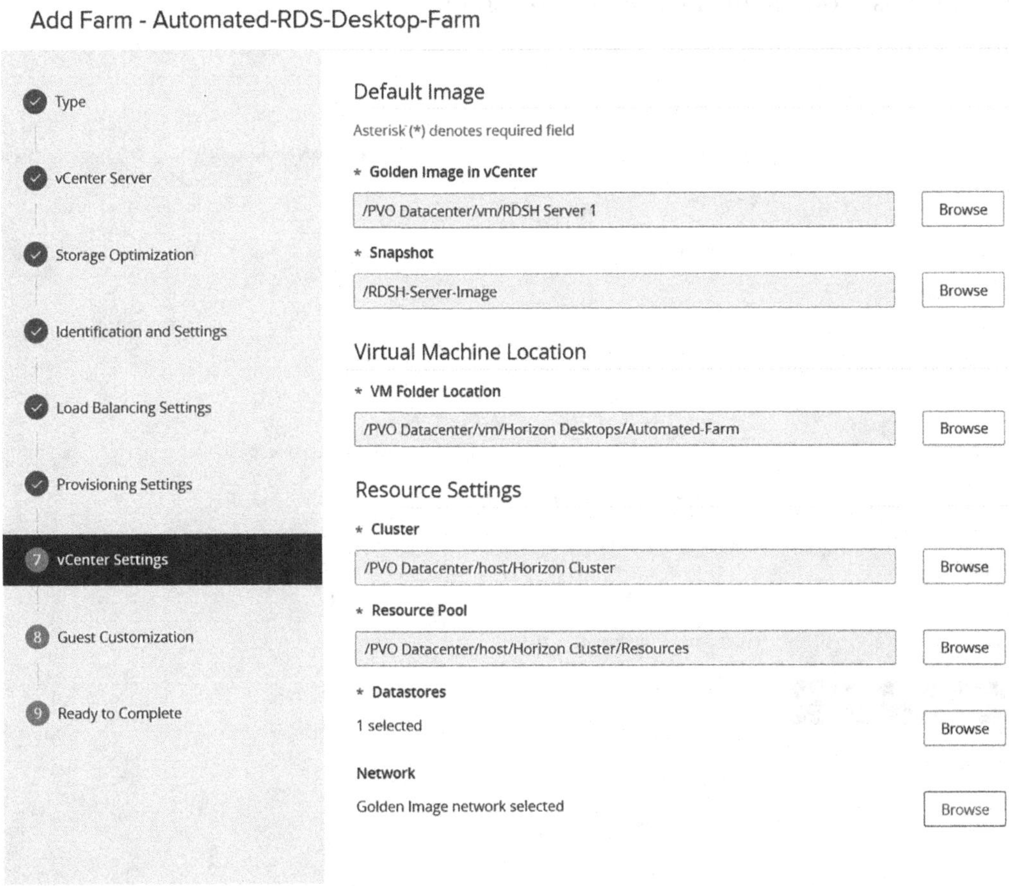

Add Farm - Automated-RDS-Desktop-Farm

✓ Type	**Default Image** Asterisk (*) denotes required field
✓ vCenter Server	* **Golden Image in vCenter**
	/PVO Datacenter/vm/RDSH Server 1 Browse
✓ Storage Optimization	* **Snapshot**
	/RDSH-Server-Image Browse
✓ Identification and Settings	**Virtual Machine Location**
	* **VM Folder Location**
✓ Load Balancing Settings	/PVO Datacenter/vm/Horizon Desktops/Automated-Farm Browse
✓ Provisioning Settings	**Resource Settings**
	* **Cluster**
⑦ vCenter Settings	/PVO Datacenter/host/Horizon Cluster Browse
	* **Resource Pool**
⑧ Guest Customization	/PVO Datacenter/host/Horizon Cluster/Resources Browse
	* **Datastores**
⑨ Ready to Complete	1 selected Browse
	Network
	Golden Image network selected Browse

Figure 12-94. vCenter Settings screen

77. Click the **Next** button.

78. You will now move on to the next step of the configuration for **Guest Customization**.

79. In the **Domain** box, click the drop-down menu and select the domain in which these virtual desktop machines are going to be created. In this example, we are using the pvolab.com domain.

80.   This is shown in the following screenshot:

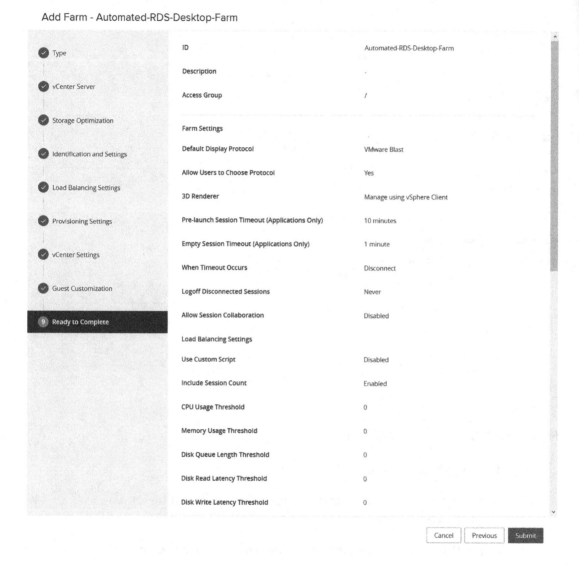

Figure 12-95.   *Ready to Complete screen*

81.   In the **AD container** box, enter the details of the OU in which the virtual machines are going to reside.

82.   You can either type directly into the box or click the **Browse** button to navigate to the desired OU.

83. The next option is the check box for **Allow Reuse of Existing Computer Accounts**. This option requires an additional computer account that resides in the same AD as the Instant Clone desktops themselves.

    Computer accounts are usually created automatically; however, you can use pre-created accounts and the additional computer account we just mentioned.

    If you enable this option, then you add this computer account in the **Image Publish Computer Account** box.

84. The final option of this configuration screen is the **Use ClonePrep** feature.

85. ClonePrep is used to customize the Instant Clone virtual machines as they are created and to ensure that the virtual machines are joined to the domain. New virtual machines will have the same SID as the gold image, and applications will also have the same GUID, as they are part of the gold image.

    ClonePrep gives you the option to run power-off and post-synchronization scripts. Both script options allow you to specify additional parameters. These script names and parameters can be entered in their respective fields.

86. Once you have configured the guest customization features, click the Next button to continue to the final section.

87. You will now see the **Ready to Complete** screen, as shown in the following screenshot:

Add Farm - Automated-RDS-Desktop-Farm

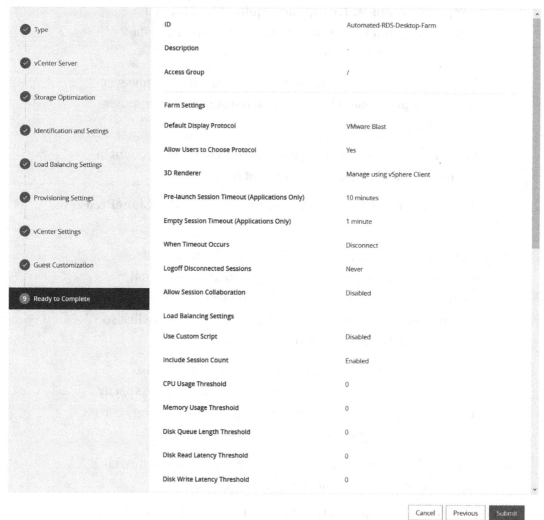

Figure 12-96. *Ready to Complete screen*

88. Once you are satisfied with the configuration, click the **Submit** button to complete the configuration.

89. You will now return to the main **Farms** screen, where you will see that the newly created farm has been added, as shown in the following screenshot:

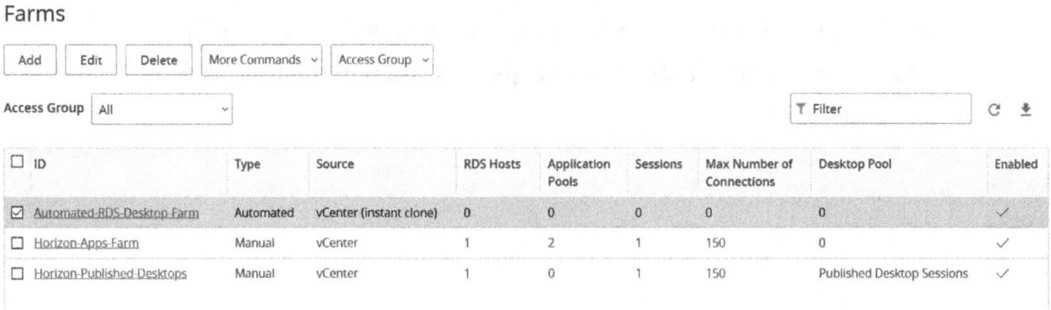

Farms

	Add		Edit		Delete		More Commands ⌄		Access Group ⌄	

Access Group All ⌄   ⊤ Filter   C̄ ⤓

☐ ID	Type	Source	RDS Hosts	Application Pools	Sessions	Max Number of Connections	Desktop Pool	Enabled
☑ Automated-RDS-Desktop-Farm	Automated	vCenter (instant clone)	0	0	0	0	0	✓
☐ Horizon-Apps-Farm	Manual	vCenter	1	2	1	150	0	✓
☐ Horizon-Published-Desktops	Manual	vCenter	1	0	1	150	Published Desktop Sessions	✓

Figure 12-97. *Automated farm successfully configured and added*

You have now successfully created an automated farm that is built using Instant Clones.

In the next section of this chapter, we are going to look at some of the management tasks for existing farms and desktop pools.

Managing Farms and Application Pools

So far in this chapter, we have looked at how to build farms consisting of RDSH Servers and how to configure application pools, so that we can create groups of applications ready to deliver to end users.

In this section, we are going to look at the tasks you can perform on these existing farms and application pools to provide ongoing management and updates.

We are going to start by looking at managing existing farms.

Managing Existing Farms

In this section, we are going to look at the tasks you can perform on existing farms. To do this, follow the steps described:

1. First, log in to the Horizon Console.

2. Now, by navigating using the options from the left-hand menu pane, expand the option for **Inventory**, then click **Farms**.

3. You will see the **Farms** configuration screen which lists the farms within the environment. In this example, we have a single farm called **Horizon-Published-Desktops**, as shown in the following screenshot:

Figure 12-98. *Farms configuration screen*

4. Select the farm you want to manage by checking the box next to the farm name. You will now have access to the icon boxes across the top of the screen. These boxes or buttons provide the following tasks:

- **Add**: Clicking this enables you to add a new farm.

- **Edit**: Opens the edit screen, where you can change the farm settings and load balancing settings.

- **Delete**: Clicking this button will delete the selected farm.

- **More Commands**: If you click this button, you will see several menu options from the drop-down list. These allow you to

- **Disable Farm**: No users can access desktop sessions.

- **Enable Farm**: Enables users to access desktop sessions.

- **Disable Provisioning**: Stops new servers from being created for automated farms.

- **Enable Provisioning**: Enables new servers to be provisioned for automated farms.

These options are shown in the following screenshot:

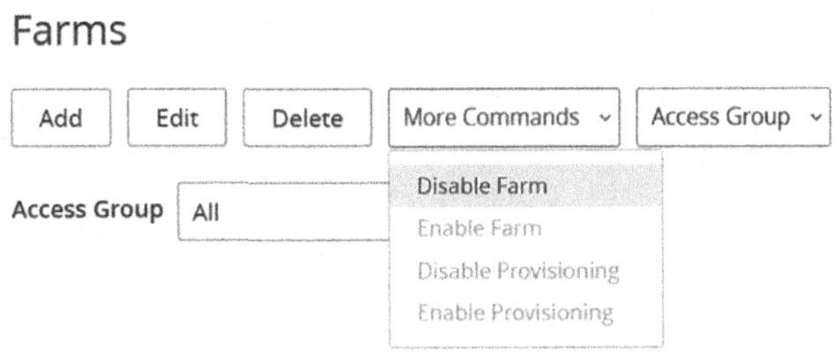

Figure 12-99. *Farms configuration screen with More Commands options*

5. The final button is for **Access Group**, as shown in the following screenshot:

Figure 12-100. *Farms configuring the access group*

6. If you click the **Access Group** button, you will see there are two options. You can create a **New Access Group**, or you can **Change Access Group**.

7. You will have also noticed on the Farms configuration screen that the name or ID of the configured farms in the list appears as links.

8. If you click the **Horizon-Published-Desktops** link, you will see the **Summary** screen showing the details of the farm configuration, as shown in the following screenshot:

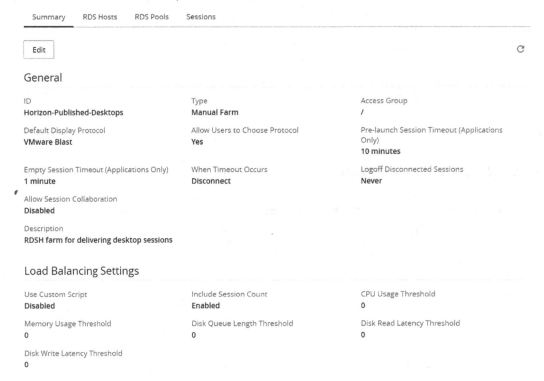

Figure 12-101. *Farms configuration summary screen*

9. Now click the **RDS Hosts** tab.

10. You will see a list of the RDS host servers that are part of this
    particular farm.

    In this example, it is the **rdsh-server.pvolab.com** server, as shown
    in the following screenshot:

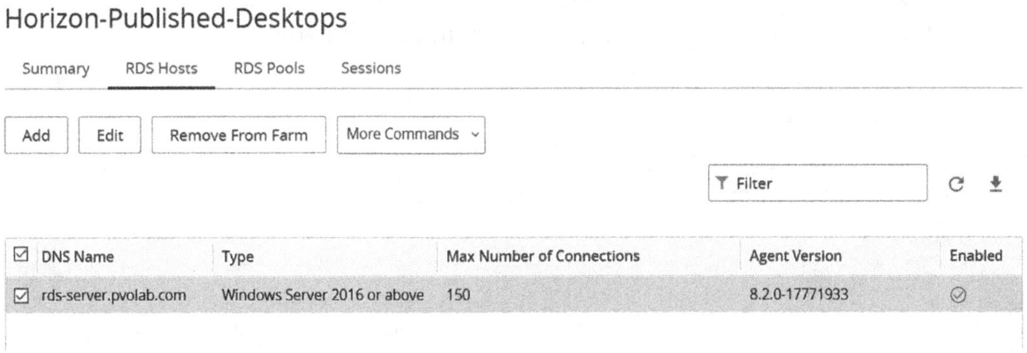
Horizon-Published-Desktops
Summary
RDS Hosts
RDS Pools
Sessions
Add
Edit
Remove From Farm
More Commands
Filter
DNS Name
Type
Max Number of Connections
Agent Version
Enabled
rds-server.pvolab.com
Windows Server 2016 or above
150
8.2.0-17771933

***Figure 12-102.** RDS Host servers in the farm*

11. You will also see that it details the type of server OS, the maximum number of connections the server can support, the Horizon Agent version, and whether the server is enabled.

12. If you check the box to select the RDS host server, you can then perform the following actions using the buttons as described:

- **Add**: Adds another RDS host server to the farm.
- **Edit**: Enables you to edit the server details.
- **Remove**: Removes this host server from the farm.
- **More Commands**: If you click this button, you will see two options from the drop-down list. These allow you to **Enable** or **Disable** the selected host server. These options are shown in the following:

More Commands
Enable
Disable

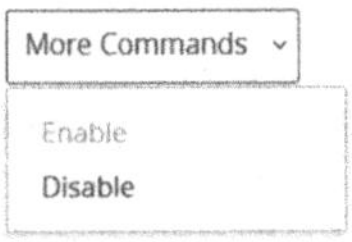

***Figure 12-103.** RDS Host servers More Commands options*

13. The next tab is for RDS Pools.

14.   If you click the **RDS Pools** tab, you will see all the desktop pools
that are assigned to this farm, as shown in the following:

Figure 12-104. Desktop pools

If you want to manage the app pools from here, then simply click the Horizon-
Published-Desktop-Pool link. We will look at managing the desktop pools in the next
section.

15.   Finally, on this farm configuration screen, you have the **Sessions**
tab, as shown in the following screenshot:

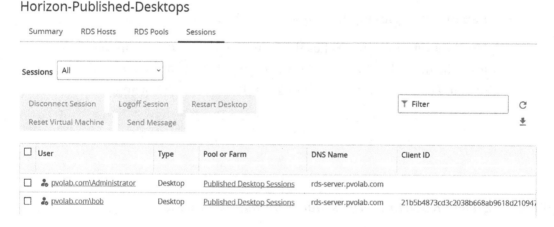

Figure 12-105. Sessions screen

16.   On this screen, you can see the current sessions. In this example,
the user called Bob is currently connected and logged on to a
desktop session.

17. If you click a user under the **User** column, this will take you to
     the Users and Groups screen for this user; if you click the link
     under the **Pool or Farm** column (in this case, Published Desktop
     Sessions), then you will be taken to the farm summary screen for
     the farm you clicked the link for.

18. You also have several other options on this screen. First, select the
     user you want to perform the tasks for. You can then perform the
     following by clicking the corresponding button, as shown in the
     following screenshot:

Figure 12-106. *Performing tasks on a user session*

19. The tasks available to perform are those that are not grayed out
     and perform the following:

- **Disconnect Session**: Disconnects the end user from their current
  session

- **Logoff Session**: Logs the end user out of their current session

- **Restart Desktop**: Restarts the desktop they are currently connected
  to – not applicable to desktop sessions

- **Reset Virtual Machine**: Resets the virtual machine – not applicable
  to desktop sessions

- **Send Message**: Allows you to send the end user a message

20. If you click the **Send Message** button, then you will see the
     following screenshot:

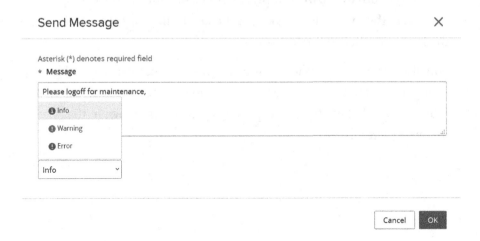

Figure 12-107. *Sending a message to the end user*

21. In the **Message** field, type in the message you want to display to
     the selected end user.

22. Then, in the **Info** drop-down box, select the type of message.
     Choose from either

• Info

• Warning

• Error

23. Click **OK** to send the message.

24. The message will appear as a pop-up message on the end user's
     desktop, sent from the VMware Horizon Administrator, as shown
     in the following screenshot:

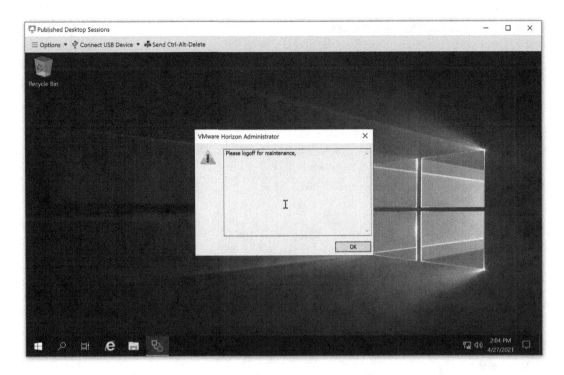

Figure 12-108. Message displayed on the end user's session

25. Now click the **Summary** tab to return to the summary screen, then click the **Edit** button, as shown in the following screenshot:

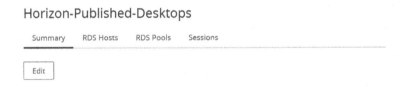

Figure 12-109. Editing the farm configuration

26. You will now see the Farm Settings configuration screen, as shown in the following screenshot:

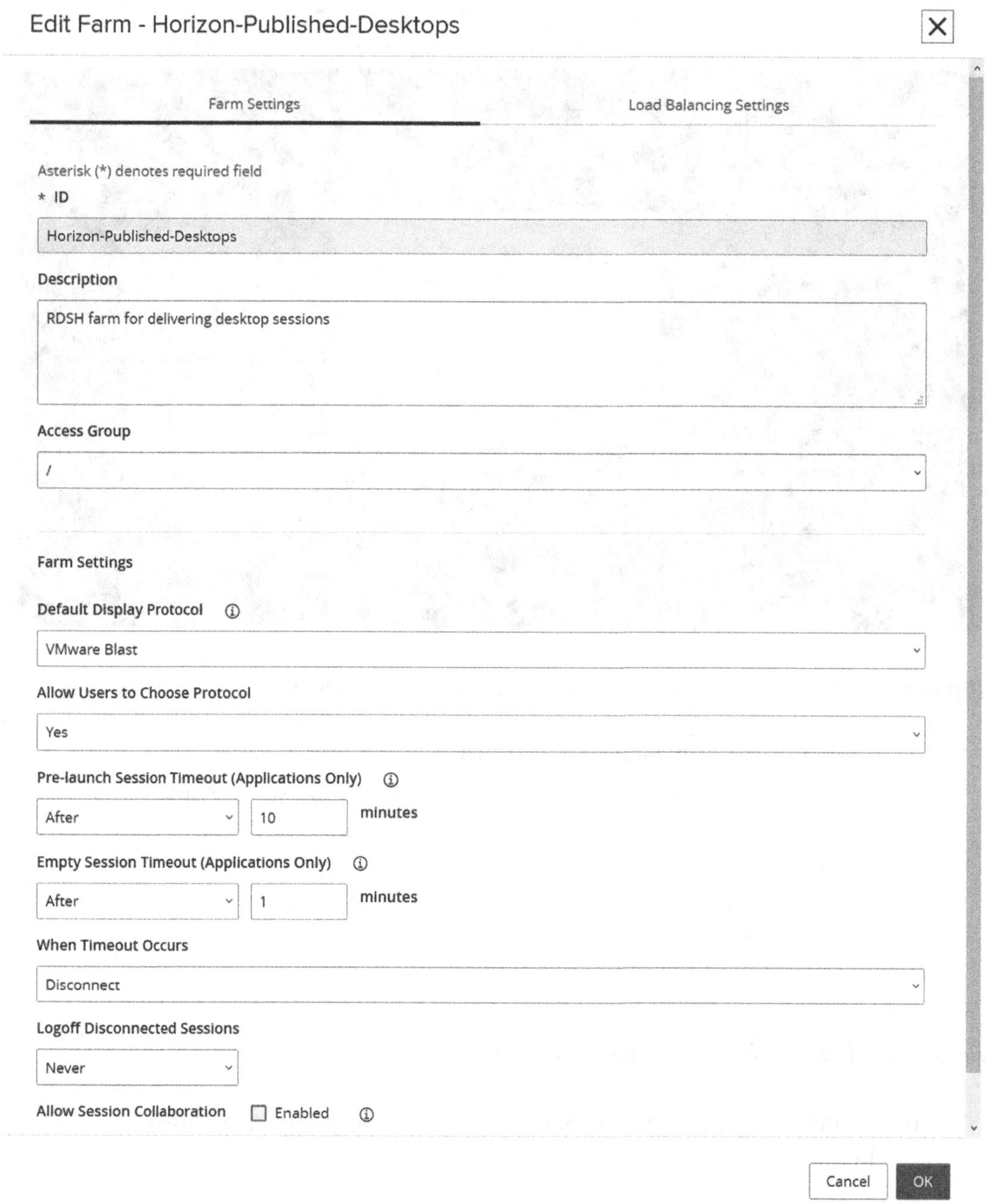

Edit Farm - Horizon-Published-Desktops   ☒

| Farm Settings | Load Balancing Settings |

Asterisk (*) denotes required field

* ID

Horizon-Published-Desktops

Description

RDSH farm for delivering desktop sessions

Access Group

/   ∨

Farm Settings

Default Display Protocol   ⓘ

VMware Blast   ∨

Allow Users to Choose Protocol

Yes   ∨

Pre-launch Session Timeout (Applications Only)   ⓘ

After   ∨   10   minutes

Empty Session Timeout (Applications Only)   ⓘ

After   ∨   1   minutes

When Timeout Occurs

Disconnect   ∨

Logoff Disconnected Sessions

Never   ∨

Allow Session Collaboration   ☐ Enabled   ⓘ

Cancel   OK

Figure 12-110. *Editing the farm settings*

27. You also have another tab for editing the **Load Balancing Settings**, as shown in the following screenshot:

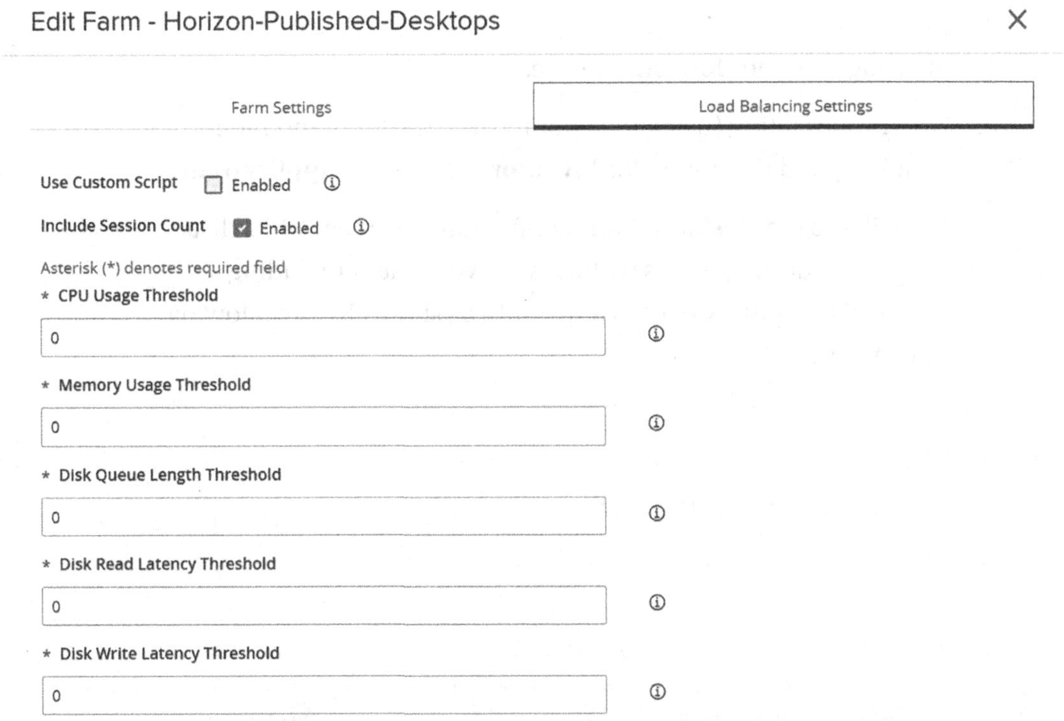

Edit Farm - Horizon-Published-Desktops   ×

Farm Settings	Load Balancing Settings

Use Custom Script   ☐ Enabled   ⓘ

Include Session Count   ☑ Enabled   ⓘ

Asterisk (*) denotes required field

* CPU Usage Threshold

| 0 | ⓘ

* Memory Usage Threshold

| 0 | ⓘ

* Disk Queue Length Threshold

| 0 | ⓘ

* Disk Read Latency Threshold

| 0 | ⓘ

* Disk Write Latency Threshold

| 0 | ⓘ

Figure 12-111. *Editing the farm settings and load balancing*

28. From here, you can edit the **Farm Settings** and the **Load Balancing Settings**.

29. Click **OK** once you have completed your edits.

We have now looked at the various tasks you can perform on existing farms. In the next section, we are going to look at the tasks that you can perform on your existing RDS desktop pools.

RDS Desktop Pool Management

In this section, we are going to look at the tasks that you can perform on existing RDS desktop pools.

1. First, log in to the Horizon Console.

2. Now by navigating (using the options from the left-hand menu pane), expand the option for **Inventory**, then click **Applications**.

3. You will see the **Desktop Pools** configuration screen, which lists the current desktop pools within the environment including both VDI and published desktop pools, as shown in the following screenshot:

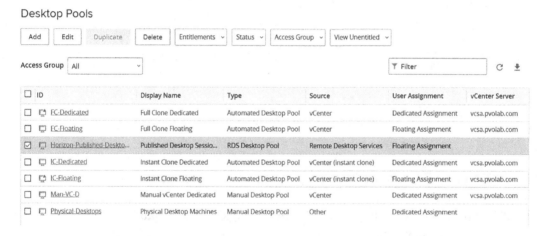

Figure 12-112. *Desktop Pools screen*

4. From the list of desktop pools on this screen, check the box next to the pool you want to perform the task on.

5. You will now see the buttons across the top are now available, each one with a different task you can perform on the selected desktop pool.

6. In this example, we have selected the **Horizon-Published-Desktop-Pool** to edit.

You can now start to perform your management tasks.

Adding a Desktop Pool

We have already covered this option several times throughout this chapter.

To add a new desktop pool, simply click the **Add** button, then complete the associated configuration screens.

Editing an Existing Desktop Pool

To edit an existing RDS desktop pool, check the box next to the pool that you want to change or update, then click the **Edit** button.

You will see the **Edit Pool - Horizon-Published-Desktop-Pool** screen and the **General** settings tab, as shown in the following screenshot:

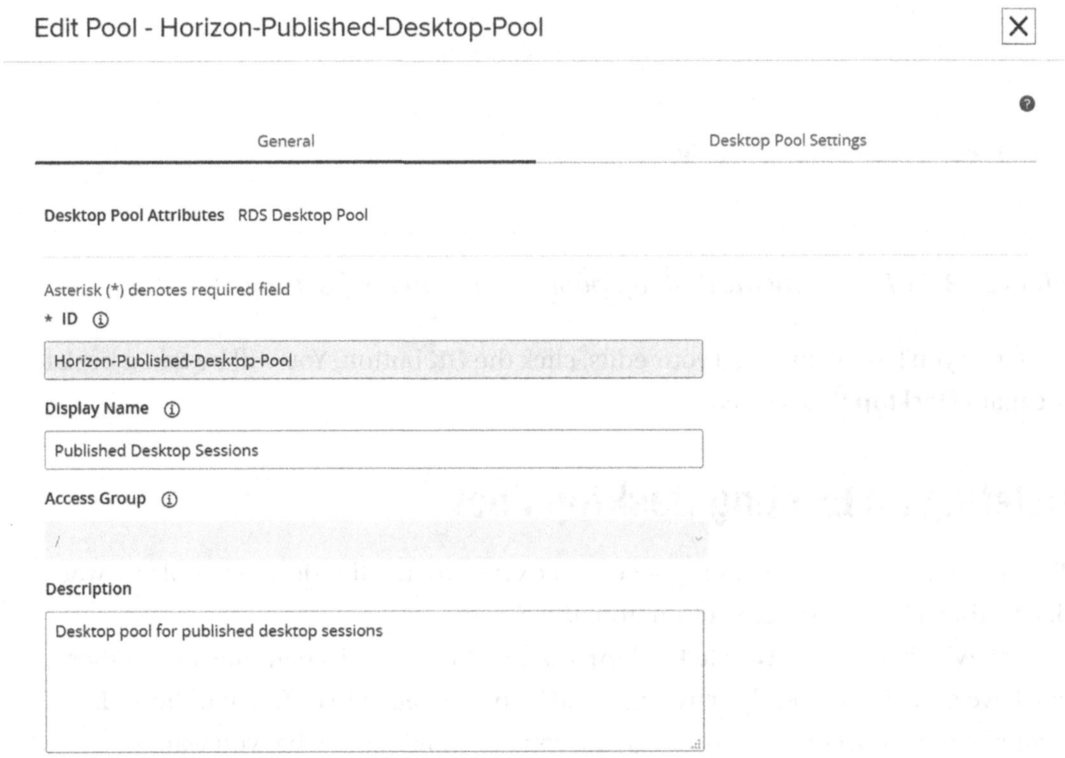

Figure 12-113. *Editing the desktop pools – General settings*

It is worth noting that you cannot edit the ID field.

The second tab is for the Desktop Pool Settings, as shown in the following screenshot:

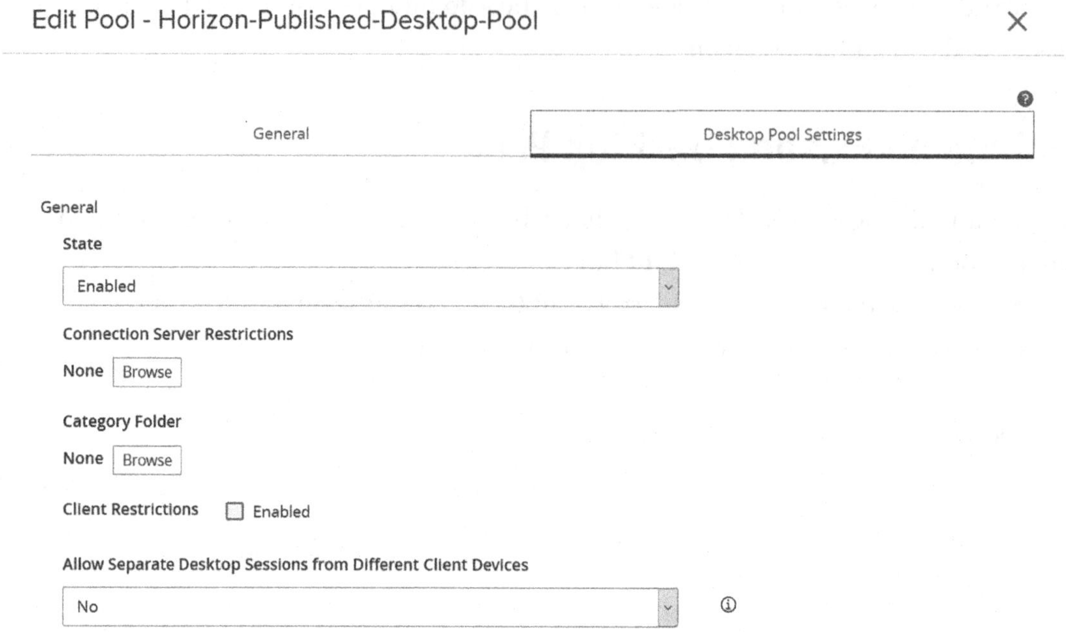

Figure 12-114. *Editing the desktop pools – Desktop Pool Settings*

Once you have completed your edits, click the **OK** button. You will be taken back to the main **Desktop Pools** screen.

Deleting an Existing Desktop Pool

To delete a desktop pool, simply check the box next to the RDS desktop pool you want to delete, then click the **Delete** button from the menu.

You will then see the **Delete Desktop Pool** warning box. Depending on whether you have a session currently active, you will be presented with different options. In this example, there is a current session, giving you the choice as to what you want to do with this session:

- **Leave active**: The session remains active until the end user logs off.

- **Terminate**: The session will be killed immediately.

This is shown in the following screenshot:

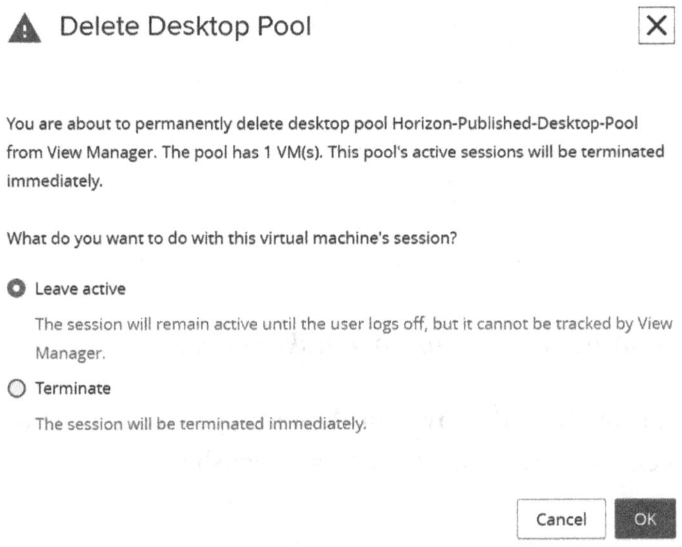

⚠ Delete Desktop Pool   ✕

You are about to permanently delete desktop pool Horizon-Published-Desktop-Pool
from View Manager. The pool has 1 VM(s). This pool's active sessions will be terminated
immediately.

What do you want to do with this virtual machine's session?

🔘 Leave active
      The session will remain active until the user logs off, but it cannot be tracked by View
      Manager.

⚪ Terminate
      The session will be terminated immediately.

                                                        Cancel   OK

Figure 12-115. *Deleting a desktop pool*

If you now click the **OK** button, the RDS desktop pool will be deleted.

Adding and Removing Entitlements

To add or remove an end-user entitlement to a desktop pool, click the **Entitlement** button from the menu, then select either **Add Entitlements** or **Remove Entitlements** from the drop-down menu as shown:

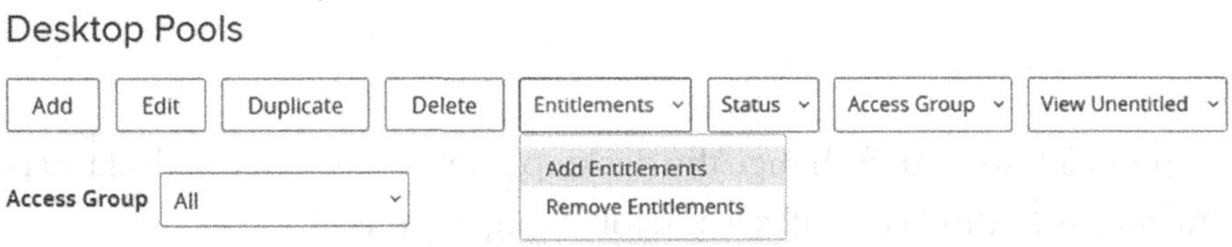

Desktop Pools

| Add | Edit | Duplicate | Delete | Entitlements ⌄ | Status ⌄ | Access Group ⌄ | View Unentitled ⌄ |

Access Group | All ⌄

Add Entitlements
Remove Entitlements

Figure 12-116. *Adding and removing entitlements to a desktop pool*

If you select the option for **Add Entitlements**, then you will see the **Add Entitlements** screen, as shown in the following screenshot:

Add Entitlements
Add new users and groups who can use the selected pool(s).
Add
Remove
Name
Domain
Email

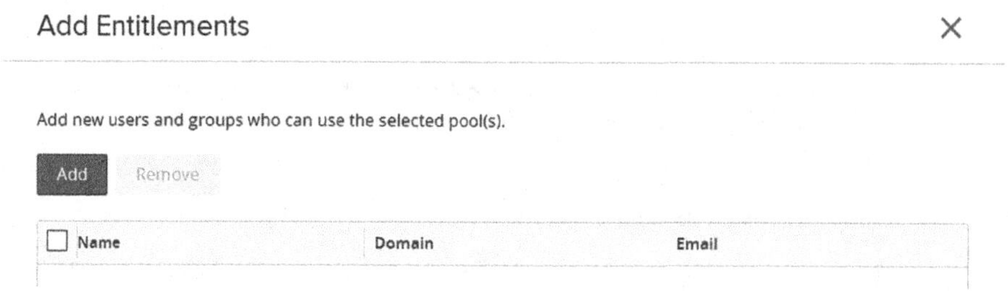

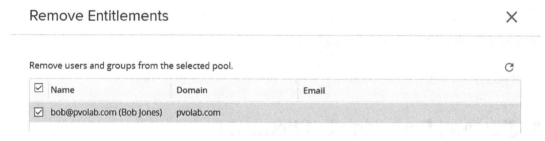

***Figure 12-117.** Adding entitlements to a desktop pool*

If you select the option for **Remove Entitlements**, you will see the **Remove Entitlements** screen, as shown in the following screenshot:

Remove Entitlements
Remove users and groups from the selected pool.
Name
Domain
Email
bob@pvolab.com (Bob Jones)
pvolab.com

***Figure 12-118.** Removing entitlements to a desktop pool*

Check the box next to the end user you want to remove from having access to this desktop pool, then click **OK**.

Status

The status option allows you to change the desktop pool status. Select a desktop pool; if you click the **Status** button, you will see the following options:

Desktop Pools

| Add | Edit | Duplicate | Delete | Entitlements ⌄ | Status ⌄ | Access Group ⌄ | View Unentitled ⌄ |

Access Group | All ⌄ |

Disable Desktop Pool
Enable Desktop Pool
Disable Provisioning
Enable Provisioning

Figure 12-119. *Desktop pool status*

This allows you to disable and enable RDS desktop pools as well as enabling and disabling the provisioning process. With an automated farm, you may want to stop new RDS host servers from being built or to prevent end users from connecting as you are performing other admin tasks on the pools.

Access Group

This option allows you to create a new Access Group for the selected desktop pool or to change the current Access Group to a different one. If you click the **Access Group** button, you will see the two options as shown:

Desktop Pools

| Add | Edit | Duplicate | Delete | Entitlements ⌄ | Status ⌄ | Access Group ⌄ | View Unentitled ⌄ |

Access Group | All ⌄ |

New Access Group
Change Access Group

Figure 12-120. *Editing the access groups*

If you select the **New Access Group** option, you will see the **New Access Group** configuration screen, as shown in the following screenshot:

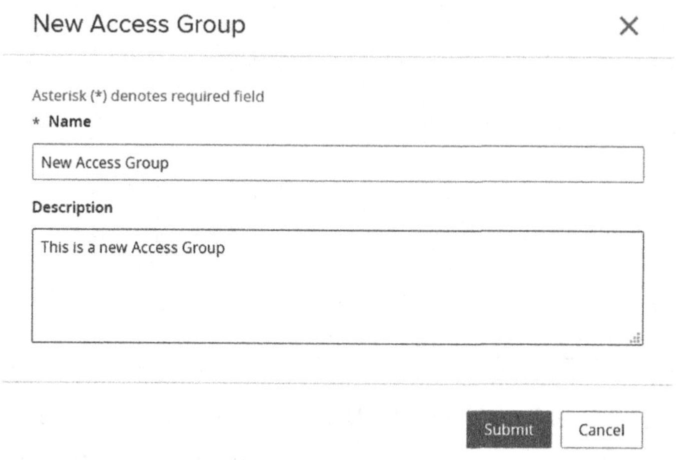

New Access Group   ✕

Asterisk (*) denotes required field
* **Name**

New Access Group

Description

This is a new Access Group

Submit   Cancel

Figure 12-121. *Creating a new access group*

Configure the details for the **Name** and **Description** for this new Access Group, then click the **Submit** button.

If you select the **Change Access Group** option, then you will see the **Change Access Group** configuration screen, as shown in the following screenshot:

Change Access Group   ✕

Access Group

/

/

Test-Group

h

OK   Cancel

Figure 12-122. *Changing to a different access group*

From the **Access Group** drop-down menu, select the Access Group that you want to change to, then click the **OK** button.

View Unentitled

The final option is to view unentitled machines or unentitled policies. If you click the View Unentitled button, then you have the two options as shown in the following screenshot:

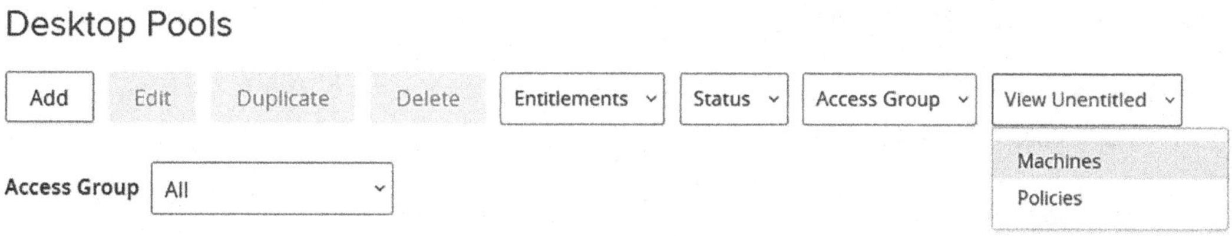

Desktop Pools

| Add | Edit | Duplicate | Delete | Entitlements ⌄ | Status ⌄ | Access Group ⌄ | View Unentitled ⌄ |

| | | | | | | | Machines |
| | | | | | | | Policies |

Access Group | All ⌄ |

Figure 12-123. *Unentitled machines and policies*

If you select **Machines**, you will see the **View Unentitled Machines** screen, where you will see a list of virtual desktop machines that are assigned to end users who are no longer entitled to the desktop pool. This scenario is only seen with desktop pools that have dedicated end-user assignments.

If you select **Policies**, then you will see the **View Unentitled Policies** screen, where you will see a list of policies that are assigned to end users that are no longer entitled to the desktop pool.

In the next section, we are going to cover the other options available, including other ways of displaying the farm and RDS desktop pool information.

Additional Management Tasks

You will have noticed on the main Desktop Pools screen, that as well as checking the box next to the name of the pool you want to edit, the pool ID also appears as a link.

If you click the link for the **Horizon-Published-Desktop-Pool** pool, you will see the following screenshot:

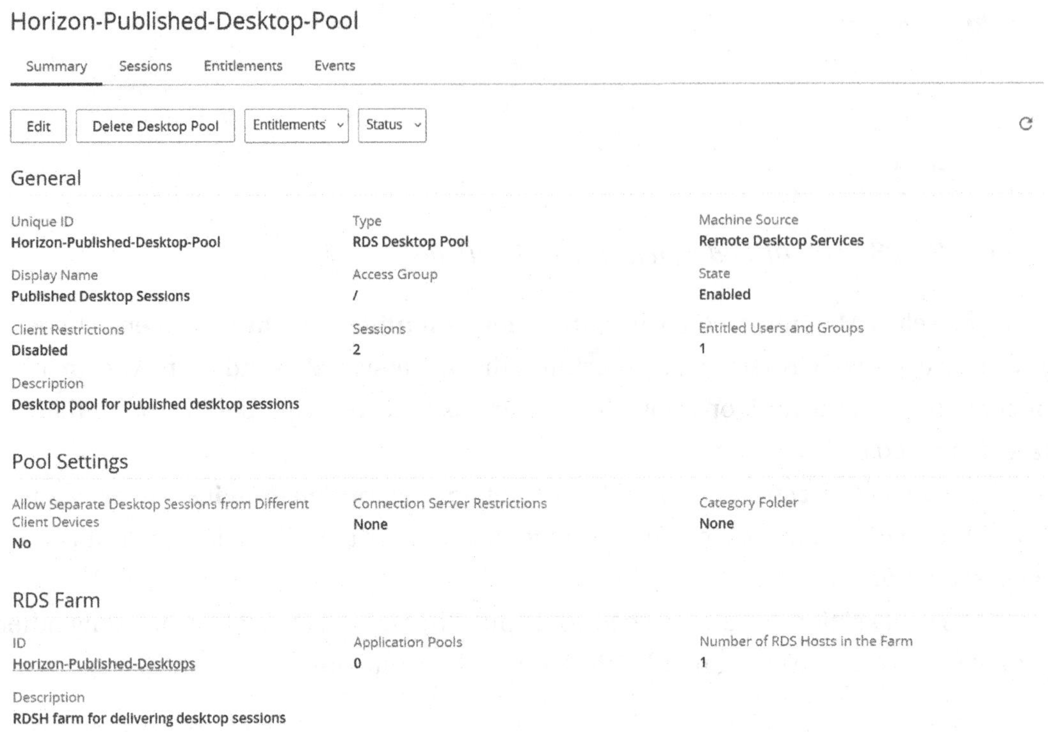

Horizon-Published-Desktop-Pool

Summary   Sessions   Entitlements   Events

| Edit | Delete Desktop Pool | Entitlements ˅ | Status ˅ | | C |

General

Unique ID	Type	Machine Source
Horizon-Published-Desktop-Pool	**RDS Desktop Pool**	**Remote Desktop Services**

Display Name	Access Group	State
Published Desktop Sessions	**/**	**Enabled**

Client Restrictions	Sessions	Entitled Users and Groups
Disabled	**2**	**1**

Description
Desktop pool for published desktop sessions

Pool Settings

Allow Separate Desktop Sessions from Different Client Devices	Connection Server Restrictions	Category Folder
No	**None**	**None**

RDS Farm

ID	Application Pools	Number of RDS Hosts in the Farm
<u>Horizon-Published-Desktops</u>	**0**	**1**

Description
RDSH farm for delivering desktop sessions

Figure 12-124. *RDS desktop pool screen*

You will see across the top that you have the same buttons for **Edit**, **Delete Desktop Pool**, **Entitlements**, and **Status**. There are also tabs for **Summary**, **Sessions**, **Entitlements**, and **Events**. We have already looked at Sessions and Entitlements, but if you click **Events**, you will see the following screenshot:

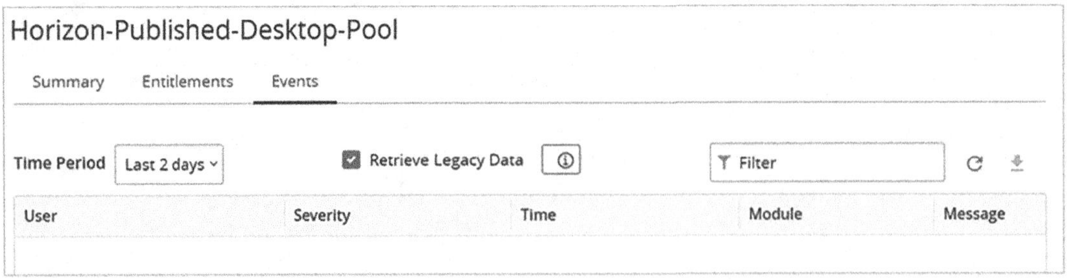

Horizon-Published-Desktop-Pool

Summary   Entitlements   Events

Time Period | Last 2 days ˅ | ☑ Retrieve Legacy Data ⓘ   ▼ Filter   C   ↧

User	Severity	Time	Module	Message

Figure 12-125. *Events tab*

Any events that are listed on this screen are stored in the Horizon events database. You can select a time period to search events, check the box to Retrieve Legacy Data, or filter the data. You also have the option to download the information.

Summary

In this chapter, we have taken a deep dive into delivering published desktop sessions using the Horizon Connection Server and configuring Horizon to broker these desktop sessions. We started the chapter by looking at the design and architecture of the solution and some of the considerations around sizing. From there, we installed and configured the RDSH Server role and prepared the infrastructure for delivering the desktop sessions to the end users. The next steps were to configure the Horizon elements of the solution, the farms and RDS desktop pools, as well as load balancing options. Finally, we looked at some of the options and management tasks that can be performed on existing farms and RDS desktop pools.

In the next chapter, we are going to look at how end users can connect to the applications and desktops using software-based solutions, such as the Horizon Client and web browsers, and also hardware-based solutions such as thin clients and zero clients.

CHAPTER 13

Connecting End Users

So far in this book, we have focused on the infrastructure side of a Horizon environment, such as designing and building out the Connection Servers and creating gold images for delivering virtual desktop machines.

Once the infrastructure was in place, we then started shifting our focus more toward the end user and how to optimize the end-user experience and how to deliver the end-user environment.

With those tasks completed, the next thing we need to look at is how the end user is going to connect to their virtual desktops and applications. By this we mean the type of device they are going to use as an endpoint. The device that will be displaying the screen contents of their virtual desktops and applications and that also provides the feedback via the keyboard and mouse movements.

In this chapter, we are going to look at the different client options available, including the software-based VMware Horizon Clients and hardware-based clients such as thin clients and zero clients, and finally connecting using a browser.

We are also going to take a closer look at the leading solutions from **IGEL** that enable you to take advantage of an OS designed specifically for accessing digital workspace environments. The IGEL solution provides a multi-platform approach that encompasses hardware, software, and the repurposing of existing devices into modern clients. All these are managed from a single management platform.

We will start with the software-based VMware Horizon Clients.

Horizon Clients

In this first section, we are going to discuss the software-based Horizon Clients that an end user will use to connect to their virtual desktops and applications.

© Peter von Oven 2022
P. von Oven, *Mastering VMware Horizon 8*, https://doi.org/10.1007/978-1-4842-7261-9_13

The Horizon Client is installed on the end user's local device and enables them to log on to the Horizon Connection Server, and then, based on the entitlement, the client will display those resources that the end user can connect to. These, as we have seen, can be full virtual desktop machines, published desktop sessions, or published applications.

Once connected and authenticated, the Horizon Client will then display the screen of the desktop or application inside the client. The client is also then responsible for keyboard and mouse interactions between the local device and the virtual desktop or application session as well as redirecting any peripheral devices such as USB web cameras, printers, or scanners.

There are several different clients available for various platforms. The first one we are going to look at in more detail is the Horizon Client for Windows end points.

Horizon Client for Windows

In this section, we are going to focus on the Horizon Client for Windows, its features, and how to install and configure it.

The Horizon Client for Windows is a Windows application that is installed on your Windows end point, such as a Windows desktop or laptop, that then allows you to connect to your Horizon delivered resources.

Using the Horizon Client for Windows ensures that you are going to deliver the best possible user experience as it enables better performance and more features.

In terms of performance, the Horizon Client for Windows takes advantage of the adaptive capabilities of the PCoIP and the VMware Blast display protocols ensuring that they are optimized for delivering the best user experience. Being adaptive ensures that even over low-bandwidth and high-latency network connections, virtual desktops and published applications remain fast and responsive.

The Horizon Client for Windows can be downloaded from the VMware website by following this link:

`https://my.vmware.com/en/web/vmware/downloads/details?download Group=CART22FQ1_WIN_2103&productId=1027&rPId=62295`

The other option is that the Horizon Client for Windows can also be downloaded by the end user if they open a browser and navigate to the address of the Connection Server from their endpoint device.

The end user will be presented with a web page that gives them the options to either **Install VMware Horizon Client** or access their resources using **VMware Horizon HTML Access**. This is shown in the following screenshot:

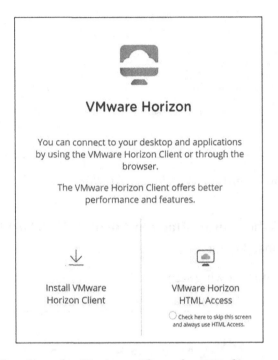

Figure 13-1. *Downloading the Horizon Client for Windows*

Now that we have looked at downloading the Horizon Client for Windows software, in the next section we are going to walk through the installation process.

Installing the Horizon Client for Windows

In this section, we are going to install the Horizon Client for Windows.

To do this, follow the steps described:

1. On the endpoint device you want to use to install the Horizon Client on, to connect to your virtual desktops and apps, navigate to the folder where you saved the downloaded installer file.

2. An example of this is shown in the following screenshot:

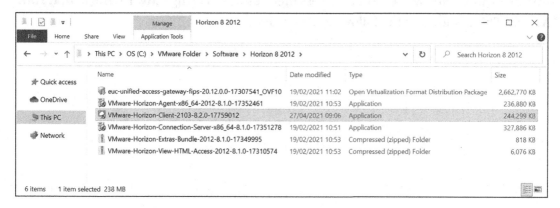

Figure 13-2. *Horizon Client for Windows installer*

3. Double-click the **VMware-Horizon-Client-2103-8.2.0-17759012** application installer file.

4. You will see the following screen:

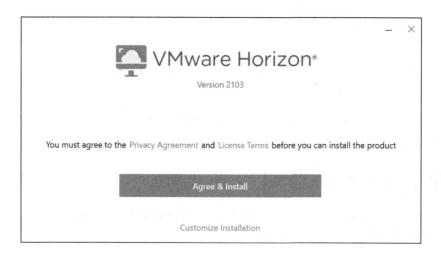

Figure 13-3. *Horizon Client for Windows installer*

5. You can either click the **Agree & Install** button to go ahead and install the Horizon Client with the default settings or click **Customize Installation** to select which features are installed. In this example, we are going to click the customize option. You will see the following screenshot:

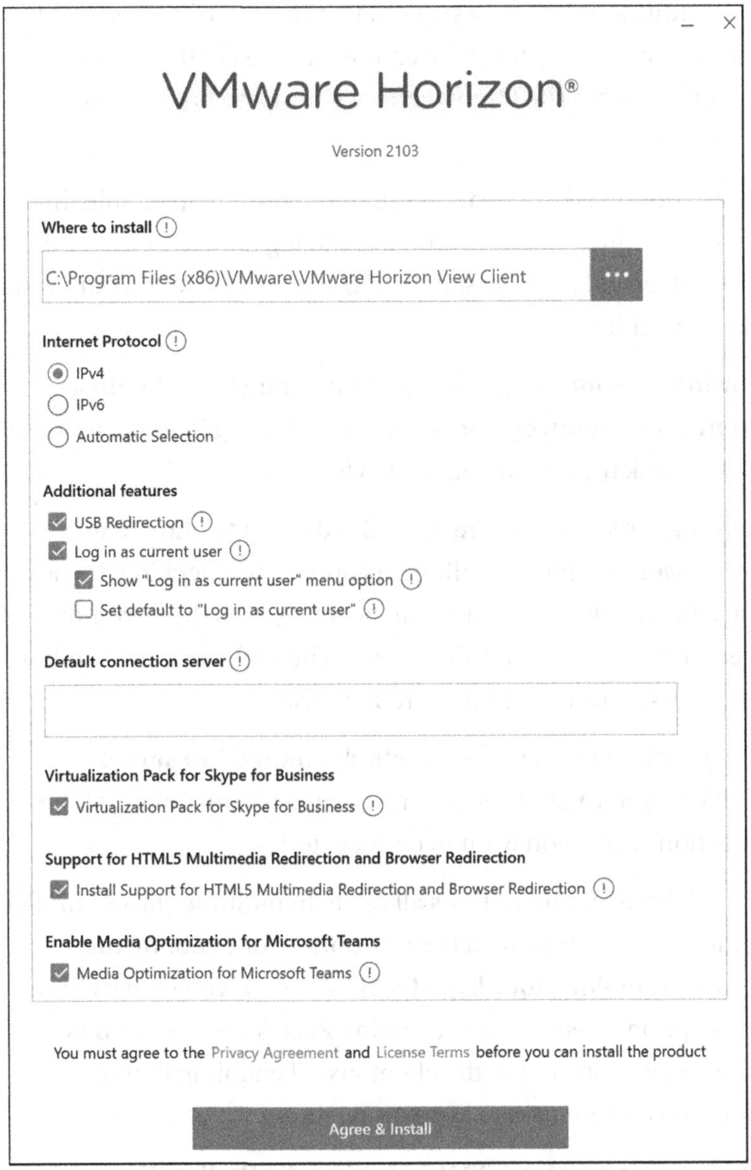

Figure 13-4. *Horizon Client for Windows installer*

6. The first option is **Where to install**. Either leave the default
    location (recommended) or click the **...** and browse to select a
    new folder location.

7. In the **Internet Protocol** section, click the radio button to select
    the protocol to use for the connection.

8. In the **Additional features** section, you can select from several additional features that can be enabled in the client. The first is whether to enable **USB Redirection**. Check the box to enable this feature.

9. The next option is for **Log in as current user**. If you enable this feature, then the credentials you used to log in to the endpoint device will be used, or passed through, as you log in to your virtual desktop machine.

10. Following on from the preceding option, the **Show "Login as current user" menu option** will display the Log in as current user option. Check the box to enable this feature.

11. Finally, in this section, there is the **Set default to "Log in as current user"** option. Enabling this option, by checking the box, means that the default setting will be to log in as the currently logged in user to the endpoint device. The end user has no other option to use alternative login credentials.

12. The next option is to enter the **Default connection server**. This allows you to prepopulate the client with the details of the connection server you want to connect to.

13. The final three feature options all relate to multimedia and unified communications apps with the first option for enabling the **Virtualization Pack for Skype for Business**. If you check the box for this option, then the Virtualization Pack for Skype for Business will be installed as part of the client install enabling better performance when using Skype for Business.

14. Next is the **Support for HTML5 Multimedia Redirection and Browser Redirection**. If you check the box to enable this feature, then HTML5 multimedia direction and browser redirection will be enabled.

15. The final feature setting is for **Enable Media Optimization for Microsoft Teams**. If you check the box to enable this feature, then the client will support optimizing the media for Microsoft Teams to ensure the best end-user experience.

16. Now click the **Agree & Install** button.

17. The Horizon Client will now be installed with the progress shown in the following screenshot:

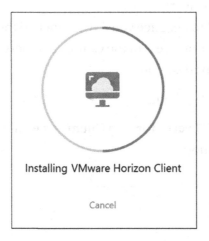

Figure 13-5. *Installing the Horizon Client for Windows*

18. Once installed, you will see the following screenshot:

Figure 13-6. *Horizon Client for Windows successfully installed*

You have now successfully installed the Horizon Client for Windows and are ready to connect to your Horizon environment and launch desktops and applications.

Connecting to Horizon Delivered Resources

In this section, we are going to look at how to connect to your Horizon environment, launch a virtual desktop or published application, as well as look at the configuration options within the Horizon Client.

The first thing you need to do, once you have launched the Horizon Client on your Windows device, is to add the address of the Connection Server that you want to connect to. To do this, follow the steps described:

1.   Launch the Horizon Client.

2.   You will see the **VMware Horizon Client** screen as shown in the following screenshot:

Figure 13-7. *Adding a new Connection Server*

3.   Now click **New Server** in the menu bar.

4.   You will see the following dialog box.

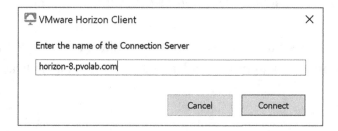

Figure 13-8. *Entering the Connection Server details*

868

5. Type the name of the Connection Server in the box. In this example, this is the Connection Server in the test environment called **horizon-8.pvolab.com**. Depending on your configuration, you might be connecting to a load balancer rather than directly to a Connection Server.

6. Now click the **Connect** button. You will see the following:

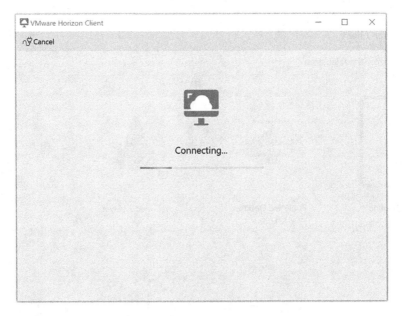

Figure 13-9. *Connecting to the Connection Server*

7. You will also see the **Login** dialog box appear as shown in the following screenshot:

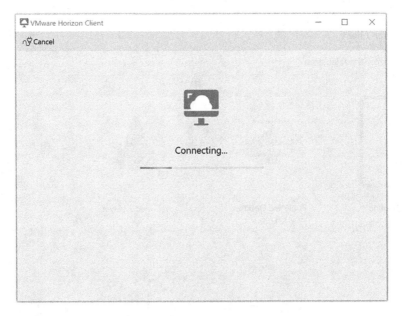

Figure 13-10. *Logging in to the Connection Server*

8. In the **User name** box, type in the name of the user that is logging in.

9. In the **Password** box, type in the password for the user.

10. Now click the **Login** button. Once successfully logged in, the end user will be presented with the resources that they are entitled to use as shown in the following screenshot:

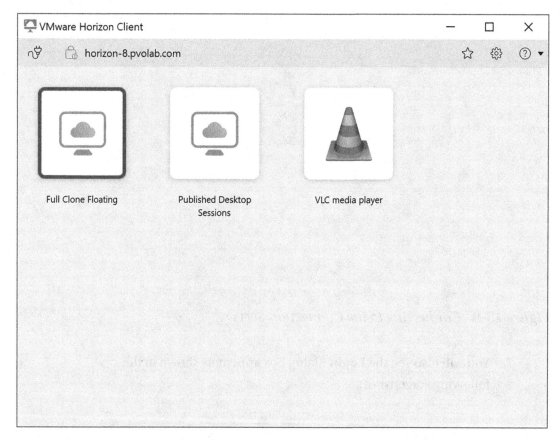

Figure 13-11. *Horizon available resources based on user entitlement*

11. The end user then double-clicks the resource they want to use, and the Connection Server will then create the connection to the virtual desktop machine or published application selected.

12. This is shown in the following screenshot which shows a desktop session connected within the Horizon Client.

Figure 13-12. *Desktop session connected and running*

The end user can now use their session, in this example a desktop, as they would use any other desktop.

Using the Horizon Client

In this section, having now looked at how to connect to a Horizon environment and launch resources, we are going to look at some of the configuration options within the client.

There are two areas which we are going to look at. The first are the client options once you have connected to a Connection Server. The next options are for how the client interacts with the virtual desktop or application you launch from the Connection Server.

Horizon Client Configuration Options

Once you have launched the Horizon Client and added the Connection Server, you will see an icon with a drop-down menu in the top right-hand corner. If you click this drop-down icon, you will see that you now have the following options as shown in the following screenshot:

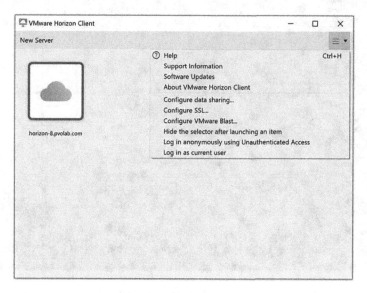

Figure 13-13. *Horizon Client menu options*

These options are as follows:

- **Help**: This takes you to the online version of the Horizon Windows Client manual.

- **Support Information**: Displays the following dialog box detailing information about the client version as shown:

Figure 13-14. *Horizon Client menu options – Support Information screen*

If you click the **Collect Support Data...** button, you will see a command prompt open, and you will see the various log files being collected as shown:

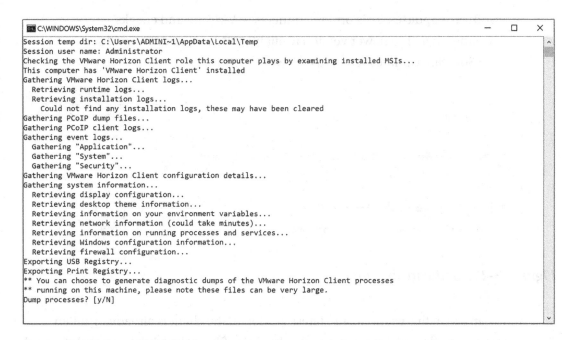

Figure 13-15. *Collecting support data*

Once collected, you then have the option to generate diagnostic dumps by pressing **Y**. You will then see the following screenshot:

Figure 13-16. *Creating a support zip file*

Once completed, press any key to close the command prompt window.

- **Software updates**: This option connects to VMware and checks whether there is a newer version available for download. You will see the Software Updates screen as shown:

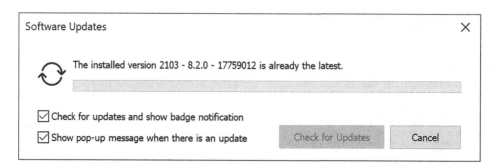

Figure 13-17. *Software updates*

As you can see in this example, the latest version of the client is already installed. There are also two other options in the dialog box. The first is the **Check for updates and show badge notification**, and the other is to show a pop-up message when an update is available.

- **About VMware Horizon Client**: Shows the details of the client version and build as shown:

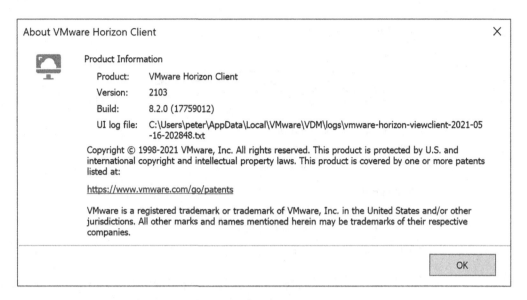

Figure 13-18. *About the Horizon Client screen*

- **Configure data sharing**: Gives you the option of switching data sharing mode on or off, by clicking the corresponding radio button. Data sharing collects anonymous data and sends it to VMware.

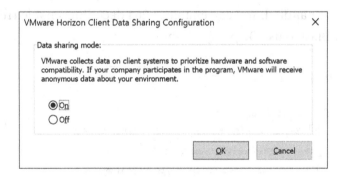

Figure 13-19. *Configuring data sharing mode*

- **Configure SSL**: Allows you to configure how SSL certificates are handled. The first option is for the Certificate checking mode. You can select, via the corresponding radio button, whether to never connect to untrusted servers, warn before connecting, or do not verify the certificate.

Figure 13-20. *Configuring SSL certificates*

The other option is to allow connection via an SSL proxy which is enabled by checking the box.

- **Configure VMware Blast**: Enables you to configure how the Blast protocol is handled. You can enable H.264 decoding, enable HEVC, or allow Blast to use OS proxy settings.

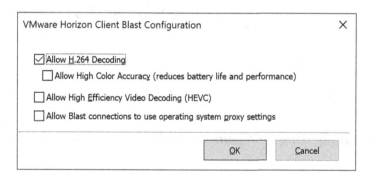

Figure 13-21. *Blast configuration settings*

- **Hide the selector after launching an item**: Enabling this setting means that the Horizon Client hides the Client window once a remote desktop or published application has been launched.

- **Login anonymously using Unauthenticated Access**: The unauthenticated access user utilizes a user alias to log in to the client. When selected, you do not need to provide Active Directory credentials or a UPN for the end user.

- **Login as current user**: This allows the client to use the credentials for the user that is currently logged in to the end point device without them having to log in to the Connection Server and enter their credentials again.

We have now covered the Horizon Client configuration options before you connect to any resources. In the next section, we are going to connect to the Connection Server and look at the configuration options available now that we are connected.

Configuration Options Once Connected

The next step of the logging in process using the Horizon Client is to connect to the Connection Server. Once connected, you will see displayed the different resources that are available for you to launch and use.

Depending on how the desktop pool has been configured, you will see different configuration options available.

Let us start with the top menu first. The following graphic shows the options available.

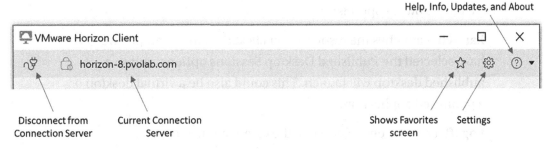

Figure 13-22. *Configuration menu options*

In this section, we are going to discuss the Settings option, which is also available by right-clicking a resource icon, as well as the other options within that contextual menu.

If you right-click one of the available resources displayed within the client, you will see the following screenshot:

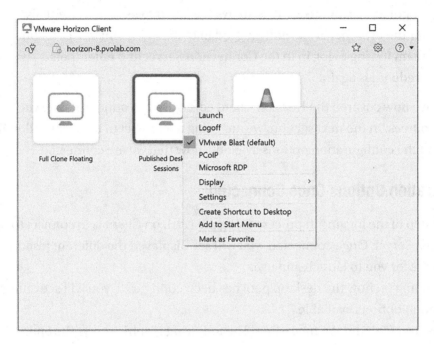

Figure 13-23. *Contextual menu options for available resources*

You have the following options:

- **Launch**: Launches the resource you clicked; in this example, we have selected the Published Desktop Sessions options, and so a published desktop will launch. This could also be a virtual desktop or a published application.

- **Logoff**: Logs the end user out of the Connection Server.

- **VMware Blast (default)**: Selects the Blast protocol to be used for this session.

- **PCoIP**: Selects the PCoIP protocol for this session.

- **Microsoft RDP**: Selects the RDP protocol for this session.

  - Depending on your pool settings, the end user may not be able to change the display protocol and therefore will not see these options.

- **Display**: Allows the end user to configure the screen size using the following options:

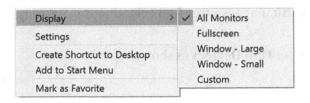

Figure 13-24. *Display settings*

Clicking the **Custom** option will display the **Custom Window Size** configuration screen, allowing the end user to select a screen size by using the slider control as shown:

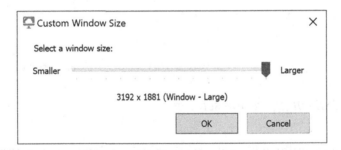

Figure 13-25. *Custom window sizing*

- **Settings**: Displays the Settings menu which we will discuss later in this section.

- **Create Shortcut to Desktop**: Places a shortcut to the resource on the desktop of the end user's device.

- **Add to Start Menu**: Adds a shortcut icon to the Start Menu on the end user's device.

- **Mark as Favorite**: Adds the icon for the resource to the Favorites screen within the client. The Favorites page is accessible by clicking the star icon from the menu on the top of the client screen.

Settings Menu Options

As we mentioned in one of the preceding bullet points, there is also a Settings menu which is accessible by either clicking the cog icon on top of the client screen or right-clicking a particular resource and selecting the Settings option from the contextual menu.

The first setting is for **USB Devices** as shown:

Figure 13-26. *USB configuration settings*

The USB Devices option will only be available if you have enabled the USB redirection feature. USB devices will be listed on this screen.

Next is the VMware Blast configuration. This is the same configuration that we looked at previously that was available from the client menu before connecting to the Connection Server and is shown in the following:

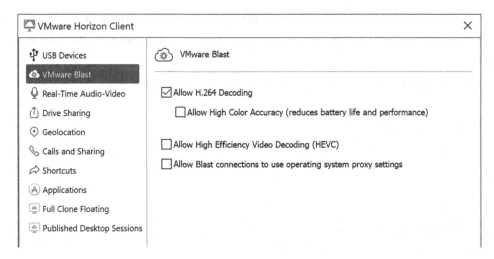

Figure 13-27. *Blast configuration settings*

On this configuration screen, you can **Allow H.264 Decoding**, **Allow HEVC**, or allow Blast to use OS proxy settings.

Next is the Real-Time Audio-Video configuration screen as shown:

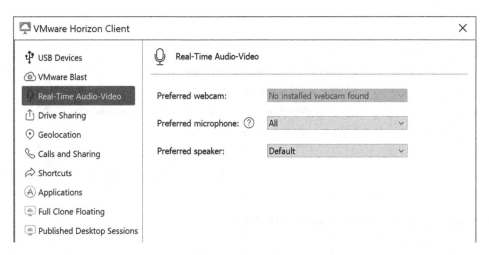

Figure 13-28. *RTAV configuration settings*

On this configuration screen, you can select your **Preferred webcam**, **Preferred microphone**, and your **Preferred speaker**. You will be able to select the device for each one from the drop-down menu if the device is installed.

The next option is to configure **Drive Sharing**. This enables you to select a folder to share between your local end point device and the virtual desktop or published desktop session.

The Drive Sharing configuration screen is shown in the following:

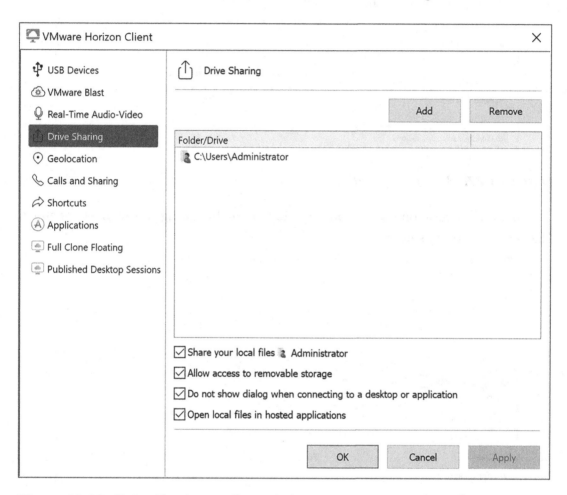

Figure 13-29. *Drive Sharing configuration*

If you click the **Add** button, then you can select a folder to share as shown by the **Browse For Folder** in the following screenshot:

Figure 13-30. *Browsing for a folder to share*

Once you have selected a folder to share, the folder called **Shared Folder** in this example, click the OK button. The folder will now appear on the list as shown in the following:

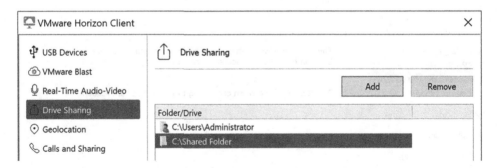

Figure 13-31. *Shared folder configured*

There are then additional four options at the bottom of the screen, all enabled via a check box. These provide the following:

- **Share your local files <username>**: If you check this box, then the C:\Users\<username> folder will be shared. In this example, as we have logged in to the end point as the administrator, the C:\Users\ Administrator folder will be shared.

- **Allow access to removable storage**: Enables access to removable storage such as an external USB/hard drive that is connected to the end point device.

- **Do not show dialog when connecting to a desktop or application**: Prevents the dialog box from being displayed when connecting to a virtual/published desktop or published applications.

- **Open local files in hosted applications**: Enables you to open files in the shared folder on the host device when running a published application.

The next option is for **Geolocation** as shown in the following screenshot:

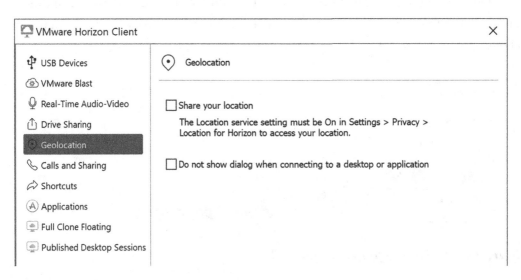

Figure 13-32. *Geolocation configuration settings*

This setting enables you to share your location information, by checking the box to enable **Share your location**. The other option is to suppress the dialog box when connecting to a virtual/published desktop or published applications.

Next is the Calls and Sharing configuration screen as shown in the following screenshot:

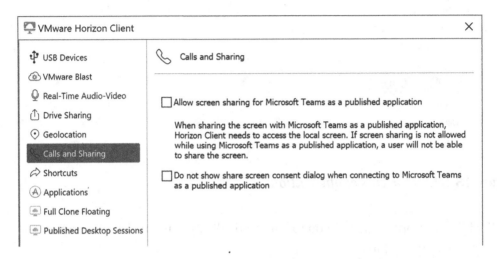

Figure 13-33. *Calls and Sharing configuration for MS Teams*

The first option on this screen is to enable screen sharing when using Microsoft Teams as a published application. You also then have the option to stop the screen sharing consent box from being displayed when using Microsoft Teams as a published application.

Next is **Shortcuts** as shown in the following screenshot:

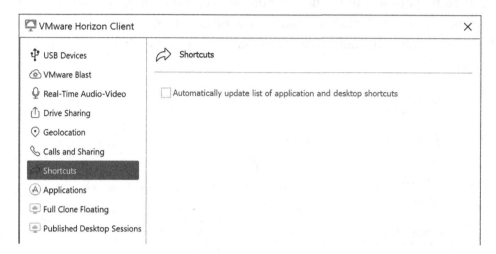

Figure 13-34. *Shortcuts configuration*

Enabling this option allows you to automatically update the list of shortcuts for desktops and applications.

The next setting, **Applications**, applies to published applications and is shown in the following screenshot:

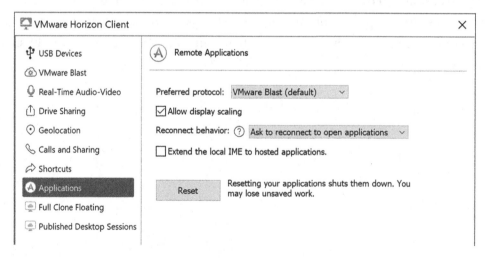

Figure 13-35. *Applications configuration*

The first option on this screen is to change the display protocol that is delivering the published desktop. Choose the protocol from the drop-down menu list if you have enabled end users to be able to change the protocol.

You then have a check box to allow display scaling to enable the screen to scale to the required size.

Next is the Reconnect behavior. This determines how you reconnect to published applications. You have the following options from the drop-down list:

- Ask to reconnect to open applications.

- Reconnect automatically to open applications.

- Do not ask and do not automatically reconnect.

Lastly in the Applications section is a **Reset** button for resetting the application session. This will shut down any published applications that are currently running.

The final two options reflect the other resources available in the client that the currently logged in end user has been entitled to. In this example, those are a Full Clone Floating virtual desktop pool and a Published Desktop Sessions pool.

Within this configuration menu, you can configure the display protocol, displays, autoconnect, display scaling, and synchronize the keypad, scroll, and caps lock. This is shown in the following screenshot:

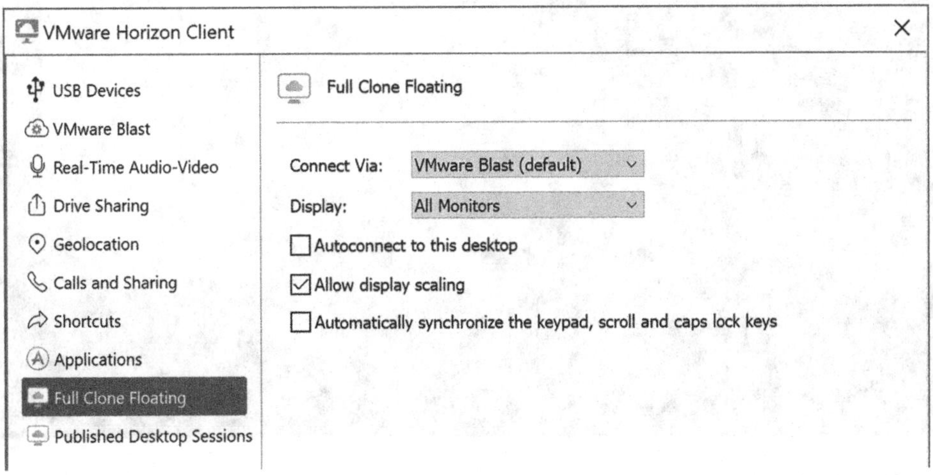

Figure 13-36. *Configuration settings for other available resources*

In the next section, we are going to explore the settings and options once you are running a virtual desktop, published desktop, or published application session.

Configuration Options During an Active Session

In this section, we are going to look at the configuration options that are available in the Horizon Client once the session has been connected.

A number of these are the same as we have already covered, and so we will highlight those new options.

Once you have connected and your session is running, either a virtual desktop machine, published desktop, or published application, you will see the following screenshot:

Figure 13-37. *Desktop session connected and running*

Across the top of the screen, you now have the following menu options:

- **Options**

- **Connect USB Device**

- **Send Ctrl-Alt-Delete**

If you click the **Options** menu, you will see the following options shown in the following screenshot:

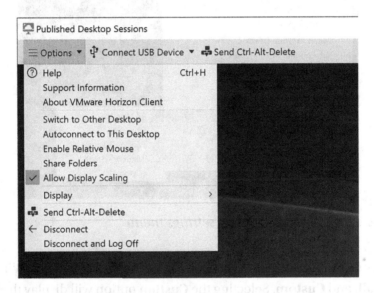

Figure 13-38. *In-session configuration menu*

The first few options, **Help**, **Support Information**, and **About VMware Horizon Client**, have already been covered in previous sections.

The next option is **Switch to Other Desktop**. This allows you to switch to another virtual desktop, desktop session, or published application.

Autoconnect to This Desktop, when enabled, means that when you launch the Horizon Client, it will automatically connect to this desktop rather than give the end user the option to choose which desktop or application they connect to.

Next is the **Enable Relative Mouse** option. This enhances the performance of the mouse in the virtual desktop or published application session. It works by translating the mouse movements as a delta from the last mouse position rather than a move to an absolute position on the screen.

We have already covered **Share Folders** and **Allow Display Scaling** as both appear in the other menus which we have already discussed.

If you click the option for **Display**, you will see that the menu expands to show several additional configuration options. These are shown in the following screenshot:

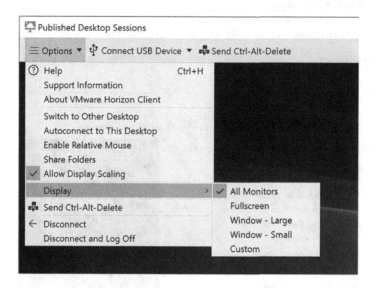

Figure 13-39. *Display configuration settings menu*

The display size options are to display on **All Monitors**, **Fullscreen**, **Window - Large**, **Window - Small**, and **Custom**. Selecting the **Custom** option will display the **Custom Window Size** configuration screen, allowing the end user to manually select a screen size by using the slider control.

Send Ctrl-Alt-Delete sends the Control-Alt-Delete keystroke to the virtual desktop or published desktop. This enables end users to access the menu where they can lock, switch user, or log out. Depending on how you have configured your virtual desktops, some of these settings may have been disabled as part of the optimization process.

The final options are for **Disconnect**, which disconnects the client from the session, but does not log the end users out of the session, and **Disconnect and Log Off** which disconnects from the session and logs the end user out of the client.

Next is the menu options for **Connect USB Device**. If you click the drop-down menu, you will see that there are two sections to the menu options displayed. The first is for configuring automatic connections, and the second section lists the USB devices that are present on the local end point device that can be redirected to the virtual session.

The menu options are shown in the following screenshot:

Figure 13-40. *USB connection menu*

For automatic connection, you can either choose to automatically connect at startup, when the session launches, or choose to redirect the USB device as soon as you plug the device into the end point device.

You can then choose which device you want to connect from those that appear on the list.

The final option is for **Send Ctrl-Alt-Delete**. This again sends the Control-Alt-Delete keystroke to the virtual desktop or published desktop.

We have now successfully installed and configured the Horizon Client for Windows and looked at the different configuration options.

In the next section, we are going to take a brief look at the Horizon Client for Linux end point device.

Horizon Client for Linux

The Horizon Client for Linux is a Linux application that is installed on your Linux end point, such as a desktop or laptop running a supported Linux distribution, with current support for Ubuntu and Red Hat Enterprise Linux (RHEL) as well as support for Raspberry Pi 4 Model B running ThinLinx and Stratodesk No Touch OS.

As with the Windows version of the client, the Linux client allows you to connect to your Horizon delivered resources using a non-Windows-based device.

Using the Horizon Client for Linux, as with the other software client versions, ensures that you are going to deliver the best possible user experience as it enables better performance and more features.

There are both 32-bit and 64-bit versions. The 32-bit version can be downloaded from the following link:

```
https://my.vmware.com/en/web/vmware/downloads/
details?downloadGroup=CART21FQ4_LIN32_2012&productId=1027&rPId=62297
```

And the 64-bit version can be downloaded from the following link:

```
https://my.vmware.com/en/web/vmware/downloads/
details?downloadGroup=CART22FQ1_LIN64_2103&productId=1027&rPId=62297
```

Next is the Horizon Client for macOS.

Horizon Client for macOS

The Horizon Client for macOS is an application that is installed on your macOS end point that enables you to connect to your Horizon delivered resources using an Apple device running the macOS.

As with the other versions of the client we have discussed previously, the macOS client allows you to connect to your Horizon delivered resources using a device such as a MacBook or iMac running the macOS.

You can download the Horizon Client for macOS from the following link:

```
https://my.vmware.com/en/web/vmware/downloads/
details?downloadGroup=CART22FQ1_MAC_2103&productId=1027&rPId=62296
```

The next client is the Horizon Client for Chrome OS device.

Horizon Client for Chrome OS

The Horizon Client for Chrome OS is an application that is installed on your Chromebook or Chromebox that enables you to connect to your Horizon delivered resources using a device running the Chrome OS.

Using the Horizon Client for Chrome OS, as with the other software client versions, ensures that you are going to deliver the best possible user experience as it enables better performance and more features.

You can download the Chrome OS Horizon Client from the following link:

```
https://my.vmware.com/en/web/vmware/downloads/details?download
Group=CART22FQ1_CHROME_2103&productId=1027&rPId=62300
```

Next, we are going to look at the Horizon Clients that are available for mobile devices, starting with Android devices.

Horizon Client for Android

As well as desktop and laptop devices, VMware also provides a Horizon Client for mobile devices such as smartphones and tablets. In this case, we are looking at those types of devices that run Android as their operating system.

The VMware Horizon Client for Android enables an end user to connect to VMware Horizon delivered virtual desktop machines and published applications and desktops using an Android-based smartphone or tablet. You can use the following versions:

- Android 32-bit and 64-bit x86-based devices

- Android 32-bit and 64-bit ARM-based devices

- Android devices from the Google Play Store

- Kindle Fire in the Amazon Appstore

A unique feature to this form factor device is the Unity Touch Sidebar. Given the smaller form factor and less screen estate than a laptop or desktop, the Unity Touch Sidebar enables users to quickly access menus as shown:

Figure 13-41. *Horizon Client for Android with Unity Touch*

To access the menu options, you would tap the circle of dots that appears in the middle right-hand side of the screen. This will then show the menu wheel as shown in the previous screenshot. From here, you can select the menu options that would normally be displayed in the menu bar across the top of the screen – options such as settings, disconnect, or send Ctrl-Alt-Del.

Removing the menu bar from the top of the screen makes the virtual desktop or application session more usable.

You can download the Horizon Client for Android from the Google Play Store by following this link:

```
https://play.google.com/store/apps/details?id=com.vmware.view.client.
android
```

The next mobile client is the Horizon Client for iOS.

Horizon Client for iOS

The Horizon Client for iOS, like the Android client, is designed to enable you to access your Horizon delivered resources using an Apple smartphone or tablet running the iOS operating system.

The following shows an example of some of the screenshots:

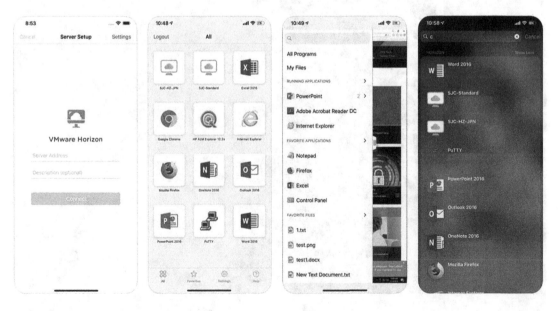

Figure 13-42. *Horizon Client for iOS*

As with the Android client, the iOS client also adopts the Unity Touch Sidebar feature to enable quick and easy access to the menus.

You can download the iOS client by following this link:

`https://apps.apple.com/gb/app/vmware-horizon-client/id417993697#?platform =iphone`

Now that we have covered the software clients, in the next section we are going to discuss hardware-based clients.

Hardware Clients

Hardware clients, as the name suggests, are hardware-based devices that are designed specifically for the task of connecting to remote resources such as virtual desktop machines and published applications.

What makes this approach different to the software-based clients is that these devices can only be used to connect to remote resources and have far less local CPU, memory, and disk resources, as they are simply not required. The processing, after all, is performed in the data center or cloud.

The operating system on these devices is also different and is typically a non-Windows OS that has been optimized for running virtual desktops and applications from the data center or cloud.

There are three types of hardware devices that we are going to discuss:

- Thin clients

- Zero clients

- Repurposed existing hardware

We will start this section by discussing the thin client options.

Thin Client Devices

A thin client, also sometimes referred to as a terminal or dumb client, is a lower hardware specification device that is used to connect to desktop and application resources that run in a data center or cloud.

These types of devices provide the ability to display the remote sessions across the network and deliver them locally for the end user. In turn, the end user uses a keyboard and mouse to drive the session, via the device, back to the data center or cloud.

Thin clients are typically hardware appliances as they can only be used to connect to remote resources and do not have the hardware resources to be able to run a full-blown desktop environment as you would on a desktop PC. The operating system they run is also a cutdown version to reflect the lower hardware resources and is typically based on a customized Linux distribution.

That provides several advantages, such as lower management overheads, less device power consumption, and devices that have a much longer life span as they do not need to be upgraded to take advantage of new operating systems and applications and they have no moving parts.

There are several thin client vendors such as LG, Dell Wyse, HP, IGEL, and 10Zig, to name but a few. It is also worth noting that each vendor will use its own version of operating system.

The next thing we are going to discuss is zero clients.

Zero Client Devices

Zero clients are almost the same as thin clients in that they are low-resource and low-powered devices designed for connecting to virtual environments, but with one big difference.

Zero clients do not have an operating system, whereas thin clients do have an operating system. Instead, a zero client has everything it needs built into firmware at the hardware layer. This means that they are typically faster to power on and boot, and as they do not have an operating system, there is no ongoing operating systems management required.

As zero clients also work at the hardware layer, then typically they offer better performance, such as more dynamic video and graphics performance. However, you need to be aware that they are not as flexible as a thin client. By that we mean that in some cases the hardware will, for example, be based on Teradici PCoIP and the Terra 2 chipset and firmware. That means it will only connect to PCoIP-based environments.

Again, there are several zero client vendors such as LG, Dell Wyse, HP, and 10Zig, to name but a few.

Repurposing Existing Hardware Devices

The final hardware-based option is to use existing hardware and to turn those devices into thin client devices. To take advantage of this option, there are several vendors that provide a solution that replaces the operating system already running on the device with the thin client operating system. We have already discussed the IGEL solution in detail earlier in this chapter.

The key use case for this option is to extend the life of existing hardware when deploying a virtual desktop or application solution. It not only extends the usefulness of the hardware, but it will also enable you to manage these devices remotely and centrally. Then, when the device naturally becomes end of life, you can replace the device with a thin or zero client.

Next-Gen Edge OS for Digital Workspaces with IGEL

In the previous sections, we have talked about specific client-based solutions such as thin clients, zero clients, and repurposing existing older hardware.

These have been point solutions for each use case; however, there is a single solution that delivers an enterprise-class managed operating system, device agnostic, for each of these use cases, complete with a centralized management platform and the ability to connect to any digital workspace whether cloud-based or on-premises.

The solution in question is IGEL. IGEL Edge OS has been built from the ground up, using a secure read-only version of Linux, optimized for connecting to remote resources such as VMware Horizon delivered virtual desktops and applications.

In addition to supporting VDI clients, IGEL OS also supports web browsers and other third-party applications and tools like unified communication clients and VPN clients. IGEL OS also supports the offloading of audio and video for unified communications which provides users with a rich experience and yet keeps management costs for IT down. IGEL also provides a single pane of glass for managing that OS across all devices as shown in the following diagram:

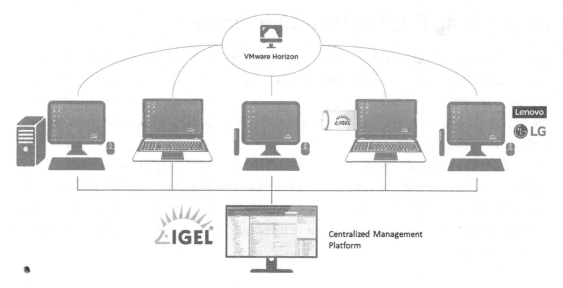

Figure 13-43. *IGEL platform for delivering digital workspace client solutions*

While IGEL also manufacture their own devices, the key to the solution lies in the Edge OS that runs not only on IGEL's own devices but the fact that the Edge OS can be deployed across several different use cases and non-IGEL devices including repurposing older x86 hardware (including other thin clients, desktops, and laptops), running as a portable USB delivered solution (UD Pocket), and hardware devices with the Edge OS already installed from vendors such as Lenovo and LG.

As a thin and lightweight operating system, devices do not require a huge amount of CPU, memory, and disk. This makes it much easier and cost-effective to manage and deploy, enabling organizations to adopt or move to a digital workspace–type environment more easily.

Another consideration is the operating system on the end points within your organization.

For example, as we are moving more and more to being online, we have discussed previously not needing to deploy expensive and powerful devices at the edge. As part of that, why do we need a full-blown Windows OS at the Edge with all the complexity that comes with managing it, maintaining it, and, more importantly, securing it when all we want to do is connect to our online environments?

We are connecting to a Windows OS typically anyway, so why double the amount of management and licensing that is required?

This is where the IGEL Edge OS and its Universal Management Suite (UMS) management platform can help reduce management overheads and costs and reduce carbon footprint as devices can last longer.

Universal Management Suite (UMS)

The IGEL UMS provides a simple and secure management platform that allows IT admins to easily manage all Edge OS endpoints, supporting tens of thousands of devices using a single pane of glass management console.

With the UMS, IT admins can manage and configure all the endpoints within your environment. They can simply create configuration profiles for the devices and then drag and drop those configurations to specific devices or groups of devices.

The following screenshot shows the VMware-specific configuration for managing the Horizon Client settings, such as the connection settings, keyboard and mouse settings, and multimedia settings.

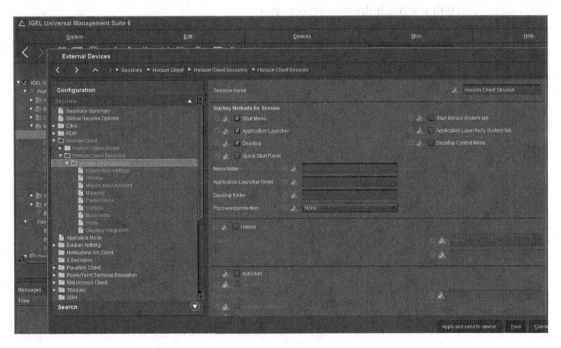

Figure 13-44. *IGEL UMS Horizon Client configuration*

As well as the basic Horizon Client settings, you can also customize the firmware of the OS and then roll that out to all clients.

Another key component to the IGEL solution enables organizations to manage devices and end users who are working remotely, either working from home, working from remote offices, or those that spend their time travelling from site to site.

The IGEL Cloud Gateway enables the UMS to manage these types of devices over the Internet, enabling them to easily gain access to their resources.

Browser-Based HTML Access

If you do not have the Horizon Client installed on the device you are using, as perhaps you are working from home using a different machine or working from a different location using somebody else's machine, then you can still access your Horizon resources using an HTML-enabled browser.

The connection process is simple, and no additional software needs to be installed on the device from which you are trying to connect.

To connect, you launch your browser and type in the address of your Connection Server, and you will see the following screenshot:

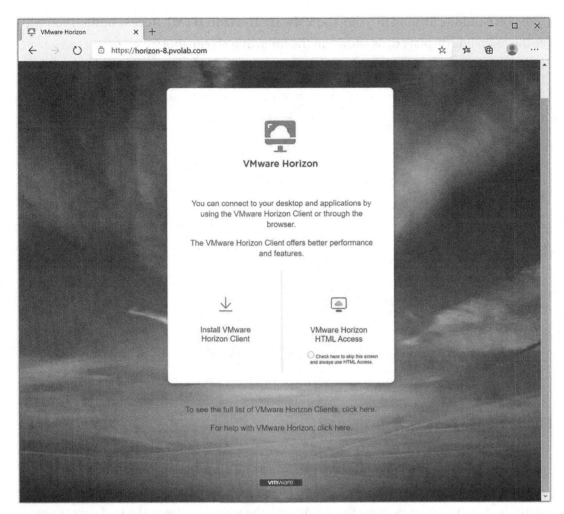

Figure 13-45. *Horizon web client portal*

On the Connection Server web page, you will see a couple of options. The first one is to install the Horizon Client. This will allow you to download and install the Horizon software client on the device.

Clicking the second option will continue the connection process using the browser. You also have the option, by clicking the radio button, to always use the HTML access to your Horizon resources.

The other options on this page are the link to the Horizon Client page on the VMware website and then the link to the online help.

If you continue logging in using the **VMware Horizon HTML Access** option, you will see the login box displayed, as shown in the following screenshot:

Figure 13-46. *Logging in to the web client*

Type in the username and then the password and click the Login button.

Once the end user has successfully been logged in, then the connection will be established with the Connection Server. As with the software client, the end user is now shown the resources that they are entitled to, as shown in the following screenshot:

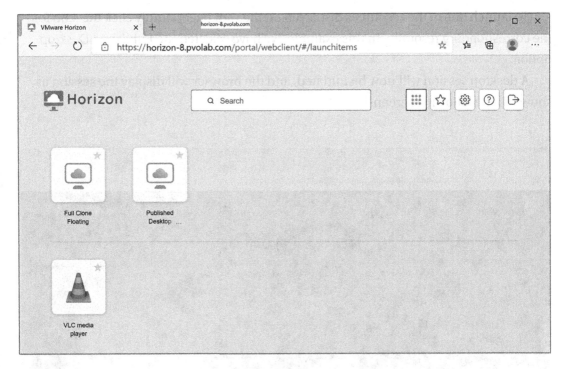

Figure 13-47. *Horizon delivered resources – portal view*

You will see several menu options as shown in the following:

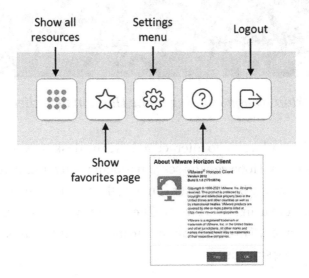

Figure 13-48. *Horizon web client menu settings*

To launch one of the resources displayed on the web page, simply click the icon for the corresponding resource. In this example, we have selected the Published Desktop option.

A desktop session will now be initiated, and the browser will display the session as shown in the following screenshot:

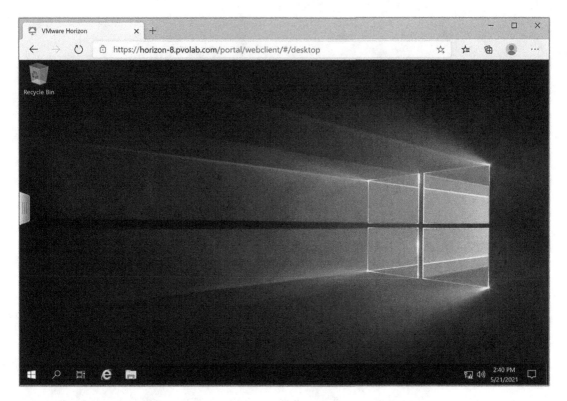

Figure 13-49. *Desktop session running in the Horizon web client*

The end user will now be able to interact and use the desktop session as they would any other desktop session. However, the session is being delivered via the browser.

As this session is running in a browser window, then there is no menu bar visible as you would see if you were using the Horizon Client. Instead, you will notice a tab on the left-hand side of the screen. This tab contains the menu options, and if you click the tab, you will see the following screenshot:

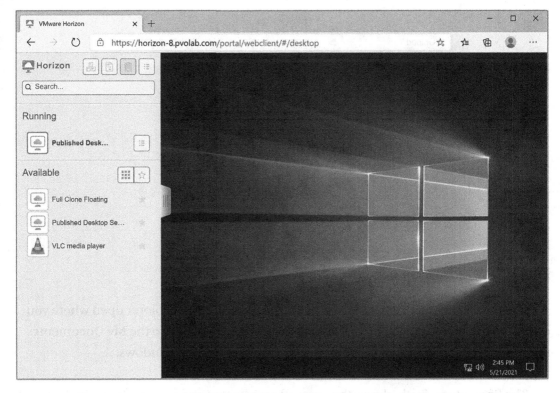

Figure 13-50. *Horizon web client menu*

The options on the tab comprise three sections. The first of these is the following menu buttons:

Figure 13-51. *Horizon web client menu buttons*

The first button is to send Ctrl-Alt-Del to the session.

Next is the File Transfer feature. If you click this button, you will see the **Transfer Files** window open as shown in the following screenshot:

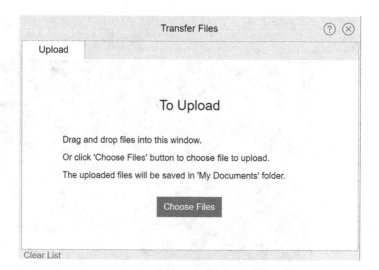

Figure 13-52. *Horizon web client file transfer window*

If you click the Choose Files button, you will see Windows Explorer open where you can choose the files you want to upload, which will be uploaded to the My Documents folder on the desktop. You can also drag and drop files into the windows.

The next button is to switch the clipboard function on or off.

The final button firstly shows the currently connected end user as shown in the following screenshot:

Figure 13-53. *Horizon web client additional menu options*

It also provides access to the settings screen, enables you to switch the session to full screen, displays the About screen, and finally allows you to log out of the session.

You then have the **Running** section which shows the current session. If you click the button on this section, you will have the option to log off or close the session as shown in the following screenshot:

Figure 13-54. *Running session options*

The rest of the options on the tab, under the heading of **Available**, show the other resources that the currently logged in user has been entitled to.

In the next section, we are going to look at how you can customize the web client page to add your own.

Customizing the Horizon Web Access Page

As the HTML access is essentially a web page, there are several customization tasks that enable you to add logos and backgrounds and prevent end users from downloading the Horizon Client.

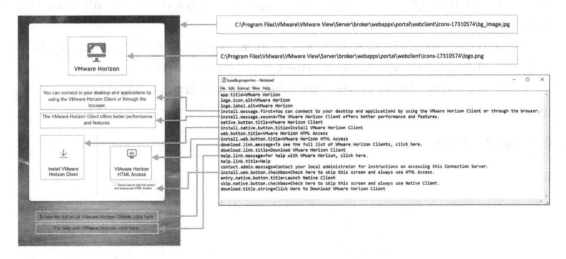

Figure 13-55. *Horizon Client web portal page outline*

The initial page that is displayed is the download page as shown in the previous screenshot. On this page, you can customize the background picture, the graphics, and the text. We will start with the background picture.

On the Connection Server, browse to the following location:

```
C:\Program Files\VMware\VMware View\Server\broker\webapps\portal\webclient\
icons-17310574\
```

Within that folder, you will find several graphics files in both JPG and PNG format. The file for the background picture is called **bg_image.jpg**. To change this background picture, just take the picture you want to use and save it as the same filename and in the same location. The image size is 2560 x 1440 px. Before you do this, it is worth taking a backup copy of the original file just in case.

Also, in this same folder, you will find the VMware Horizon logo files called **logo.png**, **logo-horizon.png**, and **logo-horizonx2.png**. If you want to use your own versions for the icon that is displayed, simply replace the files with your updated versions. It is also worth noting the image sizes of these files:

- **logo.png**: 182 x 105 px

- **logo-horizon.png**: 161 x 40 px

- **logo-horizonx2.png**: 322 x 80 px

Note it is the **logo.png** file that is used on this web page.

You can also change the text that is displayed. In the previous graphic, the location of each block of text is highlighted. You could change the text to suit your organization, with warning messages or other useful information.

The next thing we are going to look at configuring is whether the download page is displayed when the end user connects to the Connection Server web portal.

To do this, you need to locate the configuration file which you will find in the following folder on the Connection Server:

```
C:\ProgramData\VMware\VDM\portal
```

Within this folder, you will find a file called **portal-links-html-access.properties** as shown in the following screenshot:

Figure 13-56. *Horizon web client portal settings*

If you open the file using Notepad, you will see the following:

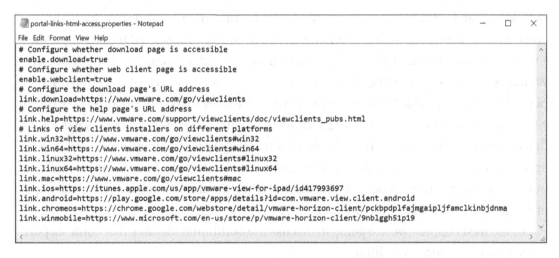

Figure 13-57. *Editing the web client configuration file*

The first line in this file is for displaying the download page. The default setting is for the download page to be displayed. To disable this and to go straight to the login page, change this line to the following:

```
enable.download=false
```

The second line is to configure whether an end user can access the web client at all. To disable the web client page, then change this line to read the following:

```
enable. webclient=false
```

Finally, within this properties configuration file, you can configure the links to the Horizon Client downloads. By default, these are configured to go directly to the VMware download page for each of the different versions. You may well, if you want to allow end user downloads, direct them to an internal page/site as you want them to use a specific version.

Once you have changed any of these configurations, you should restart the Connection Server. It is also worth noting that if you perform any upgrades, then these settings will be overwritten and reset back to the default settings.

Summary

In this chapter, we have given you a comprehensive introduction and overview to how an end user can connect to their Horizon delivered resources. We started by looking at the software clients with an in-depth overview of how to install and configure the Horizon Windows Client. As part of the Horizon Client discussion, we also looked at the other platform versions available. Next, we discussed the hardware client versions such as thin clients, zero clients, and repurposing existing hardware into client devices. As part of that discussion, we focused on the market leader in client technology, IGEL, and their approach to delivering an OS designed for the digital workspace. Finally, we looked at how to connect to Horizon delivered resources using a standard web browser and some of the additional configuration options.

In the next chapter, we are going to discuss the additional features that come as part of the Horizon Enterprise edition.

CHAPTER 14

Horizon Enterprise Edition

The focus of this book has been around the core Horizon solution to deliver virtual desktop machines, published desktop sessions, and published applications to end users with the features described as part of the Enterprise Edition of Horizon.

If you cast your mind back to Chapter 1 where we discussed the licensing options in detail, you will remember that as part of the Horizon Enterprise Edition license, a number of other complementary solutions are also included. These complementary and additional solutions include

- App Volumes

- Dynamic Environment Manager

- Workspace ONE (also included in Advanced Edition)

In this chapter, we are going to look at each of these solutions in a bit more detail and understand how they fit in to the overall digital workspace solution.

We will start by looking at App Volumes for delivering applications.

App Volumes

App Volumes is a software-based application layering technology solution that delivers applications to desktop machines.

It does this by capturing or containerizing just the application components, including the application files and settings, and saving them to a virtual hard disk. The virtual hard disk, in App Volumes terminology, is an application package or application layer. This means you have abstracted the applications from the underlying operating system, and they are now stored on their own virtual hard disk independently of the OS.

Once the application has been captured, then you can deliver back to multiple end users. To deliver an application using application layering, the virtual hard disk containing all the application runtimes, settings, and files that were captured is mounted

911

© Peter von Oven 2022
P. von Oven, *Mastering VMware Horizon 8*, https://doi.org/10.1007/978-1-4842-7261-9_14

to the virtual desktop machine. Once mounted, the application layering software will have an agent running on that virtual desktop machine that makes the application appear as if it were natively installed by layering the files and settings into the OS.

Basically, this means that it will insert or layer in settings such as registry settings and other pointers into the OS on the virtual desktop machine that ensures any calls made to the application get redirected to the virtual hard disk containing the application files. This agent also has the job of ensuring the correct files are called, especially important where DLL files are concerned.

The virtual hard disks containing the application layers are stored on a VMware datastore as VMDK files or as VHD files for non-VMware virtual desktop environment and physical desktops. As the end user logs in, the application layers they are entitled to will be mounted, therefore allowing them to run the applications.

App Volumes Use Cases

Having started the chapter with a high-level overview of what application layering is, let us now move our attention to why and where it would be used.

Application Management

Application layering came about when trying to solve the issue of delivering applications to fully stateless, or non-persistent, virtual desktops. Before the advent of application layering solutions, desktop administrators had to manage multiple virtual desktop images to accommodate all the different combinations of applications required by their end users.

One of the reasons organizations moved to a virtual desktop environment in the first place was to reduce management overheads and cut down on the number of images that they had to manage. But here we are back to managing multiple images all over again, albeit virtual images this time.

Multiple images also typically meant that a stateful or persistent virtual desktop model would be adopted, meaning every user had their own virtual desktop. Again, not very effective, and this certainly will not deliver the full benefits that virtual desktop infrastructures offer.

But the question is why was there a need to have multiple images and persistent virtual desktops? The answer is simple. So that the apps can be delivered to the end user.

In a stateless virtual desktop model, when the end users log out, either the virtual desktop gets deleted completely, or it gets reset back to a base level. Hence the reason for needing multiple images in order to deliver the different apps. If you installed apps as the user logs in via some form of scripting or allowed the end user to install apps themselves, then either way the apps could or will be lost when the end user logs out. The same is also true for the user profile as we have already discussed.

You could of course just install every app into the image, but that means you will have one big image to manage, and also you will need to license every app within the image regardless of whether the end user uses it or not. That is not very cost-effective.

With application layering, applications are abstracted away from the underlying OS of the machine and can therefore be managed independently. That immediately takes away the need to have multiple OS images for different applications, as they can now be delivered independently of the OS image. So straightaway, savings can be achieved by deploying the more cost-effective stateless desktop model and only needing to have virtual desktops available when required. This results in licensing cost savings, and also saving management time in building and maintaining multiple images, as well as lower infrastructure costs as you do not need to deploy as many virtual desktop machines up front.

When it comes to managing application lifecycles, you no longer need to build a whole new OS image just because an app has gone from v1.2 to v1.3. Instead, the app layer can be created independently and in isolation from the OS gold image, tested, and then easily delivered back to the end users.

If by any chance something goes wrong, as long as the old virtual disk with the previous version of the app layer has been kept, then it is a simple case of detaching the non-working app and going back to the known working one and allowing the end user to carry on while the problem app is remediated.

Enhanced End-User Experience

For an end user, they will have access to their applications much quicker than they would before, especially if it was an application they did not already have. No longer would they need to wait for the desktop admin team to come and install the app or give them a new virtual desktop OS image.

Instead, the desktop admins would simply entitle that end user to the apps they need. Or if the end user changes role, the desktop administrator can simply change their AD group membership, and the user will automatically inherit the apps assigned to that AD group. The apps will simply appear on their desktop as normal based on their entitlement.

In the next section, we are going to take a deeper look into how application layering works.

How Does Application Layering Work?

As we have already discussed in the introduction to this chapter, application layering provides a solution that enables desktop administrators to abstract applications from the underlying operating system, so that those applications can be managed and delivered independently.

The concept of application layering is not too dissimilar to what we have already implemented with other virtualization solutions, whether they are desktop or server based. The keyword here is abstraction.

With any virtualization solution, you are abstracting different elements. You are either abstracting the server OS or the desktop OS in the case of VDI away from the physical hardware. Application layering performs its level of abstraction at the next level up, between the OS and the applications.

Application layering forms the next part of the composite desktop model. The end-user desktop experience comprises all those elements that come together to form a complete end-user desktop experience and are abstracted, managed, and delivered back to the end users independently. Elements such as the operating system, applications, user profiles, and user authored data are all extracted from the operating system, centrally managed, and then delivered back independently in order to "reassemble" the complete desktop environment on demand. In this instance, with application layering, we are talking about the application element of this process.

Prior to this way of building the desktop experience on demand, all the desktop components would have been tightly integrated into the device operating system and therefore managed as a single entity.

Now that we have discussed what an application layer is and the use case for delivering applications using this solution, in the next section we are going to look at the App Volumes solution in more detail.

VMware App Volumes

App Volumes was the result of an acquisition of a company called CloudVolumes in August 2014. CloudVolumes enabled the real-time delivery of applications to virtual and physical desktops.

After the acquisition, VMware rebranded CloudVolumes changing the name to App Volumes and in doing so added an application layering solution to the VMware Horizon solution stack. You will still see a nod to the original product name when creating some of the virtual hard disks as they are prefixed with "CV" which points to CloudVolumes.

As an application layering solution, App Volumes works in the same way as we have described application layering in the previous section. It is designed to enable the real-time delivery of applications within a virtual desktop environment.

Application layers are captured and stored on virtual hard disks within your virtual infrastructure environment. Then, when an end user logs on to their virtual desktop machine and is entitled to use a particular application, then the virtual disk containing that application is mounted, and the application is layered into the operating system ready to be launched. The end user will see just the application icon.

When the end user logs out, the layer is removed from the OS of the virtual desktop machine, and the virtual hard disk is unmounted.

How Does App Volumes Work?

We have already discussed the general mechanics around how application layering works, so now we are going to take those principles and look specifically at the VMware implementation of those with App Volumes.

As with any other application layering solution, App Volumes sets out to address the issue of how to deliver tightly integrated applications that are essentially part of the operating system image and take away that operating system dependency so that the applications can be delivered on demand and allow VMware customers to take advantage of the full Horizon virtual desktop solution and deploy a fully stateless virtual desktop.

App Volumes provides the layer of abstraction between the operating system and the applications, allowing the applications to be delivered to the end user's virtual desktop machine on demand and based on policy. The applications are effectively containerized within a virtual disk file (either VMDK based for VMware environments or VHD based for other virtual infrastructures and physical desktop machines). These virtual hard disks or layers provide a lifecycle management–based approach to delivering applications referred to as **Simplified Application Management** or **SAM**.

In App Volumes terminology, SAM comprises **Applications**, **Packages**, and **Programs** that go to make up the application layer. The construct of this is shown in the following screenshot:

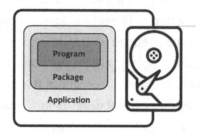

Figure 14-1. *App Volumes Application construct*

So, what do these terms actually mean when it comes to App Volumes?

Application

The first part of creating a layer is to create an **Application**. In App Volumes terminology, an application allows you to create a logical construct for an individual application or a group of applications. It is the Application that is assigned to your end users.

As part of the application lifecycle management process, an application could be made up of multiple different Packages and Programs.

The next component of the App Volumes layer is the **Package**.

Package

The Package stage is where you start the process of capturing the applications that you want to deliver.

Using a template virtual disk file from which to create the application layer, a packaging virtual machine is used to capture the installation process of the application or applications you want to include within the Package.

The packaging machine is the same as the virtual desktop machines onto which you will deliver the applications back and so will be running the same OS version. You then use the packaging machine to install your apps onto, with the files and settings that are captured during install, redirected to the virtual disk that is temporarily attached to the package machine during app installation.

When the capture process starts, initiated from the App Volumes Manager management console, a copy of the template virtual disk file is mounted on the packaging machine. Once mounted, you are prompted to install the individual applications as you would do on any other machine with the application files and settings being redirected to the virtual disk. It is like recording the installation process.

Once the installation of the applications is complete, you switch out of that record mode and the virtual disk is unmounted. It is then ready to be assigned to end users based on AD Group Policy.

A new feature introduced with App Volumes 4 is the ability to choose the package stage. This is the lifecycle of the Package, and you can select either New, Tested, Published, or Retired. It is also worth noting that only one Package inside an Application can be current at any one time.

Finally, there is the **Program** component.

Program

The **Program** elements are automatically generated based on the applications you install during the Package stage. It is made up of the actual application executables and files that were captured during the Package phase.

So now that we have covered the construct of an App Volumes application layer, how does that translate when creating the actual layers? First, we are going to look at creating an Application complete with a Package.

Creating Application Layers

Delivering application layers is a two-step process:

- Step 1: Creating and capturing the application layer

- Step 2: Delivering the application layer to the end users

917

In this section, we are going to look at the starting point for application layering, the create and capture process.

This can be summarized using the following diagram:

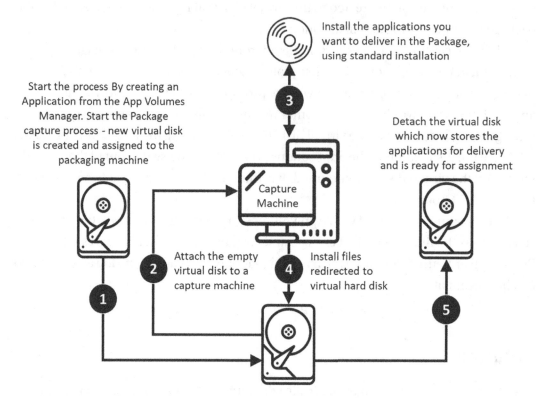

Figure 14-2. *Creating and capturing application layers*

The following describes the capture process in more detail:

- The first step is to create the **Application**. This is the part that will be assigned to the end users.

- The next step is to create the **Package**. This is where the application you want to deliver is captured. A copy of the App Volumes virtual hard disk template is taken and attached to the packaging machine.

- You can now install your apps by switching your app layering software into "record" mode and then running the application installer. As the installation files are installed, they are redirected to the virtual hard disk. These are the **Programs**.

- With the application now installed, you can switch off record mode and detach the virtual disk, which now contains your application ready to be delivered to the end users.

Delivering Application Layers

Once an application layer has been created, as described in the previous section, the resulting applications can now be delivered dynamically and on demand, based on the end-user entitlement.

The process is almost like the capture process in reverse as the virtual hard disk is again attached to the end user's virtual desktop machine as they log on, and the application files appear as if they are natively installed on the OS of the virtual desktop machine.

Under the hood, however, the application layering software is managing the access to these files, especially should a file conflict occur.

The following diagram shows what happens when an application layer is attached to an end user's virtual desktop machine:

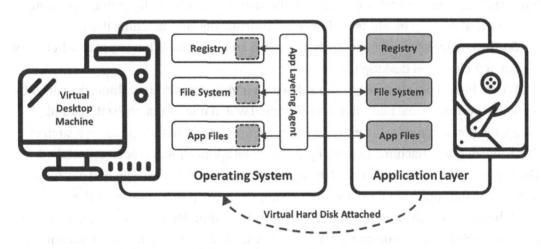

Figure 14-3. *Architecture of delivering an application layer*

When the end user logs in to their virtual desktop machine, the virtual hard disk or app layer that they have been entitled to is mounted to the operating system of the virtual desktop machine.

The application layering software on that virtual desktop machine, typically known as a filter driver or agent, temporarily inserts or layers all the files and settings that the application needs into the operating system of the virtual desktop machine. As far as the operating system is concerned, these application files and settings are installed and available locally.

This is also true for the end-user experience, with the icon for the layered application appearing on the desktop of the virtual desktop machine. They simply click it to launch it in the same way as they would for any other applications. As far as the end user and the virtual desktop operating system are concerned, then the app is actually installed locally in the virtual desktop machine.

You can see this by opening and editing the registry of the virtual desktop machine. If you did this, then you would see the layered application's registry settings present in the registry, even though in reality it has not been installed on that virtual desktop machine. The same is true for the application files.

If you open Windows Explorer, for example, and navigate to something like C:\ Program Files, there you would find all the application files, its executables, its DLL files, etc. You would see everything that references the application and to make it run; however, these files and settings reside on the virtual hard disk or layer that is mounted on the virtual desktop machine and not on the virtual desktop machine itself.

So, the end user is now running their layered applications. What happens when they log out of their virtual desktop machine?

When the end user logs out or shuts down their virtual desktop machine, the currently mounted layer, or virtual hard disk, is unmounted which means that the settings and the application files for the layered app no longer appear within the operating system of the virtual desktop machine. Essentially, it is as if the application has been uninstalled. The registry will have no mention of the application, and neither will you find any other reference to the application, its files, or its settings. It is like it was never even there!

If the end user had shut down the machine rather than logging out, and that virtual desktop machine was a non-persistent or stateless virtual desktop machine, then it would revert back to a clean state in preparation for the next user to log in.

When that next end user logs in, they may have a completely different set of applications that get layered into the operating system.

Having now covered the essentials to what application layering is, why you would need it, and how it works, in the next section we are going to discuss the lifecycle management of applications and how to manage your applications.

Managing a Single Application

Taking the SAM approach with the Application, Package, and Program elements of App Volumes, what would that look like in a real-life application lifecycle scenario?

As always, the first step is to start at the Application level. In this example, we have created an application for delivering a PDF reader. As we discussed previously, the Application is the element that gets assigned to the end users, user groups, or machines in AD.

Once the Application has been created, the next step is to capture the PDF reader by installing it on the packaging machine. The files and settings for the PDF reader are then automatically created in Programs. Once all the elements have been created, then you will have something similar to the following diagram:

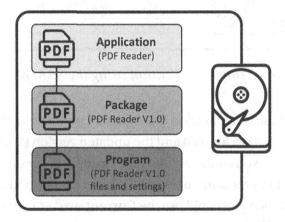

Figure 14-4. *Creating a single application using the SAM methodology*

The preceding example shows the process for a single application and a single version, but as we all know, applications do not stay on the same version for very long. So, what happens when the PDF reader updates to a new version?

When updating an Application, you don't need to create an application as we described previously. The Application for the PDF reader has already been configured and will remain assigned to the users, groups, and machines that it is already assigned to.

Instead, you go straight to the Package process and capture the new version of the PDF reader using the packaging machine and following the same process of installing the new version of the application. This in turn creates the new Program elements automatically as the files are updated to the newer versions.

Once completed, you will have updated the contents of the Application with the new version of the Package that contains the new version of the PDF reader as shown in the following diagram:

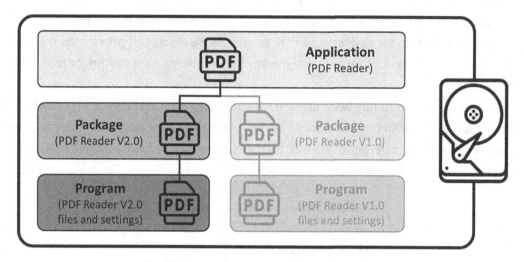

Figure 14-5. *Updating a single application using the SAM methodology*

As part of the Simplified Application Management methodology, you could now mark the old version (V1.0) as **Retired** and the updated version (V2.0) as **New** or **Published**. Alternatively, you could test the new version with a number of users to check it works, while the other users continue using the older version. Once you are happy that the application works, then you could use the **Current** marker in App Volumes to set the new version of the Application to Current, meaning that end users receive the latest and current version.

So that is how to manage an individual application. How do you manage a group of applications?

Managing a Group of Applications

Groups of applications are typically used to deploy multiple applications based on departmental use. So, for example, the finance department will have a set of specific finance-based apps, and the sales department will have a set of sales-based apps, and so on.

In this example, we are going to create an Application for the finance department which contains a PDF reader and a spreadsheet application as shown in the following diagram:

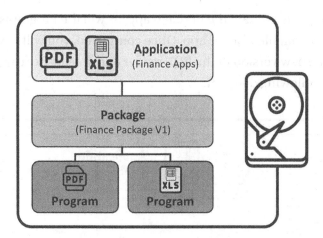

Figure 14-6. *Managing a group of applications using the SAM methodology*

So, let's run through a similar scenario as we did for single applications. First, you create the Application itself, so in this example we are going to call it something department related rather than app specific, as this Application is going to contain more than one individual application. We have chosen the finance department for this example, so we could call the Application Finance Apps.

Again, the Application is the element that gets assigned to the end users, but in this case, it means more than one application. It is a set of applications. Once the Application has been created, the next step is to capture the applications by installing them on the packaging machine. The files and settings for each individual application are then automatically created in Programs.

In this example, we have created a Package that contains Programs for the PDF reader and the spreadsheet app. To do this, it is a simple case of installing both apps while in "record" mode on the packaging machine.

The next question is how do you update the Application should there be an update to one or more of the Programs? It is the same story as we covered with updating a single app.

You do not need to create a new Application as that is already in place and assigned to end users. Instead, once you initiate the update task, the existing Package will be mounted on the packaging machine, enabling you to update the Package by capturing the new version of the application you want to update. This in turn will update the Program elements automatically. This means you could update each application independently. For example, if the PDF reader updated and the spreadsheet app did not, then you simply just update the PDF reader, capturing that update using the packaging machine.

The new package will contain the updated app, as will the Programs, which will contain the new program files for the app. Once completed, you will have updated the Application with the new version of the PDF reader and spreadsheet app, which will look something like the following diagram:

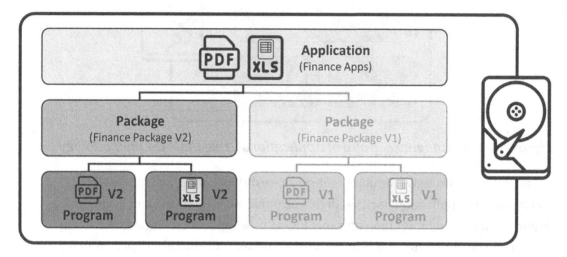

Figure 14-7. *Updating a group of applications using the SAM methodology*

So far in this chapter, we have discussed how to deliver applications to end users, to deliver a fully stateless virtual desktop environment. However, when it comes to end users, there is one other thing that they may require on their desktop, and that is the ability to install their own apps or to save their personal data.

This was typically another stumbling block for deploying stateless desktops, as anything an end user installed would be deleted when they logged out and the virtual desktop machine was deleted or refreshed back to a clean version of the gold image.

The only answer for enabling end users to install their own apps was to provide the end user with a persistent or stateful virtual desktop machine. Horizon used to have an option to attach a persistent disk; however, that no longer exists in Horizon 8.

VMware App Volumes has a solution for enabling end users to install their own apps with the Writable Volume feature.

Writable Volumes

The App Volumes Writable Volume feature enables end users to have their own dedicated virtual hard disk. This virtual hard disk is mounted to their virtual desktop machine when they log in and is used to capture anything that they install on their desktop machine.

The Writable Volume is an application layer and works in the same way as we have discussed previously with the attaching of Applications. However, it differs from that approach as it starts off as an empty disk file, save for the App Volumes components already present on the Writable Volume disk template that are required for mounting. This means that IT admins do not need to capture any application packages beforehand.

If an end user is entitled to a Writable Volume, when they install their own applications, the files and settings copied during the installation process will be redirected, by the App Volumes Agent, to the Writable Volume. Then, when the end user logs off their virtual desktop machine, the application they installed is preserved and available on a virtual disk that can then be attached and mounted to the next virtual desktop machine they log in to.

It is like having your app installed on a USB stick that you carry around with you in your pocket and plug in to each machine you use.

The following diagram shows an overview of the App Volumes solution delivering Application layers and user Writable Volumes:

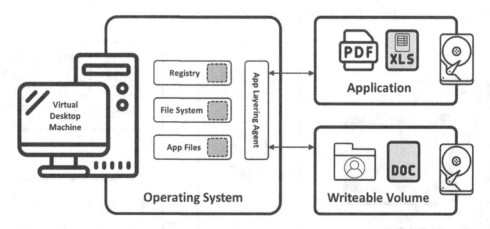

Figure 14-8. *App Volumes with Writable Volumes and Application Packages*

The other use case for Writable Volumes is for user profiles, the other component of a desktop machine that is personal to an end user.

The Windows profile delivers the end-user customization such as backdrops and other settings that are personal to the end user. With a stateless virtual desktop machine, these personalizations are deleted at the time of logoff, and so by deploying a Writable Volume, the user profile can be stored as a layer, essentially making it portable. This feature complements user environment management solutions such as VMware Dynamic Environment Manager.

Having now discussed the how part of App Volumes, in the next section we are going to discuss the why deploy App Volumes question.

Why Deploy App Volumes?

App Volumes provides a solution that enables an organization to take full advantage of deploying a fully stateless virtual desktop environment. Decoupling the apps from the underlying operating system allows IT admins to deliver applications on demand, as and when the end user requires them.

With the new Simplified Application Management methodology introduced in App Volumes 4, this also provides added benefits when it comes to updating and deploying new versions of applications all with the added bonus of not disrupting the end users. As for the end users, they will have no idea how their apps and data are delivered. All they will see are the apps on the desktop of their virtual desktop machine and that their profile has been delivered as shown in the following diagram:

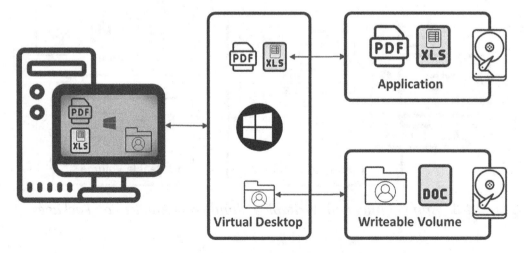

Figure 14-9. *The end-user experience using App Volumes*

The ability to manage applications independently makes it far easier for patching and updating and all without having to touch the operating system. It also means that IT can respond much quicker should security patches need to be applied quickly. It also means not having to worry about building and maintaining multiple copies of gold images. Often, an IT department has multiple copies of gold images, each containing a different set of apps to cater for the different use cases and departments.

Onboarding new users, and getting them the apps they need, is much simpler too. Applications are delivered based on an end user's Active Directory group membership or which organizational unit (OU) they are a member of. Applications can be entitled based on those groups, and therefore a user will automatically have access to the apps via that group. If they move departments, then it is a simple case of moving their group membership, and the apps will automatically follow.

If the end user needs a new application, they can, if the application has been built and configured, have that application added on the fly. That means that they do not need to wait for somebody to come and install it; once entitled, it will simply appear on their desktop.

So far in this chapter, we have focused purely on the delivery of applications, but due to the dynamic nature of App Volumes, these applications can just as easily be removed. As we have discussed, when an end user logs off their virtual desktop machine, the virtual disk containing the applications gets unmounted, and the applications appear as though they are no longer installed. If you do not want a specific end user to have access to the applications, then you simply remove them from the group.

In the next section, we are going to look at application isolation with VMware ThinApp.

ThinApp

On the surface, ThinApp and App Volumes seem to deliver the same thing, and to a certain degree, that is correct, as they both deliver applications to end users.

However, when it comes to how each solution works under the hood, they work in completely different ways and as such address very different use cases. Let us define what the ThinApp solution delivers as we have already discussed the App Volumes solution.

First and foremost, VMware ThinApp is an application virtualization solution. This means that ThinApp abstracts applications from the underlying operating system by capturing the application dependencies and files required to allow it to run, taking them, and creating a "bubble." The process is similar to the process for creating an App Volumes Package in that you capture the installation process of the application you want to run, using a clean Windows OS as the capture machine. This is typically a machine that supports the application, particularly important if you want to run an older app on a newer OS.

This bubble is referred to as a ThinApp package, which is essentially a container made up from all the elements that have been captured for the application to run.

This includes OS dependencies, captured as part of a virtual OS that is captured as part of the package, the file system, and all the application files such as the .exe and .dll files. The resultant ThinApp package is a single file, either an EXE file or an MSI file.

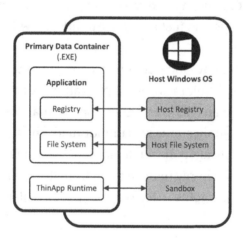

Figure 14-10. *ThinApp application package construct*

Compared to App Volumes, where App Volumes packages are virtual hard drives that contain the application files and settings that then are layered into the operating system, ThinApp is a single file that is launched on the desktop – no layering and no requirement to attach virtual hard drives. ThinApp also does not need an agent to be installed on the desktop of the machine you are delivering it to.

ThinApp is designed to eliminate application conflict and so allows you to run non-native applications on a newer operating system. For example, you could run an older version of a browser that would typically only run on an older version of Windows, package it, and then run it on the latest version of Windows as a ThinApp package. You could run an old version of Internet Explorer such as IE6 by capturing IE6 on a Windows XP desktop using the ThinApp setup capture utility and then taking the .exe file that is the ThinApp package and running that on a newer version of the Windows OS.

The ability to do this is in the way that ThinApp creates a level of isolation. As part of the package, it contains all the OS components that the app requires and therefore does not need the host machine OS. App Volumes packages do not contain any virtual OS components, just the apps.

In summary, ThinApp and App Volumes complement each other. ThinApp packages can be delivered as App Volumes layers where the layer contains a completely isolated application, allowing it to run on an OS version that ordinarily it was not designed for. Having the ThinApp package delivered as an application layer means that it does not need to be installed in the base image and can be delivered dynamically.

The next solution we are going to look at is Workspace ONE.

Workspace ONE Unified Workspace

VMware Workspace ONE is a management platform that allows IT admins to centrally manage the delivery of virtual desktops and applications to an end user's device.

This means that virtual desktops, published apps, as well as SaaS-based apps can all be aggregated into a single web page. In Workspace ONE terms, this web page is the launcher as shown in the following screenshot:

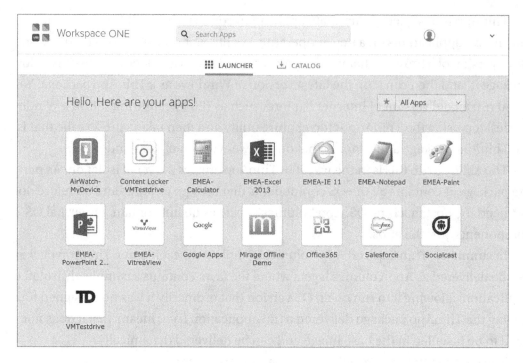

Figure 14-11. *Workspace ONE app launcher screen*

This approach allows end users to be able to have access to their corporate resources securely using smartphones, tablets, PCs, and laptops that are either personally owned or corporately owned.

As well as presenting apps in a single portal or workspace, end users are also presented with a catalog of self-service apps which they can entitle themselves to use – all under the control of the IT teams who populate the catalog with apps the end user may or may not need.

Workspace ONE unified workspace is also included in the Horizon Advanced Edition as well as the Enterprise Edition.

Summary

We have given you an overview and introduction to some of the other solutions that are provided with the Horizon Enterprise Edition. These features are also separate solutions in their own right and are all designed to deliver the best end-user experience. We looked at how App Volumes enabled dynamic delivery of applications, enabling IT teams to deploy fully stateless virtual desktop environments. Next, we looked at how to create isolated apps with ThinApp. To learn about App Volumes, you can read the Apress book entitled *Delivering Applications with VMware App Volumes 4* (`www.apress.com/gb/book/9781484266885`). Finally, we looked at Workspace ONE unified workspace for bringing together all the different resources under one simple web page from where end users can run all the apps and desktops they are entitled to. Horizon Enterprise also includes VMware Dynamic Environment Manager which we discussed in detail back in Chapter 10.

In the next chapter, we are going to discuss how to approach the upgrade process for upgrading to the latest version of Horizon and the processes involved in the upgrade.

CHAPTER 15

Upgrading Horizon

In this chapter, we are going to discuss the process of upgrading your Horizon environment to a newer or the latest version.

Depending on your current version, you need to check on some of the features that you have implemented in that current version and whether they are still available in the latest version.

For example, if you are upgrading from version 7.x, then there are several features that no longer exist in the latest 8.x versions which could affect the upgrade. These features may require you to revisit your design as they relate to specific components of the solution that you may or may not currently have deployed. We will discuss this in the "Upgrading the Connection Servers" section of this chapter.

First, we are going to highlight the key changes when upgrading to Horizon 8.2 (2103):

- **License keys**: If you are upgrading from Horizon 7.x, the license key will not work in Horizon 8.0 (2006) and newer. You will need to upgrade your license key to a Horizon 8 version.

- **Security Servers**: From Horizon 8.0 (2006) and newer, the Security Server is no longer supported, and as such you cannot install that role when installing the Connection Server software. For external connections, you should now use the Unified Access Gateway (UAG) appliance as discussed in Chapter 3.

- **View Composer**: From Horizon 8.0 (2006) and newer, View Composer and Linked Clones were deprecated, and from Horizon 8.1 (2012) and newer, they were removed completely. All editions of Horizon 8.0 (2006) now support Instant Clones. This means that you will need to build and configure new desktop pools using Instant Clones and then remove the View Composer and its associated

© Peter von Oven 2022
P. von Oven, *Mastering VMware Horizon 8*, https://doi.org/10.1007/978-1-4842-7261-9_15

database. You should also take this opportunity to review your gold image that you will use for creating Instant Clones. You will need to upgrade the Horizon Agent and other VMware agents (App Volumes and DEM).

- **Cloud Pod Architecture**: For Cloud Pod Architecture, you can upgrade pods one at a time; however, you should upgrade them all as soon as possible to avoid any compatibility issues. All Connection Servers in the pod must be online before starting the upgrade.

- **View events database**: Once you have upgraded all your Connection Servers to Horizon 8.1 (2012) or newer, you can backfill the events database with column data to improve events query performance. To do this, follow the instructions on the following KB article: `https://kb.vmware.com/s/article/80781`.

- **Persona Management**: No longer supported, instead use VMware Dynamic Environment Manager (DEM) to manage user profiles and the end-user environment.

- **Persistent disks**: No longer supported as this feature was part of Linked Clones and was used to store user settings and other user-generated data on a separate disk.

Before You Start the Upgrade

The first thing you need to do before you start the upgrade process is to disable provisioning on the Connection Servers. This will prevent any new users from requesting resources while you are performing the upgrade. Users can continue to use existing brokered resources but will not be able to launch any new ones until provisioning is enabled again.

If you have multiple desktop pools, then rather than disabling provisioning for each desktop pool you can disable the entire Connection Server. It is worth noting that if you have deployed Replica Servers within your environment, then if you have load balancing configured, users could be routed to this server as the Connection Server is offline and unavailable. This means that end users can still connect and launch their Horizon resources.

To disable provisioning on the Connection Server, follow the steps described:

1. Log in to the Horizon Console using an administrative account.

2. From the left-hand navigation menu pane, expand the option for **Settings**.

3. You will see the tabs/links across the top of the screen for **vCenter Servers**, **Gateways**, and **Connection Servers**.

4. Click **Connection Servers**.

5. You will see the following screenshot:

Figure 15-1. *Connection Servers settings screen*

6. From the list of Connection Servers shown, click the radio button for the server you want to back up.

7. Now click the **Disable** button. You will see the **Disable** dialog box
as shown in the following screenshot:

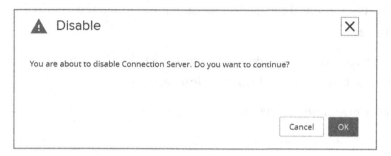

Figure 15-2. Disabling a Connection Server

8. Click the **OK** button to disable the selected Connection Server.

With the Connection Server now disabled, you can complete the next task, backing
up the Connection Server configuration.

Backing Up Your Environment Before Upgrading

Before you start upgrading, especially when it comes to the Connection Server, you
should make a backup of the configuration stored in the ADAM database.

Rather than performing this backup manually, by trying to find individual files, this
task can be performed from the Connection Server using the Horizon Console. To do
this, follow the steps described:

1. Log in to the Horizon Console using an administrative account.

2. From the left-hand navigation menu pane, expand the option for
   Settings.

3. You will see the tabs/links across the top of the screen for **vCenter
   Servers**, **Gateways**, and **Connection Servers**.

4. Click **Connection Servers**.

5.   You will see the following screenshot:

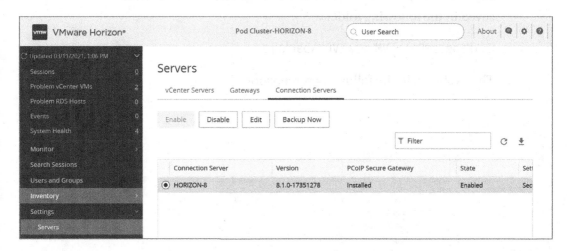

Figure 15-3.   *Connection Servers settings screen*

6.   From the list of Connection Servers shown, click the radio button for the server you want to back up.

7.   Now click the **Backup Now** button.

8.   You will see the **Backup Now** dialog box as shown in the following screenshot:

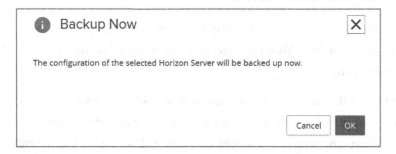

Figure 15-4.   *Backup Now dialog box*

9.   Click the **OK** button to take the backup.

10. The backup will now be taken, and the backup files will be exported using the LDAP data interchange format, or LDIF, and saved in the following folder:

    `C:\ProgramData\VMware\VDM\backups`

11. This is shown in the following screenshot:

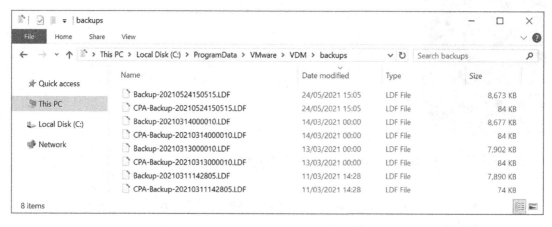

Figure 15-5. *Backups folder showing Connection Server backups*

12. In this example, you will see the backup file which is saved using the following filename format:

    `Backup-YYYYMMDDHHMMSS.LDF`

13. You will also see the CPA-Backup file as in this example environment the Cloud Pod Architecture feature has been implemented.

    As part of the backing up process, you should also ensure that things like the View events database are also backed up. If you have implemented App Volumes, as this will be part of the overall upgrade process, you should ensure you have the SQL database backed up too.

    Once these elements have been backed up, it is also worth taking a snapshot of the virtual machine, just in case.

Compatibility

As part of the upgrade process, it is also worth checking the VMware Product Interoperability Matrix to check the versions and what works with what.

For example, a new version of Horizon may now also need a newer version of ESXi or vCenter Server to take advantage of new features.

Click the following link to the Product Interoperability Matrix website:

`https://interopmatrix.vmware.com/#/Interoperability`

Once you have completed these initial tasks, you can start the upgrade process. In this chapter, we are going to start by upgrading the Connection Servers and Replica Servers.

The Upgrade Sequence

VMware recommends that the Horizon components are upgraded in a particular order. The order is as follows and is also dependent on whether you have all these components installed within your environment:

1. Horizon Clients

2. Load balancer

3. Third-party software

4. Workspace ONE Access

5. App Volumes Managers

6. Connection and Replica Servers

7. Unified Access Gateway appliances

8. vSphere components (vCenter Server and ESXi hosts)

9. VMware Tools

10. Agents (each agent also has its own installation sequence as follows)

    a. Horizon Agent

    b. VMware Dynamic Environment Manager (DEM) Agent

    c. App Volumes Agent

11. DEM Management Console

12. Active Directory – Horizon and DEM ADMX template files

13. App Volumes templates (if you are running App Volumes)

In the next sections, we are going to look at each of the specific Horizon components and how to perform the upgrade.

Upgrading Horizon Clients

Before you upgrade the Horizon Clients, it is worth noting that Horizon 8.x versions no longer support Horizon Clients 5.x and older.

With this in mind, it is a good idea to configure your client restrictions to reflect this and to prevent older clients from connecting.

The quickest and easiest way to upgrade the Horizon Client is to do it from the client itself. To do this, launch the client and click the menu button in the top right-hand corner of the screen. Now select the Software Updates option from the menu as shown in the following screenshot:

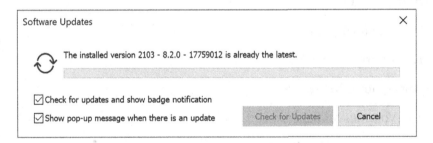

Figure 15-6. *Updating the Horizon Client*

As an IT administrator, you can also download the new Horizon Client from the VMware software download page and then deploy it using your standard software deployment tools.

Next, we are going to look at upgrading the Connection Server.

Upgrading the Connection Servers

Upgrading the Connection Server is a straightforward task. Once you have created a backup and understood the infrastructure changes, and other key differences, particularly if you are upgrading from a 7.x version, then all you need to do is download the new version onto the server and launch the installer.

The upgrade process runs as an in-place upgrade. That means all you need to do is run the Connection Server installer and click Next a couple times. The process uses the configuration that is already in place.

Once installed, you will then need to check and update the configuration from the Horizon Console. For example, if you upgraded from a deployment that used Linked Clone desktop pools, you will need to reconfigure those as Instant Clone desktop pools. You will need to update your image in any case, as you will need to upgrade the Horizon Agent.

Upgrading the Replica Server

The Replica Server provides additional Connection Server resources and is another role of the Connection Server.

That means that once you have completed the upgrade of the first Connection Server, or master server, you can complete the upgrade of your remaining Connection Servers or Replica Servers concurrently.

Upgrading the UAG Appliance

The upgrade process for the UAG is to export the configuration settings from the existing appliance, delete it, install a new version using the latest software, and then to reinstall the configuration files.

Before you start the upgrade, it is worth checking the Horizon Compatibility guide to check which version of the Unified Access Gateway is compatible with the version of Horizon you have upgraded to.

To perform the upgrade to the UAG, follow the steps described:

1. Log on to the UAG management console.

2. You will see Unified Access Gateway Appliance vxxx, where xxx is the current version number. In this example, it is v20.12 as shown in the following screenshot:

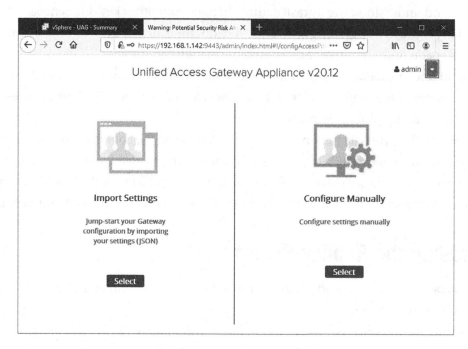

Figure 15-7. *Unified Access Gateway screen*

3. Under the **Configure Manually** section, click the blue **Select** button.

4. Now, on the configuration screen, scroll down to the **Support Settings** section as shown in the following screenshot:

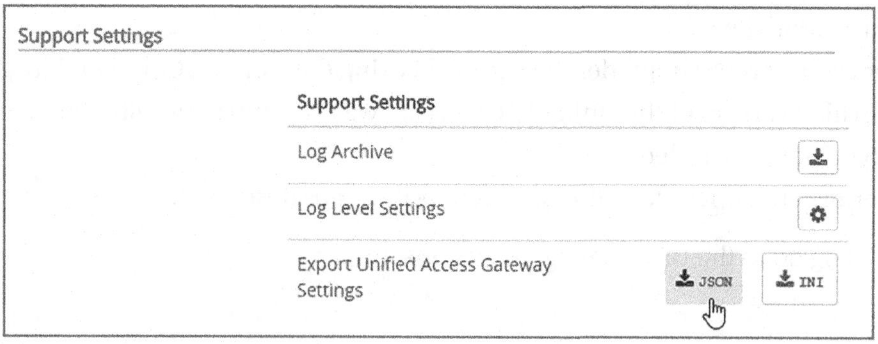

Figure 15-8. *Support Settings configuration screen*

5. Now, in the **Export Unified Access Gateway Settings** section, click the **JSON** button to export the settings.

6. The JSON file will be automatically saved to your Download folder on the machine that you used to log in to the UAG console from. You will also need the UAG certificate which is not included in the JSON export. Locate the .PFX file and save that with the JSON file as it will be required for the new UAG appliance. Or you can export a new one from Windows using the Certificate Export Wizard.

7. You can now either delete this appliance or put it into Quiesce mode and delete it once you are happy that the new UAG is operational.

8. The next step is to install your new version of the UAG appliance. For step-by-step instructions on how to do this, please refer to Chapter 4.

9. Once the new UAG appliance has been installed, log on to the management console using a browser, and from the main menu, under the Import Settings section, click the blue Select button. You will see the Import Settings screen:

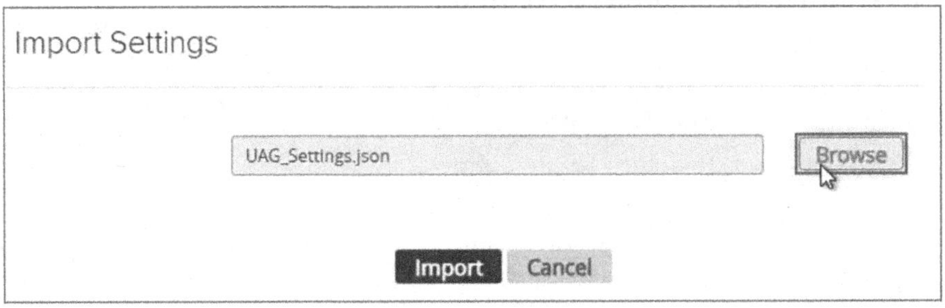

Figure 15-9. *Import Settings screen*

10. Click the **Browse** button and navigate to the location of where you saved the JSON file that you exported earlier, select the file, and click **Import**.

11. You will see a message stating **UAG settings imported successfully**.

12. Next, you need to import the certificate file. To do this, from the UAG admin console, scroll to the Advanced Settings section as shown in the following screenshot:

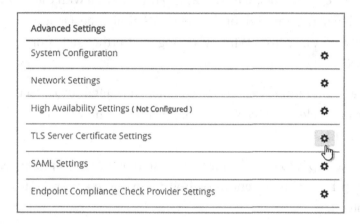

Figure 15-10. *Advanced Settings*

13. Click the **TLS Server Certificate Settings** option.

14. You will see the **TLS Server Certificate Settings** configuration box as shown in the following screenshot:

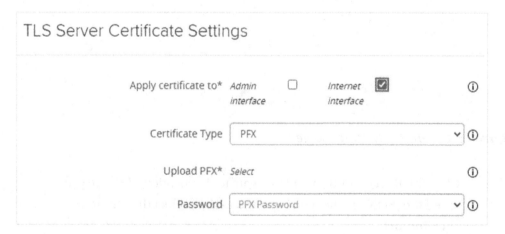

Figure 15-11. *TLS Server Certificate Settings*

15. In the **Apply certificate to** section, check the box for **Internet interface**.

16. Then in the **Certificate Type** box, from the drop-down menu, select the type of certificate. In this example, this is the PFX file we copied earlier, so select **PFX**.

17. Next, in the **Upload PFX** section, click **Select**.

18. Navigate the PFX file that was copied from the old version of the UAG appliance.

19. Finally, in the **Password** box, type in the PFX password.

20. Now click the **Save** button.

21. Reboot the UAG appliance to ensure that the configuration and the certificate have been successfully applied.

The next step is to upgrade or edit the Horizon configuration to reflect the new UAG appliance. If you have used the same gateway name for the new UAG appliance, then you can skip this step.

To do this, follow the steps described:

1. Log in to the Horizon Console.

2. From the left-hand menu pane, expand the option for **Settings** and then click **Servers** as shown in the following screenshot:

Figure 15-12. Adding the UAG in the Horizon Console

3. Now click the **Gateways** tab.

4. You will see the **Register Gateway** box as shown in the
   following screenshot:

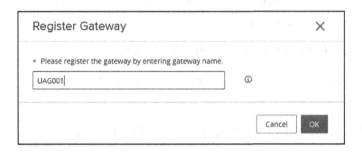

Figure 15-13. *Registering the UAG appliance with Horizon*

5. Enter the name of the UAG virtual appliance that you configured.
   In this example, we have called it **UAG001**.

6. Click **OK** to complete the configuration.

7. You will return to the **Servers** screen as shown in the following
   screenshot:

Figure 15-14. *UAG successfully registered with Horizon*

You have now successfully upgraded the UAG appliance.

Upgrading the Horizon Agent

When it comes to upgrading the Horizon Agent, there are several other things or scenarios that you need to consider as you are going to be upgrading your gold image that is used to create your Instant Clone virtual desktops from.

The first and most important thing is that Horizon Agents cannot be upgraded until you have completed the upgrade of the Connection Servers, which is why this section on upgrading the Horizon Agent comes after the Connection Server upgrade.

We are going to look at several different upgrade scenarios.

Scenario #1: Virtual Desktop Only

If your gold image is just being used as a virtual desktop image and has no other dependencies or agents installed on it, such as the App Volumes Agent, then it is just a case of downloading and installing the new version of the Horizon Agent. The upgrade runs as an in-place upgrade, and so that means it is just a case of launching the installer and following the instructions to completion.

Scenario #2: Virtual Desktop and Other Agents

In this scenario, the virtual desktop image is also running agents for App Volumes and Dynamic Environment Manager.

Before you install the new version of the Horizon Agent, you first need to uninstall the other agents. Once they have been removed, you can then perform the upgrade of the Horizon Agent.

Once upgraded, you can then reinstall the other agents, ensuring that the Dynamic Environment Manager Agent is installed before the App Volumes Agent.

Typically, you will be upgrading App Volumes and Dynamic Environment Manager if you have them running in your environment at the same time.

Scenario #3: Virtual Desktop, Other Agents, and VMware Tools

This final scenario builds on the previous scenario and now includes an upgrade to VMware Tools as maybe you have upgraded your vSphere infrastructure too.

In this scenario, you would first uninstall the Horizon Agent, DEM Agent, and App Volumes Agent. Once uninstalled, you can complete the upgrade of VMware Tools.

With the virtual desktop machine now running the upgraded version of VMware Tools, you can now reinstall the new versions of the agents, starting with the Horizon Agent, then the Dynamic Environment Manager Agent, and finally the App Volumes Agent.

Now that you have updated the gold image with the upgraded agents, the next step is to update the desktop pool to enable the newly built desktop image. This also is a good opportunity if you are building a new desktop pool based on Instant Clones in place of an existing Linked Clone desktop pool.

Pushing Out the Upgraded Instant Clone Desktop Pool Image

With the gold image updated, you can now push it out to the end users. To do this, follow the steps described in this example.

First, take a snapshot of the new image by performing the following steps:

1. Log in to the vSphere Client as an administrator.

2. Expand the vCenter Server **vcsa.pvolab.com**, expand the **PVO Data center**, then navigate to the host server on which the updated **Windows 10 Gold Image** virtual desktop machine resides. This is shown in the following screenshot:

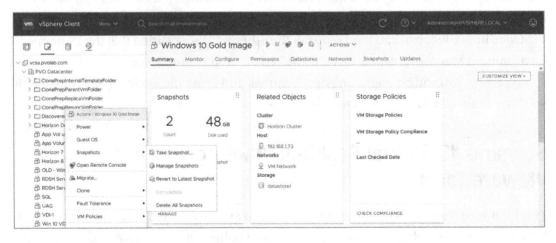

Figure 15-15. *Creating a new snapshot for the upgraded image*

3. Click to highlight the virtual desktop machine, right-click, then from the contextual menu, move your cursor onto the entry for **Snapshots**.

4. You will see the snapshot options expand, so from the list of menu options, click **Take Snapshot...**.

5. You will now see the **Take Snapshot** screen as shown:

Figure 15-16. *Taking the snapshot of the upgraded image*

6. In the **Name** field, type in a name for this snapshot. In this example, we have called it **Win 10 Gold Image - UPDATE V3**.

7. Then, optionally, add a description in the **Description** box.

8. Click **OK** to create the snapshot.

You now have a new snapshot of the gold image virtual desktop machine that can be used to update the desktop pool. The next step is to edit the desktop pool.

To do this, complete the steps described:

1. From the Horizon Console, navigate to and expand the **Inventory** option from the left-hand navigation pane, and then click **Desktops**.

2. You will see the following screenshot:

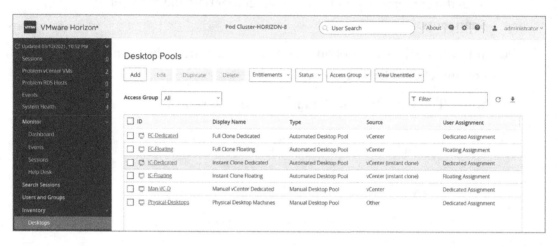

Figure 15-17. *Select the desktop pool to update*

3. From the list of desktop pools shown, click the link for the desktop pool you want to add the new and upgraded image to.

4. In this example, we are going to click the link to the **IC-Dedicated.**

5. You will now see the **IC-Dedicated** desktop pool as shown:

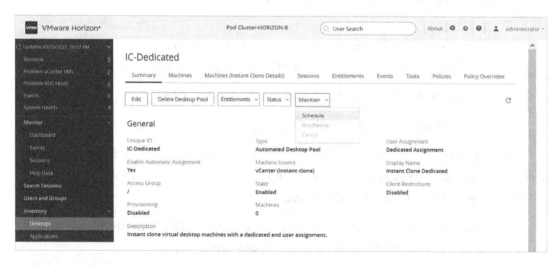

Figure 15-18. *Desktop pool configuration screen*

6. Click the **Maintain** box, and then from the drop-down menu, select the **Schedule** option as shown in the preceding screenshot.

7. You will see the **Schedule Push Image** screen as shown:

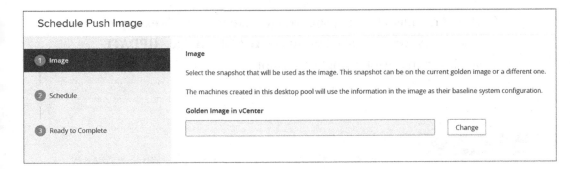

Figure 15-19. Select the new image from vCenter

8. The first step is to select the image. In the **Golden Image in vCenter** box, click the **Change** button.

9. You will see the **Select Golden Image** screen as shown:

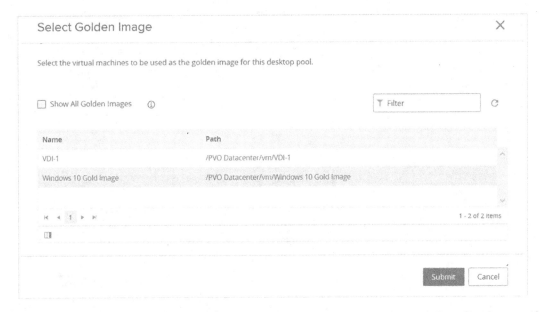

Figure 15-20. Selecting the image from the list

10. Click to select the image you want to use and then click the
     Submit button.

11. You will return to the main image screen which now lists the
     various snapshots that are available.

12. Click and highlight the snapshot you want to use. In this example,
     this is the new version called **Windows 10 Gold Image - UPDATE
     V3** as shown in the following screenshot:

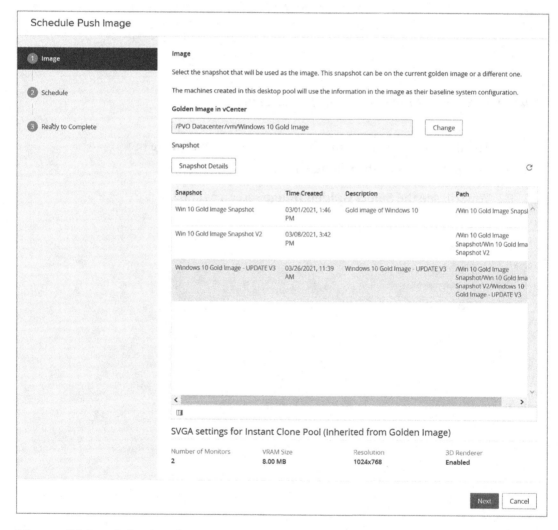

Figure 15-21. *Selecting the image snapshot*

13. Click **Next** to continue.

14. You will now see the second configuration step for **Schedule**.

15. On this configuration screen, you can configure when the update is going to be implemented to your end users.

16. The configuration screen is shown in the following:

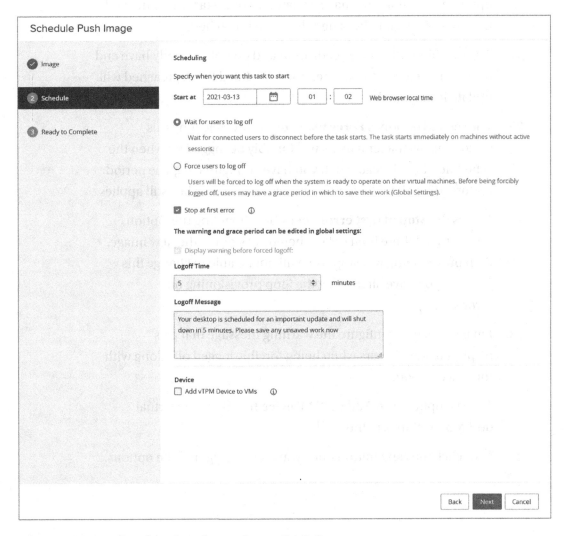

Figure 15-22. *Configuring the update schedule*

17. The first option is to configure when the update happens.

18. In the **Start at** boxes, enter the date and time of when you want to update the image.

19. Next, you then have two options to configure what happens to the end users that are currently logged in and how they are logged off so that the update can take place. The first option, selected by clicking the radio button, is **Wait for users to log off**. Selecting this option means that the image update will only start when the end user logs off, even if the scheduled time is reached.

Any machines that are already built and do not currently have end users connected to them when the scheduled time is reached will update immediately.

20. The second option is **Force users to log off**. Selecting this option means that end users will forcibly be logged off when the scheduled time is reached. If you have configured a grace period for forced logoff in the global settings, then this policy still applies.

21. Next is the **Stop at first error** check box. Enabling this option means that if there is an error when provisioning the new image, then provisioning will stop. You will not be able to change this option if you have already set the Stop provisioning on error setting.

22. Finally, you can configure the warning message that gets displayed to end users when being forcibly logged off, along with the grace period.

23. The last option is to **Add vTPM Device to VMs** to the virtual desktop machines in the pool.

24. Now click the **Next** button once you have configured the options.

25.   You will see the **Ready to Complete** screen as shown in the
following screenshot:

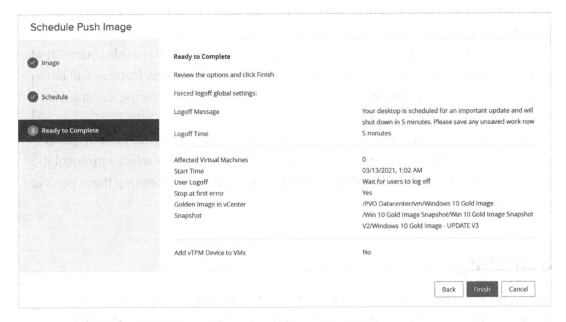

Figure 15-23. *Ready to Complete screen*

26.   Once you are happy with the configuration, click **Finish**.

In the next section, we are going to look at how to upgrade the AD components.

Upgrading AD Components

The AD components that will need to be upgraded are the Horizon Group Policy
template files or the ADMX files.

To do this, download the latest **VMware-Horizon-Extras-Bundle-xx.zip file**.

Next, extract the Horizon Extras Bundle zip file into a folder that is accessible by the
domain controller. Once extracted, copy the ADMX and ADML files into their respective
locations. For detailed instructions on how to do this, refer to Chapter 7.

Once the ADMX template files are in place, you can then check for any new policies
and configure them as a GPO and then apply them to the relevant OUs and groups in
Active Directory.

What About Upgrading the Display Protocol?

While technically there is not an upgrade for the display protocol as such, when upgrading an environment that uses the PCoIP protocol it is worth considering migrating to VMware Blast.

PCoIP is still supported within Horizon; however, given PCoIP is a third-party OEM solution from Teradici and VMware Blast is homegrown, all the new features will be available in Blast. For example, if you want to use the session shadowing feature, then that is only available when using Blast.

If you change the protocol, it is simply a case of reconfiguring your desktop pools to use Blast as the default protocol. You can still allow end users to select a protocol if required. Blast uses TCP and UDP port 22443, and so it is worth checking these ports are not blocked.

Summary

In this chapter, we have given you a walk-through of the upgrade process and how to approach it, with special attention to the order in which components should be upgraded.

In the next chapter, we are going to discuss deploying Horizon in cloud environments.

CHAPTER 16

Running Horizon in the Cloud

So far in this book, we have focused on installing, configuring, and deploying the Horizon solution for delivering apps and desktops on-premises. That is on internal infrastructure hosted within the confines of *your* data center.

However, Horizon can also be deployed in the cloud, and you would have seen a clue to which cloud providers when you installed the Connection Server as you would have seen a drop-down menu on the **Ready to Install the Program** screen as shown in the following screenshot:

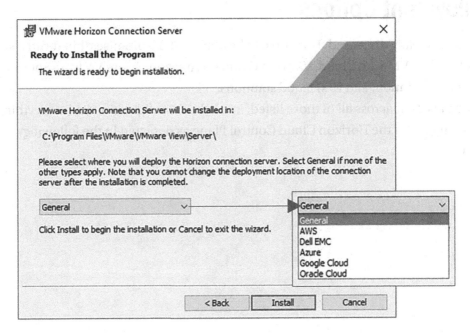

Figure 16-1. *Horizon Connection Server deployment options for the cloud*

© Peter von Oven 2022
P. von Oven, *Mastering VMware Horizon 8*, https://doi.org/10.1007/978-1-4842-7261-9_16

From the drop-down menu, you will see several different cloud options for installing Horizon.

In this chapter, rather than take a deep-dive admin approach to setting up Horizon in the cloud, we shall save that for another book; instead, we are going to cover a high-level introduction to the various cloud options that exist for running Horizon in a cloud environment.

We will also look at some of the additional features, capabilities, and components of the solution, such as

- Licensing models

- Horizon Cloud Control Plane

- Horizon JMP (DEM, App Volumes, and Instant Clones)

- Horizon Image Management Service

- Horizon Universal Broker

To start, we are going to look at the deployment options.

Deployment Options

As we have already discussed, Horizon can be deployed on-premises, but it can also be deployed on VMware Cloud, VMware Cloud on Amazon, Azure VMware Solutions, Oracle cloud solution, and IBM cloud solutions.

It can also run across all of those listed, in a hybrid configuration with everything being managed by the Horizon Cloud Control Plane as depicted in the following diagram:

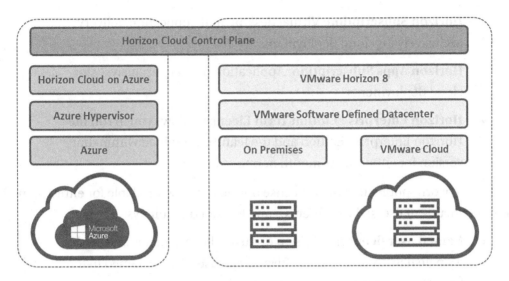

Figure 16-2. *Where to deploy Horizon Cloud*

The objective is to enable end users to have access to their apps and desktops from the cloud, wherever they are, using whatever device is appropriate.

For IT administrators, it provides a single management platform for managing the resources no matter where they are running, providing a comprehensive set of management and monitoring tools for both desktops and infrastructure that enables them to grow and scale quickly and simply.

To facilitate this ability to grow and scale, Horizon licensing, from May 2021, moved to a subscription-based model, adding the Universal option to the existing list of licenses available, which we will discuss in the next section.

Horizon Subscription-Based Licensing

With the VMware Horizon subscription licensing model introduced in May 2021, organizations can take advantage of a single and flexible entitlement to all the available Horizon technology solutions and deployment options.

This licensing model offers the following licensed options:

- **Horizon Universal**: Virtual desktop and application delivery designed for on-premises or cloud deployments

- **Horizon Apps Universal**: Application delivery designed for either on-premises or cloud deployments

- **Horizon Subscription**: Virtual desktop and application delivery exclusively for cloud deployments

- **Horizon Apps Subscription**: Application delivery exclusively for cloud deployments

- **Horizon Enterprise Edition Term License**: Allows you to run the Horizon Enterprise Edition and the feature contained within that version for either three-month or one-year terms

It is also worth noting that these license options are also available for either named users or concurrent users; the differences are described as follows:

- **Named user license**: This is an exclusive license that is assigned to a single named user of the software. The user will be named in the license agreement.

  In this model, you would need to purchase a license for each end user that would be using the software.

- **Concurrent user license**: This license model refers to the total number of people that are simultaneously, or concurrently, using the software. Ideal for organizations that have shift workers, for example, where you may have 100 end users, but only 50 will be using the software at any one time.

  In this example, you would purchase 50 concurrent user licenses rather than purchasing 100 named user licenses.

The following table lists the different Horizon subscription licenses:

Deployment	Horizon Universal Subscription	Horizon Apps Universal Subscription	Horizon Standard Subscription	Horizon Apps Standard Subscription
On-premises Deployment Option	✓	✓	✓	✓
Public Cloud Deployment Option	✓	✓	✓	✓
Hybrid & Multi-Cloud Deployment Option	✓	✓		
Single location deployment			✓	✓
vSphere and vCenter Server included (on premises deployment)	✓	✓	✓	
vSAN included (on premises)	✓			
No SDDC infrastructure option	✓	✓	✓	✓

Figure 16-3. *Deployment features for the subscription license*

When it comes to running virtual desktop machines and RDSH-based desktops and apps, then the following licenses apply:

Virtual Desktops & RDSH	Horizon Universal Subscription	Horizon Apps Universal Subscription	Horizon Standard Subscription	Horizon Apps Standard Subscription
Virtual desktops (Windows and Linux) with Instant or Full Clones	✓		Windows	
RDSH desktops and apps with Instant or Full Clones	✓	✓	✓	No Instant Clones
Linux hosted apps	✓	✓		✓
Support for Windows 10 multi-session (Azure Virtual Desktop)	✓	✓	✓	✓
VM-hosted apps (Windows 10)	✓	✓		
Remote access for Windows 10 physical desktops	✓	✓	✓	✓
Support for non-vSphere VDI or RDSH	✓	✓	✓	✓

Figure 16-4. *VDI and RDSH licensed features*

The following management features are included with each of the versions as listed in the following table:

Management	Horizon Universal Subscription	Horizon Apps Universal Subscription	Horizon Standard Subscription	Horizon Apps Standard Subscription
Access to always up-to-date control plane	✓	✓	✓	✓
VMware-managed, multi-tenant DaaS deployment option	✓	✓	✓	✓
Horizon Control Plane services: app management	✓	✓		
Horizon Control Plane services: Image Management, Monitoring, Universal Broker	✓	✓	✓	✓
Power Management	✓	✓		
REST API	✓	✓		
Help desk tool	✓	✓	✓	
App Volumes	✓	✓		
VMware ThinApp	✓	✓	✓	✓
Dynamic Environment Manager Standard			✓	✓
Dynamic Environment Manager Enterprise	✓	✓		

Figure 16-5. *Management licensed features*

The following table lists the end-user experience and access features:

End User Experience and Access	Horizon Universal Subscription	Horizon Apps Universal Subscription	Horizon Standard Subscription	Horizon Apps Standard Subscription
VMware Workspace ONE Access with VMware Verify multi-factor authentication	✓	✓	✓	✓
Unified catalog of pub-lished apps, packaged apps, virtual desktops, SaaS, and web apps with single sign-on (SSO) access	✓	✓	✓	✓
Blast Extreme, PCoIP, RDP protocol	✓	✓	✓	✓
Session Collaboration	✓			
Optimized video and audio experience for collaboration software	✓	✓	Win Client Only	Win Client Only
Secure access and edge services using multi-service proxy with VMware Unified Access Gateway	✓	✓	✓	✓

Figure 16-6. *End-user experience licensed features*

Horizon Cloud Control Plane

The Horizon Cloud Control Plane, hosted by VMware in the cloud, provides services that allow you to centrally orchestrate the management of virtual desktop machines, remote desktop sessions, and remote applications.

The control plane enables you to manage your pods. The pods can be located either on-premises, in the cloud, or on Microsoft Azure. When you log in to the cloud-based control plane console, you will see all your cloud-connected pods, enabling you to perform management tasks regardless of where the pods are located and running.

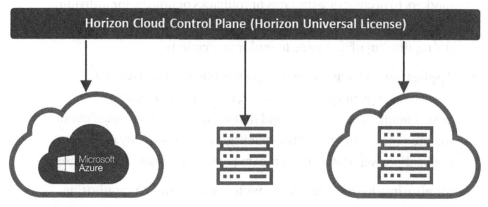

Figure 16-7. *Horizon Control Plane*

As the control plane is delivered from the cloud, a Software-as-a-Service offering, then VMware is responsible for hosting the control plane service, and as such it is their responsibility to action any feature updates and enhancements.

Horizon Cloud is a multi-tenant environment and has several regional-based control plane instances with each one corresponding to a data center within its own geographic location. When you create your tenant account, then you will specify your region at that time.

The cloud control plane also provides you with the ability to manage your environment using the browser-based Horizon Universal Console. From within this console, admins can assign a resource to end users, whether that is a virtual desktop machine, remote desktop session, or remote application. As a cloud-based console, admins can access it from anywhere and at any time.

The Horizon Control Plane provides the following features:

- **Universal brokering**: Optimize user experience and performance by intelligently connecting users to their virtual desktops and apps through a single URL to Horizon pods based on available capacity, user location, preference, and more, regardless of whether the Horizon deployment type is on-premises or in the cloud. Reduce IT management burden and costs with a global entitlement layer, eliminating the need for a global load balancing solution.

- **Image management**: Cut down image maintenance time and costs by centrally managing and distributing desktop images across Horizon environments, on-premises and in the cloud. Leverage markers to orchestrate updates or rollbacks of images for individual user groups or desktop pools, track changes of images, and automate the replication of an image to multiple locations.

- **Application management**: Simplify application delivery by packaging apps once and deploying them across Horizon environments, on-premises and in the cloud. Reduce image count, maintenance, and application packaging complexity by managing applications separately from the image with VMware App Volumes.

- **Monitoring**: Reduce downtime with real-time health monitoring of the user session, virtual desktops, and apps across Horizon environments, on-premises and in the cloud, with a single user interface. Leverage a help desk service to quickly troubleshoot user sessions with detailed metrics.

- **Lifecycle management**: Simplify initial onboarding and configuration of your Horizon environment on any cloud. Automatically install, upgrade, and scale Horizon infrastructure in environments such as Horizon Cloud on Azure with built-in automation and lifecycle management.

Horizon JMP

The Just-in-Time Management Platform (JMP) brings together all the different virtual desktop components such as OS (Horizon View with Instant Clone desktops), applications (App Volumes), and user data and profiles (VMware Dynamic Environment Manager).

This is what is sometimes referred to as the composite desktop model where all the components that go to make up the entire end-user desktop environment are abstracted from the underlying desktop machine and delivered back on demand and based on the context of the end user's entitlements, location, and device.

It acts as the orchestration layer in that it brings all these different components together and delivers them to end users on demand. The end user receives a complete desktop environment including all their applications and all their end user–specific data, all built on demand as the end user logs in. Taking this approach enables organizations to deliver a completely stateless virtual desktop environment.

JMP Orchestration Components

As you can see from the preceding description on how JMP works, there are several components that go to make up the complete solution, in addition to App Volumes. These are described in the following sections.

VMware Workspace ONE

VMware Workspace ONE is a digital workspace solution that allows IT admins to centrally manage end users' mobile devices, virtual desktops, and applications. It allows end users to access their resources securely using a device of their choice regardless of whether it is a corporate device or a personal BYOD and regardless of whether that device is joined to the corporate domain. Taking this approach also means that a VPN is no longer required.

End users access their resources from a single portal or workspace, which also provides a catalog of self-service apps that a user can access and entitle themselves to use. From an App Volumes or JMP perspective, apps accessed from the workspace could be delivered using App Volumes with the apps being delivered via either a virtual desktop, hosted desktop, or an app publishing solution.

VMware Dynamic Environment Manager (DEM)

VMware DEM is responsible for delivering the personalization of the end user's virtual desktop machine by adding their personal settings and data. The virtual desktop machine can also be dynamically configured using standard Windows policies, enabling end user–specific setting to be applied to both the OS and the apps. For example, a standard application could be delivered using App Volumes and then configured for a specific use case using DEM.

VMware Instant Clones

An Instant Clone is a feature of the vSphere platform, used by Horizon to build virtual desktop machines on demand.

It uses VMware VM Fork technology that allows you to provision virtual desktop machines very quickly from a gold image. Rather than closing a powered off virtual desktop machine and then having to power it on and customize it, with Instant Clones the clone of the virtual desktop machines is created from an already powered on and running virtual desktop machine. This means that Instant Clones are very quick to provision and deploy.

The clone shares the memory and virtual hard disk with the parent virtual desktop machine, but also has its own unique memory and delta disk file to store the changes between it and its parent.

VMware App Volumes

App Volumes provides the layer of abstraction between the operating system and the applications, allowing the applications to be packaged as virtual hard disk files (VMDK) and then delivered to the end user's virtual desktop machine on demand and based on policy.

The applications are effectively containerized within a virtual disk file (either VMDK based for VMware environments or VHD based for other virtual infrastructures). These virtual disk containers or layers were called AppStacks in previous versions of App Volumes, but this has now been replaced with a more application lifecycle management-based approach referred to as Simplified Application Management (SAM).

When it comes to end users needing the ability to install their own applications, then App Volumes has a feature called Writable Volumes. With Writable Volumes, an empty virtual hard disk is attached to the end user's virtual desktop machine, and then any application installations they initiate will be redirected to this empty disk. As this disk is "owned" by the end user, then it will be attached to each virtual desktop machine they log in to.

Horizon Image Management Service

Even though you will have deployed the composite desktop model of breaking down the desktop into individual elements such as user profile settings, applications, and OS, you still need a solution to help with the management of each of those elements.

So far, we have discussed the user environment and the applications, and so the final part is managing the operating system images that are used to build the virtual desktops and virtual RDSH host servers from as part of the Instant Clone feature.

Regardless of where the virtual machines are running, you still need to manage and patch operating system images to ensure they are secure and up to date while at the same time maintaining version control. This is an unenviable task as your environment grows both in size and complexity with the varying needs of different end users. This now becomes a greater requirement as virtual machines could be spread across multiple cloud platforms as well as on-premises. To solve this issue, VMware Horizon Cloud has a feature called the Image Management Service.

The Image Management Service enables administrators to manage and distribute operating systems used in Horizon across individual Horizon pods regardless of location. To do this, it uses infrastructure components such as vCenter to replicate and manage your images across the various platforms.

You can automate image replication across multiple locations, which in turn enables you to update virtual desktop pools or server farms, allowing them to use the new image. To help make these updates at scale, fleets of pools can easily be updated using marker tags, all using a single console.

The marker tag is a unique label used to identify a particular use case for a particular image, identifying that the image would be suitable for the use case. Image versions support having one or more markers assigned to them, meaning that an individual image can be used for several different use cases.

Virtual machine pool assignments will use these marker tags to identify which image they should use to clone and provision the virtual machines in the pool from.

The following diagram shows the process at a high level:

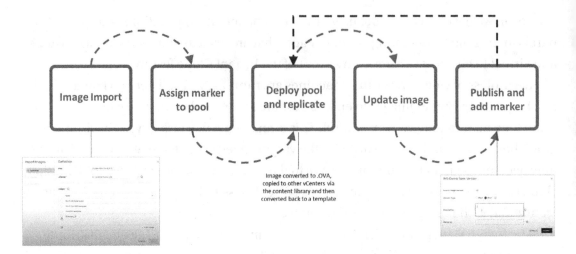

Figure 16-8. *Horizon Image Management Service workflow*

To watch a demonstration of this process, follow the link to the VMware YouTube channel:

`www.youtube.com/watch?v=NXFyrLGv4Lk`

The next component we are going to look at is the Horizon Universal Broker.

Horizon Cloud Brokering

As part of the Horizon Cloud Control Plane, you have the option to choose from two different types of connection broker: the **Universal Broker** or the **Single-Pod Broker** which is used for connecting end users in a Microsoft Azure environment.

In a hybrid cloud environment where you have deployed Horizon pods on a VMware SDDC platform and Horizon Cloud pods on a Microsoft Azure platform, each pod can have its own tenant-wide broker. You could, for example, enable the Universal Broker for your Horizon pods and the Single-Pod Broker for your Horizon Cloud pods hosted in Microsoft Azure.

It is worth highlighting that once you have selected a broker and have enabled it, the broker becomes a permanent, irreversible, tenant-wide setting for all your Horizon pods across your tenant account, which cannot be changed.

When selecting the Universal Broker option for both your Horizon pods and Horizon Cloud pods hosted in Microsoft Azure, any end-user assignment must be made up of virtual desktops from only one of these pod types. That means that the virtual desktop machine is either delivered from a Horizon pod or from a Horizon Cloud pod hosted in Azure. You cannot mix the two.

Horizon Universal Broker

The Universal Broker supports the following assignment configurations for end users:

- Multi-cloud assignment made up of virtual desktops from either one or more Horizon pods or one or more Horizon Cloud pods hosted in Microsoft Azure

- Assignments consisting of session-based desktops using Microsoft Remote Desktop Services (RDS) hosts within a single Horizon pod

- Assignments consisting of session-based desktops from RDS hosts within a single Horizon Cloud pod in Microsoft Azure

- Application assignments consisting of applications that are provisioned using RDS hosts within a single Horizon pod

- Application assignments consisting of applications provisioned by RDS hosts within Horizon Cloud pods in Microsoft Azure

- App Volumes application assignments consisting of App Volumes applications hosted on virtual desktop machines within Horizon Cloud pods hosted in Microsoft Azure

In terms of high-level architecture, the following diagram shows how the Universal Broker works:

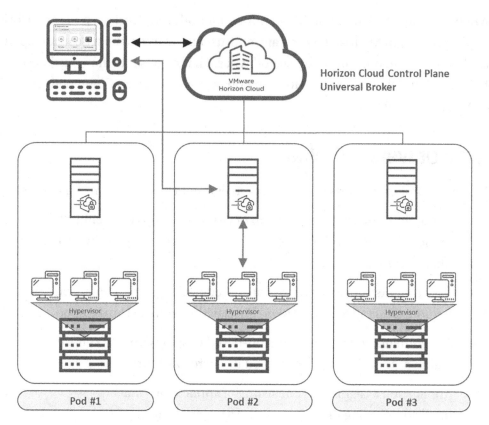

Figure 16-9. *Horizon Universal Broker*

Using the Universal Broker delivers several key benefits, including

- **Single connection FQDN to all remote resources**: This allows
  end users to be able to access multi-cloud assignments within your
  environment using a fully qualified domain name. The FQDN is
  defined within the Universal Broker configuration. Using the single
  Universal Broker FQDN, end users can access assignments from any
  participating pod from within any site across your environment. You
  do not need any internal networking between your pods to enable
  this feature.

- **Global pod connectivity and awareness**: The Universal Broker
  maintains direct connectivity with every pod within a multi-cloud
  assignment. This allows it to ensure the availability of each pod. It
  also means that the Universal Broker can manage the end user's

connection requests and route them to resources directly from these pods. As such, this removes the requirement to deploy global load balancing and removes the need for any interpod network communication.

- **Smart brokering**: The Universal Broker can broker resources from assignments to end users using the shortest network route possible. This is based on the broker having an awareness of your geographical sites and pod topology. This means that resources will be delivered from the nearest available pod to where the user connects from.

The following diagram shows the process for an end user connecting to the broker in order to access their virtual desktop machine:

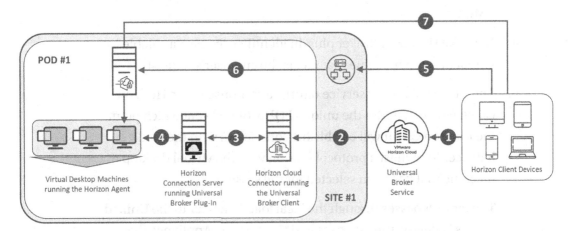

Figure 16-10. Horizon Universal Broker connection process for an end user

How Does It Work?

How does the process work when an end user logs in and requests a virtual desktop machine? The following describes the process as depicted in the preceding diagram:

1. The end user logs in to their Horizon Client, using the device of choice, and sends a request for a virtual desktop machine. This is done by connecting to the Universal Broker service through the brokering FQDN. The service then uses the XML-API protocol to authenticate the end user from the Horizon Client and to manage the connection session.

2. Based on the location of the end user, and where they are connecting from, Pod#1 located in Site#1 is determined to be the best available source from which to deliver the virtual desktop machine. The Universal Broker service then sends a message to the Universal Broker Client. The Universal Broker Client runs on the Horizon Cloud Connector that is paired with Pod#1. The Horizon Cloud Connector will be covered in the next section.

3. The Universal Broker Client then forwards the message to the Universal Broker plug-in running on one of the Horizon Connection Servers within Pod#1. The Universal Broker plug-in is installed on each of the Connection Servers, and the software can be found on the Horizon Cloud Connector download page in My VMware.

4. Next, the Universal Broker plug-in identifies the best available virtual desktop machine that meets the end user's request.

5. The Universal Broker service returns a response to the Horizon Client which includes the unique FQDN of Pod#1 at which point the Horizon Client will establish a connection with the load balancer to request a protocol session with the virtual desktop machine that has been selected for the session.

6. The request passes through the local load balancer to the Unified Access Gateway appliance for Pod#1. The UAG Appliance then validates that the request is trusted and then prepares the Blast Secure Gateway, PCoIP Secure Gateway, and the tunnel server.

7. Finally, the Horizon Client receives the specified desktop and establishes a session to it based on the configured secondary protocol, either Blast, PCoIP, or RDP.

The end user will now have access to a virtual desktop machine. Also, in the background, the virtual desktop could have been created using Instant Clones, applications added using App Volumes, and the end users' specific settings delivered with Dynamic Environment Manager.

Next, we are going to look at the Single-Pod Broker option.

Horizon Single-Pod Broker

The second type of broker is the Single-Pod Broker which is also referred to as legacy or classic brokering. The Single-Pod Broker is only available for Horizon Cloud pods that are hosted in Microsoft Azure with the following use cases:

- All your Horizon Cloud pods hosted in Microsoft Azure were deployed at pod manifest 2298.0 or later. With this use case, you must explicitly select the Single-Pod Broker to use the classic brokering method for all the pods in Microsoft Azure deployed across your tenant environment.

- At least one of your Horizon Cloud pods hosted in Microsoft Azure was deployed at earlier than pod manifest 2298.0. With this use case, you will not be able to select the broker type. The Single-Pod Broker is selected by default.

By deploying the Single-Pod Broker, you can create the following types of end-user assignments:

- A virtual desktop assignment that consists of virtual desktop machines delivered from a single Horizon Cloud pod hosted in Microsoft Azure

- Assignments consisting of session-based desktops delivered using Microsoft Remote Desktop Services (RDS) hosts within a single Horizon Cloud pod hosted in Microsoft Azure

- Assignments consisting of applications provisioned by RDS hosts within Horizon Cloud pods hosted in Microsoft Azure

- App Volumes application assignments consisting of App Volumes applications hosted on virtual desktop machines within Horizon Cloud pods hosted in Microsoft Azure

In the next section, we are going to look at the Horizon Cloud Connector and what it is used for.

Horizon Cloud Connector

The Horizon Cloud Connector is a virtual machine, deployed as an OVF within vSphere, that certifies your entitlements to the Horizon Cloud Service which in turn enables you to access the different cloud services that are delivered via the Horizon Control Plane for your Horizon pods.

A Horizon Cloud Connector must be deployed for each Horizon pod that you want to use with the Horizon subscription licenses and is shown in the architecture diagram in the "Horizon Universal Broker" section of this chapter.

The main role of Horizon Cloud Connector is to activate your Horizon subscription-based licenses; however, it also delivers the ability to monitor the health of your environment and to provide a help desk service to help with troubleshooting, all delivered from the Horizon Cloud Service management console.

You can connect multiple Horizon pods to a single Horizon Cloud Service account; however, every individual pod will need to have its own dedicated Horizon Cloud Connector.

In the final section, we are going to focus on Horizon Cloud running on Microsoft Azure.

Horizon Cloud on Microsoft Azure

Throughout this chapter, we have focused the discussions around running Horizon on-premises, in the cloud, and particularly on the Microsoft Azure platform. But the question that often gets asked is why would you run Horizon on Azure when you have Azure Virtual Desktops?

VMware has partnered with Microsoft to offer customers even greater features and functionality when it comes to running cloud-based desktops on Azure as highlighted in the following:

974

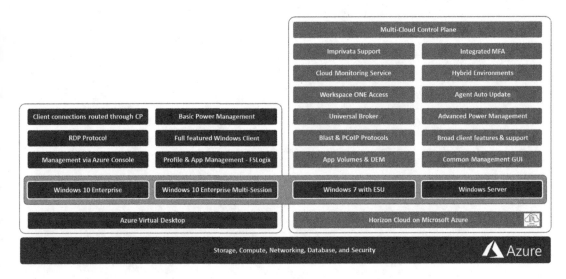

Figure 16-11. *Horizon Cloud on Microsoft Azure features*

Summary

In this chapter, we have given you an introduction to running Horizon as a cloud-based service. We started the chapter by looking at the different deployment methods before getting into the new subscription-based licensing model and the features available with each license option. Next, we looked at each of the unique components that enable you to run Horizon in the cloud and how some of those features work to give you an introduction to cloud-based deployments to help the design process when migrating to the cloud.

In the final chapter, we are going to look at some of the more common troubleshooting tips for diagnosing Horizon-related issues.

## CHAPTER 17

Horizon Troubleshooting

Although this chapter is titled Horizon Troubleshooting, we are going to also look at a more proactive approach. This will enable you to provide a more proactive approach to the monitoring of your environment and allow for you to preempt any potential issues rather than wait for them to become real-life issues that affect the performance of your end users.

The one big takeaway you should have learned by reading this book is that a successful virtual desktop or end-user computing project is made up of multiple components, and its success comes down to delivering a good user experience.

As such, you need to have the tools to enable you to diagnose and fix issues within your environment quickly and before those issues affect more users. This, if there were any, is one of the pitfalls with this type of solution. If there is an issue with the infrastructure, then it could potentially affect hundreds, if not thousands, of users, whereas with physical desktops, if a desktop breaks, it affects a single user. That is of course just so long as it isn't network related or an online service that is unavailable.

In this chapter, we are going to discuss troubleshooting tips using some of the available tools but more importantly look at how you can proactively monitor your environment. We will look at this by discussing three specific areas:

- General troubleshooting tips

- Managing specific issues

- Proactive monitoring and management

We will start by looking at some of the general troubleshooting tips before drilling down into some of the more specific information.

© Peter von Oven 2022
P. von Oven, *Mastering VMware Horizon 8*, https://doi.org/10.1007/978-1-4842-7261-9_17

General Troubleshooting

In this first section, we are going to take the cliched helicopter view of the environment and look at the entire environment to understand any potential issue before we start to look at the specifics of whether it is a CPU issue, a disk issue, or something else.

Quite often with VDI, especially when it is a new implementation, when a fault occurs VDI will become the point of blame. That then leads to the IT teams spending time trying to troubleshoot an issue with the VDI implementation rather than understanding what the issue actually is and looking at the bigger picture.

What also typically happens at this stage, particularly if it is a perceived performance-related issue, is that IT teams throw more resources at the problem. For starters, they may increase the number of CPUs and memory that the virtual desktop machine has been configured with and see if the problem goes away.

You have to remind yourself that VDI and Horizon delivered desktops and applications are just one component in a much larger solution. Quite often, it turns out that the issue is related to the network, storage, or an individual application. Moreover, the fault would have occurred in a physical environment too, and VDI and Horizon have nothing to do with it.

When a user reports an issue, or you notice an issue within the infrastructure, you will need to think logically as to which component within the infrastructure is going to be likely the cause and where you are going to start your troubleshooting journey. Maybe it is a storage issue, or maybe even it's a Windows issue and not anything to do with VDI at all!

How Many Users Are Experiencing Issues?

We have already touched on this subject, and the question you need to ask before embarking on troubleshooting is whether an individual user is experiencing the reported issue or whether it is a whole group of users being affected.

What we are trying to establish here is whether this could be infrastructure related and therefore multiple users will report the same problem or whether it is something an individual user is experiencing. If it is an individual user, then you need to understand what they were doing when they experienced the issue.

For example, are they connecting from the same location using the same device? Have they installed something or configured something on the desktop? Not that they should be able to do this, but there may be some use cases where they can.

If you suspect it is an issue with their individual desktop, then you can simply get them to log out and log back in again upon which they will be allocated and built a new desktop. This is one of the major advantages of deploying a stateless desktop model with Instant Clones and floating desktop assignments.

Should the issue continue after an OS refresh, then you would need to look at the configuration and the apps running on the desktop. If you need to apply a fix, you can update your gold image and push out an update. That will also ensure no other users will have the same issue.

Troubleshooting Performance-Related Issues

Performance issues are probably the biggest issues faced when working with and troubleshooting virtual desktop solutions, with the network likely to be blamed as the main culprit for any poor performance. However, before you then go and spend hours looking at network monitoring tools and other analyses, you need to step back and understand whether it really is the network.

As the remote desktop sessions are being delivered over the network, that is the reason the network is often seen as the issue; however, poor performance could have another root cause, and the network in this instance is just the messenger. But that is not to say there aren't network issues causing poor performance; the takeaway here is to not jump straight to blaming the network.

User Performance Issues

Most issues, in the first instance, will be reported by end users. The key thing here is to understand the issue as typically an end user will call the help desk and complain that their session is slow and no other information.

When an end user reports issues relating to poor performance, then you need to try and get them to be more specific. Ask them whether it is their session that is generally slow with everything they do or whether it is down to something like an individual application that is slow, or it is taking longer than expected to log in. The other key thing is whether this is a new issue or they have always experienced this.

It is also useful to keep a log of the issue, noting the time and date the issue occurred. If you are using some of the monitoring tools that we will cover later in this chapter, then you will be able to use these tools to reference what exactly was happening within the environment when the issue occurred.

As part of the general troubleshooting, it is also useful to understand whether the end user is doing something different. Although this may sound obvious, the end user won't usually mention the fact that all was fine when working from the office and connected to the network, but the issue occurs when they connect from home, upon where they suffer performance issues, for example.

In this example, the environment and location have changed which is a key piece of information to know before you go off examining the internal network when the issue could be down to the end user having slow home broadband. The fix may be that you change a policy setting that disables features that demand more network bandwidth.

Non-virtualized Performance Issues

By non-virtualized performance issues, we mean issues that do not relate to the virtualization layer, such as the virtual desktop machines or the hypervisor itself.

We are specifically talking about performance issues or other issues that would potentially occur on a desktop regardless of whether it is running in a virtual environment or not.

Things such as

- Logon time taking too long.

- Applications freeze or crash.

- Applications take too long to load.

- OS crashes such as blue screens.

- Applications run slowly.

- Permission errors.

These issues are not exclusive to a virtual environment; however, as they *are* running in a virtualized environment, then troubleshooting and resolution may be much easier.

Take an example of where the OS crashes or the virtual desktop machine becomes unresponsive. Rather than spend time trying to understand why, the end user can simply log out and log back in where they will receive a brand-new virtual desktop machine built from the clean image. If this issue affects more users, then consider patching your gold image, and when it has been tested, you can easily roll out the new image to all your end users.

If other changes are required, whether OS or application related, then these can very easily and quickly be rolled out.

The important point here is that you need to understand that these types of generic desktop issues will still exist whether you are running virtual or physical desktops and that you shouldn't automatically blame the virtual infrastructure as happens all too often.

As we have said, in these cases where end users experience issues, virtual desktops are your friend. Don't forget about troubleshooting general desktop support issues and spending far too much time examining your virtual infrastructure looking for issues when the answer may be as simple as a Windows OS or application issue.

Bandwidth, Connectivity, and Networking Issues

Networking issues are often some of the hardest to diagnose and can quite often be intermittent and depending on how many users are online and what they are doing at the time can all affect the network performance.

The best way to understand these usage patterns to help identify when there is an issue is to work closely with the networking teams and ensure you deploy some form of end-to-end monitoring solution.

Most of your end users will most likely be connecting over your local network or wide area network, meaning that you shouldn't have too many bandwidth issues given the network requirements were part of your overall design, and the network has been designed to deliver these requirements. If you do start to experience network performance issues, then start with looking at the following:

- Has anything on the network changed? If the network team are a separate team, have they implemented or changed something such as new firewalls, VLANS, or bandwidth restrictions?

- Is the end user connecting via a wired or wireless network? Perhaps, they are not close enough to a Wi-Fi hotspot, or their device has an older wireless protocol running.

- Have you configured QoS on your switches?

- Is the network currently reliable in general? Maybe this is not a virtual desktop–related issue, and it is just a network issue experienced by everyone.

- Are you seeing any dropped packets? This could indicate a failed switch or router or maybe a faulty cable. If it is from the client device, maybe the client has a poor Wi-Fi signal.

- Is the latency as expected?

- Check your design in terms of required bandwidth. Even on the LAN in enterprise environments, bandwidth could become an issue. Check your design and that you have configured enough bandwidth. Monitor end-user usage. Is an end user running something new that is consuming more bandwidth than your design catered for?

- Are you routing between different networks? If so, do your routers deliver suitable performance?

- Do you have any load balancers in place? Are the load balancers sized correctly for your environment, or are they causing a bottleneck?

When your end users are remote and connecting externally over the Internet, for example, it can become far more difficult to troubleshoot or guarantee connection quality and performance.

For remote or branch offices, ensure that the Internet connection is sized correctly, and wherever possible configure QoS for the protocol end to end. You should also configure the protocol to suit an environment that has reduced bandwidth. Turn off some of the higher-end graphics capabilities, for example.

It is also worth looking at the relevant log files and events databases on both the end-user client devices and the Horizon Connection Servers. This may give you an indication as to what happened and when. This can correlate with what the end user was doing at the time so you can understand whether it was an actual issue, or the end user was doing something unexpected that required more network capacity.

There are also some hard faults that end users will report, rather than just complaining about slow or poor performance. The following are some of the more common faults that an end user could report:

- **Black screen on the client device after connecting**: This is caused by the PCoIP protocol being blocked. The end user can connect to the desktop, and the login process works as expected; however, when they expect to see their desktop, instead they will see a black screen. As the desktop is delivered via PCoIP, it uses port 4172 to display the desktop. If this port is blocked, then the pixels are blocked, and the end user sees a black or blank screen. You could consider allowing end users to change the protocol so they can try again with a different protocol.

- **Disconnections**: If end users experience high latency and dropped packets, then the result will be that the end users will be disconnected from their virtual desktop machine session. To help with end users reconnecting, you should consider configuring enough time for users to reconnect before they are logged out.

- **Poor resolution images**: If there is limited bandwidth, end users may complain about the poor quality of the images displayed on their desktop. You should consider using policies to configure the image quality based on end-user location. For example, if you use PCoIP, turn off build-to-lossless over Internet connections.

Next, we are going to look at compute issues.

Compute Resource Issues with CPU and Memory

The underlying virtual infrastructure hosting your virtual desktop machines, especially when it comes to CPU and memory, can have a negative impact on end-user experience should there be any issues.

At the start of the project, you would have conducted an assessment phase which would have provided you with the data to correctly size the environment in terms of the CPU and memory resources required. With this in mind, you should have allocated enough resources, plus a little extra to cope with the workload. So that means if you are experiencing CPU and memory issues, then there is a physical fault with a host server, or something has changed.

Also, as part of that initial assessment, you would have created a baseline which would have defined the key performance characteristics of CPU and memory utilization along with deeper metrics around CPU ready times.

When troubleshooting, you should refer to these baselines to enable you to compare what is happening now to what was happening before. This should help you identify the issue. Maybe more users than planned have been added, and therefore there isn't enough CPU and memory to cope with the additional capacity. Maybe applications have been updated or added that now require more resources.

There are several tools and solutions to help with this, such as vRealize Operations for Horizon that will help you understand performance utilization over time, or maybe a third-party product such as Liquidware Stratusphere which can provide both the baseline metrics (measured during the assessment phase) and the ongoing management of the entire user experience.

When it comes to memory utilization, the best practice is not to overcommit memory. You need to carefully consider how much memory you allocate to each virtual desktop machine. Then you need to size your hosts accordingly, ensuring that your total allocated memory is less than the total in your hosts. Also take into consideration what happens if a host fails or goes offline. Can the remaining servers manage the additional workload?

If you experience performance issues related to memory, it is worth checking to see if memory is being swapped with other virtual desktop machines. Is there any memory ballooning taking place? This would potentially indicate that you don't have enough memory allocated to the virtual desktop machine as it is having to page. Consider increasing the amount of memory to resolve this issue or look further into why more memory is being required and whether that was highlighted in your assessment data.

With CPU, you need to understand the CPU Ready metrics. The acceptable CPU Ready figures within your environment will vary based on what the end users are doing. As a rule of thumb, you need to keep the CPU Ready metric below 5% per allocated CPU, with a maximum peak of around 10%. Beyond that, then you could experience performance issues. Again, it is worth looking at your baseline assessment data and data from when the issue occurred to understand why this is happening. It may be a new application has been added which requires additional CPU capacity, or you have not sized the requirements correctly.

A number of these performance-related issues, as we have mentioned, could be classed as growing pains. Once the environment is up and running and users are onboarded, quite often we don't review any of the performance data until there is an issue. Your environment will have likely moved on from where it was at the point of the initial deployment, and it could be simply down to the additional users and new and updated applications that are causing the issues.

Disk Performance Issues

Disk performance is also a key component within your environment. You need to manage your disk performance as your environment grows and the demand for building Instant Clones increases as more end users are added.

One of the metrics to monitor for storage performance is the disk latency. How much latency is acceptable within your environment depends on your end users and what they are running on their virtual desktop machines. Disk-intensive apps will obviously suffer more from performance issues.

Generally, disk latency of less than 25 ms is acceptable, but that doesn't mean that an end user that has been using a desktop with sub 25 ms latency would necessarily be happy. If a user is running disk-intensive applications, then 25 ms may be simply not acceptable regardless. It's all about what is acceptable for the application to run and the end user's perception of acceptable performance.

Troubleshooting Horizon-Specific Issues

In this book, we discussed all the different components that make up your complete Horizon infrastructure. These are generally very reliable; however, they are not immune to failure or issues.

As part of your overall design, you will have designed out failure points wherever possible, ensuring that all your Horizon components and those supporting infrastructure components such as databases and Active Directory are also highly available.

Horizon Infrastructure Issues

To monitor your environment at a high level, you will see on the Horizon Console dashboard a section for System Health. If you click the **VIEW** button on this section, then you will see the following screenshot:

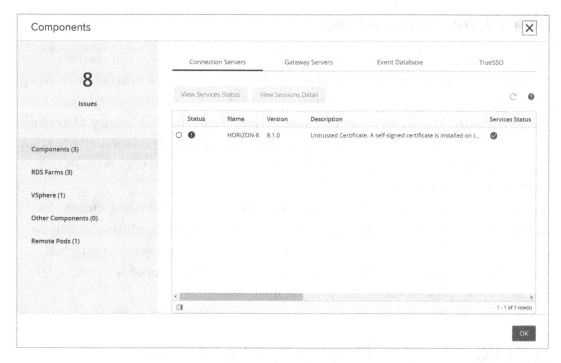

Figure 17-1. *System Health screen in the Horizon Console*

From here, you can quickly see which component has an issue from the status shown. In this example, the Connection Server called Horizon-8 has an issue with an untrusted certificate.

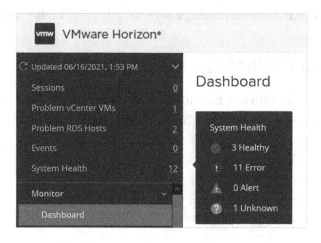

Figure 17-2. *System Health shown as red, amber, green*

Across the top, you will also see that you can check other components such as gateway servers and the event database, while down the side of the screen, you can select some of the other components such as RDS farms and your vSphere virtual infrastructure.

Connection Servers	Gateway Servers	Event Database	TrueSSO

View Services Status	View Sessions Detail				C ❓

CPU Consumption	Memory Consumption	TLS Certificate	Unauthenticated Access	Connections	Replication Status
69%	87%			0	

Figure 17-3. *System Health of a specific Horizon component*

As a starting point, when troubleshooting Horizon infrastructure, you should look at the system health information. Then from here you can start to drill down to what is causing the issue and then move on to fix the problem.

You also have the ability to look at the Horizon event database that will provide you with information about events that have occurred and been logged.

To access the event log, click Events from the first section of the top-left navigation menu pane. You will see the following example screenshot:

Events

Updated 06/16/2021, 2:11 PM

Time Period | Last 2 days ∨ | | Filter | C ⬇

User	Severity	Time	Module	Message
	ℹ️ Info	06/16/2021, 2:11 PM	Connection Server	machine Full-Clone-F-02 has been deleted
pvolab.com\administrator	☑ Audit success	06/16/2021, 2:11 PM	Vlsi	pvolab.com\administrator deleted Machine Full-Clone-F-02
	ℹ️ Info	06/16/2021, 2:10 PM	Connection Server	vCenter at address https://vcsa.pvolab.com:443/sdk has been temporarily disa
	ℹ️ Info	06/16/2021, 2:10 PM	Connection Server	vCenter at address https://vcsa.pvolab.com:443/sdk has been enabled
pvolab.com\administrator	☑ Audit success	06/16/2021, 2:10 PM	Vlsi	pvolab.com\administrator has updated database configuration
pvolab.com\administrator	☑ Audit success	06/16/2021, 2:10 PM	Vlsi	pvolab.com\administrator has attempted to change event configuration

Figure 17-4. *Example event log from the events database*

If you have configured it, then you could also have access to syslogs from a Syslog server.

As well as checking the system health in the Horizon Console, you should also not forget the simplest of troubleshooting steps when troubleshooting your Horizon infrastructure, such as

- Are all the servers, desktops, infrastructure components, and hosts contactable on the network? Can you ping them?

- Are all the required services started?

- Is there a sufficient free resource on the hosting infrastructure?

- Is the memory and CPU utilization maxed out?

Don't forget the back-end infrastructure either. Is Active Directory available for end users to be able to log in to their virtual desktop machines? What about the other services and components that Horizon depends on? These all need to be considered when troubleshooting.

As part of your overall troubleshooting and remediation process, there may be issues that fall outside those that we have discussed so far or are visible from the Horizon Console or for the end user to see. These are typically more admin-focused issues.

Unfortunately, though, sometimes the corrective actions are not so straightforward to implement and need a more advanced approach perhaps using the command-line tools that we have covered in Chapter 16.

These issues could include

- Manual removal of a Connection Server after the loss of a component or OS corruptions when a new server is deployed. It would need to be manually removed using command-line tools from the inventory.

- Manual removal of desktops within a pool or the whole pool.

- Recovery of Horizon from a backup, whether a backup of the entire VM or an automated backup of the ADAM database.

There are many different scenarios which we aren't going to cover in this chapter; however, they have been covered in Chapter 16.

In addition, there are some great knowledge base articles already available on VMware's KB site at the following address:

`http://kb.vmware.com/`

In the next section, we are going to look at the integrated Horizon Help Desk Tool.

Horizon Help Desk Feature

Horizon also has its own integrated help desk tool that enables you to search for a specific Horizon user and check their session status and the resources they are using.

The idea here is that should the end user call in to the IT help desk, you, as an IT admin, can quickly find the user and their session to quickly understand and identify the issue.

In the following example, an end user named Bob calls the help desk as he is experiencing issues with his session. As an IT admin, you would perform the following tasks:

1. Log in to the Horizon Console with the appropriate permissions to be able to use the help desk tool.

2. From the Horizon Console, expand the option for **Monitor** from the left-hand navigation pane, and then click **Help Desk**.

3. You will see the following screenshot:

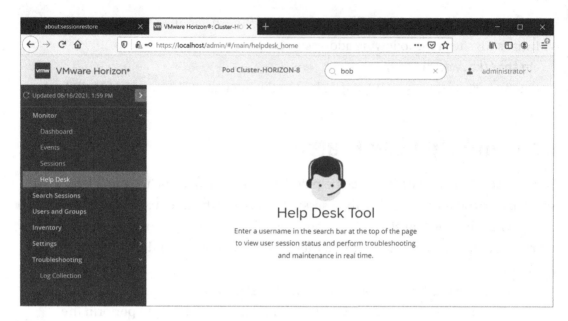

Figure 17-5. *Horizon Help Desk Tool main screen*

4. At the top of the screen, you will see a search box stating
    User Search. Type in the name of the user you want to search for.
    In this example, it is our user called **Bob**.

5. Now click the search button.

6. You will see the following screenshot that displays the results of
    the search. In this case, the user called Bob is displayed as a fully
    qualified name as shown:

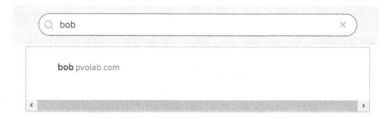

Figure 17-6. *Selecting the end user*

7. Click the name in the results box, so **bob pvolab.com**.

8. You will now see the first screen which shows the sessions for the user Bob as shown in the following screenshot:

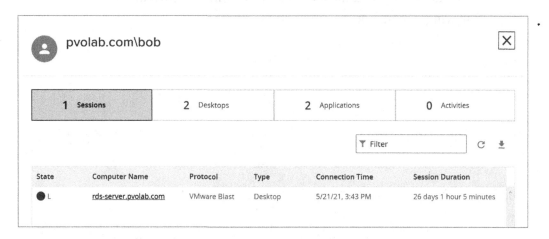

Figure 17-7. *End-user sessions displayed in the Help Desk Tool*

9. In this example, we can see that Bob has had a desktop session open and running as indicated by the green dot under the State heading. It also shows the name of the computer he is connected to and the protocol being used to deliver the session.

10. If you click the button under the **State** heading, you will be taken to a details screen for that session; the first shows the client details from where the end user is connecting as shown in the following screenshot:

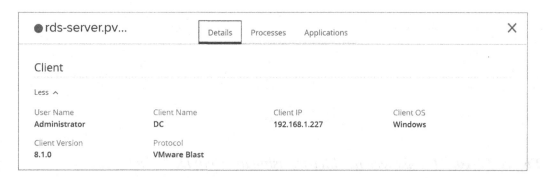

Figure 17-8. *Client information using the Help Desk Tool*

11. If you scroll down, you will see the details of the virtual machine the end user is connected to. In this case, it is an RDSH Server that is delivering a published desktop session as shown in the following screenshot:

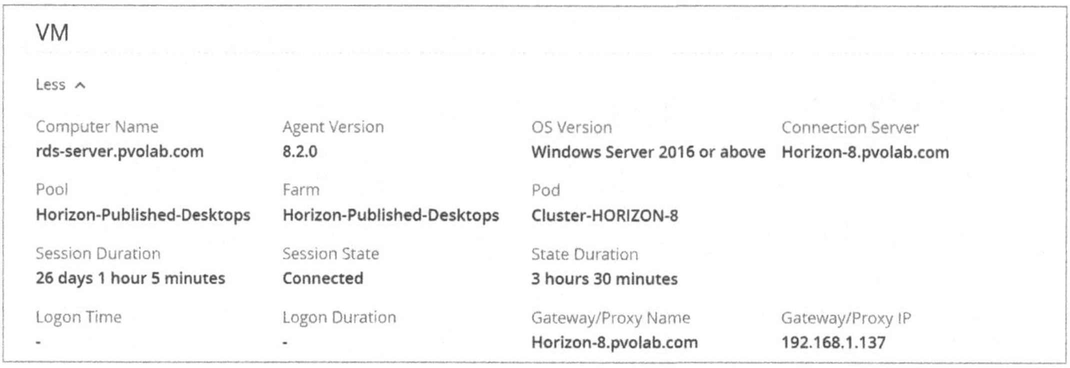

Figure 17-9. *VM information using the Help Desk Tool*

12. If you continue to scroll down, you will see the User Experience Metrics section that displays the protocol information with details on the frame rate and estimated bandwidth consumption as shown in the following example screenshot:

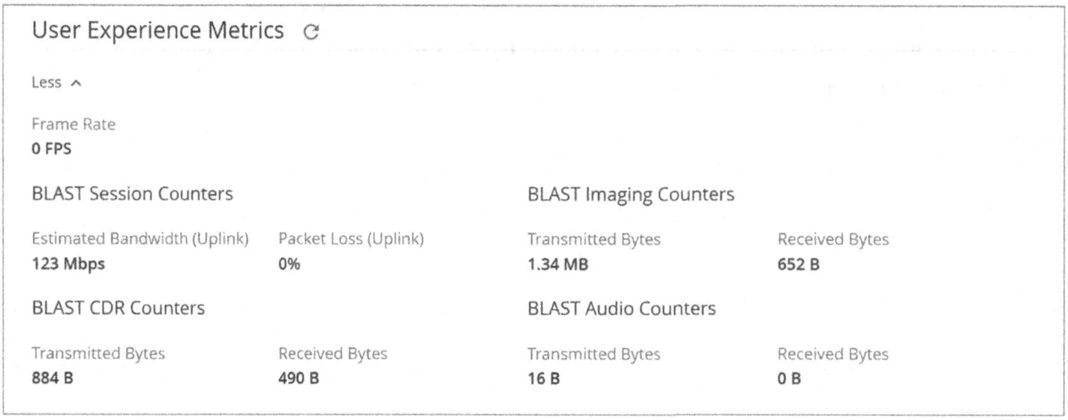

Figure 17-10. *User Experience Metrics using the Help Desk Tool*

13.   Then finally on the details screen, you can see details of the
      resource utilization, detailing CPU and memory usage and
      network and disk performance as shown in the following example
      screenshot:

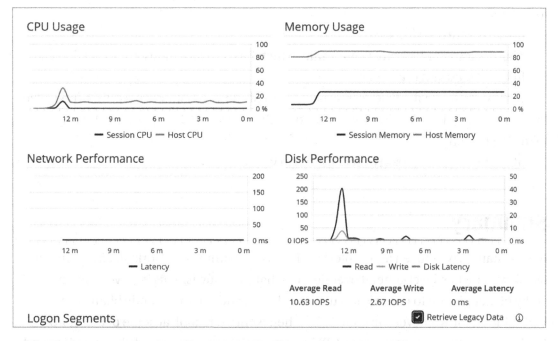

Figure 17-11. *Resource utilization using the Help Desk Tool*

There is also another free tool, the Horizon Helpdesk Utility, available from the
VMware Flings website from the following link:

`https://flings.vmware.com/horizon-helpdesk-utility`

In the next section, we are going to touch on some of the place where you can find
additional resources and information.

Additional Help and Support

In addition to the standard VMware documentation found on the VMware website, there
are a huge number of resources available that discuss Horizon that can help if you have
an issue with Horizon or just need some additional advice.

If you do however have an actual fault, then first and foremost, you should log a call with VMware Global Support Services (GSS) as soon as possible. Ultimately, VMware support will get to the bottom of any issues you are experiencing.

There are also many resources online such as blogs from experienced EUC experts. One of the most comprehensive sites is written by Carl Stalhood, and his site can be found here:

www.carlstalhood.com/

There is also the VMware Community which has a wealth of resources available at

https://communities.vmware.com

Finally, there are the EUC vExperts, a group of subject matter experts that specialize in VMware digital workspace solutions. You will find the EUC vExpert directory by following this link:

https://vexpert.vmware.com/directory/euc

Summary

In this chapter, we looked at troubleshooting issues within your Horizon environment by taking a higher-level general overview to what the issue is. This involved looking at the bigger picture to understand the issue better and not to instantly blame the VDI solution for whatever the issue is. We then went on to look at some of the more Horizon-specific elements such as CPU and memory performance, disk utilization, and networking limitations. This would help pinpoint and understand the issues the user is facing. It would help determine whether it is limited to a specific user or whether the issue is more widespread. The key takeaway here is to treat the issue like a desktop issue rather than a VDI issue. That isn't to say that the underlying cause could be down to the virtual infrastructure, but most likely that the problem would have occurred in a physical desktop environment too. Next, we looked at the Help Desk Tool that is built into the Horizon Console and how that can be used to help understand the performance and utilization of an individual end user's session.

Finally, we provided additional resources to help you solve issues and ask questions regarding the deployment of your Horizon environment.

Index

A

Active Directory (AD)
  components, 955
  group policy objects
    ADMX templates, 449–450
    features and configurations, 447
    group policy objects and link,
      453–455
    infrastructure, 142
    loopback processing, 455–458
    optimization configurations, 447
    organizational unit, 450–452
    unzipped files, 449
    virtual desktops policies, 458–460
    ZIP file, 448
  organizational units (OUs), 146
  user accounts, 146
Active Directory Application Mode
    (ADAM), 29
Administration tasks (environment)
  administrators
    access groups screen, 196
    account creation, 197
    permission, 193–194
    role screen selection, 195–196
    user account, 193
  events database
    configuration screen, 187
    editing process, 187–188
    event settings, 190

horizon events, 186
    log files, 191–192
    screenshot, 189–190
    Syslog event logging, 191
  general settings
    API session, 198
    automatic status, 200
    client restrictions, 204–206
    configuration screen, 197–200
    console session timeout, 198
    discard SSO credentials, 199
    domain list option, 201
    end user's credentials, 201
    factor re-authentication
      option, 201–202
    logoff feature, 201
    pre-login message option, 200
    security settings, 202–204
    single sign-on (SSO), 199
    windows server desktops, 201
  Instant Clones, 184–186
  license key
    dashboard screen, 175
    screenshot, 172
    serial number, 172–173
    usage screen, 173–174
  login screen, 171
  steps, 171
  vCenter desktop server
    add button, 176
    address box, 177

995

© Peter von Oven 2022
P. von Oven, *Mastering VMware Horizon 8*, https://doi.org/10.1007/978-1-4842-7261-9

G

J, K

R

Z

Printed in the United States
by Baker & Taylor Publisher Services